The Management of Business Logistics

Fifth Edition

THE MANAGEMENT OF BUSINESS LOGISTICS

FIFTH EDITION

JOHN J. COYLE
Pennsylvania State University

EDWARD J. BARDI
University of Toledo

C. JOHN LANGLEY, JR.
University of Tennessee

WEST PUBLISHING COMPANY

St. Paul   New York   Los Angeles   San Francisco

Dedicated to Dr. Robert D. Pashek
Teacher, administrator, and friend

Composition: Parkwood Composition Services, Inc.
Copyediting: Kim Kaliszewski
Text Design: John Rokusek/Rokusek Design
Illustrations: Patti Isaacs/Parrot Graphics
Cover Design: Delor Erickson/Studio West, Inc.

COPYRIGHT © 1976,
1980, 1984, 1988   By WEST PUBLISHING COMPANY
COPYRIGHT © 1992   By WEST PUBLISHING COMPANY
                     50 W. Kellogg Boulevard
                     P.O. Box 64526
                     St. Paul, MN 55164-0526

Library of Congress Cataloging-in-Publication Data

Coyle, John Joseph, 1935–
    The management of business logistics / John J. Coyle, Edward J.
Bardi, C. John Langley, Jr.–5th ed.
        p. cm.
    Includes bibliographical references and index.
    ISBN 0-314-93364-6 (hard)
    1. Business logistics. I. Bardi, Edward J., 1943–
II. Langley, C. John, 1946–   . III. Title.
HD38.5.C69 1992
658.7—dc20   CIP ∞   91-30184

CONTENTS IN BRIEF

CONTENTS

PART IV

CHAPTER 12   FACILITY LOCATION, 424

PREFACE

Most professionals in logistics agree that the 1980s was the most turbulent decade in the post-World War II era, perhaps the most turbulent ever for the areas that logistics includes. Transportation, in particular, experienced unparalleled change in the 1980s because of economic deregulation. For example, the number of motor carrier companies more than doubled to reach the present level of about 45,000. But the bankruptcy rate has also more than doubled among motor carriers, contributing to what some felt was an environment bordering on chaos. Railroads, airlines, and ocean shipping firms also experienced many changes that we will discuss in the new edition of the text.

For the logistics manager, the 1980s presented significant opportunities and challenges. Many companies experienced absolute and/or relative decreases in their logistics-related costs. Third-party logistics companies have become prevalent, offering a variety of logistics services that have provided companies the opportunity of outsourcing part or all of their logistical activities. Other developments have included strategic alliances with vendors; total quality management; more emphasis on effective management of inventory; increased awareness of customer service as an important part of competitive strategy; and more reliance on technology to improve information flows and communication, as well as to increase productivity. The list could continue. The practice of logistics management changed dramatically during the 1980s. To digest the range of changes and the dynamics of the internal and external environments for logistics is almost mind-boggling.

One should not conclude that everything has completely changed in logistics. Some things have remained constant or very close to the way they were during the 1980s. Consequently, anyone familiar with earlier editions of this text will find some of the same topics which were presented and discussed in previous editions.

However, we have made a number of important changes in this new edition. There are new chapters and some significant changes in other chapters. The total number of chapters has been reduced from seventeen to fifteen. All of these changes were made in response to changes the authors feel reflect recent developments in logistics. Also, we received excellent input from colleagues at other universities (see list below). We have attempted to respond to their suggestions, but we ultimately had to make some judgments to put everything together in a coordinated manner.

There was consensus about the need for more emphasis on international logistics. In the previous edition, a chapter treating international logistics appeared later in the sequence of chapters. In this edition, the international chapter, retitled "Global Logistics," is significantly revised. We have also repositioned it as one of the early chapters to raise awareness of the international issues that the remaining chapters address.

Supply chain management and the logistics pipeline are concepts that have entered the logistics vocabulary in recent years. A revised and retitled chapter reflects the importance of this integrated topic. While this chapter replaces two chapters from the previous edition, we have incorporated the important material from those two previous chapters into the new chapter.

As one would expect, the chapters covering the topic of transportation have been changed again. The fifth edition has only two chapters devoted to transportation, but they are comprehensive and provide excellent insights into the management of transportation within the logistics function.

We have added a new chapter on the management of quality in logistics to reflect this area's overall importance in companies today. It also shows the role of logistics quality in improving the competitive effectiveness of companies. The chapters on Organization, Logistics Strategy, and Inventory have also received special attention in the new edition.

The authors are indebted to many individuals who have provided assistance and support in the new edition of the text. Our faculty colleagues at Penn State, the University of Toledo, and the University of Tennessee have made many suggestions for improvement. Special thanks are in order for Jean Beierlein, Janet Gochberg, Chris Norek, Mary Holcomb, David Menachof, Gregory Stock, Michael Tracey, Wendy Weisberg, and the thousands of students at Penn State, the University of Toledo, and the University of Tennessee.

A very special note of thanks and gratitude is given to our wives, Barbara, Carol, and Anne, who have provided the understanding, encouragement, and support necessary for us to complete this work, and to our children, John and Susan, Susan and Pamela, and Sarah and Mercer. With you, our lives and our work have meaning.

Special thanks to the following reviewers of the manuscript for their special input:

Janice P. Bowers
University of South Alabama

Edward R. Bruning
Kent State University

Clive Cannon
George Brown College

Barry Katz
Virginia Polytechnic Institute and State University

Ruth K. Krieger
Oklahoma State University

Richard Lancioni
Temple University

Marius M. Solomon
Northeastern University

David B. Vellenga
Arizona State University

Roy Dale Voorhees
Iowa State University

Walter L. Weart
William Rainey Harper College

Kenneth C. Williamson
James Madison University

This introductory section treats four major topics, namely, the framework of logistics, the logistics environment, supply chain management, and global logistics. The first topic exposes the reader to the basic nature of logistics in an organization. Logistics is defined, and the interest in the area is explained. In addition, the systems aspect of logistics analysis is discussed, and some basic techniques of systems analysis are explored.

The second topic looks at the various environments of logistics. Initially, logistics is examined from a macro perspective and its role in the economy is explored. Then logistics is viewed from a micro dimension with consideration given to the relationship of logistics to the distribution channel members and to other functional areas within the company, such as marketing and production.

The third topic examines logistics as a supply chain and enhances the reader's understanding of materials management, customer service and distribution channels. Finally, the fourth topic considers global logistics and the managerial issues facing logistics in today's global business environment.

This introductory section of four chapters should provide the reader with the background for an in-depth study of logistics functional areas and of the integrative decision-making areas.

LOGISTICS MANAGEMENT: AN OVERVIEW

In 1988, Softsel/MicroAmerica felt the need to make changes in order to develop a new competitive advantage. Until then, the microcomputer distributor had gained a marketplace advantage with its thorough understanding of the technology associated with hardware and software for microcomputer products. But it was evident by 1988 that customers no longer wanted technology guides as much, or, for that matter, no longer needed technology guides at all. Customers seemed more interested in cost, seamless service, quick response to orders, and fast product delivery.

changing marketplace

Softsel/MicroAmerica did what appears to be, for many companies, a trend for the 1990s. They streamlined their ordering, purchasing, and distribution chain through an integrated logistics system. Their sales increased by 30 percent, and they also experienced better inventory turnover. In other words, revenues increased and costs decreased.[1]

1990s trend

Softsel/MicroAmerica is not unique in this regard. In 1988, the top management at Alpo Pet Foods, Inc., was disappointed with the distribution system of the company. The firm had fourteen warehouses located throughout the United States with reasonable proximity to the customer base. However, a survey of 400 of their major customers indicated that Alpo's service was not up to par with that of their competitors. In some cases, their service ranked below that of their rivals.

Alpo

Subsequently, Alpo revamped its distribution operation and now promises delivery anywhere in the United States within five days. They achieved this improved customer service level, not feasible with their old system, and still trimmed their distribution costs.

five-day delivery

Alpo attributed their success to reorganizing their distribution and related activities into an integrated logistics function. Other companies, including Chrysler, Land-o-Lakes Foods, Bergen-Brunswick, Coors Beer Company, Cummins Engine Company, and Sara Lee Knit Products have also achieved the type of success Softsel/MicroAmerica and Alpo attained.[2] In fact, the list could be much longer if space permitted.

other examples

THE CASE FOR LOGISTICS

Let's use Alpo to demonstrate some of the basics of what this text will discuss. For Alpo, a subsidiary of Grand Metropolitan P. L. C. of Great Britain, achieving the cost savings and service improvements the competitive 1990s marketplace dictated meant consolidating and integrating logistics activities. For example, Alpo consolidated its network of fourteen warehouses into two large distribution centers: one in the east and another in the west. Alpo also eliminated a private truck fleet and negotiated for service and rates with contract carriers. They enhanced their computer system to provide more information for logistics and for billing and sales available instantaneously throughout the company. They

Alpo's revamped system

also appointed a logistics vice president responsible for materials flow and storage of products from vendors to customers. This necessitated boundary-spanning activities including purchasing, transportation, inventory, warehousing, and customer service.

3M

Pacific Rim

While not all companies organize their logistics activities in the same way, the general approach Alpo took can result in substantial savings and in customer service improvements. For example, the 3M Company linked its U.S. logistics operations with those of its international subsidiaries to prepare for changes in the 1992 European Economic Community and for rapid expansion into countries on the Pacific Rim. Managing its logistical functions overseas in conjunction with its domestic operations has saved 3M approximately $40–$50 million per year.[3] The company expects even more savings in the future. While not all companies can achieve this level of cost reduction or savings with logistics integration, savings can be substantial; and associated service improvements can help a company develop and sustain competitive advantage in the marketplace.

new or old

The discussion thus far suggests that the logistics area is of very recent origin. In some ways this is very true, but we can argue that the study of logistics activities is quite old. Movement/transportation and storage/warehousing have concerned business enterprises for a long time. One might argue that a rudimentary interest in transportation and storage goes back to the beginning of mankind. However, the systematic analysis of logistics activities management presented in this text did not receive much attention from business until well after World War II. In fact, a number of companies still have not devoted enough attention to logistics.

Part of the overview presented in this text will explain the relatively recent interest in logistics and, in contrast, the occasional lack of interest, even today. This lack of attention, however, does not diminish the potential of logistics for many companies in the competitive marketplace of the 1990s.

ORIGIN AND DEFINITION OF BUSINESS LOGISTICS

WWII origins

We can trace origins of business logistics, as it is known today, to developments occurring in military logistics during World War II. Logistical expertise and effort were doubtlessly key factors in the outcome of the war for the Allies. Logistics, particularly critical in the European theater, also played an important role in the Pacific. The United States' ability to move and store personnel and supplies efficiently contributed much to the success of the allied war effort.

Persian Gulf War

The Persian Gulf War of 1990-91 again demonstrated the importance of logistics to a successful military effort. Some have, in fact, called the military effort in the gulf area the "Logistics War." The efforts of General Gus Pagonis, in charge of the logistical effort for Operation Desert Shield, contributed heavily to the outstanding success the United States achieved during the war's short duration.

massive military logistics

system

From mail to toilet paper, General Pagonis was in charge of everything that moved in the gulf area. He organized food service for the troops, and the transportation of supplies with a distribution network of 100,000 trucks, 50,000 workers, and massive open-air "warehouses." This integrated logistics system was critical to the military effort's overall success. While the cost approached $1 billion per day, the military managed service levels and costs from an integrated logistics perspective to most efficiently achieve the gulf effort's established objectives.

visibility of logistics

In some companies, logistics accounts for twenty to twenty-five percent total business costs. One would think that an activity as important as logistics would be as well known as marketing, sales, finance, or accounting. Surprisingly, it is not. For one thing, logistics is a relatively new area for focused management attention. Another reason is that movement does not change an item's appearance; therefore, logistics does not appear to add value to the product. Like transportation, other logistics activities, such as protective packaging, materials handling, and warehousing, are not apparent to the casual observer or the typical consumer.[4] Yet, a piece of industrial equipment manufactured in Germany but destined for Chicago, Illinois, has little value until it is available to the buyer at the right place, at the right time, and in good condition.

adds value

The logistical requirements that ensure a product's unique combination of packing, materials handling, warehousing, inventory control, and transportation may often double the product's value from the time it is manufactured or grown until it is consumed or used in a further industrial process.[5]

Given the lack of familiarity with the logistics area, we might find it useful to compare several logistics definitions. However, before looking specifically at definitions, let us discuss terminology.

Terminology

The relative newness of logistics as an area of study has encouraged writers to generate numerous terms to describe the same activities discussed in this text. The list of terms includes, but is not limited to, the following:

Physical distribution
Marketing logistics
Materials management
Logistics engineering
Industrial logistics
Business logistics
Logistics management
Integrated logistics management
Supply management
Logistics pipeline management
Distribution management
Supply chain management

Discussing why each of these terms is used, who coined the term, or any subtle differences existing among them would not appear to serve any useful purpose. One company may prefer the term *physical distribution,* for example; another may use one of the other terms listed above. Some companies, such as Pillsbury, having recently reorganized their logistical activities, have used the materials management label for logistics at the corporate level.

preference for logistics

The authors of this text prefer *logistics,* whether the term is used as business logistics, logistics management, or integrated logistics management. One can logically view materials management and physical distribution as terms describing activity subsets within the logistics function. However, when these other terms occur in this text or elsewhere, the reader can usually view them as synonyms. Logistics seems the most popular term for the 1990s, as the National

Council of Physical Distribution Management (NCPDM) changing its name to the Council of Logistics Management (CLM) would indicate.

Definitions

A number of logistics definitions will help to provide an understanding of the area's nature and importance. We could utilize each definition, given the appropriate business situation.

Seven Rs   Sometimes called the layperson's description of logistics, the Seven Rs define logistics as "ensuring the availability of the *right* product, in the *right* quantity and the *right* condition, at the *right* place, at the *right* time, for the *right* customer, at the *right* cost."[6] (See On the Line.)

multiple dimensions

These Seven Rs imply the essential activities of logistics. These concepts, emphasizing the spatial and temporal dimension (place and time, or movement and storage), provide a basic underpinning of the logistics area referred to throughout this text. The Seven Rs also emphasize cost and service. Logistics managers must continually evaluate cost and service as they investigate changes for their logistics systems.

customer focus

Another aspect emerging from this definition is the importance of meeting customer requirements. The focus upon the customer is essential for logistics, since logistics plays an important role in customer satisfaction. An additional Seven Rs element is the notion of quality, the idea that a company has to perform its task right, the first time, or the task, in a competitive marketplace, is probably not worth doing. Increasingly, U.S. companies are recognizing that quality is important not only in manufacturing a product but in all of the company's areas, especially logistics.

Inventory Perspective   One can also define logistics as the effective management and control of inventory (raw materials, goods in process, and finished goods) in motion or at rest in some facility. This somewhat simplistic definition suggests that the essence of logistics is inventory, whether moving or still. Both movement and storage are important, but in either case one deals with inventory and its related cost and service potential. The ramifications of this seemingly simple definition provide many pages of discussion and analysis. The flow and storage of materials in the logistics pipeline from vendor to customer provides a key perspective of the nature of logistics.

importance of inventory

CLM Definition   The Council of Logistics Management (CLM), the largest and best known of the professional logistics organizations, provides the definition of business logistics discussed in this section. As indicated, CLM is a new label for an older organization called the National Council of Physical Distribution Management (NCPDM), and its logistics definition changed with the organization's title. The earlier definition was used in previous editions of this text. The new CLM definition is as follows:

> Logistics is the process of planning, implementing and controlling the efficient, effective flow and storage of raw materials, in-process inventory, finished goods, services, and related information from point of origin to point of consumption (including inbound, outbound, internal, and external movements) for the purpose of conforming to customer requirements.[7]

Pressure from the Retail Floor
Retailers demand—and get—what they want, when, where, and how they want it.

It takes a lot of mayonnaise to keep Stew Leonard's customers happy. Business guru Tom Peters has dubbed Stew Leonard's Norwalk, Connecticut, supermarket one of America's outstanding customer service purveyors. And fans of the store's crabmeat salad simply can't get enough of it.

But Leonard couldn't get enough of the new light mayonnaise he wanted, to lower the salad's fat and cholesterol content for his increasingly health-conscious customers.

Best Foods, manufacturer of Hellman's mayonnaise, didn't put its light version in the five-gallon plastic jugs Leonard's salad man needed.

No problem, said Best Foods, when Leonard complained. They would have the light mayonnaise product packaged and delivered the way Leonard wanted it within two weeks.

Increasingly, retailers of all kinds are exerting pressure on manufacturers to deliver what they want when, where and how they want.

In short, they are forcing manufacturers to re-think their entire sales, ordering, purchasing and distribution chain. One manufacturer doing just that is the knit products division of Sara Lee.

"Retailers are making stringent demands on manufacturers in many different areas," said Ken Jadoff, head of customer service and logistics.

"Customers such as K-Mart are telling us that the ability to supply them quickly and efficiently weighs just as heavily in their buying decision as does public acceptance of our brand name and our merchandise quality."

K-Mart uses scanner data to order apparel products on a weekly basis; they expect their supplier to ship merchandise within five days. While the supplier makes shipments to regional distribution centers, the distribution center must pack order mix for each individual store in cartons destined for that store.

Shipping labels must carry K-Mart's bar coding so that the merchandise receives minimum handling on its way to consumers.

Frequently, store merchandise never goes into the retailer's warehoused inventory. Instead, shipments timed to arrive at a loading dock are off-loaded, checked in electronically via hand-held computer terminals that input bar code data on the shipping label, and reloaded directly onto store-bound trucks.

Such cross-docking procedures and other quick-response methods obviously require close cooperation between manufacturer and retailer.

This definition indicates that materials (raw materials, as well as semifinished and finished goods) must be transported various distances between supply points, plants, storage areas (warehouses), and markets (customers), and that the company must arrange to hold these goods safely and in quantities sufficient to meet the organization's anticipated needs.

movement

If we dissect the description even further, we will find our interest focused on two interrelated basic activities: movement and storage. *Movement* requires the selection and use of a transportation mode or modes, based upon criteria to be discussed. The modern transportation system offers numerous for-hire carriers, each offering variety of services, as well as the option of private transportation. Selecting the best transportation alternatives is often a challenging task.

The second activity, *storage,* concerns the number, size, design, type, and location of storage areas or warehouses, as well as appropriate order sizes, reorder points, stocking locations, and other inventory matters. Transportation decisions will affect category. For example, a slower and less reliable form of transportation usually requires the carrying of more inventory. Also, the number and location of warehouses will affect shipment size and perhaps the transportation modes available.

storage

Figure 1–1, representing a typical logistics system, illustrates this business logistics definition and the flow from vendor to customer.

many activities

The CLM's current definition of logistics does not list specific logistics system activities. It does, however, imply a broad range of activities. We will discuss activities that may be considered part of logistics in a later section.

managerial nature

Another dimension of the CLM definition is the managerial nature of logistics: planning, implementing and controlling. The CLM definition emphasizes the paramount role of logistics in meeting customer requirements. As indicated previously, the marketplace of the 1990s requires close attention to customer service.

SOLE Definition   The three definitions offered thus far have been both comparable and compatible in many respects. Another group interested in logistics, the Society of Logistics Engineers (SOLE), offers the following definition:

> The area of support management used throughout the life of the product or system to efficiently utilize resources assuring the adequate consideration of logistics elements during all phases of the life cycle so that timely influence on the system assures an effective approach to resource expenditures.

FIGURE 1–1   TYPICAL LOGISTICS NETWORK

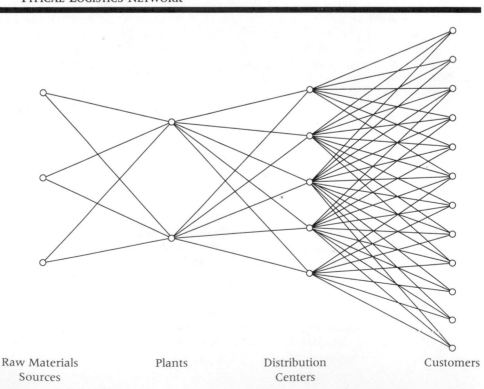

| Raw Materials Sources | Plants | Distribution Centers | Customers |

CLM versus SOLE definition

When we initially compare the CLM definition with the SOLE definition of logistical activities, little similarity appears. However, the definitions reflect a focus different as far as products. The SOLE group has been primarily interested in industrial or durable consumer products with relatively long usable lives: a generator for a power plant, for example. These products, which frequently have long lead times, require replacement parts to be available throughout their usable lives. The logistics manager's involvement in the design of such a product is very important since replacement parts and product service are critical to the product's customer service aspects. Also, SOLE definition emphasizes the inbound or materials management part of the logistics system.

life cycle

The term *integrated logistics support* (ILS), borrowed from the military, is frequently associated with the SOLE group. The military first used the life cycle definition. Figure 1–2, which illustrates the life cycle approach, provides a good contrast for the business logistics perspective, to be discussed later. Companies increasingly recognize the importance of the long-run comprehensive role of logistics SOLE defines, particularly the logistics system's inbound side.

Definition of Logistics in a Service Environment[9]

The traditional goods-related definition of logistics does not reflect the distinctive characteristics of service-producing industries. Recognizing that all companies produce both goods and services (to greater or lesser degrees), the following two-part definition of logistics reflects the major types of logistics activities that exist in all firms:

Supply Chain Logistics is the traditional process associated with the acquisition and distribution of goods.

Supply chain logistics is a major organizational element in the production and distribution of goods. It includes the functions of purchasing, transportation, inventory control, materials handling, manufacturing, distribution, and related systems. While the names may vary from company to company (e.g., procurement, supply, logistics, materials management, physical distribution), its primary focus is the physical flows and storage of materials and the system flows of related information. For many goods-producing industries, it is the largest single expenditure in the cost of goods sold and is a major critical success factor impacting profitability and competitive advantage.

Supply chain logistics also exists in service-producing industries. While important, it has a secondary role to the management, scheduling, and staffing of the network's capacity to service.

Service Response Logistics is the process of coordinating non-material activities necessary to the fulfillment of the service in a cost and customer service effective way.

Service response logistics often is at the heart of operations of service-providing organizations. It greatly impacts the network's capacity to serve. A critical element of service response logistics is the provision of inputs at the point of service delivery (e.g., ATM, desk clerk, or phone). It encompasses activities to anticipate needs, schedule the network capacity to serve, and provide for the fulfillment channels to meet customer needs. The role of service response logistics is to optimize the service providing infrastructure to coordinate and fulfill customer's needs. Generally, it is a major critical success factor for service-producing industries.

FIGURE 1-2   LOGISTICS SUPPORT IN THE SYSTEM LIFE CYCLE   SOURCE: *Ben Blanchard, "Graduate Logistics Education Requirements,"* **Spectrum** *(Winter 1981), 10.*

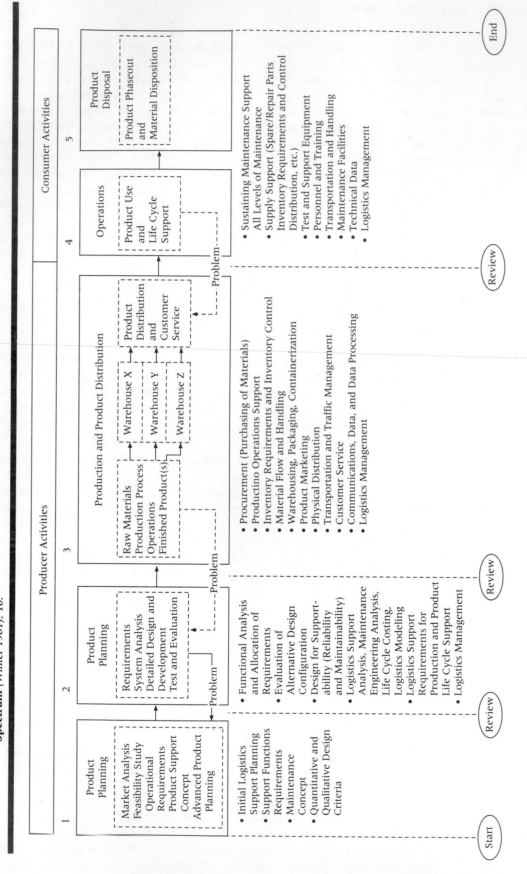

Service response logistics also exists in goods-producing industries, but is a relatively minor function with limited impact on profitability and competitive advantage.

The above definitions can be interpreted by looking at service response logistics activities which correspond to well known supply chain activities (Table 1.1). Viewing service response logistics from the traditional supply chain perspective does not give the whole story, however, since some service response activities are greatly expanded from their supply chain counterpart. Order processing and service delivery monitoring in a service-producing environment is often much more complex. When a customer applies for a bank loan, there is considerable interaction between the loan officer and the customer regarding the type of loan, timing, documentation, third parties, etc.

The Fulfillment Cycle

Both goods- and service-producing firms must perform the same basic fulfillment functions in running their business:

- Create or identify need
- Forecast and plan response
- Build capacity and/or inventory
- Accept orders and authorize for fulfillment
- Commit capacity and/or inventory to fulfill order
- Use network optimally to respond to order.

TABLE 1–1   SERVICE RESPONSE LOGISTICS FUNCTIONS

Supply chain activity	Service response activity
Sales forecasting	Services forecasting
Sourcing/purchasing	Partnership development, staff hiring, data acquisition
Production planning	Staff and equipment scheduling, distribution channel selection, capacity planning
Inbound transportation	Data collection
Inventory management	Capacity management, database management, customer record management, personnel training
Warehousing	Data/information storage, retrieval and management
Customer service	Quality measurement and management, expediting, billing
Order processing	Interfacing, assessing need, negotiating, and committing to the customer, monitoring delivery process
Distribution systems	Network layout, network planning, systems planning, channel planning
Field warehousing	Data/information storage, retrieval and control
Distribution control	Network control, communications control
Intra-company transportation	Personnel/customer movement, data/information movement transportation
Distribution administration	Network administration
Outbound transportation	Customer reporting, service engineering routing and scheduling to customer transportation sites

Source: J. J. Barry et al., *Logistics in the Services Industries* (Oakbrook, Illinois: Council of Logistics Management, 1991), 12.

Overview of Definitions

Successful logistics management in an organization requires the careful coordination of both movement and storage. It also requires knowledge of and interest in related areas such as materials handling and industrial packaging. These two areas between storage and movement deserve special attention. For example, packaging size and type affects the use of transportation equipment (stacking and use of cubic space) and warehouse space as well as the transfer between transport equipment and the warehouse.

The authors have adopted the CLM definition of logistics as the formal definition for this text. The definition indicates that a firm could include other areas, carefully coordinated to achieve overall logistics efficiency. While we will discuss those activities in detail subsequently, we will now examine the development of business logistics.

CHANGING ENVIRONMENT AND DEVELOPMENT OF LOGISTICS

Setting the Stage: 1940–1960

Top management interest in logistics has been a relatively recent phenomenon. In a classic article discussing the development of logistics, Donald J. Bowersox indicates that logistics was born of a reaction to several marketing-caused problems during the 1950s and early 1960s. However, few companies had the organizational structure to make potential trade-offs to lower costs and/or improve service.[10]

Peter Drucker

In the early 1960s, Peter Drucker, familiar to many as an author and management consultant, identified the organizational structure problem and helped companies to focus on the challenges and opportunities available in the field of logistics and distribution. In 1962, he wrote:

> We know little more today about distribution than Napoleon's contemporaries knew about the interior of Africa. We know it is there, and we know it is big, and that's about all.[11]

In the same article, Drucker argued that logistics was a last frontier for top management seeking corporate efficiency. He indicated that an examination of businesses from the beginning of the twentieth century revealed a series of evolutionary steps. Essentially, this evolution founded the development of lo-

logistics evolution

gistical organizations in companies after World War II. U.S. companies initially focused on production, then on finance, and then on marketing. What remained was a need to solve distribution or logistics problems. That is where Drucker depicted the U.S. situation in the early 1960s.

One additional factor encouraged progress in this area: the expertise in military logistics developed during World War II. The ability to deploy personnel

World War II

and material was important to Allied success in the European theater and in the Far East. If necessary, civilian industry could employ such techniques and technology. Developments in the post-World War II economy of the United States created the need.

In addition to World War II, other factors encouraged interest in the development of logistics. Part of the post-World War II environment, these factors helped set the stage for logistics development.

Product Line Expansion

Henry Ford

During the early stages of U.S. development, products were largely functional and relatively simple. Often produced in one size and one color, they were essentially identical. For example, Henry Ford based his significant automotive industry developments upon the modern concept of a production/assembly line and its related cost efficiencies. Henry Ford's Model T was black; all Model Ts looked basically the same. This was also true when Ford developed the Model A. In terms of variety, the automotive industry has certainly come a long way. This is also true of other industries. As companies became increasingly sophisticated in marketing, they recognized the competitive importance of fulfilling the needs of various market segments. Variations in color, packaging, size, and other features satisfied customer demand and enhanced sales. Variations in grade, color, and size have become very important in the market-place; these variations have spread to other sectors, including industrial goods.

increased inventory and transportation costs

Development in product line characteristics meant that manufacturers and distribution channels had to make and hold a larger variety of items which were often basically similar. This practice resulted in a lower volume per stock keeping unit, since each variation in size, color, or other characteristics required separate identification for inventory purposes. Overall, this necessitates more inventory since manufacturers are uncertain about customer preference. Larger variety also frequently results in smaller shipment size and in more frequent shipments to locations convenient for customers. Overall inventory growth and smaller shipment size significantly increased the cost to companies. These rising costs necessitated attention to logistics.

rate increases

In addition to the increasing transportation and inventory costs associated with product line expansion, transportation rates increased generally after World War II. The principle regulatory agency, the Interstate Commerce Commission, approved a series of higher rail industry rate levels which spread to other transportation sectors.

Supreme Court decisions

Another factor helped turn attention to logistics. In a series of decisions, the Supreme Court banned certain uniform delivered pricing systems in basic industries such as steel and cement. Usually aimed at price control, delivered pricing systems result in identical delivered prices among sellers at various destinations. Under this system, buyers located close to origin points often paid a premium amount for transportation; in other words, they subsidized movement to customers farther away. The limitations placed on uniform delivered pricing systems had two results. In some instances, the purchaser of basic material such as steel controlled inbound transportation costs, providing additional trade-off and coordination possibilities for a logistics manager. Also, "landed costs" increased for long-distance customers no longer subsidized by the pricing system.

overview

As suggested earlier, this particular era set the stage for logistics development. World War II, natural evolution in U.S. industrial development and factors that increased logistics-related costs in U.S. companies led to increased attention to logistics. Usually the attention emphasized controlling costs in transportation and in areas such as warehousing.

Conceptualization and Creditability: 1960–1970

In the previous stage of logistics development, many factors increased logistics awareness; but the concept of logistics needed a theoretical basis. First, total cost analysis studies analyzed "landed costs" and demonstrated that companies

total cost analysis

could reduce total cost, in some instances, by spending more money on transportation, thereby reducing costs in inventory and warehousing. In essence, a trade-off perspective developed. A company willingly spend more money in one area as long as reductions in other areas resulted in lower total costs. In-depth case studies of selected companies demonstrated the validity of the total cost concept in logistics.

Total cost analysis was an outgrowth of systems analysis or the systems concept. The latter analyzed complex relationships, examining interactions and interrelationships in order to understand the impact of selected changes on the total system. Total cost analysis was an extension of this process.

Another factor in logistics development was an increasing interest in customer service, an interest initially associated with oligopolistic market structures. A few large companies began to dominate U.S. markets during this era. In an oligopolistic setting, companies are reluctant to rely upon price competition to gain market share if several larger companies can match the price decreases. When prices are reduced, the net result is typically less sales revenue for the same unit volume of sales. Improving customer service was a more subtle form of competition. Companies increasingly realized that they could pass savings on to customers through better customer service, an activity as effective as a price cut and more difficult for competitors to discern and emulate. For example, shorter order cycle times enabled buyers to lower their average inventory, which lowered their costs.

oligopolistic markets

cost measurement

More effective cost measurement for trade-off analysis, particularly in the inventory area, also helped. We will discuss inventory costs in a later chapter. Previously, many companies considered logistics costs as part of overhead; therefore, the true cost was difficult to determine for trade-off purposes. Companies frequently lumped outbound logistics costs together under the label of distribution overhead.

shifting responsibility for inventory

A related factor was the shifting responsibility for inventory. Until now, U.S. manufacturers commonly pushed as much inventory as possible into the distribution pipeline. In other words, wholesalers, retailers, and other middlemen carried a lot of inventory while manufacturers attempted to reduce their own levels. During this era, distribution channels, recognizing the true costs of carrying inventory, attempted to save themselves some expense by pushing inventory back to the manufacturer. This practice became much more prevalent in the 1980s.

computers and models

The final factor in the era of conceptualization and creditability was the tremendous development in computer hardware. Also, quantitative techniques or models, such as those used for inventory control and location, developed, enabling companies to more realistically analyze their logistics systems. With computers and quantitative models, the emerging logistics field instituted more effective management practices to control logistics-related costs and to measure trade-offs. This second stage established a theoretical base giving logistics more creditability.

Era of Changing Priorities and Patterns: 1970–1980

The decade of the 1970s was very important in the continuing development of logistics. Several factors turned attention to logistics. One was the energy crisis of the early 1970s, associated with the Middle East oil cartel. This cartel, able to control supply, increased the prices of oil and gasoline. In early stages of the energy crisis, price increases significantly shortened gasoline supplies, disrupting logistics the United States and increasing transportation prices. Prior to this time, the United States, acting as if gasoline supplies were endless, had put little effort toward the inbound side of logistics systems to manage energy and supplies.

In addition to the oil crisis, shortages developed in basic raw materials also assumed to be readily available. The United States was increasingly importing these materials, such as iron ore, from countries whose political instability or other problems could cause temporary or long-term supply interruptions.

recession

Also during this era, a serious recession caused companies to increase attention to logistics in order to increase sales in selected market areas and to reduce costs. The inbound side of the logistics system, largely neglected during the previous two eras, received attention from many manufacturers because of potentially serious savings this area offered and because of the material shortages mentioned above.

interest rates

Increasing interest rates, which made controlling inventory levels very important, also compounded difficulties for many companies. As we will discuss in detail in a later chapter, a major component of inventory carrying costs is the cost of capital associated with the inventory. The interest rate level correlates quite closely with the cost companies assign to capital. In the 1970s, interest rates escalated above twenty percent, levels almost unheard of in the United States. This high interest cost made inventory reduction mandatory. Interest rates also helped to determine whether companies would invest in logistics-related assets such as warehouses or trucks for a private fleet. Companies explored alternatives such as public warehousing and relied more on contract trucking.

international competition

Another factor important to logistics development during this era was the tremendous growth in international competition for finished goods. Until now U.S. companies dominated sales to U.S. consumers. International competition had developed during the 1960s in some basic industries such as steel, but now international companies increasingly competed for the sales market in finished products such as automobiles, televisions, stereo equipment, and clothing. Such competition caused U.S. companies to seek cost control and sales enhancement in logistics.

demographic trends

A factor different from those previously discussed was the shift in population U.S. trends. Companies realized that knowledge of population trends was important for market competition and for maintaining labor supplies. The United States population was shifting from the Northeast and the Midwest to the Southeast, the Southwest, and the Far West. Needing to rearrange transportation and warehousing, companies adjusted logistics systems and other related areas.

New Era of Economic and Technical Change: 1980 to the Present

The previous three eras brought changes, adjustments, and, of course, recognition of the importance of logistics. These eras, however, pale by comparison to the 1980s in terms of change and development for logistics. Four extremely important factors influenced logistics organizations during the 1980s: (1) the globalization of business; (2) the changing government infrastructure; (3) structural changes in business; and (4) rapidly changing technology.[12]

The internationalization of globalization of business had a tremendous impact on the way companies operate. In companies, this globalization runs the gamut from foreign sourcing in procurement or selective sales in international markets,

internationalization

to multifaceted international manufacturing and marketing strategies encompassing international production sites, inventory multi staging, and countertrading product sales. Wherever companies operate along this scale, the logistics cost as a percentage of total costs is usually greater for international ventures; and logistics operations usually become increasingly complex in the international area. As we will discuss in transportation for example, international movement of freight is much more complicated in terms of documentation, scheduling, and standardization. As companies increasingly "go global" on both their inbound and outbound sides, logistics receives additional attention. Companies are integrating the international and domestic markets and viewing suppliers and vendors from a global perspective.

deregulation

Another major happening during the 1980s was deregulation transportation, part of the changing government infrastructure. Deregulation spurred a virtual revolution in the U.S. transportation system, resulting in many fundamental changes, some positive and some negative. Overall, it is probably safe to say that, with few exceptions the cost and quality of transportation services have improved for shippers. The deregulation started in 1977 with the deregulation of air freight and proceeded, in 1978, with the deregulation of air passenger movements.

rail and motion

In 1980, two major federal acts additionally deregulated transportation. One, the Stagger's Act, related to railroad deregulation; the other concerned motor carriers deregulation. In all instances, economic regulation was drastically reduced. In other words, transportation companies became much more like other businesses, adjusting their prices more quickly in response to the marketplace and adjusting their service in terms of markets in which they wanted to operate.

nature of regulation

Prior to this time, a very complex bureaucratic regulatory agency system required elaborate hearings to make relatively simple changes in transportation price and service. We will discuss this topic in much more detail in a later chapter. Let us say here that deregulation in the U.S. transportation system caused major changes for carriers and shippers. The reader should note, however, that regulation was not completely eliminated and that it actually increased in noneconomic areas such as safety.

banking and communications

In addition, banking and communications were also deregulated. Of the two, communications deregulation has had the most significant impact on logistics: the great emphasis on electronic data interchange and nationwide communication links will probably reverberate throughout the 1990s. In addition, we should note the deregulation of motor carrier transportation in Canada and the changes in the european economic community, which resulted in more open market structures in 1992.

organizational changes

A third factor in logistics development continuing from the 1980s has been the restructuring of business organizations through mergers, acquisitions, leveraged buyouts (LBO), employee stock ownership plans (ESOP), and spinoffs. U.S. organizations, in general became much leaner during the 1980s, a trend continuing into the 1990s. This organizational flattening has impacted in the logistics area. In some instances, firms have consolidated logistics functions to streamline the merged organizations through efficiency and reduced costs. Mergers have also led companies to seek logistics-related supplies and services from outside sources. In some mergers, however, two or more separate logistics organizations continue to operate because of company differences.

A fourth factor is rapidly changing technology, particularly in computer hardware and software. First of all, amazing price reductions in hardware allow *technology* companies to provide more powerful and smaller equipment throughout the organization, that is to decentralize computers. Managers commonly have personal desk top computers which are usually more powerful than mainframes ten years ago. In addition to inexpensive, powerful hardware, logistics-related software is available in a much greater variety than ever before. The Council of Logistics Management publishes a yearly software guide. The present size of that guide, compared to earlier years, is tremendous. The user friendly nature of much of the software enhances this variety. In addition, standard software packages such as spreadsheets have enhanced the logistics manager's ability, leading to better inventory control, improved equipment scheduling, more efficient rating of transportation movement, and better analysis of location decisions with respect to inventory and facilities. Another area to affect logistics, the interface between computers and communication technology will continue to affect the future.

All in all, the eighties were a decade of major change for logistics. In many instances, companies advanced logistics organizations and established logistics vice presidents. In the nineties level three logistics organizations are increasingly evident in many U.S. companies; another author has called them "leading edge logistics organizations."[13] We will discuss these developments at some length in a later chapter. Suffice it for now to say that the dramatic change during the eighties continues during the nineties.

LOGISTICAL ACTIVITIES

The logistics definition the Council of Logistics Management provides implies activities for which the logistics manager may be responsible.

- Traffic and transportation
- Warehousing and storage
- Industrial packaging

FIGURE 1–3   THE LOGISTICS EVOLUTION

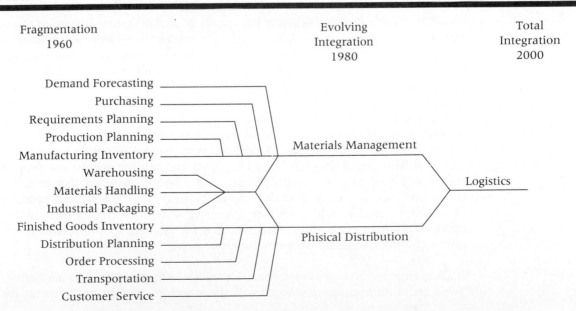

| Fragmentation 1960 | Evolving Integration 1980 | Total Integration 2000 |

Demand Forecasting
Purchasing
Requirements Planning
Production Planning
Manufacturing Inventory
Warehousing
Materials Handling
Industrial Packaging
Finished Goods Inventory
Distribution Planning
Order Processing
Transportation
Customer Service

Materials Management

Phisical Distribution

Logistics

- Materials handling
- Inventory control
- Order processing
- Customer service levels
- Demand forecasting
- Procurement
- Distribution communications
- Plant and warehouse site location
- Return goods handling
- Parts and service support
- Salvage and scrap disposal

This activities list is quite comprehensive; some companies with well-organized logistics areas may not place responsibility for all of these activities within the logistics area. For example, companies having physical distribution focus would not include procurement in their logistics organization.

Scope of Activities

The section discussing the development of interest in logistics indicated the growth in activities associated with logistics. Given the scope of this growth, we will find it worthwhile to discuss several of these activities and their relationship to logistics.

Transportation   Transportation is a necessary part of the logistics system. A major focus in logistics is upon the physical movement or flow of goods, or upon the network that moves the product. This network is composed of transportation agencies that provide the service for the firm. The logistics area is usually responsible for selecting the mode or modes of transportation used in moving the firms raw materials and finished goods or for developing private transportation as an alternative.

Storage   A second area, which has a trade-off relationship with transportation, is storage. It involves two separate but closely related activities: inventory management and warehousing. A direct relationship exists between the transportation agency used and the level of inventory and number of warehouses required. For example, if firms use a relatively slow means of transport, they usually have to keep higher inventory levels and usually have more warehousing space for this inventory. They may examine the possibility of using faster transport to eliminate some of these warehouses and the inventory stored therein. As suggested previously, several firms have reduced their total logistics cost by spending more on transportation and reducing costs in inventory and warehousing.

transportation trade-off

We will further discuss the inventory area and interest within the firm in succeeding chapters. At this point, note that internal organizational conflicts may arise over inventory level that should be held and the level and location of inventory stocks. Also note that a very close relationship exists between transportation and inventory levels and that the systems approach usually requires close coordination between these two areas.

Packaging   A third area of interest to logistics is industrial (exterior) packaging. The type of transportation selected will affect both packaging requirements for

modal impact

moving the product to the market and for the raw materials involved. In regard to the product, rail or water transportation will usually require additional packaging expenditures because of the greater possibility of damage. In analyzing trade-offs for proposed changes in transportation agencies, logistics personnel generally look for how the change influence packaging costs. In many instances, changing to a premium transport means, such as air, will reduce packaging costs. Therefore, we can argue that packaging should be responsibility of logistics because of this relationship to the transportation agency and to storage costs.

Materials Handling   A fourth area that should be considered a logistics activity is materials handling, which is also of interest to other areas in the typical manufacturing organization. It should be readily apparent that materials han-

efficiency

dling is important to the efficient warehouse operation. Logistics managers are concerned with the movement of goods into a warehouse, the placement of goods in a warehouse, and the movement of goods from storage to order picking areas and eventually to dock areas for transportation out of the warehouse. Materials handling affects such activities.

Materials handling is usually concerned with mechanical equipment for short-distance movement; such equipment includes conveyors, forklift trucks, overhead cranes, and containers. Production managers may want a particular pallet or container type which is compatible with logistics warehousing activities. Therefore, the materials handling designs must be coordinated in order to ensure congruity between the types of equipment used. In addition, the company may find it economical to use the same type of forklift trucks in the plants and in the warehouses.

Order Processing   Another activity area that logistics may control is order processing, which generally consists of activities involved with filling customer

time perspective

orders. Initially, one might question why the logistics area would concern itself directly with order processing. However, one important physical distribution factor is the time elasping from the moment a customer decides to place an order for a product to the time that those goods are actually delivered in a satisfactory condition.

The initial stage of order processing concerns some form of customer transmittal, firm's reception of the order, some designation that the order is to be shipped out, the selection and preparation of the order, and the order's actual transportation. The time lapse between communications and processing can be quite significant. Previous sections discussed trade-offs between transportation agencies and inventory and recognized the oligopolistic market structure's growing emphasis on good customer service. Consequently, a company may be forced to use a premium means of transportation, such as motor carrier or air, to meet service requirements. When order processing is a part of logistics, possible order processing improvements requiring additional expenditures could decrease transportation costs.

For example, assume that the present system takes a total lead time of eight days for transmittal, processing, order preparation, and shipping. Order processing may take four days, and order preparation may take an additional two days, which means that the goods have to be transported to the customer in two days. The short delivery time may require premium means of transportation. If order processing is considered part of the logistics system, then the company might examine order processing improvements, such as using telephone calls and more computer equipment for processing, to reduce order processing time to two days or less. This would allow the firm to use much cheaper transportation and still get the goods to the customer within eight days. Looking from a time perspective or in terms of total lead time, we can see that order processing is quite important to the logistics function.

inventory accuracy

Forecasting   Another activity that can be assigned to the logistics area is inventory forecasting. We could also question why forecasting would concern the logistics manager. Sales forecasting is based upon market knowledge as well as upon the manipulation of data with statistical techniques. Sales forecasting is frequently used with marketing logistics to facilitate deliveries to various market areas. However, logistics managers making forecasts for inventory purposes may use sales forecasts as input.

Accurate forecasting of inventory requirements and materials and parts is essential to effective inventory control. This is particularly true in companies using just-in-time (JIT) or materials requirements planning (MRP) to control inventory. Logistics personnel should develop their own forecasts in those situations to ensure accuracy and effective control. Too frequently, forecasts developed by marketing staff reflect sales objectives rather than inventory requirements.

Production Planning   Another area of growing interest for logistics managers is production planning, which is closely related to forecasting in terms of effective inventory control. Once a forecast is developed and the current inventory on hand and usage rate are assessed, production managers can determine the number of units necessary to ensure adequate market coverage. However, in multiple-product firms, production process timing and certain product line relationships require close coordination with logistics or actual control of production planning by logistics. The integration of production planning into logistics is becoming increasingly common in large corporations.

Purchasing   Purchasing, or procurement, is another activity that we can include in logistics. The basic rationale for including purchasing in logistics is that transportation cost relates directly to the geographic location (distance) of raw materials and component parts purchased for a company's production needs. In terms of transportation and inventory costs, the quantities purchased would also affect logistics cost. Including purchasing within the logistics area is primarily a matter of whether this more effectively coordinates and lowers costs for the firm. As noted previously, growing number of companies added purchasing to the logistics function during the seventies and eighties. These companies focused increasingly on the inbound side of logistics systems.

Customer Service   Another area of growing importance is customer service. Customer service is a complex topic, and one that concerns other functional company areas. Customer service levels in many ways glue together other logistics areas. Decisions about inventory, transportation, and warehousing relate to customer service requirements. While customarily the logistics area does not completely control customer service decisions, logistics plays an extremely important role in ensuring that the customer gets the right product at the right place and time. Logistics decisions about product availability in inventory lead time are critical to customer service.

Site Location Another area increasingly important to logistics is plant and warehouse site location. We will discuss this activity at some length in a later chapter. At this point, its logistics importance should be apparent. A location change could alter time and place relationships between plants and markets or between supply points and plants. Such changes will affect transportation rates and service, customer service, inventory requirements, and possibly other areas. Therefore, the logistics manager is quite concerned about location decisions. In fact, plant location, as discussed in a subsequent chapter, is frequently as important as warehouse location. Transportation cost is frequently a very important factor in deciding location.

Other Activities Other areas may be considered a part of logistics. Areas such as parts and service support, return goods handling, and salvage and scrap disposal indicate the reality of logistical activities managed in companies producing consumer durables or industrial products. Here, a very integrative approach is necessary. Logistics offers input into product design as well as into maintenance and supply services, since transportation and storage decisions affect these areas. The definitions of logistics engineering and materials management implied the importance of such activities to systematic logistics management in such companies.

APPROACHES TO ANALYZING LOGISTICS SYSTEMS

The analysis and control of logistics activities requires grouping or classifying such activities in several different ways. The introductory section noted the different terms or labels used in the logistics and distribution area. One such term, physical distribution, most appropriately associated with the movement and storage of finished goods, is of interest to the marketing area. In fact, a term often used synonymously with physical distribution is *outbound logistics*. Physical distribution, therefore, concerns the movement and storage of finished goods from the end of the production line to the customer.[14] (See Figure 1–4.)

The CLM definition of logistics indicated, however, an interest in the movement and storage of raw materials and semifinished goods, which suggests a broader view. In other words, this definition also includes an interest in the activities surrounding movement and storage up to the manufacturing point. Some authors have referred to this area as *physical supply*.[15] Another term frequently used synonymously is *materials management*. This inbound facet of logistics is of special interest to the production or manufacturing area in the firm.

Materials Management versus Physical Distribution

The classification of logistics into materials management and physical distribution is very useful to logistics management or control in an organization. Frequently, in the movement and storage of raw materials and finished products in a firm is very different. For example, a steel company may move required raw materials of iron ore and coal by barge and large rail carload. Storage may require nothing more elaborate than land where these items can be dumped and piled for future use. On the other hand, the finished steel will very often be moved by motor carrier; and the storage will require both an enclosed facility for protection against the elements and, perhaps, elaborate materials handling equipment.

FIGURE 1–4   A VIEW OF BUSINESS LOGISTICS IN A COMPANY

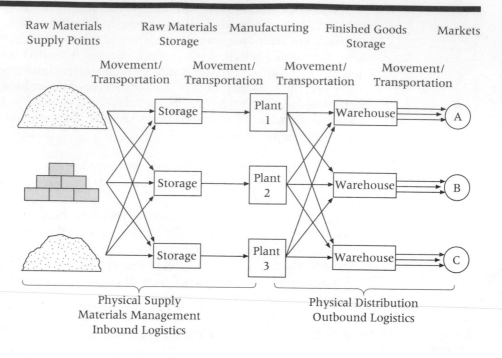

cost differences   The different logistics requirements that may exist between materials management and physical distribution may have important implications for the design of an organization's logistics system. Great differences may result in different logistics system designs for materials management and physical distribution. Companies may find it convenient to view their logistics system from these two perspectives, and somewhat different management approaches for each may result. Note, that in spite of such differences, close coordination between materials management and physical distribution is still necessary.

Additional perspectives related to viewing logistics in terms of materials management/inbound logistics and physical distribution/outbound logistics deserve consideration. In fact, from the inbound and outbound requirements perspective, we may classify companies into five different types of logistics systems.

Balanced System   Some companies have a reasonably balanced flow on the inbound and outbound sides of their logistics systems. In other words, they receive supplies from various vendors in different locations and ship to various customers in different locations. Consumer product companies such as General Foods, Pillsbury, and General Mills typically fit this description. While these companies may emphasize the physical distribution or outbound side because of the importance of customer service, both inbound and outbound logistics are important.

Heavy Inbound   Some companies have a very heavy inbound flow and a very simple outbound flow. Aircraft companies such as Boeing and McDonnell-Douglas are good examples. They use thousands of parts manufactured by hundreds of vendors to assemble and produce a finished airplane. Once the airplane is finished and tested, the company simply flies it to the customer (Delta Airlines for example), who ordered it two or three years before delivery. The process requires no warehousing, special transportation arrangements, or packaging. In contrast, the inbound side requires detailed scheduling, coordination, and planning ensure that parts arrive in time. Varying lead times for parts from vendors present a complex logistics challenge. Auto manufacturers, using twelve thousand to thirteen thousand parts per car, also fit this model. Their outbound systems while more complex than an aircraft company's are not nearly as complex as their inbound systems.

Heavy Outbound   Chemical companies like Dow offer good examples of this logistics system. Inbound crude oil by-products, salt water, and other raw materials flow from a limited number of sources and move in volume over often relatively short distances. On the outbound side, a wide variety of industrial and consumer products need storage, packaging, and transportation to the final customer. Therefore, in a company with heavy outbound, the physical distribution side of logistics system is more complex.

Out-and-Back Outbound Systems   Some companies have out-and-back systems on their logistics systems outbound side. This is true of companies producing durable products that the customer may return for trade-in, for repairs, or for salvage and disposal. Companies that produce computers, telephone equipment, and copy machines have these characteristics. Companies that deal with returnable containers also fit this model. Bringing back the original container presents some special challenges for the logistics manager.

Cost Centers

We previously mentioned the management activities many firms include in the logistics area, namely, transportation, warehousing, inventory, materials handling, and industrial packaging. We also emphasized the necessity to consider these activities highly interrelated. Examining these activities as cost centers, one can analyze possible trade-offs between and among them that could result in lower overall cost and or better service.

trade-offs   The breakdown of logistics into various cost centers or activity centers represents a second approach to the logistics system. Firms, frequently analyzed logistics on the activity center basis since reducing total logistics costs and/or improving service most frequently will occur by trading off one activity center against another. For example, shifting from rail to motor carrier may result, because of faster and more reliable service, in lower inventory costs, which will offset the higher motor carrier rate. (See Table 1–1.) Another possibility might be increasing the number of warehouses, thereby raising warehousing and inventory costs but possibly reducing the cost of transportation and lost sales enough to lower total costs. (See Table 1–2.)

The activity or cost center perspective is very useful in reviewing various trade-offs for lower cost and/or improved service to the customer or plants. However, as Table 1–2 indicates, every change does not result in lower total costs.

TABLE 1–2   ANALYSIS OF TOTAL LOGISTICS COST WITH CHANGE TO
HIGHER-COST MODE OF TRANSPORT

Cost Centers*	Rail	Motor
Transportation	$ 3.00	$ 4.20
Inventory	5.00	3.75
Packaging	4.50	3.20
Warehousing	1.50	.75
Cost of Lost Sales (1)	2.00	1.00
Total Cost	$15.00*	$13.00*

* Costs Per Unit

Nodes versus Links

A third approach to the logistics system in an organization is in terms of nodes
and links.* (See Figure 1–5.) The nodes are established spatial points where
goods stop for storage or processing. In other words, the nodes are plants and
warehouses where the organization stores materials for conversion into finished
products or goods in finished form for sale to customers (equalization of supply
and demand).

The other part of the system is the links, which represent the transportation
network connecting the nodes in the logistics system. The network can be
composed of individual modes of transportation (rail, motor, air, water, pipelines) and of combinations and variations that we will discuss later.

From a node-link perspective, the complexity of logistics systems can vary
enormously. One-node systems may use a simple link between suppliers and
combined plant and warehouse to customers in one relatively small market area.
At the other end of the spectrum are large, multiple-product firms with multiple
plant and warehouse locations. The complex transportation networks of the
latter may include three or four different modes and perhaps private as well as
for-hire transportation.

The node and link perspective in allowing analysis of a logistics system's two
basic elements, represents a convenient basis for seeking possible system improvements. As we have noted a logistics system complexity often direct relates
to the various time and distance relationships between the nodes and the links
and the regularity, predictability, and volume of flow of goods entering, leaving,
and moving within the system.

Logistics Channel

A fourth logistics approach is an analysis of the logistics channel, the network
of intermediaries engaged in transfer, storage, handling, communication, and
other functions that contribute to the efficient flow of goods.[16] We can view the
logistics channel as part of the total distribution channel, which includes, in
addition to the logistical flow, a transaction flow of specific interest to the
marketing specialist.[17]

*Some authors refer to this breakdown as a fixed points and transportation network. See, for example,
J. L. Heskett, Robert M. Ivie, and Nicholas A. Glaskowsky, Jr. *Business Logistics: Management of
Physical Supply and Distribution* (New York: Ronald Press, 1973), 43.

FIGURE 1–5   NODES AND LINKS IN A LOGISTICS SYSTEM

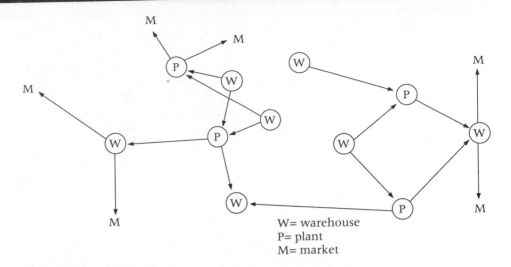

W= warehouse
P= plant
M= market

The logistics channel can be simple or complex. Figure 1–6 shows a simple channel in which an individual producer deals directly with a final customer. The control in this channel is relatively simple. The individual manufacturer controls the logistical flows since he or she deals directly with the customer.

Figure 1–7 presents a more complex, multiechelon channel, with a market warehouse and retailers. The market warehouse could be a public warehouse. In this instance, the control is more difficult because of the additional storage and transportation.

Figure 1–8, illustrates a complex, comprehensive channel. In this instance, achieving an effective logistical flow in the channel is far more formidable. This figure very realistically portrays the situation confronting many large organizations operating in the United States.

Some instances involving production of a basic good like steel, aluminum, or chemicals may further complicate the situation because companies may be

FIGURE 1–6   SIMPLE LOGISTICS CHANNEL

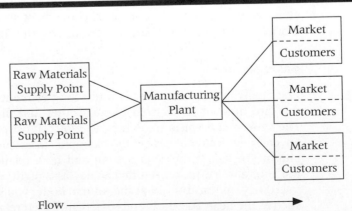

Flow ⟶

FIGURE 1–7   MULTIECHELON LOGISTICS CHANNEL

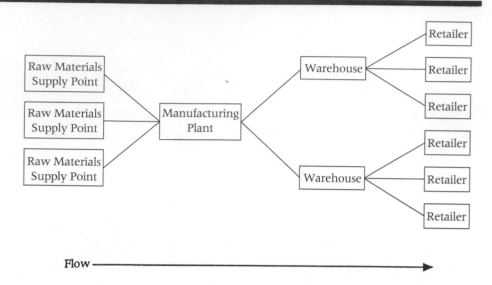

a part of more than one channel. For example, the steel may be sold to auto manufacturers, container manufacturers, or file cabinet producers. Duplication of storage facilities, small-shipment transportation, conflict over mode choices, and other problems may contribute to inefficiency in the channel. Communications problems may also exist.

In attempting to overcome the problems mentioned earlier, companies employ different strategies. For example, some organizations integrate vertically in order to control the product over several stages in the logistics channel. Some strong companies dominate the channel to achieve efficiency. In any case, we can appreciate the complicating factors of the complex channel. The various approaches to logistics should provide additional insights into relevant logistics activities. A discussion of systems analysis in logistics may further aid your understanding of logistics.

LOGISTICS AND SYSTEMS ANALYSIS

An earlier section pointed out that improvements in analysis and methodologies facilitated the development of logistics. One such improvement was systems analysis, or the systems concept. A convenient starting point for this section is a brief discussion of the basic nature of systems analysis.

Basic Nature

Concept of a system

Essentially, a system is a set of interacting elements, variables, parts, or objects that are functionally related to each other and that form a coherent group.[18] The system concept is something to which most people have been exposed at an early educational stage; for example, in science your instructor probably taught you about the solar system and how relationships among the planets, the sun, and the moon resulted in day and night, weather, and so forth. Later, in biology, in learning about the human body, you viewed the parts of the body, such as the heart and the blood vessels, and their relationships as another system.

FIGURE 1–8   COMPLEX LOGISTICS CHANNEL

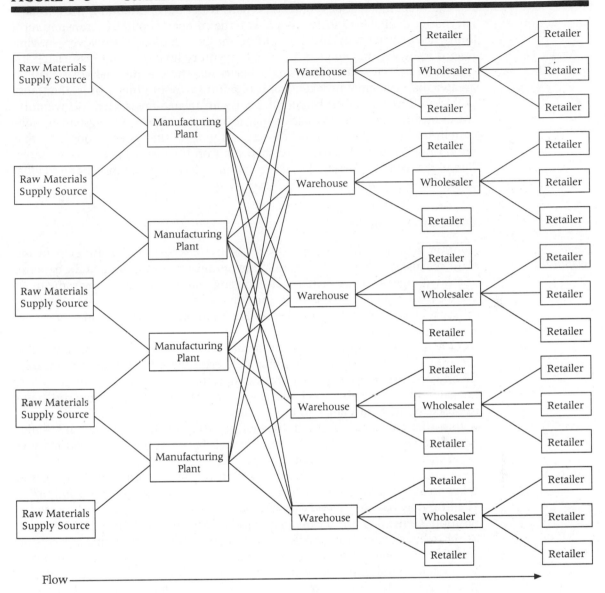

Flow ——————————————————————→

Perhaps in a power mechanics class, you learned about internal combustion engines as a system. You probably learned that engine parts, such as the pistons, could have been larger size and more efficient, but that their very efficiency may have overloaded other parts of the engine, causing it to break down. So the pistons had to be designed in harmony with other parts of the engine. In other words, the overall performance of the engine was more important than the performance of one part.

Cost Perspective

The preceding engine analogy provides insight into business system character-istics. If we measure efficiency by cost, an individual part of the system not

optimization

operating at its lowest cost may contribute to the system's overall efficiency. For example, in a logistics context, perhaps water transportation is the cheapest alternative available to some company. If the company optimizes transportation alone, then water movement would be the best approach. However, moving freight by water may require increased inventory holdings, with associated increases in warehousing space and other costs. These additional costs may be greater than the amount water transportation saves. In other words, the transportation decision has to be coordinated with related areas such as inventory, warehousing, and perhaps packaging, to optimize the overall system or subsystem, not just transportation. The general tenet of the systems concept is that we do not focus on individual variables but on how they interact as a whole. The objective is to operate the whole system effectively, not just the individual parts.

Level of Optimality

functional relationships

Another aspect of the systems concept is that *levels of optimality* exist in the firm. We just stated that a firm should not optimize transportation at the expense of related logistics areas such as warehousing and packaging. At the same time, logistics is only one subsystem in the firm; and therefore the firm should not optimize it at another area's expense. For example, the logistics manager may want to give five-day delivery service to certain customers in order to eliminate some warehouses and inventory. But this may conflict with marketing, since the firm's competitors give three-day delivery service in the same sales area. Clearly, the firm must work out some compromise after analyzing the situation. Logistics may have to accept the three-day service as a working constraint imposed because of competition, and may have to design the "best" system within this constraint. Some individual or group at the organization's senior executive level has to examine the trade-offs between marketing and logistics in terms of the total organization's efficiency or profit.

constraints

In addition to marketing, the firm has to consider production, finance, and other areas. In other words, the overall firm is a system that should be optimized. The firm may have to suboptimize internal subsystems to achieve the best overall position. Generally, this means that logistics may work within constraints such as set delivery times, minimum production run orders, and financial limits on warehouse improvements and construction. Such constraints, occasionally somewhat arbitrary, should be flexible within reason. Ideally, logistics managers should make decisions such as delivery times on a more individual or short-run basis, but organizations are sometimes too complex to make this possible from an operational standpoint. A dynamic simulation model would help to solve some of these problems and to allow more flexibility. We will say more about this point in the chapters covering management of logistics systems.

We should make one other point about optimality levels. Firms producing intermediate goods such as steel or having a multiple product line very often operate in several channels.[19] Therefore, one might consider channel optimization or the external effects of a firms decisions as higher optimality level. For example, a container or pallet designed for shipping a firm's product in a manner consistent with the firm's overall needs may not be compatible with the ordering and receiving needs of customers. Therefore, in the final analysis, such an improvement may harm the channel's overall efficiency. (See Figure 1–9.)

FIGURE 1–9   LEVELS OF OPTIMALITY

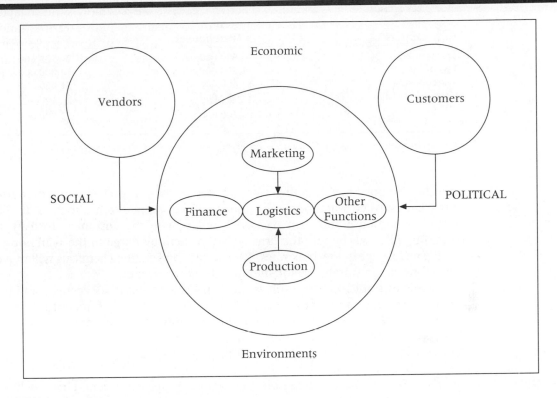

TECHNIQUES OF LOGISTICS SYSTEM ANALYSIS

In this section, we will consider total cost analysis techniques for logistics systems. We will only examine the more basic methods; more sophisticated techniques of total cost analysis are discussed in a later section. The basic approaches examined here unite some of the concepts discussed thus far and provide a background for the material discussed in the book's next section.

Short-Run/Static Analysis

We can use two general approaches in total cost analysis for business logistics. First, we can look at a short-run situation and develop costs associated with the various logistics cost centers previously described. We can develop such cost information for each alternative system considered. We would then select the system with the lowest overall cost, as long as it was consistent with constraints the firm imposed on the logistics area. Some authors refer to this short-run analysis as static analysis.[20] Essentially, they are saying that this method analyzes cost associated with a logistics system's various components at one point in time or at one output level.

Example   For an example of static analysis, see Table 1–3. In this instance, a firm is presently using an all-rail route from the plant and the associated plant warehouse to the customers. At the plant warehouse, the chemicals are bagged

Cost Centers*	System 1 3 Warehouses	System 2 5 Warehouses
Transportation	$ 850,000	$ 500,000
Inventory	$1,500,000	$2,000,000
Warehousing	$ 600,000	$1,000,000
Cost of Lost Sales (1)	$ 350,000	$ 100,000
	$3,200,000	$3,700,000

(1) Expected cost, based upon probabilities, of not having stock/inventory available when customers want it.

and then shipped by rail to the customer. A proposed second system would use a market-oriented warehouse. The goods will be shipped from the plant to the market warehouse and then packaged and sent to the customer. Instead of shipping all goods by rail, the firm will ship them by barge to the warehouse, taking advantage of low bulk rates. Then, after bagging, the chemicals will move by rail from the warehouse for shipment to the customer.

In this example, the trade-off is lower transportation costs versus some increases in storage and warehousing. If the analysis is strictly static (at this level of output), the proposed system is more expensive than the present one. So, unless analysis provided additional information more favorable to the proposed system, the firm would continue with its present system.

Rationale   We have two reasons to select the proposed system. First, we have no information about customer service requirements. The new market-oriented warehouse might provide better customer service, therefore increasing sales and profit and offsetting some of the higher cost of System 2.

Second, using a longer-run perspective (dynamic analysis) to look at the example (Figure 1–10), System 1 gives a lower cost at 50,000 units of output. But, at approximately 70,500 units of output, System 2 becomes less expensive than System 1. Therefore, a company experiencing rapid sales growth may want to plan the shift to System 2 now. The start-up time for the new warehouse may necessitate the immediate planning.

Another reason why a firm might switch to System 2, even though it is presently experiencing lower costs with another system, is that the firm expects the second system to result in lower costs in the future. Since setting up a new system usually takes time, the firm may initiate the change in the near future. If this firm is growing relatively rapidly, perhaps it will achieve 70,500 units in a fairly short time.

Long-Run/Dynamic Analysis

The second way to project the optimum system is to mathematically calculate the point of equality between the systems. In the example used here, System 1 and System 2 are equal at about 70,500 units of output. If we use a graph to determine the equality point, complete accuracy is difficult. For a mathematical solution, we simply need to start with the equation for a straight line ($y = a + bx$). In this particular case, a would be the fixed costs and b would be the variable cost per unit. The x would be the output level. If we want to solve for the point at which the two systems are equal, we can set the two equations up

FIGURE 1–10   DYNAMIC ANALYSIS

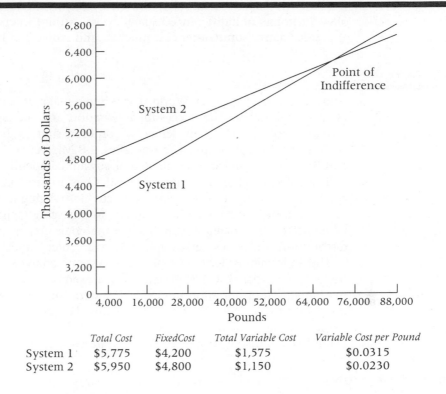

	Total Cost	FixedCost	Total Variable Cost	Variable Cost per Pound
System 1	$5,775	$4,200	$1,575	$0.0315
System 2	$5,950	$4,800	$1,150	$0.0230

as equal and plug in the cost information appropriate to solve these equations. As demonstrated here, at approximately 70,500 pounds the two systems are equal; and we see a point of indifference between the two systems:

1. System 1

   Total cost = fixed cost + variable cost/unit × number of units
   $$y = 4{,}200_1 + 0.0315x$$

2. System 2

   $$y = 4{,}800 + 0.0230x$$

3. Trade-off point

   $$4{,}800_1 + 0.0230x = 4{,}200_1 + 0.0315x$$
   $$600_1 = 0.0085x$$
   $$x = 70{,}588 \text{ pounds}$$

A particular firm may consider more than two logistics systems at one time. Many examples show a firm considering three or sometimes four systems. We can use the same basic methodology for plotting and mathematically solving for the points of indifference regardless of how many systems we analyze. Further, in a particular situation involving two systems, the cost functions may not necessarily intersect. Hence, one function will be lower than the other over the entire output range. When a firm considers three or more systems, two of them may intersect while the other occurs at a higher level in the quadrant. If we have three intersecting systems, two relevant intersection points or two relevant points of indifference usually occur. A third intersection would occur at a point above some other cost function and would not be relevant.

SUMMARY

Logistics has evolved since World War II into a major area in a growing number of U.S. companies. The successful integration and management of logistical activities, now an important element of corporate strategy, has helped companies such as Nabisco, Pillsbury, Land-o-Lakes, I.B.M., Xerox, Procter and Gamble, and Bergen-Brunswick to create and/or sustain competitive advantage.

The growth and development of logistics has occurred in four states. In many companies, logistics now encompasses activities ranging from the interface with vendors to the interface with customers. In analyzing logistics systems, we can take different approaches, including (1) materials management versus physical distribution; (2) nodes versus links; (3) cost centers; and (4) channels.

The rationale underlying logistics is systems analysis which evaluates the trade-offs associated with some change: for example, more or fewer warehouses or changing transportation modes. The systems perspective should focus upon the total firm and its channel relationships. We can analyze the trade-offs in logistics systems with some basic analysis tools demonstrated in this chapter using fixed, variable, and total costs associated with alternative systems.

STUDY QUESTIONS

1. Compare and contrast military logistics and business logistics. What is the relationship between them?

2. What types of changes occurring in the 1990s "marketplace" have led to increased emphasis upon logistics? How does logistics help companies to respond to these changes?

3. "Logistics is not as visible as company areas such as marketing or manufacturing." Do you agree with this statement? Why or why not?

4. Compare and contrast the Council of Logistics Management definition of logistics with the Seven-Rs definition. Which one do you prefer? Why?

5. What factors and conditions led to interest in logistics management after World War II? Which of these factors and/or conditions do you believe were most important? Why?

6. "In many ways, the eighties were the most important decade in the development of logistics management in the U.S." Do you agree with this statement? Why or why not?

7. Why would the logistics system of a large airplane manufacturer such as Boeing differ from that of a company such as Dow Chemical? What is the nature and scope of the differences? Why is this important?

8. Compare and contrast the node and link approach to logistics system analysis with the channels approach. Which one, if any offers most to a logistics manager?

9. Why is systems analysis so important to logistics? How is it used?

10. If you were asked to make a presentation about the importance of logistics to a new group of employees, what points would you stress and why?

NOTES

1. "Logistics: Just-Right Delivery," *Enterprise* (Summer 1990), 27–24.
2. W. David Gibson, "Logistics: A Trendy Management Tool," *New York Times,* 1989 December 24, 12 sec. F.
3. "Logistics," op cit., 27.
4. C. John Langley, Jr., "The Evolution of the Logistics Concept," *Journal of Business Logistics* 7, no. 2, 2–4.
5. Langley, "The Evolution of the Logistics Concept," 4.
6. Roy D. Shapiro and James L. Heskett, *Logistics Strategy: Cases and Concepts* (St. Paul, Minnesota: West Publishing, 1985), 6.
7. Council of Logistics Management, Oakbrook, Illinois, 1985.
8. Gerald L. Harrison, "The Acquisition Logistician," *Logistics Spectrum* (Spring 1981), 11–12.
9. J. J. Barry et al., *Logistics in the Services Industries* (Oakbrook, Illinois: Council of Logistics Management, 1991), 10–12.
10. Donald J. Bowersox, "Emerging from the Recession: The Role of Logistical Management," *Journal of Business Logistics* 4, no. 1, 21–33. In addition, there are two other articles of related interest in the same issue of the *Journal of Business Logistics:* Bernard J. LaLonde, "A Reconfiguration of Logistics Systems in the '80s: Strategies and Challenges," 1–11; and James L. Heskett, "Challenges and Opportunities for Logistics Executives in the 1980s," 13–19. Also of related interest: Bernard J. LaLonde, John R. Grabner, and James F. Robeson, "Integrated Logistics Systems, Past, Present and Future," Chapter 2 in the *Distribution Handbook* (New York: Free Press, 1985), 44–72.
11. Peter F. Drucker, "The Economy's Dark Continent," *Fortune* (April 1962), 103, 265–70.
12. Donald J. Bowersox et al., *Leading Edge Logistics Compositives Positioning for the 1990's* (Oakbrook, Illinois: Council of Logistics Management, 1989), 43.
13. Bowersox, "Emerging from the Recession,"
14. Ronald H. Ballou, *Business Logistics Management* (Englewood Cliffs, N.J.: Prentice-Hall, 1973), 67.
15. J. L. Heskett, Robert M. Ivie, and Nicholas A. Glaskowsky, Jr., *Business Logistics: Management of Physical Supply and Distribution* (New York: Ronald Press, 1973), 26.
16. Donald J. Bowersox, *Logistical Management* (New York: Macmillan, 1974), 36–37.
17. Bowersox, *Logistical Management, XX.*
18. E. J. Kelley and W. Lazor, *Managerial Marketing: Perspectives and Viewpoints* (Homewood, Irwin, 1967), 19.
19. Heskett et al., *Business Logistics,* 42.
20. Heskett et al., *Business Logistics* 454–69.

NITTANY SYSTEMS ELECTRONIC AND MISSILES GROUP

Like many organizations, Nittany Systems Electronic and Missles Group is striving to maintain a quality distribution system—one that gets the right part to the right place at the right time and at the right cost. To achieve this objective Nittany Systems has been analyzing its current logistics system.

Don Martin, vice-president of logistics, has come up with the idea of total electronic material control in order to integrate the inbound and outbound portions of the logistics system. Essentially his perspective includes three parts that can be added separately over time or all at once.

David Cox, CEO of Nittany Systems, has requested a cost analysis of the three components of the total material control program that Don Martin has developed. Bruce Grimm, System Analyst, in Don Martin's group has prepared the following cost information for the three components—(1) computer networks, (2) bar coding and (3) automated storage and retrieval for the warehouse. Bruce Grimm has presented the following data:

Level	Fixed Cost	Variable Cost/Unit
1	$16,000,000	$100
2	$30,000,000	$ 65
3	$50,000,000	$ 35

Questions:

1. Over what range of output would Level 1 be most economical?
2. Over what range of output would Level 2 be most economical?
3. At what output would Level 3 be most economical?
4. Graph the three systems and calculate the indifference points.

LOGISTICS ENVIRONMENTS

The recession of 1991 was significant for a number of reasons, one of which was that new inventory practices such as just-in-time (JIT) appeared to have passed a major test. National data showed that because inventories had not gotten out of hand during the more prosperous period preceding the recession, a modest increase in sales would result in restocking.

In previous economic ups and downs, inventories would creep up to excessive levels during the "good times;" and companies would use the inventories during the lean periods. The bad feature was that companies would not recall laid-off workers until the inventory levels came back down, prolonging the recession or the business cycle downturn. Economists sometimes call this a "double dip" recession.

But since the end of the 1981–82 recession, inventories have never really gotten far out of line. In fact, as we will demonstrate later in this chapter, inventories-to-sales ratios on a macro basis have declined.

The best reason we can offer for this phenomenon is that individual companies have adopted the new inventory management techniques (JIT, MRP, DRP) we mentioned briefly in the previous chapter and which we will explore in depth in Chapter 4. U.S. manufacturers, who have experienced intense foreign competition, have adopted these measures in response to the competitive pressure. These new inventory management approaches are an outstanding example of what companies can do to cut costs and ultimately increase profits.

We must emphasize two very relevant points here. First, logistics has an important affect on and relationship to the overall economy (macro level); and, as we will point out, inventories are not the only relevant economic factor. Second, important interaction occurs between micro level and macro level economic activities; so we need to discuss both.

As Chapter 1 indicated, the 1990s promise to be a decade of great development and interest for logistics in a wide variety of organizations both private and public. As we discussed in Chapter 1, companies have been interested in logistics since the 1960s; but, for various reasons, that growth and development will increase at an expanding rate.

In this chapter, we will focus on the environments in which logistics operates, including the macro or external environment, the intrafirm environment, and, finally, the internal environment of the logistics system itself. We should also mention an additional environment, the supply chain or interfirm environment, which includes both vendors and customers and which we will discuss in Chapter 3.

Figure 2–1 presents a conceptual view of the environments and relationships relevant to the logistics area. As indicated, the external or macro environment looks at how logistics contributes to the economy and the value that it adds to overall economic development. The intrafirm or micro perspective looks at logistics as it relates to other functional areas, such as marketing and manufacturing, and examines how logistics can add competitive advantage for the com-

FIGURE 2–1   THE ENVIRONMENTS AND RELATIONSHIPS OF LOGISTICS

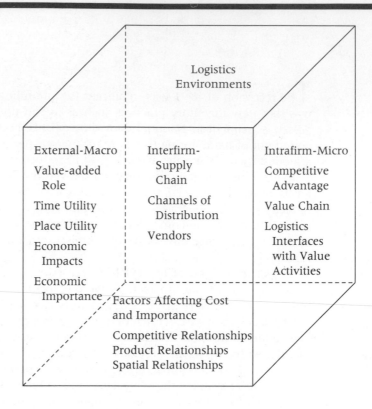

pany. We could think of the third environment, which focuses on the internal logistics system, as a subset of the second, the intrafirm or micro relationship, since logistics obviously is a part of the overall company or firm. However, given the importance of the trade-offs and relationships which exist within the logistics system itself, the third system merits separate consideration in this chapter. By examining each of these environments in detail, the reader will become familiar with issues in logistics areas and obtain a convenient background for further understanding of following chapters.

LOGISTICS IN THE ECONOMY: THE MACRO, OR EXTERNAL, ENVIRONMENT

The typical analysis of logistics systems focuses on the *micro* dimension, implying an examination from the perspective of the individual firm. This section, in contrast, looks at logistics as it relates to the economy, or the external environment. This is referred to as the *macro* dimension of business logistics.

This section covers three topics. First is a discussion of how logistics adds value to goods and services in the context of overall economic activity. Specifically, the section discusses the utility types created in the economy. Second is an overview of economic impacts that may be attributable to logistics. Finally, the section explains several facts and figures to stress the importance of logistics to a macro, or external, environment.

Value-Added Role of Logistics

types of utility   As illustrated in Figure 2–2, four principal types of economic utility add value to a product or service. Included are form, time, place, and possession. Generally, we credit manufacturing activities with providing form utility, logistics activities with time and place utility, and marketing activities with possession utility. We will discuss each briefly.

what   **Form Utility**   This type of utility refers to the value added to goods through a manufacturing, production, or assembly process. For example, form utility results when raw materials are combined in some predetermined manner to make a finished product. This is the case, for example, when a bottling firm adds together syrup, water, and carbonation to make a soft drink. The simple process of adding the raw materials together to produce the soft drink represents a change in product *form* that adds value to the product.

In today's economic environment, certain logistics activities also provide form utility. For example, bulk breaking and product mixing, which typically take place at distribution centers, change a product's form by changing its shipment size and packaging characteristics. Thus, unpacking a palletload of breakfast cereal into individual consumer-size boxes adds form utility to the product. However, the two principal ways in which logistics adds value are in place and time utility.

where   **Place Utility**   Logistics performs one role by moving goods from surplus points to points where demand exists. Logistics extends the physical boundaries of the market area, thus adding economic value to the goods. This addition to the economic value of goods or services is known as *place* utility. Logistics creates place utility primarily through transportation. For example moving farm produce

FIGURE 2–2   FUNDAMENTAL UTILITY CREATION IN THE ECONOMY

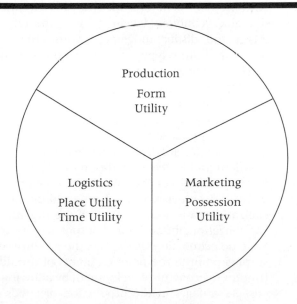

by rail or truck from production areas to areas where consumers need this produce creates place utility.

when

Time Utility   Not only must goods and services be available where consumers need them, but they must also be at that point when customers demand them. This is called *time* utility, or the economic value added to a good or service by having it at a demand point at a specific time. Logistics creates time utility through proper inventory maintenance and the strategic location of goods and services. For example, logistics creates time utility by having heavily advertised products and sale merchandise available in retail stores at precisely the time promised in the advertising copy.

To some extent, transportation may create time utility by moving something more quickly to a point of demand. For example, substituting air transportation for warehousing adds time utility.

why

Possession Utility   Logistics creates this form of utility primarily through the basic marketing activities related to the promotion of products or services. We may define *promotion* as the effort, through direct and indirect contact with the customer, to increase the desire to possess a good or benefit from a service. The role of logistics in the economy depends on the existence of *possession* utility, for time or place utility make sense only if demand for the product or service exists.

Economic Impacts

Another important topic related to the macro, or external, environment is that of economic impacts. This section highlights four major areas: economic development and specialization, variety of goods, effects on prices, and land values.

Economic Development and Specialization   The emphasis on production efficiency in the nineteenth and early twentieth centuries also resulted in considerable economic development in the form of specialization. In fact, during this period, distinct movements within the economy specialized the production of certain output types in regions possessing particular economic advantages.

specialization or division of labor

This tendency to specialize and to produce at lower costs was a normal development of economic growth as described by Adam Smith and other economists. We may question why labor specialization, potentially lowering costs and prices, did not advance more rapidly, or why the United States does not presently specialize more. We might also question why underdeveloped countries do not practice production specialization to aid in their economic development.

extent of the market

Adam Smith answered this question when he indicated that the extent of the market or the volume of demand for the product limits specialization or division of labor. In other words, an organization does not benefit from practicing specialization to a greater degree if the organization cannot sell the fruits of this specialization, the additional output, to consumers. The additional output would have no economic value unless the producer could move it from the production surplus point to the point or points of unfulfilled demand. Thus, logistics contributes to economic development by allowing firms to capitalize on comparative cost advantages in the production of goods and services by efficiently transporting goods to the market.

variety and assortment of products

Variety of Goods   In other ways, logistics has an impact on the macro environment. One contribution, for example, is the volume and variety of goods made available to consumers in areas far from production or manufacturing points, and, frequently, long after the goods were manufactured or produced. We often take for granted goods available in a wide assortment at a desired time, but satisfying this demand very much depends upon all firms in the economy effectively performing movement and storage functions (logistics). The total of these logistics operations provides the link and storage network so crucial to the functioning of a modern and progressive economy.

prices of products

Effects on Prices   By creating time and place utility, logistics activities in the economy may also contribute to lower prices. For example, if logistics extends markets for goods in both time and space, transported goods may sell for prices lower than goods produced locally. Frequently, firms base lower prices upon the greater efficiency of large scale production and the increased opportunity for trade-offs in the logistics system. As firms improve logistics systems from both a technical and managerial perspective, we are sure to observe numerous benefits on prices and on the availability of goods.

impacts on land values

Land Values   Logistics also affects other aspects of the economic system; for example, the transportation segment often affects land values when technical improvements occur. When a new major highway is built in an area, or when an existing facility is significantly enhanced, land values near the highway usually go up because of the increased accessibility to other areas.[1] The interchange areas of such highway facilities often attract manufacturing and storage facilities. Besides economic effects improved logistics systems bring about, we should consider a wide range of relevant social, political, and national defense aspects.

Economic Importance of Business Logistics—Aggregate Economic Data

U.S. business logistics costs should exceed $600 billion per year during the 1990s. Figure 2–3 summarizes logistics costs from 1980–1990, showing logistics costs in billions of dollars and as a percentage of GNP. Aggregate logistics costs have

logistics costs and GNP

been increasing since about 1983. However, logistics costs as a percentage of gross national product (GNP) have largely declined during the eighties. The end of the decade showed logistics costs stabilized around eleven percent, but this is down from a high close to fifteen percent in 1981. The projection for the nineties is that logistics costs as a percentage of GNP will again increase from the current level of about 11 percent. Table 2–1 presents the components of 1990 logistics costs. As the table indicates, the major categories are inventory costs, transportation costs, shipper-related costs, and administrative costs. The largest, transportation costs, accounted for $277 billion out of a total of $600 billion. Inventory carrying cost was a close second at $221 billion.

Figure 2–4 compares overall logistics costs, transportation costs, and inventory carrying costs as a GNP percentage from 1970–1990. The top line, which indicates overall cost, shows the previously mentioned logistics costs figure of approximately eleven percent for 1990. The second line shows transportation

trends

costs, which during the eighties, declined to about 6.3 percent of GNP from a high of about 8 percent. The third line, which shows inventory cost, also indicates a decline: costs fell to approximately four percent from a high of about six

RATIONALIZATION OF TRANSPORT—
DRIVING LOGISTICS INTO THE 1990s

In order to improve our world competitiveness, we must drive our U.S. logistics costs below ten percent of GNP and keep them there. Let's look at the fundamentals. I believe that it is possible to obtain a further ten percent reduction in transportation costs relative to GNP. I believe that more efficient and reliable transport services will support a twelve percent reduction in inventory holding costs. We must finally bring U.S. inventory efficiency into line with the achievements the Japanese have been making since 1965. Driving transportation and inventory to new levels of efficiency will require information systems that are more robust.

If the United States intends to compete in the 1990s, we need a new engine to drive our business logistics systems. We must adopt the attitude of the European Community's Committee on Single Market Benefits. What can we do to remove the barriers affecting manufacturing and trade? How can we develop economy of scale through increased competition? What available productivity can we safely implement? How can we rationalize our transport services in order to reduce empty miles and conserve energy?

We need a national freight transportation policy that is tough, consistent, unambiguous, and fair. We still have far too much protection, waste, and subsidy. We must compel our freight transportation services to provide the best value to manufacturers and distributors, and through them to the ultimate consumers of goods and services. The means that we will use to achieve that end are competition, rationalization, productivity, and efficiency.

What if we designed our new logistics engine for the 1990s to drive us to more efficient levels of transport rationalization? Our policy would not focus on accommodating the owners and operators of trucks. Instead, our policy would focus on reducing intercity ton-miles, conserving energy, lowering cost, and providing the best value for consumers of goods and services. As an example, Ross Laboratories, a leading manufacturer of health care products, ships approximately eighty truckloads a day from five plants. Most of the trucks Ross loads are operated by food manufacturers who earn income by transporting Ross products as a backhaul. Rationalization reduces transportation costs for Ross and private trucking costs for the food companies serving Ross. What would happen if all of us followed the example of Ross Laboratories and made a conscious, systematic effort to encourage rationalization of transport services throughout the United States? The bottom line is that we will not know the level of intercity ton-miles necessary to support GNP and industrial production until we pull the plug on market protection.

A single-minded focus on logistics efficiency will have its critics. You should expect that transport carriers will contest any change in the status quo. Reform legislation has been in Congress for six consecutive years. The transport lobby has prevented even a hearing from taking place. I cannot improve on the words of Court Appeals Judge Richard A. Posner in his landmark text *Economic Analysis of Law:* "Efficiency has always been an important social value. It may be the only value that a system of common-law rulemaking can effectively promote." We must not chase the changing times. We must not settle for what Milton Friedman described as "the tyranny of the status quo."

Driving logistics costs below ten percent of GNP and keeping them there is admittedly a stretch objective. But if you achieve only half of that objective, you will contribute $25 billion of real cost reduction over a period of about five years. How confident am I that we can save $25 billion? After twenty years of using the same scorecard, I guarantee it!

Robert V. Delaney, "Logistics: A New Engine for the 1990s," *Annual Conference Proceedings, Council of Logistics Management* I (7–10 October 1990), 1–31.

FIGURE 2–3   U.S. LOGISTICS COSTS SINCE 1980   *Source:* Robert D. Delaney, Cass Logistics, Inc., reprinted with permission.

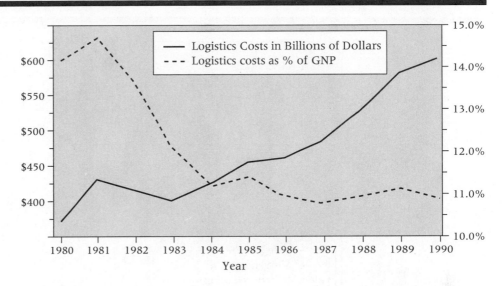

—— Logistics Costs in Billions of Dollars
- - - Logistics costs as % of GNP

percent in the early eighties. These trends in inventory and transportation costs are quite interesting on a macro basis. Many elements have reduced transportation costs, but one important factor has been the deregulation of transportation, discussed in more detail in other chapters. That transportation deregulation provided shippers more opportunities to negotiate contracts, which led to reduced transportation rates. In addition, increased competition in the transpor-

TABLE 2–1   COMPONENTS OF 1990 LOGISTICS COST

	$ Billions
Inventory Carrying Costs	
Interest	66
Taxes, obsolescence, depreciation	84
Warehousing	61
Subtotal	221
Transportation Costs	
Motor Carriers:	
Public and for hire	77
Private and for own account	87
Local freight services	113
Subtotal	277
Other Carriers:	
Railroads	32
Water carriers	21
Oil pipelines	9
Air carriers	13
Subtotal	75
Shipper-Related Costs	4
Distribution Administration	23
TOTAL LOGISTICS COST	$600

Source: Robert D. Delaney, Cass Logistics, Inc., reprinted with permission.

FIGURE 2—4   BUSINESS LOGISTICS, TRANSPORTATION, AND INVENTORY CARRYING COSTS AS A PERCENTAGE OF GNP   *Source:* Robert D. Delaney, Cass Logistics, Inc., reprinted with permission.

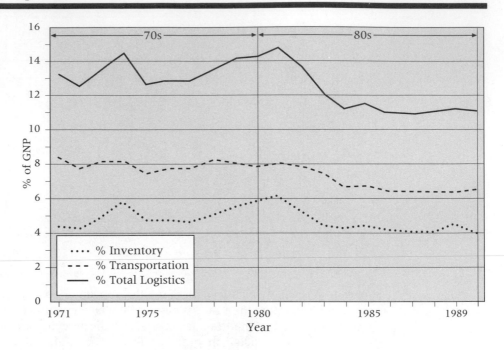

tation marketplace also led transportation companies to lower prices. To some extent, better transportation service and better overall inventory management levels, with increasing emphasis in the 1980s upon improved transportation management techniques such as just-in-time (JIT) (which we will discuss in more detail in following chapters), reduced inventory. Overall business logistics costs declined by approximately $65 billion during the eighties, with about $30 billion in savings from the inventory area and $35 billion in savings from transportation.

*business
inventories*

Figure 2—5 shows the ratio of business inventories to final sales from 1980—1990. This is a more dramatic perspective on the inventory area declines. As we can see, that ratio, which was over twenty-six percent in 1980, declined to a little less than twenty percent in 1990. This dramatic decrease of approximately twenty-two percent accounted for the $30 billion in savings mentioned previously.

transportation

Figures 2—6 and 2—7 address the transportation costs discussed previously. Figure 2—6 shows trucking costs during the seventies and eighties using 1973 constant dollars. The table presents information for both truckload and less-than-truckload costs. As we can see, both costs have declined significantly in the post-deregulation era during the eighties. The same general conclusion is apparent for railroad costs in Figure 2—7, which shows costs for the seventies and eighties. Rail costs have been declining since 1980. The reductions in motor carrier costs are more significant than those of railroad. Of the $35 billion combined total mentioned previously, trucking savings accounted for the largest share: $30 billion.

The nineties will see additional savings on a macro basis, but only in selected areas of transportation and inventory control. In other words, we are not likely

FIGURE 2–5   NOMINAL RATIO OF BUSINESS INVENTORIES TO FINAL SALES: 1980–1989   *Source:* Robert D. Delaney, Cass Logistics, Inc., reprinted with permission.

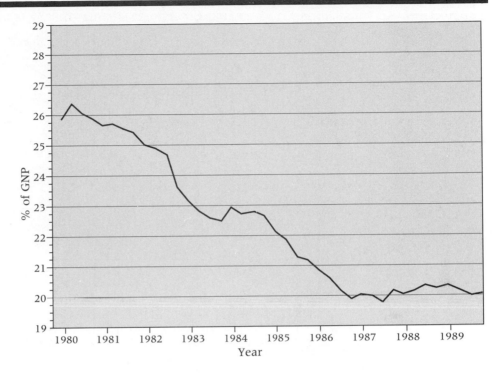

to witness the dramatic savings that occurred during the eighties, savings heavily based on transportation deregulation.

Given the importance of international logistics, which we discussed in Chapter 1 and which will be a major focal point of this book, we ought to comment about the international situation on a macro basis. Canada passed a deregulation act in 1988, the National Transportation Act. It attempted to deregulate transportation but required the concurrence of each Canadian province. The Province of Ontario deregulated its transportation system in 1989, but Quebec did not. However, the Province of Quebec allows progressive market entry procedures. Heavy traffic moves between Canada and the United States via motor carriers. U.S. carriers are allowed to deliver up to 150 miles into Canada, and U.S. motor carriers have a cost advantage over Canadian motor carriers because of the U.S. tax code, which allows investment write-offs not allowed in Canada.

international logistics

The European economic community's goal of completely eliminating by 1992 barriers affecting manufacturing and trade will have a significant impact on these countries. This elimination of barriers will increase productivity by an estimated five to seven percent and will create possibly two to five million new jobs. The removal of these barriers will also affect distribution and transportation patterns in Western Europe. Companies presently operating in the European economic community need to have plants and warehouses in each of the countries in which they wish to market their goods. With the elimination of trade barriers and tariffs among the various countries, a more regionalized approach, similar to that used in the United States, will be possible. In other words, because countries are very small, a company may have a warehouse in one country from which it will distribute to several countries, using longer, more efficient trans-

FIGURE 2–6   TRUCKING COSTS: 1973–1987   *Source:* Robert D. Delaney, Cass Logistics, Inc., reprinted with permission.

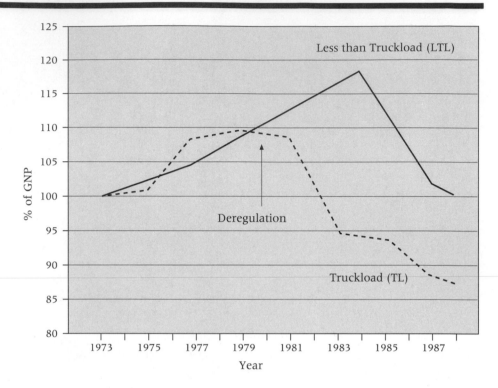

portation hauls and larger, more efficient warehouses. Likely to have a dramatic impact in Western Europe, this regionalized approach may produce potential logistics savings not unlike those experienced in the United States during the eighties.

Overall, the eighties were a period of great change in logistics and in the related areas of transportation and inventory. Dramatic cost reductions promoted efficiency in the logistics systems of many companies. The responsibilities of logistics managers grew and developed. The decade of the nineties promises additional challenges, but duplicating the savings which occurred during the eighties will be very difficult.

LOGISTICS IN THE FIRM: THE MICRO, OR INTRAFIRM, ENVIRONMENT

The third major perspective from which we must view logistics is from the perspective of the individual firm, and the specific contributions that logistics may make to the mission of the whole organization. We will first examine the micro, or intrafirm, environment by discussing the topics of competitive advantage and the value chain, and second by identifying the key relationships between logistics and other activities within the firm's value chain. The final sections of this chapter highlight factors affecting logistics cost and importance within the individual firm.

Competitive Advantage and Logistics

In his widely read book *Competitive Advantage,* Michael E. Porter identifies three generic strategies for achieving competitive advantage in the marketplace.[2]

FIGURE 2—7   RAILROAD COSTS: 1981–1988   *Source:* Robert D. Delaney, Cass Logistics, Inc., reprinted
with permission.

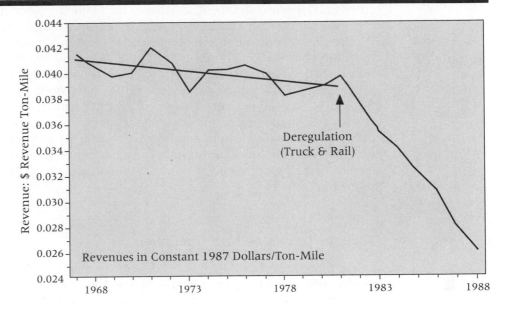

Deregulation (Truck & Rail)

Revenues in Constant 1987 Dollars/Ton-Mile

keys to competitive advantage

The first is *cost leadership,* which results directly from being the low-cost producer of a given product or service. The second is *differentiation,* in which case a firm establishes itself as unique in certain ways perceived by customers. The third strategy is *focus,* wherein a firm attempts to achieve a competitive advantage in one or more market segments, and thus strategically "focuses" its efforts.

Each of these strategies can lead to competitive advantage in the marketplace, but not all competing firms will succeed in their efforts. As a result, firms continually search for new and innovative ways to successfully implement the strategies of cost leadership, differentiation, and focus.

In response to this challenge, many firms identify the logistics function as an excellent opportunity to exploit one or more of these strategies. For example, effective logistics management may reduce the total cost of logistics to the point where the firm's low-cost logistics profile becomes a potential source of competitive advantage. Similarly, emphasis on high customer service levels and ready marketplace identification as a high-quality provider of logistical customer service, may help a firm to establish itself on this basis. Finally, as logistics managers become more aware of their area's true power and potential, the logistics function will become more of a key in determining a firm's ability to penetrate specific target markets, and to thus achieve a desired focus.

Value Chain

corporate value chain

Porter introduces the concept of a *value chain* as a basic tool that "disaggregates a firm into its strategically relevant activities in order to understand the behavior of costs and the existing and potential sources of differentiation.[3] He suggests that a firm gains competitive advantage by performing these important activities either less expensively or better than its competitors do.

value activities

Figure 2–8 illustrates Porter's concept of the value chain, dividing a firm's activities into those which are *primary* (inbound logistics, operations, outbound logistics, marketing and sales, and service), and those which are *support* (firm infrastructure, human resource management, technology development, and procurement). He describes these activities as the "building blocks by which a firm creates a product valuable to its buyers" and defines *margin* as "the difference between total value and the collective cost of performing the value activities.⁴

In this context, cost control in logistics and superior customer service levels may clearly add significant value for the firm's customers, thus generating higher profit margins for the business as a whole. To see business in general recognize the logistics functions strategic value within the firm is encouraging.

This text draws upon the value chain concept to highlight the interfaces between inbound and outbound logistics and the other primary and support activities that add value and produce margin for the firm. The following discussions center around Porter's interpretation of each area of primary and supporting activity.⁵

Logistics Interfaces with Operations

Of principal importance here are the activities relating to the manufacturing, production, fabrication, or assembly of raw materials into some other intermediate or finished product form. Also included would be ancillary activities such as packaging, equipment maintenance, and testing.

length of production runs

A classic interface area between logistics and manufacturing management regards the length of the production run. We typically associate production economies with long production runs with infrequent production line setups or changeovers. These can, however, easily result in excessive inventories of certain finished products and in limited supplies of others. Thus, the ultimate production decision requires management to carefully weigh the advantages and disadvantages of long versus short production runs. Many industries today tend toward shorter production runs, and whatever it takes to reduce the time and expense normally associated with changing production lines from one product to an-

FIGURE 2–8   THE GENERIC VALUE CHAIN   Reprinted with permission of The Free Press, a Division of Macmillan, Inc. from *Competitive Advantage: Creating and Sustaining Superior Performance* by Michael E. Porter. Copyright © 1985 by Michael E. Porter.

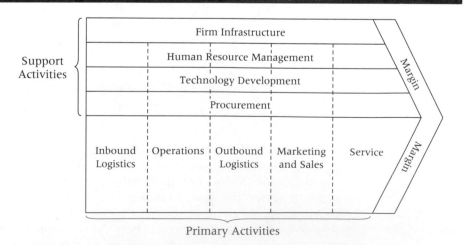

other. This is particularly true for firms employing the just-in-time approach to inventory and scheduling.

seasonal demand   The production manager is interested in minimizing the effects of seasonal demand for products. Fully anticipating such demand is not always possible, however; thus, having desired product quantities available when and where needed is not always possible. For example, cold weather and snow accumulation in various parts of the country easily influence sales of snow skis or snowmobiles. To keep costs low, to avoid overtime and rush situations, and to prepare for the sales schedule, production managers usually like to produce well ahead of the season and to produce a maximum amount. Such advance production may not be economically feasible because of inventory storage costs. However, production managers have to consider this problem in an attempt to keep production costs down. Therefore, the logistics department, in conjunction with production or manufacturing, must be prepared to accept seasonal inventory, which can start to accumulate three to six months before sales occur. For example, Hallmark Cards begins to accumulate Christmas items at its Kansas City warehouse during the summer months, so that the company will be prepared to ship to retailers and other customers during the fall months.

supply-side interfaces   Since the logistics manager is responsible for the inbound movement and storage of raw materials that will feed the production line, logistics and production also interface on the supply side. A shortage or stockout situation could result in the shutdown of a production facility or an increase in production costs. The logistics manager should ensure that available raw materials quantities and other production inputs are sufficient to meet production schedules, yet are conservative in terms of inventory carrying costs. Because of the need for this type of coordination, many firms today have shifted the responsibility for production scheduling from manufacturing to logistics management. The end result is a broadening of overall logistics responsibility.

protective packaging   Another activity at the interface of logistics and operations is packaging, which many firms treat as a logistics activity. In the context of either operations or logistics management, the principal purpose packaging serves is to protect the product from damage. This is distinct from whatever value the package may have for marketing or promotional reasons.

foreign and third party alternatives   The interface between logistics and operations is becoming more critical, given recent interest in the procurement of raw materials and other production inputs from foreign sources. Also, many firms today are making arrangements with third party manufacturers, or "co-packers," to produce or assemble some or all of the firm's finished products. These arrangements are especially prevalent in the food industry, where many firms solely manufacture food items to be sold under someone else's label.

Logistics Interfaces with Marketing

Logistics is often referred to as the other half of marketing. The rationale for this definition is that the physical distribution part of a firm's logistics system is responsible for the physical movement and storage of goods for customers, and thus plays an important role in selling a product. In some instances, physical distribution may be the key variable in selling a product; that is, your ability to provide the product at the right time in the right quantities may be the critical element in making a sale.

marketing mix   This section briefly discusses the interfaces between logistics and marketing, activities in each principal area of the marketing mix. The following material is organized according to the "4 Ps of marketing" originally identified by Professor Jerome McCarthy of Michigan State University: price, product, promotion, and place.[6] In addition, we will comment on recent trends in the interface area between logistics and marketing.

Price   Decisions concerning price usually have a direct impact on the extent to which an organization achieves financial and corporate goals. This is true where demand is relatively elastic, and even where it is relatively inelastic. Pricing decisions typically require a thorough analysis of factors including competitive products and their pricing, socioeconomic and demographic characteristics of the customer base, and prevailing general economic conditions. This analysis becomes a very critical step in developing a pricing strategy and setting market prices for individual products.

carrier pricing   From a logistics perspective, adjusting quantity prices to conform with shipment sizes appropriate for transportation companies may be quite important. We have mentioned truckload versus less-than-truckload shipments and carload shipments of varying sizes and weights. Railroads, for example, publish minimum weight requirements for carload lots—for instance, 30,000 pounds. Motor carriers typically publish four or five rates that will apply on the same commodity between two points depending upon the size (weight) of the shipment. The larger the size, the lower the unit rate charged. In other words, a price discount schedule for shipping larger volumes at one time applies because the transportation company experiences economy if the customer sends larger shipments.

matching schedules   Companies selling products also typically provide a discount schedule for larger purchase quantities. If such discount schedules relate to transportation rate discount schedules in terms of weight, then the company may be able to save itself some money or save money for customers, depending on the sale terms. For example, if a company sells on a delivered-price basis (price includes transportation charges) and if its price schedule matches the transportation shipping requirements on a weight basis, the company should be able to get lower rates with larger purchases and thus save money. So when the company calculates the number of units that it wants to sell to a customer for a particular price, it should see how the weight of that number of units compares with the weight requirement for a transportation rate. In many instances, increasing the quantity purchased in order to produce a total shipment weight that will qualify for a lower per unit transportation weight becomes advantageous. Even if the firm were selling goods on an F.O.B. (free on board) point-of-origin basis (transportation charges paid by the buyer), this approach would enable the firm's customers to qualify for the lower rate and thus save money.

Although it is not always possible or feasible to adjust prices to meet rate breaks and to have a quantity convenient to deal with, organizations should investigate such alternatives. In some organizations, entire pricing schedules conform to various quantities the company can ship by motor and railroad or by other modes of transportation. Under the Robinson-Patman Act and related legislation, transportation cost savings are a valid reason for offering a price discount.

volume relationships   In addition, the logistics manager may be interested in the volume sold under different price schedules, because this will affect inventory requirements, replacement times, and other customer service aspects. Although this is somewhat difficult to analyze, a firm may consider the logistics manager's ability to provide sufficient volumes within an attractive price schedule. Such a situation may be particularly true when price specials generate extra sales at particular times of the year. The logistics manager must be apprised of such specials so that he or she can adjust inventory requirements to meet projected demand.

impact on logistics

Product   Another decision frequently made in the marketing area concerns products, particularly their physical attributes. Much has been written about the number of new products that come on the market each year in the United States. Their size, shape, weight, packaging, and other physical dimensions affect the logistics' ability to move and store products. Therefore, the logistics manager should offer input when marketing is making the physical dimensions of new products. The logistics manager can supply appropriate information about the movement and storage of the new products. In addition to new products, firms frequently refurbish old products in one way or another to improve and maintain sales. Very often such changes may take the form of a new package design and perhaps different package sizes. The physical dimensions of products affect the use of storage and movement systems. They affect the carriers that a firm can use, equipment needed, damage rates, storage ability, use of materials handling equipment such as conveyors and pallets, exterior packaging, and many other logistics aspects.

It is very difficult to convey the frustration that some logistics managers experience when discovering a change in a product package that makes the use of standard-size pallets uneconomical, or that uses trailer or boxcar space inefficiently or in a way that could damage products. For example, when Gillette first introduced the Daisy razor, the logistics group did not learn until late in the game that they had to deal with light and bulky floor stand displays, with consequent low weight density. Not only would the floor stand displays not fit on the warehouse conveyors, but they had to be shipped at a rate 150% higher than the existing rate for the product itself. Gillette eventually corrected the situation, but it was an expensive lesson. These things often seem mundane and somewhat trivial to people concerned about making sales to customers, but they greatly affect an organization's overall success and profitability in the long run.

No magic formulas can spell out what firms should do in these cases, but we can keep in mind that interaction can allow the logistics manager to provide input about the possibly negative aspects of decisions. It may well be that logistics can do nothing and that the sale is overridingly important. But often the logistics manager can make small changes making the product much more amenable to a logistics system's movement and storage aspects while having no real effect upon the sales of the product itself.

consumer packaging

Another marketing area that affects logistics is consumer packaging. The marketing manager often regards consumer packaging as a "silent" salesperson. At the retail level, the package may be a determining factor in influencing sales. The marketing manager will be concerned about package appearance, information provided, and other related aspects; for a customer comparing several products on the retailer's shelf, the consumer package may make the sale. The consumer package is important to the logistics manager for several reasons. The consumer package usually has to fit into what is called the industrial package, or the external package. The size, shape, and other dimensions of the consumer package will affect the use of industrial packages. The protection the consumer package offers also concerns the logistics manager. The physical dimensions and the protection aspects of consumer packages affect the logistics system in the areas of transportation, materials handing, and warehousing.

example   **Promotion**   Promotion is a marketing area that receives much attention in an organization. Firms often spend hundreds of thousands of dollars on national advertising campaigns and other promotional practices to improve a sales position. An organization making a promotional effort to stimulate sales should inform its logistics manager so that sufficient inventory quantities will be available for distribution to the customer. But even when logistics is informed, problems can occur. For example, when Gillette introduced the disposable twin-blade Good News razor, the company's original plan called for three consecutive promotions. The national launch promotion was to achieve sales of twenty million units. A following trade deal promotion was to net ten million in sales, and Gillette expected a third promotional campaign to net an additional twenty million—for a total of fifty million in sales. As it turned out, the first promotion sold thirty-five million—seventy-five percent over the plan. Needless to say, this placed quite a burden on the logistics group to try to meet the demand.

push versus pull   We should look beyond the obvious relation and analyze basic promotion strategies to see how they affect the logistics department. Marketing people often classify their promotion strategies into two basic categories: push or pull. What they are implying is that they can try to "push" the product through the distribution channel to the customer, or "pull" it through. We will discuss distribution channels subsequently in more detail. Briefly, they are the institutions that handle products after manufacture but before sale to the ultimate consumer. They include organizations such as wholesalers and retailers.

channel competition   Producers frequently compete to get distribution channels to give their products the sales effort they feel their products deserve. For example, a cereal producer may want to ensure sufficient space for its product on the retailer's shelf, or to ensure that wholesalers hold product quantities sufficient to satisfy retailers and, ultimately, the final consumer product-demand will influence the retailer and the wholesaler. By selling popular products they improve their profitability. The higher the product turnover, the more likely they are to make a profit; the happier they are with a particular product, the more willing they are to give it space and a better position in the store.

pull strategy   Companies can attempt to improve their sales by *pulling* their product through the distribution channel with national advertising. Promotional advertising attempts to create or stimulate sales to customers and to get customers into the retail store asking for a product they have seen advertised in a magazine, have heard advertised on a radio, or, more likely, have seen advertised on television. The purchases will likely influence the retailer, and the retailer will influence the wholesaler, if any, from whom the retailer purchases. Some companies feel that the best approach in promoting a product is to pull it through distribution channels by directly stimulating demand at the consumer level.

push strategy   The other basic approach is the *push* method. Implied in the push approach is cooperation with the channels of distribution to stimulate customer sales—in other words, retailers or wholesalers possibly pay part of local advertising costs or have special store displays to stimulate sales. In cooperating with the wholesaler, a manufacturer may be able to offer retailers a special price at a particular time to stimulate product demand. The emphasis is upon having the distribution channel work with the company in stimulating product demand. This contrasts with the pull approach, wherein the company stimulates sales somewhat independently of the retailer by national advertising or by advertising a product on a broad regional scale.

logistics impact   We can offer many arguments both for and against these two approaches. In fact, some companies combine the two in their promotion efforts. From the logistics manager's point of view, however, "push" and "pull" are often different as far as logistics system requirements are concerned. The pull approach is more likely to generate erratic demand that is difficult to predict and that may place emergency demands upon the logistics system. Broad-scale national advertising has the potential to be extremely successful, but predicting consumer response to new products is often difficult. Such advertising may also strain the logistics system, requiring emergency shipments and higher transportation rates. Frequent stockouts may also result, requiring additional inventory. The Gillette situation is an example of such a case. On the other hand, a push approach very often has a more orderly demand pattern. Cooperation with the retailer allows manufacturers to fill the "pipeline" somewhat in advance of the stimulated sales rather than quickly, on an almost emergency basis, as retailers and consumers clamor for some successfully promoted new product.

coordination necessary   Therefore, from the logistics manager's point of view, the push approach with its more orderly filling of the pipeline in preparation for sales, is often more desirable. The pull approach can lead to tremendous demand that may cause some problems, but a logistics manager involved in coordination and planning can be better prepared to meet any emergency situation.

wholesalers versus retailers   **Place**   The place decision refers to the distribution channels decision, and thus involves both transactional and physical distribution channel decisions. Marketers typically become more involved in making decisions about transactional channels and in deciding such things as whether to sell a product to wholesalers, or to deal directly with retailers. From the logistics manager's point of view, such decisions may significantly affect logistics system requirements. For example, companies dealing only with wholesalers will probably have fewer logistics problems than will companies dealing directly with retailers. Wholesalers, on the average, tend to purchase in larger quantities than do retailers, and to place their orders and manage their inventories more predictably and consistently, thereby making the logistics manager's job easier. Retailing establishments, particularly small retailers, often order in small quantities and do not always allow sufficient lead time for replenishment before stockouts. Consequently, manufacturers often need shippers to provide expediting services or need to purchase time-sensitive transportation service at a premium price to meet delivery needs.

customer service   **Recent Trends**   Perhaps the most significant trend is that marketers have begun to recognize the strategic value of place in the marketing mix, and the increased revenues and customer satisfaction that may result from high-quality logistical services. As a result, many firms have recognized *customer service* as the interface activity between marketing and logistics, and have aggressively and effectively promoted customer service as a key element of the marketing mix. Firms in industries such as food, chemicals, and pharmaceuticals have reported considerable success along these lines.

Table 2–2 shows the results of a recent comprehensive study undertaken to develop empirical evidence about the importance of customer service. The information shows that, in general, product was the marketing variable respon-

TABLE 2–2   IMPORTANCE OF MARKETING VARIABLES BY INDUSTRY

	Food	Chem-ical	Phar-maceu-tical	Auto	Paper	Elec-tronic	Cloth/Tex.	Other Mfg.	Total Mfg.	Mer-chan-dise	Total Response
Product (quality, breadth of line, etc.)	34.8	33.0	36.9	26.8	23.2	41.3	34.7	32.6	33.2	32.9	33.3
Price (base price, competitive-ness, etc.)	25.8	34.8	29.4	29.8	35.8	26.5	22.0	33.7	30.0	27.9	29.9
Customer service	20.0	19.1	17.3	33.5	28.9	21.8	22.8	23.6	22.6	21.3	22.4
Advertising, pro-motion, sales effort	19.4	13.1	16.4	9.9	12.1	10.4	20.5	10.1	14.2	17.9	14.4
Total	100.0	100.0	100.0	100.0	100.0	100.0	100.0	100.0	100.0	100.0	100.0

Note: Survey respondents were asked to distribute 100 points among the marketing variables listed to indicate the importance of each in generating sales of product to the customer.

Source: Adapted from draft research findings to be published in Ohio State University, *Customer Service: A Management Perspective* (Oak Brook, IL: Council of Logistics Management, 1988).

dents perceived as most important. Price, customer service, and promotion followed in general order of importance. Although product and price generally perceived participating industries to be more important than customer service, Table 2–2 contains some notable exceptions. Specifically, automobile industry respondents ranked customer service most important; and paper and clothing/textile industry respondents ranked it second in importance.

sales forecasting

Finally, firms are tending to place sales forecasting activity within the logistics area, rather than within the marketing area. This not only acknowledges that timely and accurate sales forecasting is important to the firm's logistics mission, but also highlights sales forecasting as another interface area between marketing and logistics.

Logistics Interfaces with Service

Porter cites service as a primary activity in the value chain and suggests that the principal value of service is that it may enhance or maintain product value through activities such as installation, repair, training, parts supply, and product adjustment.

categories of product

If we distinguish between *core, tangible,* and *augmented* products in a classical marketing sense,[7] then the service activities cited in the preceding paragraph would constitute a large part of the augmented product. In today's competitive environment, firms seek augmented product forms that may help them to establish a competitive advantage. As a result, activities such as installation, repair, training, and parts supply lead the list of services which may satisfy such expectations.

Overall logistics responsibility includes delivering product to customers. Thus, some representative of the firm (or an agent such as a transportation company) should be able to ensure that the product reaches the customer in the desired quantity, at the right time, and in the right condition. The logistics area should be able to provide timely feedback concerning the availability of product the customer orders.

Through effectively designed customer service, logistics should also be in an excellent position to identify service needs and see that necessary services are provided. Properly executed, this responsibility can help to improve the firm's competitive position in the marketplace.

example

One example of customer service responsibility is Frito-Lay, whose company drivers make all product deliveries to retail stores. By adopting this approach, the company enables its drivers to see that retailers merchandise product properly and that retailers take full advantage of available marketing and logistics services (e.g., point-of-purchase display materials or special racks for Frito-Lay products).

establishing a competitive edge

In an industrial environment, postsale services and customer support are critical to establishing and maintaining a competitive edge. The firm that chooses to develop strength in this area can gain an advantage over its closest competitors. Once again, the firm's logistics function is in an excellent position to help implement and operate a meaningful system aimed at delivering necessary services to customer firms.

Logistics Interfaces with Procurement

Procurement is the area of the firm that acquires purchased inputs such as raw materials, component parts, supplies, and other items consumed in the production process, and durables such as equipment, machinery, and structures which support overall business needs. The term *purchasing* relates specifically to buying inputs such as those identified here, whereas *procurement* typically includes purchasing as well as activities such as warehousing and the receipt of inbound materials. We classify procurement as a "support" activity, given that purchased inputs are relevant to all other activities, both primary and support.

purchasing decisions

Typical purchasing decisions involve determining where the company will purchase needed inputs and the quantities in which the company will make purchases. Both aspects of this decision affect logistics costs. The *where* aspect is important particularly if such goods are purchased F.O.B. point of origin, since the firms must make arrangements to transport the goods to the plant. The distance from vendors to the plant will affect transportation cost. In addition, a firm may have to store or warehouse goods purchased in large quantities ultimately using them.

Purchasing decisions affect logistics costs, and the opposite is also true. For example, in adequate transportation arrangements or space for storing materials inadequate, will cause problems for the purchasing area. In some instances the relationship between purchasing and logistics is so important that purchasing responsibility may be within the overall responsibility of the logistics manager. Apparent in industry today, this trend holds true for many consumer goods manufacturing firms, as well as for many industrial manufacturing firms.

Logistics Interfaces with Technology Development

technology development

Another value activity is technology development, the broad range of technologies and processes that support all other value chain activities. As discussed by Porter, "the array of technologies employed in most firms is very broad, ranging from those technologies used in preparing documents and transporting goods to those technologies embodied in the product itself." Porter indicates that most technologies involve several different subtechnologies; for example, machining involves metallurgy, electronics, and mechanics.

The overall message is that technology development pervades the firm and its many value activities, including those which are primary and those which are support. Inbound and outbound logistics are primary value chain activities, so technology development applies entirely to processes and technologies relevant to the firm's logistics function and its individual activity areas. Since most firms have many customers, and each customer may have unique logistical needs, firms need to develop appropriate processes and technologies relating to individual customers. Thus, the logistics and technology development areas have both considerable opportunity, and a need, for meaningful interface.

Logistics Interfaces with Human Resource Management

This activity refers to the full range of personnel management decisions that are relevant to, and that cut across, all corporate functions and activities. Included are specific activities such as recruiting, hiring, training and development, and compensation matters relating to personnel at all levels within an organization.

activities

The logistics area interfaces closely with the value activity of human resource management. Aside from routine involvement such as assistance in recruiting, selecting, and hiring, logistics should seek advice and direction from human resource management in matters concerning the compensation and career growth of logistics employees.

training and development

On another level, these areas need to interface in areas of training and development. Logistics personnel at all levels need to know how to perform their jobs in manners that meet expectations. Finally, since logistics operations are frequently labor intensive, the firm's human resource management can frequently be an expert source of information and guidance for matters such as labor relations and contract negotiation with union organizations. Thus, these two important value activities need to interact.

Logistics Interfaces with Firm Infrastructure

Included here are the relationships between logistics and activities such as general management, planning, finance, accounting, legal, government affairs, and quality management. Although much of what constitutes *firm infrastructure* is difficult to attach to other specific value activities, these relationships attempt to positively affect the entire value chain. We may highlight the interface with logistics in certain specific ways and the following paragraphs describe some commonly observed interactions.

logistics planning

Planning   The strategic and business planning processes discussed throughout business literature all apply directly to the functional areas of inbound and outbound logistics. Thus, a firm's logistics area may benefit from types of planning approaches valuable for the whole business. We will pursue this topic in depth in Chapter 15.

Finance   Although operations and marketing are usually the most important other functional areas in a manufacturing organization in terms of relationships with logistics, we need to mention two specific matters relating to finance.

competition for resources

First, the organization's financial management is typically quite important. The logistics manager often competes with areas such as marketing and operations for the organization's capital. For example, a logistics study might suggest acquiring a private warehouse or a fleet of private trucks to provide better service. These are assets that require capital, which is a scarce and expensive resource. Logistics would have to justify why the company's spending money on such facilities would be more worthwhile than spending money on a new machine or a new advertising campaign, or some other investment.

inventory

The second important area is inventory. While a company expects to sell all inventories, in the short run inventory represents company capital that is "tied up," or unavailable for other uses. Given that the firm must assess some charge because capital in inventory represents an opportunity cost, the firm often has to coordinate inventory accumulation with the finance area.

need for accurate and timely cost information

Accounting Another important area is accounting, in that good cost information is essential to logistics. Without adequate cost information, accomplish the basic analysis types suggested in the previous chapter, let alone more sophisticated simulation modeling types is difficult. Very often logistics departments have problems because the firm's centralized accounting systems are designed to give good financial data for financial analysis or for tax and audit functions—not for managerial purposes. Logistics managers today critically need to receive timely and accurate cost and revenue information in a form suitable for making logistics decisions.[9]

recent studies

The Council of Logistics Management sponsored two studies of how accounting and control practices relate to transportation and warehousing within a firm's logistics function.[10] Both studies generally concluded that these areas each have very specific cost and revenue information needs which a firm must satisfy in order to maximize the results of logistics decisions.

The overall message here is that a firm accounting and control systems must customize to meet the management information needs of logistics and its component activities. A firm better able to interface and coordinate these areas will achieve the full potential competitive advantage.

focus on quality in logistics

Quality Management Given the prevalent trend in many firms today toward a companywide commitment to quality improvement, we should naturally expect a high degree of interaction between this corporate initiative and the logistics area. Since performance in the logistics area can directly affect customer satisfaction, most firms should be able to formally commit to a logistics area quality process.

When a firm has made companywide commitment and the quality improvement process is well underway, logistics area success should follow soon thereafter. Companies that have placed high priority on both corporate and logistics quality processes include Campbell Soup Company, Shell Oil, Tennessee Eastman, and Ford Motor Company, to name but a few.

Overview

"bridge" between production and marketing

Organizations can benefit from the interrelationships among marketing, production, and logistics. Some authors have described this relationship as logistics providing a "bridge" between production and marketing. Such a statement has several significant implications. One, the logistics department can transmit marketing information to production so that production, advised of market needs, will have adequate advance notice to avoid overtime or special production sequences.

logistics as an integrating mechanism

Two, having logistics effect an interface between logistics and marketing will usually lower inventory costs. Both areas may tend to build up inventories, for reasons indicated previously.

Three, logistics can provide effective coordination with purchasing and sales forecasting, which are often related to production and marketing. For example, at Clairol Corporation, the logistics organization provides the bridge from sales and marketing plans to the planning which ensures production support. This reduces the natural conflict that arises between objectives in any organization.

Four, we could include the finance area in this discussion because of its interest in the inventory investment level. The logistics area can serve as a mediating unit for fundamental conflicts between marketing, finance, and production. In other words, logistics ensures system optimality by seeking optimal trade-offs among otherwise "competing" functions.

Coordination among functional departments is difficult because individual departments try to satisfy their own interests, thereby blocking timely resolution of problems. Logistics must consider the trade-offs between areas, such as transportation cost versus customer service, and purchasing cost versus inventory cost. The overall logistical and interfunctional strategies must be consistent with overall corporate strategy.

LOGISTICS IN THE FIRM: FACTORS AFFECTING THE COST AND IMPORTANCE OF LOGISTICS

This section deals with specific factors relating to the cost and importance of logistics. Emphasizing some of the competitive, product, and spatial relationships of logistics can help to explain the strategic role of a firm's logistics function.

Competitive Relationships

Frequently, people's interpretation of competition is narrow in that they think only of price competition. While the price issue is certainly important, in many markets and circumstances customer service is a very important form of competition. For example, if a company can reliably provide its customers with its products in a relatively short time period, then its customers can often minimize inventory cost. A company should consider minimizing buyer inventory costs, just as important as lower product prices, since minimizing such costs will contribute to more profit or in turn enable the seller to be more competitive. Therefore, customer service is of great importance to the logistics area.

length of order cycle

Order Cycle   That order cycle length directly affects inventory requirement is a well-accepted principle of logistics management; stated another way, the shorter the cycle, the less inventory required.[11] Figure 2–9 shows this relationship. We will discuss order cycles in greater detail in the chapter dealing with order processing and information systems. For now, we can define order cycle as the time it takes for a customer to receive an order once he or she has decided to place it. It includes elements such as order transmittal time, order preparation time, and transportation time.

Figure 2–9 shows that longer order cycles require higher inventories. Therefore, if a firm can improve customer service by shortening customer order cycles, then its customers should be able to operate with less inventory. It follows, then, that such a cost reduction could be as important as a price reduction.

FIGURE 2–9 RELATIONSHIP BETWEEN REQUIRED INVENTORY AND ORDER CYCLE LENGTH FROM A CUSTOMER PERSPECTIVE

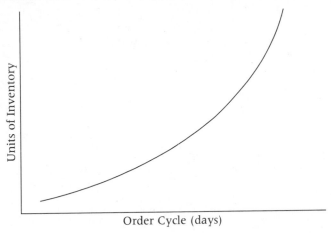

Logistics Environments

nature **Substitutability** *Substitutability* very often affects the importance of customer service. In other words, if a product is similar to other products, then consumers may be willing to substitute a competitive product if a stockout occurs. Therefore, customer service is more important for highly substitutable products than for products that customers may be willing to wait for or back order. This is one reason firms spend so much advertising money making customers conscious of their brands. They want consumers to ask for their brands, and, if their brands are temporarily not available, they would like consumers to wait until they are.

variation Product substitutability varies greatly. Usually, the more substitutable a product, the higher the customer service level required. As far as a logistics manager is concerned, a firm wishing to reduce its lost sales cost, which is a measure of customer service and substitutability, can either spend more on inventory or spend more on transportation.

relationship to lost sales **Inventory Effect** Figure 2–10 shows that by increasing inventory costs (either by increasing the inventory level or by increasing reorder points), firms can usually reduce the cost of lost sales. In other words, an inverse relationship exists between the cost of lost sales and inventory cost. However, the total cost curve shows that firms are willing to increase the inventory cost only until total costs start to go up. They are typically willing to spend increasing amounts on inventory to decrease lost sales cost by larger amounts—in other words, up to the point at which the marginal savings from reducing lost sales cost equal the marginal cost of carrying added inventory.

relationship with transportation **Transportation Effect** A similar relationship exists with transportation, we can see in Figure 2–11. Companies can usually trade off increased transportation costs against decreased lost sales costs. For transportation, this additional expenditure involves buying a better service—for example, switching from water to rail, or rail to motor, or motor to air. The higher transportation cost also

FIGURE 2–10   GENERAL RELATIONSHIP OF THE COST OF LOST SALES TO INVENTORY COST

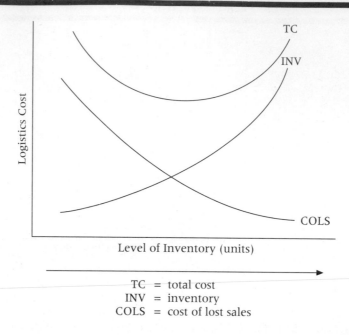

TC = total cost
INV = inventory
COLS = cost of lost sales

could result from shipping more frequently in smaller quantities at higher rates. So, as indicated in Figure 2–11, firms can reduce the cost of lost sales by spending more on transportation service to improve customer service. Once again, the total cost curve shows firms willingly do this only up to the point where the marginal savings in lost sales cost equal the marginal increment associated with the increased transportation cost.

Although showing inventory cost and transportation cost separately is convenient here, companies often spend more for inventory and for transportation almost simultaneously to reduce the cost of lost sales. In fact, improved transportation will usually result in lower inventory cost.* In other words, the situation is much more interactive and coordinated than indicated here.

Product Relationships

A number of product-related factors affect the cost and importance of logistics. Among the more significant of these are the following: dollar value, density, susceptibility to damage, and special handling.

Dollar Value A number of product aspects will have a direct bearing on logistics cost. First, the product's dollar value will typically affect warehousing costs, inventory costs, transportation costs, packaging costs, and even materials handling costs. As Figure 2–12 indicates, as the product's dollar value increases, the cost in each indicated area will also rise. The actual slope and level of the cost functions will vary from product to product.

---

*The lower inventory costs stem from smaller carrying capacity and faster transit times.

FIGURE 2–11 GENERAL RELATIONSHIP OF THE COST OF LOST SALES TO TRANSPORTATION COST

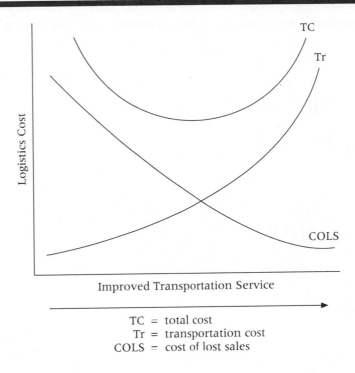

TC = total cost
Tr = transportation cost
COLS = cost of lost sales

impact on rates   Transportation rates reflect the risk associated with the movement of goods. There is often more chance for damage with higher-value goods; and damage to such goods will cost the transportation company more to reimburse. Transportation companies also tend to charge higher rates for higher-value products because their customers can typically afford to pay a higher rate for such products. A relationship exists between the product value and the rate amount in transportation rate structures.

impact on warehousing   Warehousing and inventory costs will also go up as the dollar value of products increases. Higher value means more capital in inventory, with higher total capital costs. In addition, the risk factor for storing higher-value products will increase the possible cost of obsolescence and depreciation. Also, since the physical facilities required to store higher-value products are more sophisticated, warehousing costs will increase with increased dollar value.

impact on packaging   Packaging cost will also usually increase because the firm uses protective packaging to minimize damage. A company spends more effort in packaging a product to protect it against damage or loss if it has higher value. Finally, materials handling equipment used to meet the needs of higher-value products is very often more sophisticated. Firms are usually willing to use more capital-intensive and expensive equipment to speed higher-value goods through the warehouse and to minimize the chance of damage.

impact on logistics cost   **Density** Another factor that affects logistics cost is density, which refers to the weight/space ratio. An item that is lightweight compared to the space it occupies—for example, household furniture—has low density. The Gillette

FIGURE 2–12   GENERAL RELATIONSHIP OF PRODUCT DOLLAR VALUE TO VARIOUS LOGISTICS
COSTS

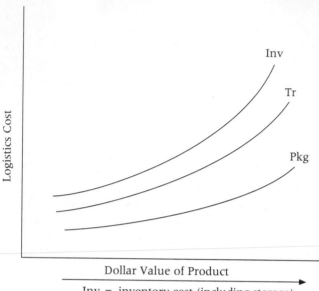

Inv = inventory cost (including storage)
Tr = transportation cost
Pkg = packaging cost

packaging situation previously described is also a good example. Density affects transportation and warehousing costs as Figure 2–13 shows. As we move from low density to high density, warehousing cost and transportation costs tend to fall.

In establishing their rates, transportation companies consider how much weight they can fit into their vehicles, since they quote their rates in terms of dollars and cents per hundred pounds. Therefore, on high-density items they can afford to give a lower rate per hundred pounds because they can fit more weight into a car. Density also affects warehousing costs. The higher the density, the more weight can fit in an area of warehouse space—hence, the more efficient the use of warehousing space. So both warehousing cost and transportation cost tend to be influenced in the same way by density.

Susceptibility to Damage   The third product factor affecting logistics cost is susceptibility to damage (see Figure 2–14). The greater the risk of damage, the higher the transportation and warehousing costs. Transportation companies expecting greater product damage, will charge higher rates, and warehousing cost will go up either because of damage or because of measures taken to reduce the risk of damage.

Special Handling   A fourth factor, related to damage susceptibility but somewhat distinct, is special handling requirements for products. Some products may require specially sized transportation units, refrigeration, heating, or stopping

Figure 2–13   General Relationship of Product Weight Density to Logistics Costs

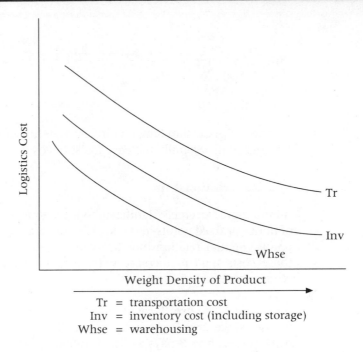

Tr = transportation cost
Inv = inventory cost (including storage)
Whse = warehousing

Figure 2–14   General Relationship of Product Susceptibility to Loss and Damage to Logistical Costs

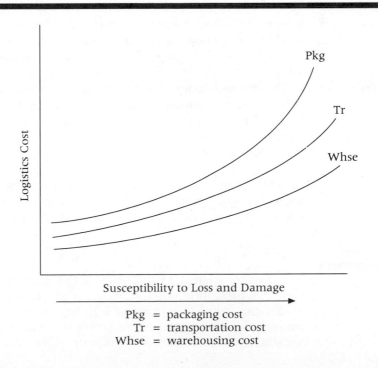

Pkg = packaging cost
Tr = transportation cost
Whse = warehousing cost

FIGURE 2–15   LOGISTICS SPATIAL RELATIONS

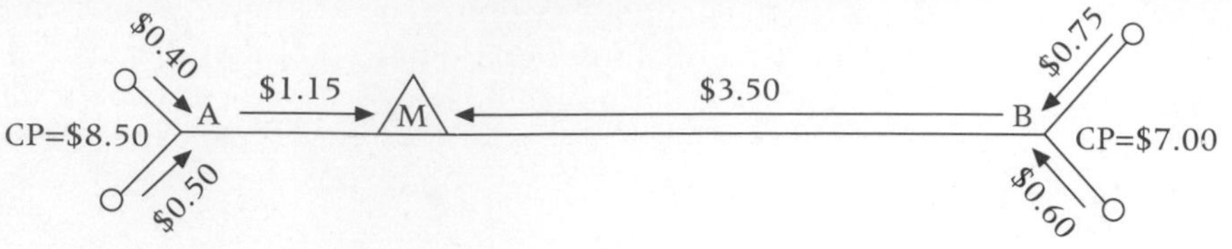

in transit. Special handling requirements, whether for transportation or for warehousing, will generally increase logistics cost.

Spatial Relationships

A final topic extremely significant to logistics is spatial relationships, the location of nodes or fixed points in the logistics system with respect to market and supply points. Spatial relationships are very important to transportation costs, since these costs tend to increase with distance. Consider the following example, which Figure 2–15 illustrates.

Example   The firm located at B has a $1.50 production cost advantage over firm A, since firm B produces at $7.00/unit as opposed to $8.50/unit for firm A. However, firm B pays $1.35 for inbound raw materials ($0.60 + $0.75) and $3.50 for outbound movement to the market, for a total of $4.85 in per-unit transportation charges. Firm A pays $0.90 for inbound raw materials and $1.15 for outbound movement, for a total of $2.05 in transportation charges. Firm A's $2.80 transportation cost advantage offsets the $1.50 production cost disadvantage. Firm B may wish to look at alternative strategies for its logistics system in order to compete more effectively at M. For example, firm B may base its $3.50/unit transportation cost for shipping to the market on less-than-truckload rates (low-volume movements). The firm may consider using a warehouse at M and shipping in higher-volume rail carload lots at lower transportation costs.

distance factor   The distance factor or spatial relationships may affect logistics costs in ways other than transportation costs. For example, a firm located far from one or more of its markets may need to use a market-oriented warehouse to make customer deliveries in a satisfactory time period. Therefore, distance can add to warehousing and inventory carrying costs. It may also increase order processing costs.

Distance or spatial relationships are of such importance to logistics cost that logistics responsibilities include site location. We will consider location, or site analysis, in some detail at a later point in the text.

SUMMARY

This chapter addresses issues relating to the three principal environments of a firm's logistics function. The first—the macro, or external, environment—includes the value-added role of logistics, as well as the economic impacts of business logistics. Aggregate economic data and specific cost and industry data substantiated the economic importance of business logistics.

The second environmental perspective is distribution channels, which characterize the interfirm environment logistics faces. Only by understanding channel separation, channel functions, and channel systems will the logistics manager be able to fully utilize opportunities in interfirm relationships.

The third environmental area is the micro, or intrafirm, environment. This chapter divided intrafirm environment discussion into two key portions. First, the text likened the logistics mission to the keys to competitive advantage Michael Porter set forth in *Competitive Advantage:* cost leadership, differentiation, and focus. Examining the relationships between inbound and outbound logistics and other primary and support activities in the firm's value chain highlighted some key interface types that must take place. Second, the text discussed specific factors affecting the cost and importance of logistics.

A sound understanding of the environments the firm's logistics function faces should provide a valuable background for studying the individual activities constituting logistics management. A familiarity with the logistics environment is also a prerequisite to identifying and implementing logistics strategies.

STUDY QUESTIONS

1. "The time utility dimension of business logistics is of utmost importance for companies operating in the global environment of the nineties." Do you agree or disagree with this comment? Why?

2. The United States has developed into a service-based economy, with manufacturing declining in importance to the overall gross national product. How will this affect time and place, the traditional utilities of logistics?

3. Some individuals argue that one advantage of better logistics systems is lower prices in the economy. Do you agree? If so, why?

4. During the eighties, overall logistics costs declined on a relative basis. What factors contributed to this decline in cost? What is the outlook for the nineties? Why does the nineties outlook differ from that of the eighties?

5. If logistics savings occur in the nineties, which area is likely to have the greatest impact: transportation or inventory? Defend your position.

6. Logistics is said to add marketplace value that can enable a company to sustain competitive advantage. How does the value chain concept contribute to understanding the value that logistics adds to products?

7. Some have referred to logistics as marketing's other half because of its close relationship to marketing on the system's outbound side. Is the relationship between logistics and marketing likely to strengthen or weaken during the nineties? Explain the rationale for your answer.

8. The value chain displays procurement as a supporting activity that cuts across an entire organization. What is the rationale for positioning procurement in this way? What rationale could you offer for positioning procurement within the logistics function?

9. The nineties have been referred to as the Decade of the Customer. How will this emphasis affect the logistics system?

10. An inverse relationship exists between logistics costs and product weight density. Why is this the case? What steps do companies take to improve the weight density of their products?

11. U.S. companies have tended to produce higher-value products in the post-World War II era. How has this affected overall logistics costs? How can companies offset these effects?

NOTES

1. C. John Langley, Jr., "Adverse Impacts of the Washington Beltway Residential Property Values," *Land Economics* 52, no. 1 (February 1976), 54–65; and Hays B. Gamble, Owen H. Sauerlender, and C. John Langley, Jr., "Adverse and Beneficial Effects of Highways Reflected by Property Values," *Transportation Research Record Number 508* (Washington, D.C.: Transportation Research Board, December 1974), 37–48.

2. Michael E. Porter, *Competitive Advantage* (New York: Free Press, 1985), 11–16.

3. Porter, *Competitive Advantage,* 33–34.

4. Porter, *Competitive Advantage,* 38.

5. Porter, *Competitive Advantage,* 36–43.

6. E. Jerome McCarthy and William E. Perrault, Jr., *Basic Marketing: A Managerial Approach,* 9th Ed. (Homewood, IL: Richard D. Irwin, 1987), 46–52.

7. Philip Kotler, *Marketing Management: Analysis, Planning, and Control,* 5th ed. (Englewood Cliffs, NJ: Prentice-Hall, 1984), 463–64.

8. Porter, *Competitive Advantage,* 42.

9. For a discussion of why traditional accounting systems fail to produce the key nonfinancial data required for effective and efficient operations, see Robert S. Kaplan, "Yesterday's Accounting Undermines Production," *Harvard Business Review* (July–August 1984), 95–101.

10. Council of Logistics Management, *Transportation Accounting and Control: Guidelines for Distribution and Accounting Management* (Oak Brook, Ill.: Council of Logistics Management, 1983); and Council of Logistics Management, *Warehouse Accounting and Control: Guidelines for Distribution and Financial Managers* (Oak Brook, Ill.: Council of Logistics Management, 1985).

11. Roy Dale Voorhees and Merrill Kim Sharp, "Principles of Logistics Revisited," *Transportation Journal* (Fall 1978), 69–84.

CASE 2–1

MACKLIN, LTD.

Heinrich Macklin, president of Macklin, Inc., had requested that the company include the Corporate Logistics Department in its strategic planning efforts. Bill End and Harold Massen, the department's two senior managers, chose to represent the logistics department in this effort.

During the initial briefing meeting, Bill and Harold received an overview of corporate goals and challenges and other related information.

The president identified the following goals for Macklin:

- Sharpen market profile and technological focus
- Improve competitive position in the marketplace

■ Improve productivity
■ Promote business unit specialization but maintain overall unity and synergy

The strategic directions team also learned about the following recent and soon-to-be announced developments in Macklin:

■ Establishment of seventeen business units with complete profit and loss specialization
■ Corporate marketing and sales decentralization at the business unit level
■ A smaller executive committee which would include the vice president of logistics

Macklin manufactures technical products ranging from semiconductors to power plants. They produce on a mass production basis as well as on a project (make-to-order) basis. In addition to their twenty plant locations worldwide, they utilize forty private and public warehouses.

For the next meeting, Bill End and Harold Massen must make a presentation to the executive committee describing the relationships between logistics and the organization's other major areas such as marketing, production, and finance, and detailing how logistics contributes value to the product. Write the presentation for them.

SUPPLY CHAIN MANAGEMENT

The Logistics Pipeline

Toys "R" Us

Toys "R" Us sells throughout the year at discount prices and maintains the largest selection of toys available nationwide. In order to maintain 18,000-item inventories at each store at the lowest cost, Toys "R" Us must make off-season purchases in large quantities, rapidly respond to developing fads, and still minimize systemwide storage and handling costs.

Toys "R" Us achieves those somewhat conflicting objectives through one of the most comprehensive and detailed logistics systems in existence. The system combines daily updates from its electronic point-of-sale cash register system with its expert system (artificial intelligence), which is linked to very sophisticated vendor/supplier information models.[1] The 350-store system of Toys "R" Us is so effective that the company knows more about toy sales than any of its suppliers/vendors.

Nabisco Foods

Logistics systems also play an extremely complex part in the foods industry, and Nabisco Foods Company is a good example of the distribution, product variety, and customer service possible with an efficiently planned and managed logistics system. At any local grocery store, you can see the tremendous variety of products that Nabisco produces and distributes. From syrup to salsa, margarine to molasses, Nabisco Foods products line supermarket shelves—in every flavor and form imaginable.

product expansion

The product line proliferation and product line extension trends that we discussed in Chapter 1 are certainly manifested in the food industry today. New products in various sizes and shapes require new manufacturing processes, expanded material and packaging requirements, and new suppliers/vendors—all of which the logistics manager must schedule and manage efficiently.

changing environment

But these changes are not limited to inbound logistics (materials management). They also occur on the outbound side (physical distribution/customer service). The channels and distribution networks of food companies have become extremely complex. Nabisco Foods serves not only grocery and food service operations but also drug mass merchandisers and wholesale clubs, to name a few. All of these distribution channels have different needs and expectations as Nabisco's customers.

The roles of the distribution channels are changing. Gone are the days when the mighty producers such as Nabisco Foods, Procter & Gamble, and General Mills could deliver whatever they wanted, whenever they wanted, to retailers and wholesalers. A company can no longer maintain competitive advantage by simply producing a quality product at a reasonable cost: intense competitive pressure forces producers and sellers alike to also maintain high customer service levels.[2]

In the wake of all these changes, Nabisco has had to reduce logistics operating costs while boosting the company's customer service level—two seemingly contradictory objectives. In prior eras, logistics managers usually expected to increase their costs in order to increase customer service levels.

Nabisco attributes its success in achieving lower costs with higher service levels to its management foresight in linking Nabisco's distribution pipeline: linking vendors to carriers to plants to warehouses to distributors to customers (see Figure 3–1.)

Once upon a time, the key to true strategic advantage or power in the marketplace lay in owning the largest resource base, manufacturing plants, and research labs. Today, superior physical facilities and even a seemingly superior product will not enable most companies to sustain a competitive advantage. Competitors can clone a company's products; they can bypass or even surpass a company's ace product. Instead, maintainable, superior competitive advantage comes from outstanding depth in particular human skills, and knowledge bases, and especially from logistics. Competitors have more difficulty reproducing these areas; such areas can lead to very demonstrable "added value" for the customer.[3]

A company at which logistics provides the key to competitive advantage is Seagate Technology, the world's leading manufacturer of hard disk drives for personal computers. In an effort to gain competitive advantage against Japanese rivals, Seagate decided to absorb the cost of delivering its products to customers *and* to guarantee delivery within four days. Because the guaranteed delivery was critical, Seagate developed a special alliance with Skyway Freight Systems to make deliveries from Seagate's California distribution center to customers all over the United States. Interestingly, the delivery costs Seagate incurred amounted to less than one percent, per unit, of each disk drive's total cost. Seagate's number of late deliveries was also significantly less than one percent.[4]

The above discussion indicates that in today's fiercely competitive business environment, customer demands require greater flexibility and faster reaction. Terms such as "quick response logistics" and "turbo logistics systems" are becoming increasingly common in business literature. Essentially, competition is compelling companies to manage their material flows better—from vendors right through the pipeline to customers (see Figure 3–2).

Effectively managing the flow of materials through the logistics pipeline requires not only faster service but also lower costs. As the Toys "R" Us and Nabisco Foods examples indicated, companies must reduce inventory levels, improve customer service levels, incorporate greater flexibility in scheduling

FIGURE 3–1   THE LINKS IN NABISCO'S DISTRIBUTION PIPELINE   *Source:* Robert Sloan, Proceeding of Council of Logistics Management, Vol. 1 (1989) 24.

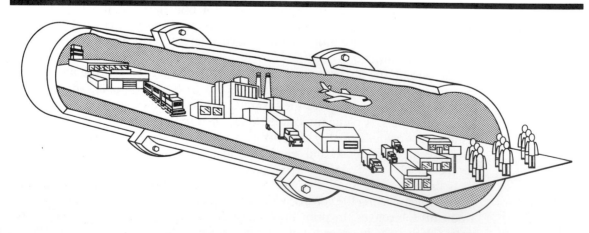

FIGURE 3–2 THE FLOW OF MATERIAL AND INFORMATION IN THE LOGISTICS PIPELINE

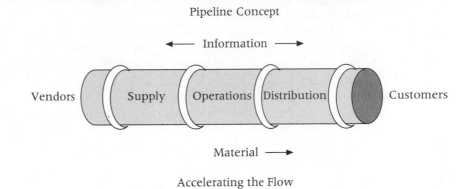

Pipeline Concept

←— Information —→

Vendors | Supply | Operations | Distribution | Customers

Material —→

Accelerating the Flow

shipments and equipment, and increase inventory velocity (turnover) in the pipeline.

Other companies who have enjoyed the benefits of effective logistics supply chain/pipeline management include:

- Procter & Gamble has saved an estimated $500 million in logistics system operating costs.
- Burgen Brunswig, a major distributor of pharmaceuticals and health care products, has achieved a remarkable twelve-hour order cycle time (the time elapsing from when the customer places the order until the customer receives it).
- Xerox has reduced inventory costs by twelve percent and increased its number of inventory turns by thirty percent.

Logistics pipeline or supply chain management involves managing the sequence of all supplier-to-customer material flow activities that add value to the final product. In essence, we are talking here about the entire logistics pipeline—the subject matter of this entire book. This chapter will focus upon the beginning and end of the pipeline, materials management and customer service, respectively and upon distribution channels.

MATERIALS MANAGEMENT

role in logistics   Figure 3–3, which portrays a manufacturing firm's function in a logistics pipeline, illustrates the role of materials management in logistics. In essence, the sourcing and inbound movement and storage of finished products (or semifin-

FIGURE 3–3 THE ROLE OF MATERIALS MANAGEMENT IN THE LOGISTICS PIPELINE

Vendors | Sourcing | Inbound Storage/ Transp. | Operations | Outbound Storage/ Transp. | Customer Distrib. | Customers

raw materials

ished products) is the materials management phase of logistics. Combining materials management and physical distribution management forms the complete logistics pipeline.

The logistics function's dichotomy should not imply that the two basic functions, materials management and physical distribution management are independent. Rather, these functions are interdependent. The demand the customer generates for finished goods sets in motion the physical distribution function and consequently signals the plant to increase production, which in turn sets in motion the materials management function. As demand for the finished good develops, the manufacturer requires raw materials to produce the products or to replenish depleted inventories. Fulfilling the demand for raw materials is the materials management function.

Materials Management Functions

We can describe *materials management* as the planning and control of a firm's inbound materials (manufacturing supplies and finished goods); such planning and control often extends to the production process. Materials management usually includes the following activities: materials planning and control, purchasing, inbound transportation, receiving, incoming quality control, warehousing, production scheduling, and salvage and scrap disposal. We will discuss each activity in the following sections. For many companies, the major materials management activity is purchasing or procurement; and we will discuss this functional area in greatest detail.

Purchasing/Procurement   *Purchasing* and *procurement* is the process of obtaining goods and services for a firm. This concept, which extends well beyond the simple act of buying, involves all the activities necessary to perform the daily and long-term functions of acquiring goods and services. To accomplish this, the purchasing manager must determine a company's material needs, locate supply sources, evaluate and select one or more suppliers, choose a buying method, establish an acceptable price and other terms of sale, monitor the purchase's status until the supplier delivers it, and evaluate the vendors' products and service.

buying

We may understand the purchasing function somewhat better by examining procurement activities. The classic definition of purchasing/procurement is buying the right quality, in the right quantity, at the right price, from the right source, at the right time.[5] This definition of purchasing addresses the major decision-making areas of purchasing: how much to buy; what quality is needed; what the cost is; from whom the goods should be purchased; and when and where should the goods be delivered.

The purchasing/procurement process involves a set of activities that are generic to most organizations. We will briefly explain these activities below.[6]

- ■ **Identify or Reevaluate Needs**
  The purchasing manager initiates a procurement transaction in response to either a new or existing need of a user, usually an individual or department within the firm. Purchasing something for which the firm has no need would make little sense. In some instances, the manager must reevaluate changing needs. In either case, once the manager identifies the need, the procurement process can begin.

- **Define and Evaluate User Requirements**

  Once the purchasing manager has determined the need, he or she must represent its requirements by some type of measurable criteria, such as weight, measurement, blueprints for production, or metallurgical requirements. Using these criteria, the procurement professional can communicate the user's needs to potential suppliers.

- **Decide to Make or Buy**

  Before soliciting outside suppliers, the buying firm must decide whether it will make or buy the product or service the user needs. Even a buying firm that decides to make a product will usually have to purchase some types of inputs from outside suppliers. The firm usually bases this decision upon a supplier's input cost and quality. However, other factors may affect the purchasing decision.

- **Identify Type of Purchase**

  The type of purchase the user needs will determine the procurement process's duration complexity. The three purchase types, from least time and complexity to most time and complexity, are (1) a straight rebuy or routine purchase, (2) a modified rebuy which requires a change in an existing supplier or input, and (3) a new buy which results from a new user need.

- **Conduct Market Analysis**

  A supply source can operate in a purely competitive market (many suppliers), an oligopolistic market (a few large suppliers), or a monopolistic market (one supplier). Knowing the market type will help the procurement professional to determine the number of suppliers in the market, where the power/dependency balance lies, and whether negotiations, competitive bidding, or some other buying method might be most effective.

- **Identify All Possible Suppliers**

  This activity involves identifying all possible suppliers that might satisfy the user's needs. Important to this activity is including in the pool of possible suppliers those that the buying firm has not used previously.

- **Prescreen All Possible Sources**

  When defining and evaluating user requirements, the procurement professional must differentiate between demands and desires. Product or service demand are critical to the user; desires are not as critical and are therefore negotiable. Differentiating reduces the pool of possible suppliers to those that can satisfy the user's demands.

- **Evaluate Remaining Supplier Base**

  After reducing the pool of possible suppliers to those that can meet the user's demands, the purchasing manager can now determine which supplier(s) can best meet the user's negotiable requirements, or desires.

- **Choose Supplier**

  This activity requires the purchasing manager to choose the supplier(s). The choice of supplier(s) also determines the relationship that will exist between the buying and supplying firm(s) and how the firms will structure and implement this relationship's mechanics. This activity also determines how the buying firm will maintain relationships with the nonselected suppliers.

- **Deliver Product/Performance Service**

  This activity occurs with the supplier's first attempt to satisfy the user's needs. This activity's completion also generates performance data that the buyer will use in the next activity.

■ **Postpurchase/Make Performance Evaluation**
Once the supplier has performed the service or delivered the product, the buying firm must evaluate the supplier's performance to determine if it has truly satisfied the user's needs. This also acts as a control activity. If supplier performance did not satisfy the user's needs, the purchasing manager must determine the causes for this variance and implement proper corrective actions.

Vendor Selection Criteria   A critical factor in this process is selecting the appropriate vendor or supplier. As we indicated above, a buying firm must critically evaluate vendors using appropriate criteria. The usual factors that firms consider include the following:

quality

The most important vendor selection factor is usually *quality*. As we indicated earlier, quality refers to the specifications a user desires in an item (technical specifications, chemical or physical properties, or design, for example). The procurement professional compares the actual quality of a vendor's product with the specifications the user desires. In actuality, quality includes additional factors such as life of the product, ease of repair, maintenance requirement, ease of use, and dependability.

reliability

Reliability comprises delivery and performance history, the second- and third-ranked factors. So as to prevent production line shutdowns resulting from longer-than-expected lead times, the buyer requires consistent, on-time deliveries. Also, the product's performance life directly affects the quality of the final product, the manufacturer's warranty claims, and repeat sales. Finally, in cases of material malfunction, the buying firm considers the vendor's warranty and claim procedure a reliability measure.

capability

The third major vendor selection criterion, *capability*, considers the potential vendor's production facilities and capacity, technical capability, management and organizational capabilities, and operating controls. These factors examine the vendor's ability to provide a needed quality and quantity of material in a timely manner. The examination includes not only the vendor's physical capability to provide the material the user needs, but also the vendor's capability to do so consistently over an extended time period. The buying firm may answer this long-run supply concern considering the vendor's labor relations record. A record of vendor-labor unrest resulting in strikes may indicate that the vendor is unable to provide the material quantity the user desires over a long time period. A firm that buys from this vendor will incur increased inventory costs storing material in preparation for likely disruptions in the vendor's business due to labor strife.

financial

Financial considerations constitute the fourth major vendor selection area. The vendor's price is, of course, a major consideration in the vendor selection process; but price may not be the most important selection determinant. Although the price a buyer pays for materials affects the cost of producing the final products, in a total cost analysis, the material's quality, reliability, and capability are more important. In addition to price, the buying firm considers vendor's financial position. Financially unstable vendors pose possible disruptions in a long-run continued supply of material. By declaring bankruptcy, a vendor that supplies materials critical to a final product could stop a buyer's production.

desirable qualities   We may group most of the remaining vendor selection factors into a miscellaneous category of desirable, but not necessary, criteria. Though the buyer might find the vendor's attitude difficult to quantify, attitude does affect the vendor selection decision. A negative attitude, for example, may eliminate a vendor from a buyer's consideration. The impression or image the vendor projects has a similar affect on vendor selection. The importance of training aids and packaging will depend on the material the buyer is purchasing. For example, packaging is important to buyers of easily damaged material, such as glass, but not important to buyers purchasing a commodity that is not easily damaged, such as coal. Training aids would be significant to a firm selecting vendors to supply technical machinery such as computers and robots, but not to a firm seeking office supplies. Likewise, a buyer would consider repair service availability more important when buying technical machinery. As we will discuss in the carrier selection section, buyers should not consider reciprocal arrangements—that is, "You buy from me, and I will buy from you" important in the vendor selection decision.

vendor location   One final vendor selection factor is geographical *location.* This question addresses the issue of whether to buy from local or distant vendors. Transportation cost is one obvious aspect of this issue. Other factors, such as the ability to fill rush orders, meet delivery dates, provide shorter delivery times, and utilize greater vendor-buyer cooperation, favor the use of local suppliers. However, distant vendors may provide lower prices, greater technical ability, greater supply reliability, and higher quality.

factor importance   The vendor selection factors' relative importance will depend upon the material the buyer is purchasing. When a buyer purchases a computer, for example, technical capability and training aids may be more important than price, delivery, and warranties. Conversely, a buyer of office supplies would probably emphasize price and delivery more than the other factors.

price, quality, and service   As we indicated earlier, one purchasing objective is to acquire materials at the lowest cost that quality and service requirements will allow. This objective emphasizes the purchase price's importance to the overall cost of doing business. The objective also indicates that product's quality and service considerations constrain its lowest price. However, the price a company pays for material directly affects the company's profitability; and, since material costs can be so significant, the purchasing manager carefully considers the price a potential vendor quotes.

commodity markets   Purchasing managers utilize four basic procedures to determine potential vendors' prices: commodity markets, price lists, price quotations, and negotiations.[7] *Commodity markets* exist for basic raw materials such as grain, oil, sugar, and natural resources including coal and lumber. In these markets, the forces of supply and demand determine the price that all potential vendors will charge. Reductions in the supply of these materials or increases in demand usually result in increased prices; the converse is true for increases in supply or decreases in demand.

price list   *Price lists* are published prices that are generally used with standardized products such as gasoline or office supplies. The vendor's catalog describes the items available and provides the price list. Depending on the status buyer's, may receive a purchaser discount from the list price. For example, a vendor may give a ten percent discount to small-volume buyers (less than $1,000 per month) and a thirty-five percent discount to large-volume buyers (more than $10,000 per month).

price quotations   Purchasers use the *price quotation* method for both standard and speciality items. It is particularly useful in promoting competition among suppliers. The process begins with the buyer sending potential vendors *requests for quotes* (RFQs). An RFQ contains all the necessary information regarding the specifications the purchaser requires and the manner in which potential suppliers are to present their offers. In turn, the vendors examine the cost they will be incur in producing the material, considering the quantity the purchaser will order, the purchases' duration, and other factors that will affect the vendor's profitability. Finally, the purchaser compares the vendor's quoted price and offer specifications with those of other vendors.[8]

negotiation   The fourth procedure, *negotiation,* is useful when the other methods do not apply or have failed. Negotiation is particularly effective when the buyer is interested in a strategic alliance or long-term relationship. The negotiation process can be time-consuming, but the potential benefits can be significant in terms of price and quality.

best price   As we stated earlier, a purchasing objective is to buy at the best price. However, the "best" price may not be the lowest price. The purchasing department must consider how other selection factors will affect the procurement process's total cost.

The purchasing function is a major component of the materials management area. A manufacturing firm spends approximately fifty to sixty percent of its sales dollar on purchased materials. The next section examines the warehousing element of materials management.

Warehousing   The *warehousing function* concerns the physical holding of raw materials until a firm uses them. Chapter 7 discusses general warehousing functions and decision areas. Though storing the raw materials a manufacturer will use in the production process is basically the same as storing finished products, raw materials storage and finished goods storage differ notably in terms of the type of facility each requires, the stored items' value, and product perishability.

facilities required   Basic raw materials such as coal, sand, or limestone normally require an open-air warehouse facility; that is, a firm would merely dump the basic raw materials on the ground. Thus, the facility cost for storing basic raw materials is lower than the facility cost for storing other materials—finished goods, components, and other semifinished products, for example—that require an elaborate enclosed structure.

The value of raw materials is usually lower than that of finished goods, since the manufacturer enhances the value of the finished material, or processed raw material, during the manufacturing process. Last, basic raw materials usually suffer less damage and loss than finished goods because raw materials have lower value and need no protection from the elements.

Chapter 7 will discuss the warehousing function and the ways in which its activities and decisions affect logistics systems.

Production Planning and Control   *Production planning and control* in a manufacturing environment involves coordinating product supply with product demand. As Figure 3–4 shows, the starting point of the production planning and control process is the demand for the finished product the company produces and sells. This demand is the process's independent variable, since the seller cannot control customer demand.

FIGURE 3–4   OVERVIEW OF PRODUCTION PLANNING AND CONTROL

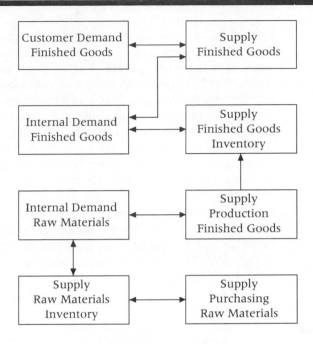

The manufacturer must forecast, or estimate, customer demand. This sales forecast should indicate the sales amount the manufacturer expects for each item and the time period the sales projection covers. After establishing this independent customer demand, the manufacturer can attain the finished product supply either from available inventory or by producing the product.

Thus, external demand establishes an internal demand for a finished product; and the manufacturer fills this demand from existing stocks or from new production.

When demand requires production, the production scheduling manager uses the sales forecast to develop a production schedule. A production planner's main concerns include the following:

- Number of units of a specified product to be produced
- Time intervals over which production will occur
- Availability of materials and machines to produce the number of units required within the specific time frame

Production control results as the production manager specifies time intervals and develops order schedules for raw materials to supply the production schedule.

For example, suppose sales forecasts estimate that a firm will sell 10,000 units of product A and 30,000 units of product B in March. The firm makes both products on the same machine, which produces 10,000 units per week. The production planner first determines how much, if any, production the firm requires to satisfy customer demand and to maintain target inventory levels. In this example, low inventory levels require the firm to produce all 40,000 units. Additionally, a special promotion has depleted product A's inventory quickly, giving product A scheduling priority. However, vendor labor strikes have made the material for product A unavailable until week 2. As a result, the production planner first schedules one week of product B, followed by one week of product A and then two weeks of product B.

inbound traffic

Traffic   The *traffic* function manages the inbound transportation of materials. Transportation originates with the materials vendor, and the movement's destination is the buyer's plant. The inbound traffic activity supports the firm's supply effort in that the inbound transportation bridges the spatial and temporal gap existing between the buyer and the vendor, or seller.

The management of inbound traffic requires transportation knowledge and expertise similar to that necessary to handle the movement of finished goods outbound from the plant. The traffic manager must decide about the transportation mode, the routes, the rates, claims handling, carrier services, cost analysis, and regulations. Chapters 9, 10, and 11 discuss these factors in detail.

vendor control

In many situations, the vendor controls inbound transportation. F.O.B. delivered terms of sale characterize such cases. When the buyer relinquishes the traffic function to the vendor, the buyer assumes that the vendor will ship the material as cost-efficiently as possible. However, such an assumption is not always true. The buyer should periodically analyze the cost effectiveness of the vendor's transportation decision.

modal choice

For basic raw materials, the traffic activity normally involves rail or water transportation, the modes companies most commonly utilize to ship large volumes of low-value, high-density products, such as coal or sand. With the advent of rail deregulation, many of these shipments are moving into plants under contract rates with the railroads. The contracts usually agree to provide a specific rate or service in return for a guarantee that the shipper will allow the carrier to ship a given amount of freight.

rush shipments

Finally, inbound traffic is normally under less pressure from "rush" shipments than is outbound traffic. The demand for raw materials is much more stable and predictable than the demand for finished goods, since economies of production dictate long production runs, which give way to fixed production schedules. However, inbound traffic must occasionally handle a rush shipment—if a plant receives damaged raw materials, for example. Also, with increased JIT use, inbound transportation requires much stricter schedules. Occasionally, when a problem develops, inbound traffic must expedite (rush) a shipment.

inspection

Receiving   The *receiving* process involves the actual physical receipt of the purchased material from the carrier. The receiving clerk, who must ensure that the goods a firm receives were those ordered and shipped, compares the material indicated on the buyer's purchase order and the vendor's packing slip with the material the buyer has actually received. If discrepancies exist, the receiving department notifies the purchasing department, the material's users, and the accounts payable department.

damaged claims

Another critical inspection during the receiving process involves examining the received material for any physical damage. As we note in Chapter 9, claims against the carrier for damage are easier to make if the receiving clerk notes on the bill of lading that the buyer received the shipment in damaged condition. When such a notation appears on the bill of lading, the carrier is presumed guilty of damaging the material. Any legal action places the burden on the carrier to prove that the carrier was not guilty of damaging the freight. Not noting damage on the bill of lading does not preclude the payment of a damage claim, but it puts an additional burden on the receiver (or owner) of the material to prove that the shipment was damaged when the carrier delivered it. Inbound traffic departments and receiving departments usually coordinate freight claims handling activities.

quality standards

Quality Control The *quality control* function, like the receiving function, attempts to ensure that the items a firm receives are those the firm ordered. However, the quality control function is directly concerned with defining the product's quality in terms of dimensions, design specifications, chemical or physical properties, reliability, ease of maintenance, ease of use, brand, market grade, and industry standard. The quality control area's specific concern is whether or not the product received meets the quality standards the buyer and seller set forth in the purchase agreement.

quality implications

The quality of the materials a manufacturer procures directly affects the quality of the finished product, and consequently affects the sale of the finished product. If a firm sells a defective product, the product's buyer will become dissatisfied and may refuse to purchase the firm's product in the future. In addition, a manufacturer who uses inferior materials in production may be legally liable for a hazardous or unreliable product. Thus, quality control function responsibilities cover the spectrum from market to legal concerns.

sample

Normally inspecting each item that a buyer purchases is neither possible nor desirable. Quality inspectors usually examine a limited sample of the items purchased. For example, a quality inspector wanting to determine whether the life of a given vendor's light bulbs met longevity specifications would test a sample of the vendor's light bulbs. The quality control department would statistically examine the results and, on the basis of the tested sample, would decide to accept or reject the order received. The increased emphasis on quality in recent years has required vendors to develop their own statistical quality control programs. Today, many buyers insist upon total or 100% quality.

Salvage and Scrap Disposal The final activity in the materials management function involves disposing of *salvage, scrap,* excess, and obsolete materials. Although primarily concerned with buying, the materials management department has assumed this selling responsibility since most marketing or sales departments must concentrate on selling the firm's finished products.

value of scrap

Scrap and salvage material that is useful to others has a certain value, and these items' disposal provides income for the firm. The recent recycling trend has provided a ready market for many scrap and salvage items. For example, companies using used oils and other scrap items such as olive pits and corncobs as fuel sources. And, as recent years of double-digit inflation have sent new equipment prices beyond many potential buyers' abilities to pay, more companies are buying or salvaging used equipment.

disposal

Certain scrap materials cannot be sold but must be disposed of in a safe and prescribed manner. One such commodity group is hazardous wastes—materials that are ignitable, corrosive, reactive (volatile), or toxic. Disposing of these hazardous materials is quite costly, and the generator of such materials is under specific legal liability to dispose of them properly.

The materials management function, as we indicated, occurs on the inbound side of the logistics pipeline. Customer service and distribution activity channels are on the pipeline's outbound side. But a firm must tightly coordinate both inbound and outbound logistics in today's highly competitive marketplace.

A good example of the importance of and potential for integrating the supply chain is the Greencastle, Pennsylvania, facility of Corning Glass's Consumer Products Division. The giant Greencastle facility, a warehouse, a packaging

QUICK RESPONSE: A LOGISTICS RECIPE FOR THE NINETIES

Here's a new recipe for you. Take a healthy portion of JIT philosophy and mix with equal measures of EDI and bar-coding technology. Then blend in a solid commitment to quality customer service from your logistics personnel. Soon you'll have something that may well be vital to business success in the 1990s. It's called Quick Response.

Pioneered by the textile and apparel industry, Quick Response is essentially where the customer and JIT meet. One consultant, in fact, defines Quick Response as the application of JIT concepts throughout the entire supply pipeline, from the manufacturer to the final consumer. Another consultant puts it slightly differently. "Quick Response is the ability to deliver 100 percent to the customers' needs," says Gene Hansen, president of Synergetics, Inc., in Sioux Falls, South Dakota. "It encompasses the ability to obtain raw materials, set up production, and deliver goods within the time constraints of the customer."

Whatever definition you use, Quick Response appears to be one hot buzzword right now. In at least one industry analyst's view, Quick Response will be to the nineties what MRP (materials requirements planning) was to the seventies and JIT was to the eighties. Born out of heightened competition in both domestic and world markets and made possible by advances in technology, the Quick Response concept may help turn American industry around as the twentieth century heads into the home stretch.

A Retailer's Dream

As a retailer, imagine the benefits of a fully integrated Quick Response system. A customer walks into your store. He selects the widget he needs off the shelf and goes to the checkout counter. The cashier takes the item, scans the bar code attached to it, and collects the money from the customer. The item goes into a bag that the clerk hands to the customer with an itemized receipt and a smile. The transaction is complete.

As the customer is leaving the store, data collected when the cashier scanned the widget's bar code is being used to order a replacement widget. Every party that plays a role in getting what replacement on the shelf is being notified electronically to get moving.

Those capabilities may sound like overkill, but industry observers insist they are fast becoming a competitive necessity. The changes in the consumer marketplace in recent years have been so profound, says one logistics industry executive, that retailers and their vendors have almost no room for error in satisfying customer needs. "There's unprecedented pressure out there today to offer customers quality, value, selection, and price," said Charles B. Lounsbury, president and CEO of Leaseway Transportation's Integrated Logistics Group in Cleveland.

Although JIT philosophy and a competitive marketplace may have given rise to the Quick Response movement, it's technology that makes it all possible. The data-collection and -recording capabilities of bar-code technology and the ability to communicate these data throughout the supply pipeline via electronic data interchange (EDI) are the tools necessary to build a Quick Response System.

The bar code's value lies in its ability to capture data accurately at the point of sale, says consultant Bonney Stamper, president of Bar Code Systems, Inc., in Atlanta. That means the supplier can replenish shelves based on what is sold, she explains, not on a forecast of expected demand. "In the past, retailers and manufacturers could rely only on analysis of historical buying patterns," she said. "Now they can respond to exactly what is selling."

Traffic Management (April 1991), 54–56. Reprinted with permission of *Traffic Management*, a Cahners Publication.

center, and a distribution center rolled into one, functions as a hub receiving about 300 million pounds of products each year and shipping about fifty million packaged sales units to its customers.

Having traditionally focused on the pipeline's customer service side, Corning Glass has in recent years recognized the importance of controlling materials management. As a part of a newly adopted JIT strategy, Corning has been reducing the number of its vendors/suppliers. The result has been an increase in inventory turns (velocity), as well as cost reductions and better quality. Customer service time has not suffered a bit; in fact, it has improved because of Corning's increased packaging line flexibility.

Corning is not unique in this regard. Many other companies, as we suggested previously, have achieved similar results by improving their inbound logistics efforts. At this point, however, a more detailed discussion of the pipeline's other end is necessary.

CUSTOMER SERVICE

As Chapters 1 and 2 indicated, business logistics involves minimizing total cost while maximizing time and place utility in goods. Much of the early work in this field highlighted new and innovative ways to achieve logistics cost savings. At the same time, however, it became obvious that most cost reduction opportunities had at least some, and often a significant, effect upon the customer service levels a firm could provide. Thus, from a managerial perspective, customer service levels provided an inherent constraint upon the firm's logistics system; and logistics costs such as transportation, warehousing, inventory, and order processing either increased or decreased depending on the service levels customers desired. As a result, it became difficult for a firm to make any rational cost reduction decision without considering the customer service level the firm needed to maintain in order to retain its competitive position in the marketplace.

Customer service is usually the most important logistics element directly related to the firm's marketing mission and marketing activities. Thus, customer service, by mixing logistics activities that provide time and place utility consistent with the customer's needs, is the output, or end product, of the business logistics function. Whether we are speaking about logistics in the sense of inbound to production/assembly or outbound to market, the end product of the logistics process is to provide certain services consistent with the customer's needs.

Xerox Canada provides an excellent example of the relationship between marketing and the logistics supply chain/piepline. In the mid-1980s, Xerox Canada, wishing to carve a more prominent niche for itself among competitor organizations, created a Supply and Logistics Division. The logistics supply chain thus became a specialty designed to improve Xerox Canada's international competitiveness. The new division's objective was to maximize customer service while optimizing the use of assets and inventory in the logistics pipeline—in other words, to cut costs and improve service. For an organization known as a marketing company, recognizing a new Division of Supply and Logistics as a top priority was a major breakthrough. The new division at Xerox has worked with marketing and sales to be responsive to customers' expectations.[9]

What is Customer Service?

Anyone who has ever struggled to define customer service will soon realize the difficulty of explaining this nebulous term. Thus, different people will understandably have different interpretations of just what *customer service* means.

levels of product   We may think of customer service as something a firm provides to those who purchase its products or services. According to marketers, there are three levels of product: (1) the core benefit or service, which constitutes what the buyer is really buying; (2) the tangible product, or the physical product or service itself;

and (3) the augmented product, which includes benefits that are secondary to, but an integral enhancement to, the tangible product the customer is purchasing. In this context, we may think of logistical customer service as an augmented product feature that adds value for the buyer. Other augmented product examples include installation, warranties, and after-sale service.[10]

competitive advantage

Extending our thinking along these lines, a firm could achieve a competitive advantage by providing superior levels of logistical customer service. Thus, a real potential benefit exists in viewing customer service as a "product" that may add significant value for a buyer.

Types of Customer Service

general types of customer support/ service

A fundamental point is to recognize that customer service is a concept whose importance reaches far beyond the logistics area. Frequently, customer service affects every area of the firm by attempting to ensure customer satisfaction through the provision of aid or service to that customer.

Examples of the various forms that customer service may take include the following:

- Revamping a billing procedure to accommodate a customer's request
- Providing financial and credit terms
- Guaranteeing delivery within specified time periods
- Providing prompt and congenial sales representatives
- Extending the option to sell on consignment
- Providing material to aid in the customer's sales presentation
- Installing the product
- Maintaining satisfactory repair parts inventories

This chapter examines the customer service focus within a business logistics mission. However, customer service can, as the list above indicated, have many interpretations throughout the firm. Customer service's numerous nonlogistical aspects may add value for the customer, and a firm should include these aspects within its overall marketing effort.

Definitions of Customer Service

levels of involvement

While customer service has no single definition, customer service, people think of customer service in three principal ways, which we think of as three levels of customer service involvement or awareness. The levels include the following:[11]

1. *Customer service as an activity.* This level treats customer service as a particular task that a firm must accomplish to satisfy the customer's needs. Order processing, billing and invoicing, product returns, and claims handling are all typical examples of this customer service level. Customer service departments, which basically handle customer problems and complaints, also represent this level of customer service.

2. *Customer service as performance measures.* This level emphasizes customer service in terms of specific performance measures such as the percentage of orders delivered on time and complete, and the number of orders processed within acceptable item limits. Although this level enhances the first one, a firm must look beyond the performance mea-

sures themselves to see that its service efforts achieve actual customer satisfaction.

3. *Customer service as a philosophy.* This level elevates customer service to a firmwide commitment to provide customer satisfaction through superior customer service levels. This viewing of customer service is entirely consistent with many firms' contemporary emphasis on quality and quality management. Rather than narrowly viewing customer service as an activity or as a set of performance measures, this interpretation involves a customer service dedication which pervades the entire firm and all of its activities.

complexity of customer service

The customer service issue has many dimensions and is truly complex. However, a firm may fully control numerous customer service elements through effective business logistics management. Successfully implemented, high levels of logistics customer service may easily become strategic ways in which a company can differentiate itself from its competitors.

Importance of Customer Service in Logistics

impacts on sales revenues

In much the same way they respond to increases or decreases in a product's price, customers will respond to changes in the customer service levels a firm provides. Generally, providing higher levels of customer service should positively affect a firm's revenue levels and, hence, its market share with respect to its competition.

This principle has some exceptions, however, as the experience of Dutch Boy Paints shows. When Dutch Boy Paints established same-day delivery service to customers, customer service levels did increase measurably but had no perceptible effect on sales. The same company found that increasing product availability to ninety-six percent (that is, filling ninety-six percent of its orders from existing stocks) generated little attention from the customer base, while reducing the level to ninety-two or ninety-three percent incited significant customer reaction.[12] However, in today's market environment, Dutch Boy's experience is an exception.

augmented product

The customer is concerned with the total product he or she is purchasing, not merely with its physical characteristics of the goods. The level of logistical customer service is important to the augmented product and may very well have effects upon customer response satisfaction similar to the effects of price and other physical characteristics. In essence, the logistics function is the final phase of the buyer-seller transaction that involves the physical transfer of goods. This transfer automatically produces some level of customer service, good or bad. Superior levels of logistical customer service will generally enhance a firm's product offering; inferior levels will generally detract from it.

cost trade-offs

Customer service is an important basis for incurring logistics costs. Economic advantages generally accrue to the customer through better supplier service. As an example, a supplier can lower customer inventories by utilizing air rather than truck transportation. Lower inventory costs result from air transport's lower transit time, but the link costs will be higher than those for truck transportation. The supplier's logistics manager must balance high service level the customer desires and the benefits the supplier may gain from possible increased sales against the cost of providing that service. The logistics manager must strike a balance among customer service levels, total logistics costs, and total benefits to the firm.

customer service mix

The customer service mix blends a number of key elements, including product availability, order cycle time, distribution system flexibility, distribution system information, distribution system malfunction, and postsale product support.[13] Table 3–1 briefly describes each and provides examples of typical measurement units. Product availability is often the single most important element of the customer service mix; for most manufacturing sectors, order cycle time is second in importance.[14] Together, these elements suggest that dependability is perhaps the single characteristic customers desire most in a firm's logistical capabilities.

food industry example

The food industry illustrates the importance of these customer service factors and how they will probably change over time. Table 3–2 lists customer service factors that are important in the food industry. The first column is for 1990; the second column projects customer expectations for 1995. As we can see, customers will have even higher expectations in 1995. We can also be certain that the 1990 data represents a customer service level higher than that for 1985.

If the table provided data from another industry, the percentages would probably be different but the upward direction of customer service standards would be the same. We may also be certain that companies both within and outside of the food industry would implement such improvements in response

TABLE 3–1   KEY ELEMENTS OF CUSTOMER SERVICE

Element	Brief Description	Typical Measurement Unit(s)
Product availability	The most common measure of customer service. Usually defined as percent in stock (target performance level) in some base unit (i.e., order, product, dollars).	% availability in base units
Order cycle time	Elapsed time from order placement to order receipt. Usually measured in time units and variation from standard or target order cycle. Note: Frequently, product availability and order cycle time combined into one standard. For example, "ninety-five percent of orders delivered within ten days."	Speed and consistency
Distribution system flexibility	Ability of system to respond to special and/or unexpected needs of customer. Includes expedite and substitute capability.	Response time to special requests
Distribution system information	Ability of firm's information system to respond in timely and accurate manner to customers' requests for information.	Speed, accuracy, and message detail of response
Distribution system malfunction	Efficiency of procedures and time required to recover from distribution system malfunction (i.e., errors in billing, shipping, damage, claims).	Response and recovery time requirements
Postsale product support	Efficiency in providing product support after delivery, including technical information, spare parts, or equipment modification, as appropriate.	Response time quality of response

Source: Bernard J. LaLonde, "Customer Service," Chapter 11 in *The Distribution Handbook* (New York: The Free Press, 1985), 244.

TABLE 3–2   CUSTOMER SERVICE FACTORS FOR THE FOOD INDUSTRY

Element	1990	1995
Product Availability	97%	98%
Order Cycle Time	10 days	9 days
Complete Orders Shipped	86%	90%
Accurate Invoices Provided	75% of invoices	91%
Damaged Products	2% damage ratio	1%

Source: A. T. Kearney, Customer Service Data for Food Industry (1991).

to market pressures and that lower costs would frequently accompany these improvements.

CUSTOMER SERVICE ELEMENTS

four main dimensions

Based on this chapter's preceding discussions, we may think of customer service for logistics as having four main dimensions: time, dependability, communications, and convenience. The ways in which these elements affect the cost centers of both buyer and seller firms are the topics this section will explore.

Time

The *time* factor is usually order cycle time, particularly from the perspective of the seller looking at customer service. On the other hand, the buyer usually refers to the time dimension as the lead time, or replenishment time. Regardless of the perspective or the terminology, several basic components or variables affect the time factor.

control over lead time

Successful logistics operations today have a high degree of control over most, if not all, of lead time's basic elements, including order processing, order preparation, and order shipment. By effectively managing activities such as these, thus ensuring that order cycles will be of reasonable length and consistent duration, seller firms have improved the customer service levels that they provide to buyers.

Order Transmittal   Order transmittal encompasses the time that elapses from the time the customer initiates the order until the seller receives the order. Order transmittal time can vary from a few minutes by telephone to several days by mail. A seller moving from slow to fast order transmittal reduces lead time but increases the cost of order transmittal.

use of computers

The computer is revolutionizing order transmittal. Computers linking buyers with sellers permit the buyer to log into the seller's computer. The buyer can determine product availability and other information, such as the probable shipping date. The buyer then selects the items he or she desires, and transfers the order electronically to the seller for processing.

The Bergen Brunswig Corporation, a drug and health care distributor, has adopted such an automated order entry system. The company maintains that this system is largely responsible for increasing the company's income from $3 million to $9.3 million between 1975 and 1980. In this example, reduced lead time made possible through reductions in order transmittal time resulted in improved customer service and increased sales income.

Order Processing   A seller requires order processing time to process the customer's order and make it ready for shipment. This function usually involves a customer credit check, transferral of information to sales records, transferring the order to the inventory area, and preparing shipping documents. Many of these functions can occur simultaneously through the effective use of electronic data processing equipment. Often, a seller's aggregate savings in operating costs will more than exceed the capital investment implementing modern technology requires.

Order Preparation   Order preparation time involves "picking" the order (see Chapter 11) and packaging the item for shipment. Various types of materials handling systems affect order filling and preparation in different ways, as we will discover in later chapters. These systems can vary from a simple manual system to a very highly automated system. Consequently, preparation time can vary considerably. The logistics manager has to consider the alternatives' costs and benefits.

productivity gains   For example, one U.S.-based manufacturer of cans and containers purchased a microcomputer system to help control order picking, labor productivity, and excessive training time at its four warehouse locations. The company has realized a considerable productivity gain in its order picking area through more efficient order picking procedures. The computer generates an order picking slip that is stamped as to time of issue. When the equipment operator completes the order selection and returns the order picking slip, the time is stamped again, measuring the operator's performance as well as the order picking time. Management easily detects inefficient, unproductive operations (operators) and implements corrective action.[10]

transit times   **Order Shipment**   Order shipment time extends from the moment the seller places the order upon the vehicle for movement until the buyer receives and unloads it. Measuring and controlling order shipment time is usually difficult when a seller uses for-hire carriage. Information from the carrier may be unreliable. Having the buyer to complete response cards permits the seller to measure for-hire carriage transit time. To reduce the for-hire carriage transit time, the seller must use a faster (lower transit time) carrier within the current mode or utilize a faster transport mode and incur higher transportation costs.

Chrysler Corporation's Service and Parts Operations Division has established an integrated private/contract carriage system and a computerized parts locating and order system to produce prompt and dependable delivery service for small, less-than-truckload shipments. The system, called Mopar Dedicated Delivery System (DDS), provides next-day delivery to most of its dealers from the company's eighteen distribution centers located throughout the United States. Mopar makes about eighty percent of its deliveries at night through a passkey operation. The company drivers receive keys to the dealer's facility, where deliveries are made to secured areas. The night deliveries reduce delays daytime highway traffic and dealer congestion normally produce.[11]

Modifying all four customer service elements may be too costly. The firm may therefore make cost modifications in one area and permit the others to operate at existing levels. For example, investing in automated materials handling equipment may be financially unwise for the firm. To compensate for its higher manual order processing time, the firm could switch from mail to telephone order transmittal than by mail and could use motor transportation instead of rail. This would permit the firm to reduce lead time without increasing its capital investment in automated materials handling equipment.

Guaranteeing a given level of lead time is an important advancement in logistics management. We may see its impact in the efficiencies that accrue both to the customer (inventory costs) and to the seller's logistics system and market position. By the concept of time, by itself, means little without dependability.

Dependability

To a customer, *dependability* is often more important than lead time. The customer can minimize his or her inventory level if lead time is fixed. That is, a customer knowing with 100% assurance that lead time is ten days could adjust his or her inventory levels to correspond to the average demand (usage) during the ten days and would have no need for safety stock to guard against stockouts resulting from fluctuating lead times.

inventory and stockout costs

Lead Time Lead time dependability, then, directly affects the customer's inventory level and stockout costs. Providing dependable lead time reduces some of the uncertainty a customer faces. A seller who can assure the customer of a given level of lead time, plus some tolerance, distinctly differentiates its product from that of its competitor. The seller that provides dependable lead time permits the buyer to minimize the total cost of holding inventory, stockouts, order processing, and production scheduling.

Figure 3–5 graphs a frequency distribution pertaining to lead time, as measured in days. The graph is bimodal. It indicates that lead time length tends to be in the vicinity of either four days or twelve days. The customer typically receives within four days orders the seller can fill from stock. Orders that the

FIGURE 3–5 EXAMPLE FREQUENCY DISTRIBUTION OF LEAD TIME LENGTH

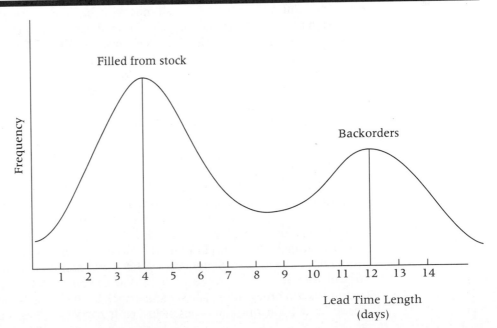

seller cannot fill from available stock, and for which the customer must place a backorder, typically result in a total order cycle time of approximately twelve days.

Dependability encompasses more than just lead time variability. More generally, dependability refers to delivering a customer's order with a regular, consistent lead time, in safe condition, and in harmony with the type and quality of items the customer ordered.

Safe Delivery   An order's safe delivery is the ultimate goal of any logistics system. As we noted earlier, the logistics function is the culmination of the selling function. If goods arrive damaged or are lost, the customer cannot use the goods as he or she intended. A shipment containing damaged goods aggravates several customer cost centers—inventory, production, and marketing.

stockout costs

Receiving a damaged shipment deprives the customer of items for sale or production. This may increase stockout costs (foregone profits or production). To guard against these costs, the customer must increase inventory levels. Thus, unsafe delivery causes the buyer to incur higher inventory carrying costs or to forego profits or production. This situation would be unacceptable for a company interested in minimizing or eliminating inventories through some form of just-in-time program. We will discuss this topic further in Chapter 7.

claims

In addition to the preceding costs, an unsafe delivery may cause the customer to incur the cost of filing a claim with the carrier or returning the damaged item to the seller for repair or credit. (Depending upon the F.O.B. terms of sale and other sales agreement stipulations, the seller, not the buyer, may be responsible for these costs.) The seller will probably be aware of these two costs, since he or she will be more or less directly involved in any corrective actions that may be necessary.

lost sales

Correct Orders   Finally, dependability embraces the correct filling of orders. A customer who has been anxiously awaiting the arrival of an urgently needed shipment often discovers upon receiving the shipment that the seller made an error in filling the order. The customer who has not received what he or she requested may face potential lost sales or production. An improperly filled order forces the customer to reorder, if the customer is not angry enough to buy from another supplier. If a customer who is an intermediary in the marketing channel experiences stockout, the stockout cost (lost sales) also directly affects the seller.

order information

The two logistics activities vital to order filling are the communication of customer order information to the order filling area and the actual process of picking out of inventory the items ordered. In the order information stage, the use of EDI (electronic data interchange) can reduce errors in transferring order information from the order to the warehouse receipt. The seller must simplify product identification such as codes in order to reduce order picker errors.

EDI can only reduce the number of errors in order filling but can also increase inventory velocity in the pipeline. Combining EDI with bar coding can improve a seller's service and lower costs. In fact, EDI along with bar coding can help a seller to improve most logistics functions.

For example, Quill Corporation, the largest independent distributor of office products in the United States, uses a bar code scanning system to effectively control the shipping of more than 12,000 cartons a day.[12] Through catalogs, customers can order any of 7,500 SKUs (stock keeping units). Data electronically transmitted from the bar codes helps with carrier routing, billing, inventory control, and a variety of other tasks. The system helped Quill to reduce transportation expenses by $1 million per year while improving customer service.

seller-customer channel

However, customer contact can be as important as accurate electronic data interchange. *Communication* with customers is vital to monitoring customer service levels relating to dependability. Customer communication is essential to the design of logistics service levels. The communication channel must be constantly open and readily accessible to all customers, for this is the seller's link to the major external constraints customers impose upon logistics. Without customer contact, the logistics manager is unable to provide the most efficient and economical service; in other words, the logistics manager would be playing the ball game without fully knowing the rules.

two-way street

However, communication must be a two-way street. The seller must be able to transmit vital logistics service information to the customer. For example, the supplier would be well advised to inform the buyer of potential service level reductions so that the buyer can make necessary operational adjustments.

In addition, many customers request information on the logistics status of shipments. Questions concerning shipment date, the carrier, or the route, for example, are not uncommon. The customer, who needs this information to plan operations, expects the logistics manager to provide answers.

Convenience

flexibility

Convenience is another way of saying that the logistics service level must be flexible. From the logistics operations standpoint, having one or a few standard service levels that applied to all customers would be ideal. But this assumes that all customers' logistics requirements are homogeneous. This is not the situation in reality. For example, one customer may require the seller to palletize and ship all shipments by rail; another may require truck delivery only, with no palletization; still others may request special delivery times. Basically, logistics requirements differ with regard to packaging, the mode and carrier the customer requires, routing, and delivery times.

different customer requirements

Convenience recognizes customers' different requirements. A seller can usually group customer requirements by factors such as customer size, market area, and the product line the customer purchasing. This grouping, or market segmentation, enables the logistics manager to recognize customer service requirements and to attempt to fulfill those demands as economically as possible.

customer profitability

We can attribute the need for convenience in logistics service levels to the differing consequences the service levels have for different customers. More specifically, the cost of lost sales will differ among the customer groups. For example, a customer purchasing 30% of a firm's output loses more sales for the firm than a customer buying less than 0.01% of the firm's output does. Also, the degree of competitiveness in market areas will differ; highly competitive market areas will require a higher service level than less-competitive market areas will. The profitability of different product lines in a firm's marketbasket will limit the service level the firm can offer; that is, a firm may provide a lower service level for low-profit product lines.

However, the logistics manager must place the convenience factor in proper operational perspective. Customer service level convenience at the extreme would provide a specific service level policy for each customer. Such a situation would set the stage for operational chaos; the plethora of service level policies would prevent the logistics manager from optimizing the logistics function. The need for flexibility in service level policies is warranted, but the logistics manager should restrict this flexibility to easily identifiable customer groups. He or she must examine the trade-off between the benefits (improved sales and profits or elimination of lost profits) and the costs associated with unique service levels in each specific situation.

The Effect of Service upon Sales

As we indicated previously, increasing customer service levels should have a positive impact on sales revenues. While the marketplace may be insensitive to varying service levels, typically we would expect higher service levels to translate into increases in revenues.

There are three fundamental approaches to analyzing the relationship between sales and service: customer surveys, modeling, and experiments and simulations.

gathering of basic information

Customer Surveys   The customer survey is perhaps the most traditional analysis method. The principal value of customer surveys is that they provide information concerning customer intentions and expected behavior patterns. A seller may use the customer survey to ask questions on topics such as how much additional product people would buy if service were to increase, the minimum acceptable customer service standards, and the principal variables that the customer considers to be part of customer service. Aside from practical concerns regarding the length of customer surveys and questionnaires, nothing limits the types and numbers of questions a seller can raise through this tool. Also, a well-designed customer survey can be an excellent vehicle for gathering information about competitors and their logistics capabilities.

Survey results frequently provide valuable insight into customer thinking and intentions. However, surveys have an inherent limitation in that people don't always do what they say they will do on the survey forms. Given this lack of reliability in customer survey results, using the results with 100% confidence for decision-making purposes is difficult. As a result, supplementing customer surveys results with managerial judgment, intuition, and marketplace knowledge will always be necessary.

Modeling Approaches   This approach involves understanding the relationship between sales and certain factors, such as customer service, that may have a causal relationship with sales. The goal of any modeling effort would be to accurately represent how logistical customer service affects sales. Then, the seller can use empirical testing to assess whether the relationships the model includes are valid.

modeling requirements

Effective modeling use requires that other marketing and nonmarketing factors that may affect sales be held constant. This is necessary for isolating and measuring the effects of logistical customer service with any degree of confidence. Modeling approaches should avoid limiting attention, for example, to how stockouts affect sales, and should consider the full range of ways in which logistics provide customer service. Frequently, a perceptible timelag will exist between service level changes and effects on sales. The modeling approach must be sufficiently versatile to account for this.

Modeling approaches offer a methodologically sound approach to analyzing sales and service. To the extent that they accurately represent the relationships between sales and service, models can provide a variety of valuable insights. Aside from the cost of developing a model, the seller will probably need to validate specific modeling approaches through fairly expensive empirical testing using historical or marketplace data. Despite these expenses, model use has become a popular means to gain insight into the relationships between sales and customer service.[13]

Experiments and Simulation   By using a controlled testing environment, a seller may be able to observe the ways in which purchase behavior changes as customer service levels vary. This technique provides the same types of insight as does test marketing a new product. By holding other factors constant, the seller may see the extent to which sales will directly vary with alternative customer service levels. While this approach can provide meaningful results, the experimental design task is a science unto itself; and its users should approach it very methodically.

risk-free experimentation and learning

Simulation is a form of experimentation that involves asking people to make decisions in a *simulated environment,* a laboratory setting that replicates real-world conditions. Using such an environment, the seller may observe the sales decisions customers would make when they encounter with varying customer service levels in the "real" world. Although, at best, a simulation simply reveals what may happen under actual market conditions, it does offer the opportunity for considerable observation in a virtually "risk-free" environment.

Expected Cost of Stockouts

A principal benefit of inventory availability, and hence customer service, is to reduce the incidence of stockouts. Once we develop a convenient way to calculate the cost of a stockout, we can then use stockout probability information to determine the expected stockout cost. Last, we can analyze alternative customer service levels directly comparing the expected cost of stockouts and the revenue-enhancing benefits of customer service.

This section examines stockout issues more directly related to finished goods inventories than to inventories of raw materials or components parts. Calculating stockout costs for finished goods is generally more formidable than calculating these costs for raw materials. We must, however, address issues relating to both of these inventory types. A subsequent section of this chapter deals specifically with inbound logistics supplies and stockout costs.

effects of stockouts

A *stockout* occurs when desired quantities of finished goods are not available when and where a customer needs them. When a seller is unable to satisfy demand with available inventory, one of four possible events may occur: (1) the customer waits until the product is available; (2) the customer backorders the product; (3) the seller loses a sale; or (4) the seller loses a customer. From the viewpoint of most companies, we have listed these four outcomes from best to worst in terms of desirability and cost impact. Theoretically, scenario 1 (customer waits) should cost nothing, this situation is more likely to occur where product substitutability is very low.

nature of cost

Backorder   A customer having to backorder a stocked-out item will incur expenses for special order processing and transportation. The extra order processing traces the backorder's movement, in addition to the normal processing for regular replenishments. The customer usually incurs extra transportation charges because a backorder is typically smaller-size shipment and often incurs higher rates. Also, seller may need to ship the backordered item a longer distance—for example, from a plant or warehouse in another region of the country. In addition, the seller may need to ship the backorder by a faster and more expensive means of transportation. Therefore, we could estimate the backorder cost by analyzing additonal order processing and additional transportation expense. If customers always backordered stocked-out items, the seller could use this analysis to estimate the cost of stockouts. The seller could then compare this cost with the cost of carrying excess inventory.

direct loss

Lost Sales   Most firms find that although some customers may backorder, others will turn to alternative supply sources. In other words, most companies have competitors who produce substitute products; and when one source does not have an item available, the customer will order that item from another source. In such cases the stockout has caused a lost sale. The seller's direct loss is the loss of profit on the item that was unavailable when the customer wanted it. Thus, a seller can determine direct loss by calculating profit on an item basis and multiplying it by the number the customer ordered. For example, if the order was for 100 units and the profit is $10 per unit, the loss is $1,000.

special explanation

We should make three additional points about lost sales. First, in addition to the lost profit, we might include an amount for the cost of the salesperson who made the initial sale. The sales effort was wasted effort and in that sense an opportunity loss. Whether including such a cost is valid would depend upon whether the company uses salespeople in its marketing effort. Second, determining the amount of a lost sale may be difficult in some circumstances. For example, numerous companies customarily take orders by telephone. A customer may initially just inquire about an item's availability without specifying how much he or she desires. If an item is out of stock, the customer may never indicate a quantity; and the seller would not know the amount of the loss. Other problems may cause difficulties but are not insurmountable. For example, though developing a system for recording lost sales in telephone-order situations is often difficult, a seller can overcome this problem through sampling techniques. Third, estimating how a particular stockout will affect future sales within other product lines is difficult.

calculation

In the likely event that a firm will sustain lost sales with inventory stockouts, the firm will have to assign a cost along the lines we suggestcd earlier. Then the firm should analyze the number of stockouts it could expect with different inventory levels. A later section offers an example of this technique. The seller should then multiply the expected number of lost sales by the profit loss plus additional assigned cost, if any, and compare the cost with the cost of carrying safety stock.

difficult nature

Customer Loss   The third possible event that can occur because of a stockout is the loss of a customer; that is, the customer permanently switches to another supplier. A supplier who loses a customer loses a future stream of income. Estimating the customer loss stockouts can cause is difficult. Marketing researchers have attempted to analyze brand switching for some time. Such analysis often uses management science techniques along with more qualitative marketing research methods.

In addition to the loss of profit, stockouts may also cause loss of goodwill. Goodwill is difficult to measure and is often ignored in inventory decisions, but it is essential to future sales and business dealings. In certain markets, it is also very important to overall company profits.

Determining the Expected Cost of Stockouts To make an informed decision as to how much inventory to carry, a firm must determine the expected cost it will incur if a stockout occurs. That is, how much money will the firm lose if a stockout occurs?

procedure

The first step is to identify a stockout's potential consequences. These include a backorder, a lost sale, and a lost customer. The second step is to calculate each result's expense or loss of profit and then to estimate the cost of a single stockout. For the purposes of this discussion, assume the following: seventy percent of all stockouts result in a backorder; twenty percent result in a lost sale for the item, and this loss equals $20.00 in lost profit margin; and ten percent result in a lost customer, or a loss of $200.00.

Calculate the overall impact as follows:

$$
\begin{array}{rcl}
70\% \text{ of } \$ \ \ 6.00 &=& \$ \ \ 4.20 \\
20\% \text{ of } \$ \ 20.00 &=& 4.00 \\
10\% \text{ of } \$200.00 &=& \underline{20.00} \\
\text{Total} = \text{estimated cost} &=& \$28.20 \\
\text{per stockout} & &
\end{array}
$$

Since $28.20 is the average dollar amount the firm can save by averting a stockout, the firm should carry additional inventory to protect against stockouts only as long as carrying the additional inventory costs less than $28.20.

A firm can easily use this information when formally evaluating two or more logistics system alternatives. For each alternative, the firm would need to estimate the potential number of stockouts and to multiply those numbers by the estimated cost of a single stockout. This would represent a way to include stockout costs in the overall decision-making process.

CUSTOMER SERVICE STANDARDS

Developing *customer service standards* requires the firm to determine the types of service its customer desire, the cost of providing alternative services, and measures for evaluating service performance. Inherent to this development is a market analysis of customers by market area, customer size, and product or product lines. Such information is the basis analyzing required customer service levels, costs, and measurement standards.

Establishing Standards

analysis of demand

The establishment of a customer service policy must start with an analysis of customer demand. The degree of product substitutability and the number of competitors determine the amount of product a firm will not sell and, consequently, the money the firm can expect to lose during a stockout. For highly substitutable products, the need to maintain high inventory levels or use premium transportation is greater than that for less-substitutable products. More specifically, the firm must determine for each product or product line whether its customers will wait until the firm replenishes stocked-out items, or if during a stockout its customers will purchase from competitors. Because factors such

costs are different

as the number of competitors and customer brand loyalty will differ among territories, the firm must determine specific service levels for specific territories.

We should also note that stockout cost is not homogeneous for all customers. Customer size, or purchase volume, determines a stockout's potential long-run cost. For example, consider the long-run profit loss a customer causes by permanently shifting to a competitor's product during a stockout. This lost profit is much greater for a customer who purchases 25% of a firm's output than for a buyer who purchases less than 0.1%. Thus, the customer's size may warrant different service policies. As a result, a firm may wish to use some form of ABC analysis to group its customers by importance. Chapter 5 discusses using ABC analysis to group individual inventory items according to importance.

operational needs

The firm must also consider the customer's operational needs. To effect efficiencies in production processes or marketing campaigns, the customer may require specific delivery dates. The seller must know such requirements in order to tailor the product offering and thereby increase or at least maintain sales and profits.

competitor's service

Finally, the market analysis must examine current competitor service levels. At the minimum, a firm must establish a service level policy that equals that of its competitors. Any firm utilizing a service level less than that its competitors provide places itself at a competitive disadvantage. The real concern is whether the firm can provide better service than competitors at a cost that does not place the firm at a price disadvantage.

This market analysis must not be a one-time function performed for the customer service level development. It must be an ongoing process to monitor changes in customer demands and competitors' performance. The continued customer service analysis provides the feedback the firm needs to evaluate and effect changes in its established policy. The marketing department can be tremendously helpful in analyzing customer service needs and competitor service levels.

Objectivity in evaluating customer service level needs, benefits, and costs is paramount. Marketing's objective of increased sales or finance's concern for reduced costs must not overshadow the customer service policy decision. The logistics department possesses objectivity necessary to recognize the marketing benefits and financial constraints and to thereby establish, implement, and control a customer service level policy that is beneficial to the whole firm.

Service Level Standards

Useful customer service level definitions must permit quantifiable measurement. Policy statements such as "ninety percent customer satisfaction" are not readily measurable and therefore are difficult to achieve and control. Ambiguous or nonquantifiable policies do not offer opportunities to evaluate a system's performance and to control customer service costs.

As a result, the logistics function must identify meaningful, measurable customer service standards. The logistics department should use these standards regularly to monitor and control the customer service levels a firm provides.

key elements of customer service

Refer again to Table 3–1, which briefly describes customer service key elements. The last column in the table lists typical measurement units for each element. For example, the table suggests that "% availability in base units" is a typical measurement unit for product availability, and that "speed and consistency" is a typical measurement unit for order cycle time.

development of standards

To develop customer service *standards,* a firm should first identify the measurement unit, and to then establish a specific target performance level. In this manner, the firm can derive customer service standards for each customer service element. The remainder of this section offers some basic advice about developing standards for each element identified in Table 3–1.

fill rates

Product Availability Firms usually measure this in terms of item fill (percentage of line items filled from stock) or order fill (percentage of orders filled from stock). The standard for this element may also combine timeliness with availability to derive a measure such as "ninety-five percent of orders to be shipped on time and complete."

Customer surveys have identified product availability as a very critical customer service element. As a result, a firm must develop standards for the number or percentage of orders correctly filled per time period.

duration of lead time

Order Cycle Time For practical applications, firms generally use standards based on the time necessary to complete the order cycle. Often, however, a firm will state these standards as a given percentage of deliveries completed within a given number of days after order receipt—for example, "ninety percent of deliveries made within three days after the seller firm receives the order." If service is consistent with this policy, then the firm will deliver ninety percent of the shipments to customers within three days of order receipt—only ten percent will take longer.

To determine whether a logistics function is meeting desired customer service time standards, the logistics manager charts the cumulative frequency distribution of the actual delivery times and compares this with the stated policy. For example, if the policy states "ninety percent of deliveries within three days of order receipt," the logistics manager would analyze order receipt information to determine how many orders the firm delivers on time and how many are late. The manager could use a random sample or comprehensive computer analysis of orders for all or particular markets to determine how well actual service time performance complies with stated policies.

Distribution System Flexibility Standards relating distribution system flexibility would probably focus on the seller firm's ability to meet special needs, such as expediting shipments when necessary. In this instance, developing a standard such as "eighty-five percent of all shipments expedited as per buyer's instructions" would be appropriate. Other measures of a shipper's ability to respond to special requests would also help a firm to provide desired distribution system flexibility levels.

Table 3–3 indicates the frequency with which various manufacturing and merchandising firms customarily use different order fill measures.

availability of information

Distribution System Information The speed, accuracy, and detail of needed information are all important to the buyer of a firm's products. For example, a firm may wish to formulate information policies and standards at the customer's request. Developing such a standard would facilitate the process of monitoring and controlling the quality of distribution system information.

service failures

Distribution System Malfunction Unfortunately, logistics systems do occasionally malfunction; and a firm must be able to control any consequences

TABLE 3–3   ORDER FILL MEASURES CUSTOMARILY USED IN VARIOUS INDUSTRIES

	Food	Chemical	Pharma-ceutical	Auto	Paper	Elec-tronic	Cloth/ Tex.	Other Mfg.	Total Mfg.	Merchan-dise	Total Response
Lines filled/lines ordered	5.6%	5.9%	51.5%	52.4%	21.4%	66.7%	36.4%	38.0%	28.7%	16.7%	28.2%
Cases shipped/ cases ordered	70.5	11.8	22.6	9.5	35.7	0.0	18.2	5.6	27.6	8.3	26.8
Dollars shipped/ dollars ordered	1.4	8.8	3.2	4.8	14.3	6.7	0.0	14.1	7.1	50.0	8.9
Promised delivery dates	7.0	52.9	6.5	14.3	21.4	6.7	45.5	22.5			
Invoices shipped complete/ total invoices	8.5	14.7	9.7	9.5	0.0	6.7	0.0	9.9	19.8 / 9.0	8.3 / 8.3	19.3 / 8.9
Other	7.0	5.9	6.5	9.5	7.1	13.3	0.0	9.9	7.8	8.3	7.9
Total	100.0	100.0	100.0	100.0	100.0	100.0	100.0	100.0	100.0	100.0	100.0

Note: Entries in this table indicate the percentage of respondents indicating primary use of each individual order fill measure listed.

Source: Adapted from B. J. LaLonde and M. Cooper, *Customer Service: A Management Perspective* (Oak Brook, IL: Council of Logistics Management, 1988).

that could have a negative effect on the customer. For example, if the firm delivers a damaged shipment, the customer cannot use it; for all practical purposes, this is equivalent to nonreceipt of the order. Resupplying the customer with a usable item requires additional time, as well as added expense to the seller. Thus, the delivery of a damaged product reduces a firm's customer service level and increases logistics costs. A similar analogy would apply when the seller firm makes errors on customer invoices, making it difficult if not impossible for the customer to ascertain the dollar amount due. On a more elemental level, a fire or strike could physically disrupt a firm's logistics operations.

Most distribution system malfunctions are very expensive to remedy. The expense of responding to a malfunction is often many times the original profit margin the seller would have earned on the sale. Such potential losses can usually justify the cost of preventative measures, even if significant.

after-sale support   **Postsale Product Support**   The logistics area has many opportunities to become involved in postsale product support activities such as equipment modification and repair parts service. For example, a firm would benefit from developing time standards for shipping needed repair parts to customers. Thus, a measurable standard such as "ninety-five percent of all repair parts shipped on the same day as order is received" would promote customer confidence in a company's commitment to this type of customer service.

Implementing Customer Service Standards

This section highlights keys for successfully developing and implementing customer service standards.

setting standards   The first point is to be wary of adopting easily achievable performance standards; such standards may be too low to be of practical value. While setting and adhering to a meaningful standard should help to differentiate your firm from the competition, setting standards at unrealistically low levels would not help to establish a competitive advantage.

levels of quality

Second, some current management philosophies—such as the Deming Method for Quality—are very critical of any acceptable quality level (AQL) set below 100%.[14] This does not mean that a firm can achieve 100% performance at all times. The expression of 100% represents an attitude more than a measurement. From a practical viewpoint, however, establishing an AQL that is less than 100% will generally limit, rather than encourage, superior performance.

communication with customers

Third, the firm should develop customer service policies and standards through customer consultation. After adopting these standards, the firm should formally communicate them to customers. Certain firms prefer to keep silent about their customer service standards and to avoid letting their customers know their exact policies and performance targets. The best approach, however, is to very openly communicate these policies and standards to customers.

control of customer service

Fourth, the firm should develop procedures to measure, monitor, and control the customer service quality the firm's performance measures and standards indicate. Using techniques such as statistical process control (SPC), obtaining feedback, and taking corrective action are essential to success.[15] When customer service standards are ineffective, the firm should not hesitate to amend or delete them as appropriate.

A NOTE ON PHYSICAL SUPPLY SERVICE LEVELS

Up to this point, we have been considering customer service levels from the physical distribution side of logistics. A brief digression into customer service levels for physical supply will reveal much similarity to those for physical distribution.

One hundred percent customer service is almost a necessity on the physical supply side. As we noted previously, disruptions in the flow of goods to the consumer aggravate the consumer's costs. However, the consumer can often substitute products; even if substitutes are unavailable, a stockout's cost in foregone sales and profits may be quite small in comparison with a stockout's cost on the physical supply side.

Short lead times usually preclude the possibility for substituting raw materials. First, raw materials suppliers are not as widely available as suppliers of finished goods. Second, a particular raw material's unique technical standards may prevent a firm from substituting even a highly similar material. In short, the lack of alternative raw materials suppliers coupled with the possible technical incompatibility different suppliers' raw materials greatly restrains a firm's ability to substitute raw materials during a stockout.

cost of physical supply stockout

Without this substitution possibility, a physical supply service disruption may result in a plant closing, temporary layoffs, and high start-up costs when the raw material finally arrives. Temporarily closing a plant may mean paying labor for a partial day's wage (depending upon union contract terms) even though no production occurs during this time. If the temporary stockout is prolonged, the firm will furlough labor, increasing future unemployment compensation rates. In addition, once the stockout is alleviated, overtime production might be necessary to replace reduced finished goods inventory or to fill finished goods backorders. If finished goods inventory is depleted, the firm will incur foregone profits as well. Last, the firm still incurs the plant's overhead costs throughout the nonproductive period.

In short, the cost of a physical supply stockout is very great. This extremely high cost greatly increases the "value" of a raw material facing stockout; that is, the item assumes an emergency value much higher than the item's price. The emergency value of raw materials requires the logistics manager to utilize movement and storage functions that he or she would not normally use.

For example, consider a possible stockout of a door handle, valued at fifty cents per handle, at a plant manufacturing auto bodies. A stockout of the fifty-cent handle would stop the auto body assembly line and incur corresponding costs for labor that reported for work but could not complete the shift. The company values this lost productivitty at $160,000 per shift (assuming 1,000 employees @ $20/hour for 8 hours). In addition, the company incurs plant overhead even though no production occurs, a cost of $200,000 per day (assumed cost). Thus the auto body manufacturer in this example values the cost of the door handle stockout at $360,000 per day.

In addition, a raw material stockout may cause intracompany and intercompany effects. The chain reaction of shortages may affect other plants that depend upon the stopped auto body plant, possibly causing work stoppages. Thus a raw material stockout at one plant may affect the operations of other manufacturing plants in the firm's system or the firm's customers.

To offset the door handle stockout, the auto body manufacturer would probably utilize air transportation. The door handle's air freight cost may be ten times the handle's value ($5 per handle for air freight, versus fifty cents for the handle itself). However, considering the potential stockout cost, the handle assumes an emergency value of $360,000 in this example, cost-justifying air freight.

For bulk raw materials such as coal, iron ore, and sand, providing uninterrupted supply service normally entails high inventory levels rather than premium transportation. Bulk commodities' physical characteristics permit the use of inexpensive warehousing facilities—an open-air facility is usually adequate—and preclude the use of air freight. In addition, the bulk material's value is relatively low, requiring a fairly low capital investment.

For example, we might find that an electric utility company utilizing coal stockpiles a 60- to 120-day coal supply. In this example, the potential costs of stockouts (the social and economic costs to all users of electricity) are astronomical. Also, the volume of coal the company uses in one day would make the use of premium transportation (air or even truck) a physical impossibility. Therefore, the potentially devastating cost of an electric supply stoppage justifies the capital investment associated with a ninety-day inventory of coal.

CHANNELS OF DISTRIBUTION

As we suggested in the Nabisco Foods discussion at the beginning of this chapter, no discussion of the end of the logistics pipeline would be complete without some reference to channels of distribution. Technically, a channel of distribution is one or more companies or individuals who participate in the flow of goods and/or services from the producer to the final user or consumer.

Many companies use other companies or individuals to distribute some or all of their products to the final consumer. Let's take the example of Nabisco Foods again. When we stop at a grocery store to pick up a bag of Oreo cookies and/or a can of Planter's peanuts and/or a jar of mustard, we are buying a relatively small quantity and often we want to buy several companies' products—Crest toothpaste from Procter & Gamble or Maxwell House coffee from General Foods, for example. We do not want to visit three different stores to purchase these products. And Nabisco does not want to operate stores in proximity to every possible buyer.

So, for cost efficiencies and customer convenience, Nabisco Foods sells in large quantities to other companies who can get the product to a location convenient for the consumer more inexpensively than Nabisco could. This does not mean that Nabisco may not sell directly to some users or customers. Large restaurants, schools, military installations, and other organizations that buy in large quantities may actually buy directly from Nabisco Foods.

Many customers, however, actually purchase Nabisco's Life Savers or Royal Pudding from another company, usually a retail store. In fact, the retail store may buy from a wholesaler or broker; so several "layers" can separate Nabisco from Mrs. Novack in Mountaintop, Pennsylvania when she purchases Nabisco's Ritz crackers for her son, Tommy.

As we pointed out in Chapter 1, certain companies only sell directly to their ultimate customer. Boeing Aircraft Company is an example. However, many companies sell some part of their product line through a distribution channel. Figure 3–6 presents an overview of the possible channel arrangements. We should keep in mind that a company such as Nabisco may use five to seven of the alternatives Figure 3–6 depicts.

An important point here is that the channel company—K-Mart, Wal-Mart, or Toys "R" Us—is the manufacturer's real customer. Therefore, a manufacturer discussing customer service is talking about Thrift Drug Stores or some other retailer, not about an individual consumer.

FIGURE 3–6   EXAMPLE CHANNELS OF DISTRIBUTION FOR THE FOOD PRODUCTS MANUFACTURING INDUSTRY

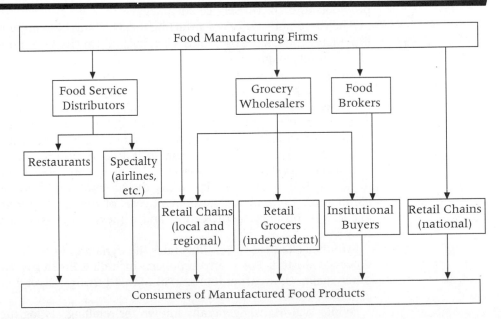

Growth and Importance of Distribution Channels[17]

Growing evidence shows that channels of distribution will assume increasing importance for many producers in the twenty-first century. For example, one study indicates that wholesaler-distributor sales are expected to grow faster than the economy throughout the 1990s. Another study found that seventy-six percent of the companies manufacturing industrial goods use intermediaries/channels to distribute their products to the ultimate user.

When we combine the growing reliance on distribution channels with the consolidation trend reshaping the $1.6 trillion wholesaling industry and large retailers' increasing demands for services such as slotting and trade allowances, we can see the power position in many distribution channels is clearly shifting. Such changes have and will continue to necessitate increasing attention across several functional areas in companies being devoted to channel management.

Channels of distribution, particularly wholesalers, are being called upon to provide value-added services. Health industry distributors provide a good example of this. In response to intense economic pressures, hospitals began to streamline their materials management operations by consolidating supply purchases, automating purchasing inventory-control systems, and seeking suppliers able to reduce ordering costs and inventory levels. They reduced their supplier bases and joined buying groups, which leverage greater transaction volume to obtain lower product prices.

Within this newly competitive environment, hospitals view the distributor's function in one of two ways. Some users—generally the large hospitals—opt for tonnage distribution, whereby they purchase large quantities of products from wholesalers at a low cost. In this basic-services distribution process, the hospital or medical facility usually handles materials management.

Other users of medical products prefer value-added distribution. The customer contracts with the wholesaler to provide services such as storage, handling, inventory management, and delivery. This permits the customer to utilize the distributor's ability to leverage asset investments and knowledge across several providers to gain cost/service advantages.

The value-added services attracting the most attention among medical service providers are the same programs receiving publicity in the automotive industry—JIT inventory management.

Under the JIT approach, a medical distributor pools stock across several hospitals rather than sending it to each facility's central storeroom. This method provides a high level of product availability at reduced total-inventory levels.

Such programs go beyond traditional JIT to eliminate—not just reduce—central storeroom inventory. In these arrangements, the distributor runs a pick-and-pack operation for the hospital as if it were running the picking operation out of the hospital's own storeroom. JIT operations offer multiple benefits for hospitals. They reduce the inventory the hospital carries while simultaneously eliminating the labor and equipment costs of running a storeroom, reduce the expense of product obsolescence, and achieve purchasing economies for the hospital.

Another example which illustrates the dynamics of the distributor's role involves Wal-Mart. For many suppliers, including Procter & Gamble, 3M, and other major U.S. corporations, Wal-Mart's buying power represents a major economic force.

While Wal-Mart is generally known for retailing, its logistics expertise may be just as impressive. The company, which considers minimizing the flow of material through the distribution network essential to controlling costs, has very specific performance standards for the arrival of inbound material. For example, Wal-Mart usually requires a single point of contact with suppliers, regardless of the number of shipping points involved, restricts the mixing of purchase orders on pallets, and strictly specifies how warehouse personnel are to identify and segregate pallets. The company aims all of this at streamlining its receiving and warehousing functions.

The 3M corporation had an established logistics system which shipped product on a first-in, first-out basis from each 3M facility. Traditionally, the system served 3M's needs very well; but it did not meet Wal-Mart's standards. 3M adapted to Wal-mart's requirements by acquiring the special value-added services of Jones Motor Company. At its terminals, Jones consolidated and sorted 3M's products for delivery to Wal-Mart. Jones also provided information to assist both 3M and Wal-Mart in scheduling inventory. In this case, the carrier obviously played a non-traditional role in using an important blend of traditional logistical and transactional activity to help a buyer and seller enhance their transactional relationship.

DISTRIBUTION CHANNELS: A COMPARISON OF MARKETING AND LOGISTICS PERSPECTIVES

In many organizations, major changes have increased the importance of logistics in general and of distribution channels in particular. More computerized links among manufacturers and channel members, the increased cost of selling directly to consumers, just-in-time inventory practices, an increase in the scope of services some intermediaries provide, and an emphasis on integrated logistics management and a supply chain perspective have increased the complexity of channel relationships for marketing and logistics managers, who need to rethink these relationships, including the logistics-marketing interface.

The Marketing Perspective

Marketers define channels as a set of interdependent organizations involved in making a product or service available for use or consumption. The channel's structure is a network of interdependent institutions, agencies, and establishments through which a product must move to reach a customer.

Channels contribute to demand satisfaction by helping to supply goods and services at the right place, in the right quantity and quality, and at the right price. Channels also help to stimulate demand through the promotional and advertising activities its member agencies perform. We can therefore view a channel as an interactive network that helps to create customer value by generating form, possession, time, and place utilities.

Intermediaries, according to traditional marketing theory, exist between producers and consumers to smooth the exchange process, to sort out goods assortment discrepancies, to make transactions routine, and to simplify search processes for both the buyer and the seller. Typical intermediary functions can include carrying inventory, selling, providing after-sale service, and credit extension. In today's environment, the traditional view of channels is too simplistic.

The service level customers require determines channel structure, and the number of intermediaries often increases with the service level customers demand. The degree of postponement and speculation existing in a channel and a producer's size and market power relative to that of other channel members also influence structure. Because of changing customer service requirements and channel member relations, the channel structure is typically dynamic.

Logistics Perspective

The marketing definition and general rationale for distribution channels are quite apropos from a logistics perspective. Logistics channel structure can develop from the delivery time requirements of a company's customer; this structure evolves and changes in response to customer requirements. The logistical flows are the tasks that physically move a product through the distribution channel. These tasks include adjustment, transfer, storage, and handling.

Traditionally, logistical channels have been composed of organizations that perform some or all of the logistical process. These organizations can be independent businesses or a producer's organizational units. The typical firm, which usually selects combinations of facilities and intermediaries to minimize channel cost, usually institutes logistical planning channelwide.

Implementing cost trade-offs in a distribution channel involves two important factors. The first is how customer service offerings affect channel members. The second is how inventory location affects total channel costs and customer service levels.

The traditional logistics treatment of channels emphasizes channel function mechanics and tends to be both static and descriptive. The dynamic issues of channel design, redesign, implementation, and strategy development generally receive little attention. As we stated when discussing the marketing perspective on channels, the traditional perspective is too limited for today's dynamic, competitive market.

SUMMARY

The supply chain or pipeline perspective for logistics is very important in today's environment. Managing the flow of materials from vendor to consumer, whether in a warehouse, plant, or a truck, has enabled companies to increase inventory's pipeline velocity, allowing companies to make better use of assets and to provide better service.

Du Pont's Polymers Division provides a good final illustration. Several years ago Du Pont adopted what they call a supply-chain business strategy to continuously improve their logistics function. Du Pont starts by assessing customer requirements, frequently basing this assessment upon a management team visit to the customer's location. After determining customer requirements, Du Pont uses these requirements to drive quality products and services through the entire logistics pipeline from vendor to customer, saving time and money in the process.[17]

STUDY QUESTIONS

1. Assume that you are currently director of logistics for Quick-Fill Foods Company and that you have been asked to provide a description of and a rationale for the ways in which Quick-Fill could use the logistics pipeline concept to reduce costs and improve service. In your description and rationale, cite examples of how other companies have used this approach.

2. How does materials management affect the logistics pipeline? How does it tie into other supply chain activities?

3. What essential activities does purchasing, or procurement include?

4. Quick-Fill's director of procurement has decided to reevaluate her current vendors. Provide her with a list of the criteria she can use to evaluate and select vendors. Be sure to explain each criterion.

5. Traffic and warehousing are two activities that are a part of the materials management function in the logistics pipeline. How do they relate to purchasing?

6. In this chapter, Corning Glass provides a good example of a company controlling the materials management function as a part of the logistics supply chain. What has Corning done in this area? How do their materials management efforts affect their customer service needs?

7. Customer service is frequently referred to as the link between logistics and marketing. Why? How has Xerox Canada changed to take advantage of this link concept?

8. As a management consultant, you have been asked to write a definition and explanation of customer service that your client can present to her company's board of directors.

9. Why are logistics managers concerned about distribution channels? Is their interest different from that of marketing managers? If so, explain the difference.

CASE 3–1

NO-TELL COMPUTER PARTS

Jerry Sandusky, vice president of logistics for No-Tell, a major producer of microcomputer parts, was in New York making a presentation to a group of potential investors. He had been asked to describe the overall company and the logistics division's role in helping No-Tell to establish a competitive advantage in the marketplace.

In producing microcomputer parts, Jerry pointed out, No-Tell operates within the biggest growth segment of the computer industry. They sell primarily to equipment manufacturers who incorporate No-Tell's products into their microcomputer systems. Founded in 1966, No-Tell currently has about 25,000 employees and had sales of $5 billion last year. No-Tell sells microprocessors, embedded controllers and memories, and microcomputer platforms. The company's goals are to be better, faster, and cheaper than competitors.

No-Tell purchases from vendors all over the world and also sells globally. In an effort to be these customers' vendor of choice, No-Tell strives to achieve on-time, damage-free, low-cost delivery to their plants and to their customers.

Jerry, feeling the increased pressure in the marketplace, reports to the investor group that No-Tell is currently investigating approaching their logistics system from a pipeline or supply chain perspective. Though the investor group is quite excited about this new approach, Jerry's description is sketchy. They request a more detailed report that includes examples. Prepare Jerry's report, being sure to describe how No-Tell could benefit from this new approach.

NOTES

1. J. B. Quinn, T. L. Doorley, and P. C. Paquette, "Beyond Products: Services-Based Strategy," *Harvard Business Review* (March–April 1990), 59–60.
2. "DRP: Key Ingredient in Nabisco's Success," an unpublished paper of STSC, Inc. (Rockville, MD, April 1991), 1–3.
3. Quinn et al., "Beyond Products: Services-Based Strategy," 60.
4. Quinn et al., "Beyond Products: Services-Based Strategy," 61.
5. Joseph L. Cavinato, *Purchasing and Materials Management* (New York: West, 1984), 259.
6. Robert A. Novack and Stephen W. Simco, "The Industrial Procurement Process: A Supply Chain Perspective," *Journal of Business Logistics* 12, no. 1 (1991), 147–49.
7. Cavinato, *Purchasing and Materials Management,* 39–40.
8. Cavinato, *Purchasing and Materials Management,* 90.
9. Fred Moody, "Examples of Excellence," *Canadian Transportation Journal* (May 1991), 17–19.
10. Philip Kotler, *Marketing Management,* 5th ed. (Englewood Cliffs, NJ: Prentice-Hall, 1990), 225–226.
11. Bernard J. LaLonde and Paul H. Zinszer, *Customer Service: Meaning and Measurement* (Chicago: National Council of Physical Distribution Management, 1976), 156–59.
12. J. L. Cavinato, "How to Keep Customers Coming Back for More," *Distribution* (December 1989), 60.
13. Patrick Galaghen, "A Fresh Cost of Paint for Sherwin-Williams," *Handling and Shipment Management* (November 1981), 31–35.
14. LaLonde and Zinszer, *Customer Service: Meaning and Management,* 171.
15. Bernard J. LaLonde, "Customer Service," Chapter 11 in *Distribution Handbook* (New York: Free Press, 1985), 243.
16. "How Advanced Customer Service Expands a Drug Distributor's Profits," *Traffic Management* (November 1981), 48.
17. John J. Coyle and Joseph C. Andraski, "Managing Channel Relationships," *Annual Proceedings of the Council of Logistics Management* I (Oak Brook, IL, 1990), 246–50.
18. "How Du Pont Forged a Quality Supply Chain," *Traffic Management* (June 1991), 55–57.

3A

CHANNELS OF DISTRIBUTION

CHANNEL FUNCTIONS AND INTERMEDIARIES

overview

As defined in the main text of this chapter, a channel of distribution is "any series of firms or individuals who participate in the flow of goods and services from producer to final user or consumer."[1] This encompasses a variety of intermediary firms, including those that we can classify as wholesalers or retailers. Since most companies find that distribution channels decisions are critical to their overall success, this topic should be an educational priority for all corporate managers. In the logistics area, understanding and appreciating the area of channels is a prerequisite to effective strategy formulation, operations, and control.[2]

The topic of distribution channels requires a firm to coordinate and integrate marketing and logistics activities in a manner consistent with overall corporate strategy. Two channels, the transaction channel and the logistical channel, are related. Effective channel management necessitates a good grasp of the management alternatives and guiding principles applicable to each of these. We should also note the four basic functions of logistical channel members: sorting out, accumulating, allocating, and assorting. We can classify channel systems as either direct or indirect, and we can further subdivide indirect channels into traditional and vertical marketing systems (VMS). With the VMS, some degree of implicit or explicit relationship exists among the firms in the channel; and firms in the channel have considerable opportunity to coordinate their activities.

content of appendix

This appendix, which elaborates further on the topic of distribution channels, covers several areas that are important to logistics managers today. The first section covers channel systems in detail. It also describes industry-specific channels of distribution to show some of the available alternatives that companies use. The second section discusses channel issues in general. The third section directs attention to factors of specific interest to service sector channels. The fourth examines the evaluation and measurement of channel effectiveness.

This appendix focuses on institutions and processes that are of direct relevance to the transactional and logistical channels. For a channel to properly perform its activities, however, it must include another important channel participant: a *facilitating* agency or institution. Examples of this type include firms that provide transportation, warehousing, and distribution services, advertising agencies and marketing research firms, and those that provide financial and insurance services.

CHANNEL SYSTEMS

example of a channel system

Figure 3A–1 presents some of the principal channels of distribution a manufacturing firm may consider to see that its products are ultimately available for purchase by consumers or industrial users. The diagram shows that a channel may consist of various levels, and it may have both *vertical* (e.g., manufacturer-wholesaler-retailer-end user) and *horizontal* (among firms at the same level) dimensions. A firm need adopt no single channel of distribution for its products. Typically, firms use a variety of channels to see that products are available for end users to purchase.

Systems Approach to Channels

systems approach

Channels are *systems* of organizations that work in a coordinated manner toward some common goal.[3] A channel must meet five criteria to qualify as a system:

1. There must be a set of cooperating institutions.
2. There must be an objective that transcends individual objectives in the performance of channel activities.
3. The channel involves a sequence of activities; orders flow toward the supplier, products flow toward the market.
4. The channel includes several different types of flows simultaneously.
5. Channel performance increases through central coordination of individual decisions of each channel member.[4]

A channel system is a complex mechanism. To meet its objectives, a successful channel system places significant demands on its member entities and requires an exceptional degree of transactional as well as logistical coordination of activities among those various firms.

Major Types of Channel Intermediaries

Institutionally, channel intermediaries, or channel middlemen, may be participants in either the wholesale or retail trade. We will discuss both here, and briefly summarize the specific alternative forms available under each.

wholesale intermediary

Wholesalers   The *1984 Industrial Outlook* describes three principal types of entities in the wholesale-distribution industry: merchant wholesalers; manufacturer's sales branches and offices; and agents, brokers, and commission merchants.[5] Merchant wholesalers account for the largest share of sales, employment, and firms and establishments.

The wholesaler's role is broad and complex. This role includes selling goods to retailers or to industrial, commercial, institutional, farm, and professional business users. In addition to selling, wholesalers frequently perform some other functions, including maintaining inventories of goods; extending credit; physically assembling, sorting, and grading goods in lots; breaking up bulk lots for redistribution in smaller lots; and various types of promotion such as advertising and label design.[6]

FIGURE 3A–1   ALTERNATIVE CHANNELS OF DISTRIBUTION   *Source:* James F. Robeson and David T. Kollatt, "Channels of Distribution," *The Distribution Handbook* (New York: The Free Press, 1985), 226. Reprinted with permission of The Free Press, a Division of Macmillan, Inc. from *The Distribution Handbook,* James F. Robeson and Robert G. House, Editors. Copyright © 1985 by The Free Press. This illustration is an adaptation by Robeson and Kollatt of one appearing in John R. Bromell, *Primary Channels of Distribution for Manufacturers,* Business Information Source (Washington, D.C.: U.S. Department of Commerce, July 1950). 3.

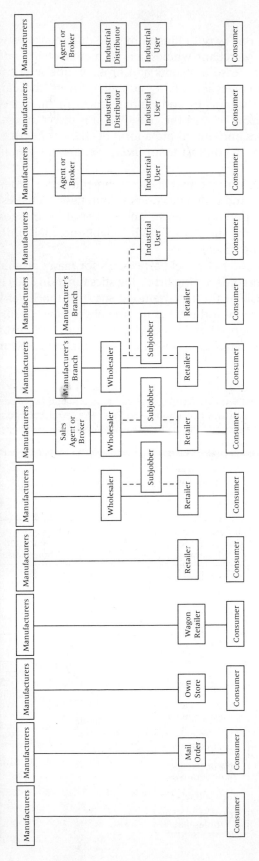

*A manufacturer's branch is owned by the manufacturer.

Figure 3A–2 shows one way of illustrating the differences between various wholesale institutions. Merchant wholesalers or merchant intermediaries take title to the goods. In the case of agents and brokers, title is not transferred— their role principally involves identifying potential buyers and earning a commission. Manufacturers' branches and outlets represent manufacturer-owned establishments which exist to give the manufacturer direct access to the marketplace. These branches and outlets are a form of channel intermediary within a *direct* channel system, in contrast to an *indirect* channel system.

retailer establishments

Retailers   The principal function retail establishments serve is to make product available for consumers and industrial users to purchase. Retail establishments may be in the form of traditional stores and places of business, as well as in innovative, nonstore forms such as selling by telephone, mail order, computer, door-to-door, or vending machine.

Retail firms are important channel participants for many products. They can significantly affect the manufacturing firm's logistics function and channel members' other activities. Given the trend among some of the large firms toward concentrating retail activity, other channel members have been pressured to absorb much of the responsibility for carrying inventory and ensuring that it is available for delivery to retail locations in a timely manner. Fortunately, many

FIGURE 3A–2   CLASSIFICATION OF WHOLESALING MIDDLEMEN   *Source:* Ralph M. Gaedeke and Dennis H. Tootelian, *Marketing Principles and Applications* (St. Paul, MN: West Publishing Company, 1983), 256; and David W. Cravens and Robert B. Woodruff, *Marketing* (Reading, MA: Addison-Wesley Publishing Company, 1986), 396.

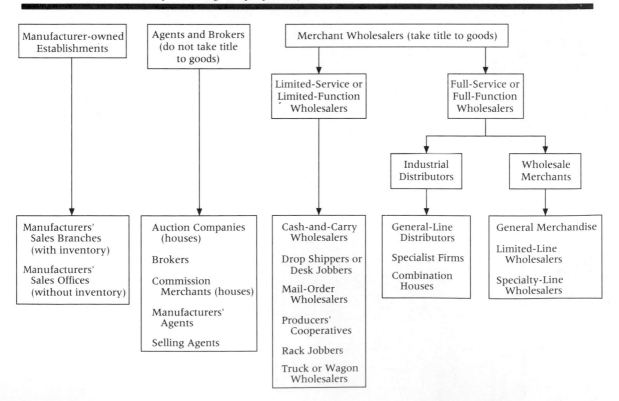

industries are developing effective vertical marketing systems, which can facilitate streamlining overall logistics and distribution activities within the channel.

Functional Shiftability

conventional versus VMS

Figure 3A–3 compares how functional activities may be performed in a conventional (traditional) channel with how they may be performed in a vertical marketing system. In a conventional channel, each participant performs a relatively standard set of activities, and these activities are likely to overlap. In contrast, in vertical marketing systems, activities or functions may be *shifted* between the manufacturer, wholesaler, and retailer in a manner most consistent with the overall interests of the channel itself.

Examples

example channels

Figures 3A–4 and 3A–5 show example channels of distribution that are applicable to the food and manufacturing and industrial gas manufacturing in-

FIGURE 3A–3   THE CONCEPT OF FUNCTIONAL SHIFTABILITY   *Source:* James F. Robeson and David T. Kollatt, "Channels of Distribution," *The Distribution Handbook* (New York: The Free Press, 1985), 226. Reprinted with permission of The Free Press, a Division of Macmillan, Inc. from *The Distribution Handbook,* James F. Robeson and Robert G. House, Editors. Copyright © 1985 by The Free Press. This illustration is from David. T. Kollatt, Roger D. Blackwell, and James F. Robeson, *Strategic Marketing* (New York: Holt, Rinehart and Winston, 1972), 14.

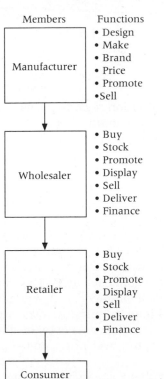

(a) A CONVENTIONAL CHANNEL

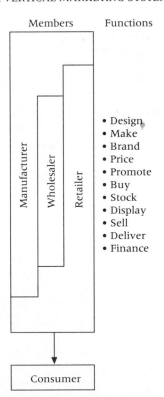

(b) A VERTICAL MARKETING SYSTEM

FIGURE 3A–4   EXAMPLE CHANNELS OF DISTRIBUTION—FOOD PRODUCTS MANUFACTURING
INDUSTRY

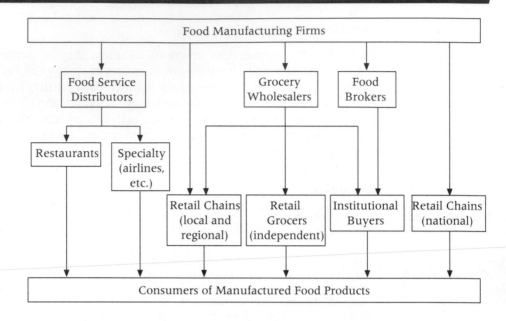

dustries, respectively. These figures provide a valuable perspective on channel
structure in relation to these specific industries.

CHANNEL ISSUES

Intensity of Distribution

desired intensity   Aside from making a general decision regarding channels of distribution, firms
must determine the distribution intensity they desire. This intensity falls into
three generic categories: intensive, exclusive, and selective.

Intensive distribution involves seeing that product is available for purchase
at as many wholesale and retail establishments as possible. The principal goal
is to achieve widespread market coverage. This decision typically requires considering a wide range of channel alternatives, and involves making logistical
and transactional arrangements with numerous firms and other entities throughout the various channels. Of the three categories, intensive distribution requires
the greatest responsiveness from the logistics function of channel members.

Exclusive distribution occurs when a manufacturer severely limits the number
of intermediaries involved in channel activities. This limitation usually applies
to both wholesale and retail establishments. It typically provides those firms
with exclusive rights to distribute the product over a particular geographical
area or sales territory. The principal advantage to the manufacturing firm is the
ability to exert considerable control over prices and ancillary services provided
to purchasers of the product.

Selective distribution falls somewhere in between the other two. To a certain
degree, it "narrows" the specific channel intermediaries authorized to handle a

FIGURE 3A–5   EXAMPLE CHANNELS OF DISTRIBUTION—INDUSTRIAL GAS MANUFACTURING
INDUSTRY

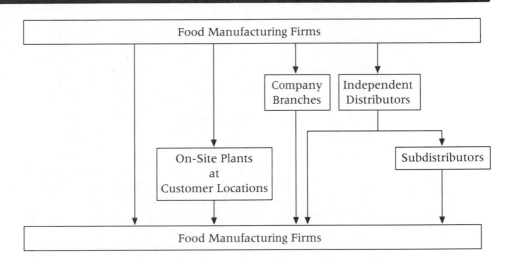

particular product. Firms choosing this alternative are interested in achieving a
breadth of market coverage, while retaining a degree of control over pricing and
services.

Cooperation, Conflict, and Competition

cooperation

Any study of distribution channels is also studies the behavior between the firms
constituting the channel. Perhaps most commonly discussed are topics relating to cooperation, conflict, and competition within and between distribution
channels.[7]

Cooperation refers to a joint effort by channel members to achieve a goal or
set of goals that are of mutual interest. For cooperation to exist, channel members
must agree that they have mutual concerns, must work together toward achieving those common goals, and must collectively be able to create logistical and
transactional channels that will enable the whole channel to be competitive in
the marketplace.

The success of vertical marketing systems requires cooperation among channel
members. Through this form of distribution channel, manufacturers, wholesalers, and retailers have the greatest chance of working together toward accomplishing their common goals.

conflict

Conflict refers to a situation where channel members may have competing
objectives, and where achieving optimal operation for the whole channel is
difficult. Channel conflict may take the form of *horizontal* conflict, in which
parallel members of a distribution channel are at odds over some issue. For
example, conflict may arise between fast-food retailers of a specific brand who
perceive that their sales territories overlap.

Of principal concern here, however, is *vertical* conflict, which may arise
among members of the manufacturer-wholesaler-retailer distribution channel.
For example, a wholesale intermediary may disagree with pricing, product availability, and other policies that the manufacturer establishes. In this instance,
conflict will likely result. From a physical supply channel perspective, a man-

ufacturer may place significant demands on the capabilities of vendors providing needed materials and supplies. If those demands do not acknowledge the overall needs of the channel and of the member firms, then conflict is likely to result.

Often, one of the firms in a distribution channel emerges as the channel activity leader, becoming the *channel captain.* This phenomenon is critical to the success of many channel relationships, where one firm takes an aggressive role in seeing that the overall channel system functions as it should. The channel captain's ability to induce change is sometimes referred to as *power,* a topic that researchers have also treated in depth. Generally, researchers treat power in conjunction with the topic of *dependence,* or the extent to which channel members depend upon one another to achieve desired results.

competition

Finally, *competition* is of significant interest. This includes competition between parallel members of distribution channels (e.g., automobile dealers selling the same brand within a given geographical area) and between various distribution channels (e.g., food supermarkets versus convenience stores). Both cases involve issues of concern from both a transactional and a logistical channels perspective.

The issues of cooperation, conflict, and competition within and between distribution channels are complex. The more we understand about these topics, the more likely we are to conceptualize and implement successful relationships in an overall channel system.

Legal Considerations

legal environment

One environment in which firms make channel decisions is the legal environment. While the advice of qualified legal counsel has no substitute, logistics and marketing managers should at least understand the fundamental legal issues that may affect decision making regarding distribution channels.[8]

Laws

The first topic relates to the laws that can directly affect marketing channels. Of particular interest are the following: Sherman Act (1890), Clayton Act (1914), Federal Trade Commission Act (1914) and Robinson-Patman Act (1936).

- *Sherman Act (1890).* The Sherman Act represents the fundamental antitrust legislation in the United States. It prohibits monopoly practices and conspiracies that restrain trade. In terms of specific effects on channels, the Sherman Act prohibits monopolistic conspiratorial practices from controlling distribution channels.
- *Clayton Act (1914).* This law strengthened the Sherman Act by outlawing price discrimination and prohibiting other practices that tend to substantially lessen competition or create a monopoly. This act affects the channels area by specifically prohibiting practices such as tying arrangements (in which a seller requires that the purchaser either buy another product from the seller or agree not to use or purchase competitor's goods, and exclusive dealing (which would limit the supply sources available to purchasers). The Celler-Kefauver Act of 1950 broadened the impact of the Clayton Act to apply to acquisitions and mergers among firms that are vertically aligned in a distribution channel, in addition to horizontal mergers and acquisitions.

- *Federal Trade Commission Act (1914).* This legislation established the Federal Trade Commission to enforce the provisions of the Clayton Act. In effect, this act forbade "unfair methods" of competition, including those identified in the Sherman Act and the Clayton Act, as well as other practices that may be injurious to competition.
- *Robinson-Patman Act (1936).* This law prohibited price discrimination on goods of "like grade and quality," unless the seller could cost-justify the difference in prices. The Robinson-Patman Act also made it illegal for buyers to set up "dummy" brokerage firms that would purchase goods at prices lower than those available to the purchaser itself. Before the passage of this act, larger firms often set up dummy firms to acquire products at prices lower than those sellers offered the firms' (smaller) competitors.

Practices

Another interesting topic regards practices that relate to the channels decision and that have legal implications. Because the list of possible practices is too broad to completely cover here, we will limit our discussion to dual distribution, exclusive dealing, full-line forcing, tying agreements, and vertical integration.

- *Dual distribution.* The many firms involved in this practice develop and maintain two or more distribution channels for their products. For example, a firm may distribute its products through a vertical marketing system as well as through traditional distribution channels. In such a case, interpretations of prevailing legislation principally protect the rights of the traditional channel's independent members.
- *Exclusive dealing.* Laws against exclusive dealing prohibit a seller from requiring the buyers either deal exclusively in that seller's product brand or refrain from buying competitor's products for resale.
- *Full-line forcing.* This practice occurs when a seller requires a buyer to carry a full line of its products in order to sell any specific product line item available from that seller. This practice becomes illegal when it prevents other suppliers from securing business with firms that have had a full line forced upon them and therefore have no capacity to handle anyone else's products.
- *Tying agreements.* These agreements occur when seller requires a buyer to purchase some other product as well, or when the buyer agrees not to buy a particular product from a competing firm. This illegal practice would tend to restrict the range of channel alternatives available for both marketing and logistics managers.
- *Vertical integration.* Firms today show a very evident trend toward developing vertical marketing systems, which involve integrating and coordinating the interests of entities vertically aligned in a distribution channel. Referring back to the Clayton Act of 1914 as amended by the Celler-Kefauver Act of 1950, it is clear that any such vertical arrangements must not substantially lessen competition or create a monopoly.

Since certain channels-related practices are illegal, managers who make distribution channel decisions need to understand the full range of relevant laws and legal issues.

CHANNELS IN THE SERVICE SECTOR

service-sector distribution

Given the recent growth of service industries in the United States, it is logical to examine the applicability of the channels concept to industries such as health care, transportation, and food retailing. Each of these industries has well-defined procurement/physical supply needs, and discussing these in the terms of the distribution channel decision is easy.

By using the university-level educational system as an example, we can examine how service industry firms *distribute* outputs and services. Universities distribute various educational programs through a number of channels. In addition to the full roster of day courses for degree students, many universities offer night and weekend course for both degree students and those seeking continuing or executive-level education. Courses are sometimes taught at remote locations either physically or through the use of state-of-the-art video and telecommunications equipment, and various courses are available on magnetic media in a self-paced educational format. We could cite similar distribution examples for firms in other service industries.

EVALUATING PERFORMANCE OF CHANNEL MEMBERS AND CHANNEL SYSTEMS

measurement and evaluation

After making and implementing a decision regarding a channel of distribution, a firm should develop some ongoing means to evaluate channel system and channel member performance. In performing this evaluation, most manufacturers use some combination of the following channel member characteristics:

- Sales performance
- Inventory maintained
- Selling capabilities
- Attitudes
- Competition
- General growth prospects

Firms may use three approaches to apply these performance criteria. The first involves developing separate performance evaluations on one or more criteria, as Table 3A–1 indicates. The second is to informally combine multiple criteria,

TABLE 3A–1   CHANNEL MEMBER PERFORMANCE EVALUATION USING CRITERIA SEPARATELY

Criterion	Frequently Used Operational Performance Measures	Procedure for Combining Measures
1. Sales performance	1. Gross sales 2. Sales growth over time 3. Sales made/sales quota 4. Market share	No attempt made to combine the operational performance measures within or among the criteria categories
2. Inventory maintenance	1. Average inventory maintained 2. Inventory/sales 3. Inventory turnover	
3. Selling capabilities	1. Total number of salespeople 2. Salespeople assigned to manufacturer's product	

Source: Bert Rosenbloom, *Marketing Channels* (Chicago, IL: The Dryden Press, 1987), 355.

and the third to formally combine multiple criteria.[9] Any of these approaches will provide information that will help a firm to evaluate the performance of individual channel members.

Figure 3A–6 provides a perspective on the overall topic of channel system performance. It suggests that the firm examine four specific areas: channel member behavior, channel structure, channel policies, and channel member performance. This figure, which goes beyond measuring individual channel members contributions, and relates to the channel system as a whole.

By utilizing any of these measurement approaches, a firm will enhance the channels decision's likelihood of producing results acceptable in terms of the company's intended goals.

NOTES

1. E. Jerome McCarthy and William D. Perrault, Jr., *Basic Marketing*, 8th ed. (Homewood, IL: Irwin, 1984), 362.

2. There are several excellent sources of information on the topic of distribution channels, including Bert Rosenbloom, *Marketing Channels*, 3d ed. (Chicago: Dryden Press, 1987): Louis P. Bucklin, *Competition and Evolution in the Distributive Trades* (Englewood Cliffs, NJ: Prentice-Hall, 1972); Louis W. Stern and Adel I. El-Ansary, *Marketing Channels*, 2d ed. (Englewood Cliffs, NJ: Prentice-Hall, 1982); Bruce Mallen, *Principles of Marketing Channel Management* (Lexington, MA: Lexington Books, 1977); and Donald J. Bowersox, M. Bixby Cooper, Douglas M. Lambert, and Donald A. Taylor, *Management in Marketing Channels* (New York: McGraw-Hill, 1980).

3. See Philip B. Schary, *Logistics Decisions: Text and Cases* (Chicago: Dryden Press, 1984), 32.

4. Schary, *Logistics Decisions*, 32.

5. U.S. Department of Commerce, *1984 Industrial Outlook* (Washington, DC: U.S. Department of Commerce, Bureau of Industrial Economics, 1984), 47-1.

6. U.S. Department of Commerce, *1984 Industrial Outlook*, 47-1.

7. Additional information and direction regarding cooperation, conflict, and competition are available in sources such as those listed in note 2.

8. Portions of this section have been adapted from Rosenbloom, *Marketing Channels*, 89–99; David W. Cravens and Robert B. Woodruff, *Marketing* (Reading, MA: Addison-Wesley, 1986), 451–54; David M. Cravens, Gerald E. Hills, and Robert B. Woodruff, *Marketing Decision Making*, rev. ed. (Homewood, IL: Irwin, 1980), 513–33; and McCarthy and Perrault, *Basic Marketing*, 126–31.

9. Rosenbloom, *Marketing Channels*, 345.

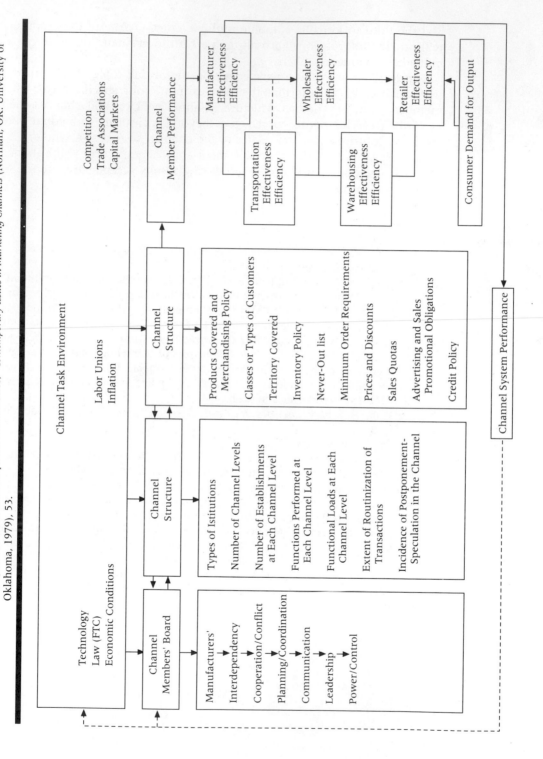

FIGURE 3A–6 AN ENVIRONMENTAL FRAMEWORK FOR CHANNEL SYSTEM PERFORMANCE *Source:* Adel I. El-Ansary, "Perspectives on Channel System Performance," *Contemporary Issues in Marketing Channels* (Norman, OK: University of Oklahoma, 1979), 53.

CHAPTER
4

GLOBAL LOGISTICS

GLOBAL BUSINESS LOGISTICS

global sourcing

global distribution

In recent years, increasing numbers of companies have become aware that the marketplace encompasses the world, not just the United States. For example, many U.S. firms have found that evaluating offshore sourcing alternatives is essential to a well-run logistics and materials management organization. Alternatively, by developing export markets, U.S. firms have highlighted the need for effective logistics systems and networks throughout the world. Conversely, companies located in other countries have also broadened their sourcing and marketing considerations geographically; like U.S. firms, they look toward global logistics strategies and operations to provide competitive advantage through efficiency, effectiveness, and differentiation.

key issues

As a practical matter, logistics managers are finding that they need to do much work in terms of conceptualizing, designing, and implementing logistics initiatives which may be effective globally. For this reason, this chapter addresses key issues and topics that are essential to the global aspects of business logistics. Logically, the development of global logistics approaches requires a high degree of coordination between logistics groups, marketing, and purchasing groups in individual companies.

This chapter deals first with the nature of global business and global logistics. Then, two successive sections deal with key global logistics trends and with changing political and legal environments. Finally, the chapter discusses transportation, channel strategies, storage and packaging, and governmental influences.

Magnitudes of Global Logistics Activity

World trade and world logistics expenditures are growing rapidly. World trade is growing nearly twice as fast as world output. As Nigel Grimwade indicates, "over the period since 1950, world merchandise exports have increased roughly ninefold in volume terms, . . . as compared with an increase in the volume of world commodity output of roughly fivefold." [1]

world trade

Figure 4–1 indicates historical and projected growth rates for various segments of world trade. Of particular interest is that regardless of trade lane (e.g. North America to the Far East, the Far East to North America, etc.) all of the recent and forecasted average annual growth rates are positive. This supports the observation that trade continues to grow between most or all major geographical trade areas.

logistics expenditures

Another interesting trend relates to worldwide logistics expenditures (see Figure 4–2). According to projections made by Temple, Barker & Sloane, Inc., worldwide logistics expenditures should rise to nearly 2.1 trillion U.S. dollars by the year 1999. This amounts to approximately sixteen percent of worldwide GNP.

FIGURE 4–1   LONG-TERM GROWTH OF WORLD TRADE   *Source: TBS/DRI World Trade Service, 1991.*

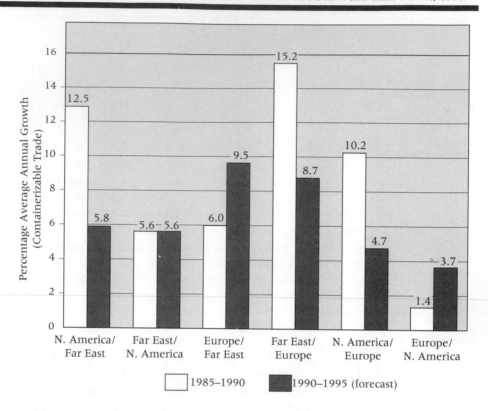

1985–1990   1990–1995 (forecast)

Figures 4–3 and 4–4 present information about the freight tonnage percentages imported to and exported from the United States. According to Figure 4–3, for example, the average percent of U.S. freight tonnage represented by import shipments is expected to reach 16.0% in 1995. And Figure 4–4 reveals

FIGURE 4–2   WORLDWIDE LOGISTICS EXPENDITURES   *Source: Temple, Barker, & Sloane, Inc., 1989.*

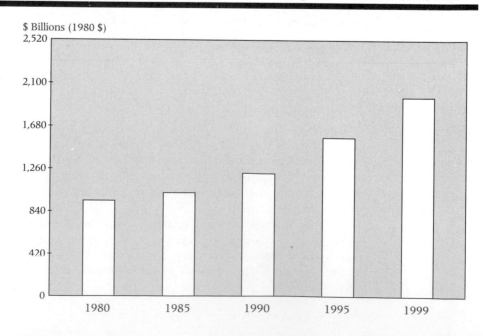

FIGURE 4–3 PERCENT OF FREIGHT TONNAGE IMPORTED TO THE UNITED STATES *Source:* Bernard J. LaLonde, Ohio State University.

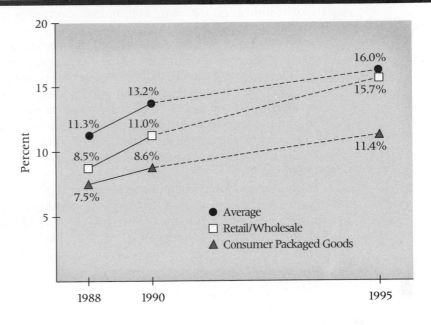

that U.S. exports as a percentage of U.S. freight tonnage should reach 15.7% in 1995.

outsourcing

In 1986 Temple, Barker & Sloane conducted an interesting study in which they asked U.S.-based multinational corporations about the importance of out-sourcing to their firms' logistics operations.[2] The study defined outsourcing as "the purchase of raw materials, semifinished components, or finished product from foreign suppliers."[3] Firms make such acquisitions in numerous ways, and

FIGURE 4–4 PERCENT OF FREIGHT TONNAGE EXPORTED FROM THE UNITED STATES *Source:* Bernard J. LaLonde, Ohio State University.

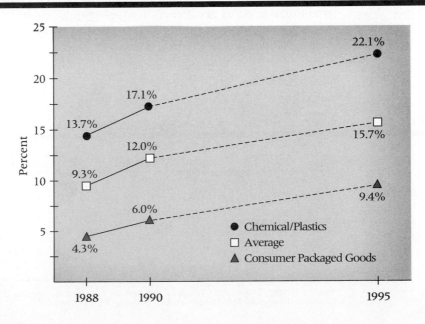

managing the outsourcing decision may be complex, depending on the circumstances surrounding the specific acquisition. The study included firms in broad variety of industries, including automotive, electronics, paper, chemicals, food, and selected general merchandise.

Table 4–1 provides information about the foreign origins of goods the firms in the study outsourced. Europe and the Far East appear to be attractive sources for outsourced raw materials and finished products, while South America seems to be a popular source of component parts and subassemblies. Geographically, component parts sources seem to be much more dispersed than raw material and/or finished product sources. Further data indicated that approximately sixty-five to seventy percent of the firms surveyed cited cost as a motive for outsourcing, twenty to thirty percent cited availability, and five to twenty percent cited quality.[4]

Many foreign firms depend on exports—or U.S. outsourcing—for a substantial portion of their revenues. In France, for example, foreign sales account for approximately thirty percent of Source Perrier's soft drink products. Of that total, the company sells over half in the United States/Canada/Caribbean Island region, requiring Perrier to ship approximately 7,000 40-foot containers per year.

Global Markets and Global Corporations

global trade

Generally, the global business environment has seen many trade barriers fall over the past decade. Whether the case involves trade between the United States and other countries or between two or more foreign countries, the trend toward facilitating, rather than constraining, global business activity is definitely accelerating. Thanks greatly to the growth and maturation of the ocean and air container shipping industries, distinct national and specific country-to-country international markets have been transformed into truly global businesses.[5]

Global markets are a direct consequence of the acknowledgement and homogenization of global needs and wants.[6] Through new and extensive communications technologies, people throughout the world learn of and express the desire to have many of the same products. As a result, people have sacrificed traditional product preferences for higher-quality, lower-priced products which are more highly standardized. This preference for non-traditional products is due to economic and cultural factors. The availability of high-quality merchandise at locally reasonable price levels is an attractor to people throughout the

TABLE 4–1   FOREIGN ORIGINS OF OUTSOURCED GOODS

	Raw Materials	Components	Finished Products
Europe	42%	—	33%
South America	5	40%	4
Far East	29	18	35
Africa	—	15	—
Indian Subcontinent	—	15	1
Middle East	1	12	1
Other	23	—	26

Source: Temple, Barker, & Sloane, Inc., *International Logistics: Meeting the Challenges of Global Distribution Channels* (Lexington, MA: Temple, Barker, & Sloane, Inc., 1987), 2.

world. In addition, the opportunity to own or use products which are used in other countries helps people to feel that they enjoy standards of living which may be comparable to those of more prosperous nations.

global product strategy

We commonly see differences in promotion and in products themselves when manufacturers market their products to potential buyers in various parts of the world.[7] Canon's marketing of a new 35mm automatic camera served as a good example. As a result of extensive customer research conducted in markets world-wide, Canon decided to create a single "world camera" that would respond to the collective preferences of a wide variety of potential purchasers. In order to customize its appeal to buyers in individual countries, however, Canon positioned the camera differently in various market areas. In the United States, Canon described the camera as easy-to-use and slanted its appeal toward the growing market of non-professional photographers who nevertheless wanted a product of reasonable quality. Alternatively, in Japan, Canon designed the camera to appeal to the consumer as a state-of-the-art example of technological advancement in the photography field. This positioning was very effective, considering many Japanese buyers' strong desire for the latest, most advanced electronic equipment.

Global Competitive Strategy

definition

An interesting distinction is that of a global company versus one whose operations are simply multi-domestic. Essentially, global companies formulate strategy on a worldwide basis in order to exploit new market opportunities.[8] Such companies, which seek to influence their industries' competitive balance, implement global strategy effectively and efficiently. In comparison, multi-domestic companies tend to operate within individual markets throughout the world, but do not emphasize coordinating individual strategies into a cohesive global strategy.

Global companies tend to be more successful at developing strategies that help them to simultaneously achieve their business objectives at locations throughout the world. These companies are likely to strategically source materials and components worldwide, select global locations for key supply depots and distribution centers, use existing logistics networks when sourcing and distributing new products, and transfer existing logistics technologies new markets.

example companies

Examples of U.S.-based global companies include Xerox, IBM, Du Pont, Kodak, Philips Consumer Electronics Corporation, Merck, Coca-Cola, Philip Morris, and McDonald's.

One key to achieving global success is to achieve global business volumes. This not only justifies entering markets and introducing new products in many areas of the world, but provides business activity sufficient to absorb the significant cost outlays essential to this level of activity.

global operating strategies

Global corporations typically design their operating strategy objectives around four components: technology, marketing, manufacturing, and logistics.[9] While initiatives in all four areas should function synchronously, the logistics system serves as the global infrastructure upon which the other systems operate. Also, firms have recognized that the global logistics system itself may provide a source of competitive advantage. For example, the availability of systems that efficiently supply and distribute original and postsale parts largely justifies the globalization of automobile assembly. Years ago, the Japanese used our domestic distribution capabilities to bring U.S. consumers television sets manufactured in Japan. More recently, Japan has transferred much of the manufacturing itself to North America.

Customer Service Strategies for Global Markets

An interesting distinction exists between the meaning of the terms "global," and "international" or "multi-national." According to Martin Christopher,

> Global marketing is as different from international or multi-national marketing as chalk is from cheese. Whereas the emphasis in multi-national marketing has been to tailor products and marketing strategies to meet perceived local needs, the thrust of global marketing is to seek to satisfy common demands worldwide. There has been a belated recognition that, for all the mythology, the customer in Bogota is little different from his counterpart in Birmingham.[10]

global competition

Christopher concludes that global competition has four prominent characteristics.[11] First, companies competing globally seek to create standardized, yet customized, marketing. Second, life cycles are shortening, sometimes lasting less than one year. This is true for certain high-tech products such as computers and peripherals, photography items, and audio-visual equipment. Third, more companies are utilizing outsourcing and offshore manufacturing. Fourth, marketing and manufacturing activities and strategies tend to converge and be better coordinated in firms operating globally.

As companies service global markets, logistics networks tend to become more expansive and complex. As a result, it is not unusual to see lead times increase and inventory levels rise. To successfully operate in a time-based competitive environment, firms emphasize managing logistics as a system, shortening lead times when possible, and moving toward the use of "focused" factories which produce limited product lines for geographically specific areas. In Europe, companies such as Unilever, Electrolux, and SKF have successfully practiced this latter strategy.

customer needs

Perhaps the most important step in designing and implementing global logistics strategies is to understand the service needs of customers in locations dispersed throughout the world. This is a prerequisite to developing effective manufacturing, marketing, and logistics strategies to satisfy the needs of the global marketplace.

CRITICAL FACTORS AND KEY TRENDS

This section first identifies significant factors that have affected the competitive positioning of companies in business environments throughout the world. Subsequently, the section briefly discusses several key logistics and transportation trends that have significantly affected the global business activity of U.S.-based firms and the activity of offshore firms doing business in the United States.

Importance of Competitive Environment

Based on a four-year study of ten countries, Michael Porter has concluded that "a nation's ability to upgrade its existing advantages to the next level of technology and productivity is the key to international (global) success."[12] He feels that a loss of global market share in advanced fields such as transportation and technology shows the United States slipping recently in international trade.

Porter's "dynamic diamond"

To explain his theories of what produces competitive advantage in a global business environment, Porter suggests a "dynamic diamond" containing four elements of competitive advantage which reinforce one another. These elements include:[13]

- *Factor Conditions:* A nation's ability to transform its basic factors (e.g., resources, education, or infrastructure) into competitive advantage;
- *Demand Conditions:* Examples include market size, buyer sophistication, and media exposure of available products;
- *Related and Supporting Industries:* May include partners in the supply chain, co-packers and/or co-manufacturers, or marketing and distribution intermediaries; and
- *Company Strategy, Structure, and Rivalry:* Market structures and the nature of domestic competition.

Porter concludes that each element is necessary for success in domestic and global markets, and he suggests that the presence of competition in domestic markets motivates individual firms to identify productive marketing, manufacturing, and logistics strategies. He advocates creating more competitive business environments, stimulating demand for innovative new products (through the provision of tax credits, for example), placing greater emphasis on research and development, and refocusing trade policies on truly unfair subsidies and trade barriers.

Critical Changes in Logistics and Transportation

In this section, we will discuss briefly five major areas of change: deregulation of the U.S. shipping industry, intermodal shipping, shipment control, trade policies, and currency fluctuations.[14]

market structure

Deregulation of the U.S. Ocean Liner Industry Perhaps the most striking result of the Shipping Act of 1984 was that U.S. ocean liner companies received greater freedom to set rates, establish services, and share shipping activities. At the same time, this legislation included steps to guard against unfair practices by foreign-flag carriers toward U.S.-flag carriers.

Direct consequences of this shift to marketplace regulation included the use of service contracts, the right of ocean carriers to take independent action concerning rates and services, and the offering of intermodal through rates in conjunction with land carriers such as railroads and motor carriers. Upcoming chapters on the topic of transportation will discuss related issues more fully.

intermodal transportation

Intermodalism Although we will discuss this too in greater detail later, it is useful to introduce this topic as one critical area which has grown recently in usage and popularity. Intermodalism refers to the joint use of two or more transportation modes; moving highway trailers or containers on rail flatcars or in container ships is an example. Figure 4–5 shows the options available to international, intermodal shippers. Those options include all-water service, mini land bridge, land bridge, and microbridge operations.

Intermodal operations represent one of the fastest growing areas in the global logistics arena. By combining the resources of two or more transportation modes, logistics services suppliers can provide a service to the shipper-customer which appears to be seamless, despite the sometimes numerous and complex operations which accompany moving the shipper's product. Among a number of firms that capably provide comprehensive logistics and transportation services, CSX Corporation serves as an excellent example (see Figure 4–6).

FIGURE 4–5   INTERNATIONAL DISTRIBUTION SHIPPING OPTIONS   *Source:* Temple, Barker, & Sloane, Inc., *International Logistics: Meeting the Challenges of Global Distribution Channels* (Lexington, MA: Temple, Barker & Sloane, Inc., 1987), 26.

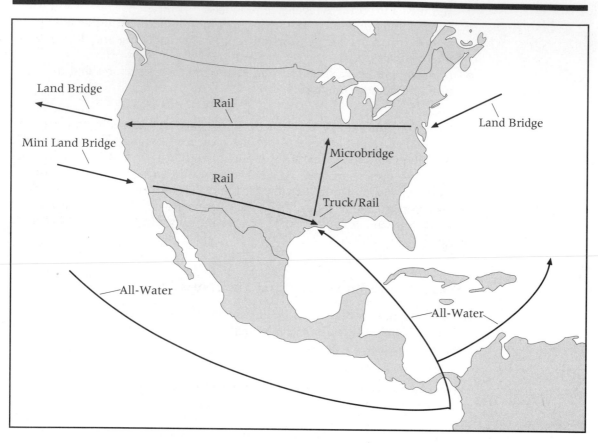

communications and control

Shipment Control   Effective communication and control systems are essential to a competitive global logistics capability. Issues concerning documentation, export-import management, and individual shipments' movements are critical to today's customers; and preferred suppliers are those who can meet these customer requirements.

Trade Policies   Although a movement toward eliminating trade barriers worldwide characterized the years following World War II until about 1975, certain countries throughout the world have recently made selective changes in trade policies. For example, Far East countries such as Japan, Korea, and China established protective trade barriers to restrict imports of goods into their home markets, even as they were experiencing sometimes significant export market growth. Such new restrictions are more the exception than the rule. As we will discuss more thoroughly below, numerous countries have taken steps to facilitate the flow of intracountry as well as international commerce.

However, we should keep in mind that official trade barriers and unofficial barriers such as customs delays may impair logistics system's ability to function effectively in terms of product supply and/or distribution.

currency exchange rates

Currency Fluctuations   Either short or long-term trends in the value of the U.S. dollar in comparison with the currencies of other nations may easily affect

FIGURE 4–6   CSX CORPORATION   *Source:* CSX, Inc., 1991.

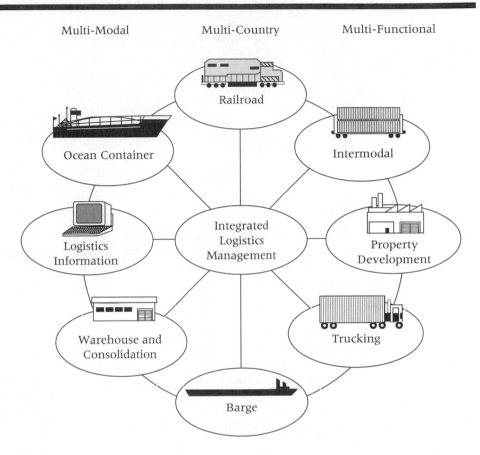

logistics decisions. When the dollar is strong, as it was during most of the 1980s, the United States tends to become a net importer of goods. This is logical, considering that when the dollar is rising in value it is less expensive for U.S. firms to buy other countries' products than it is for other countries to buy U.S. products. Conversely, when the dollar's value declines, as it did during the late 1980s and early 1990s, U.S. exports tend to rise and imports tend to fall.

Fluctuations in world currency values can significantly affect logistics decisions such as inventory positioning, plant and distribution center location, and choice of transportation mode and carrier. Buyers and sellers of logistics services sometimes agree to currency adjustment factors, which help to equalize the effect of short-term changes in relative currency values.

CHANGING POLITICAL AND LEGAL ENVIRONMENTS

As we indicated earlier, fluctuating trade policies throughout the world can significantly affect global logistics activity. This section describes several instances wherein changing political and legal environments have enhanced opportunities for trade and logistics activity.

trading partners   Before discussing examples of global logistics issues, we should note that the United States' top five trading partners include Canada, Japan, Mexico, West Germany, and the United Kingdom. Table 4–2 shows these countries' value of trade to the U.S. in billions of U.S. dollars.

TABLE 4–2   U.S. TRADING PARTNERS

Country	Value of Trade ($ in billions)
1. Canada	159.3
2. Japan	138.2
3. Mexico	52.2
4. West Germany	41.7
5. United Kingdom	39.1

Source: U.S. Department of Commerce, Statistics Canada, 1989 figures, as reported in *North American International Business* (April 1991), 25.

Single European Market

Europe 1992

In probably the most far-reaching commercial effort the world has ever seen, the twelve member nations of the European Economic Community (the EC or, more popularly, the Common Market) have agreed to move toward a single, unified European Market.[15] Instead of twelve fragmented markets in Belgium, Denmark, France, Greece, Ireland, Italy, Luxembourg, the Netherlands, Portugal, Spain, the United Kingdom, and West Germany, the single market plan would create one integrated market of more than 320 million consumers and workers. The map in Figure 4–7 shows the locations of the European Community's member nations.

The Single European Act of 1987 sought to eliminate trade barriers between EC member nations and to facilitate the free movement of goods, services, capital, and people between these nations. To achieve these goals, the act identified three general barriers for elimination:

- *Physical Barriers:* Customs controls and border formalities;
- *Technical Barriers:* For example, different health and safety standards; and
- *Fiscal Barriers:* Such as differences in value-added tax rates and excise duties.

The original target for implementation was the year 1992, and many initiatives and changes were in place sooner than that.[16] For example, considerable change occurred in areas such as documentation and customs procedures, internal trade barriers, national brands and markets, and external trade barriers. Culturally charged areas such as language and currency still require additional change.

logistics effects

Of all the changes the Single European Market concept encompasses, three affect logistics most directly.[17] The first is the facilitation of intra-country shipment procedures, most notably through the use of a single administrative document (SAD) to reduce border-crossing time. Second is the simplification of customs formalities for shipments simply "passing through" countries en route to others. This would reduce, for example, the time a container destined for Belgium would spend in customs activities at the entry port of Rotterdam, the Netherlands. Third is the introduction of common border posts, or "banalization." Essentially, this concept makes a border crossing from Spain to France, for example, a European customs entry, not a French one.

FIGURE 4–7   THE MEMBER STATES OF THE EUROPEAN COMMUNITY

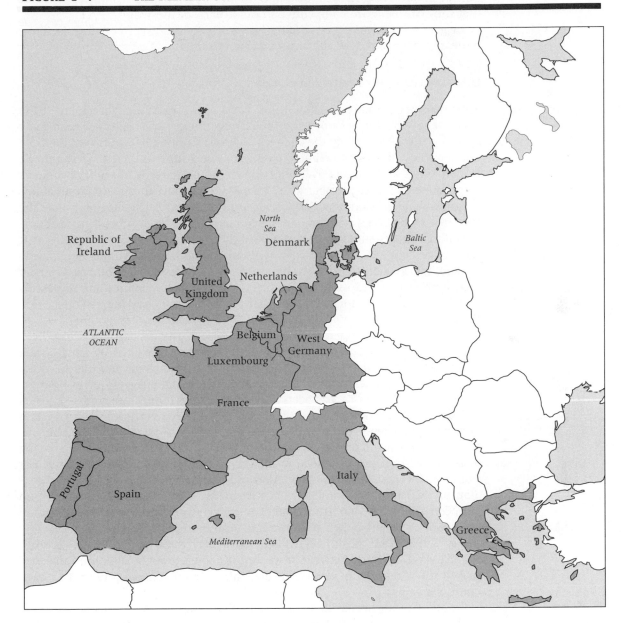

Generally, the facilitation of intercountry movements will concentrate European logistics networks of production and distribution into a more concise network of fewer facilities.

Overall, these initiatives will facilitate trade and the emergence of a more competitive business environment among EC member nations. This marketplace will likely attract new competitors, both from Europe and abroad. For example, many U.S. firms have been refining and implementing European market strategies even as this significant change has been occurring. Likewise, as the Single

European Market concept grows and matures, EC member countries will find that they can be more competitive in other parts of the world.

In general, open-market relationships such as these will certainly facilitate trade and help to reduce the cost of doing business.

U.S./Canada Free Trade Agreement

U.S./Canada FTA   Effective since January 1, 1989, the U.S./Canada Free Trade Agreement (FTA) was intended to further open the thousands of miles of border between these two countries.[18] Similar to the changes underway among EC countries, the U.S./ Canada FTA will strive to eliminate protective measures and tariffs between the United States and Canada by 1999. The overall objective is to see that shippers incorporate the least possible delay in moving product to needed destinations as quickly and efficiently as possible. Another major objective is to facilitate the flow of raw materials and components to manufacturing or processing facilities.

Both countries stand to gain significantly from the FTA. Given the fact that seventy percent of Canada's two-way international trade is with its neighbor to the south, Canadian shippers should expect to find cross-border business activity less cumbersome and more streamlined.[19] Although Canadian trade represents a smaller portion of total international commerce for the United States, U.S. shippers and receivers will also feel the FTA's benefits.

One principal benefit from the removal of these trade barriers is that both U.S. and Canadian companies should become more involved in cross-border business. This will directly reduce the supplier and product discrimination which typically accompanies more insular, protected national business environments.

remaining barriers   Even though the FTA has been in effect for some time, certain trade barriers still remain. For example, many U.S. companies have yet to recognize certain French/English requirements for packaging and ingredient labeling. Also, in- terprovincial Canadian trade still represents a source of frustration, as moving a shipment from one province to another is not always quick and easy. For example, though Canada's prohibition of interprovincial movements of Cana- dian-brewed beer has inhibited effective intra-Canada trade, this prohibition has been a source of opportunity for U.S. brewers anxious to enter the Canadian market or to enhance their position in it. Another sensitive issue as of the early 1990s is that plant closings have occurred, particularly in Canada, as a result of the liberalized trade between the countries. Even though economic efficiency may justify this type of change, it does affect labor issues significant to both countries' well-being.

In order to further facilitate U.S.-Canadian trade, leading firms are working with customs authorities to develop information-based capabilities such as elec- tronic data interchange (EDI) to facilitate tasks such as customs clearance. The end result of such efforts, coupled with a continued relaxation of trade barriers between these two countries, should be the continued growth of cross-border commerce between the United States and Canada. Like the changes occurring in Europe, the FTA should lead business in the United States and Canada to adopt a more comprehensive North American focus.

Maquiladora Operations

A concept that has become popular among U.S.-based firms is to use Mexican manufacturing/production facilities for subassembly or component manufacturing, or for final assembly of products such as electronic devices or television sets. While this has been occurring for some time, U.S. firms have only recently begun to include such Maquiladora operations (named for the region of Mexico in which many of these plant operations are located) as formal components of their manufacturing and logistics strategies.

Essentially, in a Maquiladora operation, a U.S. manufacturer either operates or subcontracts for a manufacturing, processing, or assembly activity to be performed in Mexico. Mexican production costs are lower than those in the United States, and the operations involve no local content issues. U.S. firms often send semifinished product to Mexico for final assembly, for example, and then have the finished product shipped to the United States. This concept appeals to many companies: as part of their Maquiladora operations, U.S. manufacturers operate more than 1,000 plants in Mexico.

One feature which adds to the feasibility of such approach is the concept of duty, which involves the importing, storing, manufacturing, and subsequent export of goods with virtually no net payment of customs duties or import charges.[20] Effectively, this contributes to the economic efficiency of logistics alternatives such as Maquiladora operations.

Central/South America

Generally, successful Mexican Maquiladora operations have served as role models for this concept's further exploitation in Central and South American countries. Coupled with the prospect of closer trade relations between the United States and Mexico, these alternatives offer considerable advantages to the firms utilizing them.

Asian Emergence

Far East

In perhaps the most significant trend of the past twenty-five years, Far Eastern countries have emerged as key players in the global business environment. While Japan certainly has achieved a dominant position in global financial markets, Asian countries in general account for significant portions of global trade growth. Hong Kong, South Korea, Singapore, and Taiwan have all assumed leadership positions in certain markets and product types. This trend is likely to accelerate in the future.

For U.S. firms, Far Eastern countries have become preferred sources for many raw materials and components. These countries have also become trusted suppliers of finished goods such as apparel, furniture, consumer electronics, and automobiles. Depending on the country and the specific product, the advantage of such offshore sources may lie either in low cost or high quality, or in some combination of these. Regardless, these countries and other emerging areas such as Malaysia, the Philippines, and Vietnam have become global players in overall business and logistics environments.

New Directions

"transplants"

Aside from establishing product sources in other countries, offshore companies are beginning to locate plants and/or key logistics facilities in countries that use or consume their output. For example, Japanese-based firms such as Toyota and Nissan have located "transplants" in the United States. Similarly, as part of Ford Motor Company's global logistics and manufacturing network, sole-source suppliers deliver to Ford's domestic and international plants from their own plants in those respective countries.

Although long-term change will require significant shifts in manufacturing facility locations, nearer-term strategic changes will more likely involve modifying the logistics systems that serve industries and their individual firms. These larger changes will position the manufacturing infrastructure itself for change.

U.S. and global corporations are well advised to examine sourcing and distribution strategies involving countries other than the ones with which they have been traditionally involved. In addition to the geographical areas this section discusses, new business opportunities are available in Puerto Rico and Caribbean basin countries such as Haiti and the Dominican Republic, and in areas such as Australia and Africa. Hopefully, the innovative sourcing and distribution options these locales offer will result greater logistical efficiency and effectiveness.

Soviet Union and Eastern Europe

Early in the 1990s, the prospect of developing trade with the Soviet Union and Eastern European countries received much attention. Although these areas certainly represent sources for certain materials and components, as well as fertile new market areas, opening up such new areas can offer both frustration and challenge (see On the Line).

GLOBAL TRANSPORTATION OPTIONS

Global transportation is much more complex than domestic U.S. transportation. The distances involved are greater, and the number of parties involved is typically more extensive. Because of the large expanses of water separating most regions of the world, the major modes of global transport are ocean and air. Land modes also carry significant amounts of freight between contiguous countries, particularly in Europe, where land routes are short. Each of these modes fills a specific niche in the worldwide distribution network.

Ocean

ocean shipping

Transport by ship is by far the most pervasive and important global shipment method. Table 4–3 provides an interesting perspective on the growth of ocean-going freight movements. In terms of millions of twenty-foot equivalent container units (TEU), the total volume increased from 8.5 to 36.2 million TEUs between 1974 and 1989, an increase of over 400 percent. In addition, Table 4–3 shows that ninety percent of today's liner trade is containerized and that the largest ships can accommodate nearly 5,000 TEUs, almost a doubling of capacity since 1974. Currently, sixteen percent of U.S. rail intermodal shipments have either an offshore source or destination, or both.

TABLE 4–3   GLOBAL SHIPPING TRENDS

	1974	1989
International container loads (TEUs in millions)	8.5	36.2
Containerized world liner trade	40%–50%	90%
Largest containerships	2,600 TEU	4,600 TEU
Container size	20/35/40	20/40/45/48/53
U.S. intermodal rail carloads (%)	6%	16%

Source: Temple, Barker, & Sloane, Inc., 1991.

ON THE LINE

LOGISTICS IN THE SOVIET UNION: AN AMERICAN BUSINESSMAN'S STORY

If you think your job is tough, consider the case of Levon Soorikian, former ITT international logistics executive and now a logistics consultant, who was arranging transportation of supplies from the United States to Armenia, the Soviet republic devastated by an earthquake in December 1988. Soorikian had volunteered to help expedite shipments of housing materials, donated by the Armenian Church of America, which would be used to help build a 40-building, 640-unit apartment complex that would replace the stone houses destroyed in the disaster.

Soorikian's first job was to select the best routing for the shipment. Baltic Line, a Soviet carrier, offered port-to-port service from New York to Leningrad at no charge; but that route had two big problems. The first was that although the ocean leg of the route was free, the Soviet railway insisted on payment for the rail move from Leningrad to Yerevan, the Armenian capital. Not only did the carrier want payment, it wanted rubles at official rates. Thus, the rail portion's estimated expense was 12,000 U.S. dollars for a 2,000-mile haul. The second problem was reliability: certain shipments sometimes took more than six months to arrive where they were needed.

As an alternative, Soorikian arranged ocean transport from New York through the Mediterranean to Romania through Constellation Line, a New York agent. From there, a transshipment moved the materials to the Georgian port of Poti, on the eastern side of the Black Sea. When Soorikian met a shipment of twenty-five containers in Poti, he found that the port had only a single containership slip and that it was available for only a few hours a day. Soorikian used rail and truck service from Poti for the final leg of the trip to Stepanavan. The building materials reached their destination about six weeks after leaving New York.

Soorikian's other experiences included waiting through significant delays while the Soviet KGB sorted through containers looking for weapons (there weren't any, obviously), and encountering less-than-desirable telephone service. Always an optimist, Levon Soorikian, taking these inconveniences in stride, believed that the next shipment to leave from New York "should move faster" through the Soviet Union's logistics environment.

Source: Adapted from Robert J. Kursar, "Logistics in the Soviet Union: An American Businessman's Story," *Traffic World* (25 June 1990), 43.

The Structure of Ocean Shipping Ocean shipping comprises three major categories. One is the *liner service*, which offers scheduled service on regular routes. Another is *charter vessels*, which firms usually hire on a contract basis and which travel no set routes. And finally are *private carriers*, which are part of a firm's own logistics system.

Liner trades offer common carrier service, sailing on set schedules over specific sea routes. They also offer set tariffs and accept certain standards of liability. Liners usually carry break-bulk shipments of less-than-shipload size. Most container and RO-RO (Roll-on, Roll-off) ships are liners.

liner services

Liners are the property of large steamship companies, many of which belong to shipping conferences. These conferences are voluntary associations of ocean carriers that operate over a common trade route and use a common tariff for setting rates on the commodities they handle. Conferences also work together to attract customers and to utilize member ships as effectively as possible.

In general, conferences provide excellent service with frequent and reliable schedules, published daily in the *Journal of Commerce*. Additionally, conferences help to standardize shipping on many routes by stabilizing prices and offering uniform contract rates.

Recent trends, particularly in the container-shipping business, include the quoting of intermodal through rates, service contracts, and individual carriers independently raising or reducing rates on certain routes. As a result of such actions, customers enjoy greater flexibility in individual carriers ratemaking practices, improved service levels, and, in general, a more market-driven business approach by the carrier firms themselves. This contrasts sharply with the cartel-like operation of most shipping conferences years ago.

charters

Firms contract *charter ships* for specific voyages or for specified time periods. *Voyage charters* are contracts covering one voyage. The carrier agrees to carry a certain cargo from an origin port to a destination. The price the carrier quotes includes all of the expenses of the sea voyage. *Time charters* allow the use of a ship for an agreed-upon time period. The carrier usually supplies a crew as part of the contract. The charterer has exclusive use of the vessel to carry any cargo the contract does not prohibit and assumes all expenses for the ship's operation during the charter period. *Bareboat* or *demise charter* transfers full control of the vessel terms to the charterer. The charterer is then responsible for the ship and all expenses necessary for the vessel's operation, including hiring the crew.

Chartering usually takes place through *ship brokers,* who track the location and status of ships that are open for hire. When a shipper needs to contract for a ship, he or she contacts a broker, who then negotiates the price with the ship owner. The ship owner pays the broker a commission on the charter's cost.

In a logistics system, private ocean carriers play the same role as private carriage in general. In other words, companies utilize private ocean vessels to lower their overall costs and/or to improve their transportation service control. The major differences between domestic ocean transport and international private ocean transportation would be the scale of investment, the complexity of regulations, and the greater risk international transport entails. Any company wishing to provide its own international transportation service must consider all three factors. In international operations, chartering often provides a very viable substitute for private carriage.

Air

low transit times

The low transit times air transport provide have had a dramatic effect on international distribution. The tremendous speed of airplanes combined with a high frequency of scheduled flights has reduced some international transit times from as many as thirty days down to one or two days. Recently, these low transit times have spurred the development of international courier services. These couriers offer door-to-door, next-day services for documents and small packages between most large American cities and a growing number of overseas points.

Mostly, however, the world's air carriers have concentrated on passenger service. Air cargo presently accounts for only one percent of international freight by weight. This very small volume is misleading. The nature of the cargo, mostly high-value, low-density items, brings the total value of air freight cargo up to nearly twenty percent of the world total. Air cargoes include high-valued items such as computers and electronic equipment; perishables such as cut flowers and live seafood; time-sensitive documents and spare parts; and even whole planeloads of cattle for breeding stock.

Because airlines have traditionally concentrated on passenger carriage, airfreight has taken a secondary role. Most airfreight travels as *belly cargo* in the baggage holds of scheduled passenger flights. Only a few major airlines have all-freight aircraft. One recent innovation in aircraft design is the *combi*. These aircraft have been designed with removable seats and movable partitions so that the carrier main deck's configuration can easily change between flights (see Figure 4–8) and take advantage of any variation in relative amounts of passengers and cargo.

In addition to low transit time, air transportation offers an advantage in packaging. This mode requires less stringent packaging than ocean transport since air transport will not expose the shipment to rough handling at a port, to a rough ride on the oceans, or to the weather. A firm using air transportation may also be able to use the same packaging for international shipping as for domestic shipping. In addition, shippers have developed special containers for air transport. These containers reduce handling costs and provide protection, but they also make intermodal shipments difficult. Their odd shapes usually require shippers to repack the shipment before transporting it by another mode. Recent container handling innovations have made it possible to load standard twenty-foot containers onto freight aircraft. For example, a carrier can now load

FIGURE 4–8   747–300 COMBI INTERIOR ARRANGEMENT—MAIN DECK MIXED CLASS, 10 ABREAST AT 34-INCH PITCH   *Source: Traffic World (3 November 1986), 23.*

12 Pallets

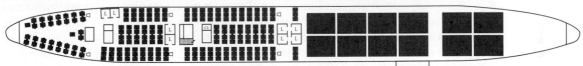

278 Passengers*
1,557 Cu Ft Passenger Baggage
12,713 Cu Ft Cargo

6 Pallets

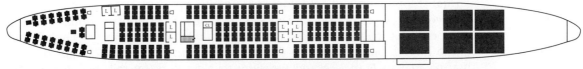

360 Passengers*
1,903 Cu Ft Passenger Baggage
8,587 Cu Ft Cargo

All Passengers

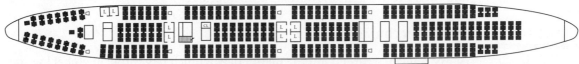

496 Passengers*
2,595 Cu Ft Passenger Baggage
3,395 Cu Ft Cargo

*Includes 69 on Upper Deck

a Boeing 747 with up to thirteen TEU containers in addition to any cargo in the belly holds.

disadvantages   A disadvantage of air carriage is high freight rates, which have prevented many shippers from transporting international shipments by air. Generally, only highly valuable, highly perishable, or urgently needed commodities can bear the higher cost of airfreight.

Motor

Companies most often use motor transport when shipping goods to an adjacent country—between the United States and Mexico or Canada, for example. It is also very common in Europe, where transport distances are relatively short. Motor also plays a large part in intermodal shipments.

advantages   The advantages of international motor transport are basically the same as those for domestic shipments: speed, safety, reliability, and accessibility to the

disadvantages   delivery site. However, motor shipment across multiple national boundaries involves a number of different import regulations. To minimize paperwork, these shipments are often made *in bond;* the carrier seals the trailer at its origin and does not open it again until it reaches its destination country.

Rail

International railroad use is also highly similar to domestic rail use. Rail's accessibility is much more limited internationally, however, because border crossing points are scarce. Differing track gauges in various countries also prevent long-distance shipments.

Intermodal container shipments are where rail is proving its value. Various *maritime bridge* concepts involve railroads both for transcontinental shipments

land bridge   and to and from inland points. For example, a shipper using a *land bridge* substitutes land transportation for part of a container's ocean voyage, taking several days off the transit time and saving in-transit inventory costs. A prime example of a land bridge occurs on the trade route between Japan and Europe. The all-water route takes anywhere from twenty-eight to thirty-one days. If the shipment travels by water from Japan to Seattle (ten days), then by rail to New York (five days), and by water from New York to Europe (seven days), we have a total shipping time of approximately twenty-two days.

mini land bridge   Two other types of maritime bridges are in use. The *mini land bridge* involves one ocean leg and one land leg, with the shipment moving between a U.S. port and a foreign port but passing through a *different* U.S. port. A shipment originating in San Francisco and traveling to New York by rail, and then on to Europe by ship, is an example of a mini land bridge. A shipment having both a land leg and a sea leg but having an inland destination or origin point is called

microbridge   a *microbridge.* A shipment starting in Pittsburgh that travels by rail to Seattle and then on to Japan by water is a microbridge.

STRATEGIC CHANNEL INTERMEDIARIES

As we indicated earlier, intermediaries play a much larger role in global logistics operations than in the domestic United States. To someone first exposed to global logistics, the scope of services intermediaries offer is almost overwhelming. However, as the following sections will explain, intermediaries play a truly strategic role in helping new and established company ventures into the global arena. Companies are all too grateful for assistance in unraveling operations involving sources and destinations in other countries.

Foreign Freight Forwarders

For a company with little international shipping expertise, the *foreign freight forwarder* is the answer. The foreign freight forwarder which employs individuals that are knowledgeable in all aspects of international shipping, supplies its experts to small international shippers who find employing such individuals in their shipping departments uneconomical.

forwarder functions

Foreign freight forwarders, like their domestic counterparts, consolidate small shipments into more economical sizes. In the international arena, these larger sizes range from containers up to entire ships. Foreign freight forwarders also perform the routine actions shipments require. The functions they supply include the following:

- Quoting steamship or other foreign carrier rates
- Chartering vessels or obtaining necessary space
- Preparing commercial invoices
- Obtaining export licenses
- Issuing export declarations for the shipper
- Preparing certificates of origin
- Obtaining and preparing consular invoices
- Compiling ocean bills of lading and checking them against packing lists, weights and measures, and other criteria
- Obtaining insurance
- Paying freight charges
- Obtaining dock receipts
- Presenting documents to the bank or forwarding them to other destinations
- Obtaining port warehouse space
- Tracing shipments in transit and expediting them through port-of-exit facilities
- Collecting and submitting money for shipments[21]

Since no two international sales are exactly alike and since shippers have varying international traffic capabilities, the forwarder usually performs the export work that the shipper cannot handle. The logistics manager must weigh the forwarder's cost against the cost of hiring personnel to perform the same tasks.

income sources

The forwarder derives income from three sources. One source is the fees charged for preparing export documentation. Another source is the commissions the forwarder receives from carriers. These commissions are based on the amount of revenue the forwarder generates for the carrier. The third type of income comes from the price difference between the rate the forwarder quotes a shipper and the lower rate per pound it receives for the consolidated shipments.

Airfreight forwarders perform the same functions as foreign freight forwarders, but for air shipments. They may own aircraft. This has led to the rise of overnight door-to-door small package service worldwide. Emery, DHL, and Federal Express are the major competitors in this field.

Non-vessel-owning Common Carriers

The *non-vessel-owning common carrier (NVOCC)* consolidates and dispenses containers that originate at or are bound to inland points. The need for these firms arose from shippers who, after unloading inbound containers at inland points, had little opportunity to find outbound turnaround traffic. Rail and truck carriers often charge the same rate to move containers whether the containers are loaded or empty.

To reduce these costs, the NVOCC disperses inbound containers and then seeks outbound shipments in the same containers. It will consolidate many containers for multiple-piggyback-car or whole-train movement back to the port for export.

The shippers and receivers of international shipments gain from the shipping expertise NVOCCs possess and from the expanded and simplified import and export opportunities. The ocean carrier gains from the increased market area the NVOCCs' solicitation services make possible.

Export Management Companies

Often a firm wishes to sell its products in a foreign market but lacks the resources to conduct the foreign business itself. An *export management company (EMC)* can supply the expertise such firms need to operate in foreign environments.

obtain orders

EMC's act as agents for domestic firms in the international arena. Their primary function is to obtain orders for their clients' products by selecting appropriate markets, distribution channels, and promotional campaigns. The EMC collects and analyzes credit data for foreign customers and advises exporters on payment terms. It also usually collects payments from foreign customers. EMCs may also supply documentation, arrange transportation, provide warehouse facilities, maintain a foreign inventory, and handle break-bulk operations.

exclusive agent

A firm usually contracts an export management company to provide its exclusive representation in a defined territory. The EMC may either purchase the goods or sell them on commission. In order to present a complete product line to importers an EMC will usually specialize in a particular product type or in complementary products.[22]

Using an export management company has several advantages. One, EMCs usually specialize in specific markets, so they understand in detail what an area requires. They will have up-to-date information on consumer preferences and will help the exporter to target its products most effectively. Two, EMCs will usually strive to maintain good relations with the governments of the importing countries. This enables them to receive favorable customs treatment when introducing new products. EMCs also remain current on documentation requirements. This helps the goods they are importing to enter with few holdups.

Export Trading Companies

An *export trading company (ETC)* exports goods and services. The ETC locates overseas buyers and handles most of the export arrangements, including documentation, inland and overseas transportation, and the meeting of foreign government requirements. The ETC may or may not take title to the goods.[23]

A trading company may also engage in other aspects of foreign trade, in which case it becomes a *general trading company.* One reason Japan has been successful in international trade is because of its large general trading companies, the *sogo shosha.* These firms, which consolidate all aspects of overseas trade into one entity, may include banks, steamship lines, warehouse facilities, insurance companies, sales forces, and communications networks.

advantages

A trading company allows small- to medium-size firms, that do not in themselves possess the resources, to engage in foreign trade. The trading company will purchase their goods and sell them on the international market, taking care of all the intermediate steps. Having all the functional areas under one control makes coordination easy and speeds response time when markets fluctuate.

antitrust constraints

The Export Trading Company Act of 1982 loosened many of the antitrust constraints that prevented the formation of American ETCs. Many different groups in the United States have formed trading companies. Multinational firms, banks, export management companies, ports, and manufacturing associations have all participated.[24]

Customs House Brokers

expert knowledge

Customs house brokers oversee the movement of goods through customs and ensure that the documentation accompanying a shipment is complete and accurate. Customs brokers also stay informed on the latest import regulation developments and on individual products' specific requirements. Customs brokers are prepared to argue for the lowest possible rates and duties for their clients. By hiring this expert knowledge, a firm can reduce importing costs.

Export Packers

rationale

Export packers supply export packaging services for shipments when the exporter lacks either the expertise or facilities. Having a specialist package the export has two distinct advantages. First, it helps the goods move through customs more easily. Many countries assess duties on the weight of the entire package, not just the contents. Export packagers, who know various countries' requirements, know what materials and methods to use in constructing the most economical crate or container.

A second reason to use an export packager is to ensure adequate protection for the goods. International shipments must withstand the rigors of handling as well as climatic variations. Potential savings in time and reduced damage outweigh the cost of using an export packager.

Ports

One of the most important decisions in the global logistics arena is port selection. Ports form the nodes of the global logistics and transportation networks. The port a firm selects for a global shipment must be appropriate to the cargo, since selecting the wrong port can add extra time and expense to the shipment's overall cost. The logistics manager must consider many factors simultaneously when selecting the best port for a particular shipment.

port authority

The term "port authority" refers to any governmental unit or authority at any level that owns, operates, or otherwise provides wharf, dock, and other terminal facilities at port locations. These institutions, which provide access to the capital needed to develop and fund such operations, market the port to the shipping public and other global logistics intermediaries.

port evaluation study

Figure 4–9 shows the results of a recently conducted study into the factors which influence shippers' selection and evaluation of individual ports and port facilities. Over 90 percent of the shippers surveyed rated equipment availability either important or very important. Factors such as cargo loss and damage frequency, and pickup and delivery times also received high rankings.

Another important aspect of port selection is the type of domestic transportation available between inland points and the port facility. As with domestic shipments, the type of transportation a firm will use depends on factors such as the shipment's weight or quantity, the cargo's value, and the product's special handling requirements, if any. With a global/international shipment, a firm must decide whether or not to containerize the product for shipment.

After choosing the transport mode, the logistics manager must ensure that the inland carrier can get close enough to the overseas vessel to minimize handling and loading expenses. The manager must also consider these factors for the destination port. Such concerns particularly apply to less-developed areas, where advanced unloading equipment may be in short supply or even entirely absent.

Also important will be the identity of the specific ocean carriers serving the origin port and the desired destination port. Logically, the logistics manager will wish to select ocean carriers that serve the origin-destination pair(s) of greatest interest to the shipper.

FIGURE 4–9   PORT EVALUATION FACTORS   *Source:* Paul Murphy, James Daley, and Douglas Dalenberg, "Some Ports Lack Shipper Focus," *Transportation & Distribution* (February 1991), 48. Copyright 1991, Penton Publishing Inc., Cleveland, OH.

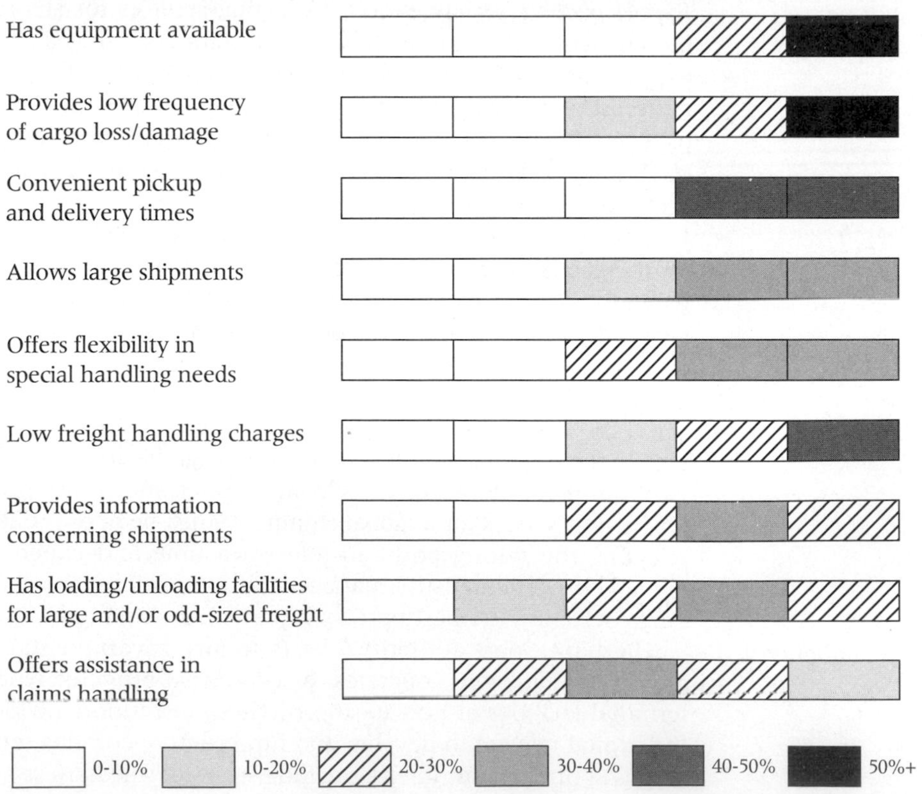

Once the consignment reaches the destination port, the shipper should load it into the vessel as quickly and as inexpensively as possible. This is where the availability of proper equipment and an adequate labor supply will work to the customer's advantage. Containerized shipments will require specialized equipment. Extra-large or outsize cargoes may also require heavy-lift cranes. These specific equipment types may be available only at certain ports.

Finally, the port selection decision should consider the facility's potential effects on overall "door-to-door" transit time and variability. Defined as the transit time from the shipment's initial origin to its ultimate destination, this door-to-door measure will certainly be longer than the ocean crossing, or port-to-port time. Ports that help to minimize the time and variability of door-to-door logistics service will be attractive to shippers who prefer a more comprehensive logistics approach.

STORAGE FACILITIES AND PACKAGING

Storage Facilities

containers

At several points during an international shipment, the goods being shipped may require storage. Storage may be necessary while the shipment waits for loading on an ocean vessel, after it has arrived at the destination port and is awaiting further transportation, or while customs clearance is being arranged for the merchandise. When packaged in a container, goods are protected from the weather, theft, and pilferage. A carrier or shipper can store containers outside between a journey's stages with little effect on the contents.

other options

Noncontainerized cargo, on the other hand, requires protection if it is to arrive in good order. Ports supply several types of storage facilities to fill this need. *Transit sheds,* located next to the piers or at the airport, provide temporary storage while the goods await the next portion of the journey. Usually, the port usage fee includes a fixed number of days of free storage. After this time expires, the user pays a daily charge. *In-transit storage* areas allow the shipper to perform some required operation on the cargo before embarkation. These actions may include carrier negotiations and waiting for documentation, packing, crating, and labeling to be completed. The carrier usually provides *hold-on-dock storage* free of charge until the vessel's next departure date, allowing the shipper to consolidate goods and to save storage costs.

When goods require long-term storage, the shipper uses a warehouse. *Public warehouses* are available for extended storage periods. These facilities' services and charges are similar to those of public warehouses in the domestic sphere. *Bonded warehouses,* operated under customs supervision, are designated by the U.S. Secretary of the Treasury "for the purpose of storing imported merchandise entered for warehousing, or taken possession of by the collector of customs, or under seizure, or for the manufacture of merchandise in hand, or for repacking, sorting, or cleaning of imported merchandise." [25] Only bonded carriers may move goods into and out of bonded warehouses.

purpose

One purpose of bonded warehouses is to hold imported goods for reshipment out of the United States. The owner can store items in a bonded warehouse for up to three years, allowing him or her to decide on the goods' ultimate disposition without having to pay import duties or taxes on them. If the owner does not reexport the goods before the three years elapse, they are considered imports and are subject to all appropriate duties and taxes.

Packaging

importance

Export shipments moving by ocean transportation require more stringent packaging than domestic shipments normally do. An export shipment receives more handling: it is loaded at the origin, unloaded at the dock, loaded onto a ship, unloaded from the ship at port, loaded onto a delivery vehicle, and unloaded at the destination. This handling usually occurs under unfavorable conditions—in inclement weather, with antiquated handling equipment, for example. If storage facilities are inadequate, the goods may remain exposed to the elements for a long time.

protection

The shipper may find settling liability claims for damage to export goods very difficult. Usually, the freight handling involves many firms; and these firms are located in different countries. Stringent packaging is the key to claims prevention for export shipments.

higher cost

Stockout costs justify more protective packaging (increased packaging cost) for export shipments. The export distance is often so great that the time (two to four months) required to receive a reordered shipment may cause the buyer and seller extremely high stockout costs. The buyer may resort to an alternative supply source, and the seller may lose business.

The package size—weight, length, width, height—must conform to the customer's instructions. Packaging dimensions usually reflect the physical constraints upon transportation in the buyer's country. For example, the 40 × 8 × 8-foot containers common in the United States may be nontransportable in certain foreign countries. The container may not be compatible with some country's existing transportation equipment, or may exceed the height and lateral clearance of highways, bridges, and overpasses. If the package cannot be transported, the shipper must repackage the shipment. This additional handling adds costs, delay, and increases risk of loss or damage to the shipment.

containers

Sellers frequently use containers for international shipping. A containerized commodity receives considerably less handling. With reduced handling comes reduced risk of loss and damage as well as greater time efficiency in the transfer among modes. The decision to use containers must reflect the savings we noted earlier, as well as the container's added cost, return freight costs on it, and any additional handling and storing costs.

marking

The package marking requirements for international shipments also differ from those for domestic shipments. On domestic shipments, package markings provide detail concerning things such as the shipment content and consignee. On export shipments, the package provides little information about the shipment. Large geometric symbols, numbers, letters, and various codes (see Figure 4–10) provide handling instructions to foreign materials handlers who often cannot read English. Using codes conceals the identity of the shipper, the consignee, and the goods so as to reduce the possibility of pilferage.

GOVERNMENTAL INFLUENCES

As Figure 4–11 indicates, the export-import process can be quite complex in terms of the various intermediaries it may involve. In addition, export-import documentation is far more complicated than it is for domestic U.S. shipments. We will address the topic of documentation as part of a more in-depth discussion of transportation later in the text.

FIGURE 4–10   SOME SYMBOLS USED FOR PACKING EXPORT SHIPMENTS   *Source:* Courtesy Air France Cargo.

keep away from heat

this way up

keep dry

use no hooks

role of government

This section addresses issues relating to the role of government in international trade. As we discussed previously, an increasing number of governments are attempting to simplify international trade and to facilitate the flow of commerce.

This section will highlight several areas in which governments can exert power over the flow of international commerce. One method is through import taxes and duties. Governments often set these at high rates to protect local firms from competition. Another approach is to place import quotas on certain goods. Quotas limit the physical amount of product that may be imported in a specific time period, usually a year. Individual nations may also enact regulations to prevent the import of dangerous items. For example many nations restrict imports of animals and plants in order to prevent the spread of disease. The importing country may base still other restrictions on safety requirements.

FIGURE 4–11 EXPORT-IMPORT FLOWCHART *Source:* John E. Tyworth, Joseph L. Cavinato, and C. John Langley Jr., *Traffic Management: Planning, Operations, and Control* (Reading, MA: Addison-Wesley Publishing Company, 1987), 388.

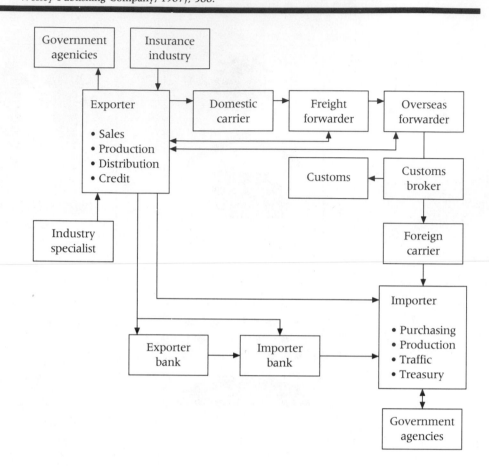

A firm must take all possible restrictions into account before it can move goods internationally. Inadequate knowledge of current regulations may cause great losses in both time and money in terms of customer delays or extra import fees.

Customs Regulation

customs National *customs regulations* have the greatest effect on the international movement of goods. Customs regulations fulfill two basic objectives: to protect domestic industry and to provide revenue.

Customs regulations protect national industries through high import duties, quotas, and restrictions on the items firms can import. If the companies involved research all of these factors before finalizing the sales contract, the shipment will encounter few problems at the actual time of entry.

import duties Regulations raise revenue through the collection of *import duties.* These duties are set by national law and are determined in three different ways.

Ad valorem duties are the most common type of import duty. They are stated as a percentage of the value of the imported goods. For example, if a good has a value of $1,000 and is subject to an import duty of 15%, the amount customs collects is $150 ($1,000 $\times$ 0.15 = $150). The value used in computing the import duty is usually the merchandise's *transaction value,* the total price paid or payable for the good. It includes the good's price at its origin, the packing costs the buyer incurred, any selling commissions, any royalty or license fees, and the cost of any modifications necessary to allow the importation of the item.

The next major type of import duty is based on a cost per unit. For example, $5 per pound or $100 per unit could be a duty. If the shipment's weight or number of items is known, this *unit duty* is easy to calculate.

The third type is the *compound duty.* This method combines the ad valorem and unit duties. Suppose that a company wishes to import 100 items with a value of $200 each, and that applicable rates for this shipment are 12% of the value and $25 per unit. We would calculate the total import duty as follows:

$$\text{Ad valorem rate: } 100 \times \$200 \times 0.12 = \$2,400$$
$$\text{Unit rate: } \quad 100 \text{ units} \times \$25 \quad = \underline{\$2,500}$$
$$\text{Compound rate: } \$2,400 + \$2,500 \quad = \$4,900$$

If the owner decides to reexport a good after importing it and the applicable duties have been paid, he or she may apply for a *drawback.* Drawbacks return ninety-nine percent of the duty paid during import. The customs service retains the other one percent as an administrative fee. To receive a drawback, one must file an application within three years of reexport.

Other Customs Functions

As well as collecting import duties, the customs service also inspects imported merchandise. These inspections, conducted before the goods may enter the country, perform the following functions:

- Determine that the goods' value is the same as that stated on the shipment's documentation. This value is used to determine the import duties.
- Ensure that the items have the correct markings. They must have all appropriate safety labels, instructions, or special marks, as well as identification of the country of origin.
- Find any items that are excluded from entry. These items include illegal drugs and weapons, and articles that do not meet national standards.
- Ensure that the shipment is correctly invoiced and that the quantities stated are correct.
- Control quota amounts.

entry procedures   The customs service collects duties and performs inspections at *entry.* Entry includes all of the legal procedures a firm requires to secure possession of imported merchandise. Entry procedures must begin within five working days of a shipment's arrival. At entry, the customs service inspects the shipment's documentation for completeness and accuracy and inspects the items themselves to ascertain the value, to ensure that all import requirements are met, and to set the amount of any duties.

Customs procedures can be very time-consuming and expensive if a company does not conduct proper research before making a shipment. Knowing customs requirements beforehand is best. The U.S. Customs Service is striving to reduce import entry complications. The increasing use of electronic data transmission provides quicker entry times and improves customs procedures' overall efficiency.

Foreign Trade Zones

Foreign trade zones (FTZs) are areas within a country that the local customs service treats as foreign territory. Shippers can land, store, and process goods within an FTZ without incurring any import duties or domestic taxes.[26] FTZs offer many advantages to parties engaged in international trade. Some of the major ones are as follows:

- Goods can be landed and stored without customs formalities, duty, or bond. FTZs offer excellent security for the merchandise because they are under customs control.
- Shippers can perform break-bulk operations on the goods before they are actually imported. Depending on the situation, this may lead to savings on duties and transportation costs.
- Imports can be processed, re-marked, or repackaged to meet local requirements before importation. This avoids any fines for importing improperly marked goods.
- FTZs can hold goods in excess of current quotas until the next quota period arrives.
- Buyers can test or sample products before import. This allows the buyer to ensure that the merchandise meets all contract stipulations before he or she accepts the goods and pays the import duties.
- The owner can reexport goods held in an FTZ at any time without having to pay any duties to the country where the FTZ is located.
- Goods can be stored indefinitely in an FTZ.

One very important aspect of a foreign trade zone is that a firm can use it for product manufacture. The manufacturer can purchase production process materials at the lowest price on the world market and bring them into the FTZ. The finished product can then be reexported or else imported using the duty on either the components or the final product, whichever is more advantageous to the importer. In addition, the manufacturer pays no duties on waste or by-products from the production process, realizing even more savings.

SUMMARY

The global business environment has opened up many new and exciting options for today's logistics managers. The firm interested in establishing competitive advantage through logistics management should not overlook opportunities for global sourcing and global distribution.

Figure 4–12 is an example of how a major U.S. company, in this instance a retailer, may prosper through the use of innovative logistics strategies. By selectively bypassing certain inbound and outbound distribution channel echelons, a company may significantly reduce transportation and inventory expenses. This represents the forward thinking which should accompany global logistics planning, operations, and control.

In general, successful global logistics approaches will involve three types of significant change:

- Broader interconnection between shipper, carrier, and customs information systems;

FIGURE 4–12   MAJOR U.S. RETAILER STREAMLINES GLOBAL LOGISTICS CHANNELS   *Source:* Temple, Barker, & Sloane, Inc., *International Logistics: Meeting the Challenges of Global Distribution Channels* (Lexington, MA: Temple, Barker, & Sloane, Inc., 1987), 26.

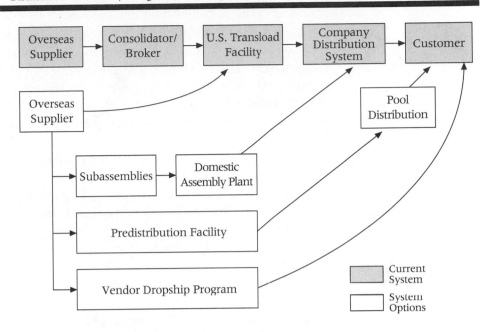

- Enhanced shipment monitoring capabilities to support global trade and sourcing; and
- Redefinition of global marketing, manufacturing, and logistics strategies.

While global logistics has many characteristics in common with domestic logistics, it is also different in many ways. The importance of global logistics will increase as more firms engage in worldwide sourcing to acquire things such as materials and components. Companies are beginning to view the entire world as a potential market, a view that leads to increased demands on current logistics systems to supply products to distant portions of the world. Users and providers of global logistics services are striving to increase efficiency by incorporating new and innovative concepts into the worldwide logistics network. The future of global logistics will be one of growth as more and more firms move into this trade arena.

STUDY QUESTIONS

1. What major trends do you see in world trade and in the significance of global logistics? Which areas of the world are projected to show the most significant increases in volumes of world trade?

2. Distinguish between domestic, multi-domestic, and global companies. What is the relationship for the global firm between logistics strategy and other corporate strategies in the areas of technology, marketing, and manufacturing?

3. Why is global logistics important to both individual companies and to the U.S. as a whole?

4. What are the elements of the "dynamic diamond" suggested by Professor Michael Porter of the Harvard Business School? Which of these do you feel are most important to the success of companies operating in the global business environment?

5. What general shifts do you see in the global business environment? What do you feel are the likely directions for the future?

6. What do you believe will be the major priorities for global logistics systems of the future? What are some of the specific directions and types of initiatives which you feel will be most relevant?

7. Briefly describe the structure of ocean shipping and the nature of the conference system.

8. Compare and contrast the services of international air, motor, and rail carriers with their domestic counterparts.

9. What are some of the key intermediaries in global logistics, and why are they important? How do freight forwarders differ from export management companies?

10. What factors should be considered in selecting ports for global logistics operations?

11. What are "bonded" warehouses, and what is their significance to global logistics operations?

12. What functions are served by customs procedures at ports of entry into various countries? What are the principal types of duties collected by customs authorities? In what general ways would you expect customs procedures of the future to differ from those which exist at present?

NOTES

1. Nigel Grimwade, *International Trade* (London: Routledge, 1989).
2. Temple, Barker, & Sloane, Inc., *International Logistics: Meeting the Challenges of Global Distribution Channels* (Lexington, MA: Temple, Barker, & Sloane, Inc., 1987), 1–6.
3. Temple, Barker, & Sloane, Inc., *International Logistics,* 1.
4. Temple, Barker, & Sloane, Inc., *International Logistics,* 3.
5. These concepts are well developed in David L. Anderson, "Logistics Strategies for Competing in Global Markets," *1985 Council of Logistics Management Annual Conference Proceedings* (Oak Brook, IL: CLM, 1985), 413–26.
6. Referenced by Anderson, "Logistics Strategies for Competing in Global Markets," 414, this source is Theodore Levitt, *The Marketing Imagination* (New York: The Free Press, 1983).
7. Anderson, "Logistics Strategies for Competing in Global Markets," 415.
8. Anderson, "Logistics Strategies for Competing in Global Markets," 415.
9. Anderson, "Logistics Strategies for Competing in Global Markets," 416.
10. Martin Christopher, "Customer Service Strategies for International Markets," *1989 Council of Logistics Management Annual Conference Proceedings* (Oak Brook, IL: CLM, 1989), 327.
11. Christopher, "Customer Service Strategies," 327–28.
12. See Michael Porter, "Why Nations Triumph," *Fortune* (12 March 1990), 54–60.
13. Porter, "Why Nations Triumph," 54–60.
14. David L. Anderson has identified and discussed several of these factors in "International Logistics Strategies for the 1980s," *1984 Council of Logistics Management Annual Conference Proceedings* (Oak Brook, IL: CLM, 1984), 355–75.

15. For an excellent overview of the significant changes among the countries of the European Economic Community (EC), see Ernst & Whinney, *Europe 1992: The Single Market* (Ernst & Whinney International, 1988).

16. Richard R. Young, "Europe 1992: The Logistics Perspective of a European-Based Multinational," *Proceedings of the R. Hadly Waters Logistics and Transportation Symposium* (University Park, PA: Penn State University, 1990), 13–26.

17. Young, "Europe 1992," 13–26.

18. Helen L. Richardson, "Canada Serves Global Markets," *Distribution* (February 1991), 16–18. Also, see Andrew Tausz, "Free Trade's Impact on Transportation," *Distribution* (May 1989) pp. 30–33; and Patricia M. Carey, "The Truth About Free Trade," *North American International Business* (April 1991), 22–26.

19. Richardson, "Canada Serves Global Markets," 16.

20. See John E. Tyworth, Joseph L. Cavinato, and C. John Langley, Jr., *Traffic Management: Planning, Operations, and Control* (Reading, MA: Addison-Wesley Publishing Company, 1987), 392.

21. Durward L. Brooks, "Exporting without Tears," *Transportation and Distribution Management* (December 1972), 44.

22. John D. Daniels and Lee H. Radebaugh, *International Business* (Reading, MA: Addison-Wesley, 1986), 465–99.

23. Evelyn A. Thomchick and Lisa Rosenbaum, "The Role of U.S. Export Trading Companies in International Logistics," *Journal of Business Logistics* 5, no. 2, 86.

24. Thomchick and Rosenbaum, "The Role of U.S. Export Trading Companies," 88.

25. Paul S. Bender, "The International Dimension of Physical Distribution Management," in *The Distribution Handbook*, edited by James F. Robeson (New York: The Free Press, 1985), 801.

26. Schary, *Logistics Decisions*, 405.

CASE 4–1

OLD BRITISH FISH 'N' CHIPS, LTD.

Based on the success of its fast-food operations in the United Kingdom, Old British Fish 'N' Chips, Ltd., was thinking of expanding its operations to other areas of the world. Old British operated forty-seven retail stores throughout England and Scotland. Of this total, thirty were franchise operations and seventeen were owned and operated by Old British itself.

Old British was committed to the high quality and low price of its retail, ready-to-eat food products. While the company specialized in fish 'n' chips, it also sold a variety of other selections, including hamburgers, fried chicken, and salads. It had recently considered, but had decided against, adding fried squid and octopus to its already well-stocked menu.

Aside from the fact that most people really liked the taste of Old British's food products and its' retail stores' general ambience, one of the company's key competitive advantages was its effective, professional ingredients supply network. Old British did business only with suppliers of consistently high-quality food products, and had arranged to have one of the United Kingdom's finest contract logistics firms manage all movements of ingredients and supplies from source to store. This supply strategy was the envy of all of Old British's competitors, who definitely regarded it as a key element of the firm's success.

In addition, Old British was in the fourth year of its formal quality process. The process was apparently working well, and franchise holders, company store operators, and headquarters personnel all perceived themselves as working toward the same goal: understanding and satisfying their customers' needs.

Case Questions   **1.** From the available information, what do you feel are the key strategic strengths of Old British 'N' Chips? How difficult do you feel it would be for a competitor to duplicate these capabilities?

2. What do you feel would be some of the key business and logistical issues Old British should address before committing itself to a market-entry strategy for the United States? For Western Europe? For Japan?

CASE 4–2

ATHLETIC CORNER

Athletic Corner is a subsidiary of a large footwear company with major distribution facilities in Phoenix, Arizona; Los Angeles, California; and Harrisburg, Pennsylvania. The parent organization, Corpus Footwear, operates its own retail outlets and once performed all its own manufacturing in the northeastern states. With the advent of much cheaper foreign labor after World War II, Corpus began to purchase more and more shoes from overseas manufacturers while continuing to manufacture twenty percent (approximately) of their total sales volume.

During the 1970s, Corpus began to investigate how to best react to the growth in athletic footwear associated with the "fitness boom." Sales of such footwear had expanded in stores where they marketed products under the Corpus name, even though a variety of vendors manufactured the shoes. Corpus decided in 1980 to set up a subsidiary, called Athletic Corner, to specifically market athletic footwear and capitalize on the fitness movement. At the same time, they decided to handle other companies' brand-name shoes in the Athletic Corner, rather than using their own label, as they did in their Corpus stores. That decision has been very successful for Corpus, and the Athletic Corner Enterprise has expanded to 275 stores nationwide.

Now, in 1992, Corpus is again considering some new directions and expanding their international sales and distribution effort. Prior to this time, their only international experience has been with procurement. They have been buying shoes and athletic footwear from Europe and the Far East, but all their sales have been in the United States.

Company president Jack Miles feels that they should expand into the European market by opening up Athletic Corner stores in European countries that have picked up the fitness craze. The big question is the logistics system. Jim Kentz, vice president of marketing, feels that they should build a larger warehouse in London and bring shoes from the Far East directly to the warehouse. Phil Cips, vice president of finance, feels that the company should distribute from the Harrisburg warehouse to the European stores through intermediaries. Dave Ketz, corporate controller, recommends building a plant/warehouse facility in Spain and producing and distributing directly in the European market.

Case Question   **1.** What is your recommendation?

SELECTED BIBLIOGRAPHY FOR PART 1

LOGISTICS MANAGEMENT

Abeles, Sir Peter. "Logistics: Where are the Professionals?" *Focus on Physical Distribution and Logistics Management* 8, no. 5 (June 1989), 2–9.

Bower, Joseph L., and Thomas M. Hout. "Fast Cycle Capability for Competitive Power," *Harvard Business Review* 66, no. 6 (November–December, 1988), 110–18.

Dumaine, Brian. "How Managers Can Succeed Through Speed," *Fortune* (13 February 1989), 54–59.

"Hewlett-Packard's Whip-Cracker," *Fortune* (13 February 1989), 58.

Langley, John. "U.S. Logistics—The State of the Nation," *Focus on Physical Distribution and Logistics Management* 8, no. 6 (July/August 1989), 28–33.

Livingston, David B. "Logistics as a Competitive Weapon: The total Cost Approach," Council of Logistics Management, *Annual Conference Proceedings* 2 (1988), 15–46.

LOGISTICS ENVIRONMENTS

Andrews, Richard A. "The Lombardi Approach to Integrated Logistics Support (ILS)," *Air Force Journal of Logistics* 13, no. 1 (Winter 1989), 1–6.

Bishop, Thomas, and Steven H. Wunning. "Third Party Logistics: A Competitive Advantage," Council of Logistics Management, *Annual Conference Proceedings* 2 (1988), 1–14.

Davis, Herbert W. "Physical Distribution Costs—Performance in Selected Industries, 1988," Council of Logistics Management, *Annual Conference Proceedings* 1 (1988), 73–82.

Edmondson, Harold E., and Steven C. Wheelwright. "Outstanding Manufacturing in the Coming Decade," *California Management Review* 31, no. 4 (Summer 1989), 70–90.

Gordon, Jay. "A Textbook Case of Adding Value," *Distribution* 88, no. 8 (August 1989), 103–105.

Horne, Robert. "Charting a Course For Integrated Logistics," *Transportation & Distribution Presidential Issue 1989–1990* 30, no. 11 (October 1989), 45–51.

"How Logistics Fits In," *Distribution* 88, no. 4 (April 1989), 28–34.

Kallock, Roger. "Develop a Strategic Outlook," *Transportation & Distribution* 30, no. 1 (January 1989), 16–18.

Kyj, Larissa S., and Myroslaw J. Kyj. "Customer Service: Product Differentiation in International Markets," *International Journal of Physical Distribution & Materials Management* 19, no. 1 (1989), 30–38.

Muller, E. J. "Logistics for Profit," *Distribution* 88, no. 6 (June 1989), 38–46.

Ohmae, Kenichi. "The Global Logic of Strategic Alliances," *Harvard Business Review* (March–April 1989), 143–54.

Watson, James F., and Herb Johnson. "The Value of Strategic Logistics Partnership," Council of Logistics Management, *Annual Conference Proceedings* 2 (1988), 277–91.

Wood, Andrew L. "Distribution Strategies for the 1990s," *Logistics World* 2, no. 2 (June 1989), 87–91.

CUSTOMER SERVICE

Ammer, Dean S. "Top Management's View of the Purchasing Function," *Journal of Purchasing and Materials Management* (Spring 1989), 16–21.

Bradley, Peter. "Global Sourcing Takes Split-Second Timing," *Purchasing* 107, no. 2 (20 July 1989), 52–58.

Burt, David N. "Managing Product Quality Through Strategic Purchasing," *Sloan Management Review* 10, no. 3 (Spring 1989), 39–48.

Cavinato, Joseph. "How To Keep Customers Coming Back For More," *Distribution* 88, no. 12 (December 1989), 60–61.

Cayer, Shirley. "Low-Key, But Savvy," *Purchasing* 107, no. 3 (17 August 1989), 49–55.

Christopher, Martin, and Alan Braithwaite. "Managing Strategic Lead Times," *Logistics Information Management* 2, no. 4 (December 1989), 192–97.

Cooke, James Aaron. "Management Briefing: Making the Handoff From Manufacturing to Distribution," *Traffic Management* 28, no. 8 (August 1989), 75–77.

Cooper, M. Bixby, and George Wagenheim. "Negotiation Preparation and Customer Service," Council of Logistics Management, *Annual Conference Proceedings* 2 (1988), 313–25.

Drucker, Peter F. "The New World According to Drucker," *Business Month* (May 1989), 48–59.

Ellram, Lisa M., Bernard J. LaLonde, and Mary Margaret Weber. "Retail Logistics," *International Journal of Physical Distribution & Materials Management* 19, no. 12 (1989), 29–39.

"Financing Customer Service," *Customer Service Newsletter* 17, no. 2 (February 1989), 1–5.

Hammant, Jeffrey. "Supply Chain Management—Vertical Integration Without Tears," *Focus on Physical Distribution and Logistics Management* 8, no. 6 (July/August 1989), 14–16.

"How Logistics Fits In," *Distribution* 88, no. 4 (April 1989), 29–34.

Keiser, Thomas C. "Neogtiating with a Customer You Can't Afford to Lose," *Harvard Business Review,* no. 6 (November–December 1988), 30–34.

Lambert, Douglas M., and Thomas C. Harrington. "Establishing Customer Service, Strategies Within the Marketing Mix: More Empirical Evidence," *Journal of Business Logistics* 10, no. 2 (1989), 44–60.

Landeros, Robert, and Robert M. Monczka. "Cooperative Buyer/Seller Relationships and a Firm's Competitive Posture," *Journal of Purchasing and Materials Management* (Fall 1989), 9–18.

Lichtenberger, H. William. "Union Carbide Won't Accept Second Place," *Transportation & Distribution Presidential Issue 1989–1990* 30, no. 11 (October, 1989), 37–43.

Loren, Allan Z. "Apple Computer Gears Up For Customer Driven 90's," *Transportation & Distribution Presidential Issue 1989–1990* 30, no. 11 (October 1989), 8–14.

"Meeting Customers on Their Turf and Yours," *Customer Service Newsletter* 17, no. 5 (May 1989), 1–3.

Muller, E. J. "The Corporate Crossroads," *Distribution* 88, no. 9 (September 1989), 28–34.

Murray, Robert E. "Outsourcing, Networking, and the Hollow Corporation," Council of Logistics Management, *Annual Conference Proceedings* 1 (1988), 171–92.

Murray, Thomas J. "Rethinking the Factory," *Business Month* (July 1989), 34–37.

Raia, Ernest. "1989 Medal of Professional Excellence," *Purchasing* 107, no. 5 (28 September 1989), 52–67.

Sellers, Patricia. "Getting Customers to Love You," *Fortune* (13 March 1989), 38–49.

Semich, J. William, and Somerby Dowst. "How to Push Your Everyday Supplier Into World Class Status," *Purchasing* 107, no. 3 (17 August 1989), 74–88.

Smith, Frederick W. "Promises to Keep," Council of Logistics Management, *Annual Conference Proceedings* 1 (1988), 1–12.

Sterling, Jay U., and Douglas M. Lambert. "Customer Service Research: Past Present and Future," monograph, *International Journal of Physical Distribution & Materials Management* 9, no. 2 (1989), 23 pp.

"10 Reasons Why You Have a Quality Problem (And What You Can Do About It)," *Customer Service Newsletter* 17, no. 3 (March 1989), 1–4.

Young, Scott T. "Prime Vendor/Hospital Purchasing Relationships," *International Journal of Physical Distribution & Materials Management* 19, no. 9 (1989), 27–30.

Zurier, Steve. "Delivering Quality Customer Service," *Industrial Distribution* 78, no. 3 (March 1989), 30–35.

GLOBAL LOGISTICS

Anderson, David L. "International Logistics Strategies for the 1980's," Council of Logistics Management, *Annual Conference Proceedings* (Oak Brook, IL: CLM, 1984), 335–75.

Anderson, David L. "Logistics Strategies for Competing in Global Markets," Council of Logistics Management, *Annual Conference Proceedings* (Oak Brook, IL: CLM, 1985), 413–26.

Boberg, Devin, David B. Vellenga, and Karen S. Gritzmacher. "Logistics Issues in the Maquiladora Operations," Council of Logistics Management, *Annual Conference Proceedings* 2 (1988), 425–35.

Christopher, Martin. "Customer Service Strategies for International Markets," Council of Logistics Management, *Annual Conference Proceedings* (Oak Brook, IL: CLM, 1989), 327.

Cooke, James Aaron. "Where to Learn About World Trade," *Traffic Management* 29, no. 9 (September 1990), 30–32.

Cooper, James, Michael Browne, and Melvyn Peters. "Logistics Performance in Europe: The Challenge of 1982," *International Journal of Logistics Management* 1, no. 1 (1990), 28–35.

Davies, G. J. "The International Logistics Concept," *International Journal of Physical Distribution & Materials Management* 17, no. 2 (1987), 20–27.

Dempsey, William A. "Recognizing and Avoiding Customer Service Problems in International Logistics," *International Journal of Business Logistics* 1, no 1 (1988), 5–12.

Fawcett, Stanley E. "Logistics and Manufacturing Issues in Maquiladora Operations," *International Journal of Physical Distribution Logistics Management* 20, no. 4, 13–21.

Gourdin, Kent N., and Richard L. Clarke. "Can U.S. Transportation Industries Meet the Global Challenge?" *International Journal of Physical Distribution & Logistics Management* 20, no. 4, 31–36.

Kallock, Roger W. "The Challenge of Managing Logistics in a Global Environment," Council of Logistics Management, *Annual Conference Proceedings* (Oak Brook, IL: CLM, 1988), 83–94.

Kyj, Myroslaw J., and Richard A. Lancioni. "International Customer Service as a New Competitive Tool" and "Is a Global Customer Service Policy Desirable?" *International Logistics: An Asia Pacific Perspective.* (Special issue of the *International Journal of Physical Distribution & Materials Management* 19, 10 (1989), 4–13.)

Macklin, Colin L. "Third Party Logistics in Europe," Council of Logistics Management, *Annual Conference Proceedings* 1 (1988), 95–122.

"Managing The Global Supply Chain," *Distribution* 88, no. 3 (March 1989), 40–42.

Morgan, Ivor P., and Peter M. Arnold. "International Logistics Management," *Journal of Business Logistics* 11, no. 2 (1990), 140–58.

Murphy, Paul R., Douglas R. Dalenberg, and James M. Daley. "Assessing International Port Operations," *International Journal of Physical Distribution & Materials Management* 19, no. 9 (1989), 3–10.

Porter, Michael E. "The Competitive Advantage of Nations," *Harvard Business Review* (March–April 1990), 73–93.

Rosenbloom, Bert. "Motivating Your International Channel Partners," *Business Horizons* 33, no. 2 (March–April 1990), 53–57.

Seguin, Vernon C. "An Introduction to the Challenge of Logistics Support for Business with the People's Republic of China," Council of Logistics Management, *Annual Conference Proceedings* 1 (1988), 161–70.

Temple, Barker & Sloane, Inc. *International Logistics: Meeting the Challenges of Global Distribution Channels* (Lexington, MA: Temple, Barker & Sloane, Inc., 1987), 1–6.

Trunick, Perry A. "The World Is Your Market," *Transportation & Distribution* 31, no. 9 (September 1990), 28–36.

van der Hoop, Hans. "Europhobia or Europhoria?" *Distribution* (October 1988), 38–46.

Wortzel, Heidi Vernon. "The Logistics of Distribution in China," *International Journal of Physical Distribution & Materials Management* 15, no. 5 (1985), 51–60.

Young, Richard R. "Europe 1992: The Logistics Perspective of a European-Based Multinational," *Proceedings of the R. Hadly Waters Logistics and Transportation Symposium* (University Park, PA: Penn State University, 1990), 13–26.

Zinn. Walter, and Robert E. Grosse. "Barriers to Globalization: Is Global Distribution Possible?" *International Journal of Logistics Management* 1, no. 1 (1990), 13–18.

II

The second part of the text examines those strategic managerial issues of information, inventory, and transportation. The cost effective development of accurate and timely information is presented in the logistics information systems chapter. Accurate and timely information is essential for effective decision-making in all logistics functional areas.

Inventory is examined in two chapters. Attention is first devoted to the general nature of inventory management and the second chapter considers how important inventory decisions are made. In this era of value added analysis, effective inventory management decisions are made in conjunction with the impact on other logistics functional areas.

The fourth chapter in this section considers transportation. Transportation is usually the largest logistics cost element for a company. In Chapter 8, the relationship of the transportation function to other functional areas is examined, a carrier selection framework is developed, and a discussion of the economic and operational characteristics of the various modes is presented within the context of the carrier selection determinants.

LOGISTICS INFORMATION SYSTEMS

Many firms today view effective logistics management both as a prerequisite to overall cost efficiency and as a key to ensuring the competitive pricing of products and services.[1] Many high-level corporate and marketing executives consider the firm's logistics strengths to be among the unique ways in which the firm can differentiate itself in the marketplace. Numerous advances in the information technology field have led firms to consider the information systems area extremely important to efficient business conduct throughout the firm.[2]

Thus, this text directs considerable attention to the topic of how the firm's logistics function and its mission have changed over time. Similarly, most firms now view information systems as an area of true strategic importance.

chapter objectives

This chapter discusses some of the fundamental ways in which a firm's logistics area can utilize the latest information technologies. The chapter focuses on the logistics information system and its principal components. Additionally, the chapter explores the latest uses of computer technology in the logistics area, discusses some new and innovative information systems that can be valuable to the logistics area, and comments about strategic information management in logistics.

link between information and customer service

Effective information management can help to ensure that a firm meets the logistical needs of its customers. Studies have shown that firms should place priority on logistical elements such as on-time delivery, stockout levels, order status, shipment tracing and expediting, order convenience, completeness of orders, creation of customer pickup and backhaul opportunities, and product substitution.[3] These activities are within the logistics manager's domain, and their successful implementation depends heavily upon a timely and accurate flow of meaningful information. The logistics area can assist significantly in meeting customer needs, and a first-class information system can facilitate the logistics mission.

QUALITY OF INFORMATION[4]

Three issues characterize information quality. The first is having the right information available to make the best possible decisions. The second is ensuring that the information is as accurate as possible. The third is the effectiveness of the various means available to communicate information.

Having the Right Information Available

relevance of information

Unfortunately, logistics managers do not always have the information they need to make effective decisions. Perhaps the most common reason is that many managers are uncertain of their information needs and that they have difficulty conceptualizing and verbalizing those needs. Another reason is that staff people charged with securing information give the logistics manager what they think is needed or what they find convenient or cost-effective to provide. Many times this is quite different from what the logistics manager truly needs.

Logistics managers need to know more about information systems and their management. Alternatively, many information system managers could benefit from a better understanding of logistics management and business in general. This indicates a need for a two-way educational process in which these areas become far more aware of and sensitive to one another's needs and capabilities.

Accuracy of Information

accuracy of information

Information available to logistics managers often leaves much to be desired, and, as a result, tends to cause less-than-perfect management decision making. This sometimes occurs because many companies use cost accounting and management control systems developed years ago in very different competitive environments. Many of these systems distort product-cost information and do not produce the information that logistics managers need to make the best decisions.

For example, many logistics managers have invested heavily in capital equipment and systems to facilitate activities in areas such as warehousing, transportation, and inventory control. As a result, some have dramatically declined labor components of total logistics cost. If firms continue to allocate overhead expenses on direct labor hours basis, as is the case in many standard cost accounting systems then the cost figures produced will not be totally helpful for management decision making.[5] The information needs of the whole company and its functional areas, not the external reporting requirements of various industry and regulatory groups, need to drive each company's internal accounting practices. A firm should place a high priority on separating data needs for internal and external purposes.

Logistics literature has raised the issue of customizing accounting practices to accommodate logistics needs.[6] We are beginning to see significant progress in this area.

Communication

effectiveness of communications

To be useful to managers, information needs effective communication.[7] This in turn requires communication in the language of the intended recipient. Otherwise, perceiving the information will be difficult for him or her. Also, communication is sometimes thwarted when people ignore unexpected information. This is sometimes referred to as *selective perception*. Finally, communication takes place only if information keys into a person's values and responds directly to the management decisions the recipient needs to make. In short, effective communication requires knowledge of what the recipient can perceive, what he or she expects to perceive, and what he or she intends to do with what he or she perceives. If the communicator misses any of these targets, communication is more difficult.

THE LOGISTICS INFORMATION SYSTEM CONCEPT

We may define the logistics information system as follows:

> An interacting structure of people, equipment, and procedures which together make relevant information available to the logistics manager for the purposes of planning, implementation, and control.[8]

definition of LIS   Figure 5–1 highlights the relationship between the logistics information system (LIS), the elements of the logistics environments, and the logistics decision-making process. The diagram shows four principal subsystems, or modules, which constitute the logistics information system: order processing, research and intelligence, decision support, and reports and outputs. Collectively, these systems should provide the logistics manager with timely and accurate information for the basic management functions of planning, implementation, and control.[9] The following major sections of this chapter discuss these systems in detail.

functional perspective   Figure 5–2 views the logistics information system from a functional, or activity-oriented, perspective. At the bottom of this illustration are listed *transaction systems,* specific responsibilities related to the logistics mission. In this diagram, for example, order entry, customer service, inventory replenishment, receiving, shipment preparation, and accounts receivable are among the key transaction systems.

Moving up to the *control reporting* level, the important modules are customer service reports, inventory management, warehouse operations, traffic, and accounting and credit. The transaction systems and the control reporting levels are most relevant to activities at the distribution center level; they involve activities that are basically *technical* in orientation.

At the *analysis* level, we find that regional or divisional managers may engage in *tactical* matters relating to marketing support, manufacturing forecasting, and finance. Finally, the overall logistics function is principally involved in the *planning* function at the divisional or corporate level, and is *strategic* in terms of importance.

The logistics information system has many dimensions, and the process of vertical aggregation (or vertical disaggregation) permits the system to serve various purposes. The following sections should enhance understanding of the logistics information system's various components.

ORDER PROCESSING SYSTEM

The order processing system represents the principal means by which buyers and sellers communicate information relating to individual orders of product.

FIGURE 5–1   LOGISTICS INFORMATION SYSTEM   *Source:* Adapted from the framework for a marketing information system suggested by Philip Kotler, *Marketing Management: Analysis, Planning, and Control,* 5th ed. (Englewood Cliffs, N.J.: Prentice-Hall, Inc., 1984), 189.

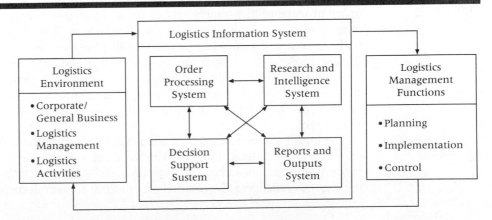

FIGURE 5–2   LOGISTICS INFORMATION SYSTEM—FUNCTIONAL PERSPECTIVE   *Source:* Perry A.
Trunick, "Computerization: The Road Ahead," *Handling & Shipping Management* (April
1981), 54.

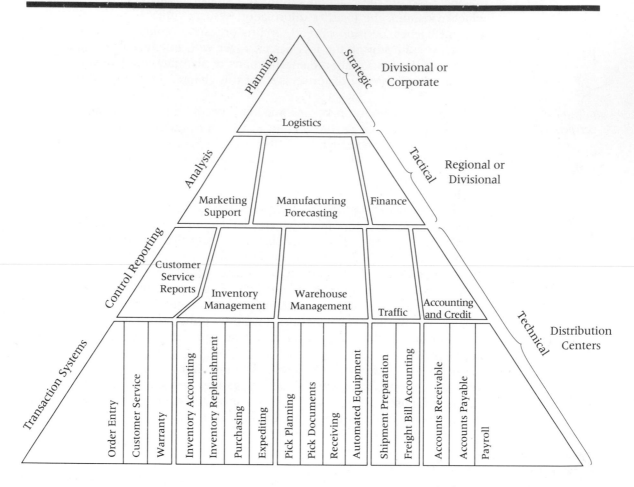

The order processing system, extremely significant to the firm's logistics area,
is also one of the most important components of the firm's overall management
information system.

*operational
efficiency and
customer
satisfaction*

Effective order processing management is a key to operational efficiency and
customer satisfaction. To the extent that a firm conducts all activities related to
order processing in a timely, accurate, and thorough manner, it follows that
other company activity areas can be similarly well-coordinated. In addition,
both present and potential customers will positively view consistent and predictable order cycle length and an acceptable response time. By starting the
process with understanding customer needs, firms can design order processing
systems that customers will view as superior to those of competitor firms. The
firm's order processing capabilities will be a factor producing a competitive
advantage.

*organizational
positioning*

The logistics area needs timely and accurate information relating to individual
customer orders; thus, more and more firms are placing the corporate order
processing function within the logistics area. This move is good not only from
the logistics function's viewpoint, but also from an overall corporate perspective.

impact of technology

Last, the order processing area has been a chief beneficiary of the enhanced computer and information systems technologies available today. In many firms, the order processing area has become an innovator in exploiting new technological advances.

terminology

Order and Replenishment Cycles

When referring to outbound-to-customer shipments, we typically use the term *order cycle;* we use the term *replenishment cycle* more when referring to the acquisition of additional inventory, as in materials management. Basically, one firm's order cycle is another's replenishment cycle. For simplicity, we will use the term order cycle throughout the remainder of this discussion.

As discussed earlier, four principal activities, or elements, constitute lead time, or the order cycle: order placement, order processing, order preparation, and order shipment. These activities appear in Figure 5–3, along with arrows indicating the principal directions in which information and product flow.

Traditionally defined, the order cycle includes only activities that occur from the time an order is placed to the time that it is received by the customer. Special activities such as backordering and expediting will affect overall order cycle length. Subsequent customer activities, such as product returns, claims processing, freight bill auditing, and so on, are not technically part of the order cycle.

order placement

Order Placement   This element is associated with the time elapsed from when the customer places the order until the order is delivered by the seller. Order placement time can vary from days by mail to minutes by phone, and instantaneously by electronic data interchange (see the discussion that follows). Company experiences indicate that improvements in order placement systems and

FIGURE 5–3   ORDER CYCLE AND ITS MAJOR COMPONENTS

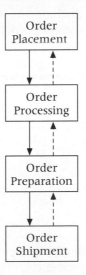

———▶ = principal product flows

- - - ▶ = principal information flows

processes offer some of the greatest opportunities for significantly reducing over-all order cycle length and variability.[10]

order entry alternatives

Table 5–1 shows the results of a study of manufacturing and merchandising firms as to how customer orders enter the firm's order processing system. In manufacturing firms, the most frequent medium for order transmittal is by phone; on-line electronic means are second; mail is third. Manual approaches rank fourth in use frequency. Aside from subtle differences among the manufacturing industries represented in Table 5–1, the general preference for the telephone is due to recent technological enhancements such as toll-free number availability, coupled with generally declining long-distance rates for such services. Also, many firms have instituted formal telemarketing programs (some-times referred to as customer service programs) to facilitate customer order entry. Finally, the availability of computers to link to buyers and sellers has increased the feasibility of electronically placing orders. We will explore this topic more fully in a later section focusing on electronic data interchange, or EDI. Finally, Table 5–1 indicates that on-line electronic means represent the most popular order transmittal form among the merchandising firms included in the study. Phone, mail, and manual approaches follow on-line electronic in use frequency.

In recent years, the popularity of placing orders through the use of fax, or facsimile transmissions, has significantly increased. Firms have also refined their ability to integrate fax and computer transmissions, tremendously enhancing the speed, efficiency, and accuracy of order processing.

order processing

Order Processing Order processing time is that required to process the customer's order and make it ready for shipment. This function usually involves checking customer credit, transferring information to sales records, sending the order to the inventory area, and preparing shipping documents. Many of these functions can occur simultaneously through the effective use of electronic data processing equipment. Improvements in computer and information systems technologies have considerably reduced the time necessary to accomplish these activities.

order preparation

Order Preparation Included here are all activities relating to picking and packaging individual customer orders. The systems involved can range from a

TABLE 5–1 How Customer Orders Enter the Firm's Order Processing Functions

	Food	Chem-ical	Phar-maceu-tical	Auto	Paper	Elec-tron-ic	Cloth/ Tex.	Other Mfg.	Total Mfg.	Mer-chan-dise	Total Response
Phone	57.3	66.9	38.4	35.9	62.6	53.0	36.8	47.5	51.4	26.7	50.2
Mail	6.3	11.5	20.1	28.0	17.0	27.6	48.2	24.1	18.4	21.0	18.5
Manual delivery by customer	.3	2.9	0.0	.2	.1	0.0	1.8	.5	.7	7.7	1.0
Manual pickup by this company	3.9	7.5	4.2	1.0	7.0	8.7	1.8	4.2	4.6	8.1	4.7
On-line electronic	32.2	11.3	37.3	34.9	13.3	10.7	11.4	23.5	24.9	36.5	25.5

Note: Entries in this table indicate the percentage of customer orders transmitted by the means indicated.

Note: The data reported in this table do not reflect the contemporary popularity and usage of facsimile, or fax, transmissions of order information.

Source: Bernard J. LaLonde, Martha C. Cooper, and Thomas G. Noordeweier, *Customer Service: A Management Perspective* (Oak Brook, IL: Council of Logistics Management, 1988), .

simple, manual system to a highly automated one. These alternatives will have dramatically different implications for response time and overall cost. Firms must carefully study the choices available.

productivity gains   For example, one U.S.-based manufacturer of cans and containers purchased a microcomputer system to help control order picking, labor productivity, and excessive training time at its four warehouse locations. More efficient order picking procedures considerably increased productivity in the order picking area. The computer generates an order picking slip that is stamped with the time of issue. When the equipment operator completes the order selection and returns the order picking slip, the time is stamped again, giving management a measure of the operator's performance and the order picking time. Management easily detects inefficient and unproductive operations (operators) and implements corrective action.[11]

transit times   **Order Shipment**   Order shipment time extends from the moment the order is placed upon the vehicle for movement until it is received and unloaded at the buyer's destination. Measuring and controlling order shipment time is usually difficult when a company uses for-hire carriage. Carrier information may be unreliable. Having the buyer complete response cards permits the seller to measure transit time of for-hire carriage. To reduce for-hire carriage transit time, the seller must either use a faster (lower-transit-time) carrier within the current mode or utilize a faster transport mode and pay corresponding increases in transportation cost.

Chrysler Corporation's Service and Parts Operations Division has established an integrated private/contract carriage system and a computerized parts locating and ordering system to produce prompt and dependable delivery service for small, less-than-truckload shipments. The system, called Mopar Dedicated Delivery System (DDS), provides next-day delivery to most of its dealers from the company's eighteen distribution centers located throughout the United States. Mopar makes about eighty percent of its deliveries at night through a passkey operation. The company drivers are given keys to the dealer's facility and make deliveries to secured areas. The night deliveries reduce delays daytime highway traffic and dealer congestion normally cause.[12]

Modifications in all four order cycle areas may be too costly. Make cost modifications in one area and operating the others at an existing level is therefore possible. For example, investing in automated materials handling equipment may be financially unwise for the firm. To balance its higher manual order processing time, the firm could switch from mail to telephone order transmittal and could use motor transportation instead of rail, reducing lead time without increasing capital investment for automated materials handling equipment.

Guaranteeing a given lead time level is an important advancement in logistics management. We may see its positive effects both on the customer (inventory costs) and on the seller's logistics system and market position. But the time concept means little without dependability.

order cycle analysis   **Length and Variability of the Order Cycle**   While traditional interest has centered more on overall order/replenishment cycle length, recent logistics interest has also focused on variability, or consistency.

One landmark customer service study incorporated a series of questions pertaining to order cycle elements of the relative time required to complete each, and total order cycle time.[13] One significant finding was that the greatest portion of total order cycle time generally occurred either before the manufacturer received the order, or after the manufacturer shipped the order to the customer. In other words, activities at least somewhat "external" to the manufacturer, and thus over which the manufacturer is likely to have less control, consume more than one-half of the total order cycle time.

order cycle length Any reduction in the length of one or more order cycle components will provide either additional planning time for the manufacturer or a shortened order cycle for the buyer. If a manufacturing firm identifies an opportunity to reduce the length of one or more order cycle components, it can then choose to either absorb the extra time into its own system (perhaps as additional planning time), or share it with the customer by shortening the order cycle in a material fashion. In competitive markets, passing such time savings along to the customer whenever possible may be critical for the manufacturer.

order cycle variability Variability of order cycle length can also safety stock levels carried by the purchasers of the firm's products. Specifically, as order cycle variability increases, needed safety stock levels also increase. Conversely, as firms reduce order cycle variability, customers may choose to carry less safety stock. In either instance, order cycle variability links directly to levels of safety stock a customer must carry.

Ideally, improvement will take the form of shorter order cycle lengths, coupled with improved consistency and reliability. Figure 5–4 illustrates a before-and-after situation in which a firm successfully reduced the length and variability of most of the activities comprising the order cycle. Aside from the improvement in each individual activity, the total order cycle time and variability have markedly decreased.

Electronic Data Interchange

EDI Electronic data interchange (EDI) most commonly represents the computer-to-computer information interchange using some standard format and the assistance of modern telecommunciations technology. One of the most significant business advances in recent years, EDI has revolutionized order processing at many companies.

> According to Temple, Barker & Sloane, Inc., ". . . logistics information consists of real-time data on company operations—inbound material flows, production status, product inventories, customer shipments, and incoming orders, among others . . . From an external perspective, companies need to communicate order shipment and billing information with vendors or suppliers, financial institutions, transportation carriers, and customers. Internal functions exchange information on production scheduling, material and product inventories, shipments among company facilities, and planning and control data—often over long distances, especially if production facilities are located in the United States."[14]

Electronic data interchange significantly improves the breadth, timeliness, and quality of data.

communications To utilize the full range of benefits EDI use offers, firms in a distribution channel must develop the capability to communicate with each other by computer. That is, effective implementation of EDI requires direct communication between the computer systems of both buyers and sellers of product.

information flow Figure 5–5 shows the major types of information flow linking buyers and sellers in a distribution channel. For the sake of simplicity, we will refer to the

FIGURE 5–4   ORDER CYCLE LENGTH AND VARIABILITY   *Source:* Adapted from Douglas M. Lambert and James R. Stock, "Using Advanced Order Processing Systems to Improve Profitability," *Business* (April–June 1982), 26.

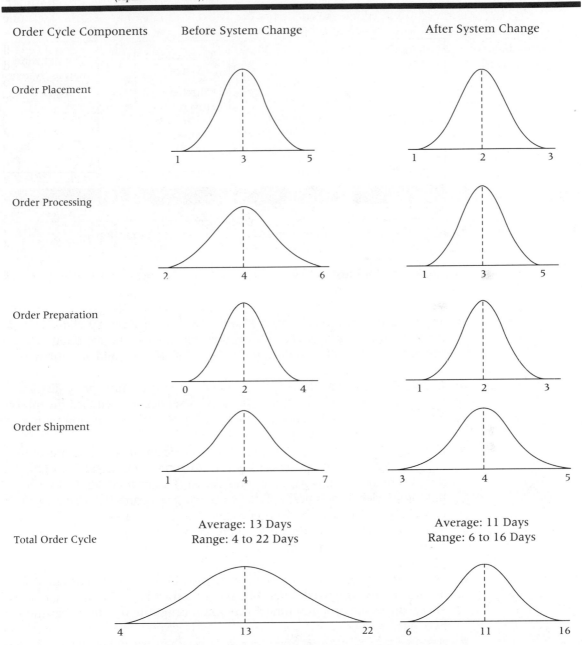

| Order Cycle Components | Before System Change | After System Change |

Order Placement

Order Processing

Order Preparation

Order Shipment

Total Order Cycle — Average: 13 Days, Range: 4 to 22 Days / Average: 11 Days, Range: 6 to 16 Days

parties in this system as Shipper A and Shipper B. The diagram indicates the relevance of planning, analysis, and transactional activity systems within each firm's logistics system. We could expand diagram to include third-party suppliers of transportation, warehousing, and information systems services.

Notable Successes Due to EDI in Logistics   The logistics literature contains numerous success stories relating to electronic data interchange use. The fol-

FIGURE 5–5   MAJOR LOGISTICS INFORMATION FLOWS LINKING COMPANIES   *Source:* David L. Anderson, *Product Channel Management: The Next Revolution in Logistics?* (Lexington, MA: Temple, Barker & Sloane, Inc., 1987), 4.

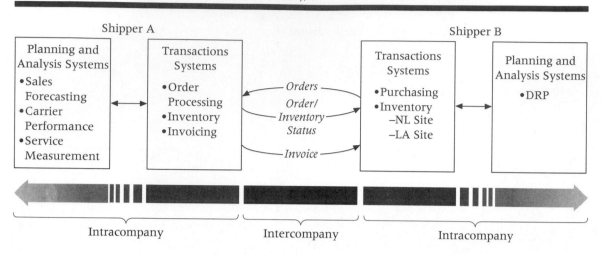

EDI examples

lowing examples illustrate situations in which EDI has created value through the timely transmission and reception of computer-to-computer communications.

- *Super-Valu Stores, Inc.*—saved $5,000–$6,000 per week by eliminating manual processing of invoices and other documents, and expected yearly savings of $600,000 by reducing the clerical staff that validates purchase orders against invoices.[15]
- *Unisys Corporation*—designed a national, same-day, third-party distribution service called Field Support Bank. This service has reduced inventory expense and reduced response time by using EDI in conjunction with a network of strategically located distribution centers.[16]
- *Burr-Brown Corporation*—manufacturers of electronic components and systems, have five computers in Tucson, Arizona; and one each in London, Edinburgh, Stuttgart, Paris, and Tokyo. This firm credits EDI with linking its global sales and logistics networks, and considers EDI a key to unlocking business in the less-restrictive European markets.[17]
- *Navistar*—reduced its inventory supply from thirty days to six days, and reduced premium payments for rapid freight shipments by ninety percent.[18]
- *McKesson Corporation*—major drug distributor, introduced customer order procedures triggered when EDI scans product bar code information. This reduces the ordering time for a typical drugstore by fifty to seventy-five percent.[19]
- *Averitt Express, Inc.*—Tennessee-based, less-than-truckload and truckload transportation firm, that developed EDI systems allowing shippers to obtain information on shipments that have been tendered, and facilitating freight invoicing and payment.[20]
- *Ralph's Grocery Company*—oldest grocery business in the western United States, developed a system which automatically resupplies stores based on information from checkout line product scanners.[21]
- *RCA*—using a third-party information network, established an electronic purchase order system at many of its facilities. Future plans include in-

creasing the number of suppliers on the system, adding new document types, and increasing the number of company facilities tied into the system.[22]

- *Volvo Transport AB of Sweden*—estimates that it avoids carrying over $28 million in excess inventory stocks each year through its EDI-based information network.[23]
- *Warehouse Information Network System (WINS)*—establishes a standard link between a company and its own or public warehouses through networks based on EDI applications.[24]

EDI standards

The EDI concept, moving forward quickly and effectively, has accelerated the move from paper documentation to electronic communication. While the progress to date has been significant, several important areas present challenges. One is the current proliferation of communications standards for use with EDI. Just as there are numerous ways to develop product bar codes, there are multiple communications standards in use today: ANS X12; EDIFACT, designed as a global standard for communicating business documents across international borders; and TDCC/EDIA.[25] For example, Figure 5–6 shows the difference between a traditional paper format and the ANS X12 format.

fiber optics

The deregulation of national communications systems, the rapid growth in fiber optics as a transmission medium, and the development of artificial intelligence/expert systems (discussed later in this chapter) should further reduce EDI costs and improve service diversity and quality over the years ahead. More incentives from cost and customer service should induce companies to introduce EDI systems into their operations.

Last, many EDI applications can utilize third-party automated clearinghouses (ACHs), which assist in transferring information from one company to another.[26] This concept, proven successful in Europe and Japan, will become critical to successful information linkages among U.S.-based firms.

Cost-Effectiveness of Order Processing Alternatives

cost-effectiveness

Figure 5–7 shows how the costs of telecommunications alternatives may vary with transferred message volume. At low volumes, for example, the least ex-

FIGURE 5–6   COMPARISON OF COMMUNICATIONS FORMATS   *Source:* Temple, Barker & Sloane, Inc., reprinted with permission.

Paper Format					ANS X12 Format
Quantity	Unit	No.	Description	Price	
3	Cse	6900	Cellulose Sponges	12.75	IT1•3•CA•127500•VC6900 N/L
12	Ea	P450	Plastic Pails	.475	IT1•12•EA•4750•VC•P450 N/L
4	Ea	1640Y	Yellow Dish Drainer	.94	IT1•4•EA•9400•VC•1640Y N/L
1	Dz	1507	6" Plastic Flower Pots	3.40	IT1•1•DZ•34000•VC•1507 N/L

FIGURE 5–7   ORDER PROCESSING SYSTEMS—COST COMPARISONS OF ALTERNATIVE APPROACHES

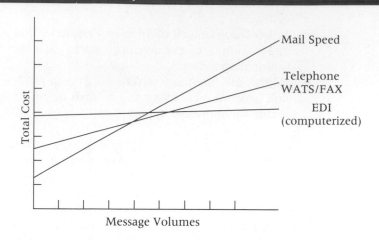

pensive alternative is to manually handle messages from customer to manufacturer through speed mail. This form of message transfer is relatively inexpensive because it involves low fixed costs. Alternatively, when message volumes are high, using telephone WATS (Wide-Area Telecommunications System) lines, fax, and EDI capabilities would be preferable. Although these approaches involve a much greater fixed costs (the LDI/EDI system being the most costly), the incremental costs of handling individual message units make them preferable at high message volumes. Also, the more manual systems would likely be slower, less consistent, and more prone to error than some of the more advanced systems. Thus, evaluating the cost-effectiveness of alternative order processing approaches necessarily involves thoroughly analyzing each available choice, fixed and variable cost.

Example of An Actual Order Processing System

example   Figure 5–8, a flowchart of the order processing system used by a particular U.S. consumer goods manufacturing firm, provides an example of a more-or-less "typical" order processing system.

Although this company centralizes its information processing capabilities the logistics vice-president has considerable influence over this particular function. While not totally responsible for the firmwide information system, he or she provides ample input into designing and implementing systems related to order processing and other types of logistics information.

order cycle   In Figure 5–8 company sales representatives or members of a broker network send orders for the company's products directly to one of the company's twenty-two district sales offices, where they are keyed in to a computer terminal linked to the general office. The mainframe computer at the company's corporate office then processes orders centrally. Following a credit check, the company sends shipment requests to plants, warehouses, and distribution centers. Product is then shipped to customers. The billing and invoicing cycle begins with information keying at the shipping points, which occurs immediately following order shipment.

This particular company, does not commit inventory to specific customer orders at the time of order placement. Rather, the company inventory commits

Figure 5–8   Example Order Processing System

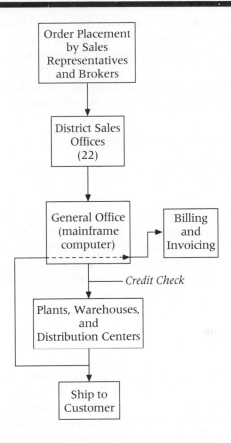

when orders are picked and shipments made. As a result, the company assures its ability to consistently allocate inventory to specific customer orders according to a priority level assigned to each customer account.

While pleased with the current efficiency of its order processing system, this company foresees providing hand-held data entry units for in-store use by company sales representatives. This kind of innovation would likely produce additional benefits to a capability already running smoothly.

Research and Intelligence System

As discussed earlier in this text, three distinct, yet related, environments should interest the logistics manager. These include (1) the macro, or external, environment; (2) the interfirm environment, as characterized by a firm's distribution channels; and (3) the micro, or intrafirm, environment. The LIS research and intelligence system scans the environment and makes observations and conclusions available throughout the logistics area and the whole firm.

strategic environmental issues

Based on the results of a thorough environmental scanning C. John Langley, Jr., and Paul E. Fulchino have identified *key issues* that logistics managers should address:[27]

- Integration of logistics planning with corporate planning
- Managing interfaces with other corporate functions

- Strategies for organization and staffing
- Integration of information technologies
- Make/buy decisions and use of third parties
- Appropriateness of logistics network form and function
- Emphasis on productivity and quality in logistics

These issues should provide a basis for effective strategic planning and for identification of successful implementation strategies.

Environmental Scanning

approaches to environmental scanning

The logistics manager may properly scan the environment in four recognized ways:[28]

- *Undirected viewing:* general exposure to information where the manager has no specific purpose in mind
- *Conditioned viewing:* directed exposure, not involving active search, to a more-or-less clearly identified area or information type
- *Informal search:* a relatively limited and unstructured effort to obtain specific information or information for a specific purpose
- *Formal search:* a deliberate effort—usually following a preestablished plan, procedure, or methodology—to secure specific information or information relating to a specific issue

We can also consider the environmental scanning process to be *irregular* (focusing on historical events and basically reactive), *regular* (and basically anticipatory, including approaches such as customer surveys), or *continuous* (generally longer lasting and representing an ongoing process, such as the use of customer advisory boards).[29]

monitoring the environment

To maximize environmental scanning results, the logistics manager should include several key information sources in a comprehensive monitoring system. First are logistics employees, as well as other people employed throughout the firm. Account executives, for example, are in an excellent position to gather strategically valuable customer-related and competitive information, once the logistics manager tells them exactly what he or she desires. Similarly, fleet drivers can frequently gather valuable information on the loading dock, if they simply know what to look for. Second, channel partners such as vendors, customers, carriers, and warehouse managers represent a valuable source of additional environmental information. These firms are usually very willing to share their environmental observations and perceptions, once asked to do so. Third, either an internal function or an outside consultant or advisory firm should perform some form of ongoing environmental monitoring and evaluation. Many firms find that selectively using outside firms to assist in this process provides an extremely objective and thorough environmental scanning and evaluation.

integration of forecasting and production scheduling

Forecasting

Firms frequently place demand forecasting responsibility with the logistics area. Figure 5–9 outlines one firm's approach to sales forecasting and its integration with production scheduling activities.

FIGURE 5−9   INTEGRATION OF SALES FORECASTING AND PRODUCTION SCHEDULING

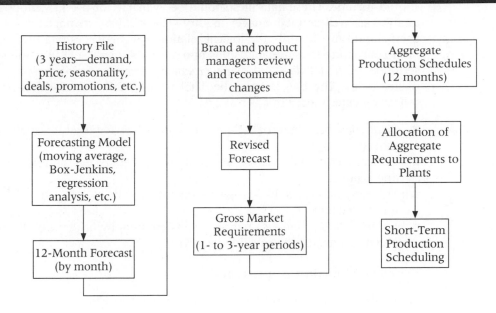

The first step is to develop a twelve-month forecast of demand by month by applying traditional approaches (moving average, Box-Jenkins, and regression analysis, etc.) to a three-year history file of data on things such as demand, price, seasonality, availability, deals, and promotions. In the second step, brand and product managers review this forecast and recommend relevant changes. The end result here is an agreed upon statement of gross market requirements for the succeeding one- to three-year periods. The third step involves developing aggregate production schedules for the next twelve-month period and allocating specific production requirements to various manufacturing facilities. Finally, the logistics function commonly assumes responsibility for scheduling production on a short-term basis, in order to coordinate finished product demand with the timing and availability of needed production inputs.

Much forecasting data gathering would be a part of the LIS's research and intelligence subsystem. Conversely, the need for forecasting models and alternative approaches to production scheduling would rely heavily upon the decision support capabilities of the LIS, discussed in the following section.

DECISION SUPPORT SYSTEM

The third major LIS component is the decision support system (DSS), an interactive computer-based system that provides data and analytic models to help decision makers solve unstructured problems—problems with many difficult-to-define variables." [30] Essentially, the DSS represents a comprehensive set of computer-oriented tools designed to help managers make better decisions.

Importance of the Database

DSS database   The need for a comprehensive database encompassing the information types logistics managers most often need to make decisions underpins the DSS concept.

Table 5–2 identifies some typical data file types that the logistics DSS database should include. These data files should be available for use in various types of analysis as well as for manager inquiry. The database management approach used should first identify the logical relationships between data file items, and then restructure those relationships into a logical database. Thus, the term descriptive *relational database management* has become very popular in the industry today. The files kept in the database may fall into one or more of the following categories:[31]

types of data files

- *Basic files:* basic internal and external data files required for analytical tool use
- *Critical factors:* key management input that defines decision making scope and guidelines
- *Policies/parameters:* basic logistics operating policies for each functional area
- *Solution files:* previous analysis results continually or periodically compared against future sensitivity analyses

Types of Modeling Approaches

Generally, we can classify models as optimizing, heuristic, or simulation. Let us discuss each briefly:

optimizing approaches

Optimizing[32]   This approach seeks the "best" answer given the way in which the problem is formulated. Techniques such as linear programming and mathematical programming are examples of optimizing approaches.

These approaches are advantageous because of their ability to provide a best solution, to handle complex model formulations and identify creative solutions, to efficiently prepare and analyze data, and to produce opportunities for cost savings or profit increases. Alternatively, optimization approaches require sig-

TABLE 5–2   DATA FILES MAINTAINED FOR LOGISTICS DSS DATABASE

Basic Files	Critical Factors
Sales—Product/Market	Planning horizon
History	Product mix
Forecasts	Scope of analysis
Transportation—Mode/Weight/Class	Other assumptions, guidelines, constraints
Shipment pattern	**Policies/Parameters**
Rates/costs	Inventory policy
Shipments	Production policy
Inventory—Item/Location	Shipment planning
Inventory levels	Service levels
Cost factors	Inventory carrying costs
Service levels	**Solution Files**
Production—Item/Plant/Line	Minimum costs
Production levels	Maximum service
Costs	Optimistic sales
Capacity	Pessimistic sales
Warehousing—Item/Location	Change in costs
Throughput	
Capacity	
Costs	

Source: Omar K. Helferich, "Logistics Decision Support Systems," Computers in Manufacturing: Distribution Management (Pennsauken, N.J.: Auerbach Publishers, Inc., 1983), p. 1.

nificant computer capacity, incorporate the most restrictive assumptions, and cannot always deal efficiently with the uncertainty of some logistics operations.[33]

heuristic approaches

Heuristic[34]   These techniques do not generate a "best" solution, but typically produce a good first approximation or "ball park" solution. In so doing, they typically involve generally lower analytical expense levels than optimizing approaches do.

Firms have successfully applied heuristic approaches in many logistics areas, including warehouse location, truck routing, and warehouse product layout. While heuristics do not always respond to a specific problem's complexities, they are typically quite good at providing useful solutions at a reasonable cost.

simulation

Simulation[35]   This category involves developing a computer representation of a logistics system, or some portion thereof, and manipulating key variables in the "risk-free" computer laboratory environment. While this approach was once expensive in terms of computer storage and processing time, the simulation of a global company's logistics operations may now take as little as two hours on a personal computer, thanks to modern technology.[36] In this type of application, simulation provides logistics managers with an exceptionally helpful test medium for evaluating alternative logistics strategies.

The logistics area may develop a completely customized simulation program or may developed a program with the assistance of one of a growing number of software packages developed specifically for this purpose. Some of the more popular packages are GPSS, Q-GERT, SIMSCRIPT, SLAM, and GASP.

Figure 5–10 arrays three logistics time horizons (strategic, tactical, and operational) against several logistics functional areas. This diagram shows that

FIGURE 5–10   LOGISTICS DECISIONS   *Source:* Richard F. Powers, "Optimization Models for Logistics Decisions," *Journal of Business Logistics,* 10, no. 1 (1989), 108.

SUBJECTS OF DECISIONS	NATURE OF DECISIONS		
	Strategic	**Tactical**	**Operational**
Forecasting	• Long range • New Products • Demographic shifts	• 6-12 months • Seasonality • Marketing impacts	• 12-16 weeks • Promotions • Trends
Network Design/ Analysis	• Plant & DC locations • Sourcing alternatives	• Public warehouses-usage and assignments • Inventory positioning	• Customer reassignments • Contingency planning
Production Planning	• Production mix • Equipment required • Equipment location	• Production Mix • Inventory vs. overtime • Crew planning	• Contingency planning
Materials Planning	• Materials and technology alternatives	• Stockpiling & contracts • Shortage analyzer • Distribution plans	• Purchasing • Inventory levels • Material releases
Production Scheduling	• Economic analyses-dedicated lines vs. multi-product	• 6-12 month production schedules	• Daily/weekly production schedules
Dispatching	• Fleet sizing and configuration	• Carrier contracts • Equipment location	• Daily/weekly loading and delivery plans • Billing

virtually every logistics area requires significant decisions in each of the three time frames. Logistics modeling needs flexible, capable approaches. The approaches discussed above could viably analyze problems such as those identified in Figure 5–10.

Other Elements of the Decision Support System

dialog subsystem

In addition to the database and the model base, a decision support system should include a dialog subsystem.[37] This DSS component facilitates interaction between the user and the system. For example, an effectively designed dialog subsystem eliminates the need for the user to be an expert programmer and incorporates user-friendly approaches to input and output.

A firm's logistics function may benefit considerably from a properly designed decision support system. The system investment is frequently significant (often $100,000 to $500,000[38]), but the results usually justify the expense. At the same time, effectively implementing the DSS concept makes it much easier for the logistics function to achieve its full potential.

Computer Applications in Logistics

In 1990, a comprehensive study at Ohio State University investigated new information technologies in logistics.[39] The study involved preparing and sending a detailed questionnaire to 200 members of the Council of Logistics Management, and the research team based results on the fifty-four questionnaires completed and returned. The respondents represented relatively diverse large manufacturing organizations with multiple plants and distribution centers. Their logistics systems varied considerably, and they served a range of retail, wholesale, and industrial markets.

computer usage

Table 5–3 tabulates the information data systems implementation expertise the survey reported. The results suggest that most of the respondent firms have reasonable experience with logistics data systems. For example, ninety-six percent have used computerized order entry/processing methods; and eighty-nine

TABLE 5–3   LOGISTICS DATA SYSTEMS EXPERIENCE

Function/System	Experienced
Order entry/processing	96%
Inventory control	89%
Freight bill payment	81%
Warehouse control	66%
Freight bill rating	57%
Shipment tracking	55%
Product recall	51%
Shipment consolidation	42%
Carrier selection	40%
Private fleet	23%

Source: Arnold Maltz and James M. Masters, "Strategies for the Successful Implementation of New Information Technology in Logistics," *Proceedings of the 1989 Annual Conference of the Council of Logistics Management* (Oak Brook, IL: CLM, 1989), 36.

percent use computers for inventory control. The table shows less computer involvement in other functions and systems.

Actually, with the exception of generally increased computer usage, these results are consistent with an earlier report from researchers at the University of Tennessee; Temple, Barker, & Sloane, Inc.; and The Pillsbury Company.[40] This study, based on telephone interviews with 100 logistics executives, indicated a greater degree of automation for routine and repetitive tasks (inventory control and order entry and inquiry, for example) than for tasks essentially involving choice or judgment (for example, shipment consolidation and carrier selection and evaluation).

The University of Tennessee study reported that firms seemed to be using local area networks (LANs) more and that they were actively linking microcomputers with mainframes. Software types most commonly used in logistics included spreadsheet applications, statistical analysis, word processing, database management, project management, and electronic mail.

Computers are valuable to overall information management in logistics. Firms are effectively integrating this technology with other logistics information system capabilities, and this integration will rapidly continue.

REPORTS AND OUTPUTS

The reports and outputs subsystem is the fourth major logistics information system component. Many logistics managers believe that most reports and other forms of output do not communicate effectively. As a result, many good ideas, many notable research results, and many managerial recommendations simply go unnoticed for lack of proper communication.

Reports may serve purposes such as planning, operations, and control. For example, planning reports may include information such as sales trends and forecasts, other market information, and economic projections of cost factors. Planning reports include both historic and future-based information.

Operating reports inform managers and supervisors about such things as current on-hand inventories, purchase and shipping orders, production scheduling and control, and transportation. Typically, these reports make information available to managers on a real-time basis.

Control reports may summarize cost and operating information over relevant time periods, compare budgeted and actual expenses, and provide direct transportation costs. They serve as a basis for strategically redirecting modifying operating approaches and tactics.

effectiveness of reports and outputs

Remember, communication occurs only if the communicated information keys into a person's values and responds directly to the decisions management personnel need to make. In actual business practice, molding people's expectations about the information contained in reports and outputs is essential. Incorporating the time-honored features of effective business communications— brevity, exception reporting, and getting at the heart of the matter—is also important. People have neither the time nor the inclination to deal with ineffective communication. In the firm's logistics area, high-quality communication through appropriate reports and outputs should be the standard, not the exception.

Whether the underlying information relates to managerial planning, operations, or control, communication effectiveness will affect how the firm's logistics function successfully achieves its mission.

ON THE LINE

BURGER KING

When the first Burger King restaurant opened in 1954, the concept was simple—sell quality food, served quickly in attractive, clean surroundings. The menu included hamburgers and milk shakes. Nearly forty years later, the concept is the same; but the logistics of carrying it out has changed. Today's fast-moving customers want it all—burgers served 100 different ways, shakes, soft drinks, french fries, chicken, salads, breakfast, lunch, and dinner—and they want it now!

And they have no patience for delays, worker shortages, or out-of-stock menu items. According to the marketing manager for Burger King Distribution Services, getting good management is becoming harder and harder. BKDS supplies food to sixty-five percent of the 5,355 Burger King restaurants in the United States.

In response to customer and competitive pressures, BKDS introduced an electronic support system (ESS) to automate supply ordering. The program's immediate goals were to provide restaurant managers with more management time and to eliminate human errors by increasing electronic data in-

terchange (EDI) use. Whereas managers previously wrote down what they needed and someone entered the lists into the computer, the ESS gives each franchisee a data terminal and an IBM-compatible PC or hand-held minicomputer.

A telephone line connects this terminal to a minicomputer at one of BKDS's twenty-one distribution centers. The manager logs onto the system, and places orders for his or her location through a menu-driven data capture procedure. The ESS helps to reduce errors and forgotten items which may be annoying and expensive. Burger King is installing sophisticated point-of-sale (POS) restaurant terminals which will directly control supply ordering, inventories, scheduling, and sales forecasting. The ESS will eventually connect to this system.

BKDS views its mission as supporting the restaurant system and improving quality, rather than centering on profit. This orientation should produce efficiency and effectiveness for BKDS and Burger King.

Source: Adapted from ''Computers: Logistics Productivity Tool,'' *Distribution* (April 1990), 66–68. Reprinted by Permission of Chilton's DISTRIBUTION Magazine, Radnor, PA.

NEW AND INNOVATIVE INFORMATION SYSTEMS FOR LOGISTICS MANAGEMENT

The preceding sections of this chapter set forth a logistics information system framework and provided details about each LIS component. Effectively implementing the LIS concept is virtually necessary to today's business environment.

This section briefly addresses four topics, each representing an innovative new information system for logistics management: artificial intelligence/expert systems, direct product profitability, product channel management, and statistical process control (SPC). This chapter simply introduces the last topic; more information on SPC is available in Chapter 13.

We should mention that new inventory management and scheduling approaches such as MRPII, MRPIII, DRP, DRPII, JIT, and other innovative information technologies are significantly affecting logistics management. We will discuss these in detail in Chapter 7.

Artificial Intelligence/Expert Systems[41]

definition   Artificial intelligence is the portion of computer science that is concerned with ''making machines do things that would require intelligence if done by humans.'' [42] An expert system is ''a computer program that mimics a human expert;

general approach

basic structure

research study

using the methods and information acquired and developed by a human expert, an expert system can solve problems, make predictions, suggest possible treatments, and offer advice with a degree of accuracy equal to that of its human counterpart."[43]

Expert systems offer an economical and practical way to capture, refine, and proliferate management skills. These systems provide a framework in which to document the questions and answers that experts use to solve analytical and operational problems. With such systems, a firm can put one expert's know-how in the hands of many workers, improving consistency, accuracy, and productivity throughout the network. These systems allow more effective management of the organization's most critical resource: knowledge.

In short, these approaches involve understanding and computerizing the human thought process. Once developers of expert systems sufficiently understand the thought process, they instruct a computer to make the same types of decisions a person would make. By observing how people make decisions, it is possible to identify decision rules and heuristics which guide the actions of logistics managers.

As Figure 5–11 shows, an expert system's principal components are the knowledge base and the inference engine. The dynamic working memory, which stores tentative conclusions, or adds information to the system's knowledge base or to the inference engine, among other functions, connects these two. The expert system also links with users and with other relevant databases.

Because of numerous successful artificial intelligence and expert systems applications, Maj. Mary Kay Allen (ret., U.S. Air Force), conducted research investigating the applicability of expert systems to logistics, specifically to inventory management.[44] Her primary objective was to identify the expert decision heu-

FIGURE 5–11   BASIC STRUCTURE OF AN EXPERT SYSTEM   *Source:* Mary Kay Allen and Omar Keith Helferich, *Putting Expert Systems to Work in Logistics* (Oak Brook, IL: Council of Logistics Management, 1990), 27.

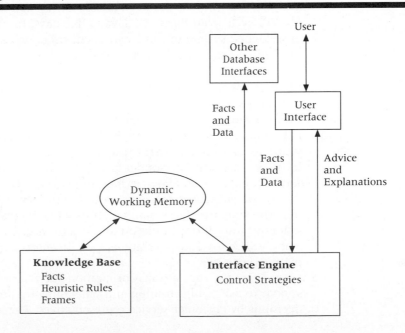

ristics that applied to a limited inventory task. A second objective was to build an expert system based on those heuristics and to measure the expert system's performance level based on the effectiveness and the efficiency of the resulting decisions.

The research methodology included a fourteen-point approach to expert systems development and testing and a joint effort with seven experts to determine the decision heuristics used in various inventory management areas. Major Allen identified 441 rules, which she used to develop an expert system related to inventory management practices. She developed the expert system at the Sacramento Air Logistics Center, a USAF facility. The Ogden Air Logistics Center was used for additional system testing.

results

Overall, inventory managers faced with complex problems, and who were assisted by the expert system experienced performance improvements of 15.1 percent to 17.73 percent.[45] In the pretesting exercise, the expert system uncovered a $600,000 error in a single item.[46] Such results helped to convince the USAF to implement many of Major Allen's recommendations.

examples

A study titled "Putting Expert Systems to Work in Logistics," recently published by the Council of Logistics Management, provides detailed case studies of six organizations that have successfully applied expert systems to logistics.[47] Let us briefly examine each:[48]

Burlington Northern Railroad uses an expert system to advise claims personnel on how to process freight relief claims. The system leads the staff through a step-by-step process, producing greater consistency and accuracy in claims handling. The system creates recovery opportunities for claims that might have gone unpaid prior to the expert system and serves as a training vehicle, allowing the more experienced customer service staff to concentrate on difficult claims problems.

Digital Equipment Corporation (DEC) uses an expert system to track work-in-process (WIP) inventories. The system ensures that an available workstation is always processing WIP and that supply and component orders are placed as soon as the need arises. The system has enabled DEC to cut its WIP cycle from thirty-six days to five days. In addition, DEC uses another expert system to route carriers distributing its products throughout the United States. This system has reduced transportation costs by twenty percent.

Eastman Kodak has implemented an expert system in its Atlantic and Dallas distribution centers to improve its workers' case-picking productivity. Developed internally, the system runs on an IBM-compatible PC. The company implemented the system in 1988 and developed it in just under one year. Kodak estimates that the system has helped to reduce training time for new warehouse personnel from several weeks to only a few days.

Federal-Mogul uses an expert system to provide advice on ordering, rescheduling, and packaging decisions, and on order entry methods and forecasting. The system reduces manual effort while increasing accuracy and consistently. Also, it uses trade-off analysis to meet emergency needs ranging from branch inventory reshipment, to inventory repackaging to vendor/plant expediting.

Sea-Land Service, Inc., a CSX Corporation subsidiary, developed an expert system to assist ships routing and scheduling by providing more consistent decisions by customer service representatives. The system also facilitates automated tracking of each shipment, significantly reducing the chances of misrouted freight.

The U.S. Navy uses an expert system to assist inventory analysis at the retail distribution center echelon. These distribution centers serve U.S. Navy customers from ships, air stations, and other supply depots. The expert system assists in processing critical stock items already on replenishment. Field tests showed manual effort reductions of over fifty percent, and the expert system can handle more than ninety percent of the decisions that need to be made. Overall, this system improves consistency, evaluates all items rather than a manually reviewed subset, and assists on-the-job training.

Figure 5–12 identifies example applications for expert systems in logistics, categorizing the applications by problem type and by decision level. Based on the successes described above, firms will increasingly emphasize the role of expert systems in logistics decision making.

Direct Product Profitability

One intriguing advance in recent years is the direct product profitability (DPP) concept, which calculates the net contribution attributable to specific projects. "DPP takes the gross margin and refines it into a net contribution for a particular

FIGURE 5–12 EXPERT SYSTEMS APPLICATION POTENTIAL IN LOGISTICS *Source:* Mary Kay Allen and Omar Keith Helferich, *Putting Expert Systems to Work in Logistics* (Oak Brook, IL: Council of Logistics Management, 1990), xvii.

| | | DECISION LEVEL | | |
		Operational	Tactical	Strategic
	Production Planning	Hazardous Chemical Advisor	Determine Sales/Market Share Impact	Predict Profit Impact for Foreign Plant Alternatives
	Plan	Job Shop Scheduler	Vehicle Dispatch Advisor	International Logistics Business Partners
PROBLEM TYPE	Operate	Suggest Retail Inventory Actions	Assist in Requisition and Desicion-Making	Monitor and Improve Logistics Performance
	Train	Instruct Inventory Managers	Train Manufacturing Staff	Instruct Buyers on Controls
	Control	Warehouse Pick Operation	Flexible Manufacturing	Maximize Worldwide Sourcing

product. It starts by assigning backhaul allowances, promotional allowances, or display allowances. Then it subtracts the costs attributable to the product, including space, handling costs, and refrigeration." [49]

value added by DPP

In effect, DPP allows corporate, marketing, and logistics managers to compare the relative profitability of parallel items in a product line. It also permits managers to examine the cost profile of each and every line item and helps to identify and isolate specific cost factors that may be unacceptable at a particular time.

opportunities for decision making

Logistics managers feel that DPP has significant logistics implications. Some specific decision that DPP analysis types will facilitate are (1) whether to deliver direct to customers or to use a channel intermediary; (2) how far a particular product's market boundary may extend before distribution becomes uneconomical; (3) where to source individual shipments; and (4) the best way to move product from origin to destination.

development of DPP concept

DPP has been around for some time, but only recently received attention when Procter & Gamble (P&G) used the concept to gain familiarity with its customers and products. [50] DPP use became popular when P&G and representatives of forty-five other manufacturers jointly developed a standardized model for industrywide use. The end result included better revenue, cost, and profit information for firms using DPP; and industry firms thought much more consistently about these topics.

actual company example

For example, the manager of materials flow systems and warehousing for the packaged products division of Scott Paper Company has been able to take advantage of the DPP approach with regard to the products of his company. [51] He said, "The materials flow cost associated with a case of towels is $3.20. That includes inbound materials, handling, storage, manufacturing process, and freight to the customer. A case of Scott towels holds thirty rolls, so you divide thirty into that and you've got over ten cents a roll in material handling costs." A penny of cost savings per roll is worth about $12,000 per year—which emphasizes the extreme importance of being sensitive to the accuracy of cost figures.

The DPP approach is gaining popularity as more firms commit themselves to better understanding their costs and profitability. If this trend continues, logistics quality and the quality of the competitive business environment will both increase dramatically.

Product Channel Management [52]

definition

A commentary entitled "Product Channel Management: The Next Revolution in Logistics," presents an innovative logistics management approach known as *product channel management.* [53] This approach "views the entire product acquisition (manufacturing or buying) and distribution process as a whole, from initial order entry through final customer delivery, with overall responsibility for product profitability placed within a single organization in a company. Rather than individually managing production or distribution activities, the product channel management organization would evaluate cross-functional tradeoffs (e.g., targeting higher margin end markets while simultaneously minimizing product acquisition and delivery costs) to maximize overall product profitability." [54]

differences from traditional approaches

The key difference between functional and product management techniques is the shift away from the management of assets such as warehouses and inventory, toward the management of processes such as product and information flow. Rather than focusing on trade-offs between corporate functional areas such as procurement, distribution, and production, product channel management evaluates trade-offs across product groups. As a result, products with greater profit potential could justify greater corporate resource commitments than could lower-end products. The product channel management process would provide the perspective necessary to analyze these cross-product trade-offs. This approach would require a firm to integrate logistics and related functions by product group and to establish a focus on end-market profitability. Key decision areas for the product channel management organization would include customer requirements, production scheduling, and inventory allocation. The goal would be to minimize product acquisition and distribution costs, while meeting customer service goals.

need for timely and accurate information

Making quality information available and accessible is perhaps the most critical operational change required to successfully implement product channel management. The approach requires sophisticated decision support systems and relational databases for internal (e.g., order entry, merchandising plans) and external (e.g., customer, supplier, carrier, warehouse manager) information needs. The process requires three decision support systems: one that organizes market or customer requirements; one that evaluates channel cost trade-offs such as production/buying, transportation, and inventory; and one that examines product profitability in the end markets.

rationalization of databases

To effectively manage their information resources, companies are rationalizing and integrating their many databases and supporting fewer databases, often reducing the absolute number from thousands to less than fifty. The product channel management concept requires fast, efficient access to critical information available through relational databases that allow for easy interfacing and data manipulation.

need for effective information systems

Successfully organizing product channel management within manufacturing or merchandising firms usually involves significantly upgrading corporate and logistics information systems. This includes improving information links between suppliers, customers, and carriers and warehouse managers and developing advanced management information capabilities in the logistics channels. Figure 5–5 presents some of these links.

opportunities for future development

In addition to the fact that many corporate and logistics information systems already provide useful product channel management information, electronic linking between suppliers, customers, and carriers and warehouse managers is beginning to develop rapidly. Many transaction processing systems in businesses today have been in place for ten to fifteen years, and cannot support current product channel management information needs. As a result, corporations interested in implementing product channel management must develop an enhanced logistics information system and high-quality capabilities in electronic data interchange. The resulting increases in transaction processing capability will also increase the likelihood of success with product channel management.

Statistical Process Control

philosophy

Finally, statistical process control (SPC) approaches offer a powerful alternative to traditional logistics management methods. These approaches are effective and innovative in providing useful logistics management information. The underlying philosophy of SPC is that to control any process, you must first understand its underlying natural, or inherent, variability. For example, to analyze delivery time from several vendors, you must know not only the mean, or average time elapsed from purchase order issuance to shipment receipt, but also how delivery times are likely to vary from the mean. This is the fundamental difference between SPC and more conventional logistics control methods. As mentioned previously, we will address this topic in much greater detail in Chapter 13.

STRATEGIC MANAGEMENT OF INFORMATION IN LOGISTICS

Three fundamental thoughts relate directly to the future of logistics information systems and to their ultimate contribution.[55]

timely and accurate information

First, firms must recognize the *strategic* value of having timely and accurate logistics information. Companies must consider the LIS strategically important to the whole firm, and they need to develop logistics information strategies, just as they would develop strategies relating to new products or capital expenditures.

coordination of efforts within the firm

Second, firms are making greater progress coordinating their information systems and logistics management personnel. Logistics managers are becoming very knowledgeable about the art and science of information systems, and information systems *specialists* exhibit a greater understanding of and sensitivity to managing challenges in an area such as logistics.

value of good information

Third, while many people consider information systems to be a *service* area within the overall business firm, good information is the key to becoming an effective player in today's competitive environment. Therefore, we should view the logistics information system not only as a major logistics component, but also as essential to competitive advantage.

SUMMARY

This chapter highlighted the purpose and strategic value of the logistics information system. It also examined its major components and subsystems, including the order processing system, research and intelligence system, decision support system, and reports and outputs system. Collectively, these capabilities provide the logistics function and the whole firm with an opportunity to achieve a competitive advantage through effectively managing and using information. Starting with the order processing system, the key link between a firm and its customers, the LIS and its many dimensions aim at providing the customer with a desired cost-service package, particularly as it relates to logistics control activities.

This chapter also provided an example of an actual company's order processing system, and discussed current computer applications in logistics. In addition, the chapter described new and innovative information systems for logistics management, including artificial intelligence and expert systems, direct product profitability, product channel management, and statistical process control. The chapter concluded by discussing strategic information management in logistics.

STUDY QUESTIONS

1. What does the "quality" of logistics information mean?
2. Discuss a "logistics information system" in terms of its purpose and its parts.
3. What are the major order placement alternatives? Which of these are most likely to prevail in the future?

4. What does "electronic data interchange", or EDI, mean? In what specific ways does EDI benefit buyers and sellers in a distribution channel?

5. What is the objective of the research and intelligence subsystem of the logistics information system? What activities does this component perform?

6. Define a *decision support system*. What general modeling applications does a logistics decision support system include?

7. What trends are evident regarding computer use in logistics?

8. Define *artificial intelligence and expert systems.*

9. Explain how *direct product profitability* would help a firm to achieve its logistics goals.

10. What is *product channel management?* In what ways is it an innovative approach?

11. In what ways will information be strategically valuable to logistics in the future?

NOTES

1. Portions of this introduction have been adapted from C. John Langley, Jr., "Information-Based Decision Making in Logistics Management," *International Journal of Physical Distribution and Materials Management* 15, no. 7 (1985), 41–42.

2. See F. Warren McFarlan, "Information Technology Changes the Way You Compete," *Harvard Business Review* 62, no. 3 (May–June 1984), 98–103.

3. For example, see Bernard J. LaLonde, Martha C. Cooper, and Thomas G. Noordeweier, *Customer Service: A Management Perspective* (Oak Brook, IL: Council of Logistics Management, 1988), 37–70.

4. This section has been adapted from Langley, "Information-Based Decision Making," 41–42.

5. Robert S. Kaplan, "Yesterday's Accounting Undermines Production," *Harvard Business Review* 62, no. 4 (July–August 1984), 95–101.

6. For example, see the following: Douglas M. Lambert and Howard M. Armitage, "Distribution Costs—the Challenge," *Management Accounting* (May 1979), 33–38; John L. Boros and R. E. Thompson, "Distribution Cost Accounting at PPG Industries," *Management Accounting* (January 1983), 54–60; and Howard M. Armitage, "The Use of Management Accounting Techniques to Improve Productivity Analysis in Distribution Operations," *International Journal of Physical Distribution and Materials Management* 14, no. 1 (1984), 95–101.

7. The issue of managerial communication in general is dealt with effectively in Peter F. Drucker, *Management: Tasks, Responsibilities, Practices* (New York: Harper & Row, 1974). This paragraph draws particularly upon the content of Chapter 38, "Managerial Communications," 481–93.

8. This definition has been adapted from the definition of a marketing information system suggested in Philip Kotler, *Principles of Marketing* 3rd ed. (Englewood Cliffs, NJ: Prentice-Hall, Inc., 1986), 87.

9. For an interesting discussion of logistics information systems, see Alan J. Stenger, "Information Systems in Logistics Management: Past, Present, and Future," *Transportation Journal* 26, no. 1 (Fall 1986), 65–82. In this discussion, logistics information consists of four groups: transaction systems; short-term

scheduling and inventory replenishment systems; flow planning systems; and network planning systems.

10. See Roy Dale Voorhees, John C. Coppett, and Eileen M. Kelley, "Telelogistics: A Management Tool for the Logistics Problems of the 1980s," *Transportation Journal* (Summer 1984), 62–70.

11. Perry A. Trunick, "Giving Warehouse Efficiency a Lift," *Handling & Shipping Management* (April 1983), 58–64.

12. Cheryl Grazulis Drugan, "DDS Delivers Parts—Not Problems," *Handling & Shipping Management* (May 1983), 72–78.

13. Bernard J. LaLonde and Paul H. Zinszer, *Customer Service: Meaning and Measurement* (Oak Brook, IL: National Council of Physical Distribution Management, 1976), 119.

14. *Logistics Data Interchange: An Emerging Competitive Weapon for Shippers* (Lexington, MA: Temple, Barker & Sloane, Inc., 1987), I–1.

15. See *Wall Street Journal,* March 6, 1987.

16. E. J. Muller, "Customized Air Service Delivers Vital Parts," *Distribution* (January 1990), 64–66.

17. Robert Bowman, "Software Success Stories," *Distribution* (May 1989), 44.

18. See *Wall Street Journal,* March 6, 1987.

19. *Logistics Data Interchange,* II–10.

20. Interview with Gary D. Sasser, President, Averitt Express, Inc., June 1, 1991.

21. *Logistics Data Interchange,* II–3 and II–4.

22. *Logistics Data Interchange,* II–4.

23. *Logistics Data Interchange,* II–5.

24. *Logistics Data Interchange,* II–7.

25. See Hank Lavery and G. A. Long, "EDI in Transportation," *Proceedings of the 1989 Annual Conference of the Council of Logistics Management* (Oak Brook, IL: CLM, 1989), 261–77.

26. *Logistics Data Interchange,* III–4 through III–8.

27. C. John Langley, Jr., and Paul E. Fulchino, "The Logistics Strategic Planning Process," a discussion document prepared for the University of Tennessee's Executive Development Program for Distribution Managers, 1987, 33.

28. Philip Kotler, *Marketing Management: Analysis, Planning, and Control,* 5th ed. (Englewood Cliffs, N.J.: Prentice-Hall, Inc., 1984), 192.

29. Liam Fahey and William R. King, "Environmental Scanning for Corporate Planning," *Business Horizons* 20, no. 4 (August 1977), 61–71.

30. Omar Keith Helferich, "Logistics Decision Support Systems," *Computers in Manufacturing: Distribution Management* (Pennsauken, N.J.: Auerbach, 1983), 1.

31. Helferich, "Logistics Decision Support Systems," 4.

32. Richard F. Powers, "Optimization Models for Logistics Decisions," *Journal of Business Logistics* 10, no. 1 (1989), 106–21.

33. John T. Mentzer "Symposium Feature: Approaches to Logistics Modeling," *Journal of Business Logistics* 10, no. 1 (1989), 104.

34. Ronald H. Ballou, "Heuristics: Rules of Thumb for Logistics Decision Making," *Journal of Business Logistics* 10, no. 1 (1989), 122–32.

35. Donald J. Bowersox and David J. Closs, "Simulation in Logistics: A Review of Present Practice and a Look to the Future," *Journal of Business Logistics* 10, no. 1 (1989), 133–47.

36. Mentzer, "Symposium Feature," 105.

37. Helferich, "Logistics Decision Support Systems," 3–4.

38. Helferich, "Logistics Decision Support Systems," 3.

39. Arnold Maltz and James M. Masters, "Strategies for the Successful Implementation of New Information Technology in Logistics: The DRP Experience," *Proceedings of the 1989 Annual Conference of the Council of Logistics Management* (Oak Brook, IL: CLM, 1989), 13–49.

40. C. John Langley, Jr., Stephen B. Probst, and Roy E. Cail, "Microcomputers in Logistics: 1987," *Proceedings of the 1987 Annual Conference of the Council of Logistics Management* (Oak Brook, IL: Council of Logistics Management, 1987) 423–428.

41. Much of this section is based on Mary Kay Allen, *The Development of an Artificial Intelligence System for Inventory Management,* (Oak Brook, IL: Council of Logistics Management, 1986).

42. Digital Equipment Corporation, Systems Manufacturing Technology Group, "What Is AI, Anyway?," Working Paper (May 1982) 1.

43. Michael Ham, "Playing by the Rules," *P.C. World* (January 1984), 34.

44. Allen, "Development of an Artificial Intelligence System for Inventory Management."

45. Allen, "Development of an Artificial Intelligence System for Inventory Management," 185.

46. Allen, "Development of an Artificial Intelligence System for Inventory Management, 128.

47. Mary Kay Allen and Omar Keith Helferich, *Putting Expert Systems to Work in Logistics* (Oak Brook, IL: Council of Logistics Management, 1990), .

48. These summaries have been taken directly from Allen and Helferich, *Putting Expert Systems to Work in Logistics,* xvi–xviii.

49. Denis Davis, "FMI Thinks DPP Is A-OK," *Distribution* (December 1985), 73.

50. Davis, "FMI Thinks DPP Is A-OK," 73.

51. Davis, "FMI Thinks DPP Is A-OK," 73.

52. Based upon David L. Anderson, *Product Channel Management: The Next Revolution in Logistics?* (Lexington, MA: Temple, Barker & Sloane, 1987).

53. *Product Channel Management,* 2. A *product* may be a broad group of similar products managed either individually (e.g., tennis racquets) or collectively (e.g., sporting goods).

54. *Product Channel Management,* 2.

55. These comments have been adapted from Langley, "Information-Based Decision Making in Logistics Management," 52–53.

CASE 5–1

PENINSULA POINT, INC.

In recent years, Peninsula Point, Inc., has become a very successful merchandiser of contemporary fashion apparel for men and women. The company publishes a high-quality catalog, which it sends to prospective customers. Customers place their orders by mail or by using a toll-free telephone number. The customer base consists principally of young couples with two incomes and no children. These customers typically receive other catalogs from competitor firms such as Land's End, Orvis, and L. L. Bean.

Although the apparel industry is fiercely competitive, the catalog business is growing. People who are "just too busy" to shop in retail stores regard it as an appealing alternative. Purchasing apparel merchandise by catalog also seems to have a certain prestige in some social circles.

Among companies of its kind, Peninsula Point is thought to offer the best product assortment, product quality, and customer service. Two critical customer service elements at Peninsula Point are that the company receives, packs, and ships orders in a timely manner and that product return procedures are "customer friendly." Although the company accommodates product returns with little or no bother to the customer, this practice is expensive and of growing concern to upper-level management.

Peninsula Point does not produce any of the merchandise it sells. Instead, it contracts with manufacturers in Korea, Hong Kong, Taiwan, and Singapore to meet its largely seasonal product line needs. The company ships container loads of labeled and pretagged merchandise by a combination of ocean transportation and domestic inland motor freight to a centralized distribution center in Nashville, Tennessee. Subsequently, UPS makes all individual customer shipments.

Peninsula Point executives consider themselves to be in the "logistics business." They feel that the company's logistical capabilities are a key to its excellent reputation in the marketplace. An area of nagging concern to the managers, however, is that consumer tastes and company product preferences are beginning to change very quickly, sometimes in the middle of a selling season. Only a continued ability to react quickly to changing marketplace needs will separate market leaders from the others.

Case Questions
1. In what ways should we consider the components of the logistics information system (as discussed in this chapter) important to Peninsula Point? What suggestions do you have for improving the company's logistics information system?
2. What macroenvironmental factors will be critical to Peninsula Point's future success? In what specific ways can the company develop logistics capabilities to address these factors?

CASE 5–2

SEA-TAC DISTRIBUTING COMPANY

Profit margins are being squeezed in the wholesale grocery business, and Michael McBee, logistics vice president for Sea-Tac Distributing Company, is under pressure to reduce unit costs and to improve customer service. Although only in business for four years, Sea-Tac enjoys an estimated eleven percent share of the Seattle-Tacoma-area wholesale grocery market and ranks fourth in total revenues among firms of its type. Sea-Tac is an aggressive marketplace competitor and is thought to be very progressive in its willingness to implement the latest available technologies.

The logistics vice president is responsible for all activities relating to product receipt, storage, and distribution, and has direct authority over the company's centralized computer system. Sea-Tac receives all of the grocery products it sells at either of its two distribution centers and makes deliveries directly from those facilities to customers' warehouses or stores. The company maintains a fleet of twelve trucks, which it uses exclusively to deliver products to customers.

All buying activities at Sea-Tac are the responsibility of the purchasing vice president, who depends on a team of eight qualified buyers, each of whom concentrates on a specific class of food and grocery items. In effect, each buyer has full authority to negotiate all sale terms (price, credit terms, and logistical responsibilities) with individual vendors. Given that the SKU number in the Sea-Tac product line exceeds 3,000, the buying function is extremely critical to the firm.

Although Sea-Tac does not integrate the purchasing and logistics functions organizations, both vice presidents feel that a high degree of coordination occurs between the two areas. Other Sea-Tac vice presidents control marketing and finance, respectively. The marketing vice president promotes and sells the company's product line, accomplishing this largely through Sea-Tac's effective advertising program and through the efforts of ten account executives. These people call on individual customers either once or twice weekly, depending on the account's importance. Customers place all orders through direct telephone contact with Sea-Tac's order entry clerks. The finance vice president provides the logistics vice president with a variety of cost-related information. Unfortunately, McBee feels uncomfortable making logistics decisions based on the average cost data provided.

Case Questions
1. Based on the content of this chapter, what suggestions would you offer the logistics vice president to help reduce unit costs and improve service?
2. What additional information would you like to have before finalizing your recommendations?

INVENTORY IN THE LOGISTICS SYSTEM

As we discussed earlier, inventory management and control is a key activity area within business logistics. Temple, Barker & Sloane, Inc., defines logistics as "the management of inventory at rest or in motion." This responsibility is critical to the satisfactory performance of the entire business logistics function.

This chapter focuses on general issues relating to the role of inventory in the logistics system. Following discussion highlighting the role of inventory, we will address inventory costs. The chapter concludes by discussing methodologies for classifying inventory and evaluating a company's inventory management approach.

Chapter 7 describes inventory management approaches that have proven effective in today's business environment. Together, these two chapters can help you understand how inventory relates to the business logistics function.

The Importance of Inventory

Although this book's principal thrust is business logistics management within the firm, understanding the importance of inventory from a broad, macroeconomic perspective is useful. We will briefly discuss how inventory relates to the overall economy and then several specific ways in which inventory is critical to the individual firm.

Inventory in the Economy

inventories in the economy

Table 6–1 summarizes the U.S. Gross National Product and the levels of manufacturing and trade inventories over the 1974–1990 time period, and calculates the ratio of inventories to GNP. Figure 6-1 shows the behavior of this calculated ratio over the seventeen-year time period.

percentage of GNP

It is apparent from Figure 6–1 that inventory as a percent of GNP has been declining in recent years, from approximately 17–20% in the 1970's, to a current level in the range of 14–16%. This decline is largely due to three factors. First, transportation deregulation resulted in greater opportunities for shippers to purchase high-quality transportation services, thus reducing to some extent the need to carry large inventories. Second, innovations and improvements in communications and information technology have helped companies to become more effective in terms of how they manage inventories. As discussed in the previous chapter, the availability of technologies such as EDI have resulted in companies being able to do business on a daily basis with less inventory. This has been referred to as "substituting information for inventory." Third, U.S. firms have become more expert at managing inventory in general, and thus have succeeded in improving "inventory velocity," or the inventory turnover rate (to be discussed later in this chapter).

TABLE 6–1   PERCENTAGE RATIO OF MANUFACTURING AND TRADE INVENTORY TO GNP

Year Ending	In Current Dollars		Ratio of Inventory to GNP
	GNP ($ trillion)	Inventory ($ billion)	
1974	1.43	286	20.00
1975	1.55	288	18.58
1976	1.72	319	18.55
1977	1.92	351	18.28
1978	2.16	397	18.38
1979	2.42	444	18.35
1980	2.63	483	18.37
1981	2.94	520	17.69
1982	3.07	520	16.94
1983	3.31	510	15.41
1984	3.78	546	14.44
1985	4.00	645[a]	16.13
1986	4.24	657[a]	15.50
1987	4.53	683[a]	15.08
1988	4.87	735[a]	15.09
1989	5.23	780[a]	14.91
1990	5.46	810[a]	14.84

Data Source: *Survey of Current Business;* U.S. Statistical Abstract; U.S. Department of Commerce; and Robert V. Delaney, reprinted with permission.

Methodology: Heskett, Ivie, and Glaskowsky *Business Logistics,* 2d ed. (New York: Ronald Press, 1973), 19–21.

[a]Change in method of measuring manufacturing and trade inventories increased values retroactively in April 1987.

Inventory in the Firm

Experience shows that recent inventory trends have a relevant impact on inventory management at the level of the individual firm. This section discusses topics highlighting the importance of inventory within the firm.

product line proliferation

Growth in Inventory Cost   Increased product line variety has increased inventory levels for many firms. For example, if Procter & Gamble were to estimate future baby diaper sales at 500,000 boxes, it must also break down this figure by color (e.g., pink versus blue), package size, and absorbency before making final production and inventory decisions. Rather than carrying a basic inventory of 500,000 boxes plus an additional 40,000 to 50,000 boxes of safety stock, the company may need a total inventory (base plus safety stock) of 700,000 to 750,000 boxes to accommodate safety stock for each line item variety.

From another perspective, the inventory investment often represents a significant percentage of a company's total assets. While this may vary from company to company, inventory investment may often equal or exceed fifty percent of a company's asset base. This is true at many retail supermarkets and department stores.

inventory carrying cost

To illustrate how increased inventory affects costs, consider a hardware discount store which carries $1 million in average inventory. As explained later in this chapter, firms generally calculate annual inventory carrying costs as a percentage of average inventory dollar value. Assuming that this percentage has been calculated at twenty percent, the annual cost of carrying the $1 million in

FIGURE 6–1 PERCENTAGE RATIO OF MANUFACTURING AND TRADE INVENTORY TO GNP (IN CURRENT DOLLARS) *Source:* Data adapted from Table 6–1, and Robert V. Delaney, reprinted with permission.

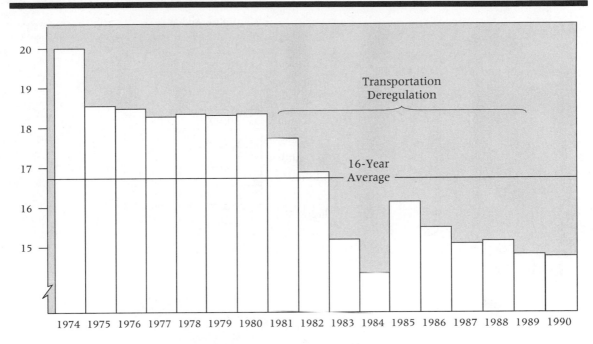

inventory is \$1 million × .20 = \$200,000. If average inventory levels rise to \$1.5 million, the annual carrying cost would increase from \$200,000 to \$300,000.

Assuming that this example company has an overall profit margin equal to five percent of sales, sales would have to increase by \$2 million to offset an average inventory increase of \$100,000 (i.e., \$100,000 ÷ 5% = \$2,000,000).

Inventory as a Percent of Value Added One way of looking at a firm's inventory investment is to calculate inventory expense as a percent of value added. Figure 6–2 shows approximate logistics costs as a percentage of value added for typical companies in several industries. For example, logistics costs range from thirty to forty percent of value in industries such as food and general merchandise retailing, petroleum, and chemicals, to ten percent or less for industries such as electrical equipment, textiles, apparel, furniture, and tobacco.

Current Trends Toward Shifting Inventory in the Distribution Channel Although the overall inventory levels needed to support U.S. manufacturing and trade operations have declined in recent years, the effect on individual companies is frequently uneven. For example, many retailers and wholesalers reduced their inventory levels in response to cost increases during the seventies and eighties. These reductions placed real pressure on many suppliers and vendors forced to carry much of the inventories their customers previously held. Rather than resolving the problem, reducing retail and wholesale inventory simply shifted the problem to other firms in the distribution channel.

Since suppliers in such situations ultimately need to recoup the costs of carrying additional inventory, this expense will inevitably pass through to customers in terms of higher product prices. A preferable solution, and one gaining

FIGURE 6–2   LOGISTICS COSTS AS A PERCENTAGE OF VALUE ADDED   *Source:* James E. Morehouse, "Improving Productivity in Logistics," *Handling & Shipping Management* (Presidential Issue, 1984–85), 12.

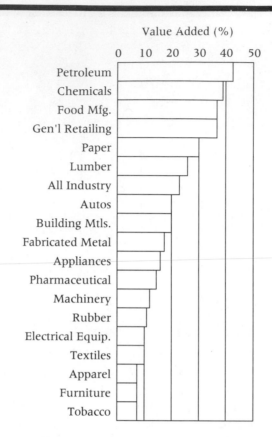

popularity today, is to identify an inventory strategy that effectively represents a "win-win" proposition for both buyers and sellers of goods. In Chapter 7, we will discuss some recent approaches that have successfully reduced cost in the entire system.

Overall, firms should be realistic as well as open-minded in terms of savings opportunities through inventory cost reduction. As we will discuss in this chapter and throughout the text, a company should seek innovative solutions which will reduce expense and improve service. They may not always be obvious, but these solutions are very effective once identified.

The next example should illustrate some of the strategic and daily operating issues relating to inventory management.

THE NEED FOR EFFECTIVE INVENTORY MANAGEMENT—THE MUNICIPAL WATER AUTHORITY CASE

As business demands fluctuate, a municipality experiences fluctuations in water demand. A daily fluctuation occurs because people use less water at night. During the day, most people use water for bathing, cooking, and other purposes. Consequently water demand increases sharply in the morning—and continues to increase throughout the day. Demand even varies during the day, at mealtimes, for example, and in the evening when many people prepare for bed.

The Problem of Peak Demand

summer versus winter

Summer and winter water demands also differ significantly in many sections of the country. In summer, consumers spend more time watering their grass, filling their swimming pools, washing their cars, and bathing. In the winter months, people perform some of these activities infrequently or not at all.

pumping capacity

One problem the municipality faces is the pumping capacity it requires. Should the capacity be sufficient to meet peak demand on that hot July day when the temperature is 100° and the relative humidity is ninety-five percent? If the municipality builds pumping capacity to meet peak demand many times during the year its pumping facility will operate at ten percent of capacity or less, which is very costly. In some instances the facility may even have to shut down during the night, which is also very expensive.

The Need for Storage

production smoothing

Most municipalities have a water storage facility that enables them to use their pumps more uniformly; that is, they do not need the productive capacity to meet peak demand. The storage facilities supply water during peak demand times. When water demand is low the municipality pumps the excess water into the storage facility so that it is ready when needed. The water storage facility allows the municipality to anticipate demand with consequent efficiencies; it allows the municipality to reduce production facility size; finally, it provides better customer service during peak periods.

Comparisons with Business Situations

personal or peak demand

Business firms face situations similar to that of the municipal water authority. If a firm sets production capacity to meet peak demand, then certainly the firm will sometimes underutilize the available capacity. Because this can be quite expensive, most business firms approach capacity planning very seriously.

An example would be companies which experience sixty to seventy percent of their yearly sales during the two to three-month Christmas season. Many toy manufacturers and specialty-item producers secure warehousing or storage facilities in which they temporarily store excess product, thus avoiding both excessive production capacity and overtime labor expenses during peak activity periods. Alternatively, more firms today are carefully synchronizing manufacturing and distribution, and identifying workable strategies for doing business without accumulating excess inventories. This latter approach explicitly recognizes that excess inventory carrying costs can be significant and quite unnecessary.

service industries

Also, more businesses today provide services, rather than tangible products, to their customers. Nevertheless, the service companies have very real inventory management needs. For example, transportation, health care, legal/professional, and financial companies need supplies and capital items. Thus, they experience inventory management and control opportunities. Although these companies find it largely impossible to inventory their services for future use, their day-to-day business requires expertise to effectively manage capacity and to ensure that services are available when and where customers need them. As a result, underlying inventory management issues in such industries often translate into exceptionally challenging problems for logistics managers. Effectively resolving these problems, however, can provide competitive advantage for the firms themselves.

RATIONALE FOR CARRYING INVENTORY

Although modern firms increasingly tend to minimize or eliminate inventory whenever possible, understanding why businesses hold or accumulate inventory can be useful. After discussing materials inventories and physical distribution inventories, we will direct attention toward a general framework for viewing various functional inventory types. This section concludes by summarizing the importance of inventory to functional business areas other than business logistics.

Materials Inventories

The first inventories we will consider are those which support a firm's processing, manufacturing, or assembly functions. Among the principal reasons for accumulating such inventories are the following: purchase economies, transportation savings, safety stock, speculative purchase, seasonal supply, and supply source maintenance.

discount versus storage cost

Purchase Economies   One reason for accumulating raw materials inventory is that the company may be able to realize purchase economies. For example, firms may buy raw materials in large quantities because of available price discounts. Although the company will need to store what it does not immediately use, the increased inventory costs may be less than what the company saves by buying in large quantities. This is becoming important to firms involved in offshore sourcing, which may secure significant quantity discounts. In such cases, companies are trading off between a purchase price discount and storage costs. As long as the amount saved on the purchase price exceeds storage costs, these companies are willing to accumulate raw materials inventory.

carload/truckload savings

Transportation Savings   A second reason for accumulating physical supply inventory may be transportation savings. Frequently, firms associate transport savings with the purchase economies discussed earlier. A firm purchasing large quantities can ship large quantities. Many firms ship raw materials in carload, truckload, or bargeload lots to decrease transportation costs. In some instances, firms make shipments in multiple carloads or even trainloads at even lower rates per hundredweight.

impact on selling price

The transportation cost usually represents a significant part of the final selling price of raw materials. Because volumes moved and are large and transportation is so important, even a small reduction in the per-hundredweight rate often can be quite important. At the same time, raw materials usually incur relatively low inventory and warehousing costs. For example, a firm can often dump a raw material such as coal on the ground without any storage shelter. Consequently, reducing transportation costs through increased volume movement often reduces total costs, since inventory and warehousing costs may not increase as much as the transport cost decreases. This situation will vary depending upon the item's value. Auto manufacturers may, for example, find raw material inventory costs to be too high to justify accumulating large supplies of such materials prior to their use.

*production
shutdown*

Safety Stock   A third reason for physical supply inventory would be to prevent an emergency production shutdown. In other words, many firms hold a certain amount of inventory as buffer or safety stock in case of shipping delays or some problem in filling orders. Shutting down an assembly line because raw materials are out of stock may cost thousands of dollars per hour. The amount of raw materials held depends upon the probability of delayed delivery and upon the volume of raw materials the firm utilizes. Like previous examples, this involves a cost trade-off analysis—namely, the inventory holding cost (safety stock) measured against the cost of a stockout. However, it also involves using probability theory to develop expected safety stock and stockout costs.

*future
uncertainties*

Speculative Purchase   A fourth possible reason for physical supply inventory is for speculative purchases or hedging against future price increases, strikes, changing political policies, delayed deliveries, rising or falling interest rates, or currency fluctuations in world markets. Also, the future supply of raw materials to some firms may be uncertain. For example, a threat of a steel industry strike leads the automobile industry to accumulate steel in case the strike occurs. And Japanese consumer goods manufacturers sometimes stockpile finished product inventories in the United States because they fear the United States will institute tariffs, quotas, or other import barriers.

*interruption in
supply*

Seasonal Supply   Seasonal supply availability is a fifth reason for accumulating physical supply inventory. Agricultural products such as wheat or other grains are good examples of items available only at certain times of the year. With such products, firms may need an accumulation of supply to meet demand throughout the year. In some cases, the transportation means may affect seasonal availability. For example, iron ore moves across the Great Lakes or down the St. Lawrence River. Ice closing the waterways interrupts the iron ore supply each winter. The steel firm trades off the inventory and accumulated ore inventory warehousing cost against lower balanced production costs—that is, being able to produce throughout the year without the higher costs of alternative transportation.

Maintenance of Supply Sources   A sixth reason for holding physical supply inventory is to maintain supply sources. Large manufacturing firms very often use small vendors or suppliers who manufacture subassemblies or semifinished goods for the large firm even when the firm can produce such items itself. They may use the vendor or supplier in much the same way a company uses a public warehouse; when they do not have enough productive capacity to meet their peak demands, they buy from the vendor or supplier.

One problem with this approach is that small vendors or suppliers may be "captive." In other words, their only customers may be one or two large manufacturers. The large manufacturer choosing not to buy from the small vendor during certain times of the year could completely cut the small vendor off, forcing it to close down and lay off its employees. When the large manufacturer again needs materials, the small vendor must try to hire its employees back again. This could cause costs to rise, or it could cause quality to drop if the vendor has to hire new employees. So the large manufacturer may choose to give the small vendor off-season business to keep it operating—at least at partial capacity. Such action would mean a certain amount of inventory accumulation, but this may be less expensive than changing vendors or getting a small vendor started up again. The trade-off in this instance is usually lower vendor prices and/or higher quality against the inventory holding cost.

Physical Distribution Inventories

The second inventory type consists principally of finished goods awaiting shipment to customers. Reasons for accumulating physical distribution inventories include transportation savings, production savings, seasonal demand, customer service, stable employment, and providing goods for resale.

carload/truckload discount

Transportation Savings   One reason companies may accumulate physical distribution inventory, or finished goods, resembles a reason for accumulating raw materials: transportation economies. By shipping in carload or truckload quantities rather than in less-than-carload or less-than-truckload shipments, a company may experience lower transportation rates. As long as transportation costs less than warehousing costs, the firm will ship more economically in larger quantities. Also, the company may experience better service, such as faster transit times, thereby reducing other costs, such as in-transit inventory cost and lost sales costs.

market-oriented warehouses

Firms frequently associate physical distribution inventory transportation economies with using market-oriented warehouses. Companies ship from their plants to strategically located market-oriented warehouses in carload or truckload quantities. The company can then ship the items shorter distances to customers in less-than-truckload quantities to minimize costs.

Traditionally, firms have associated lower rates and better service with larger shipments, but today many shippers can negotiate lower rates and higher service levels for smaller shipments as well. Transportation companies are generally willing to customize their rates and services to meet individual shippers' needs. Shippers should carefully identify their price and service needs and negotiate terms of sale with the transportation companies most capable of satisfying those needs.

production runs

Production Savings   A second reason for firms to accumulate physical distribution inventory is to achieve production economies. As the water tank analogy indicates, a firm may minimize its per unit product cost for an item by having long uninterrupted production runs for that item. This means that the company will sometimes produce in advance of demand; that is, it will not immediately sell all the items it produces. The firm would trade off lower production costs and perhaps better quality against increased inventory costs.

Alternatively, more industries now produce to order rather than to stock. This commonly results in shorter production runs, but many companies have learned to minimize frequent line changeover expense. Production to order virtually eliminates the need to carry finished product inventories, and this benefit is often financially considerable. For example, Ping produces golf clubs to order, and a production backlog of two to three months is not uncommon.

Seasonal Demand   A third reason for accumulating finished goods is that a company may have seasonal demand for its product. Having productive capacity to meet the peak seasonal demand may not be efficient, and the company would be better off producing more regularly throughout the year with a smaller plant.

Such a strategy would require warehousing facilities to store finished goods during low-demand periods, so as to ensure a lower per-unit production expense. Once again, the firm would trade off inventory cost against lower production costs and perhaps decreased plant investment. This is also similar to the water supply illustration.

substitutability   **Customer Service**   A fourth reason, very important from a marketing view point, is that a firm may hold physical distribution inventory to improve customer service or to reduce lost sale costs. We previously discussed substitutability and its effect on sales and cost. Where substitutability is high, firms may locate finished goods inventories reasonably close to their customers to allow expedient deliveries. The trade-off is between the cost of lost sales and inventory cost.

skilled labor   **Stable Employment**   A fifth reason for holding physical distribution inventory is to maintain stable employment. This is particularly important if the company does not want to lose skilled labor. The trade-off is against long-run labor cost and product quality. Although holding inventory to stabilize employment is not feasible for long periods, companies may find it expedient as a short-term tactic to produce cost efficiencies.

customer service   **Goods for Resale**   A sixth reason for holding finished goods inventory is to meet timely customer needs. A firm would be wise to have on-hand inventories sufficient to satisfy demand as it occurs. At the same time, however, the firm holding the inventories should work closely with its customers to avoid incurring extra expenses through unnecessarily high inventory levels.

Functional Types of Inventory

Thus far, this section has addressed reasons that may justify a firm holding inventory as part of its materials management or physical distribution responsibility. Another way to view inventory is in the context of its seven principal functions. We will address these in the following discussions.

cycle stock   The first functional type of inventory is *cycle stock,* the portion of a company's inventory depleted through normal sale or use and replenished through the routine ordering process. This inventory type also refers to the amounts of product the firm regularly consumes during normal business activity. As we will discuss in the next chapter, firms hold cycle stock to respond to demand or usage occurring under certainty of demand and lead time length.

in-process stock   The second type of inventory includes *goods in process,* because of the time necessary to manufacture goods, and *goods in transit.* Sometimes called *work in process,* or *WIP,* goods in process, or semi-finished goods, are important in a manufacturing situation. Inventory in transit refers to inventory that a carrier is transporting to a buyer. Because the purchasing firm sometimes has an ownership interest in goods that are in transit, carrying this inventory holds relevant financial implications. In-transit inventory also may refer to inventory that the selling firm still owns while the goods are being transported to the customer. Appendix 7A addresses the topic of in-transit inventory in detail.

safety stock   The third functional type of inventory is *safety stock,* or *buffer stock,* which protects against uncertainties in demand rate, lead time length, or both. Firms hold safety stock in addition to cycle stock, for the purpose of protecting against such uncertainties and their consequences. Holding safety stock helps a firm to avoid the negative, customer-related consequences of being out of stock when demand increases unexpectedly.

Estimating stockout cost using the procedure we discussed previously is a prerequisite to determining the appropriate amount of safety stock. Having estimated stockout cost, a firm should carry additional safety stock only if doing so does not cost more in dollars than the stockout the firm is averting.

seasonal stock

The fourth type of inventory is *seasonal stock,* which the firm accumulates and holds in advance of the season during which the firm will need it. Industries typically requiring significant seasonal stock include apparel, sporting goods, and automotive. In addition, firms may ship many Christmas toys manufactured overseas between January and June to the United States during the spring and summer months, and inventory the toys in the summer and early fall months before moving them to U.S. retail stores. Firms may also inventory products such as tomato juice before sale to accommodate seasonal growing and harvesting.

promotional stock

The fifth inventory type is *promotional stock,* held so that a firm's logistics system may respond quickly and effectively to a marketing promotion or price deal that a firm intending to pull a product through the distribution channel offers to customers. Firms frequently accumulate products such as televisions, VCRs, tires, and many tobacco products for such purposes. The success of many marketing promotions depends heavily on the capability of the firm's logistics system to infuse large amounts of product into the marketplace on relatively short notice.

speculative stock

The sixth type of inventory is *speculative stock.* Most commonly associated with materials needed by companies involved in manufacturing or assembly operations, this inventory protects against price increases or constrained availability. For example, U.S.-based firms stockpile component parts and subassemblies purchased from firms in areas such as Korea, Japan, and Singapore. This protects these U.S. firms against the uncertainties mentioned earlier and against others such as import quotas and tariffs. In addition, many food companies, such as Hershey Chocolate Company, Pillsbury, and Kraft General Foods, must actively participate in the world futures markets for ingredient commodities essential to their products.

dead stock

The seventh inventory type, "dead" stock, has no value for normal business purposes. A firm may ship dead stock to a company location where the product has real business value, sell or distribute it into overseas markets, or dispose of it in a manner which meets company and environmental standards.

More than 200 firms interested in deriving economic value from dead stock now belong to the Investment Recovery Association. This group explores effective ways for organizations to sell off or transfer used or surplus supplies, and results among its members have been impressive. For example, the income and/or savings from such programs may be ten to fifteen times the average cost of administering the programs.

Specific examples include Weyerhauser Co., whose fifteen-year-old investment recovery program has evolved into a full-fledged retailing operation. The stores offer used lumbering equipment and other gear, and even stock other companies' surplus goods. Mead Corporation markets surplus mill equipment to firms having similar needs. After trying to find uses for surplus items inside the company, Phillips Petroleum Co. opens its 66,000 square-foot warehouse (its "showroom") to the public one day every other month to sell off excess merchandise.

The Importance of Inventory in Other Functional Areas

functional interface

An earlier chapter explored how inventory interfaces with an organization's other functional areas, such as marketing and manufacturing. Nowhere is the interface usually more prominent than in the inventory area. As background for analyzing the importance of inventory in the logistics system, we should examine how logistics relates to other functional business areas on inventory matters.

■ *Marketing* desires high customer service levels and well-replenished inventory stocks in order to assure product availability and to meet customer needs as quickly and completely as possible.

■ *Manufacturing* desires long production runs and the lowest procurement costs as well as early production of seasonal items in order to minimize manufacturing costs and to avoid overtime payments.

■ *Finance* desires low inventories in order to increase inventory turnover, reduce current assets and to receive high capital returns on assets.

The preceding statements clearly show why other functional areas are interested in inventory. Also, finance area objectives may obviously conflict with marketing and manufacturing objectives. A more subtle conflict sometimes arises between marketing and manufacturing, although high inventory levels interest both areas. The long production runs that manufacturing may demand could cause shortages of some products needed by marketing to satisfy customer demand. For example, manufacturing may want to continue a particular production run up to 5,000 units at a time when marketing needs another product currently in short supply.

arbitrator role of logistics

Many companies can make a case for using a formal logistics organization to resolve these inventory objective conflicts. Inventory has an important impact on logistics, and in many logistics organizations, inventory is the pivotal activity. The logistics manager analyzes inventory trade-offs not only with other logistics areas but also with the functional areas discussed here. In some instances, this can almost be an arbitrator's role.

Proper inventory management and control affects customers, suppliers, and the organization's major functional departments. In spite of the many inventory advantages possible in a logistics system, the inventory holding costs are a major expense; and the logistics system should emphasize reducing inventory levels.

Logistics' role in the inventory area is important to the success of most companies, since all movement and information flows relate directly to inventory. In addition, much of the company's internal and external product flows center on inventory.[1]

INVENTORY COSTS

importance of inventory costs

Inventory costs are important for three major reasons. First, inventory costs represent a significant component of total logistics costs in many companies. Second, the inventory levels that a firm maintains at points in its logistics system will affect the level of service the firm can provide to its customers. Third, cost trade-off decisions in logistics frequently depend upon, and ultimately affect inventory carrying costs.

This section provides basic information concerning the costs that logistics management should consider when making inventory policy decisions. The major types include inventory carrying costs, order/setup costs, expected stock-out costs, and in-transit inventory carrying costs.

Inventory Carrying Cost

In a major research project, Douglas M. Lambert cited four major components of inventory carrying cost: capital cost, storage space cost, inventory service cost, and inventory risk cost.[2] Each cost type has a very unique nature, and the particular calculation for each includes different expenses or costs.

capital cost

Capital Cost   Sometimes called the *interest* or *opportunity* cost, this cost type focuses on what having capital tied up in inventory costs a company (in contrast to using capital in some other financially productive way). Stated differently, "What is the implicit value of having capital tied up in inventory, instead of using it for some other worthwhile project?"

The capital cost is generally the largest part of inventory carrying cost. A company usually expresses it as a percentage of the dollar value of the inventory the company holds. For example, a capital cost expressed as twenty percent of a product value of $100 equals a capital cost of $100 × 20%, or $20. Similarly, if the product value is $300, then the capital cost will be $60.

calculating capital cost

In practice, determining an acceptable number to use for capital cost is no small task. In fact, most firms find that determining capital cost may be more of an art than a science. One way of calculating capital cost for inventory decision making requires identifying the firm's *hurdle* rate, the minimum rate of return expected of new investments. In this way, the firm may make inventory decisions in much the same way as it decides to spend money for advertising, building new plants, or adding new computer equipment.

example calculation

For example, assume that a company has $300,000 worth of items in inventory. This inventory is a capital asset for the company, like a machine or any other capital investment. Therefore, if the company bases its capital cost on a fifteen percent hurdle rate and its average inventory value throughout the year is $300,000, then the capital cost is $45,000 ($300,000 × 15%) per year.

accurate inventory costing

The inventory valuation method is critical to accurately determining capital cost, and is subsequently critical to determining overall inventory carrying cost. According to Stock and Lambert, "the opportunity cost of capital should be applied only to the out-of-pocket investment in inventory. . . . This is the direct variable expense incurred up to the point at which inventory is held in storage."[3] Thus, the commonly accepted accounting practice of valuing inventory at the fully allocated manufacturing cost is unacceptable in inventory decision making because raising or lowering inventory levels financially affects only the variable portion of inventory value, and not the fixed portion of allocated cost. Including inbound transportation costs in inventory value, however, is consistent with this advice, and firms should include such cost measurements whenever possible.

storage cost

Storage Space Cost   This category includes handling costs associated with moving products into and out of inventory, and storage costs such as rent, heating, and lighting. Such costs may vary considerably from one circumstance to the next. For example, firms can often unload raw materials directly from rail cars and store them outside, whereas finished goods typically require safer handling and more sophisticated storage facilities.

fixed versus variable

Storage space costs are relevant to the extent that they either increase or decrease as inventory levels rise or fall. Thus, firms should include variable rather than fixed expenses when estimating space costs as well as capital costs. Perhaps we can clarify the issue by contrasting public warehouse use with private warehouse use. When a firm uses public warehousing, virtually all handling and storage costs vary directly with the magnitude of stored inventory. As a result, these costs are all relevant to decisions regarding inventory. When a firm uses private warehousing, however, many storage space costs (such as depreciation on the building) are fixed, and, as such, are not relevant to the inventory carrying cost.

insurance and taxes

Inventory Service Cost   Another component of inventory carrying cost includes insurance and taxes. Depending upon the product value and type, the risk of loss or damage may require high insurance premiums. Also, many states impose a tax on inventory value, sometimes on a monthly basis. High inventory levels resulting in high tax costs can be significant in determining specific locations where firms inventory product. Insurance and taxes typically vary considerably from product to product, and firms must consider this when calculating inventory carrying costs.

risk and obsolescence

Inventory Risk Cost   This final major component of inventory carrying cost reflects the very real possibility that inventory dollar value may decline for reasons largely beyond corporate control. For example, goods held in storage for some time may become obsolete and thus deteriorate in value. Also, fashion apparel may rapidly deteriorate in value once the selling season is actively underway or over. This phenomenon also occurs with fresh fruits and vegetables when quality deteriorates or the price falls. Manufactured products may face similar risks, although typically not to the same degree.

Any calculation of inventory risk costs should include the costs associated with obsolescence, damage, pilferage, theft, and other risks to inventoried product. The extent to which inventoried items are subject to such risks, will affect the inventory value and thus the carrying cost.

Calculating the Cost of Carrying Inventory

valuation of inventory

Calculating inventory carrying costs for a particular item stored in inventory involves three steps. The first is to identify the value of the item stored in inventory. According to traditional accounting practices, the three most widely recognized approaches include valuing inventory on first-in/first-out (FIFO) basis, last-in/first-out (LIFO) basis, or average cost. The most relevant value measure for inventory decision making is the cost of goods sold or the variable manufactured cost of product currently coming into the firm's logistics facilities. Again, this is because raising or lowering inventory levels affects only the variable, not the fixed, portion of inventory value.

carrying cost percentages

The second step is to measure each individual carrying cost component as a percent of product value, and to add the component percentages together to measure inventory carrying cost. Thus, carrying cost is typically expressed as a percentage of value. In computing storage space, inventory service, and inventory risk costs, it may be helpful to first calculate these costs in dollar terms and then to convert to percentage figures.

*calculation of
carrying cost*

The last step is to multiply overall carrying cost (as a percentage of product value) by the value of the product. This will measure the annual carrying cost for a particular amount of inventory.

example

Example Suppose a company manufactures hard disks for personal computers at a variable manufactured cost of $100 per unit. Table 6–2 lists the carrying cost components as a percentage of product value. The annual cost of carrying a single hard disk in inventory is calculated as follows:

$$\$100 \times 25\% = \$25.00 \text{ per year.}$$

Nature of Carrying Cost

Items with basically similar carrying costs should use the same estimate of carrying cost per inventory dollar. However, items subject to rapid obsolescence or items that require servicing to prevent deterioration may require separate cost estimates. The estimate of carrying cost per inventory dollar expressed as a percentage of the inventory value carried during the year will reflect how carrying costs change with inventory value. Table 6–3 indicates this relationship.

*concept of
average inventory*

Cost Relationships Table 6–3 shows that as average inventory increases (i.e., as the inventory level increases), annual carrying cost increases, and vice versa. In other words, carrying cost is variable and is directly proportional to the number of average inventory units or the average inventory value.

Order/Setup Cost

A second cost affecting total inventory cost is ordering cost or setup cost. Ordering cost refers to the expense of placing an order for additional inventory, and does not include the cost or expense of the product itself. Setup cost refers more specifically to the expense of changing or modifying a production or assembly process to facilitate product line changeovers, for example.

types of cost

Order Cost Ordering or acquisition costs have a fixed and a variable component. The fixed element may refer to the information system and facilities available to facilitate order placement. This cost remains constant in relation to the number of orders placed.

Alternatively, placing each individual order incurs a variable expense. The following activities typically bring about this type of expense: 1) reviewing the inventory stock level; 2) preparing and processing an order requisition or purchase request; 3) selecting a supplier, which may involve comparing several alternatives; 4) preparing and processing the purchase order; 5) preparing and

TABLE 6–2   EXAMPLE CARRYING COST COMPONENTS FOR COMPUTER HARD DISKS

Cost	Percentage of Product Value
Capital	12
Storage space	6
Inventory service	4
Inventory risk	3
Total	25

TABLE 6–3   INVENTORY AND CARRYING COST INFORMATION FOR COMPUTER HARD DISKS

Order Period	Number of Orders per Year	Average Inventory* Units	Average Inventory* Value†	Total Annual Inventory Carrying Cost‡
1 week	52	50	$ 5,000	$ 1,250
2 weeks	26	100	10,000	2,500
4 weeks	13	200	20,000	5,000
13 weeks	4	650	65,000	16,250
26 weeks	2	1,300	130,000	32,500
52 weeks	1	2,600	260,000	65,000

*One week's inventory supply is 50 units.

†Value per unit is $100

‡Percentage carrying cost assumed to be 25%

processing receiving reports; 6) checking and inspecting stock; and 7) preparing and processing payment. Some personnel and/or supply costs may seem trivial, but they become important when we consider the total activity range associated with placing and receiving an order.

production changeover

Setup Cost   Production setup costs may be more obvious than ordering or acquisition costs. Setup costs are expenses incurred each time a company modifies a production line to produce a different item for inventory. The setup cost fixed expense might include use of the capital equipment the company needed to change over production facilities, while the variable expense might include the personnel costs the needed changeovers incur.

Nature of Cost   Separating the fixed and variable portions of order/setup cost is essential. Just as calculations should emphasize the variable portion of inventory capital cost, calculating cost here should emphasize the variable portion of order/setup expense. As we will discuss in Chapter 7, this emphasis becomes central to developing meaningful inventory strategies.

general relationship

When calculating yearly order costs, firms usually start with the cost or charge associated with each individual order or setup. Correspondingly, the yearly number of orders or setups affects total order cost per year; this number is inversely related to individual order size or to the number of units manufactured (production run length) within a simple setup or changeover. Table 6–4 shows this general relationship.

As we can see in Table 6–4, more frequent order placement results in customers placing a larger number of smaller orders per year. Since both small and large orders incur the variable expense of placing an order, total annual order cost will increase in direct relation to the number of orders placed per year. As long as yearly sales and demand remain the same, total annual order or setup cost will relate directly to the number of orders or setups per year, and inversely related to individual order size or individual production run length.

Carrying Cost versus Order Cost

trade-off perspective

As Table 6–5 shows, order cost and carrying cost respond oppositely to changes in order number or size. Total cost also responds to the changing order size.

TABLE 6–4   ORDER FREQUENCY AND ORDER COST FOR COMPUTER HARD DISKS

Order Frequency	Number of Orders per Year	Total Annual Order Cost*
1 week	52	$10,400
2 weeks	26	5,200
4 weeks	13	2,600
13 weeks	4	800
26 weeks	2	400
52 weeks	1	200

*Assuming a cost per order of $200

Close examination indicates that order costs initially decrease more rapidly than carrying costs increase, which brings total costs down. In other words, a positive trade-off occurs, since the marginal savings in order costs exceed the marginal increment in inventory costs. However, this relationship begins to change, and total costs start to increase. Here a negative trade-off occurs because the marginal order cost savings are less than the marginal carrying cost increase. We can view this set of relationships in cost curve terms as shown in Figure 6–3.

Expected Stockout Cost

Another cost critical to inventory decision making is stockout cost—the cost of not having something available when a customer demands or needs it. When an item is unavailable for sale, a customer may purchase (or substitute) a competitor's product, directly taking profit from the firm experiencing a stockout. If the firm permanently loses the customer to its competitor, the profit loss will be indirect but longer lasting. On the physical supply side, a stockout may result in no new materials or in semifinished goods or parts, meaning idle machine time or even shutting down an entire manufacturing facility.

TABLE 6–5   SUMMARY OF INVENTORY AND COST INFORMATION

Order Period	Number of Orders per Year	Average Inventory* (Units)	Total Annual Order Cost†	Change in Total Order Cost	Total Annual Inventory Carrying Cost‡	Change in Total Carrying Cost	Total Cost
1 week	52	50	$10,400		$ 1,250		$11,650
				−5,200		+ 1,250	
2 weeks	26	100	5,200		2,500		7,700
				−2,600		+ 2,500	
4 weeks	13	200	2,600		5,000		7,600
				−1,600		+11,250	
13 weeks	4	650	800		16,250		17,050
				− 400		+ 16,250	
26 weeks	2	1,300	400		32,000		32,900
				− 200		+ 32,500	
52 weeks	1	2,600	200		65,000		65,000

*Assume sales or usage at 100 units per week.
†Order cost is $200.
‡Value is $100 per unit and carrying cost is 25%.

FIGURE 6–3   INVENTORY COSTS

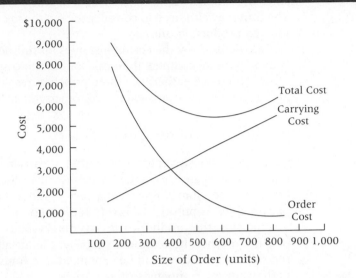

Safety Stock Most companies facing a stockout possibility will allow for *safety, or buffer, stock* safety, or buffer, stock to protect against uncertainties in demand or the lead *stock* time necessary for resupply in case of shortage. The inventory decision maker's difficulty is deciding how much buffer, or safety, stock to have on hand at any time. Having too much will mean excess inventory, whereas not having enough will mean stockouts and lost sales.

carrying cost Developing information for deciding what level of safety stock to maintain is a difficult task. Measuring the carrying cost associated with different safety stock levels can be similar to measuring carrying cost in general. First determine a percentage carrying cost that includes capital cost, storage space cost, inventory service cost, and inventory risk cost. Then multiply this percentage figure by the dollar value per unit and the number of units involved.

We should make two points here. First, although the safety stock carrying cost is likely the same as the carrying cost for cycle stock, safety stocks are inherently riskier, and implicitly more costly to carry than cycle stock. For simplicity, this text assumes that the same inventory carrying cost applies to both safety stock and cycle stock. Second, most decisions determining recommended safety stock levels involve probability analysis. The next chapter highlights this in a discussion of inventory decision making in the case of uncertainty.

stockout costs **Cost of Lost Sales** Determining safety stock inventory carrying cost may be relatively straightforward. Determining the cost of not having an item available for sale, however, may be much more challenging. For a company dealing with raw materials or supplies for a production line, a stockout may mean wholly or partially shutting down operations. Such operations cutbacks are particularly critical for firms involved in just-in-time manufacturing or assembly operations, for example, which we will discuss in the next chapter.

To best decide how much safety stock to carry, a manufacturing firm should thoroughly understand the cost consequences of shutting down its operation if needed input parts or materials were unavailable. The firm should first determine the hourly or daily production rates, and then multiply this rate by the profit loss on the number of units not produced. For example, if a plant with an hourly production rate of 1,000 units and a per-unit profit of $100 shuts down for four hours, the loss would be \$400,000. This figure is possibly conservative, however, since the firm may have to pay wages to workers despite a temporary shutdown. The firm may also need to consider the overhead costs often assigned or allocated to each production unit.

Calculating how the cost of lost sales for finished goods will affect a customer is usually more complex than calculating the cost for a raw materials stockout. As we discussed earlier, the three principal results of a finished goods stockout are backorders, lost sales, and lost customers, ranked from best to worst desirability.

Inventory in Transit Carrying Cost

F.O.B. terms

Another possible inventory cost is that of carrying inventory in transit. This cost may be less apparent than the three previously discussed. However, under certain circumstances, it may represent a very significant expense. For example, a company selling its product F.O.B. ("free-on-board") destination is responsible for transporting the product to its customers, since title does not pass until the product reaches the customer's facility. Financially, the product though still in the seller's inventory, will be contained in a transportation company vehicle or perhaps in the company's private truck.

trade-offs

Since this "moving" inventory is company-owned until delivered to the customer, the company should consider its delivery time part of its carrying cost. The faster delivery occurs, the sooner the company can collect the bill. Since faster delivery typically means higher-cost transportation, the company may want to analyze the trade-off between transportation cost and the cost of carrying inventory in transit. Appendix 7 specifically addresses this situation.

comparison with warehouse inventory

Determining Cost An important question at this point is how to calculate the cost of carrying inventory in transit—that is, what variables should a firm consider? An earlier discussion in this chapter focused on four major components of inventory carrying cost: capital cost; storage space cost; inventory service cost; and inventory risk cost. While these categories are all valid, they apply differently to the cost of carrying inventory in transit.

First, the capital cost of carrying inventory in transit generally equals that of inventory in the warehouse. If the firm owns the inventory in transit, the capital cost will be relevant.

Second, storage space cost generally will not be relevant to inventory in transit, since the transportation service supplier typically includes equipment and necessary loading and handling within its overall price or rate.

Third, while taxes generally would not be relevant to inventory service costs, the need for insurance requires careful analysis. For example, liability provisions for using common carriers are fairly specific, and a firm using a common carrier may not need to consider additional insurance (with the exception of certain "umbrella" coverages, for example). Firms using private fleets or writing contracts with for-hire carriers may place greater value on making suitable arrangements for insurance.

Fourth, obsolescence or deterioration are lesser risks for inventory-in-transit, because the transportation service typically takes only a short time. Thus, this inventory cost is less relevant here than it is for inventory in the warehouse.

Generally, carrying inventory-in-transit typically costs less than carrying inventory in the warehouse. However, a firm seeking to determine actual cost differences most accurately should examine the details of each inventory matter in depth.

ON THE LINE

COST CONTROL MEANS LOWER INVENTORIES: THE CASE OF VOLVO GM HEAVY TRUCKS

A clear message is sounding throughout the business community: "Measure and control costs." Complicating matters is the demand to maintain high service levels. These two goals have focused top management attention squarely on transportation and distribution.

In reevaluating capital deployment, corporate and financial officers are examining the size of their inventory investment. Controlling inventory levels can be a real key to controlling the size of this investment. Unfortunately, however, our financial systems sometimes encourage companies to build, rather than to reduce, inventories. This happens, for example, when companies focusing on savings in operating costs and expenses such as labor end up producing goods at a rate which inadvertently raises finished product inventories.

According to Richard Sherman, industry marketing logistics manager for Digital Equipment Corporation, measuring inventory cost and service performance requires a systematic inventory management approach. This approach makes it easier to evaluate exactly the inventory carrying costs and production timing and to break down related costs such as transportation and warehousing.

As an example of a concerted commitment to effective inventory management, Volvo GM Heavy Trucks carefully examined its options when consolidating parts operations for White, General Motors, and the Volvo lines it handles. It improved parts receiving and parts storage, and reduced outbound freight using a single central parts distribution location. It also found that, since the location was near customers and suppliers, inbound freight costs were less.

Volvo GM calls its approach cost-effective logistics. Consolidating the three parts lines and opening a truck assembly plant uncovered some interesting facts. One was the realization that logistics costs were higher than direct labor costs. That was one reason for not heavily automating the assembly plant. Volvo GM chose to concentrate on materials and material control to manage costs. The company regularly picks up parts from its vendors, consolidates, and ships

the parts in truckload quantities to its new Westerville, Ohio, parts DC.

Their approach to cost-effective logistics also caused Volvo GM to look closely at plans to open a distribution center to serve another assembly plant. Creating a warehouse within a warehouse at the central parts redistribution center allowed Volvo GM to avoid a planned warehouse construction that would have cost $7–8 million. They also found that work-in-process inventories were $2 million lower than expected.

Volvo GM set inventory goals for its five parts levels based on the parts' value. A separate service level exists for what Volvo GM calls truck-off-road. Otherwise, Volvo picks dealer stock orders received through a dealer communications network once a week. Component value sets stocking levels and turns. Parts valued over $18,000 (A items) should turn 25 times per year; B items 18 times per year; C items 8; D items 3; and E items 1.5 times per year.

An important part of Volvo GM's cost-effective logistics approach is the interface established with carriers and consolidators. They make every effort to eliminate less-than-truckload freight by consolidating into truckload on a daily basis. Parts coded for a storage carousel or outbound carrier arrive at the DC from 2,000 vendors. The parts DC can also ship directly to the use point within a Volvo GM assembly plant.

At the Volvo GM assembly plant in Orrville, Ohio, components not received directly at a use point are received onto a conveyor and pass by a computer station for identification. Those materials are then stored in a warehouse area under the same roof as the assembly plant. The entire receiving and warehousing area is 5,000 square feet.

Business can achieve much in inventory management by coordinating efforts across functional boundaries. In the future, more "inventory in motion" will place emphasis on transportation to provide high service levels at reasonable cost.

Source: Adapted from Perry A. Trunick, "Cost Control Means Lower Inventories," *Transportation & Distribution* (April 1989): 16–17. Copyright 1989, Penton Publishing Inc., Cleveland, OH.

CLASSIFYING INVENTORY

Multiple product lines and inventory control require companies to focus on more important inventory items and to utilize more sophisticated and effective inventory management. Inventory classification is usually a first step toward efficient inventory management. While we could have saved classification for the next chapter, which deals with the tools of inventory control, we will cover the topic now because it demonstrates an important aspect of most inventory decisions.

ABC Analysis

ranking system

Ford Dicky of General Electric was one of the first to recognize the need to rank inventory items in terms of importance.[4] He suggested that GE classify items according to relative sales volume, cash flows, lead time, or stockout costs. He used what we now refer to as ABC analysis for his particular classification scheme. This system assigns items to three groups according to appropriate criteria. The most important items became the "A" group, and the "B" and "C" classifications contained less important items.[5]

Pareto's Law

Actually, ABC analysis is rooted on Pareto's Law, which separates the "trivial many" from the "vital few."[6] In inventory terms, this suggests that a relatively small number of inventories items account for considerable importance within a firm's inventories.

Illustration   Figure 6–4 demonstrates ABC classification. This diagram shows that over seventy percent of company A's sales volume is associated with twenty percent of its product line items, and that over ninety percent of its sales volume

FIGURE 6–4   ABC ANALYSIS OF COMPANY A

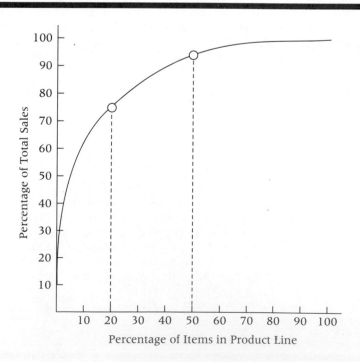

Percentage of Items in Product Line

is associated with fifty percent of its product line items. Thus, a relatively small number of items account for much of the company's sales volume and inventory value. This is typical for most companies.

80–20 rule

The "80–20 Rule" The "80–20 rule" prevails in many situations. For example, marketing research might find that twenty percent of a firm's customers account for eighty percent of its sales; or a university might find that twenty percent of its courses generate eighty percent of its student credit hours. Or a study might find that twenty percent of a city's people account for eighty percent of its crime. Whatever the example, something like the 80–20 rule usually applies.

Figure 6–5 applies the 80–20 rule to inventory management. The diagram indicates that only twenty percent of the product line items account for eighty percent of total sales. This may be because a firm with very successful new products must retail old, slower-moving products to maintain sales. In other instances, perhaps because their customers expect it, some companies maintain a complete array of items even though some are not large contributors to sales. Sometimes the C items are necessary for A and B item sales, or C items may be new products the company expects to be successful in the future. In some cases, the C items can be very profitable, despite small sales.

Decision Steps ABC classification is relatively simple. The first step is to select some criterion, such as sales revenue, for developing the ranking. The next step is to rank items in descending order of importance according to this criterion and to calculate actual and cumulative total sales revenue percentages for each item. This calculation should group the items into ABC categories.

FIGURE 6–5   ABC ANALYSIS OF COMPANY B

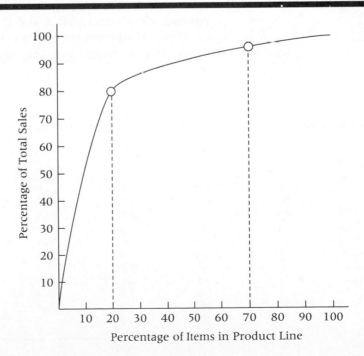

Table 6–6 shows how to base an ABC inventory analysis on sales revenue generated per line item. The first column identifies the ten items in the Big Orange product line. Then, the second and third columns show the annual sales and percent of total annual sales each item represents. The fourth and fifth columns show sales and items, respectively, as percentages of total. From these columns emanate statements like "twenty percent of the items account for eighty percent of the sales." The last column places each item into ABC classification on the basis of annual item sales revenues.

This last step assigns the items into ABC groups. This step is the most difficult, and no simple technique is available. The decision is largely arbitrary, requiring subjective judgement on the decision maker's part. As one examines item rankings, significant natural breaks sometimes appear. But this is not always the case and the decision maker will have to consider variables such as the item's importance and the cost of managing individual item types.

Also, we should note that the data in the fourth and fifth columns of Table 6–6 are the basic data points from which Figure 6–5 was constructed. This should bring our understanding of ABC inventory analysis full circle.

Increased Categories Although ABC implies three categories, using more than three inventory item subgroups is common and quite acceptable. In fact, some companies usually add a fourth category: D items, which may be "dead" items which the company should eliminate from its product line or inventory. Although companies sometimes segment inventory into five subgroups, this is not generally as cost-effective using three subgroups.

management tool   **Effective Decision Making** The 80–20 rule is an effective tool for organizing an overall inventory management approach. ABC analysis identifies natural line item subgroups which should receive similar inventory management. For example, a company might target A items for ninety-eight percent in-stock performance, B items for eighty-five percent, and C items for seventy percent.

A common mistake is to assume that B and C items are far less important than A items, and to exclude them from further consideration. Some firms have learned the hard way that they need to effectively manage all inventory clas-

TABLE 6–6   ABC Analysis for Big Orange Products, Inc.

Item Code	Annual Sales ($)	Percent of Annual Sales	Cumulative Percent		Classification Category
			Sales	Items	
64R	$ 5,000	50.0%	50.0%	10.0%	A
89Q	3,000	30.0	80.0	20.0	A
68J	400	4.0	84.0	30.0	B
37S	340	3.4	87.4	40.0	B
12G	300	3.0	90.4	50.0	B
35B	240	2.4	92.8	60.0	B
61P	220	2.2	95.0	70.0	B
94L	200	2.0	97.0	80.0	C
11T	160	1.6	98.6	90.0	C
20G	140	1.4	100.0	100.0	C
	$10,000	100.0%			

sifications and that specific items may be very important despite their category. For example, even though a particular item may be slow moving and have a high value, it may be important because its use is complementary to a certain A or B item.

Critical Value Analysis

Some companies find that ABC analysis is not entirely satisfactory for inventory control because some C items may receive insufficient attention. For example, shoelaces may be a C inventory item to a shoe distributor or wholesaler, but a shoelace stockout could cause loss of shoe sales. In the manufacture of sophisticated consumer products like refrigerators or automobiles, some small bolt or other part may be a C item based upon cost or usage; and yet a stockout could shut down the production line. Therefore, some companies utilize a military approach called *Critical Value Analysis* (CVA).[7]

Example Critical Value Analysis classifies inventory items by assigning point values for three to five categories. An example would be as follows:

1. Top priority: no stockouts—critical item
2. High priority: essential, but limited stockouts permitted
3. Medium priority: necessary, but occasional stockouts permitted
4. Low priority: desirable, but stockouts allowed

subjective nature   **CVA and ABC** Critical Value Analysis is more subjective than the straightforward quantitative approach of ABC analysis. Those assigning values must take care, because sometimes items tend to receive too high a priority. Using the critical value approach to classify an inventory of 10,000 items or more would be a formidable undertaking. Therefore, companies usually survey various inventory items in order to decide which ones are vital according to the established criterion; these items would receive an A classification. This approach is more consistent, less awkward, and more objective than Critical Value Analysis used alone.

EVALUATING THE EFFECTIVENESS OF A COMPANY'S APPROACH TO INVENTORY MANAGEMENT

A product buyer must be confident that suppliers and vendors have that product available when and where the buyer needs it. Similarly, a product seller's ability to effectively manage inventory should translate into a more satisfied customer base. Thus, both buyers and sellers should identify several questions when evaluating the effectiveness of a firm's inventory management approach.

customer satisfaction   The first question to raise is whether the company's customers are satisfied with existing customer service levels. Insight into this issue can be gained by inquiring into matters such as customer loyalty, order cancellation experience, and stockouts, and evaluating the company's general relationships with all channel partners. If there are areas where customer service levels need to improve, perhaps using more dependable transportation suppliers would enhance customer satisfaction.

*backordering/
expediting*

The second question is how frequently a need for backordering or expediting occurs. The more frequently these occur, the less effective an inventory system is presumed to be. The company's inventory management approach may not respond promptly to signals for reordering and resupplying inventory levels. Or the company may need an ABC inventory system or faster and more dependable transportation services to see that inventory is available when and where the customer needs it.

*inventory
turnover*

A third question involves inventory turnover measures calculated for an entire product line and for individual products and product groupings. Buyers and sellers should question whether these measures are increasing or decreasing and how they vary among different stocking points in the firm's distribution system.

Inventory turnover, sometimes referred to as inventory velocity, is calculated by dividing annual sales in dollars by average inventory measured in dollars. Assuming that the inventory valuation bases are equivalent (e.g., both are valued in retail price terms or cost of goods sold), the resulting figure measures how many times per year average inventory turns over.

For example, assume that a firm values its yearly products sales at $50,000 and calculate its average on-hand inventory to be $10,000. The number of inventory "turns" per year would be $50,000 ÷ $10,000, or five. The firm could either say that average inventory turns five times per year or that, on the average, an inventory item stays on the shelf for one-fifth of a year—or 10.4 weeks.

Inventory turnover varies widely between firms in different industries, and also between firms in similar industries. Inventory turnover typically ranges from five to ten turns for many manufacturing firms and from ten to twenty turns for wholesale and retail firms, through whose systems inventory moves rapidly. In either case, buyers and sellers must have specific details about a firm and its logistics system before estimating inventory turnover. (We should not view the percentages cited here as industry standards, but only as representing certain firms in the industries identified.)

While more inventory turns per year often implies more effective inventory management, customer service sometimes suffers if turnovers cause needed inventoried items to be unavailable. A firm interested in increasing its inventory turns while maintaining customer service levels should switch to faster and more reliable transportation services or improved order processing systems, which will justify lowering its safety stock investment, and therefore its overall inventory levels. Examining inventory turnover by individual products or facilities may help to identify trouble spots in a firm's logistics system.

As Table 6–7 indicates, as inventory turnover increases, average inventory and the cost of carrying the average inventory both decrease.

*ratio of inventory
to sales*

A fourth question to raise is whether overall inventory as a percentage of sales rises or falls as a company's sales increase. Generally, given effective inventory management, this figure should decline as sales increase. If a firm's inventories are rising at a rate equal to or faster than its sales, the firm may need to reconsider its overall inventory policies. Commonly, many firms experiencing a growing demand for their products will "overinventory" those products where customers are concentrated. A more suitable alternative might be to centralize supplies of such items and to depend upon capable transportation suppliers and enhanced order processing systems to provide timely product delivery to customers. *Distribution* or *pooling* may also help transportation to achieve customer service objectives more cost-effectively.

TABLE 6–7   RELATIONSHIP BETWEEN INVENTORY TURNOVER, AVERAGE INVENTORY, AND INVENTORY CARRYING COSTS

Inventory Turnover	Average Inventory	Inventory Carrying Cost*	Incremental Savings in Carrying Cost	Cumulative Savings in Savings Cost
1........	$20,000,000	$6,000,000	—	—
2........	10,000,000	3,000,000	$3,000,000	$3,000,000
3........	6,666,667	2,000,000	1,000,000	4,000,000
4........	5,000,000	1,500,000	500,000	4,500,000
5........	4,000,000	1,200,000	300,000	4,800,000
6........	3,333,333	1,000,000	200,000	5,000,000
7........	2,857,143	857,143	142,857	5,142,857
8........	2,500,000	750,000	107,143	5,250,000
9........	2,222,222	666,667	83,333	5,333,000
10........	2,000,000	600,000	66,667	5,400,000

*Assume that inventory carrying cost equals 30%.

SUMMARY

This chapter introduced some fundamental inventory management concerns in the context of overall logistical responsibility. The early part of the chapter stressed how inventory is important to both the economy and the firm. Inventory is a critical topic, whether considered an expense item, an asset, or an important component of value added.

Succeeding discussions highlighted reasons for carrying inventories and identified the functional types and costs of carrying inventory. The chapter concluded by describing two commonly used inventory classification methods and questions that buyers and sellers may use to evaluate how effectively a particular firm is managing its inventories.

A good grasp of the material contained in this chapter is essential to thoroughly understanding the content of Chapter 7, which addresses alternative approaches used to make inventory decisions.

STUDY QUESTIONS

1. What benefit does calculating inventory expense as a percentage of value added offer over calculating inventory expense as a percentage of sales revenues?

2. How would the inventory of a steel company be similar to that of a water authority?

3. Select a company and discuss its inventory holding reasons in terms of materials management inventory and physical distribution inventory.

4. Identify the major functional inventory types. Discuss the basic difference between cycle stock and safety stock.

5. What are the major components of inventory carrying cost? How would you suitably measure capital cost for making inventory policy decisions?

6. How can inventory carrying cost be calculated for a specific product? What suggestions would you offer for determining the measure of product value to be used in calculations of inventory carrying cost?

7. Explain the differences between inventory carrying costs and order costs.

8. Why is it generally more difficult to determine the cost of lost sales for finished goods than it is for raw materials inventories?

9. Discuss the cost of carrying inventory in transit.

10. You have been called in as a consultant to a large drugstore chain which has 24,000 inventory line items. Explain how inventory classification could help this company to better control its inventory.

11. What key questions would you raise when judging the effectiveness of a company's inventory management approach? If the calculated value of inventory as a percentage of sales appears to be rising, would this concern you? Explain.

NOTES

1. Warren Rose, *Logistics Management* (Dubuque, Iowa: Brown, 1979), 142–43.
2. Douglas M. Lambert, *The Development of an Inventory Costing Methodology: A Study of the Costs Associated with Holding Inventory* (Chicago: National Council of Physical Distribution Management, 1976).
3. James R. Stock and Douglas M. Lambert, *Strategic Logistics Management*, 2d ed. (Homewood, IL: Irwin, 1987), 372–73.
4. Robert Goodell Brown, *Advanced Service Parts Inventory Control*, 2d ed. (Norwich, VT: Materials Management Systems, 1982), 155.
5. David P. Herron, "ABC Data Correlation," in *Business Logistics in American Industry*, edited by Karl Ruppenthal and Henry A. McKinnel, Jr. (Stanford, CA: Stanford University, 1968), 87–90.
6. Thomas E. Hendrick and Franklin G. Moore, *Production/Operations Management*, 9th ed. (Homewood, IL: Irwin, 1985), 173.
7. Rose, *Logistics Management*, 153.

CASE 6–1

BELLWETHER CORPORATION

Eighty-Eight Enterprises, Inc., has just acquired the Bellwether Corporation. Eighty-Eight is a diversified manufacturer of sporting goods and casual furniture. It feels that Bellwether's high-quality line of tennis racquets and related products can help even out seasonal imbalances in Eighty-Eight's product line.

Martha Rodino, senior vice president of logistics at Eighty-Eight, has been asked to evaluate the effectiveness of Bellwether's logistics system, with particular emphasis on inventory management. She agrees that this task will provide her company with valuable insight as it considers merging the operations of the two companies.

As she begins her preliminary analysis of Bellwether, Rodino finds that the company produces a full line of tennis racquets, from all-aluminum models at the lower end to graphite-based composition models at the upper end. Each model is available in a number of sizes and colors, and the total number of SKUs (stock-keeping units) is forty-eight. The company also sells related items such as towels, bags, and caps, which contribute an additional 120 SKUs. Rodino has been told that the tennis racquet line accounts for approximately sixty percent of the company's gross revenues, but only thirty-five percent of its net income.

Bellwether inventories its products at three distribution centers located strategically throughout the United States, and sells them through tennis specialty shops, department stores, mass merchandisers, and catalogs. After touring the three distribution centers, Rodino feels that Bellwether's average inventory levels might be unnecessarily high.

Case Questions
1. What additional information should Rodino gather before finalizing her evaluation of Bellwether's inventory system?
2. What critical issues should Eighty-Eight address before deciding to merge its logistics operations with Bellwether's?

CASE 6–2

OK JEANS

At OK Jeans, inventory control blends the big and the small. This maker of children's apparel is enjoying some good times. Its nearly fifteen percent annual growth rate has significantly increased traffic volumes between its corporate distribution center in Harrison, Arkansas, and its twelve manufacturing locations.

Largely responsible for smooth merchandise flow is a battery-powered microcomputer which a bar code wand and an FM radio receiver connect to the host mainframe. As a result, warehouse workers have a truly personal computer; and order pickers communicate with the computer without leaving their trucks.

Inventory handling at OK Jeans has improved measurably since the company installed this new equipment, largely because bar-coded labels replaced printed forms and other cumbersome paperwork. And by utilizing real-time inventory tracking, OK Jeans has eliminated its quarterly physical inventory counts, which used to shut down operations for two days. The computer also forces order pickers to follow the company's first-in, first-out selection process. By streamlining operations and reducing inventory reporting inaccuracies, computers are improving OK Jeans' growth rate.

Source: Adapted from Bruce Heydt, "Inventory Casebook: Oshkosh B'Gosh," *Distribution* (May 1987), 38–39. Reprinted by Permission of Chilton's DISTRIBUTION Magazine, Radnor, PA.

Case Questions
1. What additional benefits do you feel OK Jeans probably derived from its computer equipment investment?
2. What cost tradeoffs are inherent in this situation? What factors would be important to a company considering greater computerization of its inventory procedures?
3. What other initiatives and priorities might OK Jeans examine when considering future growth?

INVENTORY DECISION MAKING

Chapter 6 developed the rationale for inventory in a logistics system and addressed several fundamental aspects of inventory management. An important part of that chapter analyzed major cost categories that are relevant to the inventory decision: inventory carrying costs, order/setup costs, and expected stockout costs.

This chapter places the content of Chapter 6 in an operational context by describing a number of the more progressive and commonly used inventory management approaches. While minimizing cost is a key to developing an appropriate inventory strategy, customer service requirements have received much recent attention. Thus, this chapter blends and balances important considerations regarding both customers and cost.

FUNDAMENTAL APPROACHES TO MANAGING INVENTORY

basic issues

Historically, managing inventory involved two fundamental questions: *how much* to reorder, and *when* to reorder. By performing a few simple calculations, an inventory manager could easily determine acceptable solutions to these issues. Today, questions regarding *where* inventory should be held, and *what* specific line items should be stored at specific locations challenge the creativity and analytical abilities of inventory decision makers.

managing inventories

Each question is still relevant, but managing inventory in today's business environment is complex and usually involves selecting an appropriate approach from a relatively broad range of alternatives. At the same time that inventory decision making has become more complex, firms have pressured logistics managers to streamline physical supply and distribution systems and to manage their inventories effectively. In practice, the difficulty of identifying an acceptable approach will depend upon the circumstances under which the company operates, and the logistics manager's willingness to accept certain simplifying assumptions. Generally, the more complex the circumstances, the more sophisticated the inventory model required. The remainder of this chapter treats this issue at greater length.

balancing cost with service

Regardless of the approach selected, inventory decisions must consider issues relating to cost and to customer service requirements. Figure 7–1, which illustrates the relationship between inventory and customer service levels, shows that increasing inventory amounts are necessary to produce increasingly higher customer service levels. This information highlights the importance of producing the cost and service mix which will create the most value for the external customer.

Key Differences among Approaches to Managing Inventory

Before discussing individual approaches and techniques for managing inventory, let us elaborate briefly on several important ways in which these approaches

FIGURE 7–1   RELATIONSHIP BETWEEN INVENTORY AND CUSTOMER SERVICE LEVEL

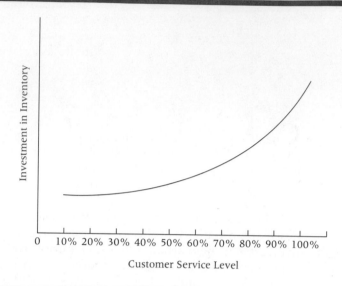

differ from each other. These differences include dependent versus independent demand, pull versus push, and systemwide versus single-facility solutions to inventory management issues.

nature of demand **Dependent versus Independent Demand**   This distinction is important to selecting an appropriate inventory management approach. According to Joseph Orlicky, "Demand for a given inventory item is termed 'independent' when such demand is unrelated to demand for other items—when it is not a function of demand for some other inventory item. . . . Conversely, demand is defined as 'dependent' when it is directly related, or derives from, the demand for another inventory item or product." [1] For example, the demand for finished automobiles is independent; the demand for tires is dependent on the desired quantity of finished automobiles. Orlicky suggests that this dependency may be *vertical* (such as when a product's assembly requires a component part) or *horizontal* (for example, when an instruction booklet must accompany a finished product).

Thus, for many manufacturing processes, basic demand for most raw materials, component parts, and subassemblies *depends* upon demand for the finished product. In contrast, demand for many end-use items, which are typically warehoused and inventoried, is *independent* of the demand for any other higher-order manufactured item.

An important point to remember is that developing inventory policies for items exhibiting independent demand will require forecasting expected demand for these items. Alternatively, forecasting is unnecessary for items having dependent demand, since the needed quantities of these items entirely depend upon the demand for the end product being manufactured or assembled. For items having dependent demand, needed quantity projections and receipts timing will rely wholly on the forecast needs for the end product.

Pull versus Push [2]   Another important distinction between inventory management approaches is the issue of pull versus push. Sometimes called a "reactive" system, the pull approach relies on customer demand to "pull" product through a logistics system. In contrast, the "push," or proactive, approach uses inventory replenishment to anticipate future demand.

examples

As an example, a fast-food system such as McDonald's basically runs on a pull system, while a catering service basically operates on a push system. McDonald's cooks hamburgers generally in response to current demand. In effect, individual purchases "trigger" more food item production. In contrast, the catering service tries to have a picture-perfect idea of what customers will need and when, and pushes food items to where customers need them, at the right time and in the right quantity.[3]

hybrid systems

While this distinction may seem simple enough, the McDonald's pull system may be quite effective in a downtown location with a steady stream of customers, but may suffer in a high-traffic, peak-demand location such as a major airport concourse. In this instance, a pull and push system hybrid would be appropriate.

A principal pull system attribute is that it can respond quickly to sudden or abrupt changes in demand. Alternatively, a push meets systemwide inventory needs in accordance with some master plan in an orderly and disciplined way. In general, the pull system applies more to independent demand, and the push system to dependent demand. A deficiency of many pull systems is that product orders are typically triggered at individual stock keeping locations; thus, the need for similar or identical items at parallel network facilities is uncoordinated. In contrast, push systems adapt better to the coincident needs of parallel logistics network facilities. Finally, pull systems sometimes involve only one-way communications between point of need and point of supply, while push systems tend to involve more two-way communications between point of need and point of supply.

environmental conditions

Bowersox, Closs, and Helferich,[4] summarizing ideal environmental conditions for each approach suggest that the pull, or reactive, approach would be most suitable when either order cycle time or demand levels are uncertain, or when market-oriented warehouses or distribution centers have capacity limitations. The push, or planning-based, approach is most appropriate for highly profitable segments, dependent demand, scale economies, supply uncertainties, source capacity limitations, or seasonal supply buildups. In general, push systems are more prevalent among organizations having greater logistics sophistication.

Systemwide versus Single-Facility Solution   A final inventory management issue is whether the selected approach represents a systemwide solution, or whether it is specific to a single facility, such as a system warehouse or distribution center. Each approach has advantages and disadvantages. The principal factors associated with the *systemwide* approach are the time and expense of developing a truly comprehensive solution to a network's inventory problems, and also the question of whether or not it will work, once developed and implemented. The *single-facility* approach is less expensive and more straightforward in development terms. Its inherent risk is that it may produce optimal single-facility results which may be suboptimal from a systemwide perspective.

comprehensiveness

Overall, those choosing an approach must carefully consider its comprehensiveness. The two extremes offer very different perspectives on the problem. Those choosing must gain an early understanding of the specific advantages and disadvantages of each, given any specific inventory problem. Such understanding will reveal important trade-offs and provide information sufficient for a rational choice between the available alternatives.

Principal Approaches and Techniques for Inventory Management

In many business situations, the variables affecting the decision are almost overwhelming. Therefore, models developed to aid in the decision process are frequently abstract or represent a simplified reality. In other words, models generally make simplifying assumptions about the real world they attempt to represent.

The model complexity and accuracy relate to the assumptions the model makes. Typically, the more the model assumes, the easier the model is to work with and understand; however, simple model output is often less accurate. The model developer or user must decide upon the proper balance between simplicity and accuracy. The best advice is to seek out models that are as simple and direct as possible but that do not assume away too much reality.

alternative approaches

The remainder of this chapter contains an in-depth treatment of approaches and techniques that professional inventory managers commonly use today. The highlighted approaches include the fixed order quantity approach under conditions of certain and uncertain demand and lead time length (also known as the economic order quantity, or EOQ, approach); the fixed order interval approach; just-in-time (JIT); materials requirements planning (MRP); and distribution resource planning (DRP). The chapter concludes by discussing how inventory needs will change as one moves from using a single facility to using multiple stocking locations to accomplish the same logistics objectives.

These discussions cover the fundamentals of each major approach and provide numerical examples to illustrate the various concepts. Further detail is available in the sources listed in the selected bibliography at the end of this section of the text.

FIXED ORDER QUANTITY APPROACH (CONDITION OF CERTAINTY)

As its name implies, the *fixed order quantity* model involves ordering a fixed amount of product each time reordering takes place. The exact amount of product to be ordered depends upon the product's cost and demand characteristics and upon relevant inventory carrying and reordering costs.

EOQ approach

Firms using this approach generally need to develop a minimum stock level to determine when to reorder the fixed quantity. This is usually called the *reorder point.* When the number of items in inventory reaches the predetermined level, the fixed order quantity (also called the economic order quantity, or EOQ) is "automatically" ordered. In a sense, the predetermined ordering level triggers the next order.

triggering orders for inventory reorder point

Sometimes firms call the fixed order quantity approach a *two-bin* system. When the first bin is empty, the firm places an order. The stock amount in the second bin represents the inventory quantity the firm needs until the new order arrives. Both notions (trigger and bin) imply that a firm will reorder or produce stock when the amount on hand decreases to some predetermined level. Again, the amount ordered depends upon the product's cost and demand, along with inventory carrying and reordering costs. The stock ordering level (number of units) depends upon the time it takes to get the new order and upon the product demand or sales rate during that time—for example, how many units the firm sells per day, or whatever per week. For example, if a new order takes two weeks to arrive and a firm sells ten units per day, the reorder point will be 140 units (14 days × 10 units/day).

Inventory Cycles

inventory cycles

Figure 7–2 shows the fixed quantity model. The figure shows three inventory cycles, or periods. Each cycle begins with 4,000 units, the fixed quantity ordered or produced; and reordering occurs when inventory on hand falls to a level of 1,500 units. Assuming that the demand or usage rate and the lead time length are constant and known in advance, the length of each cycle will be a constant five weeks. This is an example of a fixed quantity model application in the case of certainty.

As we suggested earlier, establishing a reorder point provides a trigger or signal for reordering the fixed quantity. For example, most people have reorder points for personal purchases such as gasoline. On a trip, one may customarily stop to fill the tank when the gauge indicates one-eighth of a tank. Or, similarly, one may wait until a dashboard light indicates that the gas supply has reached some minimum point.

sensitivity to demand changes

Business inventory situations base the reorder point upon lead time or replenishment time, the time it takes to replenish an order or manufacture the fixed quantity. The constant monitoring necessary to determine when inventory has reached the reorder point makes the fixed quantity model somewhat expensive, although a computer can monitor inventory at little marginal cost per transaction. Generally, this approach can be sensitive to demand without carrying too much excess inventory.

Simple EOQ Model

assumptions of the simple EOQ model

The following are the principal assumptions of the simple EOQ model:

1. A continuous, constant, and known demand rate
2. A constant and known replenishment or lead time
3. The satisfaction of all demand

FIGURE 7–2   FIXED QUANTITY MODEL

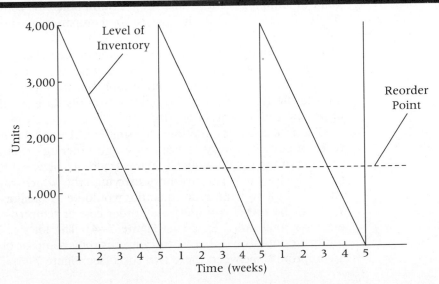

4. Constant price or cost that is independent of the order quantity or time (e.g., purchase price or transport cost)

5. No inventory in transit

6. One item of inventory or no interaction between items

7. Infinite planning horizon

8. No limit on capital availability

certainty

The first three assumptions are closely related and basically mean that conditions of certainty exist. Demand in each relevant time period (daily, weekly, or monthly) is known, and its usage rate is linear over time. The firm uses or depletes inventory on hand at a constant rate and knows the time needed to replenish stock. In other words, lead time between order placement and order receipt is constant. This means that neither demand nor the time it takes to produce or receive replenishment stock will vary. As a result, the firm has no need to be concerned about stockouts and, consequently, stockout costs.

Some individuals feel the assumptions of certainty make the basic model too simplistic—and, consequently, the output decisions too inaccurate. Although this charge is true in certain cases, several important reasons justify using the simple model. First, in some businesses demand variation is so small that making the model more complex is too costly for the extra accuracy achieved. Second, firms just beginning to develop inventory models frequently find the simple EOQ model convenient and necessary because of the limited data available. (This discussion presents this form.) Some firms get caught up in sophisticated models with simple data, and the end results are probably no more accurate than they would have been if the firm had used the simple model form. Third, simple EOQ model results are somewhat insensitive to input variable changes. That is, variables such as demand, inventory carrying cost, and ordering cost can change without significantly affecting calculated value of the economic order quantity.

no in-transit inventory

The assumption about no inventory in transit means that the firm purchases goods on a delivered-price basis (purchase price includes delivery) and sells them F.O.B. shipping point (the buyer pays transportation charges). On the outbound side, this means that title to the goods does not pass until the buyer receives them. On the outbound side, title passes when the product leaves the plant or shipping point. Under these assumptions, the company has no responsibility for goods in transit; that is, the company pays no in-transit inventory carrying costs.

The assumption about constant cost means essentially that the firm offers no volume price discounts. It also means that prices are relatively stable.

Capital availability may be important, but this decision is sometimes made outside the logistics area. If capital constraints do exist, this may result in an upper limit on inventory lot size.

inventory and ordering costs

Given the listed assumptions, the simple EOQ model considers only two basic types of cost: inventory carrying cost and ordering or setup cost. The decision reached in the simple model analyzes trade-offs between these two costs. If the model focuses only on inventory carrying cost, which varies directly with increases in lot size, the order quantity would be as small as possible (see Figure 7–3). If the model considers only order cost or setup cost, large orders would decrease total order costs (see Figure 7–4). The lot size decision attempts to minimize total cost—that is, carrying cost plus setup or order cost by reaching a compromise between these two costs (see Figure 7–5).

FIGURE 7–3   INVENTORY CARRYING COST

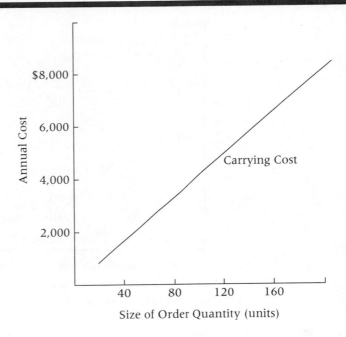

Size of Order Quantity (units)

Mathematical Formulation We can develop the EOQ model in standard mathematical form, using the following variables:

R = annual rate of demand or requirement for period (units)
Q = quantity ordered or lot size (units)
A = cost of placing an order or setup cost ($ per order)
V = value or cost of one unit of inventory ($ per unit)

FIGURE 7–4   ORDER OR SETUP COST

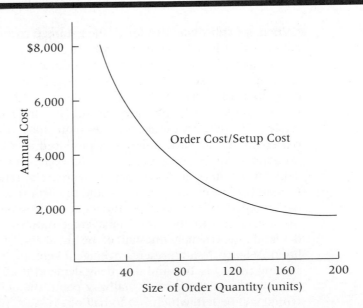

Size of Order Quantity (units)

FIGURE 7–5   INVENTORY COSTS

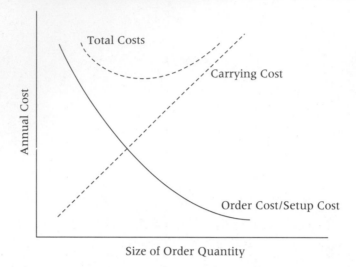

Total Costs

Carrying Cost

Annual Cost

Order Cost/Setup Cost

Size of Order Quantity

W = carrying cost per dollar value of inventory per year (% of product value)
S = VW = storage cost per unit per year* ($ per unit per year)
t = time (days)
TAC = total annual cost ($ per year)

Given the previous assumptions, we can express the total annual cost in either of the following forms:

$$\text{TAC} = \frac{1}{2}\,QVW + A\frac{R}{Q}$$

or

$$\text{TAC} = \frac{1}{2}QS + A\frac{R}{Q}$$

*When we substitute VW for S, then storage cost becomes a function of price paid per unit bought—namely, volume.

inventory carrying cost   The first term on the right-hand side of the equation refers to inventory carrying cost; it states that these costs equal the average number of units in the economic order quantity during the order cycle (½Q) multiplied by the value per unit (V) multiplied by the carrying cost (W). In Figure 7–6, called the sawtooth model, the equation's logic becomes more apparent. The vertical line labeled Q represents the amount ordered or produced at a given time, and the amount on hand at the beginning of each order cycle. During the order cycle (t), a firm depletes the amount of product on hand at the rate the slanted line represents. Demand is known and constant, and the firm uses inventory at a uniform rate over the period. The average number of units on hand during this period affects the inventory carrying cost. The average number on hand, given the constant demand rate, is simply one-half of the initial amount (Q). The broken horizontal line in Figure 7–6 represents average inventory. The logic is very simple. Assuming that Q is 100 and that daily demand is 10 units, 100 units would last 10 days (t). At the period's halfway point, the end of the fifth day, fifty units would still be left, which is one-half of Q (½ × 100).

FIGURE 7–6   SAWTOOTH MODEL

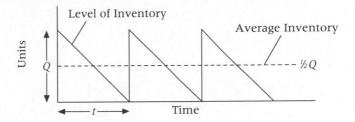

order size and inventory

Determining the average number of units is not enough, as the equation indicates. Knowing the value per unit, which depends upon the product is still necessary. Knowing the percentage carrying cost, which depends upon the product and the firm's warehousing operations, is also necessary. The larger the Q, the higher the inventory carrying cost will be. We described this general relationship earlier: increasing carrying cost accompanies larger inventory lots or orders. As the present context shows, larger inventory order quantities will last longer, thereafter increasing carrying costs. Given constant demand, average inventory will increase as the economic order quantity increases [see Figures 7–7(a) and 7–7(b)].

ordering cost

The second term in the equation refers to order cost or setup cost. Again, we assume order cost to be constant per order or setup. Therefore, if the size of Q increases, the number or orders per year will be smaller since annual demand is constant. It follows then that larger order quantities will lower annual order costs.

Although we have explained the general nature of carrying cost and order cost, determining Q, the economic order quantity is still necessary. As we indicated previously, this involves trading off inventory carrying cost and order cost. We can determine Q by differentiating the TAC function with respect to Q, as follows:

$$\text{TAC} = \frac{1}{2}QVW + A\frac{R}{Q}$$

$$\frac{d(\text{TAC})}{dQ} = \frac{VW}{2} - \frac{AR}{Q^2}$$

Setting $d(\text{TAC})/dQ$ equal to zero and solving for Q gives

$$Q^2 = \frac{2RA}{VW}$$

or

$$Q = \sqrt{\frac{2RA}{VW}}$$

or

$$Q = \sqrt{\frac{2RA}{S}}$$

FIGURE 7–7   SAWTOOTH MODELS

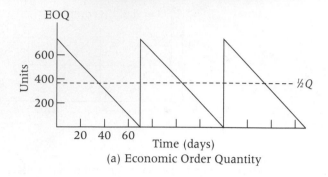

(a) Economic Order Quantity

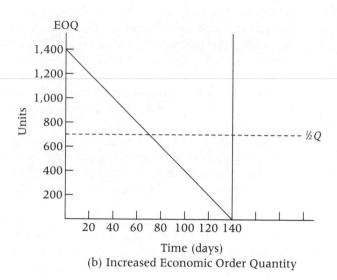

(b) Increased Economic Order Quantity

example   The following assumptions illustrate how the formula works in actual practice:

V = $100 per unit
W = 25%
S = $25 per unit per year
A = $200 per order
R = 3,600 units

To solve for Q, the example proceeds as follows:

$$Q = \sqrt{\frac{2RA}{VW}} \qquad\qquad Q = \sqrt{\frac{2RA}{S}}$$

$$= \sqrt{\frac{(2)(3,600)(\$200)}{(\$100)(25\%)}} \qquad = \sqrt{\frac{(2)(3,600)(200)}{\$25}}$$

$$= 240 \text{ units} \qquad\qquad = 240 \text{ units}$$

Analysis   Table 7–1 and Figure 7–8 show the preceding solution's trade-offs and logic. The illustrations show how inventory carrying cost and total cost vary as Q ranges from a low of 100 units to a high of 500 units.

TABLE 7–1   TOTAL COSTS FOR VARIOUS EOQ AMOUNTS

Q	Order Costs AR/Q	Carrying Cost $\frac{1}{2}QVW$	Total Cost
100	$7,200	$1,250	$8,450
140	5,140	1,750	6,890
180	4,000	2,250	6,250
220	3,270	2,750	6,020
240	3,000	3,000	6,000
260	2,770	3,250	6,020
300	2,400	3,750	6,150
340	2,120	4,250	6,370
400	1,800	5,000	6,800
500	1,440	6,250	7,690

quantity/cost relationships

As the table shows, the lower Qs incur high order costs, as expected; but carrying costs are low. As Q increases to 240, ordering costs decrease because the number of orders per year decreases, but carrying costs increase because of the higher average inventories. Beyond 240 units, the incremental increase in carrying cost exceeds incremental decrease in order costs; so total costs increase.

By defining the optimum Q in total cost terms, the information in Table 7–1 shows that a Q of 240 is optimal. Figure 7–8 also demonstrates this: the TAC curve between EOQ values of 180–200 and 300–320 is quite shallow. This means that the inventory manager can alter the EOQ considerably without significantly affecting TAC.

Reorder Point

reorder point

A previous discussion indicated that knowing when to order was as necessary as knowing how much to order. The *when*, generally called a reorder point,

FIGURE 7–8   GRAPHICAL REPRESENTATION OF EOQ EXAMPLE

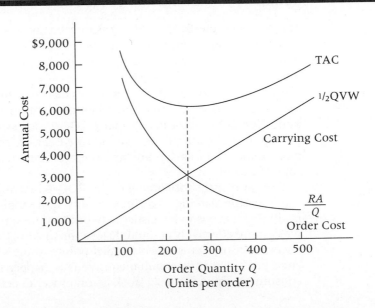

depends on inventory level—that is, some number of units. Under the assumptions of certainty, a firm needs only enough inventory to last during the replenishment time or lead time. Therefore, given a known lead time, multiplying lead time length by daily demand determines the reorder point.

Replenishment time consists of several components: order transmittal, order processing, order preparation, and delivery. The time involved depends on factors such as the order transmittal means between the buyer and seller, whether the vendor must produce the order to order or can fill it from available stock, and the transportation mode used. We will discuss the many variables affecting lead time later in this text.

example calculation

Using the previous example, assume that order transmittal will take one day; order processing and preparation, two days and delivery, five days. This results in a total of eight days for replenishment time or lead time. Given that demand is ten units per day (3,600 ÷ 360), the reorder point will be eighty units (8 days × 10 units per day).

A Note Concerning the Min-Max Approach

One widely used adaptation of the fixed order quantity approach is the *min-max* inventory management approach. With the traditional fixed quantity approach, inventory will implicitly deplete in small increments, allowing a firm to initiate a replenishment order exactly when inventory reaches the reorder point.

demand patterns

The min-max approach applies when demand may be larger and when the amount on hand may fall below the reorder point before the firm initiates a replenishment order. In this case, the min-max approach increments the amount ordered by the difference between the reorder point and the amount on hand. In effect, this technique identifies the *minimum* amount that a firm should order so that inventory on hand will reach a predetermined *maximum* level when the firm receives the order. While the min-max system is very similar to the EOQ approach, individual order amounts will tend to vary.

Summary and Evaluation of the Fixed Order Quantity Approach

Traditionally, the EOQ-based approach has been a cornerstone of effective inventory management. While not always the fastest way to respond to customer demand, the fixed order quantity approach has been a useful and widely used technique.

recent emphasis on push systems

Recently, however, many companies have become more sophisticated in their use of EOQ-based approaches, adapting them to include a push as well as a pull orientation. As a result, many EOQ-based systems effectively blend both push and pull concepts. As we indicated earlier, push, or proactive, inventory management approaches are far more prevalent in firms having greater logistics sophistication.

shortcomings

One principal shortcoming of the EOQ-based approach is that it suits inventory decision making at a single facility more than it suits decision making at multiple locations in a logistics network. (Some approaches we will discuss later work more effectively at multiple locations.) Also, the EOQ approach sometimes encounters problems when parallel points in the same logistics system experience peak demands simultaneously. This happens, for example, when many consumers simultaneously stock up on groceries before a major snowstorm. The

EOQ system alone, reacting only to demand levels as they occurred, would be too late to replenish needed inventory.

relaxing assumptions

We stated at the outset that the simple EOQ approach, though somewhat unrealistic because of the number of assumptions it required, was still useful because it illustrated the logic of inventory models in general. Actually, firms can adjust the simple model to handle more complex situations. More than 200 variations now assist inventory-related decision making in various areas. Appendix 7A covers EOQ approach applications in four special instances: (1) when a firm must consider the cost of inventory in transit; (2) when volume transportation rates are available; (3) when a firm uses private carriage; and (4) when a firm utilizes in-excess rates.

independent demand

Typically, firms associate EOQ-based approaches with independent, rather than dependent, demand. The overall approach explicitly involves carrying calculated average inventory amounts; the tradeoffs between inventory, order/ setup, and expected stockout costs justify carrying these amounts. As we refine our ability to design flexible and responsive logistics systems and to significantly reduce marginal ordering and setup expenses, the value of this trade-off-based approach will diminish. Therefore, we will focus attention away from approaches such as the EOQ toward other inventory management approaches.

FIXED ORDER QUANTITY APPROACH (CONDITION OF UNCERTAINTY)

certainty

Under the assumptions used until now, the the reorder point was based on amount of stock remaining in the warehouse. We assumed that the usage or sales rate was uniform and constant. After selling the last unit of a particular EOQ amount, a firm received another order or batch, thus incurring no stockout costs (lost sales). Although assuming such conditions of certainty may be useful, these conditions do not represent the usual operating situation for most organizations.

demand variations

Most companies would not find conditions of certainty normal for a variety of reasons. First, customers usually purchase products somewhat sporadically. The usage rates of many items vary depending on weather, social needs, psychological needs, and a whole host of other factors. As a result, sales of most items vary day by day, week by week, or season by season.

transit time variations

In addition, several factors can affect lead time or replenishment time. For example, transit times can and do change, particularly for distances over 500 miles, despite carrier efforts. In fact, for a firm deciding what transportation mode or agency to use or choosing a particular transportation company within a particular mode, the reliability of expected carrier transit times is an important factor.

order processing time variations

Another factor that can cause variations in lead time or replenishment time is order processing and transmittal. Mailed orders can cause delays. Clerks can overlook a particular order or develop undesirable backlogs. Problems in this area have led firms to develop and enhance computer systems for order processing and associated activities.

For a firm producing or manufacturing an item to order, production schedules can vary for a number of reasons. Other factors that could have an effect on lead time or replenishment time have been discussed throughout the preceding chapters.

damage

In addition to varying demand rates and replenishment times, the logistics manager can experience problems with merchandise lost in transit or damaged, in which case the firm would have to reorder the goods. Even though the carrier would usually be liable, the damage could cause a short-run stockout situation, resulting in lost sales. Figure 7–9 shows the inventory model under conditions of uncertainty.

probability distributions

Sometimes the inventory situation may seem hopeless. Fortunately, this is not the case. Statisticians refer to these variables as *stochastic,* or random variables. Experience with a particular company and associated study will enable the manager to develop probability distributions for these variables and to apply expected-value analysis to determine the optimum reorder point.

safety stock

The manager may choose several approaches to solving the problem. An essential factor in any approach is the level of safety stock, or buffer stock, a firm requires to cover variations. Logistics managers must analyze requirements very carefully so as not to maintain too much safety stock because it incurs excess inventory cost. On the other hand, a company without enough safety stock will experience a stockout, with consequent loss of sales.

Reorder Point—A Special Note

reorder point with safety stock

As we noted previously, the reorder point under the basic model is the inventory level sufficient to satisfy demand until the order arrives. Calculating the reorder point is straightforward, since demand or usage is constant, as is lead time. Therefore, a firm can multiply daily demand or usage by lead time in days and place an order for the determined quantity when inventory reaches the reorder point. Under uncertainty, the firm must reformulate the reorder point to allow for safety stock. In effect, the reorder point becomes the average daily demand during lead time plus the safety stock, as Figure 7–9 graphically depicts. The following discussion clarifies this recalculation.

Uncertainty of Demand

Dealing first with only one factor that may cause uncertainty would probably be easiest. The best and most common example would be the sales rate or usage

FIGURE 7–9   INVENTORY MODEL UNDER CONDITIONS OF UNCERTAINTY

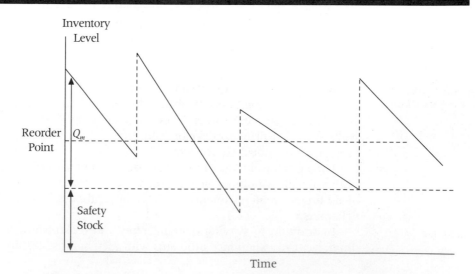

rate. As we focus on this variable, the following assumptions about the EOQ model still apply:

1. A constant or known replenishment or lead time
2. Constant price or cost that is independent of order quantity or time (e.g., purchase price or transport cost)
3. No inventory in transit
4. One item of inventory or no interaction between items
5. Infinite planning horizon
6. No limit on capital availability

balancing cost

In discussing uncertainty in sales, logistics managers emphasize balancing safety stock carrying costs and stockout (lost sales) costs.

In a fixed quantity model with an established reorder level, introducing uncertainty into the analysis initially affects inventory level needs to cover sales during lead time. Recall that in the previous example, conditions of certainty resulted in an EOQ amount of 240 units and a reorder point of 100 units. In other words, the inventory period began with 240 units on hand; and reordering occurred when inventory reached a level of 100 units.

The fact that sales may vary—and that the time elapsing between a level of 240 units and 100 units may also vary—is not critical to the inventory problem when conditions of uncertainty exist. Determining whether 100 units is the best amount to have on hand at the start of the lead time or replenishment cycle is critical. Thus, raising the reorder level accounts for safety stock. However, raising it too high will leave too much stock on hand when the next order arrives. Setting it too low will cause a stockout.

example

Using the previous problem, assume that the hypothetical firm's demand during lead time ranges from 100 units to 160 units, with an average of 130 units. Furthermore, assume that demand has a discrete distribution varying in ten-unit blocks and that the firm has established probabilities for these demand levels (see Table 7–2).

In effect, the firm must consider seven different reorder points, each corresponding to a possible demand level listed in Table 7–2. Using this information, we can develop the matrix that appears as Table 7–3.

While Table 7–3 shows many of the possible situations confronting the hypothetical firm, it does not use information from the probability distribution of demand. Using the probability distribution of demand would permit the firm with seven possible reorder points to determine the expected units "short" or "in excess" during lead time at each point.

TABLE 7–2   PROBABILITY DISTRIBUTION OF DEMAND DURING LEAD TIME

Demand	Probability
100 units	0.01
110	0.06
120	0.24
130	0.38
140	0.24
150	0.06
160	0.01

TABLE 7–3   POSSIBLE UNITS OF INVENTORY SHORT OR IN EXCESS DURING LEAD TIME WITH VARIOUS REORDER POINTS

Actual Demand	Reorder Points						
	100	110	120	130	140	150	160
100	0	10	20	30	40	50	60
110	10	0	10	20	30	40	50
120	20	10	0	10	20	30	40
130	30	20	10	0	10	20	30
140	40	30	20	10	0	10	20
150	50	40	30	20	10	0	10
160	60	50	40	30	20	10	0

Assume that the firm experiences a stockout cost (k) of $10 per unit whenever a customer demands a unit that is not in stock. The profit lost on the immediate sale and future sales is an opportunity cost.

We calculate inventory carrying cost associated with safety stock in the same way as we calculated carrying cost for the simple EOQ model. We still assume the value per unit of inventory to be $100, and the percentage annual inventory carrying cost is 25%. Remember that the percentage figure is for annual cost of inventory in the warehouse. Therefore, the $25 we derive by multiplying 25% by $100 is the annual cost per unit of inventory in the warehouse. The $25 contrasts with the $10 stockout cost, which is a unit cost per cycle or order period. Therefore, as Table 7–4 shows, multiplying the $25 by the number of cycles or orders per year puts this cost on an annual basis.

Table 7–4 develops expected units short or in excess by multiplying actual demand across the matrix by the probabilities associated with each demand level. We can add the numbers below (shorts) and above (excesses) the horizontal line, as the lower portion of Table 7–4 shows, to find the number of units the firm expects to be short or in excess at each of the seven possible reorder points. The calculation variables are as follows:

e = expected excess in units
g = expected shorts in units
k = stockout cost in dollars per unit stocked out
$G = gk$ = expected stockout cost per cycle
$G\dfrac{R}{Q}$ = expected stockout cost per year
eVW = expected carrying cost per year for excess inventory

After performing the calculations indicated in Table 7–4, we may determine the total cost for each of the seven reorder levels. In this instance, the lowest total cost corresponds to the reorder point of 140 units. Although this number does not guarantee an excess or shortage in any particular period, overall it gives the lowest expected total cost per year: $390.

Note that the number of orders per year used in step 5 of Table 7–4 came from the preceding problem with conditions of certainty. That number was the only information available at that point. Now, we can expand the total cost model to include the safety stock cost and stockout cost. The expanded formula would appear as follows:

TABLE 7–4   EXPECTED NUMBER OF UNITS SHORT OR IN EXCESS

Actual Demand	Probabilities	Reorder Points							
		100	110	120	130	140	150	160	
100	0.01	0.0	0.1	0.2	0.3	0.4	0.5	0.6	
110	0.06	0.6	0.0	0.6	1.2	1.8	2.4	3.0	
120	0.24	4.8	2.4	0.0	2.4	4.8	7.2	9.6	
130	0.38	11.4	7.6	3.8	0.0	3.8	7.6	11.4	
140	0.24	9.6	7.2	4.8	2.4	0.0	2.4	4.8	
150	0.06	3.0	2.4	1.8	1.2	0.6	0.0	0.6	
160	0.01	0.6	0.5	0.4	0.3	0.2	0.1	0.0	

Calculation of Lowest-Cost Reorder Point

	100	110	120	130	140	150	160	
1. Expected excess per cycle (of values above line)	0.0	0.1	0.8	3.9	10.8	20.1	30.0	(e)
2. Expected carrying cost per year	0	$ 2.50	$ 20.00	$ 97.50	$270	$502.50	$750	(VW)
3. Expected shorts per cycle (of values below line)	30.0	20.1	10.8	3.9	0.8	0.1	0.0	(g)
4. Expected stockout cost per cycle	$ 300	$ 201	$ 108	$ 39	$ 8	$ 1	$ 0	(gk) = G
5. Expected stockout costs per year	$4,500	$3,015	$1,620	$585	$120	$ 15	$ 0	$\left(G\dfrac{R}{Q}\right)$
6. Expected total cost per year (2 + 5)	$4,500	$3,017.50	$1,640	$682.50	$390	$517.50	$760	

$$\text{TAC} = \frac{1}{2}QVW + A\frac{R}{Q} + (eVW) + \left(G\frac{R}{Q}\right)$$

Solving for the lowest cost gives

$$\frac{d(\text{TAC})}{dQ} = \left[\frac{1}{2}VW\right] - \left[\frac{R(A + G)}{Q^2}\right]$$

Setting this equal to zero and solving for Q gives

$$Q = \sqrt{\frac{2R(A + G)}{VW}}$$

Using the expanded model and the computed reorder point of 140 units, we can determined a new value for Q as follows:

$$Q = \sqrt{\frac{2 \cdot 3{,}600 \cdot (200 + 8)}{100 \cdot 25\%}}$$
$$= 242 \text{ (approximately)}$$

Note that Q is now 242 units with conditions of uncertainty. Technically this would change the expected stockout cost for the various reorder points in Table 7–4. However, the change is small enough to ignore in this instance. In other cases, recalculation may be necessary. The optimum solution to the problem with conditions of uncertainty is a fixed order quantity (EOQ) of 242 units, and the firm will reorder this amount when inventory reaches a level of 140 units (the calculated reorder point).

Finally, the situation requires a recalculation of total annual cost:

$$
\begin{aligned}
\text{TAC} &= \frac{1}{2}QVW + A\frac{R}{Q} + eVW + G\frac{R}{Q} \\
&= \left(\frac{1}{2} \cdot 242 \cdot \$100 \cdot 24\%\right) + \left(200 \cdot \frac{3{,}600}{242}\right) \\
&\quad + (10.8 \cdot \$100 \cdot 25\%) + \left(8 \cdot \frac{3{,}600}{242}\right) \\
&= \$3{,}025 + \$2{,}975 + \$270 + \$119 \\
&= \$6{,}389
\end{aligned}
$$

The \$6,389 figure indicates what happens to total cost when we introduce conditions of uncertainty with respect to sales into the model. Introducing other variations, such as the lead time variable, would increase costs even more.

Uncertainty of Demand and Lead Time Length

This section considers the possibility that both demand and lead time may vary. It builds upon the preceding section in attempting to make this inventory approach more realistic. As expected, however, determining how much safety stock to carry will be noticeably more complex now than when only demand varied.

demand during lead time

As in the previous section, the critical issue is just how much product customers will demand during the lead time. If demand and lead time are constant and known in advance, calculating the reorder point (as we did in the section covering case of certainty) would be easy. Now that both demand and lead time may vary, the first step is to study the likely distribution of demand during the lead time. Specifically, we must accurately estimate the mean and standard deviation of demand during lead time.

normal distribution

Figure 7–10 illustrates three key properties of a normal distribution. The normal distribution is symmetrical, and its mean (average) equals its mode (highest point). Approximately 68.26% of the area under the normal curve lies within one standard deviation (1σ) from the mean, 95.44% within two standard deviations (2σ), and 99.73% within three standard deviations (3σ). Figure 7–10 also shows the areas under the curve that lie to the left and right of one, two, and three standard deviations from the mean.

After calculating values for the mean and standard deviation of demand during lead time, we can describe the stockout probability for each particular reorder point. For example, imagine that Figure 7–10 represents demand distribution during lead time. Setting the reorder point equal to $X + 1\sigma$ will result in an 84.13% probability that lead time demand will not exceed the inventory amount available. Increasing the reorder point to $X + 2\sigma$ raises the probability of not incurring a stockout to 97.72%; reordering at $X + 3\sigma$ raises this probability to 99.87%. Note that in the case of uncertainty, increasing the reorder point has the same effect as increasing the safety stock commitment. A firm must ultimately find some means to justify carrying this additional inventory.

calculations

We may calculate the mean and standard deviations for lead time demand using the following formulas:[5]

$$
\overline{X} = \overline{R}(\overline{X}_{LT})
$$

and

$$
\sigma = \sqrt{\overline{X}_{LT}(\sigma_R)^2 + \overline{R}^2(\sigma_{LT})^2}
$$

FIGURE 7–10   NORMAL DISTRIBUTION

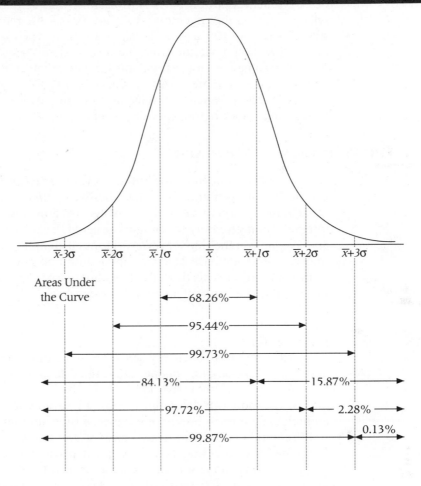

where

$\overline{X}$ = mean (average) demand during lead time

σ = standard deviation of demand during lead time

$\overline{X}_{LT}$ = mean (average) lead time length

σ_{LT} = standard deviation of lead time length

$\overline{R}$ = mean (average) daily demand

σ_R = standard deviation of daily demand

example   For example, if the mean and standard deviations of daily demand are twenty and four units, respectively, and if the mean and standard deviations of lead time length are eight and two days, respectively, then we will calculate the mean and standard deviations of demand during lead time as follows:

$$\overline{X} = \overline{R}(\overline{X}_{LT})$$
$$= 20(8)$$
$$= 160$$
$$\sigma = \sqrt{\overline{X}_{LT}(\sigma_R)^2 + \overline{R}^2(\sigma_{LT})^2}$$
$$= \sqrt{8(4)^2 + 20^2(2)^2}$$
$$= \sqrt{1728}$$
$$= 41.57, \text{ or } 42$$

Using the procedure suggested earlier, setting the reorder point at $\overline{X} + 1\sigma$, or 202 units reveals an 84.13% probability that demand during the lead time will not exceed the inventory available. Stated differently, the probability of a stockout is only 100% − 84.13%, or 15.87%, when we set the reorder point at one standard deviation from the mean. Table 7−5 shows these figures and the ones computed for setting the reorder point at two and three standard deviations from the mean. A firm should thoroughly compare the financial and customer service benefits of avoiding stockouts with the cost of carrying additional safety stock before choosing a reorder point.

FIXED ORDER INTERVAL APPROACH

The second form of the basic approach is the *fixed order interval* approach to inventory management, also called the *fixed period* or *fixed review period* approach. In essence, this technique involves ordering inventory at fixed or regular intervals; and generally the amount ordered depends on how much is in stock and available at the time or review. Firms customarily count inventory near the interval's end and base orders on the amount on hand at the time.

lower cost of monitoring inventory

In comparison with the basic EOQ approach, the fixed interval model does not require close surveillance of inventory levels; thus, monitoring is less expensive. A firm can order low-valued items infrequently and in large quantities, checking only infrequently to determine exactly how much is on hand at any particular time.

In other instances, delivery schedules or salespeople's visits necessitate this approach. This happens frequently in retail food stores, where deliveries may be daily for some items, weekly or biweekly for others, and monthly for still others. The store can determine a desired inventory level in advance and order enough each time to bring the number of units up that level.

If demand and lead time are constant and known in advance, then a firm using the fixed order interval approach will periodically reorder exactly the same amount of inventory. If either demand or lead time varies, however, then the amount ordered each time will vary, becoming a result of demand as well as lead time length. For example, as Figure 7−11 indicates, a company starting each period with 4,000 units and selling 2,500 units before its next order will have to reorder 2,500 units plus the units it anticipates selling during the lead time to bring inventory up to the desired beginning level of 4,000 units. Figure 7−11 shows an instance where the amount ordered differs from one five-week period to the next.

As with the fixed order quantity approach to inventory management, the fixed order interval approach typically combines elements of both the pull and push philosophies. This shows again how firms, in an effort to anticipate de-

TABLE 7−5   REORDER POINT ALTERNATIVES AND STOCKOUT PROBABILITIES

Reorder Point	Probability of No Stockout Occurring	Probability of a Stockout Situation
$\overline{X} + 1\sigma = 202$	84.13%	15.87%
$\overline{X} + 2\sigma = 244$	97.72%	2.28%
$\overline{X} + 3\sigma = 286$	99.87%	0.13%

FIGURE 7–11   FIXED INTERVAL MODEL (WITH SAFETY STOCK)

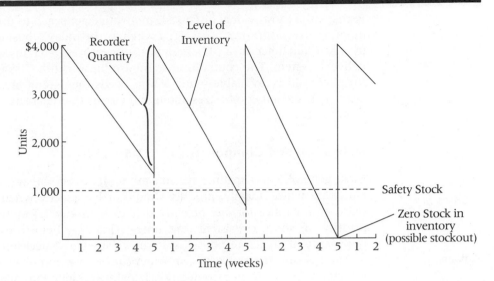

mand, rather than simply react to it, are developing systems that incorporate the push philosophy.

SUMMARY AND EVALUATION OF TRADITIONAL APPROACHES TO INVENTORY MANAGEMENT

relationship to ABC analysis

Some authors have argued that there are really four basic forms of the inventory model: fixed quantity/fixed interval, fixed quantity/irregular interval, irregular quantity/fixed interval, and irregular quantity/irregular interval. In a firm knowing demand and lead time length with certainty, then either the basic EOQ or the fixed order interval approach will be the best choice (and would produce the same answer). If either demand or lead time varies, however, approach selection must consider potential stockout consequences. In instances involving A items, a fixed quantity/irregular interval approach may be the best. The irregular quantity/fixed interval approach might be the best when C items are involved. Only under very restrictive circumstances could a firm justify using the irregular quantity/irregular interval approach to inventory management.

importance of trade-offs

The fixed order quantity (EOQ) and fixed order interval approaches have proven to be effective inventory management tools when demand and lead time are relatively stable, as well as when significant variability and uncertainty exist. Most importantly, studying these approaches requires us to gain familiarity with the inherent logistics trade-offs critical to inventory policy decision making.

new concepts

In today's business environment, however, firms expanding beyond the basic order quantity and order interval approaches have had considerable success with newer concepts such as just-in-time, MRP, and DRP. Thus, the remaining sections of this chapter focus on these topics. Throughout these discussions, we should understand that trade-offs are critical to successful inventory policy decisions regardless of the approach used. Thus, while the EOQ-based approaches have some obvious deficiencies when compared with the newer approaches, they continue to be very useful learning tools.

Just-In-Time Approach

Perhaps the most widely discussed, innovative approach to inventory management is the *just-in-time*, or JIT, approach. In today's business environment people often refer to a JIT manufacturing process, JIT inventories, or a JIT delivery system. The commonsense phrase "just-in-time" suggests that inventories should be available when a firm needs them—not any earlier, nor any later. This section emphasizes additional factors that characterize a true just-in-time system.

Definition and Components of JIT Systems

Most generally, just-in-time systems are designed to manage lead times and to eliminate waste. Ideally, product should arrive exactly when a firm needs it, with no tolerance for late or early deliveries. Many JIT systems place a high priority on short, consistent lead times. This may help to explain the recent popularity of "quick response" systems for inventory decision making.

Kanban   The just-in-time concept is an Americanized version of the Kanban system, which the Toyota Motor Company originally developed in Japan. *Kanban* refers to the informative signboards attached to carts delivering small amounts of needed components and other materials to locations within Japanese plants. Each signboard precisely details the necessary replenishment quantities, and the exact time when the resupply activity must take place.

JIT operations   Production cards (*kan* cards) establish and authorize the amount of product to be manufactured or produced; requisition cards (*ban* cards) authorize the withdrawal of needed materials from the feeding or supply operation. Given a knowledge of daily output volumes, these activities can be accomplished manually, without the need for computer assistance. Finally, an *Andon* system, or light system, is used as a means to notify plant personnel of existing problems— a yellow light for a small problem, and a red light for a major problem. Either light can be seen by personnel throughout the plant. In this way, workers are advised of the possibility of an interruption to the production/manufacturing process, if the problem warrants such action.[6]

Experience to date indicates effectively implementing this concept can dramatically reduce parts and materials inventories, work in process, and finished product. In addition, the Kanban and just-in-time concepts rely heavily on the quality of the manufactured product and components, and also on a capable and precise logistics system to manage materials and physical distribution.

fundamental concepts   Four major elements underpin the just-in-time concept; zero inventories; short lead times; small, frequent replenishment quantities; and high quality, or zero defects. JIT, a modern approach to distribution, production, inventory, and scheduling management, is an operating concept based on delivering materials in exact amounts and at the precise times companies need them—thus minimizing inventory costs. JIT improves quality and minimizes waste, and can completely change the way a firm performs its logistics activities.

similarity to two-bin system   The JIT system operates in a manner very similar to the two-bin or reorder point system. The system uses one bin to fill demand for a part; when that bin is empty (the stimulus to replenish the part), the second bin supplies the part. Toyota has been very successful with this system because of its master production schedule, which aims to schedule every product, every day, in a sequence that intermixes all parts. Producing these products in small quantities through short production runs also creates a relatively continuous demand for supplies and component parts. In theory, the ideal lot size or order size for a JIT-based system is one unit. Obviously, this encourages firms to reduce or eliminate setup costs and incremental ordering costs.

reducing lead times

By adhering to extremely small lot sizes and very short lead times, the just-in-time approach can dramatically reduce lead times. For example, when manufacturing forklift trucks, Toyota experienced a cumulative material lead time of one month, top to bottom, including final assembly, subassembly, fabrication, and purchasing. American manufacturers of forklift trucks cited lead times ranging from six to nine months.[7]

pull system

Just-in-time is a pull system in that firms place orders for more inventory only when the amount on hand reaches a certain level, thus pulling inventory through the system as needed. JIT also relates to the concept of dependent demand in that the demand for individual parts and items typically depends on the demand for the finished product. Finally, although the just-in-time approach can apply to systemwide problems, it predominantly applies to inventory management at a single facility.

JIT versus Traditional Approaches to Inventory Management

Table 7–6 highlights key ways in which the JIT philosophy differs from traditional inventory management in U.S. firms. This section discusses the critical differences.

reduce inventories

First, JIT attempts to eliminate excess inventories for both the buyer and the seller. Some people feel that the JIT concept simply forces the seller to carry inventory that the buyer previously held. However, successful JIT applications will significantly reduce inventory for both parties.

shorter production runs

Second, JIT systems typically involve short production runs and require production and manufacturing activities to change frequently from one product to the next. Historically, U.S. manufacturing operations have benefited from the economies associated with lengthy production runs. Controlling and minimizing frequent changeover cost is critical to a JIT program's success.

TABLE 7–6 TRADITIONAL VERSUS JIT ATTITUDES AND BEHAVIORS

Factor	Traditional	JIT
1. Inventory	Asset	Liability
Safety Stock	Yes	No
2. Production Runs	Long	Short
Setup Times	Amortize	Minimize
Lot Sizes	EOQ	1-for-1
3. Queues	Eliminate	Necessary
4. Lead Times	Tolerate	Shorter
5. Quality	Important	100%
Inspection	Parts	Process
6. Suppliers/	Adversary	Partners
Customers	Multiple	Single
Supply Sources	Instruct	Involve
Employees		

Source: Adapted from William M. Boyst, Jr. III, "JIT American Style." Conference proceedings for the American Production & Inventory Control Society (1988), 468.

minimize waiting lines

Third, JIT minimizes waiting lines by delivering materials and components when and where firms need them. U.S. automobile manufacturers using the JIT approach, for example, typically have replenishment inventory delivered exactly where the manufacturer needs parts for finished product.

short, consistent lead times

Fourth, the JIT concept uses short, consistent lead times to satisfy the need for more inventory in a timely manner. This is why suppliers tend to concentrate their facilities within a radius near manufacturing facilities planning to use the JIT approach. For example, once the Saturn Corporation, a wholly owned subsidiary of General Motors Corporation, decided to locate its plant in central Tennessee, many potential suppliers planned to locate new facilities in the surrounding area.

quality

Fifth, JIT-based systems rely on high-quality incoming products and components and on exceptionally high-quality inbound logistics operations. The fact that JIT systems synchronize manufacturing and assembly with timely, predictable receipt of inbound materials reinforces this need.

win-win relationships

Sixth, the JIT concept requires a strong, mutual commitment between the buyer and seller, one that emphasizes quality and seeks win-win decisions for both parties. JIT success requires a concern for minimizing inventory throughout the distribution channel (or the supply channel); JIT will not succeed if firms only push inventory back to another channel member.

Examples of JIT Successes

inventory savings

Implementing the JIT concept has resulted in notable successes in the United States.[8] One such success occurred at Apple Computer's Macintosh plant in Fremont, California, where the company's goal of achieving twenty-five annual inventory turnovers translated into a reduction in float from ten weeks to two weeks, and a payback for the $20 million plant in just eighteen months. During the mid-1980s, General Motors Corporation credited JIT for the fact that its total raw material, work in process, and finished goods inventory increased by only six percent over two years, while production levels increased 100 percent.

rail example

Other examples include a thirty-two-car minitrain Conrail operates between a parts facility in Kalamazoo, Michigan, and a General Motors Oldsmobile plant in Lansing, Michigan.[9] The operation involved no rail car switching, and Conrail has successfully met its customers' pickup and delivery times.

motor carriers

Innovative motor carriers have designed supply systems that effectively fulfill JIT requirements. For example, Ryder Distribution Resources provides all inbound logistical support for direct materials moving into Saturn Corporation's plant in Spring Hill, Tennessee.[10] Similarly, Averitt Express, a Tennessee-based provider of high-quality regional and interregional freight transportation services, designed and operates a system for Saturn to ensure that indirect materials moving into the same plant meet JIT-based priorities.

Based on the availability of high-quality, dependable transportation services which can fit a JIT-based production system's precise demands, various automobile manufacturers have justified eliminating several previously significant freight consolidation systems. The functions of these centers have been replaced by the delivery of needed parts precisely when and where manufacturers need them.[11]

Figure 7–12 shows how a firm can use a transportation strategy known as the orderly pickup concept to meet JIT-based manufacturing needs. The diagram shows how a firm may use time-sequenced motor carrier pickup from suppliers in conjunction with rail-motor intermodal service to meet JIT requirements.

FIGURE 7–12 ORDERLY PICKUP CONCEPT *Source:* Charles B. Lounsbury, Leaseway Transportation Corp., reprinted with permission.

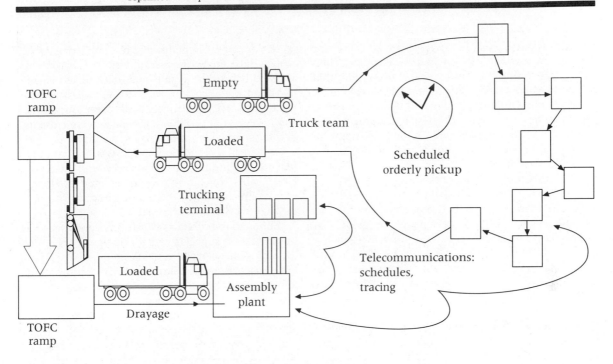

Summary and Evaluation of JIT

The just-in-time concept can enable logistics managers to reduce unit cost and to enhance customer service. A close examination of JIT-based approaches shows that they resemble the more basic reactive systems such as the EOQ and fixed order interval approaches.

comparison with traditional approaches

The principal difference between JIT and the more traditional approaches is the JIT commitment to short, consistent lead times and to minimizing or eliminating inventories. In effect, it saves money on downstream inventories by placing greater reliance on improved responsiveness and flexibility. Ideally, the use of JIT helps to synchronize the system so thoroughly that its functioning doesn't depend on inventories strategically located at points throughout the logistics system.

interface with manufacturing

Successful JIT applications also place a high priority on efficient and dependable production and manufacturing processes. Since JIT systems require the delivery of parts and subassemblies when and where the need arises, they rely heavily on the accuracy of the forecasting process used to anticipate finished product demand. In addition, timely JIT system operation demands effective and dependable communications and information systems, as well as high-quality, consistent transportation services.

Business firms gaining additional experience with JIT-based approaches to manufacturing and logistics are sure to increasingly accept this concept.

MATERIALS REQUIREMENTS PLANNING

Another inventory and scheduling approach that has received much recent attention is *materials requirements planning,* or MRP. Originally popularized

HOW GM-CANADA MAKES JIT GO

Because auto manufacturers have championed America's fascination with Just In Time production out of necessity, it should come as no surprise that General Motors is spending almost $2 billion to make its Oshawa, Ontario, plant one of the most efficient JIT facilities anywhere. The Oshawa Autoplex will have an annual capacity of 730,000 vehicles, and will utilize the latest in robotics and automated production systems.

The thrust behind JIT is to reduce inventory, because less inventory translates into substantial savings. In 1984, before JIT. GM attained twenty-four inventory turns at its Oshawa plants. Using JIT, GM expected to reach fifty inventory turns in 1988.

"Each inventory turn is worth $1 million in savings," said Joseph A. Pegg, GM-Canada's director of materials management. A veteran with thirty-one years of experience as a plant manager for both cars and trucks, Pegg stressed that JIT materials management is much more than just inventory reduction for the sake of capital costs. "Inventory costs are just the tip of the iceberg," he said. "The Japanese understood very early that if you centered decision making, plant layout and your whole process around absolute minimum inventories, then you solve a lot of problems and become more efficient."

For instance, warehousing parts in the plant is on the way out. Instead, carriers deliver shipments in small lots to point-of-use receiving docks. A carrier is instructed electronically to send a load to one of the forty-two receiving docks located around the Autoplex perimeter. Carriers then move the parts as needed from the receiving dock to the production line point that needs them.

Before JIT, all receiving docks were at the back of the plant. A carrier would unload material at one spot, and it would be moved to a central storage area. Later, the parts would be picked up and moved to the assembly line.

The point-of-use receiving system, explained Pegg, eliminates this extra cargo handling. Since inventory arrives just before its use, the only storage it needs is that directly adjacent to the line. "We didn't want to build storage," said Pegg. "The system frees floor space and you manage by sight. It becomes very obvious if you run out of material because there should be two skids of material beside the line at all times." Storage has become the responsibility of the supplier or the carrier, depending on the arrangement.

At this stage, GM planned to have only one day's worth of material at its assembly sites. This did not apply to items such as nuts and bolts, but to larger parts and metal components. "In the next two or three years, we have targeted sixty-five turns in a year," Pegg said. "To do that, we'll be very close to keeping inventories to one day's material."

As part of its transition to JIT, GM dramatically reduced the number of carriers serving its five Oshawa plants from fifty to five. GM entered into long-term contracts with the remaining truckers to ensure the high service level required JIT.

Although the contracts which GM signed with its transportation suppliers contain no penalty clauses, the arrangements reflect certain improvements. Since timing is critical these firms obtain schedules and information from all over North America through GM's mainframe computer in Oshawa.

"We piloted an electronic communications system that allows us to be on-line with suppliers," Pegg said. "It gives accurate information and we don't have to send pieces of paper back and forth." GM expected its carriers and suppliers to provide their own computer hardware, but paid for dedicated transmission line use.

For JIT to work well, a company has to attain a high level of quality. "JIT eliminates waste," he said. "We used to have so many waste operations. With the improvement in quality, you do away with all the sorting and processing of reject material, and the shipping back and forth and haggling over who should pay for it."

Due to its large scale, the automotive industry relentlessly pursues cost efficiency. JIT is one component in the quest, automation is another, and so is world sourcing. "We look everywhere for cost competitiveness," Pegg explained. GM seat belts and wiring harnesses come from Ireland, radios and engines from Mexico, and aluminum wheels from West Germany. Once the cargo is in North America, GM relies more and more on trucks for transport. Rail's unit costs are lower, but the accumulation of large inventories doesn't blend well with JIT manufacturing.

Source: Adapted from Andrew Tausz, "How GM-Canada Makes JIT Go," *Distribution* (March 1988), 38–40. Reprinted by Permission of Chilton's DISTRIBUTION Magazine, Radnor, PA.

by Joseph Orlicky,[12] MRP deals specifically with supplying materials and component parts whose demand depends upon the demand for a specific end product. MRP's underlying concepts have existed for many years, but only recently computers and information systems have permitted firms to benefit fully from MRP approaches.

Definition and Operation of MRP Systems

computing net requirements

According to Orlicky, "a material requirements planning (MRP) system, narrowly defined, consists of a set of logically related procedures, decision rules, and records designed to translate a master production schedule into time-phased 'net requirements,' and the planned 'coverage' of such requirements for each component inventory item needed to implement this schedule. . . . An MRP system replans net requirements and coverage as a result of changes in either the master production schedule, inventory status, or product composition."[13] Orlicky writes that "MRP systems meet their objective by computing net requirements for each inventory item, time-phasing them, and determining their proper coverage."[14]

goals of MRP system

The goals of an MRP system are to (1) ensure the availability of materials, components, and products for planned production and for customer delivery; (2) maintain the lowest possible inventory level; and (3) plan manufacturing activities, delivery schedules, and purchasing activities.[15] In so doing, the MRP system considers current and planned quantities of parts and inventory products, as well as the time used for planning.

exploding demand for component parts

MRP begins by determining how much end product customers desire, and when they need it. Then MRP "explodes" the timing and need for components based upon the scheduled end product need. Figure 7–13 shows how an MRP system operates. We will discuss each key element in this section.

master production schedule

Master Production Schedule Based on actual customer orders as well as demand forecasts, the master production schedule, or MPS, drives the entire

FIGURE 7–13   MRP System

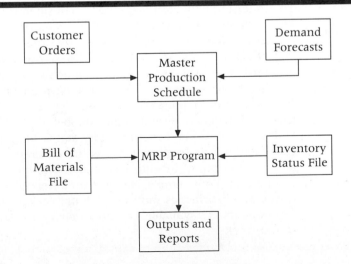

MRP system. The MPS details exactly what end products a company must manufacture or assemble, and when the customers need them.

bill of materials file

Bill of Materials File   Just as a recipe specifies the ingredients needed to bake a cake, the bill of materials file specifies the exact amount of raw materials, components, and subassemblies needed to manufacture or assemble the end product. Besides identifying gross requirements as needed quantities, the bill of materials file tells when the individual inputs must be available. This file also identifies how the various inputs to one another relate and shows their relative importance to producing the end product.

inventory status file

Inventory Status File   This file maintains inventory records so that the company may subtract the amount on hand from the gross requirements, thus identifying the net requirements at any time. The inventory status file also contains important information on things such as safety stock needs for certain items and lead times.

MRP program

MRP Program   Based on the end product need specified in the master production schedule and on information from the bill of materials file, the MRP program first explodes the end product demand into gross requirements for individual parts and other materials. Then the program calculates net requirements based on inventory status file information and places orders for inputs necessary to the production/assembly process. The orders respond to needs for specific quantities of materials and to the timing of those needs. The example in the next section clarifies these MRP program activities.

outputs and reports

Outputs and Reports   After a firm completes the MRP program, several basic outputs and reports will help managers involved in logistics, manufacturing, and assembly. Included are records and information related to the following: (1) quantities the company should order and when, (2) any need to expedite or reschedule arrival dates or needed product quantities, (3) cancelled need for product, and (4) MRP system status.

Example of an MRP System

MRP example

To understand the MRP approach, consider a company that assembles egg timers. Assume that according to the master production schedule, the company desires to assemble a single, finished egg timer for delivery to a customer at the end of eight weeks. The MRP application would proceed as described below.

Figure 7–14 shows the bill of materials for assembling a single egg timer. The gross requirements for one finished product include two ends, one bulb, three supports, and one gram of sand. Figure 7–14 also shows that the company must add the gram of sand to the bulb before assembling the finished egg timer.

Table 7–7 displays the inventory status file for the egg timer example and calculates the net requirements as the difference between gross requirements and the amount of inventory on hand. The table notes the lead time for each component. For example, the lead time needed to procure supports and bulbs is one week, whereas sand needs four weeks and ends require five. Once all components are available, the time needed to assemble the finished egg timer is one week.

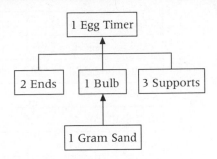

Finally, Figure 7–15 is the master schedule for all activities relating to ordering and receiving components and assembling the finished egg timer. Because the company must have the single egg timer assembled and ready for customer delivery at the end of eight weeks, appropriate parts quantities must be available in the seventh week. The upper portion of Figure 7–15 shows this requirement.

Working backward from the need for parts in the seventh week, the lower portions of Figure 7–15 identify strategies for ordering and receiving component inventories. For example, for two ends requiring a lead time of five weeks, the company must place an order in the second week. For the one additional support requiring a lead time of a single week, the company should release an order during the sixth week. Finally, the company must order the bulb in the sixth week for delivery in the seventh, and order the sand in the second week for delivery in the sixth.

This example illustrates how the MRP-based approach relates to inventory scheduling and inventory control. In effect, the MRP program itself would perform the calculations involved in Figure 7–15. Once the program develops the master schedule, reports present this information in a format suitable for manager use. The company would place orders for needed parts in quantities and at times described.

In actual practice, MRP is exceptionally suitable for planning and controlling the ordering and receipt of large numbers of parts and products that may interact during assembly or manufacture. With the exception of very simple problems such as the egg timer example, computerization is virtually a prerequisite to using MRP-based applications. Only through the processing speed and manipulative capabilities of modern computer systems can a firm perform MRP's inner workings cost-effectively.

TABLE 7-7   INVENTORY STATUS FILE: MRP EGG TIMER EXAMPLE

Product	Gross Requirements	Inventory On Hand	Net Requirements	Lead Time (in weeks)
Egg timers	1	0	1	1
Ends	2	0	2	5
Supports	3	2	1	1
Bulbs	1	0	1	1
Sand	1	0	1	4

FIGURE 7–15   MASTER SCHEDULE: MRP EGG TIMER EXAMPLE

EGG TIMERS (LT=1)	1	2	3	4	5	6	7	8
Quantity Needed								1
Production Schedule							1	

ENDS (LT=5)	1	2	3	4	5	6	7	8
Gross Requirements							2	
Inventory On Hand	0	0	0	0	0	0	0	
Scheduled Receipts							2	
Planned Order Releases		2						

SUPPORTS (LT=1)	1	2	3	4	5	6	7	8
Gross Requirements							3	
Inventory On Hand	2	2	2	2	2	2	2	
Scheduled Receipts							1	
Planned Order Releases						1		

BULBS (LT=1)	1	2	3	4	5	6	7	8
Gross Requirements							1	
Inventory On Hand	0	0	0	0	0	0	0	
Scheduled Receipts							1	
Planned Order Releases						1		

SAND (LT=4)	1	2	3	4	5	6	7	8
Gross Requirements						1		
Inventory On Hand	0	0	0	0	0	0		
Scheduled Receipts						1		
Planned Order Releases		1						

Summary and Evaluation of MRP Systems

Having established the master production schedule, the MRP program develops a time-phased approach to inventory scheduling and inventory receipt. Because it generates a list of required materials in order to assemble or manufacture a specified number of finished products, MRP represents a "push" approach.

Correspondingly, this encourages purchase order and production order development. Typically, MRP applies primarily when parts and materials demand depends on the demand for some specific end product. MRP can deal with systemwide material supplies.

responsiveness

Since actual demand is key to establishing of production schedules, MRP systems can react quickly to changing demand for finished products. Although some JIT proponents feel that a "pull" approach is inherently more responsive than a "push" approach such as MRP, the reverse is sometimes true. MRP systems can also help firms to achieve other typical JIT objectives, such as those pertaining to lead time management and eliminating waste. In short, MRP can achieve objectives more commonly associated with the JIT-based approaches, while at times decisions made through the pull concept do not reflect the future events for which the JIT policies are intended.

strengths

The principal *advantages* of most MRP-based systems include the following:

- They try to maintain reasonable safety stock levels, and to minimize or eliminate inventories whenever possible.
- They can identify process problems and potential supply chain disruptions long before they occur and take necessary corrective action.
- Production schedules are based on actual demand as well as on forecasts of end product needs.
- They coordinate materials ordering across points in a firm's logistics system.
- They are most suitable for batch or intermittent production or assembly processes.

limitations

Shortcomings of MRP-based approaches include the following:

- Their application is computer intensive and making changes is sometimes difficult once the system is in operation.
- Both ordering and transportation costs may rise as a firm reduces inventory levels and possibly moves toward a more coordinated system of ordering product in smaller amounts to arrive when the firm needs it.
- They are not usually as sensitive to short-term fluctuations in demand as are order point approaches (although they are not as inventory intensive, either).
- They frequently become quite complex, and sometimes do not work exactly as intended (Cavinato states that "MRP only works in twenty to twenty-five percent of the situations people try to force it into").[16]

A Note Concerning MRPII Systems

advanced approaches

In recent years, *manufacturing resource planning,* or MRPII, a far more comprehensive set of tools than MRP alone, has become available. Although MRP is a key step in MRPII, MRPII allows a firm to integrate financial planning and operations/logistics.

MRPII serves as an excellent planning tool, and it helps describe the likely results of implementing strategies in areas such as logistics, manufacturing, marketing, and finance. Thus, it helps a firm to conduct "what if?" analysis and to determine appropriate product movement and storage strategies at and between points in the firm's logistics system.

Gattorna and Day state that "MRPII is a technique used to plan and manage all the organization's resources . . . one which reaches far beyond inventory or even production control, to all the planning functions of an organization."[17] They suggest that MRPII is a holistic planning technique of the future, one that can draw together all of the corporate functional areas into an integrated whole. Ultimate MRPII benefits include improved customer service through fewer shortages and stockouts, better delivery performance, and responsiveness to demand changes. Successfully implementing MRPII should also help to reduce inventory costs and the frequency of production line stoppages, and create more planning flexibility.[18]

Newer, more responsive approaches are rapidly developing. The integration of MRPII and JIT (known as MRPIII), for example, is a development potentially valuable to logistics, manufacturing, and the whole firm.[19]

DISTRIBUTION RESOURCE PLANNING

similarity to MRP

Fundamentally, *distribution resource planning,* or DRP, applies MRP principles and techniques to the flow and storage of finished products destined for the marketplace. Thus, where MRP sets a master production schedule and then "explodes" into gross and net requirements, DRP begins with customer demand, classified as independent demand, and works backwards toward establishing a realistic and economically justifiable systemwide plan for ordering the necessary finished products. Using the best available forecasts of finished product demand, DRP develops a time-phased plan for distributing product from plants and warehouses to points where it is available to customers. In practice, DRP allocates available inventory to meet marketplace demands, thus, it is a push approach.

customer inventories

DRP is far more responsive than MRP to real marketplace needs in terms of product availability and receipt timing. The most noticeable difference between MRP and DRP is that DRP can adjust and readjust its ordering patterns to accommodate dynamic, changing inventory needs. The DRP approach also responds better to systemwide inventory needs, as opposed to just those specific to a single facility.

DRP in practice

A study at Ohio State University uncovered some interesting results pertaining to the use and benefits of DRP.[20] Based on the results of a survey sent to 200 members of the Council of Logistics Management, the study commented on current and projected trends at fifty-four major companies representing a variety of industries. Often respondents used DRP regularly. These firms reported that, in all instances, DRP had equalled or exceeded their expectations for improving customer service and reducing inventory expense. The companies using DRP reported improvements in transportation and in plant shipping productivity.

DRPII

Recently, firms have integrated the most progressive DRP applications with MRPII capabilities to produce DRPII (see Figure 7–16). The master production schedule is based on actual as well as forecast demand, and the MRPII program responds directly to this schedule. The DRP program then allocates inventory to stocking points in quantities based on market needs forecasts and on scheduled production outputs. The MRPII system pulls parts and materials to the point of production or assembly; DRP then allocates, or pushes, the inventory through the distribution channels to points where customers need it. Digital Equipment Corporation, for example, has successfully applied DRPII.[21]

FIGURE 7–16   RELATIONSHIP BETWEEN MRPII AND DRP

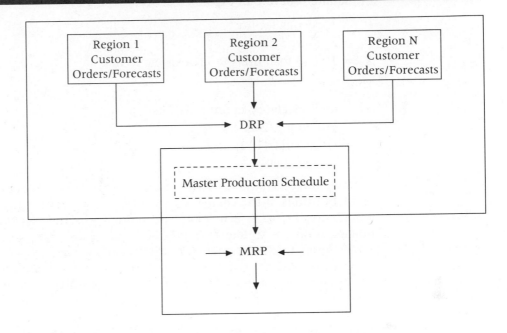

INVENTORY AT MULTIPLE LOCATIONS—THE SQUARE ROOT RULE

increased number of stocking points

To enhance customer service, or perhaps to make customers perceive that service has been enhanced, firms sometimes shift from a single centralized distribution facility to multiple market-oriented distribution centers. A firm analyzing the benefits and drawbacks of such a move must consider how the decision would affect overall inventory levels.

approach/ calculations

Assuming that total demand remains unchanged, the firm should ask whether such a move would necessitate increased systemwide inventory levels, or whether the total inventory systemwide would simply equal the amount originally located in the single facility. Answering this question requires understanding the *square root rule*, which states that a firm may approximate the aggregate inventory at multiple facilities by multiplying the square root of the number of facilities by the inventory the firm previously stored at a single facility. We may quantify this relationship as follows:

$$X_2 = (X_1)(\sqrt{n_2/n_1})$$

where

n_1 = number of existing facilities
n_2 = number of future facilities where $n_2 > n_1$
X_1 = total inventory in existing facilities
X_2 = total inventory in future facilities

example

To illustrate this, consider a company that presently distributes product to its customers throughout the southeastern United States from a single facility located in Atlanta, Georgia. The company is considering opening a second facility in Nashville, Tennessee, to help serve the same market. Assume that average inventory levels at the Atlanta facility are approximately 10,000 units. Using the square root rule as explained above,

n_1 = 1 existing facility
n_1 = 2 future facilities
X_1 = 10,000 total units in the existing facility

Thus,

X_2 = total inventory in future facilities
   = $(10,000)(\sqrt{2/1})$
   = $(10,000)(1.4142)$
   = 14,142 units

Based on this analysis, the two facilities would carry a total average inventory of 14,142 units. If the company designed them to be of equal size, then each would carry 14,142 ÷ 2, or 7,071, units. Similarly, if the company contemplated moving from one to four facilities, the required inventory would double from 10,000 units to 20,000 units. (Use the formula to check this.)

Based on data from an actual company, Table 7–8 shows the total average units of inventory implied by specific numbers of warehouses in the system. For example, as stocking locations increase from one to twenty-five, the total average inventory increases from 3,885 units to 19,425 units. This is consistent with application of the square root rule. Table 7–8 also shows the percentage change in inventories as the number of system warehouses increases.

If demand at each of the future facilities is independent of demand at the other facilities, this procedure accurately calculates both cycle stock and safety stock. The underlying theory is that total inventory requirements at multiple facilities will be proportional to the square root of the ratio between the number of future and existing facilities. Logistics personnel could easily modify the approach to reduce, rather than increase, the number of facilities within a given market area.

SUMMARY

This chapter discussed many current approaches to inventory management and formulating inventory policy. It provided details concerning the more traditional

TABLE 7–8   EXAMPLE IMPACTS OF SQUARE ROOT LAW ON LOGISTICS INVENTORIES

Number of Warehouses (n)	$\sqrt{n}$	Total Average Inventory (units)	Percent Change
1	1.0	3,885	—
2	1.41	5,494	141%
3	1.73	6,729	173%
4	2.00	7,770	200%
5	2.24	8,687	224%
10	3.16	12,285	316%
15	3.87	15,047	387%
20	4.47	17,374	447%
23	4.80	18,632	480%
25	5.00	19,425	500%

fixed order quantity (EOQ) and fixed order interval approaches. It also covered some more comprehensive approaches becoming very popular today, including materials requirements planning (MRP), manufacturing resource planning (MRPII), and distribution requirements planning (DRP).

Inventory management approaches differ from each other in three important ways. These approaches represent dependent versus independent demand, push versus pull, and systemwide versus single facility solutions. Table 7–9 summarizes the EOQ, JIT, MRP, and DRP approaches in terms of these categories. These approaches are very complex, however; and the generalizations in Table 7–9 contain an element of risk. Thus, the use of information in this table should be accompanied by careful rereading of relevant portions of the chapter.

The inventory manager's underlying responsibility is to identify a firm's logistics goals and to design inventory strategies to achieve those goals. Whenever possible, the chosen approaches should have systemwide capabilities and should consider the full range of logistics trade-offs. The inventory decision will be critical to the ultimate success of any logistics operation, and logistics personnel must use actual problems and company situations to evaluate the advantages and disadvantages of specific approaches.

STUDY QUESTIONS

1. In what major, fundamental ways may inventory management approaches differ? What is the key distinction between the push and pull approaches?

2. Explain the importance of the assumptions used in the simple EOQ model.

3. What basic trade-off does the simple EOQ approach to managing inventory consider? How do we calculate average inventory when using this methodology?

4. What does *uncertainty* mean?

5. What significance does the reorder point have in the basic EOQ model? How does this differ when using the EOQ under the condition of uncertainty, in contrast to using it under the condition of certainty?

6. Compare the advantages and limitations of the fixed order quantity and the fixed order interval approaches to inventory management.

7. What are the basic components of the just-in-time approach? In what critical way is JIT very different from traditional reorder point approaches?

TABLE 7–9   SUMMARY OF MAJOR INVENTORY APPROACHES

	Push versus Pull	*Dependent versus Independent Demand*	*Systemwide versus Single Facility*
EOQ	Pull/push	Independent	Single facility
JIT	Pull	Dependent	Single facility
MRP	Push	Dependent	Systemwide
DRP	Push	Independent	Systemwide

8. Under what conditions would materials requirements planning be appropriate for managing inventory and scheduling?

9. What are the components of an MRP system? How do they work together to accomplish MRP goals?

10. What is the purpose of distribution requirements planning? In what ways are DRP and MRP similar? In what ways are they different? When used together, what common goal do they help to accomplish?

11. Characterize the following approaches as push, pull, or some combination of push and pull: EOQ-based, JIT, MRP, and DRP. Are firms tending to develop inventory mangement systems that incorporate more of the push, rather than the pull, philosophy? Explain.

12. In general terms, explain the square root rule.

13. Perkalater Carriers employs a large fleet of trucks. To keep fleet operations running smoothly, it must order 540 tires annually at a cost of $200 per tire. The company orders the tires by telegram from the Midland Tire Company. Each order costs $48. Perkalater stores the tires in a central warehouse in Pittsburgh, Pennsylvania, which is the company's headquarters. The estimated carrying cost for holding the tire inventory is 25%.

    a. Assuming 360 days per year, what is the firm's optimum EOQ for tires?

    b. What is the total annual ordering and storage cost if Perkalater purchases the tires in EOQ-size lots?

    c. If the total lead time for the tires is six days, what is the reorder point (ROP)?

14. A retail department store manager would like to determine an appropriate EOQ-based inventory policy for an item that is stocked and available for sale. The retailer estimates that demand for the item will be 2,000 units per year. The cost per order is $80, the item value is $40, and inventory carrying cost is 20%. The retailer is open for business 250 days per year. The lead time necessary to receive additional supplies of the item is ten working days.

    a. Using the fixed order quantity approach, what is the EOQ for this item?

    b. What is the total annual ordering and inventory carrying cost if the store procures this item in EOQ-size lots?

    c. What is the reorder point?

15. Using the information from question 14, assume that demand varies somewhat. The following table shows a probability distribution of demand during the lead time:

Demand	Probability
60	.1
70	.2
80	.4
90	.2
100	.1

    a. Assuming that stockouts cost $5 per occurrence, what reorder point value will minimize the sum of the expected stockout costs and the cost of carrying safety stock?

b. Calculate the revised EOQ.

c. What revised total annual inventory cost do the new reorder point and EOQ suggest? Include all relevant costs in your calculations.

NOTES

1. Joseph Orlicky, *Materials Requirements Planning* (New York: McGraw-Hill, 1975), 22.

2. Portions of the following discussion have been adapted from David J. Closs, "An Adaptive Inventory System as a Tool for Strategic Inventory Management," *Proceedings of the 1981 Annual Meeting of the National Council of Physical Distribution Management* (Chicago, IL: National Council of Physical Distribution Management, 1981), 659–79. Also, see John W. Hummel and Alan J. Stenger, "An Evaluation of Proactive vs. Reactive Replenishment Systems," *International Journal of Physical Distribution and Materials Management* 18, no. 4, 3–13.

3. This analogy has been drawn from Uday Karmarkar, "Getting Control of Just-In-Time," *Harvard Business Review* (September–October 1989), 122–31.

4. Donald J. Bowersox, David J. Closs, and Omar K. Helferich, *Logistical Management,* 3d ed. (New York: Macmillan, 1986), 227.

5. Use of these formulas requires that demand and lead time length be independent, meaning *unrelated* in a statistical sense. If they are not independent, then a formula must be modified slightly to produce the statistical precision and accuracy desired. Note that we have simplified the discussion in this section. A recommended source for further study is Robert G. Brown, *Smoothing, Forecasting and Prediction of Discrete Time Series* (Englewood Cliffs, N.J.: Prentice-Hall, 1962), 366–67.

6. Walter E. Goddard, "Kanban or MRPII—Which Is Best For You?" *Modern Materials Handling* (5 November 1982), 42.

7. Goddard, "Kanban or MRPII—Which Is Best For You?" 45–46.

8. "How Just-in-Time Inventories Combat Foreign Competition," Special Report, *Business Week* (14 May 1984), 176E.

9. Joan M. Feldman, "Transportation Changes—Just-in-Time," *Handling and Shipping Management* (September 1984), 47.

10. Details concerning Ryder's involvement with Saturn Corporation may be found in Ray A. Mundy, Judy A. Ford, Paul E. Forney, and Jerry Lineback, "Innovations in Carrier Sourcing: Transportation Partnership," *Proceedings of the 1989 Annual Conference of the Council of Logistics Management* (Oak Brook, IL: CLM, 1989), 109–114.

11. For additional ideas, see Daniel Goldberg, "JIT's Next Step Moves Cargo and Data," *Transportation & Distribution* (December 1990), 26–29.

12. See Orlicky, *Materials Requirements Planning.*

13. Orlicky, *Materials Requirements Planning,* 21.

14. Orlicky, *Materials Requirements Planning,* 45.

15. Richard J. Tersine, *Production/Operations Management: Concepts, Structures, and Analysis,* 2d ed. (New York: Elsevier Science, 1985), 498.

16. Denis J. Davis, "Transportation and Inventory Management: Bridging the Gap," *Distribution* (June 1985), 11.

17. John Gattorna and Abby Day, "Strategic Issues in Logistics," special issue of the *International Journal of Physical Distribution and Materials Management* 16, no. 2 (1986), 29.

18. For additional information concerning MRPII, see Oliver W. Wight, "MRPII: Manufacturing Resource Planning," *Modern Materials Handling* (September 1979); or Lee J. Krajewski and Larry P. Ritzman, *Operations Management,* 2d ed. (Reading, Massachusetts: Addison-Wesley Publishing Company, 1990), 567–73.

19. More in-depth comparisons of MRPII and JIT are included in Karmarker, "Getting Control of Just-In-Time."

20. Arnold Maltz and James M. Masters, "Strategies for the Successful Implementation of New Information Technology in Logistics: The DRP Experience," *Proceedings of the 1989 Annual Conference of the Council of Logistics Management* (Oak Brook, IL: CLM, 1989), 13–49.

21. Richard G. McGee and John J. Fontanella, "DRPII: Operational Considerations," *Proceedings of the 1989 Annual Conference of the Council of Logistics Management* (Oak Brook, IL: CLM, 1989), 125–42.

CASE 7–1

TRUMP RAILCAR CORPORATION

Trump Railcar Corporation was one of the premier railroad car builders of the late 1980s and early 1990s. As a matter of fact, it was said that Trump's covered hopper grain cars were the envy of the business and that the transportation equipment Trump manufactured was the finest available anywhere. In an attempt to modernize its procurement and ordering practices, Trump's vice president of logistics, Craig Janney, incorporated trade-off analysis into his next purchase of journal bearings.

Before his analysis, Janney had been purchasing high-quality journal bearings on a monthly basis. Usage rates were fairly consistent for this needed part, and so Trump's policy was to order sixty cases every month. Each case contained eight individual bearings; each bearing weighed 32.5 pounds and cost $40. Current freight bill information showed that the transportation cost for each sixty-case shipment was $814. According to Tommy Trump, the company's CFO (chief financial officer), the best figure for inventory carrying cost was twelve percent per year.

As an alternative, Janney considered ordering only once every three months, at which time he would obtain 180 cases of bearings. This idea seemed interesting, particularly because Janney projected the inbound transportation expense to be $1,300 for each 180-case shipment, rather than $814 for each 60-case monthly shipment.

Case Questions
1. How would you evaluate the apparent trade-off between inventory carrying and transportation cost? Which alternative would you prefer, and why? Be sure to support your conclusions with appropriate analysis.

2. Overall, what do you think of Trump's approach this inventory decision? What approaches do you feel might be more effective than trade-off analysis? What are their advantages and disadvantages?

CASE 7–2

CONSOLIDATED MOTORS

Consolidated Motors is one of the largest vehicle manufacturers in the United States. It specializes in the assembly of passenger automobiles, as well as light and heavy trucking equipment. Consolidated also manufactures many of the components and parts used in these vehicles, including engines and transmissions. The company's six major manufacturing and assembly facilities are located principally in the midwestern and northeastern states.

Recently, Consolidated committed itself to the just-in-time concept in order to reduce unit costs, improve inventory performance, and enhance the quality of the company's finished products. An integral part of the overall plan is Consolidated's Preferred Supplier program. This program reduces the list of approved suppliers of all types, in exchange for a serious commitment from each to provide high-quality materials and component parts. In the two years since implementing the just-in-time concept, Consolidated reduced the number of suppliers from over 2,000 to just under 600. The goal is to reduce the total to approximately 200.

A key reason for the Preferred Supplier program's success is that Consolidated explains to each supplier what the company needs and seeks suppliers' ideas while developing suitable evaluation procedures. Also, many approved suppliers have competed actively for Consolidated's Supplier of the Year awards. Finally, Consolidated continually seeks advice from its suppliers on matters relating to model changeovers, new vehicle ideas, and so on. Through this exchange Consolidated gains valuable information early in a new concept development.

Having experienced a measure of success with the just-in-time concept, the company felt it could perform all logistics, materials management, and manufacturing/assembly activities more efficiently if more accurate end-product demand forecasts were available. Thus, with the marketing department's assistance, Consolidated developed a system to provide more accurate and timely information regarding forecast demand and actual orders received.

Consolidated is now considering implementing some form of MRP (materials requirements planning) to better coordinate materials management and manufacturing/assembly. The parts and materials the company needs at its various plants overlap considerably, and it seems that MRP could coordinate the inputs commonly needed at the multiple facilities. The company suspects that MRP would not necessarily be the best approach for all of the items needed at all six plants; thus, it has been recommended that the final system integrate aspects of both just-in-time and MRP.

Case Questions

1. Do you agree that Consolidated should consider some combination of just-in-time and MRP at this time? If so, how would you implement the integrated approach?

2. Assuming that Consolidated would procure some parts using the just-in-time approach, and some using MRP, how would you determine which approach to use for each part? In other words, what product and vendor characteristics would be more suitable for just-in-time? For MRP?

3. What additional information would you like to have before moving forward with the plan to integrate just-in-time and MRP at Consolidated?

SPECIAL APPLICATIONS OF THE EOQ APPROACH

ADJUSTMENT OF THE SIMPLE EOQ MODEL FOR MODAL CHOICE DECISIONS— THE COST OF INVENTORY IN TRANSIT

Chapter 1 mentioned the trade-off possibilities between inventory costs and transportation decisions regarding choice of mode. Implied in this discussion was the idea that longer transit times resulted in higher inventory costs. This is because in-transit inventory carrying costs will be incurred by the firms having ownership of the goods while they are being transported. In effect, the carrying costs on inventory in transit will be similar to the carrying costs of inventory in the warehouse. There are differences between inventory in transit and inventory in the warehouse, but basically the company is responsible for inventory in both instances. There is always some cost attached to having inventory, whether it is sitting in a warehouse or plant, or moving to another point. Therefore, if modes of transportation having different transit times and different rates (prices) with other variables being equal, then the trade-off between transportation rates and the inventory cost associated with the transit times should be examined. The transportation rates are usually easy to obtain, since carriers publish the rates for their services. However, to calculate the cost of carrying inventory in transit, it will be necessary to modify the basic or simple EOQ model.

transit times
Recall that the simple EOQ model considered essentially only the trade-off between order or setup costs and the carrying cost associated with holding inventory in a warehouse. To consider how different transit times affect transportation, the company must relax one basic EOQ model assumption and adapt the model accordingly.

F.O.B. assumption
One simple EOQ model assumption was that inventory incurred no cost in transit because the company either purchased inventory on a delivered-price basis or sold it F.O.B. plant. If conditions changed so that the company makes purchases F.O.B. origin or sells products on a delivered-price basis, then considering the cost of carrying inventory in transit will be necessary. Figure 7A–1 depicts a modified sawtooth inventory model; the lower half shows the inventory in transit.

256

FIGURE 7A–1   SAWTOOTH MODEL MODIFIED FOR INVENTORY IN TRANSIT

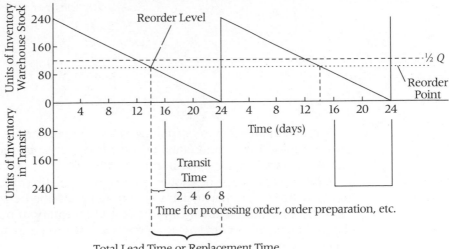

The Sawtooth Model: Adjusted

part of cycle period

Comparing the lower half of Figure 7A–1 with the upper half, which depicts inventory in the warehouse, we can see two differences relevant for calculating the appropriate costs. First, inventory is usually in transit for only part of the cycle. Typically, the number of inventory shipping days would be less than the number of days inventory from the preceding EOQ replenishment would be in the warehouse. Second, inventory in transit is not used up or sold; warehouse inventory may be used up or sold.

cost development

Since inventory in transit has these two distinctive characteristics, the cost of carrying inventory in transit will differ from that of storing inventory in the warehouse. We can calculate this cost in several ways. If a daily inventory in transit carrying cost were available, we could multiply it by the number of days in transit. We could calculate this daily cost by multiplying the inventory in transit value by a daily opportunity cost. After multiplying this cost by the number of transit days, we could multiply it by the number of orders per year or cycles per year. This would give an annual cost of inventory in transit. In effect, this resembles the procedure we followed when calculating the cost of inventory in the warehouse.

Consider the following:

Y = cost of carrying inventory in transit
V = value/unit of inventory
t_m = inventory transit time
M = average number of units of inventory in transit

We calculate the value of M as follows:

$\dfrac{t_m}{t}$ = percentage of time inventory is in transit per cycle period

Therefore,

$$M = \frac{t_m}{t} Q$$

We could rewrite this as follows:

$$t(\text{days in cycle}) = \frac{360 \ (\text{days in year})}{R/Q \ (\text{cycles per year})}$$

$$t = 360 \ \frac{Q}{R}$$

$$M = \frac{(t_m Q)}{360} \ \frac{R}{Q}$$

$$M = \frac{t_m}{360} R$$

The two approaches to calculating M give the same result, given the preceding assumptions. The second equation for M, however, frequently is more useful since the variables are given in the problem.

Now that we have developed a way of calculating the average number of units in transit, all that remains is to multiply this figure by the value per unit and the percentage annual carrying cost of inventory in transit. The result will be a dollar cost for inventory in transit that compares to the dollar cost of inventory in the warehouse:

$$\frac{t_m}{t} QVY$$

We could write the new total inventory cost equation in either of the following forms:

$$\text{TAC} = \frac{1}{2}QVW + A\frac{R}{Q} + \frac{t_m}{t}QVY$$

or

$$\text{TAC} = \frac{1}{2}QVW + A\frac{R}{Q} + \frac{t_m}{360}RVY*$$

Modal Selection Example

We can measure the trade-off between transit times and transportation cost using the total cost formula developed in the preceding section. First review the information provided in the Chapter 7 example to demonstrate the simple EOQ model:

R = 3,600 units (annual demand)
A = \$200 (cost of one order or setup)
W = 25% (cost of carrying inventory in warehouse)
V = \$100 (value per unit)
Q = 240 units (this would remain the same)

Now consider that a hypothetical company is choosing between two transportation modes (rail or motor) and that the following information is available:

Rail: 8 days in transit time
$3 per hundred pounds
Motor: 6 days transit time
$4 per hundred pounds

---

*Differentiating this equation and solving for Q with the expanded total cost formula results in the same equation as the previous one, since the last term added is not a function of Q; that is,

$$Q = \sqrt{\frac{2RA}{VW}}$$

Next assume that the company will ship the same amount, 240 units, regardless of mode. If each unit weighs 100 pounds, this represents 24,000 pounds, or 240 hundredweight. The cost of carrying inventory in transit (Y) is 10%. Given the preceding variables, we may examine the two alternatives using the formula developed previously:

The first step is to look at the product's total inventory cost if the company decides to ship by rail:

$$\text{Total inventory cost (rail)} = \left(\frac{1}{2} \cdot 240 \cdot \$100 \cdot 25\%\right) + \left(\$200 \cdot \frac{3,600}{240}\right)$$
$$+ \left(\frac{8}{24} \cdot 240 \cdot \$100 \cdot 10\%\right)$$
$$= \$3,000 + \$3,000 + \$800$$
$$= \$6,800$$

If we add the transportation cost to the inventory cost, the total cost would be

$$\text{Total cost (rail)} = \$6,800 + \left(\$3 \cdot 240 \cdot \frac{3,600}{240}\right)$$
$$= \$6,800 + \$10,800$$
$$= \$17,600$$

The next step is to determine the total inventory cost if the company ships the items by motor:

$$\text{Total inventory cost (motor)} = \left(\frac{1}{2} \cdot 240 \cdot \$100 \cdot 25\%\right) + \left(\$200 \cdot \frac{3,600}{240}\right)$$
$$+ \left(\frac{6}{24} \cdot 240 \cdot \$100 \cdot 10\%\right)$$
$$= \$3,000 + \$3,000 + \$600$$
$$= \$6,600$$

Once again we should add the transportation cost to the inventory costs:

$$\text{Total cost (motor)} = \$6,600 + \left(\$4 \cdot 240 \text{ cwt} \cdot \frac{3,600}{240}\right)$$
$$= \$6,600 + 14,400$$
$$= \$21,000 \text{ by motor}$$

trade-off

Given these calculations, the rail alternative would be less costly, and thus preferable. Before leaving this section, we should examine the trade-offs more closely. As you can see, the rail alternative has a higher inventory cost because of the slower transit time, but the transportation cost savings offset this. The net effect is an overall savings by rail.

Finally, we should note that the procedure suggested in this section is based on conditions of certainty. If transit times varied, we would need to establish probabilities and approach the solution in a more sophisticated manner.

ADJUSTMENT OF THE SIMPLE EOQ MODEL FOR VOLUME TRANSPORTATION RATES

lower rate for larger volume

The basic EOQ model previously discussed did not consider the possible reductions in transportation rates per hundredweight associated with larger volume shipments. For example, the hypothetical company in the previous illustration decided that 240 units was the appropriate quantity to order or produce. If we assume again that each unit weighed 100 pounds, this would imply a shipment of 24,000 pounds. If the rate on a shipment of 24,000 pounds (240 cwt) was $3 per hundred pounds (cwt) and the rate for a 40,000-pound shipment was $2 per cwt, knowing whether to ship 400 units (40,000 pounds) instead of the customary 240 units would be worthwhile.

total cost equation

Shippers transporting a specified minimum quantity (weight) or more commonly publish volume rates on carload (rail) and truckload (motor carrier)* quantities. Therefore, in inventory situations, the decision maker responsible for transporting goods should consider how the lower volume rate affects total cost. In other words, in addition to considering storage (holding) cost and order or setup cost, the decision maker should consider how lower transportation costs affect total cost.

Cost Relationships

Sometimes the economic order quantity suggested by the basic model may be less than the quantity necessary for a volume rate. We can adjust the model to consider the following cost relationships associated with shipping a volume larger than the one determined by the basic EOQ approach.

- *Increased inventory carrying cost for inventory in the warehouse.* The larger quantity required for the volume rate means a larger average inventory ($\frac{1}{2}Q$), and consequently an increased inventory carrying cost.
- *Decreased order or setup costs.* The larger quantity will reduce the number of orders placed and the ordinary costs of order placement and/or order setup.
- *Decreased transportation costs.* The larger quantity will reduce the cost per hundredweight of transporting the goods, consequently lowering transportation costs.
- *Decreased in-transit inventory carrying cost.* Carload (CL) and truckload (TL) shipments usually have transit times shorter than less-than-carload (LCL) or less-than-truckload (LTL) shipments, and the faster time generally means a lower cost for inventory in transit.

sensitivity test

Figure 7A–2 represents the cost relationships and considers possible transportation rate discounts (volume rates versus less-than-volume rates). The total cost function "breaks," or is discontinuous, at the quantity that permits a company to use the volume rate. Therefore, we cannot use the cost function for the transportation rate discount or discounts in the original EOQ formulation. Rather, we must use sensitivity analysis, or a sensitivity test, to determine whether total annual costs are lower if the company purchases a quantity larger than the basic EOQ amount. Note that although Figure 7A–2 indicates that using the volume rate will lower total cost, this does not necessarily have to be the case. For example, if the inventory dollar value was very high, then the increased storage (holding) costs could more than offset order and transport cost reductions.

---

*Motor carriers often publish different LTL rates and two TL rates on quantities of 500; 2,000; and 5,000 pounds.

FIGURE 7A–2   EOQ COSTS CONSIDERING VOLUME TRANSPORTATION RATE

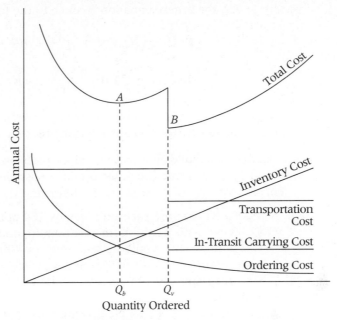

A=total cost at basic EOQ (Q_b)
B=total cost at quantity associated with transportation volume rate

Mathematical Formulation

Although there are several ways to analyze opportunities for using volume transportation rates, a useful method is to calculate and compare the total annual costs of the EOQ-based approach with the volume-rate-based approach. The following symbols will be useful in this analysis:

TAC = inventory carrying cost + order cost + transportation cost + in-transit inventory carrying cost
TAC_b = total annual cost at basic EOQ
TAC_v = total annual cost at volume rate quantity
Q_b = basic EOQ
Q_v = volume rate quantity
t_m = time in transit for less-than-volume shipment
t_n = time in transit for volume shipment
H = less-than-volume rate (high rate)
L = volume rate (low rate)

We calculate each total annual cost as follows:

$$TAC_b = \frac{1}{2}Q_bVW + A\frac{R}{Q_b} + HQ_b\frac{R}{Q_b} + \frac{t_m}{t}Q_bVY$$

$$TAC_v = \frac{1}{2}Q_vVW + A\frac{R}{Q_v} + LQ_v\frac{R}{Q_v} + \frac{t_n}{t}Q_vVY$$

Noting that $HQ_b\dfrac{R}{Q_b}$ can be written simply as HR and that $LQ_b\dfrac{R}{Q_b}$ can be written simply as LR, then these equations reduce to the following:

$$TAC_b = \frac{1}{2}Q_bVW + A\frac{R}{Q_b} + HR + \frac{t_m}{t}Q_bVY$$

$$TAC_v = \frac{1}{2}Q_vVW + A\frac{R}{Q_v} + LR + \frac{t_n}{t}Q_vVY$$

Transportation Rate Discount Example

An example that builds upon the previous problem will illustrate in this section how transportation rate discounts produce possible annual cost savings.

For this new example, assume the following variables:

H = \$3.00/cwt (assume each unit weighs 100 pounds)
L = \$2.00/cwt with a minimum of 40,000 pounds (with each unit weighing 100 pounds, this would be 400 units, or 400 cwt)
t_n = 6 days (time in transit for volume movement)
Y = 10% (carrying cost of inventory while in transit)
Q_v = 400 units
t_v = 40 days (length of a single inventory cycle for Q_v = 400 units)

From the previous problem, we know that

R = 3,600 units (3600 cwt)(annual sales)
A = \$200 (cost of placing an order or cost of setup)
V = \$100/cwt/unit (value per unit)
W = 25%
Q_b = 240 units (240 cwt, or 240,000 pounds)
t_m = 8 days (time in transit for LTL movement)
t = 24 days (length of a single inventory cycle or period)

Solving for TAC_b and TAC_v:

$$TAC_b = \left[\frac{1}{2} \cdot 240 \cdot \$100 \cdot 25\%\right] + \left[\$200 \cdot \frac{3,600}{240}\right]$$
$$+ [\$3 \cdot \$3,600] + \left[\frac{8}{24} \cdot 240 \cdot \$100 \cdot 10\%\right]$$
$$= \$17,600$$
$$TAC_v = \left[\frac{1}{2} \cdot 400 \cdot \$100 \cdot 25\%\right] + \left[\$200 \cdot \frac{3,600}{500}\right]$$
$$+ [\$2 \cdot \$3,600] + \left[\frac{6}{40} \cdot 400 \cdot \$100 \cdot 10\%\right]$$
$$= \$14,600$$

Since TAC_b exceeds TAC_v by \$3,000, the most economical solution is to purchase the larger quantity, 400 cwt. Ordering, transportation, and in-transit inventory carrying cost reductions offset the increased cost of holding the larger quantity.

We may modify this analysis to consider potential volume discounts for purchasing in larger quantities. The same procedure of calculating and comparing total annual costs under the various alternatives applies, providing we make minor modifications to the equations.

ADJUSTMENT OF THE SIMPLE EOQ MODEL FOR PRIVATE CARRIAGE

Many companies that use their own truck fleet or lease trucks for private use assess a fixed charge per mile or per trip, no matter how much the company ships at any one time. In other words, since operating costs such as driver expense and fuel do not vary significantly with weight and since fixed costs do not change with weight, many companies choose to charge a flat amount per trip rather than differentiate on a weight basis. Therefore, since additional weight costs nothing extra, it is logical to ask what quantity the company should ship.

fixed cost per trip
The basic EOQ model can handle this analysis, since the fixed trip charge is comparable to the order cost or setup cost. Therefore, the decision maker must trade off the prospect of a smaller number of larger shipments against the increased cost of carrying larger average inventory amounts.

If T_c represents the trip charge, then we can write the formula as follows:

$$\text{TAC} = \frac{1}{2}QVW + \frac{R}{Q}A + \frac{R}{Q}T_c$$

We can derive the basic model as

$$\text{EOQ} = \sqrt{\frac{2R(A + T_c)}{VW}}$$

From the previous example, we can add a charge of $100 per trip:

$$\begin{aligned}
\text{EOQ} &= \sqrt{\frac{2 \cdot \$3,600 \cdot (\$200 + \$100)}{\$100 \cdot 25\%}} \\
&= \sqrt{\frac{\$2,160,000}{\$25}} \\
&= \sqrt{86,400} \\
&= 293.94
\end{aligned}$$

The EOQ size has been increased to 293.94 units because of additional fixed charges associated with private trucking costs.

ADJUSTMENT OF THE SIMPLE EOQ MODEL TO THE ESTABLISHMENT AND APPLICATION OF IN-EXCESS RATES*

We can apply the basic inventory analysis framework discussed in Chapter 7 to utilizing an in-excess rate. Through in-excess rates, carriers encourage heavier shipper loadings. The carrier offers a lower rate for weight shipped in excess of a specified minimum weight. A logistics manager must decide whether the company should use the in-excess rate and, if so, the amount the company should include in each shipment.

Consider the following example: The CBL Railroad has just published a new in-excess rate on items that the XYZ Company ships quite often. CBL's present rate is $4/cwt with a 40,000-pound minimum (400 cwt). The in-excess rate just published is $3/cwt on shipment weight in excess of 40,000 pounds up to 80,000 pounds. The XYZ logistics manager presently ships in 400-cwt lots. The manager wants to know whether XYZ should use the in-excess rate, and, if so, what quantity the company should ship per shipment.

*Source: Adapted from James L. Heskett, Robert M. Ivie, and Nicholas A. Glaskowsky, *Business Logistics* (New York: Ronald Press, 1964), 516–20.

XYZ supplied the following data:

R = 3,200,000 pounds (32,000 cwt) (annual shipments)
V = \$200 (value of item per cwt)
W = 25% of value (inventory carrying cost/unit value/year)

Each item weighs 100 pounds.

XYZ should use the in-excess rate as long as the annual transportation cost savings offset the added cost of holding a larger inventory associated with heavier shipments. That is, realizing the in-excess rate transportation cost savings will increase XYZ's inventory carrying cost. The optimum shipment size occurs when annual net savings are maximal, that is, when annual transport savings minus the annual added inventory carrying cost are the greatest.

In developing the savings and cost functions, we will use the following symbols:

S_r = savings per cwt between present rate and new in-excess rate
Q = optimum shipment quantity in cwt
Q_m = old minimum shipment quantity in cwt

The annual net savings equals the annual transport savings minus the annual added inventory carrying cost, or $N_s = S_y - C_y$.

The annual transport savings equals the number of shipments per year times the savings per shipment, or

$$S_y = \frac{R}{Q}S_r(Q - Q_m)$$

where R/Q is the number of shipments per year, $Q - Q_m$ is the amount of shipment weight the company will ship at the lower in-excess rate, and $S_r(Q - Q_m)$ is the transportation savings per shipment. Rewriting the equation for S_r results in the following:

$$S_y = RS_r\left(1 - \frac{Q_m}{Q}\right)$$

The annual added inventory carrying cost, C_y, equals the added inventory carrying costs of the consignor (shipper or seller) and the consignee (buyer). The calculations must consider the consignee's added inventory, since the seller must pass these savings on as a price discount to encourage the buyer to purchase in larger quantities; or the seller will incur this cost if the shipment goes to the seller's warehouse or distribution center, for example.

We calculate the added average inventory—the difference between the average inventories with the larger shipment quantity and the smaller (present) shipment quantity—as follows:

$$\text{Consignor's added inventory} = \frac{1}{2}Q - \frac{1}{2}Q_m$$

$$\text{Consignee's added inventory} = \frac{1}{2}Q - \frac{1}{2}Q_m$$

$$\text{Total added inventory} = 2\left(\frac{1}{2}Q - \frac{1}{2}Q_m\right) = Q - Q_m$$

The $C_y = WV(Q - Q_m)$, where $V(Q - Q_m)$ equals the value of added inventory and W equals the inventory carrying cost per dollar value. Table 7A-1 and Figure 7A-3 show the savings and cost relationships developed here.

TABLE 7A–1   ANNUAL SAVINGS, ANNUAL COST, AND NET SAVINGS BY VARIOUS QUANTITIES USING INCENTIVE RATES

Q	S_y	C_y	ANS
400	0	0	9
410	781	500	281
420	1,524	1,000	524
430	2,233	1,500	733
440	2,909	2,000	909
450	3,556	2,500	1,056
460	4,174	3,000	1,174
470	4,766	3,500	1,266
480	5,333	4,000	1,333
490	5,878	4,500	1,378
500	6,400	5,000	1,400
505	6,654	5,250	1,404
510	6,902	5,500	1,402
520	7,385	6,000	1,385
530	7,849	6,500	1,349
540	8,296	7,000	1,296
550	8,727	7,500	1,227
560	9,143	8,000	1,143
570	9,544	8,500	1,044
580	9,931	9,000	931
590	10,305	9,500	805
600	10,667	10,000	667
610	11,017	10,500	517
620	11,355	11,000	355

The function that maximizes annual net savings is

$$N_s = S_y - C_y = RS_r\left(1 - \frac{Q_m}{Q}\right) - WV(Q - Q_m)$$

Taking the first derivative, setting it equal to zero, and solving for Q results in the following:

$$\frac{d(N_s)}{dQ} = RS_r\frac{Q_m}{Q^2} - WV = 0$$

$$WV = \frac{RS_rQ_m}{Q^2}$$

$$Q^2 = \frac{RS_rQ_m}{WV}$$

$$Q = \sqrt{\frac{RS_rQ_m}{WV}}$$

Now, taking the data from the problem posed in this example, we find the solution as follows:

$$Q = \sqrt{\frac{(32,000)(\$1.00)(400)}{(0.25)(\$200)}} = \sqrt{256,000} = 506 \text{ cwt}$$

The conclusion is that the XYZ Company should use the in-excess rate and should ship 50,600 pounds in each shipment.

FIGURE 7A–3   NET SAVINGS FUNCTION FOR INCENTIVE RATE

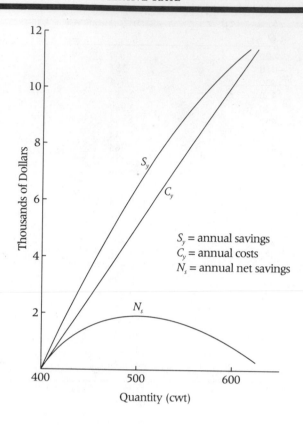

S_y = annual savings
C_y = annual costs
N_s = annual net savings

SUMMARY

The four adjustments to the basic EOQ approach discussed in this appendix all relate to decisions important to the logistics manager—modal choice, volume rates, private trucking, and in-excess rates. We could include other adjustments, but these four should be sufficient in most cases. While all of the adjustments discussed here assume a condition of certainty, other adjustments may require modifying the model for conditions of uncertainty.

THE TRANSPORTATION SYSTEM

The transportation system is the physical link connecting a company's customers, raw material suppliers, plants, warehouses, and channel members—the nodes. The nodes are fixed points in the logistics system where some activity temporarily halts the flow of goods in the logistics pipeline. The transportation companies utilized to connect these nodes affects not only the transportation costs but the nodal operating costs.

This chapter is concerned with the transportation system, or link, in the logistics system. We will focus on the fundamental relationship between the link and the node, the carrier selection decision, and the characteristics of alternative transportation providers.

THE ROLE OF TRANSPORTATION IN LOGISTICS

bridge over buyer-seller gap

Conceptually, a company's logistics system is a series of nodes (fixed points where the goods come to rest) and links (transportation companies). The transportation link permits goods to flow between the various nodes and bridges the buyer-seller gap. The transportation carrier a company utilizes to perform the link service is a decisive factor in determining the efficiency of operating the node and partially determines the company's competitive edge and product demand in a given market area.

value added

Transportation system knowledge is fundamental to the efficient and economical operation of a company's logistics function. Transportation is the physical thread connecting the company's geographically dispersed operations. More specifically, transportation adds value to the company by creating time and place utility; the value added is the physical movement of goods to the place desired and at the time desired.

For a firm to function without the aid of transportation is virtually inconceivable in today's global economy. Most companies are geographically divorced from their supply sources, thereby making them dependent upon transportation to connect the supply source to the consumption point. Labor specialization, mass production, and production economies normally do not coincide with the area where demand for the good exists. Thus, transportation is necessary to bridge this buyer-seller spatial gap.

global impact

As supply chains become increasingly longer in our global economy, the transportation function is connecting buyers and sellers that may be tens of thousands of miles apart. This increased spatial gap results in greater transportation costs. In addition, operations within this international marketplace require more transportation time, which necessitates higher inventories and resulting higher storage costs. Therefore, the greater the buyer-seller gap, the greater the transportation and storage costs.

importance in economy

The total dollars spent in the U.S. to move freight reveal the importance of transportation in the economy. In 1989, the U.S. spent an estimated $327.5

billion to move freight, or 6.26 percent of the GNP.[1] This total expenditure included shipper costs of $3.6 billion for loading and unloading freight cars and for operating and controlling the transportation function.

importance in company

As an example of transportation's relative importance in a company, a study of 1990 physical distribution (outbound only) costs revealed that total distribution costs represented 7.2 percent of sales and that outbound transportation cost amounted to 3.13 percent of sales, or 43.5 percent of total distribution costs. Warehousing cost was 1.78 percent of sales; customer service and order processing accounted for 0.34 percent of sales; administration was 0.32 percent of sales; inventory carrying cost was 1.61 percent of sales; and other distribution costs accounted for 0.02 percent of sales.[2] Outbound transportation was clearly the largest component of total physical distribution costs.

To say that transportation is logistics implies that transportation operates independently of other logistics functions. Nothing could be further from the truth because transportation directly affects a node's operation. The quality of the transportation service provided over a link bears directly upon inventory costs and stockout costs at a node as well as upon the cost of operating the node.

cost-service trade-off

For example, if a company switches from rail to air transportation to move raw materials from a vendor to the plant, the air carrier's increased speed, or lower transit time, permits the company to hold lower inventories to meet demand during transit time and to use less warehousing space and less-stringent product packaging. But the company realizes these advantages at the expense of higher transportation costs. Thus, a firm cannot make the transportation decision in a vacuum; applying the total cost or systems approach requires a company to consider how the transport decision will affect other logistics system elements.

THE TRANSPORT SELECTION DECISION

As indicated above, the transportation expenditures companies incur involve significant dollar amounts; and the carrier's service quality affects other logistics operating costs and the demand for the company's product. The company controls these expenditures and service levels through the transportation decision.

This section will focus on the carrier selection decision process and factors relevant to that decision. The carrier selection decision process provides the framework for the discussion of the different types of transportation providers that follows this section.

The Link-Node Relationship

The carrier selection decision is a specialized purchasing process whereby a firm purchases the services of a carrier to provide the necessary link among logistics nodes. The carrier selected directly affects the operation of the logistics node and other logistics system functions.

scope of transport selection decision

The carrier selection decision, then, entails more than merely evaluating the prices different transportation methods charge. It must also consider the other costs associated with how the transport method's service affects the nodal operation. The transit time different methods incur will affect the inventory level the nodes require; that is, the longer the transit time, the greater the inventory level the company requires to protect the nodes against stockouts until the next shipment arrives. The transport method's dependability and the degree of safe delivery also affect the inventory levels held at a node, the utilization of materials handling equipment and labor, and the time and cost of communicating with the carrier to determine shipment status or to seek reparations for goods damaged in transit.

A company's knowledge of carrier prices and pricing practices can simplify the carrier selection decision. Measuring and evaluating the logistical implication of the carrier cost determinant is much easier than measuring carrier service performances; logistics personnel know carrier rates and can easily compute an alternative's direct transportation cost. However, basing transport method selection upon lowest transport costs, or direct link costs, does not guarantee the least-cost decision for the whole logistics system.

The Carrier Selection Decision

specialized purchasing process

As we have noted, the carrier selection decision is a specialized purchasing process whereby a firm selects a carrier to link its logistics nodes. As with any procurement decision, vendor price (carrier rate) is not the only selection criteria the firm considers. True, the carrier rate is an important factor in the decision; but the firm must consider the quality of the link service and how this service affects nodal operation costs.

modal choice

Carrier selection is a twofold process, as Figure 8–1 indicates. First, the firm selects a transportation mode. The choices include the basic nodes of rail, water, truck, air, and pipeline. In addition, intermodal transportation, which uses two or more modes to provide service over a given link, is available. The most common forms of intermodal transportation include rail-truck (piggyback), truck-air, and rail-water.

specific carrier choice

The second step in the decision is to select a specific carrier from within the chosen mode or intermodal form. The specific carrier selection requires the firm to choose the legal carrier type: common, contract, exempt, or private. The number of alternative carriers is much greater in the specific carrier selection phase than in the modal phase. For example, while the basic modal choice is

FIGURE 8–1   THE CARRIER SELECTION DECISION

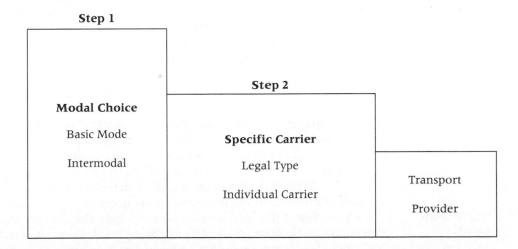

limited to five alternatives, the number of regulated motor carriers from which a firm may choose is approximately 40,000.

repetitive decision

Generally, a firm considers the carrier selection decision a repetitive purchase decision. That is, a company deciding to use motor carriers does not review this decision every time it selects a carrier to provide link service. The decision to use trucks remains in effect until the firm makes a major review of overall transportation costs and/or makes a major change in its logistics system. This repetitive decision characteristic also applies to the specific carrier decision. The firm uses the selected carrier repeatedly until the carrier's service level or rate becomes unacceptable.

The modal selection phase has received a great deal of attention. This usually involves evaluating the rates and service levels of alternative modes and intermodal forms. The firm selects the mode or intermodal form that occasions the lowest total logistics costs for both nodes and links and then applies this analysis to the specific carriers within the selected mode (or intermodal). Given today's deregulated transportation environment, carrier rates and service performance do vary among carriers within the same mode.

service

Most carriers in a given mode have the technical characteristics to provide the same level of service, but these services levels can and do vary greatly from one carrier to another. Also, since the cost structures are essentially the same for carriers in a given mode, the rates of alternative carriers in that mode are quite similar for a given movement. But, given the market and operating conditions different carriers face, the rates carriers within a given mode charge may vary somewhat. Thus, allowing for slight rate disparities, the transport rate is not the most important criterion in selecting a specific carrier; but the rate is important in modal selection. Carrier service performance, then, becomes the relevant determinant for selecting a specific carrier from one mode.

Carrier Selection Determinants

What, then, are the criteria firms use to evaluate the alternative modes and carriers? According to the carrier selection literature, the salient selection determinants are carrier costs and service performance. The relevant service performance determinants are transit time, reliability, capability, accessibility, and security. We will now discuss how carrier cost and service determinants interact in the firm's logistics function.

transportation cost

Transportation cost was the predominant carrier selection determinant in early carrier selection works. The transportation cost includes the rates, minimum weights, loading and unloading facilities, packaging and blocking, damage in transit, and special services available from a carrier—for example, stopping in transit.

Transportation cost analysis is oriented toward evaluating alternative mode, since the rates, minimum weights, loading and unloading facilities, packaging, and blocking will vary from one mode to another. However, the importance of transportation costs receded somewhat with the advent of the business logistics concept, which now focuses attention upon the cost trade-offs existing between the service a carrier provides and nodal operation costs. Even so, the transportation cost disparities prevalent in today's deregulated environment remain an important criterion in the carrier selection decision.

transit time and reliability

Transit time is the total time that elapses from the time the consignor makes the goods available for dispatch until the carrier delivers same to the consignee. This includes the time required for pickup and delivery, for terminal handling, and for movement between origin and destination terminals. *Reliability* refers to the consistency of the transit time a carrier (the link supplier) provides.

inventory and stockout costs

Transit time and reliability affect the nodal costs of inventory and stockouts (lost sales or forgone productivity). Lower transit times result in lower inventories, while more dependability causes lower inventory levels or stockout costs. With a given level of lead time, a firm can minimize inventories at a node and consequently inventory carrying costs. But, if the transit time is not consistent, the firm must increase the node's inventories above the level that a consistent transit time would require. More specifically, the node now must hold larger amounts of inventory as a safety factor against stockouts that could arise from inconsistent link service.

product differentiation

The marketing implication of reliable transit time is product differentiation and a competitive advantage in the marketplace. Thus, if your firm can provide a customer with a lower and more dependable transit time than your competitor, the customer can reduce inventory or stockout costs and your firm can increase sales. Sales are quite sensitive to consistent service, and the logistics manager must concentrate on carrier transit time and reliability to differentiate a firm's product in the marketplace.

capability and accessibility

Capability and accessibility determine whether a particular carrier can physically perform the transport service desired over a link. *Capability* refers to the carrier's ability to provide the equipment and facilities the movement of a particular commodity requires. Equipment that can provide controlled temperatures or humidity and special handling facilities are examples of capability factors. *Accessibility* considers the carrier's ability to provide service over the link in question—that is, the availability of carrier routes and terminals in shipping location proximities. Accessibility refers a carrier's physical access to the nodes. The geographic limits of a carrier's route network (rail lines or waterways) and the operating scope regulatory agencies authorize constrain a carrier's accessibility. A carrier's inability to provide the desired capability and availability service requirements can eliminate the carrier from consideration in the carrier selection decision.

security

Security concerns the arrival of goods in the same condition they were in when tendered to the carrier. Although the common carrier is held liable for all loss and damage, with limited exceptions, the firm does incur nodal costs when the carrier loses goods or delivers them in a damaged condition. Unsafe link service results in opportunity costs of forgone profits or productivity because the goods are not available for sale or use. To guard against these opportunity costs, a firm will increase inventory levels, with resulting increased inventory costs. The continued use of an unsafe carrier will adversely affect customer satisfaction and, consequently, sales.

A firm using a common carrier holds the carrier liable for damage to the lading. To recover the damage value, the shipping firm must file a claim with the carrier. This entails a claim preparation and documentation cost, as well as legal fees if the firm has the claim settled through the courts. Therefore, frequent damage to the commodities also aggravates the nodal cost associated with claim settlement.

The Pragmatics of Carrier Selection

transit time reliability

Figure 8–2 gives the relative importance of the carrier selection determinants for firms selecting motor carriers in today's deregulated environment. The most important criterion is the quality of the link service the carrier provides, that is,

FIGURE 8–2   IMPORTANCE RANKING OF CARRIER SELECTION DETERMINANTS   *Source:* Edward J. Bardi, Prabir Bagchi and T. S. Raghunathan, "Motor Carrier Selection in a Deregulated Environment," *Transportation Journal,* Vol. 29, No. 1, Fall 1989, 4–11.

Determinant	Rank
Transit time reliability or consistency	1
Door-to-door transportation rates or costs	2
Total door-to-door transit time	3
Willingness of carrier to negotiate rate changes	4
Financial stability of the carrier	5
Equipment availability	6
Frequency of service	7
Pickup and delivery service	8
Freight loss and damage	9
Shipment expediting	10
Quality of operating personnel	11
Shipment tracing	12
Willingness of carrier to negotiate service changes	13
Scheduling flexibility	14
Line-haul services	15
Claims processing	16
Quality of carrier salesmanship	17
Special equipment	18

transit time reliability. The impact of reliable transit time and total transit time (importance rank three) on inventory and stockout costs and customer service is of paramount importance today.

carrier rates

Transportation deregulation has provided transportation users with increased opportunity to negotiate both rates and services with carriers. This greater reliance on the marketplace has increased interest in the transportation rate the carrier charges. Shippers are generally utilizing fewer carriers in order to become more important to the carrier and thereby to increase their negotiating power with the carrier.

limited carriers

financial stability

Transportation rates, the carrier's willingness to negotiate rate changes, and the carrier's financial stability reflect the negotiating strategy inherent in the deregulated environment. Today's shippers utilize their economic buying power in the marketplace to realize lower transportation rates from carriers. But this highly competitive motor carrier industry has experienced over 10,000 bankruptcies since 1980. The heightened possibility of bankruptcy increases the service disruption risk; and the magnitude of this risk increases as firms implement a reduced carrier strategy.

Shippers give capability and accessibility average importance as the factors ranked from six to fifteen show. The security criterion of freight loss and damage ranks ninth in importance, and the claims processing factor ranks sixteenth.

sales rep

special equipment

Less important selection determinants are the quality of carrier salesmanship and special equipment. Shippers making the carrier selection decision give little importance to the quality of the carrier sales representative. Special equipment is not an important selection determinant for shippers who require standard equipment, but for those requiring special equipment the carrier who has it is the only one the shipper will use.

THE BASIC MODES OF TRANSPORTATION

The basic modes of transportation available to the logistics manager are rail, motor, water, pipeline, and air. Each mode has different economic and technical structures, and each can provide different qualities of link service. This section examines how each mode's structure relates to the cost and quality of link service possible with the basic modes—the basis for the modal selection analysis.

Distribution of ton-miles (an output measurement combining weight and distance, or tonnage multiplied by miles transported) among the modes shows each mode's relative importance. Table 8–1 shows this distribution. These data suggest that the relative importance of rail transport has lessened and that motor and pipeline importance has increased substantially. Air transport has continued to advance in property movement. On the surface, these data suggest that shipping firms increasingly use "premium" transportation—motor and air—to provide a desired customer service level by trading off higher transportation costs (motor and air, as compared with rail and water) for lower nodal costs. In 1989, motor carriers received 77.6 percent of the U.S. freight expenditures; rail, 9.0 percent; air, 3.4 percent; water, 6.9 percent; and oil pipeline, 2.6 percent.[3]

Railroads

All for-hire railroads in the United States are classified as common carriers* and are thus subjected to the legal service obligations we will discuss later. Since the Interstate Commerce Commission imposes no legal restraints or operating authority regulations, regarding the commodities railroads may transport, railroads have a distinct advantage in availability and in the ability to provide service to "all" shippers. This is not to imply that railroads can transport any product anywhere, for the accessibility of rail transportation does have limita-

capability

tions. But with respect to the ability to transport a wide variety of goods, the railroads have a distinct advantage over other common carriers in the different modes. Railroads are not restricted as to the cargo type they may transport; rather, all railroads are legally, as well as physically, capable of transporting all commodities tendered for transportation.

limited number of carriers

The railroad industry consists of a small number of large firms. In 1987, there were 18 Class I carriers (railroads with $50 million or more annual gross op-

*Several years ago, the ICC exempted from economic regulation railroad movement of fresh fruits and vegetables, piggyback freight, and boxcar traffic.

TABLE 8–1   DISTRIBUTION OF INTERCITY FREIGHT BY MODES (FOR-HIRE AND PRIVATE) (BILLIONS OF TON-MILES)

	Rail		Motor		Pipeline		Water		Air	
	Amt	%	Amt	%	Amt	%	Amt	%	Amt	%
1940	379	61.3	62	10.0	59	9.5	118	19.1	0.02	0.00
1960	579	44.1	285	21.8	229	17.4	220	16.7	0.89	0.07
1970	771	39.7	412	21.3	431	22.3	219	16.5	3.3	0.17
1980	932	37.5	555	22.3	588	23.6	407	16.4	4.8	0.20
1987	976	36.5	666	24.9	587	22.0	435	16.3	8.7	0.34

Source: Transportation in America, 4th ed. (Washington, D.C.: Transportation Policy Associates, 1988), 6.

erating income) and 481 Class II and III carriers (railroads with less than $50 million annual gross operating income).[4] This rather limited number of carriers may suggest limited rail service availability, but the railroads are required to provide through service which makes rail service available to points beyond a particular carrier's geographic limits.

market structure

This mode's economic structure partly accounts for the limited number of rail carriers. Railroads, which fall within that infamous group of business undertakings labeled as "natural monopolies," require a large investment in terminals, equipment, and trackage to begin operation; and the accompanying huge capacity allows the railroads to be a decreasing-cost industry. As output (ton-miles) increases, the average per-unit production cost decreases. Thus, having fewer railroads in operation in a given area and permitting those few firms to realize inherent large-scale output economies is economical and beneficial to society.

Through mergers, seven railroads—Burlington Northern, ConRail, CSX Transportation, Norfolk Southern, Santa Fe, Southern Pacific, and Union Pacific—have evolved as the dominant carriers in the industry. Many of these carriers have acquired nonrail transportation companies such as trucking and water carriers, permitting one organization to provide multimodal transportation service to shippers.

long-distance and large-volume

Railroads are primarily long-distance, large-volume movers of low-value, high-density goods. The reason for these long-distance, large-volume rail movements is ingrained in the mode's economic and technical characteristics. The railroad's decreasing cost structure suggests that large-volume, long-distance movements lower the average production cost by increasing output (ton-miles) and thereby spreading the fixed costs over a greater output base.

A major advantage of using railroad transportation is the long-distance movement of commodities in large quantities at relatively low rates. Products of forests, mines, and agriculture are the major commodities railroads transport. For these low-value, high-density products, transportation costs account for a substantial portion of their selling price. As Table 8–2 shows, rail transportation has one of the lowest revenue per ton-mile levels of all modes, with rail having the lowest revenue per ton-mile of the modes capable of transporting general commodities domestically—rail, motor, and air.

low accessibility

Low accessibility is one primary disadvantage of rail transport. Accessibility refers to the carrier's ability to provide service to and from the nodes in a particular situation. The rail carrier cannot deviate from the route rail trackage follows. If a shipper or consignee is not adjacent to the rail right-of-way, rail

TABLE 8–2   AVERAGE REVENUE PER TON-MILE (IN CENTS)

Year	Rail*	Motor*	Water†	Oil Pipeline	Air
1970	1.43	8.50	0.303	0.271	21.91
1975	2.04	11.60	0.518	0.368	28.22
1980	2.85	18.00	0.770	0.999	46.31
1984	3.09	22.16	0.818	1.272	50.20
1988	2.72	23.17	—	—	113.6

*Class 1 rail and motor carrier.

†Barge lines.

Source: *Transportation in America*, 4th ed. (Washington, D.C.: Transportation Policy Associates, 1986), p. 11. Jay Gordon, "Shippers Contain Transport Goods," *Distribution* (July 1990), 26.

transport is not easily accessible. To use rail service, a shipper or consignee not adjacent to the track must utilize another transport mode—namely, truck—to gain access to the rail service. Thus, rail service may not be advantageous in logistics situations such as the ultimate delivery of consumer goods to retail outlets.*

long transit times

Rather long transport time is another rail transport disadvantage. The problem occurs in the classification yard, where the carrier *consolidates* boxcars or marshalls them into train units. This huge physical task, which requires consolidating boxcars going in a similar direction and breaking out cars that have reached their destination or that the carrier must transfer to another train unit, adds to the overall slow speed of rail transport.

reliability and safety

Railroad favorably provide other service qualities important to the logistics manager—reliability and safety. Weather conditions disrupt rail service less than they disrupt the service of other modes; such conditions cause only minor fluctuations in rail transit time reliability. Rail safety incurs greater costs. Moving goods by rail requires considerable packaging and resultant packaging costs. This stems from the car classification operation, in which the carrier couples cars at impacts ranging from one to ten miles per hour, and from the rather rough ride steel wheels running on steel rails provide. But these service qualities differ among particular carriers, and the logistics manager must research such qualities carefully.

Today's railroad industry is changing considerably in response to the economy and deregulation. Traditional railroad markets (e.g., steel and mining) are depressed, causing rail traffic from these market segments to decline or, at best, to remain stagnant. In addition, deregulation has increased the competitive pressures for railroads to lower rates; and the railroads have responded through the contract rate-making provisions of the Staggers Act.

Traffic reduction coupled with lower rates has compressed the revenue-cost gap: profit. To increase profitability, the industry has attempted to reduce costs and increase productivity. To improve productivity and profitability, railroads are abandoning unused tracks, reducing the work force, and modifying labor work rules. Increased computer use is enabling the industry to improve train movement efficiency, saving fuel and labor costs.

intermodal

Rail carriers are attempting to increase freight traffic by entering new markets, primarily the intermodal freight market (*intermodal traffic* is freight traditionally moved by motor carriers). Many carriers have improved existing facilities or added new intermodal facilities to handle increased piggyback and container traffic volume. Rail intermodal rates and services for certain freight now compete with those of trucking companies.

Motor Carriers

The motor carrier is very much a part of any firm's logistics system; almost every logistics operation utilizes the motor truck, from the smallest pickup truck to the largest tractor-semitrailer combination, in some capacity. The United States' sophisticated highway network permits the motor carrier to reach all points of

---

*Railroads are using *piggyback* (trailer-on-flatcar) service to overcome inaccessibility. A rail flatcar moves a motor truck trailer between origin and destination terminals, but a truck transports the trailer over the highways to the consignor and consignee. We will discuss piggyback service in greater detail in a later section of this chapter.

the country. Therefore, the motor carrier can provide transportation service to virtually all shippers. Table 8–1 points out that motor carriers have made great inroads into the number of ton-miles carriers transport in the United States. Figure 8–3 offers an overview of the motor carrier industry.

types of legal carriers

Unlike the railroads, the regulated for-hire portion of the motor carrier industry consists of both common and contract carriers. Exempt for-hire carriers and private carriers are also available. Approximately forty percent of the intercity ton-miles of truck-transported freight moves through regulated carriers—common and contract. Exempt and private carriers transport the remaining sixty percent.

The exempt carrier primarily transports agricultural, fish, and horticultural products—the exempt commodities to which the next section refers. While private carriers transport a variety of products, private truck transportation most commonly moves high-value, high-rated traffic and commodities requiring "personalized" service such as driver-salesperson operations.

large number of small carriers

The regulated motor carriers consist of a large number of relatively small firms. In 1988, there were approximately 38,000 regulated motor carriers. Of this total, only two percent had annual revenues greater than $3 million; approximately ninety-four percent had annual revenues less than $1 million.

This large number of carriers is due in part to the low capital entering the trucking business requires. High variable cost and low fixed cost characterize the cost structure. The motor carrier does not require extensive terminal and equipment investment and does not invest in its own highway. The government builds and maintains the highway, and the carrier pays for highway use through fees such as use taxes and licensing charges. These variable expenses contribute to the high-variable-cost structure.

The large number of motor carriers suggests a high availability. For example, many more motor carriers than railroads are available in an area. However, the

FIGURE 8–3   OVERVIEW OF INTERSTATE MOTOR CARRIER INDUSTRY   *Source:* Adapted from John J. Coyle, Edward J. Bardi, and Joseph L. Cavinato, *Transportation,* 3rd ed. (St. Paul, MN: West Publishing Co., 1990), 71.

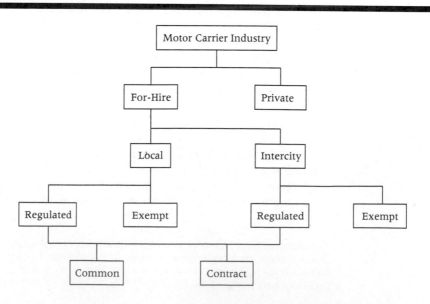

availability and operating authority

operating authorities granted particular carriers limit motor carrier availability somewhat. These operating grants limit the type of commodity a carrier may transport and the area within which the carrier may provide service. A common motor carrier of property may have operating authority to transport only general commodities, household goods, heavy machinery, liquid petroleum products, building materials, or explosives, for example. Regulation precludes it from transporting any other commodity unless the Interstate Commerce Commission gives specific authorization. The carrier's authorized service area may be a broad regional area, particular states, or particular cities; and the authorization may restrict the carrier's service provision over regular routes or irregular routes. A carrier's ICC-defined ability to transport given commodities between particular points, rather than the number of carriers serving an area, determines regulated motor carriers availability.

high accessibility

The controls regulating the commodities transported and the areas served directly affect the accessibility of particular carriers. But the major advantage of motor transport over other modes is its inherent ability to provide service to any location. Truck transportation need not provide service only to customers located adjacent to a track, waterway, or airport. For the logistics manager, the motor carrier is the most accessible transportation mode existing to serve domestic markets today.

transit time

Motor carrier operations do not involve coupling trailers together to form long "train" units, because each cargo unit (trailer) has its own power unit and can be operated independently. Thus, on truckload movements, the shipment goes directly from the shipper to the consignee, bypassing any terminal area and consolidation time. Such technical and operational characteristics enable the motor carrier to provide transit times lower than rail and water, but higher than air.

reliability

Weather conditions and highway traffic can disrupt motor service and thus affect transit time reliability. These factors affect the dependability of all motor carriers. A specific carrier's reliability relates to the operating efficiency the carrier achieves for a given link; this reliability may vary among the given carrier's links.

manufactured goods

While some motor carriers transport low-value products, such as coal and grain, and move products over long distances, motor carriers transport primarily manufactured commodities over relatively short distances. Characterized by high value, manufactured commodities include textile and leather products, rubber and plastic products, fabricated metal products, communication products and parts, and photographic equipment.

small shipment size

The physical and legal constraints on carrying capacity make motor transport somewhat amenable to small shipments. This directly affects inventory levels and the shipment quantity necessary for gaining a lower truckload (volume discount) rate. Because of the smaller shipment size coupled with lower transit times, the logistics manager can reduce inventory carrying costs while maintaining or improving customer service levels.

safety

Generalizing the other relevant service attribute, safety, is difficult for motor carriers. The packaging required for motor carrier movements is less stringent than that required for rail or water; pneumatic tires and improved suspension systems make the motor carrier ride quite smooth. Again, the degree of safety for a given link depends upon the actual operations of individual carriers.

high cost

The logistics manager must consider the relatively high motor carrier cost. As Table 8–2 points out, the average truck revenue per ton-mile is approximately eight times that of rail and twenty-four times that by water. This again suggests that commodities shippers move by truck must be of value high enough to sustain the transportation costs, or that trade-offs in inventory, packaging, warehousing, or customer service costs must warrant the use of this higher-cost mode.

Since passage of the Motor Carrier Act of 1980, for-hire motor carrier industry competition increased tremendously. The easing of regulatory entry controls has permitted thousands of new carriers to enter the industry and to compete for existing freight. To gain a market share, the new carriers, as well as the existing carriers, offer lower rates and improved service. Rate discounts are the norm today; some carriers offer shippers discounts as high as fifty to sixty percent. Lower fuel and labor costs help many carriers to sustain these large rate discounts.

The competitive environment has been a mixed blessing to shippers. On the positive side, lower motor carrier rates have enabled shippers to reduce transportation costs and improve profitability. On the negative side, the downward pressure on rates has contributed to approximately 10,000 carrier bankruptcies since 1980. These have caused logistics disruptions ranging from minor delivery delays for freight caught in the bankrupt carrier's system to temporary halting a firm's transportation function until the firm can find a carrier to replace a key link provider.

Water Carriers

Water transportation, a major factor in U.S. development, remains an important factor in today's economy. In the early stages of U.S. development, water transportation provided the only connection between the United States and Europe, the market area for U.S. agricultural production and the source of manufactured goods. Thus, many larger, industrial cities in both the United States and Europe are located along major water transport routes.

Domestic Domestic commodity movements take place along the Atlantic, Gulf, and Pacific coasts, as well as inland along internal navigable waterways such as the Mississippi, Ohio, and Missouri rivers and the Great Lakes. As Figure 8–4 indicates, water carriers are classified as internal water carriers, Great Lakes carriers, and coastal and intercoastal carriers. Internal water carriers operate on the internal navigable waterways. Great Lakes carriers operate on the Great Lakes and provide service to shippers along the northern border of the United States. Coastal carriers operate between points on the same coast, whereas intercoastal carriers operate between points on the Atlantic and the Pacific via the Panama Canal.

legal carrier types   All four legal classifications of carriers exist in water transportation. Regulated for-hire common and contract carriers transport approximately five percent of the intercity ton-miles for water-transported freight, and exempt and private carriers transport the remaining ninety-five percent.

cost structure   Rather low capital entry restraint and operations exempt from federal economic regulation account partly for a large portion of the unregulated domestic traffic transported by water. To begin operation, a water carrier, requires no investment for the right-of-way— nature provides the "highway" and public expenditures maintain the facility. The water carrier requires only the entry capital necessary for equipment. Thus, the investment does not preclude private water transport as it does private rail transport. Exemption exists for the trans-

FIGURE 8–4   OVERVIEW OF DOMESTIC WATER CARRIER INDUSTRY   *Source:* From John J. Coyle, Edward J. Bardi, and Joseph L. Cavinato, *Transportation,* 3rd ed. (St. Paul, MN: West Publishing Co., 1990), 143.

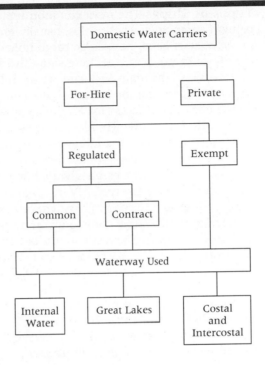

portation of bulk commodities or bulk oil products, and these are the major commodities shippers transport by water.

service characteristics

Water carriers are primarily long-distance movers of low-value, high-density cargoes that mechanical devices easily load and unload. Mineral, agricultural, and forest products are the major commodities transported. Carriers ship these products in large quantities: one barge can transport about 1,500 tons.

The principal advantage of using water transport is its low cost. Table 8–2 shows that the average revenue per ton-mile for water carriage is lower than that for rail, motor, and air. Thus, water transport is most advantageous for commodities with a low value-to-weight relationship, or for commodities in which the transportation cost is a significant portion of the selling price.

long transit time

In return for this low rate, the shipper receives a slow movement method. Possibly water transport provides the highest transit time of all modes. Weather conditions affect internal and Great Lakes operations—ice and low water levels disrupt service. In addition, water transport has greatly restrained accessibility.

low accessibility

Only shippers adjacent to the waterway can use water transport directly. In other situations, water carriage use requires a prior or subsequent land transport movement. Thus, the major water transport disadvantages are long transit times and low accessibility.

International   As indicated previously, transport by ship is by far the most widely-used international shipment method. In 1986, ocean carriage accounted for approximately sixty percent of worldwide freight movements. Companies ship almost any conceivable cargo type by sea, but most ocean cargo consists of low weight-to-value commodities such as petroleum, minerals, and dry bulk items.

general cargo

Types of Ships   The most common type of ocean vessel in use today is the *general cargo ship*. These ships, usually engaged to transport shipload cargoes on a contract basis, have large cargo holds and are equipped to handle a large variety of cargo. Many of these ships also have what is called a *tween deck,* a deck between the main deck and the main holds in which the carrier commonly stows palletized cargo. Some carriers equip cargo ships with large side doors which allow easy access for forklifts loading pallets. Most carriers equip cargo ships with derricks which allow them to load and discharge cargo at ports that lack up-to-date cargo handling equipment. This feature is very important for ships transporting goods to less-developed portions of the world.

bulk

Bulk carriers carry cargoes with low value-to-weight ratios, such as ores, grain, coal, and scrap metal. Very large openings on these ships' holds allow easy loading and unloading. Watertight walls dividing the holds allow a ship to carry more than one commodity at a time.

tanker

Tankers carry the largest amount of cargo by tonnage. These ships range in size from World War II-era tankers of 18,000 tons of VLCC's (very large crude carriers), some of which top 500,000 tons. Tankers are constructed in much the same way as bulk carriers, but with smaller deck openings. Considering the oil spill problem, the use of double-hulled tankers has become preferable to the more conventional, single-hulled tankers. Another, less common type of tanker ship, referred to as an LNG ship, carriers liquified natural gas. The largest of these vessels can carry enough natural gas to heat New York City for a winter week.

container

Container ships are becoming increasingly more important in today's market. These ships are specially-designed to carry standardized containers, which are commonly rated in TEU's (twenty-foot equivalent units) or FEU's (forth-foot equivalent units). Some of the larger containerships today carry upwards of 5,000 TEU's on board a single vessel. Also, containerships can carry a wide variety of cargo, including many products which require special handling, temperature control, etc.

The containers are preloaded at their origin and then placed aboard ship, allowing lower port loading and unloading costs. Containers allow direct access to inland points through intermodal arrangements but require specially designed heavy-lift derricks for loading and unloading. Many smaller ports cannot afford the investment required to handle this type of cargo.

RO-RO

Roll-on-roll-off (RO-RO) vessels are another type of ship proving its value in international trade. RO-ROs are basically large ferry ships. The carrier drives the cargo directly onto the ship using built-in ramps and drives or tows it off at its destination. Toyota currently operates several RO-RO ships to carry automobiles from Japan to the United States and Europe. Each ship can transport 2,000 or more cars at a time. On the return trip, the vessels carry grain or coal for use in Japan.

RO-ROs allow carriers to use standard highway trailers to transport cargo. This can be an advantage in less-developed areas where ports lack container handling facilities. RO-ROs can also carry oversized cargoes such as large earth-moving equipment or cranes, which carriers can drive directly onto the ship.

Combination RO-RO/container ships are also becoming common. The rear of these ships have built-in ramps. They also have movable decks and inner

OBO

partitions. The carrier can change the ship configuration so that it may carry various combinations of containers and RO-RO cargo.

Oil-Bulk-Ore (OBO) vessels are multi-purpose bulk carriers that are able to carry both liquid and dry bulk products. The development of these vessels allowed the shipowner to carry cargoes on most legs of a voyage, whereas previously, the vessel may have had to transit in ballast (empty) due to the trade patterns of the products shipped.

barges

Ocean-going-barge vessels are prominent in the U.S. to Puerto Rico trade and in the Hawaiian inter-island trade. In practice, these vessels are towed by an ocean-going tug, as opposed to being pushed like barges on the inland waterways. Compared to the RO-RO vessels, the ocean-going-barge is very inexpensive. Currently, the largest of these barges measures 730 feet long and 100 feet wide, and has a capacity of 512 trailers on three decks.

Air Carriers

Passenger movement is the air carrier's principal business; passenger revenue accounts for the majority of air carrier business. In the movement of freight, air transport is somewhat nascent, accounting for less than one percent of the total intercity ton-miles of freight.

The air carrier industry is highly concentrated in a limited number of carriers. The major carriers earn nearly ninety percent of the industry's revenue; the revenue these carriers generate is primarily from passenger transport.

The type designations used for air carriers differ somewhat from those used for rail and motor. For-hire air carriers are classified as follows:

- *Certificated:* carrier holding a certificate to operate large aircraft
- *Noncertificated:* carrier that does not hold a certificate to operate because it operates aircraft with a maximum payload of 18,000 pounds and sixty seats
- *All-cargo:* carrier that transports cargo only
- *International:* certificated carrier that operates between the United States and a foreign country
- *Air taxi:* noncertificated carrier that will fly anywhere on demand with a maximum payload of 18,000 pounds and sixty passengers
- *Commuter:* noncertificated carrier that operates with a published timetable
- *Major:* carrier with annual revenues greater than $1 billion
- *National:* carrier with annual revenues between $100 million and $1 billion
- *Large regional:* carrier with annual revenues between $10 million and $100 million
- *Medium regional:* carrier with annual revenues less than $10 million

The logistics manager may use any of the preceding air carrier classes to transport freight.

cost characteristics

The air carrier cost structure consists of high variable costs in proportion to fixed costs, somewhat akin to the motor carrier cost structure. Like motor and water carriers, air carriers do not invest in a highway (airway). The government builds terminals and carriers pay variable lease payments and landing fees for their use. The equipment cost, though quite high, is still a small part of the total cost.

ON THE LINE

THE LARGEST, LONGEST DOUBLE-TRUCK HAUL

Kirscher Transport of Virginia, Minnesota, recently completed the largest, longest double-truck haul in the country, according to company spokespeople. Kirscher transported a seventy-ton piece of drilling equipment 1,600 miles, from the Great Lakes port of Duluth, Minnesota, to Edmonton, Alberta, Canada.

To accomplish this haul, two seventy-foot-long trucks moved down the highway side-by-side with the seventy-ton cylindrical piece of drilling equipment lying across their two unattached lowboy trailers. To distribute the load, each eight-axle truck unit had a total of thirty tires. The gross weight of the load and trucks was 224,000 pounds.

"We don't know any other company in the country that double-trucks loads like this," said John Tucker, Kirscher terminal manager-dispatcher. "Our company has logged over 600,000 miles double-trucking." He estimates that the trucks averaged thirty miles per hour, even though their maximum legal speed limit is forty miles per hour.

Reprinted by West Publishing Company with permission from

COMMERCIAL CARRIER JOURNAL   October 1989, 302.

Major commercial air carrier freight movement started as a passenger business by-product. Excess capacity existed in the plane's "belly", offering potential room for freight movement. As cargo demand grew, the carriers began to seriously consider this business arena. Now, the scheduled carriers have dedicated equipment specifically to freight movement and operate freight service to meet freight shippers' ever-growing needs. The all-cargo lines have always concentrated upon cargo transportation.

low transit time

The major advantage of using air transportation is speed. Air transport affords a distinct advantage in low transit time over long distances. Thus, air transport is necessary for moving emergency shipments or shipments that are highly perishable both in spoilage terms and in terms of lost sales or productivity.

high cost

Cost is the major disadvantage of using air transportation, and it precludes many shippers from utilizing this mode. The average revenue per ton-mile for air carriers is approximately 41 times that of rail and 5 times that of motor transport (see Table 8–2). Commodities with high value-to-weight relationships can sustain this high transport cost because transportation is a smaller portion of the commodity's selling price than is inventory holding cost. In this shipping situation, the logistics manager can reduce inventory levels and inventory costs and can rely upon air transport speed to meet nodal demand.

limited accessibility

Air transport accessibility is somewhat limited. Most firms using air carriers must rely upon land carriers to transport freight to and from the airport. The most common and feasible mode is the motor carrier; firms utilize both local for-hire and private motor carriage to overcome air carrier inaccessibility.

reliability

Air transport reliability is also somewhat of a disadvantage. Weather conditions interrupt air service. These conditions result in increased transit time and adjusted higher inventory levels. But the advent of instrument flying and the adoption of these devices at a greater number of airports is minimizing this service interruption.

international   Air transport has become a very viable alternative to water (ocean) transport for international shipments. The reduced air transit time, delay and port handling cost reductions, and reduced packaging costs enable exporters and importers to reduce overall logistics costs and improve customer service. Again, the logistics manager must trade off the high air transport rate against other logistics cost reductions in order to justify using this method.

Pipelines

The pipeline industry refers to oil pipelines, not natural gas pipelines, though the Federal Energy Regulatory Commission, which regulates all oil pipelines, of which there are approximately 140, also regulates natural gas pipelines, just as it regulates any other public utility.

limited capability   Pipeline transportation is not suitable for general commodity transportation; rather, its use is restricted to the movement of liquid petroleum products. Some firms have attempted to move commodities such as coal in a slurry form, but moving such commodities by pipeline has not been a viable alternative to other modes—namely, water and rail.

limited accessibility   Pipeline accessibility is limited. Only shippers adjacent to the pipeline can use this mode directly. Shippers not located adjacent to the pipeline require another more accessible mode such as water, rail or truck to transport products to or away from the pipeline. The speed is quite slow, typically less than ten miles per hour, resulting in long transit times; however, weather conditions do not disrupt pipeline service.

cost characteristics   The pipeline cost structure is one of high fixed costs and low variable costs, quite similar to that existing for the railroads. The investment in the line, terminals, and pumping stations contributes most to this cost structure.

low cost   Low cost, as compared with other modes, is the major advantage to using oil pipelines. However, the inability to transport solids limits its usefulness in the logistics system of a firm manufacturing durable goods.

Performance Rating of Modes

The logistics manager bases the transportation mode decision upon cost and service characteristics. Table 8–3 summarizes each mode's relative advantages and disadvantages. Note that the ratings in this table are generalizations; the exact relationship among specific carriers of different modes may vary.

| TABLE 8–3 | PERFORMANCE RATING OF MODES BY SELECTION DETERMINANT |

| Selection | Modes | | | | |
Determinants	Railroad	Motor	Water	Air	Pipeline
Cost	3	4	2	5	1
Transit time	3	2	4	1	—
Reliability	2	1	4	3	—
Capability	1	2	4	3	5
Accessibility	2	1	4	3	—
Security	3	2	4	1	—

1 = best, lowest; 5 = worst, highest.

LEGAL CLASSIFICATIONS OF CARRIERS

Transportation firms engaged in interstate transportation of property are classified into four categories: common, contract, exempt, and private. The first three are for-hire carriers; the last is not. The firm wishing to move its goods in its own vehicles provides private transportation, and the firm does not make private carrier service available to other shippers of regulated goods.

Common Carrier

definition

The common carrier is a for-hire carrier that serves the general public at reasonable charges and without discrimination. Economically common carrier is the most highly regulated of all the legal carrier types. The economic regulation imposed upon these carriers acts to protect the shipping public and to ensure sufficient transport service within normal limits. Using a common carrier in the logistics system requires the logistics manager to know how those regulations affect the type and quality of common carrier transport.

service requirements

The essence of this regulation is located in the legal service requirements under which the common carrier operates: to serve, to deliver, not to discriminate, and to charge reasonable rates. These service requirements contain the underlying principle of public protection, for the common carrier is a business enterprise affecting public interest. To guarantee the transportation service the economy requires, the federal government has imposed regulatory controls on common carriers. The government does not impose these legal service requirements upon the other types of carriers.

serve the public

To meet its public service requirement, the common carrier must transport all commodities offered to it. The common carrier cannot refuse to carry a particular commodity or to serve a particular point within the carrier's scope of operation. The logistics manager's transportation service supply seems assured, since the common carrier cannot refuse to transport the firm's commodities, even if the movement is not profitable for the carrier. However, this service requirement has two qualifications: one, the carrier must provide service up to its physical capacity limits, where the plant level necessary to meet normal carrier demand determines capacity; and two, the common carrier must serve shippers within the carrier's shipping public.

defined by ICC operating authority

The Interstate Commerce Commission regulates entry into the common carrier transportation sector for rail, motor, and water transport; and the Department of Transportation (DOT) regulates air transport entry. A common carrier must prove to the regulatory agency that the public needs the proposed service and that the proposed service's provision will be a public convenience. The Motor Carrier Act of 1980 and the Airline Deregulation Act of 1978 have eased the entry requirements for common carrier trucking and airline companies.

liability for damage

The delivery requirement refers to the common carrier's liability for the goods in its care. The common carrier must deliver goods in the same condition they were in when the carrier received them at the shipment's origin. More specifically, the common carrier is liable for all goods lost, damaged, or delayed while in its care. This absolute level of liability has limited exceptions: acts of God, acts of public enemy, acts of public authority, acts of the shipper, and defects inherent in the goods. The logistics manager, then, can transfer the risk of cargo damage, or the bearing of this risk, to the carrier when using a common carrier over a link.

no discrimination   The shipping public finds additional protection in the requirement that the common carrier not discriminate among shippers, commodities, or places. *Discrimination* is when a carrier charges different rates or provides different service levels for essentially similar movements of similar goods. There are, however, permissible forms of discrimination. For example, common carriers may favor larger-volume shippers by charging lower rates for volume movements and higher rates for less-than-volume movements. Cost difference justifies quoting different rates for volume and less-than-volume movements.

charge reasonable rates   Finally, the duty to charge reasonable rates constrains the carrier from charging excessively high or low rates. This requirement has two protective dimensions: it protects the shipping public from rates that are too high, and it protects the carrier from charging rates that are too low. The second protective dimension ultimately protects the public by ensuring continued transportation service.

In summary, we might consider the common carrier the backbone of the transportation industry. The common carrier makes itself available to the public, without providing special treatment to any one party and operates under rate, liability, and service regulations. Most logistics systems use the common carrier extensively.

Contract Carrier

definition   The *contract carrier* is a for-hire carrier that does not serve the general public, but rather serves one or a limited number of shippers with whom it is under specific contract. The contract carrier also operates under economic regulations, but has no legal service obligations imposed upon it. The contract contains terms pertaining to the carrier's rates, liability, and type of service and equipment. Usually, a contract carrier rates are lower than those of common carriers. The government entry controls into this transportation sector but does not require the contract carrier to prove public convenience and necessity.

tailored service   The contract carrier provides a specialized type of service to the shipper. Because the carrier does not serve the general public, it can tailor its services to meet specific shippers' needs by utilizing special equipment and arranging special pickups and deliveries. In general, the logistics manager may assume that contract carriage is essentially similar to private transportation, at least in service level terms.

scope of operations   One serious problem with the contract carrier exists: availability. Unlike the common carrier, which must be available to all, the contract carrier is available only to shippers with whom the carrier has signed a contract. Thus, the contract carrier is not as readily available as the common carrier. Arranging contract carrier service for a firm requires the logistics manager to assist the carrier in obtaining a contract carrier authority.

Exempt Carrier

definition   The *exempt carrier* is a for-hire carrier exempt from economic regulation regarding rates and services. The laws of the marketplace determine the rates, services, and supply of such carriers. The only controls over entry into this transport industry sector are capital requirements, which do not seriously restrict some modes.

service   An exempt carrier gains this status by the commodity it hauls or by the nature of its operation. For example, a motor carrier is an exempt carrier when transporting agricultural products, newspapers, livestock, and fish; and a rail carrier is exempt when hauling fresh fruit. Carriers whose operation type provides exemption include motor carriers whose operations are primarily local; water carriers that transport bulk commodities such as coal, ore, grain, or liquid; air carriers that haul cargo; and rail carriers that transport piggyback shipments.

The limited number of exempt carriers—that is, the limited number of situations in which carrier exemption is possible—restrict the availability of such service. But for moving commodities such as agricultural products, where exempt carriage is possible, firms make significant use of these carriers. The primary reason for using an exempt carrier is lower transport rates. For the movement of industrial commodities, the exempt carrier does not provide viable link service.

Private Carrier

definition

A *private carrier* is essentially a firm's own transportation. The private carrier is not for-hire and not subject to federal economic regulations. More specifically, private carriage involves any person who transports in interstate or foreign commerce property of which such person is the owner, lessee, or bailee, when such transportation is for the purpose of sale, lease, rent, or bailment, or in furtherance of any commercial enterprise. A private carrier's crucial legal distinction is that transportation must not be the controlling firm's primary business; stated differently, the carrier owner's primary business must be some commercial endeavor other than transportation. As of 1980, private motor carriers may charge 100%-owned subsidiaries an intercorporate hauling fee.

primary business

The most prevalent private transportation type is by motor vehicle; private carrier is nearly synonymous with private motor carrier. The relative ease of meeting motor transport capital entry requirements and the high degree of accessibility by motor vehicle have made this mode most advantageous to shippers wishing to provide their own transportation. We should point out that private transportation by water primarily moves bulk raw materials. To a much lesser extent, private rail carriers move bulk products short distances within a plant, between plants, or from plants to rail sidings. Firms use private aircraft extensively to move company personnel and, to a lesser degree, to move emergency property shipments.

rationale

The basic reasons for a firm to enter into private transportation are cost and service. When for-hire carrier rates increase, many firms find private transport a means of controlling transportation costs. Basically, a firm can reduce private transportation costs by conducting the private carrier operation as efficiently as a for-hire operation. If this same efficiency is possible, private transport theoretically should cost less, since the firm pays no for-hire carrier profit. However, one major operational problem, the empty backhaul,* may elevate profit.

advantages

By using private transportation, a firm gains greater control and flexibility in responding to buyer and plant demands. This increased control and flexibility may result in lower inventory levels, greater customer satisfaction, and greater efficiency at the loading and unloading docks. The firm can also use private equipment as an advertising medium.

disadvantages

Private transportation does contain some disadvantages. The main ones are large capital requirements and problems in labor and management. The capital

---

*The *empty backhaul* refers to a vehicle going from origin to destination loaded, and returning empty.

the firm invests in the transport fleet has alternative uses in other firm operations, and this capital must provide a return that at least equals other investment opportunities. The labor problems arise from the firm's dealing with a new labor union. Administrative problems may arise when the firm utilizes existing managers to manage a private transport operation. Finally, the current deregulated environment has produced substantially lower for-hire carrier rates, occasionally making private transportation more costly.

INTERMODAL TRANSPORTATION

definition

Intermodal transport services refers to the use of two or more carriers of different modes in the through movement of a shipment. Carriers offer such services to the public by publishing a rate from origin to destination for one carrier of each available mode. In other situations, the logistics manager, through routing, uses different modes to get a product to its final destination.

rationale

The logistics manager often must utilize different transport modes to service a given link. While intermodal services are necessary for numerous reasons, the basic reasons are the various modes' service characteristics and costs. For example, the limited accessibility of air transport requires coordination with a land carrier to make the pickups and deliveries. Similar inaccessibility applies to rail, water, and pipeline, but not to motor, which has a definite advantage here. By manipulating the modes, a logistics manager can overcome a given mode's service disadvantages and retain the mode's basic advantage, usually low cost. This is the primary motivation for combining rail and water to move coal or grain: the rail segment improves water transport's accessibility, and the water portion permits savings by providing low-cost service for the long-distance portion of the move.

Intermodal services maximizes the primary advantages inherent in the combined modes and minimizes their disadvantages. The combined services will have both the good and the bad aspects of the utilized modes. For example, the coordination of rail and water will have a lower total cost than an all-rail movement, but a higher cost than all-water. Likewise, the combined system's transit time will be lower than that of an all-water movement but higher than that of intermodal all-rail. The decision to use combined modes must consider the decision's affect on total logistics costs.

types

Various service types exist, as Figure 8–5 shows. The most prevalent forms have been truck-rail, truck-water, and truck-air. However, rail-water, pipeline-water, and pipeline-truck also occur.

FIGURE 8–5   TYPES OF INTERMODAL SERVICES

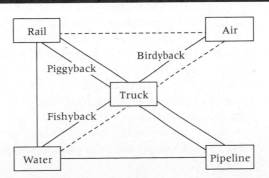

We can attribute extensive motor carrier use in intermodal service to the extremely high accessibility motor transport allows. Birdyback, fishyback, and piggyback services are examples of coordination in which a carrier physically transfers the motor carrier trailer, with the cargo intact, in another mode. Birdyback combines the accessibility of motor with the speed of the airline; fishyback couples motor accessibility with the low cost of water carriage; and piggyback adds the truck's accessibility to the low cost of rail service. In each case, the combined service suffers the disadvantages of one of the modes involved; for example, birdyback has the disadvantage of air transport high cost.

transportation company

The ultimate intermodal service is the transportation company, which provides all modal services. That is, it makes rail, motor, water, air and pipeline transportation services available to the public. The advantages of such a transportation company lie in its ability to utilize the most efficient and economical modal services to meet shipper needs. Thus far, regulatory constraints have prevented the transportation company concept from materializing; but recent mergers with nonrail carriers at Burlington Northern, CSX, Norfolk Southern and other rail companies indicate that the transportation company may soon appear.

limitations

One substantial stumbling block to intermodal service is that carriers are reluctant to participate. The ICC can require rail and water carriers to cooperate, but the commission does not hold the power over other modal pairs. The carriers coordinate willingly, even eagerly, to move a product that any one carrier could not transport in its entirety. But, when one carrier can transport the commodity the entire distance over its own lines, the carrier is hesitant to coordinate with other carriers.

Another problem with intermodal services is the transfer of freight from one mode to another. This creates time delays and adds to transportation costs. Some forms of coordination eliminate this problem by transferring a motor carrier trailer to another transport mode. The motor carrier trailer's transferability is a special coordination form termed *containerization,* the trailer being a container.

Containerization

Simply stated, a container is a large rectangular box into which a firm places commodities to be shipped. After initial loading, the commodities per se are not rehandled until they are unloaded at their final destination. Throughout the movement, the carrier handles the container—not the commodities; the shipper can transfer the container from one mode to another, eliminating the need to handle the commodities each time. Reducing commodity handling reduces handling costs, the damage cost, theft and pilferage, and the time required to complete the modal transfer.

Containerization changes materials handling from a labor-intensive to a capital-intensive operation. Handling containerized freight requires less labor because the container is too large and too heavy for manual movement. Many firms, who modify their materials handling systems to include cranes, forklift trucks, and other equipment capable of handling the large, heavy containers, have found containerization to be a desirable avenue for increasing productivity and controlling materials handling costs, especially in periods of continually increasing labor costs.

Containerization has gained notable acceptance in international distribution. The service reduces the time and cost associated with shipment handling at ports and curtails damage and theft. Some firms containerizing shipments to foreign markets have reduced costs from ten to twenty percent and have increased the service level they provide to these markets.

land bridge

As discussed earlier, a unique type of intermodal service using the container is the *land bridge,* which utilizes rail transportation to link prior and subsequent container moves by water transportation. For example, containers destined for Europe from the Far East move to the West Coast of the United States by water transportation. The containers move by rail to the East Coast, where a carrier loads them onto an oceangoing vessel for the final transportation to Europe. The rail movement provides the intermodal bridge between the two water moves and permits an overall transit time shorter than that of an all-water shipment.

Piggyback

Piggyback, or trailer-on-flatcar (TOFC), is a specialized form of containerization in which rail and motor transport coordinate. In piggyback, the carrier places the motor carrier trailer on a rail flatcar, which moves the trailer by rail for long distances. Motor carrier then moves the trailer for short-distance pickups and deliveries. This service combines the long-haul, low-cost advantage of rail with the accessibility of motor.

Recently, deregulated, piggyback service mostly moves under contract. Generally, five basic piggyback plans are available. The groups able to utilize each plan are restricted as follows:

- Plan I: All motor carrier.
- Plan II: All rail.
- Plan III: Shipper provides trailer.
- Plan IV: Shipper provides trailer and rail flatcar.
- Plan V: Joint railroad and motor carrier.

The vast majority of piggyback shipments move under Plans II. Since Plans III and IV require an investment in or lease of equipment, shippers do not use these plans to any great extent. Motor carriers use Plan I to reduce load pattern imbalances. Plan V generates very little volume since it requires the joint efforts of a railroad carrier and a motor carrier. If the shipment does not require this coordination, it will occur only when both parties benefit.

International Shipments

Almost every international shipment travels on more than one mode from its origin to its destination. Recent efforts have attempted to reduce shipping times and costs by increasing the various modes' compatibility and by trying new mode combinations.

In the early 1950s, Sea-Land's introduction of containers that trucks as well as ships could carry began the current revolution in shipping. Containers now come in several sizes and supply the major portion of break-bulk overseas shipping.

advantages

Containerized shipments have several advantages. Reduced loading times allow carries to utilize their equipment more efficiently. Shippers benefit from shorter transit times and the reduced risk of pilferage and damage during loading

disadvantages

and unloading. Savings may also result from reductions in required packing materials and insurance.

Containers also have several disadvantages. Not every port is equipped to handle containers, limiting the number of shipping routes available. Finding cargo for the container's backhaul may be difficult. Additionally, the carriers at the origin and destination are not always able to take advantage of the speed available in loading and unloading containers, decreasing the mode's efficiency.

Maritime bridges are prime examples of the savings available by combining modes. Using *double-stack* trains, which stack containers two high on railway flatcars, allows the railroads to operate their equipment more efficiently and to pass these savings on in the form of special intermodal rates, reducing overall shipping costs.

A very recent innovation is the *air/sea combination,* where carriers combine ocean and air transport to move a shipment. This method is most commonly used to ship high value-to-weight items from the Far East to Europe by way of the West Coast of the United States.

Shipping air/sea has two advantages. One, the cost of the combined modes is less than that of an all-air movement. Two, it is much faster than any of the available all-surface modes. Modern container ships can make the Pacific crossing from Japan to Seattle in ten days. When we combine this with the air leg from Seattle to Europe, total transit time will range from ten to fourteen days. This is approximately one-third of the all-ocean transit time and one-half of the land bridge time. The in-transit inventory savings will outweigh the increased cost of the premium modes.

Carriers also commonly use *roll-on-roll-off* in international trade. RO-RO is very similar to container shipping, except that the carrier uses standard truck trailers instead of containers, towing them onto the vessel at the port of origin and off at the destination. RO-RO, which transports automobiles and large mobile equipment such as bulldozers, has proven extremely useful for shipments to less-developed areas of the world where modern port facilities are unavailable. While RO-RO's advantages are basically the same as those of container shipping, RO-RO does not require special loading equipment.

INDIRECT AND SPECIAL CARRIERS

The transport methods in this category offer specialized or intermediary transportation service. In some cases, these carriers have line-haul equipment; in others, they merely provide pickup and delivery and consolidate the service.

Moving shipments of less than 500 pounds creates serious operational problems for the major modes. To make the move economical, the carrier must consolidate the small shipments into larger ones, adding time and cost for the carrier and increasing transit times and transportation charges.

Small-Package Carriers

A number of transportation companies—namely, bus, express, and package carriers—have concentrated upon small freight movements. Bus lines move small packages in their vehicles' luggage compartments. These carriers have cargo capacity only in the space passenger luggage does not require, and therefore do not require large shipments to make this service profitable. Coupled with frequent schedules, the bus lines offer a viable alternative to the logistics manager who must distribute many small-package shipments.

United Parcel Service

A common carrier motor firm, United Parcel Service (UPS), has made great strides in the efficient movement of small shipments. UPS, an innovator in terminal handling and in pickup and delivery scheduling, can transport small shipments profitably while providing better service and lower transit time than other major modes. Regulations limit the type of package a shipper can transport by UPS; at present, these restrictions are (1) a maximum weight of fifty pounds per package and (2) a maximum length and girth of 108 inches.

Other express companies offer air transportation. Federal Express, the largest air express package delivery firm, utilizes a fleet of aircraft and ground vehicles to provide next-day delivery of small packages and envelopes through the United States and internationally. Its operation, like that of most air express companies,

hub

centers around a *hub* package distribution center. Typically, Federal Express picks up packages in the late afternoon, delivers them to the local airport, and flies them to the Memphis hub airport, where they arrive in the late evening hours. Federal Express then sorts the packages according to destination and reloads them onto aircraft scheduled for predawn arrival at the destination airport, where the service loads the packages onto ground vehicles for morning delivery to the consignee.

The major advantage of using air express companies is speed—the speed required to get needed parts, equipment, documents, sales literature, and specimens to destination the next day. But the high cost of such service generally prohibits the non-emergency shipment of low-value, high-density commodities.

Freight Forwarders

The domestic surface freight forwarder collects small shipments from shippers, consolidates these shipments into large loads, and presents the consolidated shipments to railroads or motor carriers for intercity movement. At destination,

consolidator

the freight forwarder breaks the load down into individual shipments and delivers them to the correct consignee. The domestic freight forwarder realizes its revenue from the difference between the high less-than-volume rate the shipper pays and the lower volume rate the for-hire carrier charges the freight forwarder. The main advantage of using a freight forwarder is lower transit time for small shipments.

Shippers Associations

An indirect form of transportation known as the *shippers association* moves small shipments for shipper members. The shippers association consolidates shipments, presents the larger loads to for-hire carriers, and pays a lower rate for the larger-volume movement. The association passes on the lower-volume rate to its members.

Brokers

intermediary

The freight *broker* is a person or firm that acts as an intermediary between the shipper and carrier. The broker acts as the carrier's sales agent and as the shipper's traffic manager. That is, the broker represents a number of carriers that need loads to move in given directions. With this carrier capacity knowledge, the broker contacts the shippers and solicits freight to meet the carriers' needs.

types

The broker typically charges the shipper the carrier's published rate, deducts seven to ten percent, and then remits the net amount to the carrier.

There are two types of brokers: licenses and unlicensed. The *licensed* broker is licensed by the ICC and may arrange freight transportation with ICC-regulated carriers. The licensed broker operates under ICC-administered regulations, including entry control. An *unlicensed* broker who does not require ICC licensing, may arrange freight transportation for exempt transportation such as local distribution, agricultural commodities, and piggyback. Many private fleet managers utilize broker services, seeking exempt commodity movement to eliminate the empty backhaul.

Since 1980, the number and use of brokers have dramatically increased. The Motor Carrier Act of 1980 reduced the entry requirements for brokers and motor carriers. The broker provides new, small trucking companies a marketing channel with a sales force capable of generating shipments from local shippers. At the same time, the broker offers the shippers access to these new, generally lower cost carriers. In addition, brokers may offer consolidation services that afford the shipper additional savings.

selection criteria

A logistics manager selecting a broker should consider the broker's authority, liability, and billing. First, the manager should review the ICC broker license to make certain the broker is in fact licensed and subject to ICC regulations. Second, since the broker is not legally liable for damage a common carrier causes while transporting goods, the logistics manager must determine whether the broker will assist in filing claims with the carrier and whether the carrier the broker uses can pay damage claims. Finally, the manager should determine if the broker's fees are included in or are in addition to the carrier's rate.

Shipper's Agents

piggyback

Shippers' agents consolidate freight primarily for piggyback movements. The shippers' agent arranges for the piggyback transportation only; the carriage contract is between the shipper and the carrier. Usually, the shipper pays the freight charges to the shippers' agent, who in turn pays the carrier.

consolidation

The primary advantages of using a shippers' agent are cost savings, consolidation, and improved transit time. The shippers' agent normally consolidates enough freight to fill two piggyback trailers (the number of trailers loaded onto one railroad flatcar), thereby reducing the time the carrier holds the freight before moving it. The lower rate the carrier's charge the shippers' agent for the consolidated load is, in part, passed on to the shipper. Given the economic power consolidation affords, the shippers' agent may be able to negotiate lower rates and thereby lower transportation costs for the shipper.

The primary disadvantage of using a shippers' agent is in liability for freight charge payment. The shipper normally pays the freight charges to the shippers' agent. Should the shippers' agent fail to pay the carrier, the shipper is ultimately liable for paying the charges. The shipper should investigate the shippers' agent before use.

In addition to the indirect and special carriers discussed in this section, there are several types of intermediaries which are more closely-related to the international shipping industry. Chapter 4 contains a description of the nature and importance of the foreign freight forwarder, non-vessel-owning common carriers, export management companies, export trading companies, customs house brokers, and ports.

SUMMARY

This chapter considered the carrier selection decision and the characteristics of alternative transportation service providers. The determinants the logistics manager uses to evaluate and select a transportation carrier consist of direct transportation costs plus carrier service qualities that affect node operating costs.

The carrier selection decision involves selecting a transportation mode and then selecting a specific carrier from four legal carrier classifications. The major carrier selection determinants include the transportation rate, transit time, consistency of transit time, capability, accessibility, and security. Transit time consistency is generally the most important selection determinant.

The alternative transportation suppliers include the basic modes plus intermodal, legal types, and indirect and special carriers. The chapter examined these alternative suppliers' characteristics in light of the carrier selection determinants.

STUDY QUESTIONS

1. When purchasing transportation services, the carrier with the lowest rate is usually not the carrier offering the lowest total cost. Explain.

2. What are the major advantages and disadvantages of each of the basic modes?

3. Normally, a firm delivers a low-cost part to its assembly plant via railroad. But, when the plant is facing a stockout, the firm sends the part via airplane. What cost justification can the firm give for using air?

4. Why would a company use a common carrier when contract and exempt carriers offer lower rates?

5. Under what conditions is intermodal transportation advantageous?

6. Water transportation dominates international shipment. Explain.

7. What role does the container play in domestic and international shipments?

8. Under what circumstances would a firm utilize indirect or special carrier services?

9. Describe the role of economic regulation in the carrier selection decision.

10. What transportation mode would a shipper likely use to transport basic raw materials? heavy manufactured goods? lightweight consumer goods? electronic products? Why?

NOTES

1. Frank A. Smith, "Transportation in America," Eno Foundation for Transportation, Inc., as reported in Jay Gordon, "Shippers Contain Transport Costs," *Distribution* (July 1990), 27.
2. *Davis Database* 15, no. 5 (Englewood Cliffs, NJ: Herbert W. Davis and Company, October 1990), 1.
3. Frank A. Smith, "Transportation in America."
4. *Traffic World* (5 December 1988), k.

NATIONAL APPLIANCE, INC.

Bob Reard, director of corporate transportation for National Appliance Inc., just hung up the phone after a lengthy discussion with Susan Jameson, vice president of logistics. National Appliance, Inc. had just acquired an appliance distributor located in Paris, and the logistics department had two months to develop an operating process to support this European distributor with National Appliance products. The shipments to Paris would begin in approximately five months, and Mr. Reard was to prepare a transportation operating plan for these shipments.

National Appliance, Inc. was a medium-size U.S. manufacturer of refrigerators and electric ranges. During the past fifteen years, National Appliance increased its share of the refrigerator and electric range market from less than two percent to twenty percent. Part of the reason for this tremendous growth was that National Appliance offered high-quality products at low prices. In addition, National Appliance vertically integrated both its supply and marketing channels. National believed that quality products resulted from actually owning and managing key component vendors and that quality marketing and sales efforts resulted from directly managing distributors and retail appliance outlets.

It surprised Mr. Reard to learn that National Appliance purchased control of an European appliance distributor. There had been many rumors about expansion into the European market, but Mr. Reard had felt that National Appliance would merely develop a contractual relationship with a distributor in Europe, not purchase a distributor.

Purchasing the Paris distributor was the first major international business venture for National Appliance in its thirty-five year history. During the late 1980s, the company unsuccessfully attempted to market refrigerators in both Canada and Mexico; Mr. Reard personally managed the truck shipments to both countries. Consequently, Mr. Reard and his staff had very limited international experience. They did, however, possess considerable expertise in domestic transportation, having successfully controlled both transportation costs and service during the company's rapid growth in the past fifteen years.

Given the emphasis on quality products and service, top management mandated consistent, low lead times. National Appliance delivered domestic distributor orders in less than five days from the order date; the company allowed no exceptions to this service policy. Truck transportation, including a private fleet, was the primary mode the company used for both inbound and outbound shipments. Spare parts were normally shipped by ground express, but the company would use air express when the distributor or dealer needed a special part immediately. Ms. Jameson established a logistics quality control program that measured carrier performance and used Mr. Reard's managerial skills to assure acceptable performance from National Appliance carriers.

Having had little experience in international transportation, Mr. Reard felt a bit out of his element in developing an international transportation plan. Ms. Jameson assured him that transportation was transportation and that the only difference between international and domestic transportation was distance.

Distance was going to be a major factor since National Appliance had plants located in Memphis, Minneapolis, and Omaha. This long distance from the European market would contribute to two basic problems: high transport costs and long lead times. Moving the products from the plants to the Atlantic or Gulf ports would require some form of ground transportation. Ocean carrier shipment would be long, and Mr. Reard would have to arrange to move the product from the French entry port to Paris. And Mr. Reard was sure that he could hire an international transportation manager, but at a considerably high salary.

With the logistics planning meeting set for the next morning at 8:00 A.M., Mr. Reard prepared the following transportation plan for Ms. Jameson:

1. Finished product from all three plants would be shipped by truck to New York/New Jersey ports.
2. Water transportation would be used from New York/New Jersey to Le Havre, France.
3. Trucks would transport the products from Le Havre to the Paris distributor.
4. From Paris, the distributor would arrange transportation to the ultimate customer.
5. An international transportation manager would be hired.

Mr. Reard estimated that the total transit time required for this move would be approximately four weeks.

Case Questions
1. Assess the strengths and weaknesses of Mr. Reard's international transportation plan.
2. Develop an alternative international plan to present to Ms. Jameson and provide justification sufficient to support its adoption.

SELECTED BIBLIOGRAPHY FOR PART 2

LOGISTICS INFORMATION SYSTEMS

Allen, Mary Kay. *The Development of an Artificial Intelligence System for Inventory Management* (Oak Brook, IL: Council of Logistics Management, 1986).

Allen, Mary Kay, and Omar Keith Helferich. *Putting Expert Systems to Work in Logistics* (Oak Brook, IL: Council of Logistics Management, 1990).

Allen, Mary Kay, and James M. Masters. "The Application of Expert Systems Technology to the Operation of a Large Scale Military Logistics Information System," *Journal of Business Logistics* 9, no. 2 (1988) 103–16.

Ballou, Ronald H. "Heuristics: Rules of Thumb for Logistics Decision Making," *Journal of Business Logistics* 10, no. 1 (1989), 122–32.

Bookbinder, James H., and David M. Dilts. "Logistics Information Systems in a Just-in-Time Environment," *Journal of Business Logistics* 10, no. 1 (1989), 50–67.

Bowersox, Donald J., and David J. Closs. "Simulation in Logistics: A Review of Present Practice and a Look to the Future," *Journal of Business Logistics* 10, no. 1 (1989), 133–47.

Brickell, Geoff. "Logistics and the Single Market," *Logistics Information Management* 3, no. 2 (June 1990), 79–82.

Burbridge, John J. "Strategic Implications of Logistics Information Systems," *The Logistics and Transportation Review* 24, no. 4 (December 1988), 368–83.

Carter, Joseph; Robert Monczka; Keith Clauson; and Thomas Zelinski. "Education and Training for Successful EDI Implementation," *Journal of Purchasing and Materials Management* (Summer 1987), 13–20.

Closs, Steve M.; Omar Keith Helferich; and Steven J. Young. "KBS: Potential for Logistics?" *Logistics World* 2, no. 2 (June 1989), 75–79.

Cook, Robert Lorin. "Expert System Use in Logistics Education: An Example and Guidelines for Logistics Educators," *Journal of Business Logistics* 10, no. 1 (1989), 68–87.

de Leeuw, Kees. "Computers in the 1990s and the Impact on Logistics," *International Journal of Business Logistics* 1, no. 2 (1988), 21–29.

Fox, Mary Lou. "Integrating Forecasting and Operations Planning in Promotion Driven Companies," Council of Logistics Management, *Annual Conference Proceedings* (9–12 October 1988), 67–80.

Harrington, Lisa H. "The ABCs of EDI," *Traffic Management* 29, no. 8 (August 1990), 49–52.

Kling, James A., and Curtis M. Grimm. "Microcomputer Use in Transportation and Logistics: A Literature Review with Implications for Educators," *Journal of Business Logistics* 9, no. 1 (1988), 1–18.

LaLonde, Bernard J.; Martha C. Cooper; and Thomas G. Noordeweier. *Customer Service: A Management Perspective* (Oak Brook, IL: Council of Logistics Management, 1988).

Langley, C. John. "Information-Based Decision Making in Logistics Management," *International Journal of Physical Distribution & Materials Management* 15, no. 7 (1985), 41–55.

Langley, C. John. "Microcomputers as a Logistics Information Strategy," *Application of New Technologies, Methods and Approaches to Logistics* (James M. Stock, ed.), special issue of the *International Journal of Physical Distribution & Materials Management* 18, no. 6 (1988), 11–17.

Langley, C. John; Stephen B. Probst; and Roy E. Cail. "Microcomputers in Logistics: 1987," *Annual Conference Proceedings* (Oak Brook, IL: Council of Logistics Management, (1987), 423–28.

Lavery, Hank, and G. A. Long. "EDI in Transportation," Council of Logistics Management, *Annual Conference Proceedings* (Oak Brook, IL: CLM, 1989), 261–77.

LeMay, Stephen A., and Wallace R. Wood. "Developing Logistics Decision Support Systems," *Journal of Business Logistics* 10, no. 2 (1989) 1–23.

McFarlan, F. Warren. "Information Technology Changes the Way You Compete," *Harvard Business Review* 62, no. 3 (May–June 1984), 98–103.

Mentzer, John T.; Camille P. Schuster; and David J. Roberts. "Microcomputer versus Mainframe Usage in Logistics," *The Logistics and Transportation Review* 26, no. 2 (June 1990) 115–32.

Monczka, Robert M., and Joseph R. Carter. "Implementing Electronic Data Interchange," *Journal of Purchasing and Materials Management* (Spring 1989), 26–33.

Powers, Richard F. "Optimization Models for Logistics Decisions," *Journal of Business Logistics* 10, no. 1 (1989), 106–21.

Sease, Gary J. "Innovative Use of Information Management Models in Distribution," *Annual Conference Proceedings* 2 (Oak Brook, IL: Council of Logistics Management, 1987), 149–66.

Seeds, James S. "ShipSmart," *Distribution* (January 1988), 78–80.

Stenger, Alan J. "Information Systems in Logistics Management: Past, Present, and Future," *Transportation Journal* 26, no. 1 (Fall 1986), 65–82.

Temple, Barker & Sloane, Inc. *Logistics Data Interchange: An Emerging Competitive Weapon for Shippers* (Lexington, MA: Temple, Barker & Sloane, Inc., 1987).

INVENTORY

Anderson, David L., and Robert J. Quinn. "The Role of Transportation in Long Supply Line Just-in-Time Logistics Channels," *Journal of Business Logistics* 7, no. 1 (1986), 68–87.

Ansari, A., and Jim Heckel. "JIT Purchasing: Impact of Freight and Inventory Costs," *Journal of Purchasing and Materials Management* (Summer 1987), 24–28.

Bagchi, Prabir K. "Management of Materials Under Just-in-Time Inventory System: A New Look," *Journal of Business Logistics* 9, no. 2 (1988), 89–102.

Bagchi, Prabir K., and Frank W. Davis. "Some Insights into Inbound Freight Consolidation," *Application of New Technologies, Methods and Approaches to Logistics* (James M. Stock, ed.), special issue of the *International Journal of Physical Distribution & Materials Management* 18, no. 6 (1988), 27–33.

Bregman, Robert L. "Enhanced Distribution Requirements Planning," *Journal of Business Logistics* 11, no. 2 (1990), 49–68.

Cavinato, Joseph. "What Does Your Inventory Really Cost?" *Distribution* (March 1988), 68–72.

Chapman, Stephen N., and Phillip L. Carter. "Supplier/Customer Inventory Relationships Under Just in Time," *Decision Sciences Journal* 21, no. 1 (Winter 1990), 35–50.

Closs, David J. "An Adaptive Inventory System as a Tool for Strategic Inventory Management," *Proceedings of the 1981 Annual Meeting of the National Council of Physical Distribution Management* (Chicago: National Council of Physical Distribution Management, 1981), 659–79.

Closs, David J. "Inventory Management: A Comparison of a Traditional vs. Systems View," *Journal of Business Logistics* 10, no. 2, 90–105.

Eppen, Gary D., and R. Kipp Martin. "Determining Safety Stock in the Presence of Stochastic Lead Time and Demand," *Management Science* 34, no. 11 (November 1988), 1380–91.

Frazier, Gary L.; Robert E. Spekman; and Charles R. O'Neal. "Just-in-Time Exchange Relationships in Industrial Markets," *Journal of Marketing* 52, no. 4 (October 1988), 52–67.

Gomes, Roger, and John T. Mentzer. "A Systems Approach to the Investigation of Just-In-Time," *Journal of Business Logistics* 9, no. 2 (1988), 71–88.

Ho, Chrwan-jyh. "Distribution Requirements Planning: A Generalized System for Delivery Scheduling in a Multi-Sourcing Logistics System," *International Journal of Physical Distribution & Logistics Management* 20, no. 2, 3–8.

Hummel, John W., and Alan J. Stenger. "An Evaluation of Proactive vs. Reactive Replenishment Systems," *International Journal of Physical Distribution & Materials Management* 18, no. 4, 3–13.

Karmarkar, Uday. "Getting Control of Just-In-Time," *Harvard Business Review* (September–October 1989), 122–31.

Krajewski, Lee J., and Larry P. Ritzman. *Operations Management*, 2d ed. (Reading, MA: Addison-Wesley Publishing Co. 1990).

Krajewski, Lee J.; Barry E. King; Larry P. Ritzman; and Danny S. Wong. "Kanban, MRP and Shaping the Manufacturing Environment," *Management Science* 33, no. 1 (January 1987), 39–57.

Maltz, Arnold, and James M. Masters. "Strategies for the Successful Implementation of New Information Technology in Logistics: The DRP Experience," Council of Logistics Management, *1989 Annual Conference Proceedings* (Oak Brook, IL: CLM, 1989), 13–49.

Maskell, Brian H. "Distribution Resource Planning," *Management Accounting* 66, no. 1 (January 1988), 18–20.

McGee, Richard G., and John J. Fontanella. "DRPII: Operational Considerations," *Council of Logistics Management, 1989 Annual Conference Proceedings* (Oak Brook, IL: CLM, 1989), 125–42.

Mundy, Ray A.; Judy A. Ford; Paul E. Forney; and Jerry Lineback. "Innovations in Carrier Sourcing: Transportation Partnership," Council of Logistics Management, *1989 Annual Conference Proceedings* (Oak Brook, IL: CLM, 1989), 109–114.

Orlicky, Joseph. *Materials Requirements Planning* (New York: McGraw-Hill, 1975).

Pinnock, Alison. "Direct Product Profitability," *Management Accounting* 67, no. 9 (October 1989), 18–19.

Ronen, David. "Inventory Centralization/Decentralization—The Square Root Law Revisited Again," *Journal of Business Logistics* 11, no. 2 (1990), 129–38.

Trunick, Perry A. "Cost Control Means Lower Inventories," *Transportation & Distribution* 30, no. 4 (April 1989), 16–17.

Walter, Clyde Kenneth. "The Inventory Carrying Cost Methodology," *Logistics Spectrum* 22, Issue 2 (Summer 1988), 25–32.

Zemke, Douglas E., and Douglas M. Lambert. "Utilizing Information Technology to Manage Inventory," *Annual Conference Proceedings* (Oak Brook, IL:, 1987), 119–40.

Zinn, Walter, and Howard Marmorstein. "Comparing Two Alternative Methods of Determining Safety Stock Levels: The Demand and the Forecast Systems," *Journal of Business Logistics* 11, no. 2 (1990), 95–110.

Zinn, Walter; Michael Levy; and Donald J. Bowersox. "On Assumed Assumptions and the Inventory Centralization/Decentralization Issue," *Journal of Business Logistics* 11, no. 2 (1990), 138.

TRANSPORTATION SYSTEM

Anderson, David L., and Robert J. Quinn. "The Role of Transportation in Long Supply Line Just-In-Time Logistics Channels," *Journal of Business Logistics* 7, no. 1 (1986), 68–87.

Archambault, Michael. "Intermodalism and Liner Shipping Intermodal Approaches," *Transportation Practitioners Journal* 56, no. 2 (Winter 1989), 151–63.

Arthur D. Little, Inc. *Direct Store Delivery: Store-Level Study* (Cambridge, MA: Arthur D. Little, Inc., 1987).

Babcock, Michael W., and H. Wade German. "Changing Determinants of Truck-Rail Market Shares," *The Logistics and Transportation Review* 25, no. 3 (September 1989), 251–70.

Bachmann, Gwen R.; James C. Johnson; and Kenneth C. Schneider. "The 1980 Motor Carrier Act Ten Years Later: Do Trucking Company CEOs Love It or Hate It?" *Transportation Practitioners Journal* 57, no. 2 (Winter 1990), 163–87.

Beier, Frederick J. "How Will Transportation Carriers Differentiate Their Services in the Future Deregulated Economy?" in *Logistics: Contribution and Control,* ed. Patrick Gallagher *Proceedings of the 1983 Logistics Resource Forum* (Cleveland, OH: Leaseway Transportation Corporation, 1983), 137–47.

Boberg, Kevin B., and Frederick M. Collison. "International Air Transportation Trends in the Pacific Basin," *Transportation Journal* 28, no. 3 (Spring 1989), 24–34.

Chow, Garland, and Richard F. Poist. "The Measurement of Quality of Service and the Transportation Purchase Decision," *The Logistics and Transportation Review* 20, no. 1 (1984), 25–44.

Crum, Michael R., and Benjamin J. Allen. "Shipper EDI, Carrier Reduction, and Contracting Strategies: Impacts on the Motor Carrier Industry," *Transportation Journal* 29, no. 4 (Summer 1990), 18–31.

Daniels, John P., and Stan Cunningham. "Selected Legislation of the 1990s and the Effects on the Trucking Industry: A Systems Perspective," *Transportation Practitioners Journal* 57, no. 3 (Spring 1990), 298–303.

Ernst & Whinney, *Transportation Accounting & Control: Guidelines for Distribution and Financial Management* (Oak Brook, IL: National Council of Physical Distribution Management, 1983).

Glaskowsky, Nicholas A. *Effects of Deregulation on Motor Carriers* (Westport, CT: Eno Foundation for Transportation, 1986).

Grimm, Curtis M.; Thomas M. Corsi; and Judith J. Jarrell. "U.S. Motor Carrier Cost Structure Under Deregulation," *The Logistics and Transportation Review* 25, no. 3 (September 1989), 231–49.

Heijmen, Ton C. M. "Private Carriage Market Place: Changing Times Reflect a New Purchase Logic," National Council of Physical Distribution Management, Annual Conference Proceedings (1983), 892–938.

Higginson, James K., and James H. Bookbinder. "Implications of Just-in-Time Production on Rail Freight Systems," *Transportation Journal* 29, no. 3 (Spring 1990), 29–35.

Jerman, Roger E., and Ronald D. Anderson. "Intermodalism: Shipper and Carrier Views," *Transportation Practitioners Journal* 57, no. 2 (Winter 1990), 187–97.

Kling, Robert W. "Deregulation and Structural Change in the LTL Motor Freight Industry," *Transportation Journal* 29, no. 3 (Spring 1990), 47–53.

Langley, C. John Jr., and Wallace R. Wood. "Managerial Perspectives on the Transportation Equipment Leasing Decision," *Transportation Journal* 18, no. 3 (Spring 1978), 36–48.

Lieb, Robert C. *Transportation: The Domestic System,* 3d ed. (Reston, VA: Reston Publishing, 1985).

Lieb, Robert C., and Robert A. Millen. "The Responses of General Commodity Motor Carriers to Just in Time Manufacturing Programs," *Transportation Journal* 30, no. 1 (Fall 1990), 5–11.

Locklin, D. Philip. *Economics of Transportation,* 7th ed. (Homewood, IL: Richard D. Irwin, 1972).

Milne, A. M., and J. C. Laight. *The Economics of Inland Transportation,* 2d ed. (London: Sir Isaac Pitman and Sons, 1963).

Nincent, Daniel, and Dinos Stasinopoulos. "The Aviation Policy of the European Community," *Journal of Transport Economics and Policy* XXIV, no. 1 (January 1990), 95–100.

Pegrum, Dudley F. *Transportation Economics and Public Policy,* 3d ed. (Homewood, IL: Richard D. Irwin, 1973).

Phillips L. T. "Structural Change in the Airline Industry: Carrier Concentration at Large Hub Airports and Its Implication for Competitive Behavior," *Transportation Journal,* 25 (Winter 1986), 18–29.

Rakowski, James P.; R. Neil Southern; and Lynn R. Godwin. "Recruiting and the Truck Driver Shortage: Is the Industry Reactive or Proactive?" *Transportation Practitioners Journal* 56, no. 4 (Summer 1989), 381–92.

Robeson, James F., and Robert G. House, eds. *The Distribution Handbook* (New York,: The Free Press, 1985).

Sampson, Roy J., and Martin T. Farris. *Domestic Transportation Practice, Theory, and Policy,* 4th ed. (Boston: Houghton Mifflin, 1979).

Sheffi, Yosef. "Carrier/Shipper Interactions in the Transportation Market: An Analytical Framework," *Journal of Business Logistics* 7, no. 1 (1986), 1–27.

Stephenson, F. J., Jr. *Transportation USA* (Reading, MA: Addison-Wesley Publishing Co., 1987).

Sweeney, D. J.; C. J. McCarthy; S. J. Kalish; and J. M. Cutter, Jr. *Transportation Deregulation* (Washington, D.C.: NASSTRAC, 1986).

Taff, Charles A. *Commercial Motor Transportation,* 7th ed. (Centerville, MD: Cornell Maritime Press, 1986).

The objective of Part III is to acquaint the reader with the economic and operational characteristics of transportation management, warehousing and materials handling and packaging. Chapter 9 addresses the managerial aspects of transportation management and the impact of transportation regulation upon the utilization of carrier services and logistics control. Attention is directed to transportation pricing and to the functions involved in traffic management.

In Chapter 10 warehousing activities are examined. The inventory decisions presented in Part II must be made in conjunction with warehousing. In particular, such questions as the use of private versus public warehousing, contract warehousing, and the number of warehouses required to meet the company's storage needs are considered in light of the effect on inventory costs. Warehouse management issues are also given consideration.

The final chapter in this part considers materials handling and packaging. The two topics provide an important integration with transportation and storage decisions. Efficient warehouse operations depend on materials handling systems and the effective interchange between the warehouse and the carrier. Packaging interacts with transportation and warehousing in terms of protection afforded the product and the utilization of the transportation and storage facilities.

TRANSPORTATION MANAGEMENT

Transportation costs, which represent approximately forty to fifty percent of total logistics costs and four to ten percent of the selling price for many companies, may represent logistics management's major concern. Transportation decision directly affect the total logistics costs, costs in other functional areas of the firm, and costs within other logistics channel members. This chapter focuses on the daily transportation management activities in today's deregulated transportation environment, focusing specifically on transportation regulation, carrier pricing, services and documentation. We will first direct our attention toward transportation management philosophy.

MANAGEMENT PHILOSOPHY

The passage of the transportation deregulation acts in 1977 and 1980 drastically changed the business climate within which the transportation manager operated. Before them, the climate emphasized the ability to operate effectively within regulation confines. Good transportation managers were those who worked within the system to ensure that competitors were not getting better rates or services; that is, to achieve regulatory parity among transportation users.

regulatory orientation

The bureaucratic red tape of transportation regulation placed a stranglehold on management initiative. Pre-deregulation-era managers commonly defined activities regulations prohibited in the transportation field so as to achieve regulatory parity and to prevent other shippers from achieving favorable rates and services from a carrier. Managerial transportation innovations were difficult to develop because of regulatory constraints. By necessity, transportation managers armed themselves with a list of "thou shalt nots" that would squelch any and all suggestions company managers put forth.

current philosophy

Since 1980, the transportation environment has changed. The regulations shackling management decisions are gone. A transportation manager can no longer utilize the regulatory constraints to prevent a competitor from gaining a competitive advantage when a carrier offers the competitor better rates and services. In fact, contracting and the publication of individual carrier tariffs will probably prevent the transportation manager from knowing what rates and services a carrier is providing to competitors.

proactive

With the regulatory safety net gone, the transportation manager must rely on traditional management techniques, using a proactive approach to identify and solve transportation problems and to provide the company with a competitive advantage in the marketplace.

problem solving

A proactive management approach seeks to identify transportation problems and to postulate solutions that benefit the whole company. Without regulatory rule book, transportation management is free to concentrate on innovative solutions to today's logistics and transportation challenges. Only managers' ability and creativity and normal business law constraints limit the benefits of this proactive business strategy.

For example, a firm's sales decline in a particular market result from longer and less dependable lead times than those the competition in that market provide. If the firm makes a modal switch from rail to truck, the increased cost of truck service would force the firm to increase prices or to incur a loss, neither outcome being acceptable. Negotiating with carriers, establishing carrier contracts with prescribed service levels, or modifying loading procedures are alternatives that the transportation manager may explore to improve services and sales while maintaining acceptable costs.

negative versus positive approach

Today, the transportation manager actively participates in solving company problems. Companies no longer look upon transportation as a necessary evil; rather, transportation contains fundamental solutions to problems that plague a company's functional areas. Thus, today's transportation manager must understand other functional areas as well as the entire company, so as to seek logistics strategies that support other departmental and corporate strategies.

Reduce Number of Carriers

market power

By reducing the number of carriers it uses, a shipping firm increases the freight volume and freight revenue that it gives to a carrier, thereby increasing its ability to have the carrier provide the rates and services the shipper needs. As the shipper concentrates its freight business in a limited number of carriers, the shipper becomes more important to each carrier; and each carrier, in becoming more dependent on the shipper's business, is more willing to negotiate with the shipper.

For example, Martin-Marietta's Electronic Missile Systems Group uses twelve inbound carriers, four nationwide motor carriers, two regional motor carriers, an airfreight carrier, two air express carriers, two freight forwarders, and one international airfreight forwarder.[1] Mack Truck reduced the number of carriers it utilizes at its Baltimore distribution center from between forty and fifty to seven and uses these seven carriers for both inbound and outbound moves. From 1986 to 1987, Mack realized a 17.5 percent saving in freight cost.[2]

Being one of the carrier's largest customers gives the shipper significant negotiating power: the fear of losing the shipper's business motivates the carrier to comply with the shipper's demands for better rates and service levels. In essence, the shipper who is one of the carrier's A customers (part of the twenty percent of the carrier's customers who provide eighty percent of the carrier's sales revenue) possesses market power with the carrier.

strategic alliance

This concentration of freight in a limited number of carriers not only increases market power, but also permits a company to develop a strategic alliance with the carriers it uses. In a strategic alliance, the shipper and the carrier, recognizing their mutual dependency, strive to be efficient so that both can survive and prosper. In addition to reducing transportation costs, the improved working relations within the strategic alliance reduce other logistics costs such as information processing, inventory, and warehousing.

balanced loads

Reducing the number of carriers a firm uses also may increase the possibility of providing a carrier with balanced loads of raw materials inbound and finished goods outbound. By reducing excess capacity a balanced load pattern enables the carrier to reduce its costs and to offer lower rates. In addition, providing the carrier with balanced loads may increase the carrier's service level.

risks

A negative risk associated with concentrating business in a limited number of carriers is the firm's increased dependency on the carrier it uses. A shipper who uses only ten carriers is much more vulnerable to shipment disruptions and resulting customer service declines than is a shipper who uses 100 carriers. With the 100-carrier strategy, losing one carrier requires the shipper to reallocate only one percent of its freight volume among the remaining ninety-nine carriers, which should pose no problem to carrier capacity and customer service levels. In the ten-carrier scenario, however, losing one carrier requires the shipper to secure shipping capacity equivalent to ten percent of the shipper's volume, which the remaining nine carriers may not have capacity to handle. This will force the shipper to use carriers unfamiliar with the shipper's freight, shipping procedures, and customer service requirements, will normally disrupt operating systems and customer service levels, and, possibly, will lead to higher transportation costs since crisis stage allows the shipper little market power to negotiate favorable rates.

CARRIER NEGOTIATION

Following transportation deregulation, transportation management expanded to include carrier negotiation. Before deregulation, transportation management gave carrier negotiation little attention since the economic controls regulating common carriers permitted little rate freedom. The common carriers adhered to the rate bureau's prevailing rate, and rate negotiation was a fruitless exercise for the transportation manager.

Today, carrier negotiation is the norm, and, in some situations, a daily function. The transportation manager must possess negotiating skills sufficient to secure the desired service level at the least cost. Successful carrier negotiation has enabled many companies either to remain competitive in the market or to increase competitive advantage through improved carrier service levels.

Market forces and regulatory constraints determine the negotiable factors between the carrier and the shipper. Generally, the negotiated factors resolve around the rates and services the carriers provide; and the remaining economic regulations, the ICC (see following section) and antitrust scrutiny, impose upon the truck and rail common carriers govern the negotiated rates and services; air carrier negotiations are subject to antitrust scrutiny only.

The marketplace determines the negotiable factors assuming that these factors violate no regulatory constraints. The shipper's operational needs, customer demands, and company objectives determine the areas where negotiations will begin. The shipper brings these needs to the carrier, who decides (negotiates) whether these needs are realistic. More than likely the carrier will respond with a counterproposal that offers something less than what the shipper requested.

At other times the carrier will initiate negotiations. The carrier, who may have a specific need to eliminate an empty backhaul, specify pickup times, or increase tonnage, entices a shipper to respond usually by offering a concession, a reduce rate. The shipper will analyze the carrier proposal and either accept or reject the offer or request a greater concession.

market power   Throughout this negotiation, the marketplace power each party enjoys influences the outcome. The shipper possesses market power in terms of the transportation business available in a given time period and the shipper can increase this market power by limiting the number of carriers it uses. The carrier possesses market power in terms of the carrier's importance to the shipper—that is, the availability of equal or better-quality service substitutes.

Carrier Contracting

advantages

The Motor Carrier Act of 1980 and the Staggers Act of 1980 increased shippers' ability to enter into contracts with carriers. Contracting enables the shipper to eliminate the uncertainties in rates and services common carriers provide. Through the contract terms, the shipper can specify the rate and level of service that the carrier will provide and can dictate noncompliance penalties, thereby fixing service levels during the contract period.

specialized services

Contracting permits shippers that desire specialized services to purchase a unique or tailored service level that may not be legally available from the common carrier. The common carrier must provide service to all shippers without discrimination or preferential treatment. Recognizing the shipping public's need for specialized contract transportation, as opposed to a basic service level, Congress established the contract motor carrier classification in the Motor Carrier Act of 1935. However, the act restricted the number of shippers the contract motor carrier could serve (the rule of eight) and converted the contract carrier's authority to common carrier if the number of shippers under contract exceeded the maximum.

truck

With the elimination in 1980 of the restriction on the permitted number of contracts, many contract carriers now have fifty to sixty contracts in effect. Truck leasing companies provide contract motor carrier service to firms that formerly leased their equipment. In addition, many private carrier operations have become for-hire contract carrier subsidiaries which provide tailored service to the parent firm as well as to other shippers.

rail

Rail transportation has widely adopted contracting. A railroad negotiation normally establishes a contract rather than the rate discount common to motor carrier negotiations. Rail contracts normally specify a rate, the type of equipment the carrier will provide, and the service level the shippers expect (a fifteen-day maximum transit time on shipments from Chicago to Seattle, for example). The contract also dictates a minimum or guaranteed quantity that the shipper will tender to the carrier during the contract life.

JIT

Companies implementing the just-in-time (JIT) system use contracting to ensure safe, consistent, and fast service. The JIT system emphasizes low inventory levels and a reliance upon transportation to deliver goods as customers and logistics nodes need them. Transportation delays decrease production, increase inventory costs, and disrupt operations, which defeats JIT's objectives. Contracting with all transportation modes ensures the required transportation service level.

Consolidation Shipments

benefits

The freight volume a shipper tenders to a carrier directly relates to the freight rate the carrier charges. By consolidating shipments, the transportation manager can reap the benefits of the lower rates carriers charge for larger shipment volumes. That is, the manager may increase the weight of the shipment the shipper tenders to the carrier to the level that will enable the carrier to use TL (truckload) or CL (carload) rates. In addition, the motor carrier tariffs provide rate discounts at multiple weight levels such as 1,000 pounds, 2,000 pounds, and 5,000 pounds, thus encouraging shippers to consolidate small shipments into larger ones.

shipment size

As a general rule, carriers charge lower rates for shipping larger quantities. Carrier cost per weight unit transported (pound, cwt, or ton) decreases as the shipment weight increases. For example, the carrier pickup cost does not vary with shipment size. The per-pound carrier pickup cost for a 2,000-pound shipment is 50% of that for a 1,000-pound shipment. (If the pickup cost is $50, the pickup cost per pound is $0.05 for the 1,000-pound shipment and $0.025 for the 2,000-pound shipment.) TL rates requiring 25,000- to 30,000-pound shipments may be 30% to 60% lower than LTL rates.

price discounts A shipper may utilize freight consolidation to support a competitive price marketing strategy. By consolidating shipments, the transportation manager realizes a lower carrier rate; and the shipper can translate this lower transportation cost per unit into a lower price for buyers purchasing the larger quantity. Thus, shippers can coordinate the quantity discounts they offer buyers with the rate reductions possible with consolidated shipment sizes.

Monitor Service

product differentiation Transportation service can differentiate a company's product, thereby providing the company with competitive market advantage. An ability to get the product to the customer on a consistent, timely, and undamaged basis reduces the buyer's inventory and stockout costs. Thus, product differentiation through the transportation service a company provide is a significant nonprice marketing strategy.

service/cost trade-off However, a trade-off exists between transportation service and cost. The transportation manager must compare the service level finished product buyers require and against the level the shipper currently provides. If the buyers require three-day transit time and the shipper provides two-day transit time the transportation manager is providing a better and more costly service level than the buyers demand. The transportation manager might correct the service level by negotiating a lower rate with the carrier in return for a longer transit time (three-day delivery instead of two-day delivery) or utilizing a slower but lower-cost mode of transportation.

A fundamental element for implementing this strategy is information. The transportation manager must have information regarding the customer service demands and the service level current carriers provide. Without this information, the transportation manager cannot make a rational transportation service/cost decision that meets the shipper's established logistics and corporate goals.

transport documents Normal transportation documentation—the bill of lading, freight bill, customer shipping document, and so on—does not contain transportation service data. These source documents do not indicate the number of days the shipment is in transit, the transit time consistency, or the frequency and extent of shipment damage. The transportation manager must obtain these data directly from the shipment's receiver.

transit time The bill of lading, freight bill, and customer shipping document indicate the date the shipper dispatched the shipment to the carrier, but not the date the consignee received it. To obtain the delivery date, the transportation manager could attach a return postcard to the shipment asking the consignee to indicate the reception date. Another method, which is more costly but more effective, is to conduct a phone survey. Some transportation managers have asked the sales force to request delivery service information from customers during sales calls.

Figure 9–1 is an example of a carrier evaluation report which bases its evaluation criteria upon the carrier selection factors we discussed in Chapter 8. The figure assigns each criterion a weight indicating the criterion's importance to the company and gives the carrier's performance in each service and financial areas a numerical rating. The criterion rating multiplied by the criterion importance gives a weighted rating; the sum of the weighted ratings provides an evaluation score for each carrier.

Using a carrier evaluation system like the one Figure 9–1 depicts provides the transportation manager with information that is vital to the achievement of the transportation, logistics and corporate customer service strategies and goals.

FEDERAL REGULATION*

Federal regulation of transportation has been with us since the Act to Regulate Commerce passed in 1887. The years immediately preceding the enactment of this law were full of turmoil, for both shippers and carriers. Inland transportation was basically by railroad, and the carriers charged high rates when possible and discriminated against small shippers. Control over the transportation industry was important to U.S. economic growth and to assure a stable transportation service supply compatible with an expanding society's needs.

public interest
We find the basis for federal economic regulation of transportation in transportation's significance to the overall economy of the United States. Transportation enables business to accomplish the very foundation of economic activity—the exchange of commodities from areas of oversupply to areas of undersupply. The transportation activity benefits all citizens; thus, we could argue that the government should provide transportation, just as it provides public interest functions such as the court system and national defense.

Traditionally, however, private enterprise has provided freight transportation. Through the dollars shippers spend, the marketplace identifies the resources that transportation companies commit to various transportation services and considers this resource allocation to be more efficient than that a governmental, political allocation could produce. Since the free enterprise marketplace has imperfections that may allow monopolies to develop, government control of transportation attempts to allocate resources in the public's interest by maintaining and enforcing the competitive market structure.

Overview of Federal Regulation

granger laws
Before passage of federal economic regulation, several midwestern states had passed granger laws regulating transportation in their respective states. These laws attempted to correct the railroads monopolistic price and service practices after Civil War. However, in 1886, the Supreme Court held that a state could not regulate interstate traffic. This decision created an interstate transportation regulation vacuum, which the federal government corrected in 1887 by passing the Act to Regulate Commerce.

legal service duties
The following common carrier legal service duties best describe the public interest aspect of federal regulation: to serve, to not discriminate, and to charge reasonable rates (see Chapter 8). These common carrier legal service duties reflect the original and subsequent transportation acts. Government regulations essentially attempt to ensure that common carriers provide transportation service to all shippers without discrimination, and that they charge reasonable rates.

ICC
Congress established the Interstate Commerce Commission (ICC) as an independent regulatory agency to administer the transportation laws. To accom-

---

*For a thorough discussion of transportation regulation, see John J. Coyle, Edward J. Bardi, and Joseph L. Cavinato, *Transportation,* 3rd ed. (St. Paul, MN: West, 1990), chapters 3, 15, 16.

FIGURE 9–1   CARRIER EVALUATION REPORT

Carrier: _____   Time Period: _____

Criteria Import	Evaluation Criteria	Carrier Rating	Weighted Rating	Comments
	Meets Pick-up Schedules			
	Meets Delivery			
	Transit Time			
	Overall			
	Consistency			
	Claims			
	Frequency			
	Timely Settlement			
	Equipment			
	Availability			
	Condition			
	Driver			
	Customer Acceptance			
	Courteous			
	Attitude			
	Scope of Operations			
	Operating Authority			
	Computer			
	EDI			
	Electronic Billing			
	Billing			
	Errors			
	Timeliness			
	Tracing Capabilities			
	Problem Solving			
	Innovativeness			
	Management			
	Attitude			
	Trustworthiness			
	Financial			
	Operating Ratio			
	Cash Flow			
	Profitability			
	Rates			
	Accessorial Charges			
	Handles Rush Shipments			
	Total Weighted Rating		_____	

Evaluator: _____   Date: _____

plish its administration charge, the ICC exercises legislative, judicial, and executive powers. For example, enforcement of statutes is an executive function, adjudicating the reasonableness of rates is a judicial function, and establishing rules is a legislative function. The ICC is limited by regulatory authority and is subject to review by the courts.

initial period

The 1887 act required carriers (railroads) to charge reasonable rates and to publish rates in tariffs that they were to make available to the public and file with the ICC. The act precluded personal discrimination and undue preference or prejudice (charging one person more or less than another for similar transportation service). The act also prohibited long- and short-haul discrimination, or charging less for a longer haul than a shorter one when the longer haul includes the shorter one, and made pooling agreements, in which carriers shared traffic or revenues, illegal.

amendments

From 1887 to 1920, amendments made to the original act increased the ICC's control and enforcement power. This period of negative regulation restricted the carriers from providing rates and services that were not in the public's best interest. The Elkins Act of 1903 strengthened the laws governing personal discrimination by providing criminal penalties for carriers and shippers who failed to follow the published tariff rate (filed rate doctrine) and to offer and accept rebates.

In 1906, the Hepburn Act gave the ICC the power to prescribe maximum rates and to control joint and through rates. The Hepburn Act contained the commodities clause, which prevented the railroads from hauling their own commodities and which brought pipelines under ICC jurisdiction. The Mann-Elkins Act of 1910, gave the ICC the power to suspend proposed rates and in 1912, the Panama Canal Act made it illegal for a railroad to own common water carriers with which the railroad competed, unless the ICC approved.

promotional

After 1920 regulatory policy became more carrier promotional. This change emanated from the financial chaos the railroads experienced because of severe intramodal competition and the emerging motor carriers' intermodal competition. The new regulations attempted to promote the carriers' viability.

The Transportation Act of 1920 allowed the ICC to establish minimum rates. At this point, reasonable rates became compensatory to the carrier. The Emergency Transportation Act of 1933 permitted cooperative actions (e.g., joint facility use) among railroads to achieve economies of operations, and gave the ICC power over railroad mergers. By giving the ICC the authority to establish the minimum rate level, Congress indirectly attempted to protect the public by somewhat assuring a stable supply of transportation.

other modes

From 1935 to 1942, transportation regulation expanded to other modes, imposing regulation that was basically the same as that under which the railroads operated. The Motor Carrier Act of 1935 brought for-hire motor carriers and brokers under ICC control; the act controlled motor carrier entry by requiring new carriers to secure a certificate of public convenience and necessity. The Civil Aeronautics Act of 1938 established economic regulations over air carriers and created the Civil Aeronautics Board (CAB) as an independent regulatory agency to administer the regulations. In 1940, regulation similar to that for motor carriers brought domestic water carriers under ICC control. Finally, Congress passed economic regulation for domestic freight forwarders in 1942.

regulatory agencies

Today, the ICC administers the federal economic regulations for railroads, motor carriers, and domestic water carriers. Domestic surface freight forwarders were deregulated in 1986. The Federal Maritime Commission administers ocean shipping regulations, and the CAB administered federal economic controls for air carriers until air carrier deregulation abolished the CAB in 1985 and transferred the remaining minimal economic regulations to the Department of Transportation. The Federal Energy Regulatory Commission administers pipeline economic regulations.

deregulation
　　Beginning in 1976, a number of transportation laws reduced the regulation imposed on transportation. Under these deregulation laws, transportation was to rely more on marketplace control over rates and services. We will discuss these deregulation amendments in the following section.

Deregulation

air carriers
　　In 1977, Congress completely deregulated air cargo transportation. Air cargo carriers are no longer subject to convenience and entry controls and air cargo rates are regulation free.

trucking
　　The Motor Carrier Act of 1980 "reregulated" rate controls over trucking; rather, the act provided greater rate-making freedom and encouraged rate competition among the carriers. Beginning in 1984, motor carriers could not collectively (through the rate bureau process) vote on or discuss single-line rate proposals. However, the carriers may discuss or vote on general rate increases or decreases.

zone of flexibility
　　The Motor Carrier Act of 1980 allowed the carriers greater freedom to set rates in response to demand by establishing the *zone of flexibility*, which permits the carrier to raise or lower a rate by fifteen percent per year without ICC intervention; the ICC presumes the rate to be reasonable if it is within the zone of flexibility. Furthermore, the act allowed a carrier and shipper to negotiate a reduced rate in return for a limited liability on the property the carrier transported.

railroads
　　In 1976, the Railroad Revitalization and Regulatory Reform Act, which established a zone of reasonableness initially introduced railroad rate deregulation. The *zone of reasonableness* permitted a railroad to raise or lower rates by seven percent from the rate level in effect at the beginning of the year. The act also allowed the ICC to grant exemptions from commodity traffic regulations when public interest did not require those regulations. This exemption has eliminated rate controls over the movement of piggyback traffic and fruit shipments, for example.

maximum rates
　　Finally, the Staggers Act of 1980 permitted rail carriers greater rate freedom by limiting ICC maximum rail rate jurisdiction to rates where railroads exercise market dominance, defined initially as rates that exceed 160% of variable costs (180% by 1984). A zone of rate flexibility permitted rail rates increase by six percent a year through 1984, and four percent per year thereafter. The act limits collective rate-making to carriers who can practically participate in the joint movement. Railroads may establish contract rates for a specific shipper. Rail rate increases take effect in twenty days, and rate reductions take effect in ten days.

　　In summary, rate deregulation has been complete for air cargo and certain rail traffic types—piggyback, for example. For trucks and railroads, deregulation has increased rate-making flexibility and rate competition among the regulated carriers. However, a 1990 Supreme Court decision, *Maislin Industry* v. *Primary Steel*, has generated a considerable amount of confusion regarding the extent of deregulation for common carrier marketplace-determined rates. In the Maislin

filed rate doctrine
case, the Supreme Court held that a common carrier must charge the rate filed with the ICC—the filed rate doctrine the Elkins Act of 1903 contains. Following the carrier's (Maislin's) bankruptcy, the shipper (Primary Steel) was held liable

for the difference between the negotiated rate and the filed rate. A negotiated rate with a common carrier is not a legal rate unless it is published in the carrier's tariff and the carrier files the tariff with the ICC. Shippers continue to negotiate rates with common carriers, but the transportation manager must make sure that the negotiated rate is published in the carrier's tariff and that the carrier has filed the tariff with the ICC.

DOCUMENTATION—DOMESTIC

Domestic transportation utilizes a number of different documents to govern, direct, control, and provide information about a shipment. This section focuses on the bill of lading, freight bill, claims, and F.O.B. terms of sale—the documentation that is most prevalent in interstate transportation.

Bill of Lading

contract receipt

The *bill of lading* is probably the single most important transportation document. It originates the shipment, provides all the information the carrier needs to accomplish the move, stipulates the transportation contract terms, acts as a receipt for the goods the shipper tenders to the carrier, and, in some cases, shows certificate of title to the goods. Figure 9–2 shows a typical motor carrier bill of lading.

All interstate shipments by common carriers begin with the issuance of a properly completed bill of lading. The information on the bill specifies the name and address of the consignor and consignee, as well as routing instructions for the carrier. The bill also describes the commodities in the shipment, the number of items in each commodity description, and the commodity's class or rate. Many shippers provide their own bills of lading (short form), which show the shipper's preprinted name and describe the commodities the company most commonly ships. This reduces the time filling out the bill requires, thereby eliminating delays at the shipper's loading facilities.

nonnegotiable

Straight Bill of Lading   The *straight bill of lading* is a nonnegotiable instrument, which means that endorsement of the straight bill cannot transfer title to the goods the straight bill names. For firms using the straight bill of lading, the terms of sale upon which the buyer and seller agreed the buyer and seller generally dictate where title to the goods passes. The carrier does not require presentation of the straight bill's original copy to effect delivery; the carrier must simply deliver the goods to the person or firm as consignee the straight bill of lading names.

negotiable

Order Bill of Lading   The *order bill of lading* is a negotiable instrument showing certificate of title to the goods it names. Using the order bill of lading enables the consignor to retain security interest in the goods; that is, the consignee pay the goods' invoice value before the carrier will deliver them.* The carrier cannot deliver the goods until the consignee, or rightful owner, presents the original copy of the order bill of lading to the carrier.

---

*When using a straight bill of lading, the shipper can retain security interest in the goods by using the C.O.D. (cash on delivery) service carriers offer. With a C.O.D. shipment, the carrier collects the invoice price of the shipment before deliverying the shipment to the consignee.

FIGURE 9–2   BILL OF LADING   *Source:* Courtesy of Jones Transfer Company.

†The fibre boxes used for this shipment conform to the specifications set forth in the box maker's certificate thereon, and all other requirements of Consolidated Freight Classification.   ††Shipper's imprint in lieu of stamp; not a part of bill of lading approved by the Interstate Commerce Commission.

STRAIGHT BILL OF LADING - SHORT FORM
ORIGINAL - NOT NEGOTIABLE

Shipper's No.   12345

CARRIER: **JONES TRANSFER COMPANY - JTRC**   July 1,   19 88   Carrier's No.

RECEIVED, subject to the classifications and tariffs in effect on the date of the issue of this Bill of Lading,
the property described below, in apparent good order, except as noted (contents and condition of contents of packages unknown), marked, consigned, and destined as indicated below, which said carrier (the word carrier being understood throughout this contract as meaning any person or corporation in possession of the property under the contract) agrees to carry to its usual place of delivery at said destination, if on its route, otherwise to deliver to another carrier on the route to said destination. It is mutually agreed, as to each carrier of all or any of said property over all or any portion of said route to destination, and as to each party at any time interested in all or any of said property, that every service to be performed hereunder shall be subject to all the terms and conditions of the Uniform Domestic Straight Bill of Lading set forth (1) in Official, Southern, Western and Illinois Freight Classifications in effect on the date hereof, if this is a rail or a rail-water shipment, or (2) in the applicable motor carrier classification or tariff if this is a motor carrier shipment.
Shipper hereby certifies that he is familiar with all the terms and conditions of the said bill of lading, including those on the back thereof, set forth in the classification or tariff which governs the transportation of this shipment, and the said terms and conditions are hereby agreed to by the shipper and accepted for himself and his assigns.

TO:			FROM:	
Consignee	Ajax Machine Company		Shipper	ABC Manufacturing Company
Street	1 Anyplace Street		Street	300 Main Street
Destination	Toledo, OH 43601 Zip		Origin	Detroit, MI 48201 Zip

Route ___ JTRC ___   Car or Vehicle Initials   JTRC   No. 1234

No. Packages	H.M.	KIND OF PACKAGE, DESCRIPTION OF ARTICLES, SPECIAL MARKS, AND EXCEPTIONS	*WEIGHT (Sub. to Cor.)	Class or Rate	Ck. Col.	
5		Ctns Nuts or Bolts, NOI, Iron or Steel	600			Subject to Section 7 of Conditions of applicable bill of lading, if this shipment is to be delivered to the consignee without recourse on the consignor, the consignor shall sign the following statement:
3		Plts Hardware, NOI, Iron or Steel	325			The carrier shall not make delivery of this shipment without payment of freight and all other lawful charges.
						ABC Manufacturing Co
						(Signature of consignor)
						If charges are to be prepaid, write or stamp here, "To be Prepaid."
						PREPAID
						Received $ to apply in prepayment of the charges on the property described hereon.
8		TTL Pieces	925			
		Send Freight Bill To: Associated Motors Corporation				Agent or Cashier.
		P. O. Box 123				Per
		Columbus, OH 43201				(The signature here acknowledges only the amount prepaid.)
						Charges advanced: $

*If the shipment moves between two ports by a carrier by water, the law requires that the bill of lading shall state whether it is carrier's or shipper's weight.
NOTE–Where the rate is dependent of value, shippers are required to state specifically in writing the agreed or declared value of the property.
The agreed or declared value of the property is hereby specifically stated by the shipper to be not exceeding ___ per ___

						Notification of arrival	
						Begin loading	
Shipper ABC Manufacturing Company *John Smith*	Agent (Carrier) JTRC	Per *Joe Jones*				Complete loading	
P. O. Box 777	7/1	Ⓢ				Vehicle released	
Detroit, MI 48201 Permanent post office address of shipper	Date of pickup	No. of pieces (or SL & C)				**DETENTION RECORD**	

HM - HAZARDOUS MATERIALS

1

Figure 9–3 shows the procedure for using the order bill of lading. The consignor completes the order bill of lading, gives a copy to the carrier, and forwards the original copy to the consignor's bank, where a sight draft in the amount of the shipment's invoice price is attached. The consignor's bank then sends the sight draft to the consignee's bank. After payment of the sight draft, the consignee receives the original copy. The bank transfers the funds to the consignor. After presenting the original copy to the carrier, the consignee receives the goods.

If the original consignee cannot pay the sight draft, the consignor retains title to the goods and can seek out a new buyer. If either the consignee or original consignee sold the goods to another party, the carrier could not legally make delivery to the original consignee. In both situations, the party possessing the properly endorsed original copy would have title to the goods; and the carrier would make delivery to this new owner.

Using the order bill of lading to retain security interest in goods requires a fairly long transit time, to permit a bank to process the sight draft. For example, if a shipment's transit time were two days and the bank required four days to

FIGURE 9–3   PROCEDURE FOR USE OF ORDER BILL OF LADING

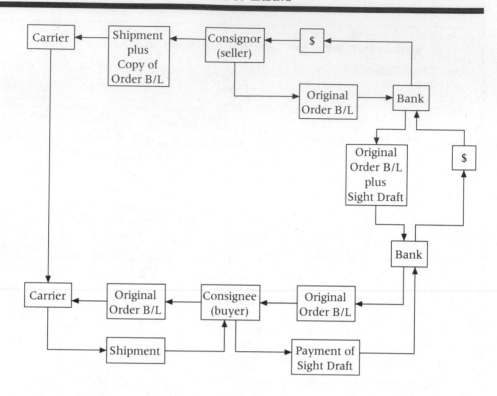

process the order bill of lading, the shipment would arrive before the original copy of the order bill of lading. Since the consignee would not have the original copy, the carrier would be unable to make delivery. When the original copy did arrive, the consignee could face an additional transportation charge for a second delivery.

Contract Terms The bill of lading contains the *terms of contract* for movement by common carrier. The contract is between the shipper and the common carrier for the movement of the freight the bill of lading identifies to the consignee the bill identifies. The bill of lading contract contains nine sections. Section 1, delineating the extent of the carrier's liability, is a primary contract term.

The major terms of the carrier's contract of carriage as found in the bill of lading sections are as follows:

1. *Carrier liability.* The carrier is held liable for all loss, damage, or delay to the goods except for the following:

exceptions to liability

> *Act of God*—loss resulting from any unavoidable natural catastrophe. If the carrier had sufficient opportunity to avoid the catastrophe, the carrier is liable and cannot use this exception.
> *Act of public enemy*—loss resulting from armed aggression against the United States.
> *Act of shipper*—loss resulting from shipper's improper loading, packaging, or concealment of goods being shipped.

Act of public authority—loss resulting from public agencies taking or destroying goods by due process of law.

Inherent nature of the goods—the normal or expected loss of the products (e.g., evaporation).

delay

2. *Reasonable dispatch.* The shipper holds the carrier liable for the actual loss or damage that results from an unreasonable delay in transit. No specific rule exists for determining reasonable time. The shipper examines the shipment's specifics to see if the delay was unreasonable under given circumstances.

3. *Cooperage and baling.* The owner pays such costs. The carrier may compress cotton or cotton linters and may commingle bulk grain shipments destined to a public elevator with other grain.

4. *Freight not accepted.* The carrier may store at the owner's cost any property the consignee does not remove within the free time. After notifying the consignor, the carrier may sell at public auction property the consignee refuses.

5. *Articles of extraordinary value.* The carrier is not obligated to carry documents or articles of extraordinary value unless the classification or tariff specifically rates such items. This is one area where a common carrier can refuse to provide service.

6. *Explosives.* The shipper shall give the carrier full written disclosure when shipping dangerous articles. If there is no disclosure, the shipper is held liable for any damage such goods cause.

7. *No recourse.* The carrier has no legal recourse back to the shipper for additional charges after making delivery. If the shipper signs the no recourse clause and the carrier delivers the shipment, the carrier has recourse only to the consignee for additional freight charges for the shipment.

8. *Substitute bill of lading.* When a bill of lading is an exchange or substitute for another, the subsequent bill of lading shall encompass the prior bill's statements regarding shipment value, election of common law liability, and consignor's signature.

9. *Water carriage.* If water transportation is involved, the water carrier is liable for negligence in loading, and is responsible for making the vessel seaworthy and for outfitting and manning the vessel.

10. *Alterations.* The carrier's agent must note any changes, additions, or erasures to make such alterations enforceable.

In essence, this brief discussion of the bill of lading contract terms describes the contract of carriage with a common carrier. The various rules and regulations the carrier's tariffs contain and those the ICC issues provide the finer detail in the contract. These contract terms are subject to regulatory scrutiny for compliance to common carrier duties and other transportation regulations.

Freight Bill

definition

The *freight bill* (see Figure 9–4) is the carrier's invoice for the charges the carrier incurs in moving a given shipment. ICC regulations stipulate the credit terms that common carriers may offer the shipper or consignee. Regulating credit terms precludes discrimination; for example, it prevents the carrier from dis-

FIGURE 9–4   FREIGHT BILL   *Source:* Courtesy of Jones Transfer Company.

All claims for loss or damage must be reported immediately. By ruling of the Interstate Commerce Commission extension of credit is limited to seven (7) days. We must request your compliance.

PREPAID ORIGINAL FREIGHT BILL

REMIT TO: ↓↓

JONES TRANSFER COMPANY–JTRC
ALPHA CODE
P.O. BOX 717
MONROE, MICHIGAN 48161
CARRIER CODE J-8400 & D.U.N.S. 005418645
PHONE AREA CODE (313) 241-4120

DATE: 7/1/88   NO. 1234567
SHOW THIS NUMBER ON YOUR REMITTANCE

SUMMARY OF CHARGES

WEIGHT	RATE	PREPAID
600	540	32.40
325	677	22.00
1000		
75	540	4.05
925 TTL	PAY THIS AMOUNT	$ 58.45

INTERCHANGE POINT   CARRIER   DIVISION

EXCEPTIONS MUST BE NOTED HERE

PAY FROM THIS INVOICE, NO STATEMENT RENDERED

UNLOADING RECORD	CONSIGNEE SIG.	TIME
DRIVER #1	NOTIFICATION OF ARRIVAL	
DRIVER #2	BEGIN UNLOADING	
	COMPLETE UNLOADING	
DELIVERY DATE PIECES	VEHICLE RELEASED	

DRIVER INFORMATION

FIRM

BY
RECEIVED PROPERTY DESCRIBED HEREON IN GOOD CONDITION EXCEPT AS NOTED

AJAX MACHINE COMPANY
1ANYPLACE STREET
TOLEDO, OH 43601

CONSIGNEE

SHIPPER
ABC MANUFACTURING COMPANY
300 MAIN STREET
DETROIT, MI 48201

POINT OF TRANSFER

CARRIER AND PRO

SHIPPER NUMBER   12345   INITIAL   THJ

PIECES	PKG	HM	DESCRIPTION OF COMMODITIES
5	CTN		NUTS OR BOLTS, NOI, IRON OR STEEL
3	PLT		HARDWARE, NOI, IRON OR STEEL
		AS DEF	
8	TTL PCS		

SEND FREIGHT BILL TO:

ASSOCIATED MOTORS CORPORATION
P O BOX 123
COLUMBUS, OH 43201

criminating against a particular shipper by extending that shipper credit times shorter than those it grants others. Shippers must comply with the credit payment periods.

credit terms   The ICC permits railroads and motor common carriers to extend credit terms of fifteen to thirty days as published in their tariffs; that is, the shipper must pay freight charges within fifteen to thirty days of receiving the freight bill. Carriers may allow discounts for prompt payment and may add service charges

prepaid or collect

for late payment. The carrier may require prepayment of the charges if, in the carrier's opinion, the commodity's value is less than the freight charges.

Freight bills may be either prepaid or collect. The prepaid or collect basis determines when the carrier will present the freight bill, not necessarily whether the shipper will pay the charges in advance or after the movement's completion. On a *prepaid* shipment, the carrier presents the freight bill on the effective day of shipment. On a *collect* shipment, the carrier presents the freight bill on the effective day of delivery. In both cases, the shipper must pay the bills within the maximum days of credit from presentation; but on the collect basis, the carrier extends the payment due date by the transit time length.

auditing

Traffic personnel may perform freight bill auditing internally. Internal auditing requires personnel with extensive carrier tariff and rate expertise. For companies lacking in-house expertise, external auditors, who usually receive a percentage of the overcharge claims paid, are available. The shipper must file overcharge claims with the carrier within three years of the shipment delivery date.

Claims

definition

The *freight claim* is a document (with no prescribed format) the shipper files with the carrier to recoup monetary losses resulting from loss, damage, or delay to the shipment or to recover overcharge payments. As we noted earlier, the common carrier is liable, with limited exception, for all loss, damage, or delay.

nature of claims

The shipper must file in writing freight claims with the carrier (originating, deliverying, or on whose line damage occurred) within nine months of delivery, or, in the case of loss, within nine months of reasonable delivery. The carrier must acknowledge in writing the receipt of the claim within thirty days and must inform the claimant within 120 days after receipt whether the carrier will pay or refuse the claim. If the carrier does not dispose of the claim within 120 days, the carrier must notify the claimant of the reasons for failure to settle the claim at the end of each succeeding sixty days. If the carrier disallows the claim, the filing party has two years from the time of disallowance to bring legal action through the courts against the carrier.

damage claims

Damage may be either visible or concealed. Visible damage, usually discovered at delivery, is that the consignee detects before opening the package. Concealed damage is not detected until the consignee opens the package. A problem arises with determining whether concealed damage occurred while the goods were in the carrier's possession or in the consignee's possession. Many carriers stipulate that the shipper must file concealed damage claims within fifteen days of delivery. This does not overrule the nine-month limitation, but the carrier will look more favorably upon the claim if the shipper files it within the stated policy period.

supporting document

To support a claim, the claimant must submit the original bill of lading, the original paid freight bill, and some indication of the commodity's value (an invoice or price catalog, for example). If the consignee notes on the bill of lading that the goods were damaged when the carrier tendered them for delivery and the carrier indicated no such damage when picking up the shipment, the claimant has a prima facie case against the carrier. The original paid freight bill determines the amount the carrier will reimburse the claimant, since the courts have concluded that the carrier is liable for the commodity's market value at destination less any unpaid freight charges.

The following principle establishes the damage claim's value: The claim shall restore the claimant to a condition as good as that in which the claimant would have been had the carrier safely delivered the goods. To determine this value, the claimant utilizes the original invoice, price catalog, and other factors to show the commodity's market value at destination. For commodities that do not have a ready market value, such as one-of-a-kind items, the claimant may use cost accounting records to determine value.

F.O.B. Terms of Sale

The *F.O.B. terms of sale* determine the logistics responsibility that the buyer and seller will incur. Originally, *F.O.B.* referred to the seller's making the product free of transportation charges to the ship, or "free on board." More specifically, the F.O.B. terms of sale delineate (1) who is to incur transportation charges, (2) who is to control movement of the shipment, and (3) where the title passes to the buyer.

The F.O.B. term specifies the point to which the seller incurs transportation charges and responsibility and relinquishes title to the buyer. For example, *F.O.B. delivered* indicates that the seller incurs all transportation charges and responsibility to the buyer's destination and that title passes to the buyer at delivery. *F.O.B. plant* means the opposite: the buyer incurs all transportation charges and responsibility, and title passes to the buyer at the shipment's origin.

The terms a firm utilizes to sell its products or to purchase its raw material directly affect the magnitude of the transportation function. A firm that purchases raw materials F.O.B. origin and sells its finished product F.O.B. delivered would require extensive transportation management. In such a situation, the firm controls carrier selection and warehousing and also incurs transportation charges for all commodity movements. The firm can pass this responsibility on to the buyer or supplier by altering the terms of sale, thereby lessening its transportation management requirements.

The F.O.B. term also defines the party responsible for filing a damage claim. The party that possesses title to the goods, must file the claim. If damage occurs after the shipment reaches the named point, the buyer would be responsible for filing the claim. Conversely, if damage occurred before the shipment reaches the named point, the seller would file the claim.

DOCUMENTATION—INTERNATIONAL

more complicated

Export documentation is far more complicated than the documentation domestic shipments require. Since the transaction involves different nations, political as well as economic considerations affect the documentation required. Specific documentation requirements vary widely from country to country. It is necessary to complete each document accurately, for a mistake may delay the shipment's delivery.

For discussion purposes, we will group the various documents into two categories: sales and transportation. Much of the information the documents require is similar, but each document serves a different purpose.

Sales Documents

sales contract

The *sales contract* is the initial document in any international business transaction, and export sales contracts exhibit little uniformity. To reduce time and cost, the export sales contract should completely and clearly describe the commodities, price, payment terms, transportation arrangements, insurance requirements, the carrier, and any special arrangements the agreement may require.

letter of credit

After negotiating the sales contract, the parties involved must determine the method of payment. The *letter of credit*, the most common payment method, provides a high degree of protection. The other payment forms include cash, consignment, and open account. The letter of credit is a bank's assurance that the buyer will make payment as long as the seller meets the sales terms (export sales contract terms) to which the parties agreed. When the seller complies with the sales conditions the letter of credit states and presents a draft drawn in compliance with the letter of credit, the buyer makes payment to the exporter.

A letter of credit is drawn up and used in the following manner.

1. The buyer and seller make a contract for the sale of goods
2. The buyer arranges for its bank to issue the seller a letter of credit in the sale amount
3. The buyer's bank places amount in the seller's bank
4. The seller prepares a draft against the deposit and attaches the draft to the following documents:
   —Clean, negotiable bill of lading
   —Certificate of insurance
   —Seller's invoice
   —Letter of credit
5. The seller endorses the order bill of lading to the bank and receives the money
6. The seller's bank endorses the bill of lading to the buyer's bank
7. The buyer's bank endorses the bill of lading to the buyer
8. The buyer takes the bill of lading to the carrier and picks up the shipment

Terms of Sale

A very important point in international transport is the *terms of sale.* Unlike domestic shipments, where buyers and sellers primarily use F.O.B. origin and F.O.B. destination terms, the international arena has a multitude of different terms.

importance

The specific terms affect all aspects of a specific shipment, partly determining the type of transportation used, the required documentation and insurance, and, most importantly, where the buyer assumes risk for the shipment. Most of the terms limit the liability of the seller and the shipper, who both try to shift the risk involved to the buyer as early as possible. Let us briefly discuss the most commonly used terms of sale and the most important aspects of each.

origin

Ex Works The term *ex works (EXW)* stipulates that the price the seller quotes applies only at the point of origin. The buyer agrees to take possession of the shipment at the point of origin and to bear all of the costs and risk transporting the goods to the destination involves.

quote lower price

Using ex works allows the seller to quote a selling price lower than would be possible if he or she had to arrange the shipment's export. This is particularly important when the seller has little or no international trade expertise. The buyer assumes all shipment costs, but also completely controls shipment's movement. This may be important when the buyer has access to favorable shipping conditions and also knows international shipping procedures better than the shipper does.

Free on Board   The term *free on board (F.O.B.)* has the same meaning as it does in domestic operations, but it has many more possible exchange points. For example, *F.O.B. carrier* means the seller is responsible for delivering the shipment to a specific carrier, after which the buyer assumes all responsibility. The F.O.B. term may also stipulate a specific port of export, a specific vessel to which the seller must deliver the shipment, and even a point within the country of importation at which the buyer and seller will exchange control. Between them, the parties decide the shipment exchange point, which depends on the price of the goods, the desired shipment method, and, most importantly, each party's ability to handle the international shipments many portions. As with domestic shipments, the F.O.B. term may also specify freight prepaid or freight allowed, depending on the sales contract's specifics.

Free Alongside   Under *free alongside (FAS)* terms, the seller agrees to deliver the goods to the dock alongside the overseas vessel that will carry the shipment. The seller pays the costs of getting the shipment to the dock, where possession and responsibility pass to the buyer. The buyer is responsible for contracting the ocean carrier, obtaining the necessary documentation, and paying all costs involved from that point to the destination.

price includes freight

Cost and Freight   With *cost and freight (C&F)* terms, the seller quotes a price that includes the cost of transportation to a specific named point. The shipper is responsible for acquiring required export documentation and contracting for the overseas shipper. The buyer assumes responsibility for loss and damage as soon as the goods pass "the ship's rail" (when the goods are actually loaded onto the overseas vessel). The buyer is also responsible for purchasing any required insurance, acquiring any documentation the country of origin requires, and paying the shipment's movement costs within the country to which it is imported.

price includes freight and insurance

Cost, Insurance, Freight   The term *cost, insurance, freight (CIF)* is very similar to C&F. The major difference is that the price quote includes the marine insurance cost along with the freight cost. Risk again passes at the ship's rail, and the parties' other responsibilities remain the same.

Others   Several newer terms are becoming increasingly important in international trade. *F.O.B. airport (FOA)* has the same meaning for air transport as F.O.B. has for ocean shipments. The seller agrees to deliver the goods to a specific air carrier, at which point all risk and responsibility for transportation cost transfer to the buyer.

Free carrier (FRC) applies mainly to intermodal shipments. Each party's responsibilities are similar to those under F.O.B. terms, with the transfer point being delivery to an agreed-upon carrier.

Transportation Documents

export declaration

After the buyer and seller reach an agreement as to sales and credit terms, the exporter files with exit port customs an *export declaration* (see Figure 9–5),

FIGURE 9–5   SHIPPER'S EXPORT DECLARATION

FORM NO. 7525-V (SEPT. 15, 1971) *(See Instructions on Reverse Side)*	U.S. DEPARTMENT OF COMMERCE – BUREAU OF THE CENSUS – BUREAU OF INTERNATIONAL COMMERCE **SHIPPER'S EXPORT DECLARATION** OF SHIPMENTS FROM THE UNITED STATES Export Shipments Are Subject To U.S. Customs Inspection	Form Approved O.M.B. No. 41-R0397 **CONFIDENTIAL** – For use solely for official purposes authorized by the Secretary of Commerce. Use for unauthorized purposes is not permitted. (Title 15, Sec. 30.91(a) C.F.R.; Sec. 7(c) Export Administration Act of 1969, P.L. 91-184)

READ CAREFULLY THE INSTRUCTIONS ON BACK TO AVOID DELAY AT SHIPPING POINT

For shipments to foreign countries, where authentication of the Shipper's Export Declaration is required, the export declaration must be presented to and authenticated by Customs and a copy so authenticated delivered to the exporting carrier prior to exportation.

Declarations Should be Typewritten or Prepared in ink

Customs Authentication (For Customs use only)

DO NOT USE THIS AREA	DISTRICT	PORT	COUNTRY (For Customs use only)

File No. (For Customs use only)

1. FROM (U.S. Port of Export)	2. METHOD OF TRANSPORTATION (Check one):
	☐ VESSEL (Incl. ferry) ☐ AIR ☐ OTHER (Specify) _____

2a. EXPORTING CARRIER (If vessel, give name of ship, flag and pier number. If air, give name of airline.)

3. EXPORTER (Principal or seller – licensee)	ADDRESS (Number, street, place, State)
4. AGENT OF EXPORTER (Forwarding agent)	ADDRESS (Number, street, place, State)
5. ULTIMATE CONSIGNEE	ADDRESS (Place, country)
6. INTERMEDIATE CONSIGNEE	ADDRESS (Place, country)

7. FOREIGN PORT OF UNLOADING (For vessel and air shipments only)	8. PLACE AND COUNTRY OF ULTIMATE DESTINATION (Not place of transshipment)

MARKS AND NOS. (9)	NUMBERS AND KIND OF PACKAGES, DESCRIPTION OF COMMODITIES, EXPORT LICENSE NUMBER, EXPIRATION DATE (OR GENERAL LICENSE SYMBOL) *(Describe commodities in sufficient detail to permit verification of the Schedule B commodity numbers assigned. Do not use general terms. Insert required license information on line below description of each item.)* (10)	SHIPPING (Gross) WEIGHT IN POUNDS° (REQUIRED FOR VESSEL AND AIR SHIPMENTS ONLY) (11)	SPECIFY "D" OR "F" ᵇ (12)	SCHEDULE B COMMODITY NO. (13)	NET QUANTITY SCHEDULE B UNITS (State unit) (14)	VALUE AT U.S. PORT OF EXPORT (Selling price or cost if not sold, including inland freight, insurance and other charges to U.S. Port of Export) (Nearest whole dollar; omit cents figures) (15)

16. WAYBILL OR MANIFEST NO. (of Exporting Carrier)	17. DATE OF EXPORTATION (Not required for shipments by vessel)

18. THE UNDERSIGNED HEREBY AUTHORIZES _____
TO ACT AS FORWARDING AGENT FOR EXPORT CONTROL AND CUSTOMS PURPOSES.

(Name and address – Number, street, place, State)

EXPORTER _____ BY (DULY AUTHORIZED OFFICER OR EMPLOYEE) _____

▶ 19. I CERTIFY THAT ALL STATEMENTS MADE AND ALL INFORMATION CONTAINED IN THIS EXPORT DECLARATION ARE TRUE AND CORRECT. I AM AWARE OF THE PENALTIES PROVIDED FOR FALSE REPRESENTATION. (See paragraphs I (c) and (e) on reverse side.)

SIGNATURE _____ FOR _____
(Duly authorized officer or employee of exporter or named forwarding agent) (Name of corporation or firm, and capacity of signer; e.g., secretary, export manager, etc.)

ADDRESS _____

▶ Declaration should be made by duly authorized officer or employee of exporter or of forwarding agent named by exporter. ᵃIf shipping weight is not available for each Schedule B item listed in column (13) included in one or more packages, insert the approximate gross weight for each Schedule B item. The total of these estimated weights should equal the actual weight of the entire package or packages. ᵇDesignate foreign merchandise (reexports) with an "F" and exports of domestic merchandise produced in the United States or changed in condition in the United States with a "D." (See instructions on reverse side.) All copies of the export declaration, bill of lading, and commercial invoice must show a destination control statement, when required. (See Department of Commerce Export Control Regulations.)	*DO NOT USE THIS AREA*

which provides the Department of Commerce with information concerning the export shipment's nature and value. The required information usually includes a description of the commodity, the shipping weight, a list of the marks and numbers on the containers, the number and dates of any required export license, the place and country of destination, and the parties to the transaction.

export license

A company requires an *export license* to export goods from the United States. These licenses fall into one of two categories. The *general license* allows the export of most goods without any special requirements. The commodities this license covers are general in nature and have no strategic value to the United States. On the other hand, certain items whose export the government wishes to control require a *validation export license.* Commodities include military hardware, certain high-tech items such as microprocessors and supercomputers, and other goods for which control is in the national interest.

commercial invoice

The *commercial invoice,* which the seller uses to determine the commodity's value less freight and other charges is basically the seller's invoice for the commodities sold. The letter of credit and companies or agencies often require this invoice to determine the correct value for insurance purposes and assessing import duties. Some countries have special requirements (language, information requested, etc.) for the commercial invoice. Many countries also require a special

consular invoice

form called a *consular invoice* for any incoming shipments. The consular invoice, which allows the country to collect import statistics, is usually written in the importing nation's language.

carnet

When a seller makes a shipment in a sealed container, a *carnet* is often issued. A carnet indicates that the shipment has been sealed at its origin and will not be opened until it reaches its final destination. The container may then pass in transit through intermediate customs points without inspection. Carnets are very useful for intermodal shipments and for containers crossing several national boundaries between origin and destination. Much of the overland shipping in Europe travels under carnet.

import duties

A destination country that has made a treaty agreement to give favorable import duty treatment to certain U.S. goods often requires a *certificate of origin,* which certifies that the goods' origin is the United States. This prevents a shipper from applying the favorable import duty to foreign goods that the shipper merely reshipped from the United States.

bill of lading

The initiating document for any international shipment is the *bill of lading (B/L).* One bill of lading, the *export bill of lading,* could govern the domestic portion of the move (from plant to port of exit), the intercountry portion (by ocean or air), and the foreign portion (from port of entry to final destination in a foreign country). In practice, most shipments move under a combination of domestic and ocean (or air) bills of lading.

terms

The *ocean bill of lading* is similar to the domestic bill of lading we discussed earlier. The ocean bill of lading serves as the contract of carriage between the carrier and the shipper. It sets down the terms of shipment and designates the origin and destination ports. It also supplies shipment information, such as the quantity and weight, the freight charges, and any special handling requirements. The ocean bill of lading is hardly uniform. The carrier is able to add conditions to the bill of lading as long as the additions are not contrary to law.

negotiable

Bills of lading, sometimes called *order bills of lading,* also provide evidence of ownership. Sellers can use these negotiable documents to transfer title of the goods.

clean bill of lading

The carrier issues a *clean bill of lading* when the cargo arrives aboard ship in good condition. If the goods show evidence of damage, the carrier will note this on the bill of lading and will not issue a clean B/L. After processing all the bills of lading, the carrier prepares a *ship's manifest,* which summarizes the cargo aboard the ship, listed by port of loading and destination.

The primary bill of lading contract terms concern the ocean carrier's liability. The Carriage of Goods by Sea Act of 1936 states that the ocean carrier is required to use due diligence to make its vessel seaworthy and is held liable for losses resulting from negligence. The shipper is liable for loss resulting from perils of the sea, acts of God, acts of public enemies, inherent defects of the cargo, or shipper negligence. Thus, the liability of the ocean carrier is less than that imposed upon a domestic carrier.

liability

The terms of sale may also require a *certificate of insurance.* This certificate will state that the buyer or seller has obtained insurance adequate to cover any losses resulting during transit.

After the carrier has delivered the goods at the dock, the steamship agent issues a *dock receipt* indicating that the domestic carrier has delivered the shipment to the steamship company. This document can be used to show compliance with a letter of credit's payment requirements and to support damage claims.*

dock receipt

Another increasingly important document is the *universal airway bill,* a standardized document that air carriers use on all international air shipments. By reducing required paperwork to one document, the carrier reduces processing costs. Having a standardized document also helps to speed shipments through customs.

airway bill

Improving Documentation

International transportation can become a paperwork jungle. A single shipment typically generates as many as forty-six different documents with 360 copies requiring forty-six working hours to process. Extreme cases may require as many as 158 documents with 790 copies.[3] Documentation costs may be as high as ten percent of the value of foreign trade.

electronic transmission

Several groups are trying to reduce the amount of documentation international transportation requires. The National Council on International Trade Documentation (NCITD) has developed a system to relay information electronically and to ultimately transit documents to a shipment's destination so that the buyer may inspect them before the goods arrive. This reduces the time required for customs processing. And, by developing export-import document format standards, both NCITD and the United Nations Conference on Multimodal Transport are working to simplify the form of the documentation.

EDI

Electronic data interchange (EDI) is also entering common use. Various nations and organizations are standardizing documentation and electronic requirements to create an international system for transmitting export-import information. Simplified documentation and electronic interconnecting will dramatically reduce information processing and transmission time, leading to savings and providing incentive to increase international trade.[4]

CARDIS

The U.S. Customs Service has developed a system utilizing many of these innovations to clear shipments at several large U.S. ports. The Customs Service developed this system, called the *Cargo Data Interchange System (CARDIS),* using NCITD guidelines. It provides the following basic functions:

---

*Marine insurance is an integral part of ocean shipping, since the ocean carrier's liability is rather limited. For a discussion of marine insurance, see Kenneth U. Flood, Oliver G. Callson, and Sylvestor J. Jablonski, *Traffic Management,* 4th ed. (Dubuque, Iowa: Brown, 1984), 450–53.

- *Shipment file maintenance* that contains all the data needed to move a shipment under one bill of lading
- *Electronic links* between all the parties involved in the shipment
- *Documentation* that produces documents needed to complete a specific shipment
- *Tracing* to provide a shipment's status until it reaches its destination and to supply provisions for updating the files
- A *statistical and summary report* that the system generates from the database
- *Government and company interfaces* to exchange data about shipments[5]

Using CARDIS will provide several advantages to American companies. First, the quicker data exchange will reduce cargo warehousing and handling costs by allowing earlier review of the customs documents. Second, automation and the reduced number of documents will greatly reduce clerical costs. Third, faster transmittal times will help to shorten shipment times, allowing quicker clearance of letters of credit. This will give a company savings on in-transit inventory costs.

Harmonized Code   Finally, an international classification system, the *Harmonized Commodity Description* and Coding System, has been developed to identify specific products with an internationally accepted identification number. The Harmonized Code permits consistent classification for transportation elements such as documentation and duties.

BASES FOR RATES

As we saw previously, the carriers, not the regulatory agency, establish the rates they charge. This section directs attention toward the bases carriers use or the factors they consider in determing rates. The following factors usually affect the rate: (1) the cost and value of service, which affect the different rates the carrier establishes for different commodities; (2) distance; and (3) the volume or weight of the shipment.

Cost of Service

definition   Basing rates upon the *cost of service* considers the supply side of pricing. The cost of supplying the service establishes the floor for a rate; that is, the supply cost permits the carrier's viability by providing the rate's lower limit (see Figure 9–6).

cost concepts   A continual problem of what cost basis to use has plagued this area. Carriers have used fully allocated (average total) costs, as well as average variable costs and out-of-pocket (marginal) costs. In essence, this problem set up subfloors to the lower rate limit: the carrier will base the higher limit upon fully allocated costs and will base the lower limit upon out-of-pocket costs. The ICC use of these bases has varied and depends upon the particular circumstances surrounding the case in question.*

common costs
joint costs   Common and joint costs also increase the problem of using service cost as a basis for rates. The carrier incurs common and joint costs when producing

---

*See John J. Coyle, "The Compatibility of the Rule of Ratemaking and the National Transportation Policy," *ICC Practitioners' Journal* (March–April 1971), 340–53.

FIGURE 9–6   LIMITS ON RATES

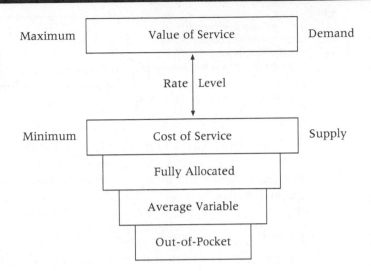

multiple units of output; the carrier cannot directly allocate such costs to a particular production unit. (*Joint cost* is a particular type of common cost in which the costs a carrier incurs in producing one unit unavoidably produce another product. For example, moving a commodity from A to B unavoidably produces the movement capacity and cost from B to A—the backhaul.) The procedure the carrier uses to assign these costs determines the cost basis permitting latitude for cost variations and, consequently, for rate variations.

Value of Service

definition

Value of service pricing considers the demand side of pricing. We may define value of service pricing as "charging what the traffic will bear." This basis considers the transported product's ability to withstand transportation costs. For example, in Figure 9–7, the highest rate a carrier can charge to move producer A's product into point B is fifty cents per unit. If the carrier assesses a higher rate, producer A's product will not be competitive in the B market area. Thus, value of service pricing places the upper limit upon the rate.

rationale

Generally, rates vary by transported product. The cost difference associated with various commodity movements may explain this, but this difference also contains the value of service pricing concept. For higher-value commodities, transportation charges are a small portion of the total selling price. From Table 9–1, we can see that the transportation rate for diamonds, for a given distance and weight, is 100 times greater than that for coal; but transportation charges

FIGURE 9–7   EXAMPLE OF VALUE OF SERVICE PRICING

Maximum Rate = $0.50

A ———————————————————————————————— B

A's Production Cost = $2.00   B's Production Cost = $2.50

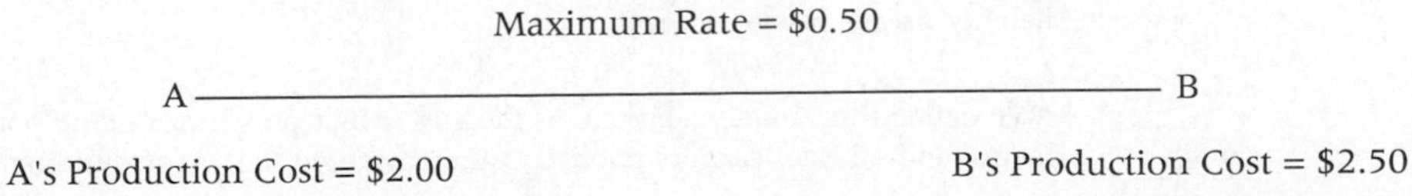

TABLE 9–1   TRANSPORTATION RATES AND COMMODITY VALUE

	Coal	Diamonds
Production value per ton*	$30.00	$10,000,000.00
Transportation charge per ton*	10.00	1,000.00
Total selling price	$40.00	$10,001,000.00
Transportation cost as a percentage of selling price	25%	0.01%

*Assumed.

amount to only 0.01% of the selling price for diamonds, as opposed to 25% for coal. Thus, high-value commodities can sustain higher transportation charges; and carriers price the transport services accordingly—a specific application of demand pricing.*

Distance

Rates usually vary with respect to *distance;* that is, the greater the distance the commodity moves, the greater the cost to the carrier and the greater the transportation rate. However, certain rates do not relate to distance. One example of these is a *blanket rate.*

blanket rate   A blanket rate does not increase as distance increases; the rate remains the same for all points in the blanket area the carrier designates. The postage stamp rate is one example of a blanket rate. No matter what distance you ship a letter, your cost as shipper (sender) is the same. In transportation, carriers have employed blanket rates for a city's commercial zone,* a given state region, or a number of states, for example. In each case, the rate into or out of the blanket area will be the same no matter where the origin or destination is located in the blanket area.

tapering rate   Most transportation rates do increase as distance increases, but the increase is not directly proportional to distance. This relationship of rates to distance is known as the tapering rate principle. As Figure 9–8 shows, the rate increases as distance increases, but not linearly. The rate structure tapers because carriers spread terminal costs (cargo handling, clerical, and billing) over a greater mileage base. These terminal costs do not vary with distance; as the shipment's movement distance increases, the terminal cost per mile decreases. The intercept point in Figure 9–8 corresponds to the terminal costs.

Weight of Shipment

Carriers quote freight rates in cents per hundredweight (actual weight in pounds divided by 100 = hundredweight, or cwt) and determine the total transportation charge by the total weight of the shipment in cwt, and the appropriate rate per cwt. The rate per cwt relates to the shipped volume: carriers charge a lower rate for volume shipments and a higher rate for less-than-volume quantities. In

*We could argue that for high-valued goods the carrier bears a higher cost because of the increased liability risk in case of damage.

*We define the commercial zone as the city proper plus surrounding points, determined by population, and all rates carriers publish to the city apply to the surrounding points within this limit.

FIGURE 9–8   EXAMPLE OF TAPERING RATE PRINCIPLE

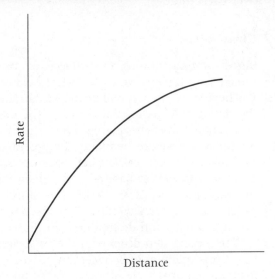

essence, carriers offer a quantity discount for shipping large volumes (buying link service in a large quantity).

quantity discount   Railroads term these quantity discounts carload (CL) and less-than-carload (LCL); motor carriers call them truckload (TL) and less-than-truckload (LTL). The CL and TL rates represent the lower, volume rates; and the LCL and LTL rates denote the higher, less-than-volume rates.

One noteworthy exception to the rate-volume relationship is the any-quantity (AQ) rate, which bears no relationship to volume shipped. The rate per cwt remains constant regardless of the volume a firm tenders to the carrier for shipment; that is, no quantity discount is available.

THE TRANSPORTATION PRICING SYSTEM

One of the most difficult and confusing logistic manager responsibilities will be determining the prices of various transportation services available for a logistics system's use. Determining how much it will cost to move a barrel of pickles from Toledo, Ohio, to New York City is not always easy.

To appreciate the problem, consider the nature of a transportation service. It would be simple if carriers sold all transportation service on the basis of ton-miles; that is, if we had to pay X dollars to move one ton of a product one mile. But carriers do not sell transportation services in ton-miles; rather, carriers sell transportation services for moving a specific commodity (stereos) between two specific points (Toledo and New York City). This fact gives us a glimpse of the enormous magnitude of the transportation pricing problem. There are over 33,000 important shipping and receiving points in the United States. Theoretically, the number of different possible routes would be all the permutations of the 33,000 points. The result is in the trillions of trillions. In addition, we must consider the thousands and thousands of different commodities and products that firms might ship over any of these routes. On top of that, we must consider the different modes and the different companies within each mode. We may also need to consider each commodity's specific supply-and-demand situation over each route.

Class Rates

Since quoting trillions and trillions of rates is impossible, the transportation industry has taken two major steps toward simplification.

shipping points

The first was to consolidate the 33,000 shipping points into groups by dividing the nation into geographic squares. The most important shipping point (based on tonnage) in each square serves as the *rate base point* for all other shipping points in the square, reducing the potential number of distance variations for rate-making purposes. The railroads determined the distances from each base point to every other base point and filed them with the ICC for publication in the National Rate Basis Tariff. The distance between any two base points is called the *rate basis number*. This first simplifying step reduced the number of possible origins and destinations for pricing purposes.

rate basis number

The second step deals with the thousands and thousands of different items that firms might ship between any two base points. The railroads have established a national scale of rates, placed on file with the ICC, which gives a rate in dollars per hundredweight (cwt) for each rate basis number. These rate scales are the basis for a simplified product classification system.

classification procedure

Classification simply means grouping together products with similar transportation characteristics so that one rating can be applied to the whole group. The four primary classification characteristics are density, stowability, ease or difficulty of handling goods, and liability. High demand and high value items might be placed in Class 100, which means that carriers will charge them 100% of the *first class rate*. Low-value items, such as coal, might be placed in a Class 20, which means carriers will charge them 20% of the first class rate. This percentage number is a *class rating*, the group into which carriers place a commodity for rate-making purposes.

Now the number of possible pricing situations is small enough to allow the formation of a transportation pricing system. We determine the price of moving a particular item between two particular points as follows: First, look up the rate basis point for the origin and for the destination. Then determine the rate basis number between the two base points. Next, determine the classification rating (class rating) for the particular product to be shipped. Then find the rate in the class rate tariff that corresponds to the appropriate rate basis number and class rating. Finally, multiply this rate, which is in cents per cwt, by the total shipment weight in cwt to determine the cost to move that specific product between those two points.

tariff

The word *tariff* commonly means almost any publication that a carrier or a tariff publishing agency produces, which concerns itself with the pricing or service the carrier performs. All the information a shipper needs to determine the cost of a move is in one or more tariffs.

example

Now look at an example of the mechanics involved in determining the class rate charges for a motor carrier shipment. A firm wishes to ship 4,000 pounds of rust preventive pipeline coating in metal cans from Reading, Pennsylvania, to Washington, D.C.

1. The rate basis number Table 9–2 contains is 98 (at the intersection of Reading, Pennsylvania, and Washington, D.C., in the vertical and horizontal portions of the tariff, respectively).

TABLE 9–2   TABLE OF RATE BASIS NUMBERS

To Rate Groups	From Rate Groups							
	Allentown, Pa.	Altoona, Pa.	Bellefonte, Pa.	Reading, Pa.	Scranton, Pa.	State College, Pa.	Williamsport, Pa.	York, Pa.
	Apply Rate Basis Numbers							
Baltimore......Md.	84	73	86	62	64	92	76	98
Barnesville.....Md.	103	94	122	96	95	132	102	117
Newark .......N.J.	98	90	96	101	92	113	84	76
Newark .......N.Y.	61	76	60	76	76	76	60	77
New York .....N.Y.	96	92	92	101	96	111	87	73
Washington....D.C.	109	96	111	98	90	118	103	122
Wilmington....Del.	98	66	98	84	66	107	83	101

Source: MAC Tariff 2-M.

2. The class ratings and minimum weight, found in the classification for rust preventive pipeline coating in metal cans (see Table 9–3), are LTL = 60, TL = 35, and minimum weight = 36,000 lb. Since this shipment weighs less than 36,000 piounds, we use the LTL rating of 60—the higher, less-than-volume rating.

3. The table of class rates gives the applicable rate (see Table 9–4); the intersection of the horizontal line of rate basis number 98 (92 to 99 group) and the vertical line of class 60 determine this rate. Since the 4,000-pound shipment falls between weight groups 2,000 and 5,000, we must compute the charges under both weight groups to determine the lowest cost. The appropriate rates are $2.52/ctw for 2,000 pounds and $1.93/cwt for 5,000 pounds.

4. We find the transportation charge by multiplying the rate per cwt by the number of cwt in the shipment, or

$$4,000 \text{ lb} = \frac{4,000}{100} = 40 \text{ cwt}$$

The firm could ship the 40 cwt under the 2,000-pound rate of $2.52 or under the 5,000-pound rate of $1.93, as follows:

$$40 \text{ cwt} @ \$2.52 = \$100.80$$
$$50 \text{ cwt} @ \$1.93 = \$\ 96.50$$

In this case, the shipper would elect the 4,000-pound shipment as a 5,000-pound shipment—in essence, shipping 1,000 pounds of phantom freight—and pay $96.50 rather than $100.80.

weight break

We can compare the cost of shipping at a volume higher than actual weight to realize a lower rate and lower shipping cost with the cost of shipping at the actual weight by determining the *weight break*. The weight break is the shipment size that equates the transportation charges for different rates and weight groups. That is,

$$\text{LV rate} \times \text{WB} = \text{HV rate} \times \text{MW}$$

TABLE 9–3 NATIONAL MOTOR FREIGHT CLASSIFICATION

Item	Articles	Classes		Min. Wt.
		LTL	TL	
149500	PAINT GROUPS: Articles consist of Paints, Paint Material			
150090	Plasticizers, paint, lacquer, varnish, gum, resin or plastic;			
	Solvents, paint, lacquer, varnish, gum, resin, plastic or rubber;			
	Compounds, paint, lacquer, varnish, gum, resin or plastic increasing, reducing, removing, thickening or thinning:			
Sub 1	In barrels, boxes, five-ply paper bags or Packages 33 or 727, or in solid mass in Package 601; also TL, in tank trucks, see item (rule) 370	55	35	36
Sub 2	In plastic carboys	70	40	30
Sub 3	In carboys other than plastic	100	45	24
150110	Putty, in containers in barrels, boxes or crates, or in bulk in barrels, steel putty drums, kits, pails or tubs, or steel-lined drum or tubs with metal or wooden covers	55	35	36
150150	Rust Preventive Pipeline Coating, asphaltum coal tar or pitch base, other than asphaltum or coal tar paint or varnish:			
Sub 1	In metal cans in barrels or boxes....................	60	35	36
Sub 2	In bulk in barrels, or in bulk in metal drums, in boxes, or solid in packages	55	35	36
150170	Smalts, painters', in barrels, boxes or double bags	55	35	36
150180	Solvent, spray paint, see Note, item 150182, in boxes ..	70	40	30
150182	Note: Applies only on paint solvent in aerosol cans plus plastic liners for hand pumps not in excess of 20% of canned solvent.			

Source: National Motor Freight Classification A-10.

where

LV rate = lesser-volume rate
WB = weight break
HV rate = higher-volume rate
MW = minimum weight for higher-volume rate

Plugging in the numbers from the example used here, we find the weight break to be

$$\$2.52 \times WB = \$1.93 \times 50 \text{ cwt}$$
$$WB = 38.3 \text{ cwt}$$

Next, can establish a simple decision rule for shipping clerks to use to determine when it is economical to ship a shipment at a volume higher than the volume a firm is actually shipping. In this example, the decision rules are as follows:

shipping decision rules

1. If the shipment weighs between 2,000 and 3,830 pounds, ship the actual weight at the 2,000-pound rate of $2.52/cwt.

TABLE 9–4   CLASS TARIFF

Rate Basis No.	Weight Group	Classes										
		100	85	70	60	55	50	45	40	35	30	27½
		Rates in Cents Per 100 Pounds										
60 to 67	500 LTL	408	358	312	273	256	239					
	1,000 LTL	361	314	268	236	223	207					
	2,000 LTL	297	255	216	189	175	161					
	5,000 LTL	216	184	151	130	119	108					
	Truckload	169	144	120	103	95	89	82	73	64	57	52
76 to 83	500 LTL	470	410	355	311	291	270					
	1,000 LTL	421	365	310	273	256	238					
	2,000 LTL	356	304	256	223	208	191					
	5,000 LTL	271	230	190	163	149	136					
	Truckload	223	191	158	135	125	116	107	97	84	74	66
	TL 30,000	221	189	156	133	123	114	101	90	80	69	60
84 to 91	500 LTL	496	432	374	325	304	282					
	1,000 LTL	449	388	330	288	271	251					
	2,000 LTL	385	329	278	241	223	205					
	5,000 LTL	304	258	213	182	167	152					
	Truckolad	263	223	187	159	147	136	125	113	98	87	79
	TL 30,000	261	221	185	157	145	134	118	105	93	81	71
92 to 99	500 LTL	514	448	386	336	314	291					
	1,000 LTL	467	404	342	299	281	260					
	2,000 LTL	403	345	290	252	233	214					
	5,000 LTL	322	274	225	193	177	161					
	Truckload	285	242	201	171	158	147	136	122	106	94	85
	TL 30,000	283	240	199	169	156	145	129	114	101	86	78
100 to 109	500 LTL	566	492	423	367	343	317					
	1,000 LTL	519	448	379	330	310	286					
	2,000 LTL	455	389	327	283	262	240					
	5,000 LTL	374	318	262	224	206	187					
	Truckload	342	290	240	206	188	170	165	149	130	112	107
	TL 30,000	342	290	240	206	188	170	156	139	121	106	97
110 to 125	500 LTL	598	519	444	387	361	334					
	1,000 LTL	549	474	399	349	326	302					
	2,000 LTL	484	413	345	299	278	255					
	5,000 LTL	399	339	279	239	219	200					
	Truckload	365	310	254	219	200	185	177	159	138	119	116
	TL 30,000	365	310	254	219	200	185	168	152	131	113	103

Application of weight groups: 500 LTL; Applies on LTL or AQ shipments weighing 500 pounds or more but less than 1,000 pounds. 1,000 LTL: Applies on LTL or AQ shipments weighing 1,000 pounds or more but less than 2,000 pounds. 2,000 LTL: Applies on LTL or AQ shipments weighing 2,000 pounds or more but less than 5,000 pounds. 5,000 LTL: Applies on LTL or AQ shipments weighing 5,000 pounds or more. Truckload: Subject to minimum weights in NMFC (Note A). TL 30,000: Applies on truckload shipments where actual or billed weight is 30,000 pounds or more (Note A).
Note A: Where the charge under the rates for TL 30,000 pounds is lower than the charge under the rates for TL shipments subject to minimum weights of less than 30,000 pounds.

2. If the shipment weighs between 3,830 and 5,000 pounds, ship at 5,000 pounds (minimum weight) at the 5,000-pound rate of $1.93/cwt.
3. If the shipment weighs more than 5,000 pounds but less than the truckload minimum weight, ship the actual weight at the 5,000-pound rate of $1.93/cwt. (*Note:* a weight break exists between the 5,000-pound rate and the truckload rate.)

Exception Ratings (Rates)

The classification and class rate system are the backbone of the transportation pricing system, but only about ten percent of all volume (CL to TL) freight moves under this pricing system. The remaining ninety percent moves under either an exception rating (rate) or commodity rate. These two rate types complicate the class rate structure's inherent simplification.

Carriers publish exception ratings when the transportation characteristics of an item in a particular area differ from those of the same article in other areas. For example, large-volume movements or intensive competition in one area may require the publication of an exception rating; the exception rating supersedes the classification. The same procedures described earlier apply to determining the exception rate, except now we use the exception rating (class) instead of the classification rating. Table 9–5 gives an example of an exception tariff.

Continuing with the earlier example, an exception rating is available under item number 10700 of the exception tariff for the rust preventive pipeline coating moving from Reading, Pennsylvania, to Washington, D.C. It lists a class rating for truckload (TL) quantities only, a rating of 27½. This means that in order to use the exception rating of 27½, the rust preventative company needs to ship 36,000 pounds (see Table 9–3, item 150150, sub 1). Since the shipment under consideration is 4,000 pounds, the company would need to ship 32,000 pounds of phantom freight. The cost comparisons are as follows:

$$\text{Class rate:} \quad 50 \text{ cwt @ } \$1.93 = \$ 96.50$$
$$\text{Exception rate:} \quad 360 \text{ cwt @ } \$0.78^* = \$280.00$$

For truckload shipments (36,000 pounds or more), the exception rating will result in lower transportation charges than will the classification rating. That is, the class rate for shipping 36,000 pounds of rust preventive pipeline coating from Reading, Pennsylvania, to Washington, D.C., is $1.01/cwt (see Table 9–4) as compared with the exception rate of $0.78/cwt; the exception rate offers a 22.7% savings for truckload shipments.

Commodity Rates

commodity specific

direction specific

O-D (origin-destination) specific

Carriers can construct a commodity rate on a variety of bases. The most common is a specific rate concerning a specific commodity or related commodity group between specific points and generally by specific routes. Commodity rates are complete in themselves and are not part of the classification system. If the rate does not specifically state the commodity you are shipping, or if the origin-destination is not that the commodity rate specifically spells out, then the commodity rate does not apply for your particular movement. A published commodity rate takes precedence over the class rate or exception rate on the same article between the specific points.

Carriers offer this type of rate to commodities that firms move regularly and in large quantities. But such a pricing system, which completely undermines the attempts to simplify transportation pricing through the class rate structure, has caused transportation pricing to revert to publishing a multiplicity of rates and adds greatly to the pricing system complexity.

---

*We find the exception rate for class 27½ in Table 9–4 at the intersection of class 27½ and rate basis 92 to 99 for TL 30,000.

TABLE 9–5   EXCEPTION TARIFF

Exceptions to National Motor Freight Classification					
	Classes (Ratings)				
Item	*Articles*		*AQ*	*LTL*	*TL*
	PAINTS GROUP:				
	Kalsomine, dry, or Cold Water Paints, dry, in packages . . .		. . .	. . . .	27½
	Lead, silicate; Litharge, when shipped dry and not in oil,				
	Lithopane; red Lead, when shipped dry and not in oil;				
	Sublimed Lead, when shipped dry and not in oil;				
	Titanium Composite Pigments, dry; Titanium Pigments,				
	dry; White Lead, when shipped dry and not in oil; Zinc				
	Oxice; Zinc Sulfate; Zinc Sulfide; Zinc Sulfide Pigments,				
10700	dry; Zinc Composite in Pigments, dry; in packages		. . .	. . . .	27½
	Paint, earth, dry, in bulk, in paper bags, paper lined bags,				
	or double cloth bags, in barrels or in bulk (Note)		. . .	. . . .	27½
	Rust Preventive Pipe Line Coating, asphalt, coal tar or				
	pitch base (other than asphaltum or coal tar paint or				
	varnish), in metal cans in barrels or boxes or in bulk in				
	barrels or drums		. . .	. . . .	27½

Source: MAC Tariff 10-V.

Table 9–6 gives an example of a commodity tariff. Using the rust preventive pipeline coating shipping example, we find a commodity rate exists in item 15020 in Table 9–6. Item 15020, which applies to classification items 149500 to 150230, includes rust preventive pipeline coating since rust preventive pipeline coating is item 150105 in Table 9–3. Note that the commodity rate specifies a route from Reading, Pennsylvania, to Washington, D.C., the example problem's origin and destination. Again, however, Table 9–6 lists only a TL rate with a minimum weight of 30,000 pounds.

We can compare the class, exception, and commodity rates for the movement of rust preventive pipeline coating from Reading, Pennsylvania, to Washington, D.C., in truckload quantities (36,000 pounds or more) as follows:

$$\text{Class rate} = \$1.01/\text{cwt}$$
$$\text{Exception rate} = \$0.78/\text{cwt}$$
$$\text{Commodity rate} = \$0.71/\text{cwt}$$

TABLE 9–6   COMMODITY TARIFF

Commodity Rates in Cents per 100 Pounds					
Item	*Commodity*	*From*	*To*	*TL Rate*	*Min. Wt.*
15020	PAINTS GROUP, as	Reading . . Pa.	Baltimore . . . . . Md.	68	23M
	described in		Beltsville . . . . . Md.	71	30M
	NMFC Items		Washington . . . D.C.	71	30M
	149500 to				
	150230, rated				
	Class 35.				

Source: Mac Tariff 2-M.

As we can see from this comparison, the commodity rate is the lowest, 30% less than the class rate and 8.9% less than the exception rate. The exception rate offers a 22.7% savings over the class rate.

zip code

Motor carrier have introduced a unique commodity rate that uses U.S. postal service zip codes to identify origins and destinations. The *zip code commodity rates* specify rates for named commodities from a specific origin to multiple destinations identified by a three-digit zip code prefix. Table 9–7 contains an excerpt from a general commodity zip code tariff where the origin is zip code 430 (Columbus, Ohio, area). The rates apply from the 430 zip code origin to multiple zip code destinations in the state of Indiana. The table gives rates for various shipment weights subject to a minimum charge (M/C column) of $20.00. The rate per cwt to ship 5,500 pounds from zip code 430 to zip code 464 is $4.46, and the total shipping charge is $245.30 (55 cwt @ $4.46/cwt).

Other Rates

In addition to class rates, exception rates, and commodity rates, many special rates have developed over the years to meet very specific situations. The most prevalent and most important of these special rates are all-commodity, released-value, actual-value, deferred, multiple-vehicle, incentive, and innovative rates.

All-Commodity Rates. All-commodity rates, also known as freight-all-kinds (FAK) rates, are a recent development in which the carrier specifies the rate per shipment either in dollars per hundredweight or in total dollars per shipment with a specified minimum weight. The shipped commodity or commodities are not important. These rates tend to price transportation services by cost rather than by the value of service, and are used mostly by shippers who send mixed-commodity shipments to a single destination.

released value
actual value

Value Rates Of a whole host of value rates, released-value rates and actual-value rates are the most important. The degree of liability (commodity value) the carrier assumes determines these rates. Generally, a common carrier is liable for the actual value of any goods lost or damaged while in the carrier's custody. Carriers base a released-value rate on the assumption of a certain fixed liability, usually stated in cents per pound. Usually this fixed liability is considerably less than the actual value of the goods. As a result of this limited liability, the shipper receives a lower rate.

TABLE 9–7   ZIP CODE TARIFF

From OH Zip 430 (Columbus, Ohio, area) to Indiana									
Dest. Zip Code	M/C	<500	500	1,000	2,000	5,000	10,000	20,000	30,000	40,000
460–462	20.00	10.59	8.49	6.15	5.01	3.57	3.31	1.96	1.58	1.42
463–464	20.00	12.39	9.95	7.37	6.07	4.46	4.12	2.43	1.95	1.74
465–466	20.00	11.35	9.13	6.72	5.45	3.99	3.68	2.19	1.75	1.57
467–468	20.00	10.19	8.24	5.94	4.78	3.39	3.14	1.79	1.43	1.30
469	20.00	10.59	8.49	6.15	5.01	3.57	3.31	1.96	1.58	1.42
470	20.00	10.08	8.08	5.74	4.68	3.32	3.07	1.77	1.41	1.28

Source: ICC JTRC 5006 Tariff, Jones Transfer Company.

Carriers use released-value rates extensively in the shipment of household goods and use actual-value rates when goods considered to be the same commodity—jewelry, for example—vary greatly in value. In these cases, a single rate is not desirable because some shipments have a high liability potential whereas other shipments have a low liability potential. The actual-value rates make allowances for this potential difference, and the rate the carriers charges reflects the liability difference. The 1980 deregulation acts reduced the ICC constraints on motor carrier and railroad use of value rates. Today, carriers may offer value rates without ICC approval.

Deferred Rates   Deferred rates are most common in air transportation. In general, they allow the carrier to charge a lower rate for the privilege of deferring a shipment's arrival time. For example, Federal Express offers a one-to-two-day two-pound package delivery rate that is forty-six percent lower than the rate for early-morning next-day delivery. A deferred rate allows the carrier to move shipments at the carrier's convenience as long as the shipment arrives within a reasonable time or by the scheduled deferred delivery date. This allows the carrier to use the deferred-rate shipments as "filler freight" to more fully load its vehicles.

Multiple-Vehicle Rates   Carriers offer multiple-vehicle rates as a special incentive rate to firms shipping multiple vehicle loads of a particular commodity at one time to a single destination. Motor carriers first used these rates to overcome the fact that a rail car holds more than a truck. By publishing lower multiple-vehicle rates, the motor carriers competed more effectively with the railroads. Multiple-vehicle rates also reduce commodities' transportation costs, thus allowing those commodities to move to more distant markets. The savings carriers achieve by economies of scale justify lower rates. The railroads can often demonstrate savings in multiple-vehicle pickups. Multiple-vehicle rates have progressed to the unit train rates rail carriers give for whole trainloads of commodities such as coal, ore, and grain.

in-excess rates   **Incentive Rates**   A carrier publishes incentive rates, or in-excess rates, to encourage heavier loading of individual vehicles so the carrier can improve its equipment utilization. One rate covers all cargo up to a certain minimum weight, and a lower rate covers all cargo in excess of the minimum weight.

Innovative Rates   Shippers commonly negotiate rates with carriers. The negotiated rate could take the form of (1) a discount from the prevailing rate, a situation common to shippers that ship small shipments under class rates; (2) a commodity rate for TL shipments that move in large volumes, on a regular basis—for example, 40,000 pounds per day, seven days per week; and (3) a contract rate (rail) for very large freight volumes—for example, 800 carloads (80,000 tons) per year.

The following rates partially list the rate reduction types shippers and carriers have negotiated since the passage of the deregulation laws:

■ *Exception rating.* Individual carriers have the option of publishing an exception rating to the classification rating.
■ *Density-based rating.* A lower rating (classification or exception) is possible when the shipper increases product density; the increased product

ON THE LINE

WHAT TO DO ABOUT MAISLIN?

My wife is an excellent shopper, and she prides herself on that quality. So when I saw several department store bags on the bed, I knew what to expect—a "how much?" guessing game for each item.

Her shameless pride beams through as she explains that this outfit was "regularly $33, 40% off, plus another 10% off today only. And I got another five dollars off—see the snag?—I think I can fix it, so I paid $11.50."

And she smiles that I-did-very-well-and-I-know-it smile.

Most of you are professionals, more specialized than she in buying and selling transportation services. Since 1980, you buyers have been able to smile that I-did-very-well-and-I-know-it smile.

That is because you carriers have had to sell at just about whatever price to even have a chance to stay in business.

But you can't sell at that price to everybody, so you forget to file the tariff. Nobody's the wiser until the carrier goes bankrupt. By that time you're shooting pool, or working for someone else.

Buyers couldn't afford to grow complacent since your competition was getting just about the same deals transportation-wise. You could see if their deals were better when your orders began to fall off.

And, you big buyers, well, there must have been a certain thrill the first few times you squeezed those sellers for deals. They went along because (you thought) you had convinced them that their prices were out of line.

You could use someone else and your sellers know it. What they didn't know was that you would rather stick with them, at least at first, as long as you got some kind of reasonable deal.

Then, you must have cringed the first time you squeezed harder than you had any right to. Instead of walking, the trucker gave you what you asked for.

You realized that trucker was not long for this world and there must be something wrong with the system. But that just made you push harder.

It is amazing how far the little truckers would go, like paying for their gas and a burger, but you didn't think about that. You had a job to do—buy transportation at the best price possible, just like your competitors.

Truck deregulation wasn't about this. It was about letting truckers serve where they wanted, at prices they could live with and would charge to everyone. Tariffs still were required, and rates had to be reasonable and nondiscriminatory.

This is Justice Brennan's starting point in *Maislin, Ind.* v. *Primary Steel, Inc.* It almost has to follow that a carrier has to announce its prices and can't deviate from its tariff. And the agency must enforce it.

That's exactly what the Interstate Commerce Commission did not do for an entire decade, which is the biggest part of why we are where we are.

The immediate problem is not just how to deal with the hundreds of millions of dollars in past claims, but now the ICC can shout loud enough that tariffs **will be enforced** from now on. That is the ending point for Maislin.

Except that Congress is now involved. Maybe it should wipe out about half the past claims if it can, and tell the ICC to get busy. And it should get busy itself, finding a better way to prevent cutthroat discounts (predatory pricing), particularly in transportation.

Some antitrust types—even the Supreme Court—work on it. We get answers such as cutthroat pricing never happens, or happens rarely (*Matsushita* v. *Zenith Radio*).

Tell that to the thousands of truckers who have gone out of business. Or tell it to Braniff, or Eastern, or the dozen other airlines that had to merge rather than go under.

Which brings me back to my wife, who has come to recognize a desperate price when she sees one, what with so many stores having hit bottom recently.

I imagine you can spot a cutthroat price too. As a lawyer, all I can say is take it. But make sure it's filed.

Adapted from Michael G. Roberts, "What to Do About Maislin?" *Inbound Logistics* (October 1990), 16. Reprinted with permission from INBOUND LOGISTICS, 5 Penn Plaza, New York, NY 10001 212-629-1560.

density permits heavier loading of the carrier's vehicle, thus spreading the cost over a larger number of weight (pricing) units.

- *Specific description.* Shippers seek a specific commodity description for a commodity that does not fit an existing classification description; for example, defective goods being returned to the plant have a lower value, liability, and so forth than if perfect, and thus should receive a lower rating.
- *Incentive rate.* In return for shipping heavier volumes per shipment, the shipper must realize a lower rate to compensate the shipper and consignee for larger inventory (shipment) holding costs.
- *Released-value rate.* By lowering the value for which the shipper will hold the carrier accountable in case of damage to the goods, the carrier will experience a lower liability cost in case of shipment damage. In return for this lower liability, the shipper seeks a lower rate.
- *Loading and unloading allowance.* The carrier is responsible for loading and unloading LTL-size shipments. If the shipper and consignee perform this function, the carrier realizes a lower cost and passes it on to the shipper and consignee.
- *Aggregate tender rate.* The carrier gives a lower rate to the shipper who presents multiple shipments at one time. The carrier realizes a lower pickup cost per shipment, while the shipper delays delivery by aggregating shipments before dispatch.
- *Mileage rate.* This rate is quite common for truckload-type freight; carriers base it upon the number of miles the shipment moves, regardless of the commodity or the shipment's weight.
- *Contract rate.* Railroads may negotiate a specific rate with a shipper for moving a given commodity volume between specified points. These rates which require large volumes, 600 cars or more per year, are appropriate for the movement of bulk commodities or manufactured products that move regularly between specific points in large volumes. The shipper may specify service constraints and penalties for noncompliance.

Ocean Freight Rates   Carriers set ocean freight rates at a level that will cover all the expenses of operating the ship, the ship's capital cost, and any charges specific to the voyage. The rates cover items such as fixed costs for crew, maintenance, repair, and insurance, and variable costs such as fuel, port fees, dockage, and cargo handling. The carrier and the shipper balance these factors against the cargo type, as well as the voyage's length and special requirements, to arrive at an agreeable price.

TRANSPORTATION SERVICES

The preceding material did not entirely delineate the nature of the transportation service. Carriers may seem to merely provide commodity movement service between two nodes; in reality, the carrier provides terminal and line-haul services as well as basic link service. For some services, but not all, the carrier charges no additional fee. The transportation manager must recognize and take advantage of these "extra" services.

Terminal Services

Although carrier terminal operations fall outside the logistics manager's direct control, exploring the nature of this operation provides the logistics manager with some knowledge of the constraints carrier terminals impose upon the provision of link service.

Terminal Functions Essentially, the carrier's terminal performs five basic functions: concentration, dispersion, shipment service, vehicle service, and interchange.[6] Performing these functions requires time, and therefore affects the total transit time a carrier provides.

consolidation
    Concentration is the consolidation of many less-than-volume shipments into one large shipment that the carrier can transport economically. Thus, if a shipper tenders a 2,000-pound shipment, the carrier will combine this shipment with other small shipments before dispatching it on toward destination. *Dispersion* is just the opposite; when a consolidated shipment arrives at the destination

break-bulk
terminal, the carrier must break down the many shipments in the vehicle (break-bulk) for dispatch to the individual consignees.

shipment service
    Through *shipment service,* the carrier provides freight handling services for consolidation and dispersion and performs the clerical, billing, routing, and other functions for the shipment. *Vehicle service* essentially maintains a sufficient vehicle supply. The carrier must constantly review vehicle distribution among terminals to ensure a supply sufficient to provide the transport service the shipping public and regulatory requirements demand. Finally, *interchange* provides freight-exchange facilities for carriers coordinating to provide through service.

pickup
delivery
    In addition to the preceding functions, the carrier's terminal provides pickup and delivery service. Pickup and delivery involve picking up movement-ready freight at shipper's plant or making ultimate shipment delivery at the consignee's plant. Carriers may or may not charge for this service; the shipper must consult the carrier's tariff.

Loading and Unloading The concentration function embraces the carrier's obligation to load and unload small shipments. For TL- and CL-size shipments, the shipper is required to load the vehicle and the consignee is required to unload it; but, if a firm wishes, the carrier will perform these services at an added cost. The shipper must consult the carrier's tariff to determine loading (or unloading) requirements.

demurrage and
detention
    The carrier grants the shipper or consignee a specified amount of free time to load or unload a vehicle and assesses charges for holding the vehicle beyond the free time; these are known as *demurrage* (rail) and *detention* (motor). For railroads, the free time for loading or unloading a boxcar is twenty-four to forty-eight hours, Saturdays, Sundays, and holidays excluded. The demurrage charge per rail car per day held varies by carrier.

    The motor carrier industry has no standard detention rules and charges. Consequently, a shipper must consult each carrier's tariff to determine free time and detention charges. As a general rule, detention charges for holding the power unit and driver beyond the free time are higher than for holding the trailer only.

short-term
warehousing
    Carriers use demurrage and detention charges to discourage shippers and consignees of using the carrier's vehicle as a short-term warehouse. Many consignees whose permanent storage capacity is fully utilized use these vehicles as

convenient temporary storage facilities. However, the logistics manager must weigh the demurrage and detention charges against the short-term warehousing cost, vehicle utilization, and carrier costs.

Shipment Monitoring As we noted earlier, carriers quote transportation rates in terms of cents per cwt. Thus, the carrier the shipment's exact weight determined so that the carrier realizes the appropriate revenue and the shipper pays the correct charges. The carriers maintain weighing devices that the regulatory commissions control. A shipper may request a carrier to reweigh a vehicle and its contents if the shipper feels the original weight is in error. For some commodities, the carrier's tariff specifies an agreed weight per package, case, carton, or other container; the carrier and shipper jointly determine this weight which is subject to regulatory scrutiny. If an agreed weight is in effect, the number of shipped packages times the agreed weight determines the total shipment weight.

weighing

In many situations, the transportation manager must know where a shipment is or when it will arrive at its destination. Such information eliminates customer ill will and stockouts and improves the utilization of materials handling equipment and labor. Carriers provide this monitoring function, known as tracing and expediting. *Tracing* is tracking a shipment's movement to determine its location in the link pipeline. *Expediting*, which utilizes the same procedure as tracing, has the objective of getting the shipment to destination quicker than normal. Some motor carriers use satellites to monitor a vehicle's exact location.

tracing
expediting

Line-Haul Services

Carriers also provide line-haul services that permit the logistics manager to effect changes in the original shipping order and to realize savings in transportation costs. The line-haul services are reconsignment and diversion, pool car (or truck) service, stopping in transit, and transit privilege.

definition

Reconsignment and Diversion Carriers use reconsignment and diversion interchangeably to mean a change in the shipment's destination and/or consignee with the shipper paying the through rate from origin to final destination. There is, however, a technical difference between the two. Reconsignment permits the shipper to change the destination and/or consignee after the shipment has reached its original destination but before the carrier has delivered it to the original consignee. Diversion enables the shipper to effect the same changes while the shipment is enroute and before it reaches the original destination.

benefit

Shippers use reconsignment and diversion extensively in the movement of perishable products (fruits, etc). and for movement in which the original consignee refuses the shipment or cancels the order. Shippers may start perishable products in movement before they have a buyer, using the time in transit to obtain a buyer. Having found a buyer, the shipper issues a reconsignment or diversion order with the buyer named as consignee. When the original buyer decides not to accept an order, the shipper can utilize a reconsignment or diversion order to change the shipment's destination to a new buyer location or to have the shipment stopped and returned to the seller's location. These services permit the shipper to amend the original contract (bill of lading) with the carrier and to realize the benefits of the lower through rate (tapering rate principle) from origin to new destination.

Pooling   Pool car or pool truck service permits the shipper to combine many LCL or LTL shipments into one CL or TL shipment and to send it to one destination and one consignee. The lower CL or TL rate applies to the combined shipments and thus effects savings for the shipper. Since the service requires one destination and one consignee, the shipper is usually sent the shipment to a warehouse or drayage firm,* which breaks down or disperses the consolidated shipment into individual shipments and delivers them to the appropriate consignees. The warehouse manager or drayage firm assesses a fee for this service. For inbound movements, the opposite is possible: the warehouse manager can combine small shipments from a firm's suppliers and present them to a carrier, who delivers them to the firm's plant under a lower high-volume rate.

Stopping in Transit   Another service, stopping in transit, allows the shipper to complete loading or to partially unload freight, and to pay on the highest weight in the vehicle at any time the lower TL or CL rate between the most distant origin-destination nodal pair. The shipper assesses a stop-off charge for each intermediate stop, but not for the final destination. Figure 9–9 shows an example stopping-in-transit service. The shipper at N_1 has two customers, located at N_2 and N_3, that have purchased 25,000 pounds each.

   The shipper has two shipping options for these two shipments: (1) as two LTL shipments and (2) as one stopping-in-transit shipment. The cost of each is as follows:

1. Two LTL shipments
   N_1 to N_2 = 250 cwt @ \$3.00 = $ 750.00
   N_1 to N_3 = 250 cwt @ \$4.00 = 1,000.00
                     Total cost = \$1,750.00

2. Stopping in transit shipment
   500 cwt @ \$2.50   = \$1,250.00
   Stop-off charge   =   35.00
                     Total cost = \$1,285.00

Use of the stopping-in-transit service saves \$465.00.

Transit Privilege   The final line-haul service is the transit privilege, which permits the shipper to stop the shipment in transit and to perform some function

FIGURE 9–9   EXAMPLE OF STOPPING-IN-TRANSIT SERVICE

N_1	————————	N_2 ————————	N_3
50,000 lb. (total shipment)		25,000 lb.	25,000 lb.

Rates per cwt

	LTL	TL	Minimum Weight
N_1 to N_2	\$3.00	\$2.00	50,000 lb.
N_2 to N_3	\$4.00	\$2.50	50,000 lb.

Stop-off charge = \$35.00 per stop-off

*A *drayage firm* is a motor carrier specializing in providing pickup and delivery service.

that physically changes the product's characteristics. With this privilege, carriers charge the lower through rate (from origin to final destination), rather than the higher combination of rates from origin to transit point and from transit point to final destination. Carriers have established the transit privilege for grain milling, steel fabrication, lumber processing, and storage of various commodities for aging.

SUMMARY

This chapter examined transportation management, the knowledge of which is fundamental to the logistics system's efficient operation, specifically to operating and controlling the link activities. The transportation function is a daily activity in any logistics system and requires considerable expertise with carrier tariffs, regulation, and service.

Embracing a proactive management philosophy, transportation management finds solutions to problems in the logistics system. Companies reduce the number of carriers they use, negotiate and contract with carriers for lower rates and desired service levels, consolidate shipments to realize lower costs, and monitor carrier service levels.

Transportation deregulation has set the stage for transportation management to negotiate more aggressively with carriers, but considerable economic regulation controls common carrier actions. Economic regulation influences common carrier rates and the documentation required for both domestic and international shipments. Now, in the post-deregulation environment, marketplace forces shape carrier ratemaking.

STUDY QUESTIONS

1. Describe the transportation management philosophy existing today, pointing out the major strategies firms use. Compare it to the pre-deregulation era.

2. Although Congress passed laws deregulating transportation, considerable economic regulation exists today. Comment.

3. International documentation is far more complicated than domestic documentation. Describe these differences and the reasons for these differences.

4. How do the terms of sale affect transportation management?

5. Define the purpose and function of the following domestic ratemaking factors: classification, rate basis point, minimum weight, rating, rate basis number, and exception.

6. Determine the lowest possible class rate charge for shipping 30,000 pounds of rust preventive pipeline coating in bulk in metal drums from Altoona, PA, to Newark, NJ.

7. Discuss the economic role of value of service and cost of service pricing.

8. Since 1980, carriers have developed numerous innovative rates. Describe both the carrier's and the shipper's economic rationale for these innovative rates.

9. What is the economic and service affects a carrier's terminal services have?

10. Under what circumstances would a company utilize a carrier's line-haul services?

NOTES

1. James Aaron Cooke, "Computers Lead The Way to Total Inbound Control," *Traffic Management* (January 1990), 50–53.
2. James J. Callari, "Fewer Carriers Mean Lower Freight Costs," *Traffic Management* (July 1988), 42–45.
3. Philip Schary, *Logistics Decisions* (New York: Dryden Press, 1984), 397.
4. Paul S. Bender, "The International Dimension of Physical Distribution Management," in *The Distribution Handbook*, edited by James F. Robeson (New York: The Free Press, 1985), 796.
5. Bender, "The International Dimension of Physical Distribution Management," 809–810.
6. Roy J. Sampson and Martin T. Farris, *Domestic Transportation*, 4th ed. (Boston: Houghton Mifflin, 1979), 124.

CASE 9–1

SPECIALTY METALS COMPANY

During the past two months, Thomas Train, vice president of transportation for Speciality Metals Company, a metals servicing company with operations in ten midwestern states, has been soliciting bids for the movement of tool steel, a speciality steel used for manufacturing tools and related products. Tom's goal is to reduce the shipping cost of this high-value steel. The supplier is located in Weirton, WV, 350 miles from Speciality's Toledo, OH, service center. Steel Haulers, Inc., a regional contract motor carrier currently moves the tool steel under contract. Steel Haulers' current rates are incremental: $2.80/cwt for shipments weighing less than 150 cwt, $2.60/cwt for shipments between 150–250 cwt, $2.40/cwt for shipments between 250–400 cwt, and $2.25/cwt for shipment weight in excess of 400 cwt up to a maximum of 450 cwt. The carrier submitted $2.25/cwt rate for weight in excess of 400 cwt two hours before the carrier proposals submission deadline.

For various equipment, financial, and/or management reasons, Tom has eliminated all but two carrier proposals. One of the two remaining carrier proposals is from Flatbed, Inc., a contract motor carrier that has an excellent reputation for providing specialized steel hauling service. Flatbed submitted a rate of $2.60/cwt with a minimum weight of 100 cwt; the carrier gives no discounts for larger shipments. The second carrier under consideration is the Middlewest Railroad, which submitted a piggyback rate of $2.45/cwt with a minimum of 200 cwt; the rate is for Plan 2, door-to-door piggyback service with a maximum shipment weight of 400 cwt per load. Both motor carriers will provide one-day transit time, while the piggyback transit time is three days.

The final proposal Tom is considering is a private trucking proposal the transportation department submitted. The estimated total private fleet operating cost (including overhead and depreciation) is $50,000 per year; the investment the vehicles require is $85,000. This annual operating cost equates to $2.50/cwt with a minimum of 400 cwt per shipment and fifty shipments per year. The private truck proposal recognizes Speciality's inability to provide a load for the backhaul from Toledo to Weirton. But, given environment today's deregulated, the proposal assumes the private fleet will be able to solicit return loads from other Toledo shippers thirty percent of the time and generate $15,000 in annual backhaul revenue.

Specialty has a contract with the steel mill to purchase two million pounds of tool steel per year. Last year, tool steel shipments averaged 250 cwt per order. Tool steel has a purchase value of $250/cwt. Unloading costs would be the same under each proposal.

The chief financial officer estimates Specialty's annual inventory carrying cost per dollar of average inventory stored to be twenty percent (fifteen percent for the cost of money and five percent for the cost of insurance, taxes, and handling); he estimates the cost to place an order to be $75. The inventory-in-transit cost is fifteen percent per year.

Case Question   1.   Tom indicated that he would decide on the bid proposals today. Given the facts of the different proposals, what would you advise Tom to do?

WAREHOUSING DECISIONS

The 1980s were notable for many business changes. One such change has been wholesalers' and retailers' increased power in channels of distribution. The balance of power has shifted from manufacturers to large wholesalers and retailers such as K-Mart, Wal-Mart, and The Gap.

In seeking the most efficient product distribution pipeline, the large retailers, in particular, want more cooperation, better service, and shorter lead times from their suppliers. This pressure is forcing manufacturers to rethink their logistics/distribution chain.

One such company that had to gear up for this new environment was Sara Lee Knit Products of Winston-Salem, North Carolina. K-Mart informed Sara Lee that making product available quickly was just as important as product quality. K-Mart ordered on a weekly basis and expected Sara Lee to ship orders within five days. Sara Lee examined its entire logistics/distribution channel to make its procedures, particularly in logistics, meet its customers' expectations.

A key factor in Sara Lee's success was the company's three warehouses and the inventory management in those warehouses. Sara Lee redesigned and automated the warehouses, reducing lead time to customers and lowering costs. Sara Lee is not alone in recognizing the importance of warehousing in today's competitive environment.

The inventory cost analysis in this text included a warehousing cost component when a firm calculated the cost of carrying inventory in a warehouse. However, the warehousing component focus was very static. In other words, warehousing and materials handling require much more comprehensive coverage, especially with contract warehousing and the global nature of most businesses. The synergistic relationship between warehousing and inventory management also needs additional discussion.

NATURE AND IMPORTANCE OF WAREHOUSING

We often define warehousing as the storage of goods before their use.[1] Broadly interpreted, this definition includes a wide spectrum of facilities and locations that provide warehousing, including the storage of iron ore in open fields, the storage of finished goods in the production facility, and the storage of raw materials, industrial goods, and finished goods while they are in transport. It also includes highly specialized storage facilities such as bean and grain elevators, tobacco warehouses, potato cellars, and refrigeration facilities. Every product manufactured, grown, or caught is warehoused at least once during its life cycle (from creation to consumption). Given this fact, we can easily understand why warehousing is of national economic importance. In 1989, warehousing costs in the U.S. totalled $60 billion dollars, as Table 10–1 indicates. The United States spent a total of $581 billion dollars on logistics, which equalled 11.1 percent of the nation's entire gross national product (GNP).

creating time
utility

In a macroeconomic sense, warehousing performs a very necessary function. It creates time utility for raw materials, industrial goods, and finished products. The proximity of market-oriented warehousing to the customer allows a firm to serve the customer with shorter lead times. More important, warehousing increases the utility of goods by broadening their time availability to prospective customers. In other words, by using warehouses, companies can make goods available *when* and *where* customers demand them. This warehousing function continues to be increasingly important as companies and industries use customer service as a dynamic, value-adding competitive tool.

The quantity and variety of commodities that require storage determine the basic warehousing demand. Thus, warehousing exists because companies inventory commodities. We can divide inventories into two general categories—*physical supply* (raw materials and/or components) and *physical distribution* (finished goods). Firms store both inventory types for some of the same reasons. The reasons for holding inventory are essentially the same as the rationale for warehousing. Briefly reviewing the rationale for holding warehouse inventory will aid our discussion the role of warehousing in a logistics system.

Rationale for Holding Warehouse Inventory

transportation

In almost all companies, transportation cost savings are a reason for creating inventories. A company can realize rate savings, for example, by transporting commodities in bulk, since carload and truckload rates average approximately 80% to 110% lower than less-than-carload and less-than-truckload rates. The cost savings in transportation alone are sufficient to cause some companies to warehouse inventories.

TABLE 10–1   COMPONENTS OF 1989 LOGISTICS COST

		$ Billions
Inventory Carrying Costs		
Interest		72
Taxes, obsolescence, depreciation		96
Warehousing		60
	Subtotal	228
Transportation Costs		
Motor Carriers		
Public and for hire		72
Private and for own account		84
Local freight services		100
	Subtotal	256
Other Carriers		
Railroads		30
Water carriers		21
Oil pipelines		9
Air carriers		11
	Subtotal	71
Shipper Related Costs		4
Distribution Administration		22
	TOTAL LOGISTICS COST	$581

Source: Robert Delaney, Cass Logistics.

safety stock

In contrast to these price savings, stopping the production line is usually prohibitively expensive. To never shut down the line for lack of raw materials is a common rule in many companies. To avoid production stoppages, a company must maintain adequate stocks of raw materials and/or components. Efficient and balanced production runs for different products also dictate sufficient warehouse space for finished goods. However, as we discussed in a preceding chapter, a firm must monitor safety stock level closely. Just-in-time inventory systems drive safety stock levels as close to zero as possible, but not all companies can use JIT systems.

purchase economies

Companies warehouse raw materials for other significant reasons. Offering quantity discounts a prevalent pricing strategy, makes volume purchases advantageous, thus making it necessary to store the commodities until needed. For companies subcontracting or purchasing from suppliers, maintaining these supplies' viability is necessary. For a firm making purchases, maintaining the suppliers can become as important as realizing cost efficiencies for the firm. This is particularly true when the company is an important customer for the supplier, or when a company needs the supplier's products only seasonally.

seasonality

Seasonal variability in obtaining required raw materials also necessitates storage. Many situations can alter the timing of replenishment. Some are expected, such as the seasonality of agricultural commodities and poor transportation conditions during winter. All are important reasons, depending upon the company, for maintaining warehouse facilities for raw materials.

customer service

A more elaborate customer service rationale is one reason for the extensive use of inventories and warehouses in finished goods. Since World War II, companies have increasingly relied on customer service as a competitive tool. By increasing their finished goods inventories and warehouses, companies reduce their stockout risk and improve customer service. Firms sometimes design logistics systems to minimize the time between the customer's order and receipt of the product. Company customer standards may include never being stocked out, one-day delivery time, and a ninety-eight percent customer service level. These stringent goals increase inventory and warehousing requirements dramatically. Each company's service philosophy determines the number of market-oriented warehouses and production facility warehouses necessary to serve a national market. One firm felt that 350 different warehouse locations were necessary to meet its customers service requirements.[2] The continued emphasis on customer service will pressure companies to increase finished goods inventories.

other factors

The industry, a firm's own philosophy, the particular product's characteristics, the economy, and various production processes can all affect the forgoing reasons for storing inventory. Many industries are radically different in their inventory orientation. For example, the distribution characteristics of the chemical and retail industries are individual and unique. Also, firms within an industry can have different marketing philosophies—for example, Avon and Max Factor in the cosmetics industry. Numerous product characteristics, such as size, perishability, product lines, substitutability, intended market, obsolescence, dollar density and weight density, affect the distribution system a firm requires. An economic change can quickly alter a manufacturer's inventory policy.

Various production processes place different and unusual demands on the inventory and warehouse system. For companies marketing seasonal products such as Christmas lights, lawn mowers, and packing cans, finished product storage assumes added importance. We can readily see that a multitude of variables cause tremendous changes in inventory methods, patterns, and warehousing philosophy.

The Role of the Warehouse in the Logistics System—A Basic Conceptual Rationale

The warehouse is a fixed point or node in the logistics system where a firm stores or holds raw materials, semifinished goods, or finished goods for varying periods of time. Holding goods in a warehouse stops or interrupts the flow of goods, adding cost to the product or products. Some firms have viewed warehousing cost very negatively; in short, they sought to avoid it if at all possible. This view is changing due to the realization that warehousing can add more value than cost to a product. Other firms, particularly distributors or wholesalers, went to the opposite extreme and warehoused as many items as possible. Neither end of the spectrum is usually correct. Firms should hold or store items only if possible trade-offs exist in other areas.

transportation consolidation

The warehouse serves several value-adding roles in a logistics system: transportation consolidation, product mixing, service, contingency protection, and smoothing. As we indicated previously and as Figure 10–1 demonstrates, companies will sometimes face less-than-truckload and less-than-carload shipments of raw materials and finished goods. Because shipping goods long distances at LTL or LCL rates is more costly than shipping at full truckload or carload rates, by moving the LTL and LCL amounts relatively short distances to or from a warehouse, warehousing can allow a firm to *consolidate* smaller shipments into a large shipment (carload or truckload), with significant transportation savings. For the physical supply system, the warehouse would consolidate different suppliers' LTL or LCL shipments and ship a volume shipment (TL or CL) to the firm's plant. For the physical distribution system, the warehouse would receive a consolidated volume shipment from various plants and ship LTL or LCL shipments to different markets.

FIGURE 10–1   TRANSPORTATION CONSOLIDATION

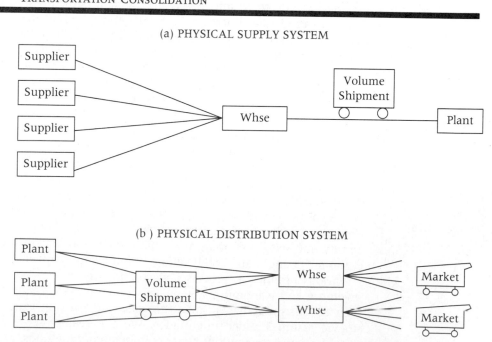

(a) PHYSICAL SUPPLY SYSTEM

(b) PHYSICAL DISTRIBUTION SYSTEM

mixing

A second warehousing function may be customer order *product mixing.* Companies frequently turn out a product line that contains thousands of "different" products, if we consider color, size, shape, and other variations. When placing orders, customers will often want a product line mixture—for example, five dozen four-cup coffee pots; six dozen ten-cup coffee pots with blue trim and ten dozen with red trim; and three dozen blue salad bowl sets. Because companies often produce items at different plants, a company that did not warehouse goods would have to fill orders from several locations, causing differing arrival times and opportunity for mix-ups. Therefore, a product mixing warehouse for a multiple-product line leads to efficient order filling (see Figure 10–2). By developing new mixing warehouses near dense urban areas, firms can make pickups and deliveries in smaller vehicles and schedule these activities at more optimum times to avoid congestion.

Figure 10–2   Supply and Product Mixing

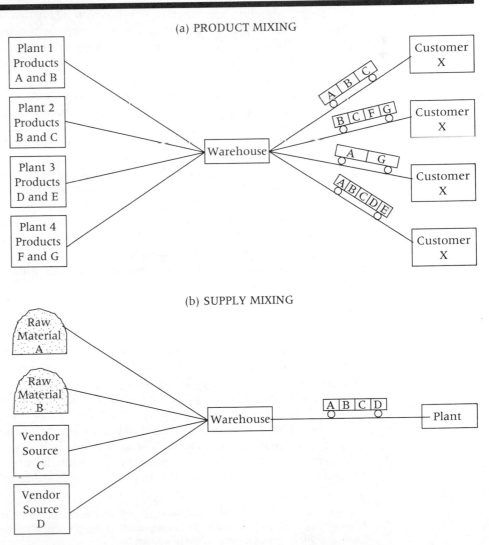

(a) PRODUCT MIXING

(b) SUPPLY MIXING

In addition to product mixing for customer orders, companies using raw materials or semi-finished goods (e.g., auto manufacturers) commonly move carloads of items mixed from a physical supply warehouse to a plant (see Figure 10–2). This strategy not only reduces transportation costs from consolidation, but also allows the company to avoid using the plant as a warehouse. This strategy will become increasingly popular as increased fuel expenses raise transport costs. For firms using sophisticated strategies such as MRP (materials requirements planning) or JIT (just-in-time) systems, supply warehouse use is essential.

service

A third warehouse function is to provide *service.* The importance of customer service is obvious. Having goods available in a warehouse when a customer places an order, particularly if the warehouse is in reasonable proximity to the customer, will usually lead to customer satisfaction and enhance future sales. Service may also be a factor for physical supply warehouses. However, production schedules, which a firm makes in advance, are easier to "service" than customers: while customer demand is often uncertain, physical supply stockout costs sometimes seem infinite.

contingencies

A fourth warehousing function is *protection against contingencies* such as transportation delays, vendor stockouts, or strikes. A potential trucker's strike will generally cause buyers to stock larger inventories than usual, for example. This particular function is very important for physical supply warehouses in that a delay in the delivery of raw materials can delay the production of finished goods. However, contingencies also occur with physical distribution warehouses—for example, goods damaged in transit can affect inventory levels and order filling.

smoothing

A fifth warehousing function is to *smooth* operations or decouple successive stages in the manufacturing process. Previous discussions mentioned seasonal demand and the need for production run length sufficient to ensure reasonable cost and quality. These are examples of smoothing—that is, preventing operations under overtime conditions at low production levels. In effect, this balancing strategy allows a company to reduce its manufacturing capacity investment.

As we can see, warehousing functions can make important contributions to logistics systems and company operations. However, we must also view warehousing in a trade-off context; that is, warehousing's profit contribution must be greater than its cost.

BASIC WAREHOUSING DECISIONS

private versus public warehousing

A number of important decisions or choices including ownership, number, size, location, and stocking, relate to warehousing management. The first item we will consider is *ownership.* In arranging warehousing space, an organization has two basic alternatives: *private* ownership of facilities or use of *public* warehouses.* To choose between the two or to combine them is a major warehousing decision. Many firms combine public and private warehousing because of varying regional market conditions and other factors, such as seasonality.

A firm has to approach the ownership decision in a trade-off framework. Certain operations lend themselves to private warehousing, whereas others lend

---

*A third alternative is *leased* warehousing. Generally this means leasing a complete facility at a fixed fee per year. The basic nature of this arrangement closely resembles private warehousing, so we will treat them synonymously in this discussion.

themselves best to public facilities where a firm rents space or contracts on a shorter-term basis according to need. We will examine each alternative's cost variations, favorable use conditions and advantages in a later section.

Related to the private warehousing decision are decisions concerning warehouse design and layout. A firm deciding to use a private warehouse must make a number of decisions about how to utilize the facility most effectively, which we will discuss later in the text.

centralized versus decentralized warehousing

Another important warehousing decision is whether the firm will use a *centralized* approach or a *decentralized* approach in providing warehousing facilities. This decision essentially concerns how many warehouses the firm should provide. In some instances, the decision will be relatively simple because of the firm's size. That is, small and medium-size firms with a single regional market area often will need only one warehouse. Usually, only large firms with national or international market areas need to examine the question in detail.

As with the private versus public warehousing decision, a firm has to use a trade-off framework in analyzing the need for warehouses in various areas. A particular firm's demand and supply conditions will make one alternative more attractive than others. For example, a firm manufacturing or distributing a highly competitive and substitutable product on a national basis may need to use decentralized warehousing to give rapid service in its market area.

A firm has to closely coordinate the decision about *number* of warehouses with its decision about transportation (link) alternatives. For example, air freight makes possible rapid national market coverage from one or two strategically located warehouses. Although the cost of air freight is relatively high, a company can nevertheless trade it off against savings in warehousing and inventory costs. As the next section explains, a number of link or transportation alternatives make the decision about warehouse numbers a real challenge, particularly when we consider this decision in conjunction with the public-private warehouse alternative.

warehouse size and location

Very closely related to the warehouse number decision and the centralized versus decentralized question are two other warehousing decisions: warehouse *size* and warehouse *location*. If a company is using public warehousing, the size question is important; but such a company can usually expand or contract space according to its needs at different times. Similarly, the location decision becomes less important when a company uses public warehousing. Although the firm has to decide where to use public warehousing, the exact location is fixed; and the firm can change its decision if necessary.

As with other logistics decisions, a firm must examine location in a trade-off perspective. The firm must achieve a desired customer service level at the least possible total distribution cost. By analyzing the warehouse's intended function, a firm can determine general locations, such as high-service facilities near markets, raw materials mixing close to production, or a combination of other factors. The choice of an exact location must rely on factors such as transportation, the market, and local characteristics. These decisions, once implemented, may be very costly to change, especially in private warehousing; therefore, proper consideration of all factors is essential.

layout

Size and location questions are of paramount importance to firms using private warehousing and, in particular, to firms that have to provide national or international market coverage. In addition to making the five warehouse decisions we cited earlier, firms have to decide how to lay out the warehouse's interior. In other words, the firm has to make decisions about aisle space,

items stocked

shelving, equipment, and all the other physical dimensions of the interior warehouse. Another decision is how to arrange stock most efficiently in the warehouse.

Still other warehousing decisions involve what items the firm should stock and how much stock the firm will assign to various warehouses, but these questions are relevant only if the firm has multiple warehouse locations. A firm having a number of locations must decide whether all warehouses will carry the entire product line, whether each warehouse will specialize to some extent, or whether the warehouses will combine specialization and general stocking. Some aspects of this decision, particularly when a firm knows location of warehouses, size, and demand, make a convenient linear programming decision.

employee safety

Other concerns, such as employee risks due to the monotonous and dangerous work in many traditional warehouses as well as to hazardous materials handling and sanitation, will also influence efficiency improvement decisions. Efficiency also involves the interaction with materials handling equipment, as we will discuss later in the text.

Warehousing decisions are important and require close attention. Improving efficiency and productivity will be a major management focus in warehousing operations. Properly utilizing space through carefully planned inventory management and distribution operations will be more important in the future than building additional facilities. Moreover, warehouse decisions interact very closely with other areas of the logistics system. We will explore some of these decisions in detail in this chapter. Before addressing these questions, we will discuss the warehouse and its basic functions in the logistics system.

BASIC WAREHOUSE OPERATIONS

movement

The basic warehouse operations are *movement* and *storage.* Storage is probably the most obvious warehouse operation, whereas movement may seem incongruous. However, movement is a very vital aspect of warehousing; and we can divide this aspect into four somewhat distinct operations: (1) receiving goods into the warehouse from the link or transport network; (2) transferring goods into a particular location in the warehouse; (3) selecting particular combinations of goods for customer orders or raw materials for production; and (4) loading goods for shipping to the customer or to the production line. All four involve short-distance movement.

The movement function characterizes distribution or market warehouse for finished goods. Goods brought to distribution or market warehouses "move" through the warehouse rapidly; that is, there is rapid inventory turnover. Of the reasons for rapid stock turnover, the most fundamental is the high cost of holding finished goods inventory for long time periods. Recall the inventory cost formulation and the inventory cost examples. Finished goods have high value, need more sophisticated storage facilities, and have greater risks for damage, loss, and obsolescence, all contributing to higher inventory costs. So moving goods quickly and efficiently through the market or distribution warehouses is almost mandatory. A distribution warehouse visitor can sense the activity level almost instantly. Although modern materials handling technology has made movement more orderly in many warehouses, the movement is still quite obvious.

storage

The other very important warehousing function is more obvious—the storage or holding of goods. In some warehouses, the storage or holding function is very temporary or short-term. In fact, some items will "turn" in twenty-four to forty-eight hours. Firms often associate holding goods for longer time periods (over ninety days) with raw materials or semifinished goods, because they have a lower value, involve less risk, require less sophisticated storage facilities, and may involve quantity purchase discounts.

Note, however, that warehouses may hold even finished goods for time periods longer than the preceding comments suggest. In some instances, the longer time is for very obvious reasons. For example, a winemaker or distiller may have to store certain alcoholic beverages, which may be considered finished after processing, for conditioning or aging purposes.

In addition, for firms facing very erratic demand for their goods, accurately forecasting inventory requirements is quite difficult. If substitutability is an associated problem, then the firm may need to carry relatively large inventories to preclude stockouts. Although such an approach is costly, it is sometimes necessary. Such a problem occurs in fashion goods; here, firms pass on the higher inventory cost in the form of higher prices.

seasonal demand   One common reason for holding finished goods longer than ninety days is that seasonality of demand enters the picture, and the distribution channels for distributing the goods to the ultimate consumer may be relatively long. For example, manufacturers of Christmas cards, paper, and accessories will start to accumulate inventory for the Christmas season in late June or July and will often complete the production of such items by November. The products will start moving out to wholesalers and other intermediaries in early September or even in late August. But the manufacturers will retain some stock until mid-November or possibly later to satisfy stockouts by shipping quickly and directly to retailers. Other companies are in very similar situations; although they may not need to store items as long as Christmas item manufacturers do, they nevertheless hold finished goods for longer than thirty days, very often for 90 to 120 days. Firms may store seasonal goods for relatively longer periods as a trade-off against increased production costs. In other words, by lengthening production runs and eliminating overtime, a firm can usually trade off reduced production costs against increased storage costs.

All warehouses provide both movement and storage. One function is usually more accentuated, depending on the warehouse's orientation in the system. Thus, the movement function characterizes market-oriented or distribution warehouses storing finished goods. Goods move through the warehouse rapidly and may be held for only twenty-four to forty-eight hours. Very often, firms decentralize such warehouses to serve specific market areas. Storage warehouses very often hold raw materials, semifinished goods, and seasonal finished goods for much longer time periods; and their design, location, and orientation reflect this fact.

The facility's layout affects a warehouse's basic or emphasized operations. While no magic formula states exactly what layout design a firm should use, we should consider the basic aspects.

WAREHOUSE LAYOUT AND DESIGN

space requirements   To understand warehouse layout and design, some background information on a typical warehouse's basic space requirements is necessary. This discussion of space requirements relates quite closely to the discussion of basic warehouse operations. Before looking specifically at the types of space a firm needs, we will comment briefly about determining how much space a firm requires.

forecast   The first step in determining warehouse space requirements is to developing demand forecast for a company's products. This means preparing an estimate in units for a relevant sales period (usually thirty days) by product category.

Then the company will need to determine each item's order quantity, usually including some allowance for safety stock. The next step is to convert the units into cubic footage requirements, which may need to include pallets and which usually include an allowance of ten to fifteen percent for growth over the relevant period. At this point, the company has an estimate of basic storage space requirements. To this the company must add space needs for aisles and other needs such as offices, lavatories, and meeting rooms. Warehouses commonly devote one-third of their total space to nonstorage functions. Many companies make these space decisions through computer simulation. The computer can consider a vast number of variables and can help predict future requirements; good software packages are available.

link interface   One additional space warehouse requirement provides an interface with the link part of the logistics system—*receiving and shipping*. While this can be one area, efficiency usually requires two separate areas. In considering these space needs, a firm must consider whether to use the dock area outside the building or to unload goods out of the vehicle directly into the warehouse. The firm will have to allow for turnaround space and possibly for equipment and pallet storage. Also important are areas for staging goods before transportation and for unitizing consolidated shipments. In addition, this area may need space for checking, counting, and inspecting. The volume and frequency of the throughput will be critical in determining space receiving and shipping needs.

order selection space   Another space requirement in physical distribution warehouses is for *order picking* and *assembly*. The amount of space these functions need will depend upon order volume and the product's nature, along with the materials handling equipment. This area's layout is critical to efficient operations and customer service. We will discuss this aspect later in an analysis of layout requirements.

storage space   A third type of space is the actual *storage* space. In a warehouse, a firm must use the full volume of the cubic storage space as efficiently as possible. A firm can derive the amount of storage space from the analysis we described earlier in this section, and it will be the largest single area in the warehouse. As with the order picking area, a firm will have to consider storage area layout in detail. We will cover this topic in a subsequent section.

other types of space   A firm must consider three additional types of space. First, many physical distribution warehouses have space for *recoupering*—that is, an area to salvage undamaged parts of damaged cartons. Second, administrative and clerical staff generally require *office space*. Finally, rest rooms, an employee cafeteria, utilities, and locker rooms require *miscellaneous* space. The amount of space these last three categories require will depend on a number of variables. For example, the average amount of damaged merchandise and the feasibility of repacking undamaged merchandise will determine recoupering space needs. The space requirement for a cafeteria and locker rooms will depend on the number of employees.

Layout and Design Principles

While the discussion thus far has delineated a typical warehouse's various space needs, we need to consider layout in more detail. We will first consider some general layout design principles and then examine layout in the context of the space categories discussed previously.

one-story straight-line   The most commonly accepted warehouse design and layout principles are as follows: First, use a one-story facility wherever possible, since it usually provides more usable space per investment dollar and usually is less expensive to construct. Second, use straight-line or direct flow of goods into and out of the warehouse, as Figure 10–3 illustrates, to avoid backtracking and inefficiency.

efficient handling   A third principle is to use efficient materials handling equipment and operations. The next chapter explores materials handling fundamentals. Among other benefits, materials handling equipment improves efficiency in operations.

storage plan   A fourth principle is to use an effective storage plan in the warehouse. In other words, the firm must place goods in the warehouse in such a way as to maximize warehouse operations and to avoid inefficiencies. Stated simply, we are trying to utilize existing space completely and effectively as possible while providing both adequate accessibility and protection for the goods we are storing.

aisle space   A fifth principle of good layout is to minimize aisle space within the constraints the size, type, and turning radius of materials handling equipment impose. We must also consider the products, the constraints they impose.

height   A sixth principle is to make maximum use of the building's height—that is, to utilize the building's cubic capacity effectively. As the next chapter points out, this usually requires integration with materials handling. Though vehicles capable of maneuvering in small aisles and stacking higher than conventional vehicles can are very expensive, such equipment offers potentially large overall systems savings because using height costs only one-fifth the cost of building the same cubic footage horizontally. What's more, a high-rise building (forty to fifty feet high) attains almost the same cubic footage as a building twenty-five feet high, with less than half of the floor space, thus cutting land costs.

With these general principles in mind, we can focus upon the design requirements of some of the warehouse's basic space areas. With regard to the shipping and receiving areas, a firm will have to consider whether to place stock temporarily in these areas and whether to store equipment here. The turning requirements of materials handling equipment will also influence needs in this area. The firm must also analyze the number of bays, as well as their size and shape. The type of carrier the firm utilizes, product characteristics, and materials handling equipment will influence the bay requirements.

In regard to the order picking and preparation area, we must keep in mind that, in a physical distribution warehouse, nearly constant movement characterizes this section. Utilizing cubic space effectively, is difficult because of the need to keep items within order pickers' reaching distance. While utilizing materials handling equipment can overcome this problem to some extent, a firm

FIGURE 10–3   BASIC WAREHOUSE CONFIGURATION

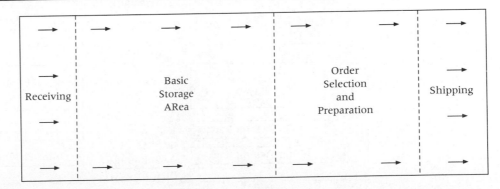

will never completely resolve the problem, because constant movement requires more open space.

layout for order picking and preparation

There are three basic ways to lay out the order picking and preparation area. One is to use the general area approach, which basically mixes the order picking and preparation area with the storage area, with appropriate racks and order preparation equipment (see Figure 10–4).

The second basic layout for order picking and preparation is the modified area approach, which provides separate storage and order preparation areas (see Figure 10–5). To allow better access, the order picking bays are usually smaller than the storage bays. The firm will stock the order picking bays on a regular basis and will usually make provision for partial and full boxes. Separating order picking from storage reduces picking time and distance but also reduces the facility's flexibility. The third basic layout for order picking and preparation is the reserve/active area approach (see Figure 10–6). This approach which is

FIGURE 10–4   GENERAL AREA CONFIGURATION FOR ORDER PICKING

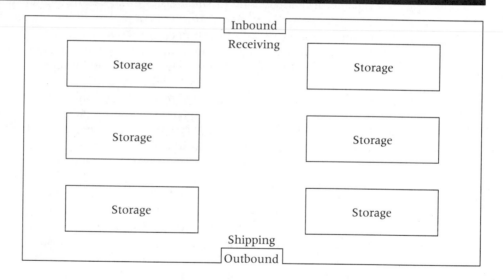

FIGURE 10–5   MODIFIED AREA CONFIGURATION

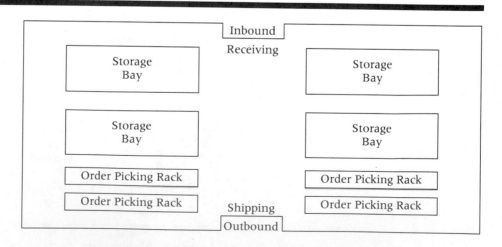

more complex than the modified area approach, subdivides the storage area into two more areas: (1) reserve storage and (2) active or forward storage. The reserve storage area would be located next to the inbound receiving area. The active or forward storage area would be located next to the order picking and preparation area. When the inventory in the active storage location falls to a certain level, warehouse personnel replenishes the inventory with items from the reserve storage area. With the reserve/active system, the active storage area racks usually flow directly into the order picking areas.

Layout and Design Objectives

capacity utilization

As we stated previously, an underlying layout design principle in the warehouse's storage area is to fully use the cubic capacity. One storage area design feature that lends itself to this objective is the use of larger storage bays having more limited access. The turnover or throughput level will affect storage bays' actual size. For example, when turnover is very low, as in physical supply warehouses, the bays can be wide and deep with limited access; and the aisles can be narrow. Increased turnover necessitates better access, and, consequently, smaller bays and wider aisles. The customer service requirements of the physical distribution warehouse necessitate quick access (see Figure 10–7).

protection

Warehouse layout's protection and efficiency objectives provide a good framework for determining the use of warehouse space. Looking first at the protection aspect, we can develop some general guidelines. First, warehouse space utilization should separate hazardous materials such as explosives, flammable items, and oxidizing items from other items so as to eliminate the possibility of damage. Second, the firm should safeguard products requiring special security against pilferage. Third, the warehouse should properly accommodate items requiring

FIGURE 10–6   RESERVE/ACTIVE AREA APPROACH

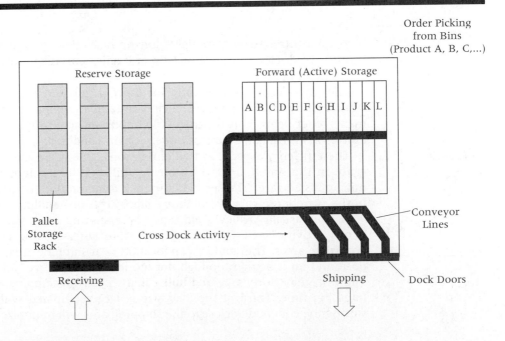

Order Picking
from Bins
(Product A, B, C,...)

FIGURE 10–7   TYPICAL SMALL WAREHOUSE   *Source:* From General Services Administration, *Warehouse Operations* (Washington, D.C.: U.S. Government Printing Office, 1964).

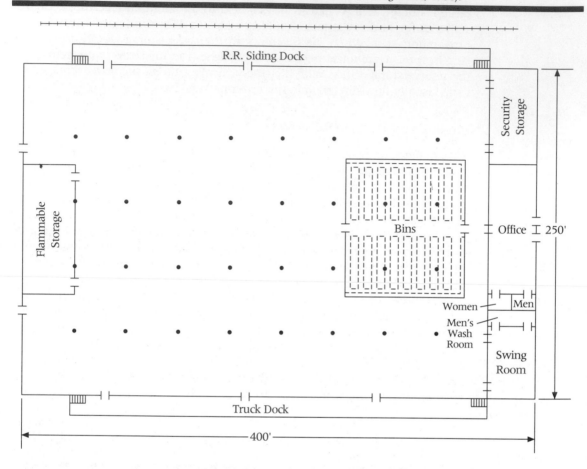

physical control such as refrigeration or heat. Fourth, warehouse personnel should avoid stacking or storing light or fragile items near other items that could cause them damage.

The government has recently increased regulation of the movement and storage of hazardous materials, including radioactive materials, explosives, and many other items. This is particularly important since any product can be hazardous in certain situations or under certain conditions.

efficiency   The efficiency aspect has two dimensions. One is the effective *utilization of space* in the warehouse, which means utilizing the facility's height and minimizing aisle space. The second efficiency dimension is the *placement of stock* in the warehouse so as to minimize labor costs or handling costs.

A firm usually achieves efficiency by analyzing three variables. First is an item's activity level. The firm should store faster-moving items in the most accessible areas. This could mean location near shipping areas or simply a shelf position that is neither too high nor too low. Second, size can affect efficiency. The firm may store large and bulky items near the shipping area to minimize handling time. Third, if the load size is large compared with the order size, storing the commodity close to the shipping area will minimize handling costs.[3]

mechanization   Though mechanized systems are not the solution for every warehouse, these systems frequently offer great potential to improve distribution efficiency. Careful planning should consider all the risks of investing in automation. These risks include obsolescence due to rapid technological change, market fluctuations, and return on the large investment. The planning stages of mechanization also call for an operations analysis. Mechanization generally works best when items are regularly shaped and easily handled, when order selection is the middle range of activity, and when product moves in high volumes with few fluctuations. The next chapter looks into the various types of mechanized equipment available.

productivity   A company should not make these decisions once and then take them for granted; rather, the company should monitor productivity regularly during warehouse operations. While monitoring methods vary widely, the company should set goals and standards for costs and order handling efficiency and then measure actual performance in an attempt to optimize the warehouse's productivity. By improving productivity, a company can improve its resource use; increase cash flow, profits, and return on investments; and provide its customers with better service. Warehouse costs constitute six to eight percent of the sales dollar, so any improvement in warehouse costs through productivity increases would flow quickly to the bottom line.

To begin a productivity program, a company should divide warehouse operations into functional areas and measure each area's productivity, utilization, and performance, focusing on improvements in labor, equipment, and facilities and making comparisons with standards if they exist; repeating measurements can show relative trends. There is no single measure of warehouse productivity, but the method the company chooses must have the following attributes: validity, coverage, comparability, completeness, usefulness, compatibility, and cost effectiveness.

resources   The inputs a warehouse uses when measuring productivity are labor, facilities, equipment, energy, and financial investment. In a company-owned warehouse, the functions the company measures are receiving, putaway, storage, replenishment, order selection, checking, packing and marking, staging and order consolidation, shipping, and clerical and administration.

improvements   Kenneth B. Ackerman recommends four methods for improving warehouse productivity.[4] First, reduce distances traveled through the warehouse by examining the planning of facility stock location, data handling, and materials handling. Second, increase the size of the units the facility handles, possibly by working with marketing to encourage larger customer orders. Third, seek round-trip use for warehouse equipment. Finally, improve cube utilization by increasing the storage space. The firm may also improve productivity by improving the lighting, clearing blocked aisles, changing task orientations, and efficiently handling information.

Firms could also view productivity in a customer service perspective. Such measurements could include the percentage of orders the company filled correctly, lost records, or stockouts. No matter the criteria the company should utilize this information as feedback to correct any problems in materials storage and movement.

We can cite a number of commonsense warehouse layout principles: do not exceed specified floor loads, keep aisles straight and clear of obstructions, rotate stock. At this point, we have sufficient background to turn our attention to the major warehousing decisions. The first of these is ownership.

THE OWNERSHIP DECISION

The introductory comments for this chapter stated that one important warehousing decision is whether to use private or public warehousing. In other words, should the company purchase or build its own warehouse or warehouses; or should it rent public warehouse space on an as-needed basis? Both approaches have advantages and disadvantages. Companies usually resolve the decision in cost terms (i.e., which alternative or combinations thereof will result in the lowest total cost). Figure 10–8 presents a simplistic view of the costs involved.

variable cost   Figure 10–8 shows a general cost comparison between a public warehouse and a private warehouse. As we can see, the public warehouse is all variable cost. As the volume of throughput in the warehouse increases, the company has to rent more space. This space is available at a specific charge per square foot or per cubic foot. Thus, the cost will rise proportionately to the amount that the company stores in the warehouse. The cost function is linear in this instance. As the next section explains, obtaining lower rates for larger volumes in a public warehouse may be possible; but the curve will taper off at the upper end. The general relationship will remain the same.

fixed cost   The private warehouse, on the other hand, has a fixed cost element, which we can attribute to elements such as property taxes and depreciation, in its cost structure. The variable warehouse operating cost would usually increase more slowly than the cost of the public warehouse because of the profit and the cost of marketing the public facility. Consequently, at some point the two cost functions will meet, or be equal. Generally, at lower output volumes, the public warehouse is the best alternative. As volume increases, we are able to use private facilities more efficiently; that is, we can spread the fixed costs over the large output volumes.

As Figure 10–8 shows, a firm can make the ownership decision using the same technique we used to solve total cost problems earlier in the text. The difference would be that the public warehouse, as depicted, would have zero fixed costs for the equation $y = a + b(x)$. The decision maker could therefore find a solution to the problem by solving for the equality point between the two cost functions.

FIGURE 10–8   COST COMPARISON BETWEEN PRIVATE AND PUBLIC WAREHOUSING

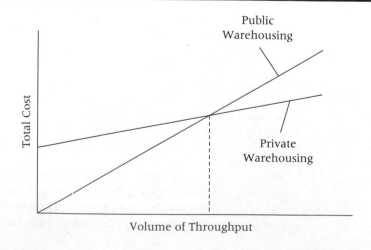

This is a somewhat simplistic view of the situation confronting many firms, particularly large multi-product-line companies that may be involved with anywhere from five to one hundred warehouses. However, for two reasons, such a simplistic perspective may be fairly realistic even for more complex situations. First, companies often add warehouses one at a time; and, because of different market and cost circumstances, the choice in each new instance could be between private and public. Second, even when a company is adding more than one warehouse, the locational circumstances are often quite different and require the company to analyze each warehouse in terms of the ownership question.

At this point it would be appropriate to investigate some characteristics of firms and their products that result in their using private or public warehousing. From Figure 10–8, we can deduce some of these characteristics or factors.

throughput volume

Because of fixed costs, the private warehouse situation requires a relatively high throughput volume to make the warehouse economical. Since the fixed costs occur irrespective of use, the company must have a volume sufficient to "spread out" the fixed cost so that the private warehouse's average cost (fixed plus variable) is lower than the public facility's. This analysis implies two assumptions. One assumption, as Figure 10–8 indicates, is that the variable cost per unit (the slope of the function) for the private warehouse is less than the variable cost per unit for the public warehouse. Otherwise the private warehouse would never be less expensive. The other assumption is that the usage rate or throughput is stable throughout most of the year. If this is not true, then we will have problems with the size decision and will be unable to utilize our space efficiently.

stable demand

Stability is often a critical factor in private warehousing, as it is in private trucking. Many products have seasonal sales. However, many large firms and some smaller firms have multiple product lines; and this helps to stabilize the warehouse throughput to build the volume necessary for an economical private warehouse. Examples would be companies like General Foods or General Mills. When coffee sales drop off in the summer, they sell more tea for iced-tea drinkers.

dense market area

Another factor conducive to private warehousing is a dense market area relatively close to the warehouse or numerous vendors relatively close to a physical supply warehouse. As a previous section indicated, small shipment rates (LTL or LCL) are relatively high per mile. Therefore, paying the relatively high small-shipment rates quickly uses up the savings that usually accrue by shipping in bulk (CL or TL) to a warehouse. Consequently, in low-population-density areas, firms often find using several public warehouses in different locales more economical than "putting together" enough volume for a private warehouse and having to serve a rather broad geographical area.

control

An additional reason why a private warehouse might benefit a firm more is for control purposes. This can encompass physical control for such things as security or refrigeration and service control for customers or plants. Certain raw materials and finished goods are highly susceptible to theft or to loss of value from damage or spoilage. Although public warehouses are usually reputable firms and must exercise care in storing goods, the chances of loss may be higher than with private warehouses. Even if the public warehousing company pays for losses, the loss of customer goodwill or production efficiencies may be too great. In some regions, public warehousing firms will not store particular products because of their hazardous nature or for some other reason. If a firm manufacturing such products decides that storage in that region is important, the only option will be to use a private facility. Customer service competition is another control factor favoring private warehousing. Although this rationale can lead to too much private warehousing, it nevertheless has become an increasingly important justification for private warehousing. This is particularly true with more sophisticated computer-based information systems that coordinate inventory control and order processing. Competition through customer service is an increasingly viable force that will justify varying strategies.

multiple use   One final justification for private warehousing may be combining this facility's use with the firm's other regional needs. For example, sales representatives and customer service representatives can have offices in the same building, with a lower total cost than having offices in two local facilities. The firm would have to combine this consideration with other cost justifications.

Companies currently using or contemplating using private warehousing find that the preceding characteristics interact to justify their use of private warehousing. Because they have volume, stability, dense markets, and the need to exercise control, firms with multiple product lines often find private warehousing particularly economical for physical distribution. And because they usually have multiple plant operations, they also find private warehousing most economical for physical supply.

At this point, we might ask if public warehousing is ever economical; the answer is yes. In fact, if we reflect on the characteristics that made private warehousing economical, we can find many firms for whom public warehousing is most economical. A firm wishing to use public warehousing should know the various services such warehousing offers, as well as such things as regulation and pricing practices. Before covering these topics, the next two sections examine the importance of public warehousing.

PUBLIC WAREHOUSING

The previous section mentioned the growth of private warehousing in conjunction with customer service competition. This does not mean that public warehousing had declined or even maintained the status quo. Instead, public warehousing has grown and prospered, and has been a very dynamic and changing industry. In particular, general merchandise public warehousing, which most companies would use most frequently, has grown rapidly. The largest users of public warehousing are retail chain stores, because of their product volume and their use of warehousing with other functions, such as purchasing and transportation to various outlets.[5] A company with no large inventory accumulations or a very seasonal need for warehousing space could not utilize a private warehouse consistently and efficiently. A company shipping in small quantities for long distances (to dispersed customers or plants) would also usually find a public warehouse more economical, as would a firm entering new market area where the sales level and stability are uncertain. Such conditions will usually necessitate using a public warehouse until the firm effectively penetrates the market. If the market venture is successful and experience shows the necessary volume and stability, then the firm can institute private warehousing.

Marketing changes since World War II have enhanced the importance of all types of warehousing. Product proliferation and customer service have been the two driving forces. Today's larger and more varied product lines use a market strategy different from that of their one-product ancestors. For each product manufactured, a firm needs to maintain differentiation inventories. The increased customer service emphasis has increased the warehousing necessity for companies. Using a national warehousing company offers one-stop shopping for storage at multiple locations and increased leverage for negotiating rates and services.[6]

A combination of factors has increased warehousing use in recent years. The oil crisis and truckers' strikes have caused more companies to maintain higher inventory levels. And higher inventories create a demand for added warehouse space. Such factors will continue to contribute to more growth in public warehousing.

Additional Rationale for Public Warehousing

limited capital investment

The first and most significant financial reason for using public warehousing is that it requires no or limited capital investment of the company. The company must accomplish any capital investment only after careful planning. Even though interest rates have dropped, they remain highly volatile; and this will have a considerable effect on a project's return on investment. When a company builds, it establishes a long-term financial commitment. Therefore, the firm incurs capital payback risks through continued profitable use or sale of the facility. This assumes that the firm has adequately forecast and located consumer demand and concentration, and that technological breakthroughs in construction, transportation, or warehouse systems will not make the facility obsolete. For automated warehouses, the consideration of facility obsolescence becomes even more acute. A firm having made in accurate predictions might have to sell or lease a warehouse to continue capital payback. By using public warehousing, companies can avoid the capital investment and financial risks of owning their own warehouses.

flexibility

A second public warehousing advantage is flexibility. A firm can rent space for thirty-day periods, enabling the firm to react quickly to movements in demand or changes in the quality of transportation services. Exploring new markets requires location flexibility. Public warehousing enables a firm to immediately launch, expand, or pull out in new, untried markets without lingering distribution costs.[7]

Public Warehousing Services

Public warehouse personnel can perform such tasks as testing, assembly, price marking, and lot number marking. Contract warehousing, a public warehousing subdivision, provides these highly specialized services only to major or special accounts. Contract warehousing can offer a feasible alternative to private warehousing. We will discuss this concept further in the next section.

The great diversity of product characteristics, distribution systems, customer demand, and company operations and philosophy require that the public warehouse consider each customer's needs individually. The former president of the American Warehousemen's Association, Don Haslett, recognized this challenge:

> Now, we and our customers and potential customers think in terms of the total physical distribution concept in which there is no perfect pattern, no set of rules, that applies to every situation. The intelligent distribution executive plans carefully to make use of every possible tool in the distribution field to accomplish the effective distribution of his company's products. Public warehousing is one of these tools. The key to the importance of public warehousing as a tool is service.[8]

Mr. Haslett went on to discuss the competitive importance of service:

More and more, business is placed with a public warehouse, or not placed with a public warehouse, on the basis of whether, first of all, any public warehouse in a particular area provides the proper location for a needed service, followed by the consideration of which public warehouse can best and most efficiently provide that service on a regular basis.[9]

These statements indicate the increasing importance of varying public warehousing services. The general storage and handling services that have long been public warehousing mainstays must expand in order for public warehousing to remain competitive against private warehouse operations.

In addition, a public warehouse or a public warehouse manager at a private facility can offer two traditional public warehousing services: a bonding service and field warehousing. In both instances, the public warehouse manager is responsible for goods, issues a receipt for them, and cannot release the goods unless the requester meets certain conditions.

bonded warehousing

In bonded warehousing, the user is usually interested in delaying the payment of taxes or tariffs, or even avoiding their payment altogether. Because taxes are relatively high on certain items such as cigarettes and liquor, the seller, who is liable for the taxes, may want to postpone paying them until the goods are immediately ready for sale. The same may be true of imported items that a seller needs to hold in inventory before sale. If a public warehouse holds the items in custody, the seller does not have to pay the tax or tariff until the warehouse releases the items, at which time, or even before the service's user must usually pay what is appropriate.

In special cases, items may be imported and later exported without entering the "stream of commerce." In such instances, if a warehouse holds the items in bond, the seller may avoid the tariff altogether. The alternative would be to apply for a rebate after exporting the goods. Using free trade zones or free port areas accomplishes essentially the same thing. Sellers can import goods to these points and pay no tariff if they later reexport them.

field warehouse

A field warehouse situation occurs when a firm requests a receipt for goods stored in a public warehouse or under a public warehouse manager's supervision in a private warehouse. The firm usually plans to use the warehouse manager's receipt as collateral for a loan. The receipt is a negotiable instrument whereby title to the goods is transferable. This service is attractive to individuals or companies that have accumulated inventory and that need working capital. While most attractive to small and medium-size companies, it is a potentially valuable service for all companies.

All in all, public warehousing today offers many valuable services, from the traditional storage function to complete inventory management and associated customer services. A dynamic dimension of the logistics industry, public warehousing offers the logistics manager many possible alternatives. An additional public warehousing area is legal control, which we will consider in the next section.

Public Warehousing Regulation

In spite of public warehousing's for-hire or public nature, the government has exercised very little control over this industry's affairs. This is in sharp contrast to the transportation industry's for-hire segment, particularly the common carrier. There are probably a number of reasons for the regulatory control difference, but the underlying cause is that the warehousing industry has never caused public clamor for regulation by discriminating against its users, as was the case in the nineteenth-century rail industry.

liability

Several regulatory acts have affected public warehousing. The most comprehensive and important was the *Uniform Warehouse Receipts Act of 1912.* This act did several things. First, it defined the warehouse manager's legal responsibility. The public warehouse operator is liable only for exercising *reasonable* care. So if the public warehouse manager refused to pay for damages he or she felt was basically beyond his or her control, the user would have the *burden of proof* to attempt to show that the warehouse manager was liable.

Once again, this contrasts sharply with the common carrier situation, wherein the carrier bears burden of proof when damage occurs and has only several allowable excuses from liability. This does not mean that the public warehouse assumes no responsibility for damage or loss—that is, liability. Rather the situation is one of relative degrees of liability; and the comparison simply shows the transportation industry's special case.

receipts

In addition to establishing the public warehouse manager's legal responsibility, the Uniform Warehouse Receipts Act defined the types of receipts that the public warehouse manager can issue for items stored. The act recognized two basic types of receipts—negotiable and nonnegotiable. As we indicated previously, if the receipt was negotiable, then the title to the goods the public warehouse manager held was transferable. So, in effect, the "holder" of the receipt owned the goods; or, in other words, the holder could sign over the receipt like a check.

The act also set forth certain receipts information requirements, required information included the warehouse location, the receipt's issuance date, warehousing service rate, a description of the goods, signatures of the parties, and the instrument type. These requirements primarily protect the public warehousing user and anyone taking advantage of the receipts' negotiable aspects.

While public warehouse managers regulation and service is important, the logistics manager is also very much interested in public warehousing rates or charges, which is the topic of the next section.

Public Warehousing Rates

The public warehouse sells service in terms of a facility with fixed dimensions. The warehouse usually sells the service on a space basis per time period—for example, dollars per square foot per time period. Although the warehouse company in a sense has a less complicated pricing structure than a transportation company does, the logistics manager should basically understand the factors affecting rate, keeping in mind that rates are negotiable.

Value As we indicated previously, a public warehouse has a certain legally defined liability for goods stored. The risk increases with higher-valued goods, and rates generally reflect the higher risk of higher-valued goods.

The logistics manager may be able to reduce his or her rate by using protective packaging to decrease the chance of damage, and also by marking packages to specify care in handling and perhaps in position. If the public warehouse believes that these efforts diminish risk, the rates will be reduced.

Fragility   Warehouse rates must consider commodities' general susceptibility to damage because of the risk to the warehouse company. The logistics manager may reduce the risk of damage by using protective packaging, and consequently reduce the warehouse rates. Once again, the trade-off is between the warehouse rate reduction and the increased packaging cost.

Damage to Other Goods   In a public warehouse setting, incompatible stored goods always run the risk of damaging each other. In a sense, this is a two-way risk. Your product may damage another, or your product may be particularly susceptible to damage from some other product. Chemicals and food are obvious examples, but other more subtle ones exist. For example, automobile tires may have an adverse effect on certain products, even causing color change in some instances. Using proper packaging may reduce the risk, but once again the logistics manager should view this in a trade-off context.

Volume and Regularity   While the cost of using a public warehouse is generally variable, the warehouse company itself will experience fixed costs. Therefore, use volume and regularity will influence the rates, since the company can "spread" its fixed costs; that is, volume and regularity will help achieve efficiencies in terms of lower per-unit costs. Many public warehouse users, who may use public warehouses to handle peak seasonal demands on their own facilities, may be unable to offer regular use. In other cases, a logistics manager may be able, by proper planning, to use the public warehouse systematically, consequently reducing the warehouse rates.

Weight Density   Warehouses generally set rates in terms of space, usually, square footage. However, warehouses will sometimes base charges on weight density. In other words, like transportation carriers, warehouses will assess charges on a hundredweight basis. Therefore, the warehouse manager will have to assess higher charges for light and bulky items. Even users whose charges the warehouse does not assess in this fashion should be concerned about weight density because it affects their ability to efficiently use the space they rent. For example, light weight assembled items will use up a lot of space per unit of weight. Perhaps the seller could store the same number of items in a smaller space if the items were packaged unassembled.

Services   Public warehousing is a comprehensive and sophisticated industry today, willing and able to offer a variety of services beyond the general storage function. Such services have associated charges—and the more service, usually the higher the charge. However, having the public warehouse provide the services may be less costly, particularly in low-sales-density areas, than providing them privately.

As the preceding discussions show, logistics managers can influence their public warehouse rate levels. While these rate-influencing opportunities require analysis to prove their economic justification, the logistics manager should explore the options nevertheless.

Lately, public warehouse managers are becoming more aggressive in their search for business. This is evident in recent appeals to firms' sales, marketing, and executive departments. One public warehouse official said, "Public warehousemen have to sell the advantages of public warehousing to the right people. Our selling has historically been directed at traffic managers and traffic departments [the firms] who use public warehouses. We now feel that much of our selling time could be better directed to a vast, untapped pool of companies not using public warehouses—many because they have never been approached and do not know the functions and advantages of public warehousing."[10] This selling of public warehousing to upper management and new firms is getting AWA support, in the belief that such awareness may make logistics managers more knowledgeable about public warehousing opportunities.

CONTRACT WAREHOUSING

A growing public warehousing trend is the use of contract or third-party warehousing. Contract warehousing is a customized version of public warehousing in which an external company provides a combination of logistics services that the firm itself has traditionally provided. The contract warehousing company specializes in providing efficient, economical, and accurate distribution services.

The logistics manager must differentiate contract warehousing from general public warehousing. Firms desiring "above average" quality and service should use contract warehousing. These warehouses are designed to adhere to higher standards and specialized handling needs for products such as pharmaceuticals, electronics, and high-value manufactured goods. On the other hand, firms desiring average product handling service levels use public warehousing. In essence, contract warehousing is a partnership between the manufacturer and the warehousing firm. Because of these partnerships, contract warehousing companies service a smaller client base than traditional public warehousing companies do. The contract warehouse provides space, labor, and equipment tailored to handle a client's specific product needs.

The contract warehousing company makes a marketbasket of customized logistics services available to a limited number of warehouse users. Examples of these services include storage, break-bulk, consolidation, order assortment, spot stocking, in-transit mixing, inventory control, transportation arrangement, logistics information systems, and any additional logistics support services a user requires. Rather than providing only storage, the contract warehousing firm provides the logistical services package the user requires to support a firm's logistics channel.

Even though contract warehousing and distribution has grown substantially, the concept is still in its infancy in terms of overall understanding and use. In the past, companies needing to cut costs turned to the manufacturing operations. Companies contracted out component or subassembly production or outsourced overseas where labor costs were lower. Presently, companies are turning to logistics operations for potential cost reductions. By using contract warehousing services, a company can also outsource its logistics operations. By contracting out their secondary business functions, firms can concentrate on manufacturing and marketing.

Contract warehousing has many strategic, financial, and operational reasons advantages over private or traditional public warehousing. The main reason is the cost reduction. We will elaborate this reason in the next section. Other important reasons include the following: to compensate for seasonality in products; to gain geographical coverage, flexibility in testing new markets, management expertise and dedicated resources, and offbalance sheet financing; and to reduce transportation costs.

CATERPILLAR CREATES A NEW COCOON

Caterpillar, Inc. is one of the world's largest manufacturers of materials handling equipment. In recent years, Caterpillar, Inc. created a subsidiary, called Caterpillar Logistics Services, Inc. (CLS), as a spinoff of the parent corporation's own logistics department. "We felt that distribution was something Caterpillar did well," explained Robert L. Evans, vice president of CLS, "so we decided to find other people to serve."[10] The international CLS is equipped to handle industrial goods, component and replacement parts, and nonperishable products through its twenty-three distribution centers located in eleven countries.[11] The services CLS provides include warehousing, transportation, information systems, and consulting.

Compensate for Seasonality in Products A contract distributor can handle the peaks and troughs typical in seasonal industries more effectively than a private distributor can. For example, a contract distributor may have several contracts with companies having peak sales in the winter and virtually no sales in the summer. To offset this cycle, the distributor also contracts with companies having peak sales in the summer and virtually no sales in the winter. This alternate pattern of peak sales allows the contract distributor to utilize their equipment and capacity more effectively throughout the year than could a private warehouse handling one-season products.

Increased Geographical Coverage Contract distribution can increase a company's geographical market coverage through a network of facilities. A company could have warehouse locations in different regions without investing in numerous private facilities. Ideally a contract warehouse firm would have strategically located facilities and services, enabling the customer to deal with one warehousing mangement and one set of warehousing logistics service standards in different warehousing locations.

The reason for the decline in private warehousing is due, in part, to the rising use of contract warehousing. Many companies are reducing their private warehouses down to only a few centralized facilities and contracting out regional market coverage to a contract warehousing firm. With this private and contract warehousing network, a company can remain in direct control of the centralized facilities, while using the contract warehouses to lower direct labor costs and increase geographic market coverage.

Flexibility in Testing New Markets Contract logistics flexibility can enhance customer service. Firms promoting existing products or introducing new ones can use short-term contract distribution services to test market demand for the products. When a company wants to enter a new market area, building a new distribution facility could take years. However, by using a contract distribution network, the company could immediately use an existing facility to service customers in the new area.

ON THE LINE

LONG-RANGE SUCCESS WITH CUSTOMIZED WAREHOUSING FOR DAKIN, INC.

Although the use of contract or customized warehousing has dramatically increased in recent years, some companies have been contracting out their warehouse needs for over two decades. One such company is Dakin, Inc. which began using customized warehousing for its product lines in 1963. When the demand for Dakin's stuffed animal line began to increase, their present warehousing and distribution facility located in Brisbane, California, could not handle the East Coast market areas. Dakin had two options for meeting the increased demand. First, it could build a new private warehouse on the East Coast, requiring a large capital investment in the facility, materials handling equipment, and labor force. The second option was to contract out its warehousing and distribution needs. Dakin chose the latter option and entered into a contract with Stafford Enterprises, Inc., a customized warehouse company headquartered in Hauppage, New York. Utilizing the services of Stafford Enterprises enabled Dakin to:

1. Immediately meet the East Coast market demand by using Stafford's existing contract facilities;
2. Forego the capital investment in a private warehouse; and
3. Gain the valuable expertise and experience of professional warehouse managers.

Dakin was able to concentrate on their primary business as one of the nation's leading manufacturers and marketers of stuffed toys and other gifts. These concentrated efforts increased Dakin's sales from $800,000 in 1968 to over $150 million 1989.[12]

Management Expertise and Dedicated Resources Contracting out is a unique opportunity to hand a company's logistics function over to a team of managers who are distribution experts. These experts can provide innovative distribution ideas and cost-reducing product handling procedures. For some contracts, the contract distributor will dedicate space, workers, and materials handling equipment exclusively to client's products. In this way, the contract warehouse represents several different private warehouses under one roof.

Offbalance Sheet Financing Hiring a contract distributor to perform distribution operations can increase a company's return on investment (ROI), allowing the company to invest only in those assets that support its primary business. Physical distribution assets for a private warehouse yield the lowest ROI of all corporate assets, tie up corporate funds, and sometimes are not fully utilized. In addition, these assets represent an opportunity cost to invest funds elsewhere. Contracting out the distribution services takes these assets off the balance sheet, increasing a company's ROI. Even though these assets would be on the contractor's balance sheet, they would be dedicated to the company's logistics needs.

Reduce Transportation Costs Because they handle a high volume of products from different client accounts, contract warehouses offer significant freight savings by consolidating freight into full truckloads (TL).

Along with its advantages, contract warehousing has some disadvantages. The major one is losing control of the logistics function. Other obstacles include contract costs possibly exceeding private costs and remaining unjustified, management and union acceptance problems, lack of product volume, incompatibility with company needs, and insufficient understanding of contract warehousing and its value. Table 10–2 shows the results of a survey logistics on reasons to outsource a company's logistics functions or not.

Loss of Control   Losing direct control of operations is one of a company's greatest fears when considering the use of contract distribution services. With contract warehousing, the company exerts less control over personnel, hiring practices, policies, and procedures. On the same line, companies with high-value products such as pharmaceuticals must be very cautious to reduce employee theft as much as possible. Hiring an outside company to handle products is more risky than using a private facility.

Contract versus Private Warehousing

The overriding question a company must ask when comparing an internal private warehouse with an external contract warehouse is "Can the contract warehouse provide higher service performance for the same or less money than our private warehouse?" If the answer is yes, the contract warehouse should be the optimum choice. If the answer is no, then the company must evaluate the trade-offs between the better service's higher costs. A company can quantitatively measure a contract warehouse's service performance level by measuring the number of cases the warehouse ships per hour, attainment of a standard fill rate percentage, and percentage of on-time deliveries.

The answer to the above question is more often yes because contract distributors whose management focuses on maximizing warehouse efficiency can run their operations more cheaply than privately operated ones. In addition, contract warehouse wage rates and benefits are lower than those in a manufacturer's privately owned warehouse. When companies combine these reasons, the cost of contract warehousing may be up to thirty-seven percent less expensive than private warehousing.[13] Table 10–3 shows the percentage breakdown of private

TABLE 10–2   REASONS FOR AND AGAINST OUTSOURCING

Reasons for outsourcing	
Cost reduction	60%
Lower labor costs	49%
Flexibility	31%
Better information systems	30%
Improved delivery/service	23%
Obstacles to outsourcing	
Loss of control	18%
Not cost justified	11%
Management/union acceptance	6%
Lack of volume	6%
Inflexible/incompatible	5%
Don't understand/recognize value	4%

Source: Arthur D. Little, *Traffic Management.* Survey on third-party logistics (October 1988), 6.

Table 10–3   Private Warehousing Costs for 1989

Category	
People, including fringe	51.8%
Space, including taxes, insurance and maintenance	25.8%
Energy (heat, light and power)	6.1%
Equipment (lease, depreciation, maintenance)	3.9%
Material for packing and shipping	7.5%
Other	5.1%
Total	100.0%

Source: Davis Database (August 1989), 2. Herbert W. Davis and Company, Herbert W. Davis, President.

warehousing costs for 1989. At 51.6 percent, the labor (people) category comprises over half of the total costs.

Privately owned warehouses tend to operate as cost centers, while contract distributors operate their facilities as profit centers. The private warehouse option might seem favorable in that this cost structure has no added profit built in. However, the contract distributor has to make a profit in order to run its operations. This profit orientation motivates the contract distributor to operate as efficiently as possible. User fees reimburse the distributor for operating costs *and* provide a profit margin. In contrast, a company's product sales pay *only* for a private warehouse's operating costs.

Cost Comparisons

A company choosing between private warehousing and contract warehousing must compare each options' operating costs. In order for this comparison to be as accurate as possible, the company must access a complete and comparable cost analysis for both warehousing options. For example, an analysis that excludes the private warehouse's cost of depreciation would underestimate the true operating costs and bias the analysis. All warehouse types (public, private, and contract) generally incur the same cost elements. The differences are due to variations in the accounting methods a company uses to calculate each cost element.

Performing a cost comparison analysis is complex. We can further divide two main warehouse expenditures, direct handling and direct storage, to illustrate this complexity. Direct handling expenses refer to all costs a company incurs when moving products into, through, and out of the warehouse (variable expenses). Direct handling activities include unloading inbound/loading outbound vehicles, palletizing/sorting goods, placing goods in storage, and filling orders. Direct storage expenses occur regardless of product volume (fixed expenses). Table 10–4 shows a complete breakdown of these expenditures, along with examples of each.

In addition to determining the least costly warehousing option, the interested company should visit a contract warehouse to observe the facility, operations, equipment, personnel, and management.

The Contract

Before using third party services, the user or company purchasing an outside distribution company's services negotiates a contract with the contract facility

TABLE 10–4   BREAKDOWN OF DIRECT STORAGE EXPENSES

I. DIRECT HANDLING EXPENSE
  A. Warehouse Labor
    1. Direct payment to employees (wages, bonuses)
    2. Compensated fringe benefits (pension, insurance)
    3. Compensated time off (holidays, sick pay)
    4. Statutory payroll taxes (worker's compensation)
    5. Purchased labor (temporary labor)
    6. Fees and compensated time (training)
  B. Handling Equipment
    1. Lift trucks and attachments (fuel, parts maintenance)
    2. Special purpose handling equipment (shrinkwrap equipment, conveyors)
  C. Other Handling Expenses
    1. Pallets (to load/store products)
    2. Supplies (small tools, tape, printed forms)
    3. Detention/demurrage (transportation carrier charges for unloading delays)
    4. Recouping warehouse damage
    5. Trash hauling (recycling)
II. DIRECT STORAGE EXPENSE
  A. Facility
    1. Rent or depreciation and interest
    2. Real estate taxes
    3. Insurance
    4. Exterior maintenance (building itself)
  B. Grounds (areas surrounding facility)
  C. Storage Equipment (racks, shelving)
  D. Facility Modification (to accommodate a change in product line/operations)
  E. Utilities (heat, electricity)
  F. Interior Maintenance (painting, repairs)
  G. Security (alarm systems, guard service)

Source: DCW-USA, Inc., *How To Determine Total Warehousing Costs* (1990), 24.

operator. A legal agreement between the two parties, the contract specifically states the following information: the time period the contract covers, the operator's service fee, the specific services upon which the parties have agreed, terms and conditions, responsibilities, performance measurements, and default clauses. The user must provide large amounts of "sensitive" information, such as customers, vendors, and sales, to enable the third party to function effectively within the parameters the contract establishes. Companies use state-of-the-art information transfer technology to achieve third party warehousing efficiencies in accurately filling specific customer orders.

A primary contract element is space. A company can contract space through a lease, flexible space rental, or a sublease agreement. With a lease agreement, the user purchases the facility for a certain time period, usually one year. The fee includes fixed costs such as lighting, heat, and property maintenance, while the user provides labor. A flexible space rental agreement occurs when the warehouse charges the user only for the space or actual square footage the company uses. Warehouses charge user costs on a per unit basis: costs per pallet, per hundredweight (cwt), or per cubic foot, for example. In a sublease agreement, the contract facility provides both the management and labor for the user. In all three agreements, the user may promise to conduct a minimum monetary or volume amount of business with the contract warehouse during the contract's life.

Other factors that a company should consider when accessing needed services and cost allocations include materials handling equipment and clerical or office services. The type and amount of materials handling equipment a company will use depends on the inbound and outbound transportation mode, unit size (item, case, pallet), and product variety, of the number of stock keeping units (SKUs). Clerical or office services refers to processing documents such as bills of lading, purchase orders, and inventory records. The contract should state which party is responsible for these functions.

Liability

When drawing up a contract, a company and a warehouse must include the liability issue. With respect to public warehousing, the Uniform Commercial Code (UCC) states that the warehouse operator is liable for any damage, loss or injury to the goods his failure to exercise reasonable care might cause. Unless the warehouse and its client agree otherwise, the warehouse operator is not liable for unavoidable damages. If unavoidable damages occur, the company owning the goods assumes the liability. However, in a contract arrangement, the warehouse operator can choose to assume the risk for unavoidable damages. To compensate for this added responsibility, the warehouse operator will charge the user a higher contract rate, usually basing the liability price on a percentage of the product value's storage rate.

Transportation Companies

By diversifying their regular operations, transportation companies have begun to provide third party logistics services. Leaseway Transportation Corporation, a national motor carrier service, now offers warehousing services such as packaging and light assembly. The Contract Distribution Division of Federal Express has taken third party logistics one step further by providing services such as freight audits, order entry system operation, inventory management, and picking and packing goods. This type of system is replacing some manufacturers' in-house logistics departments at a lower operating cost.

A company finalizes its decision to utilize a third party distributor by comparing the total cost with the third party to the total cost without this service. The logistics manager must weigh the third party's advantages against its disadvantages. The third party system's total cost will be the determining factor.

THE NUMBER OF WAREHOUSES

One of the logistics manager's most important tasks is to decide how many warehouses to have in the system. As was the case when examining private versus public warehousing, evaluating the general cost trade-offs in such decisions would probably be best.

increasing the number of warehouses

Figure 10–9 depicts how increasing the number of warehouses in a logistics system affects important physical distribution costs. As the number of warehouses increases, transportation cost and the cost of lost sales decline, whereas inventory cost and warehousing cost increase.

Consolidating shipments into carload or truckload lots with lower rates per hundredweight decreases transportation costs. On the outbound side, increasing

FIGURE 10–9   LOGISTICS COST RELATED TO THE NUMBER OF WAREHOUSES

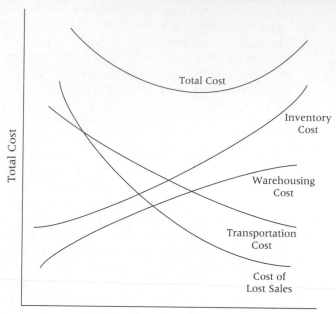

Number of Warehouses

the number of warehouses brings the warehouses closer to the customer and market area, reducing both transportation distance and costs.

Warehousing costs increase because the total amount of space always increases with a larger number of warehouses. For example, a firm with only one warehouse that has 200,000 square feet would not be able to operate at the same sales level with two facilities having 100,000 square feet each. Maintenance, offices, lavatories, lunchrooms, and other facilities need a certain, almost fixed amount of space. Also, aisles use up a higher proportion of space in smaller warehouses.

In addition, since a company increasing its number of warehouses carries more total inventory, inventory cost increases. The larger amounts of inventory require more total space. More inventory is necessary because the difficulty of predicting demand may force a company with two or more warehouses to maintain overly high levels of a product line's slower-moving items at each facility. Moreover, as companies increase their number of warehouses, growing product lines will likely require more total space, even at the same sales volumes.

As Figure 10–9 indicates, as the number of warehouses increases, total cost will generally decline. However, total costs begin to rise as increasing inventory and warehousing costs offset decreasing transportation costs and cost of lost sales. Of course, the total cost curve and the range of warehouses it reflects will be different for each company.

decreasing the number of warehouses

Companies often increase their number of warehouses to improve customer service, to reduce transportation costs, and to provide storage for increased product volumes. Surprisingly, decreasing a system's number of warehouses is becoming the preferred way to meet the same needs. Warehouse building and operating costs are great. In contrast, by reducing the number of warehouses, a company can eliminate those unproductive facilities that incur wasteful costs.

Combining the utilization of fewer warehouses with a reliable transportation system can improve customer service and lower transportation costs through consolidation opportunities. With fewer warehouses and move greater volumes of product, a company must increase throughput rates or inventory turns. By increasing its number inventory turns, a company will lower its inventory carrying costs.

The next section explores factors that affect the number of warehouses. Keep in mind that a company has to consider a total cost framework when deciding its number of warehouse facilities.

Factors Affecting the Number of Warehouses

customer service
One factor affecting the number of warehouses is the need for customer service. The need for rapid customer service in local market areas usually correlates strongly with the degree of product substitutability. If competitors are giving a market area rapid service, a company with inferior customer service lead times will lose sales volume. The company may waste sales promotion and advertising efforts if customers are unable to purchase the product when they want it.

Another closely related factor is inadequate transportation. In other words, if a company needs rapid customer service (low lead times), fast transport service is a possible alternative. If adequate transportation service is unavailable, the company may add another warehouse. Logistics managers who feel that transportation service is deteriorating often investigate warehouses as an alternative.

small-quantity purchases
An additional factor favoring decentralized warehousing is small-quantity buyers. The cost of shipping many LCL and LTL shipments from a centralized warehouse to customers would be much higher than that of shipping CL or TL to decentralized warehouses and then shipping LCL or LTL to customers in the local market. As we indicated previously, retailers and wholesalers, increasingly conscious of the cost of maintaining inventory, often wish to buy smaller quantities more frequently. If they desire the same approximate lead time, then a company may need to warehouse goods in a closer location. This suggests the distribution channel's importance to warehousing requirements. If small retailers and wholesalers are a part of the channel, then the company can expect small orders and a possible need for more warehouses.

A final factor favoring decentralized warehousing would be instances when customers allow insufficient lead times before being stocked out. Also, if demand is erratic, decentralized warehousing will help a company to prevent stockouts.

computers
Many firms are using warehouse computers to solve problems and make decisions. Functions for which a firm can effectively use computers include sales and cost analysis, calculating order cycle time, inventory control, traffic management, and layout planning. A firm's customer service program can also use them to inform customers and internal managers of order progress, damage situations, and transportation. Terminals located at various distribution stages can quickly provide order status information (see Figure 10–10). Companies can also retain operational control through computer links with a public or contract warehouse.

Computers can do more than enter orders and control inventory. Companies can use these systems to make the most of warehouse resources such as labor, space, and handling equipment. In the labor area, the computer can plan the staffing for various activity periods or motivate an employee by measuring his or her performance. Indeed, computer use could potentially allow all workers

FIGURE 10–10 THE COMPUTERIZED WAREHOUSE

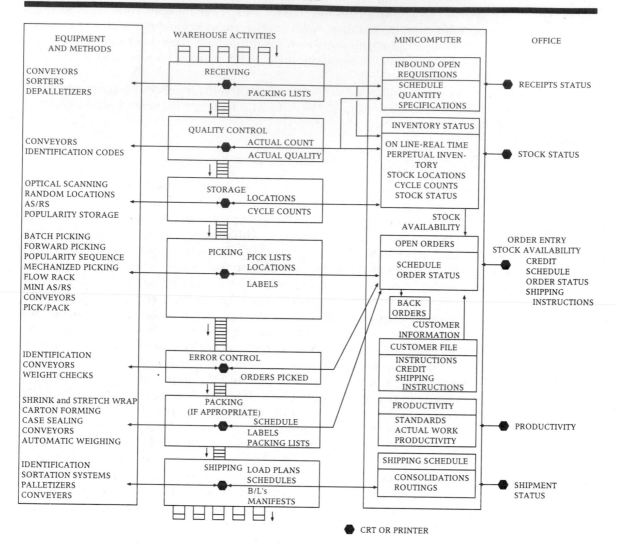

to improve their daily operating tasks.[14] Such operational benefits include improved space utilization, improved warehouse productivity, improved customer service levels, reduced error rates, and more efficient control of mechanized equipment operations.

SUMMARY

Because of logistics's strategic importance and the focus on controlling costs while offering outstanding customer service, many companies in the nineties have reevaluated their warehousing systems. Consequently, in terms of analyzing trade-offs, warehousing has become a much more dynamic component of inventory carrying cost. Also, the influence of warehousing in customer service has sparked much corporate interest.

Because of the options available with existing and additional facilities, warehousing offers the logistician a fertile area of cost-and-benefits analysis. This chapter attempted to provide insight into the whole warehousing area.

The chapter initially focused upon the reasons for carrying warehouse inventories and upon the role of warehousing in logistics systems. The chapter then investigated basic warehousing decisions and operations. Warehouse layout and design received attention because of its importance to effective warehousing in today's competitive environment.

The chapter covered public and contract warehousing extensively both because of their current importance and because of their anticipated growth in importance throughout the nineties.

The next chapter will explore the topics of materials handling and packaging. Both are closely related to warehousing, especially materials handling.

STUDY QUESTIONS

1. During the nineties, many companies will focus upon the logistics pipeline to meet their customers' needs for shorter lead times or response times. How can warehousing help companies to achieve quicker response times?

2. Some managers argue that warehousing can aid companies in providing value-added service for their customers. What is your view of this statement?

3. Inventory models and macro presentations of logistics costs generally consider warehousing to be a component of inventory carrying costs. Some individuals feel that this approach understates the importance of warehousing. What do you think?

4. The CBL Products Company, a toy manufacturer, has recently hired you as a consultant to investigate their logistics system, with particular emphasis upon warehousing. Your first assignment is to prepare a concise report that outlines the major reasons for warehousing, with a particular focus upon CBL.

5. Public warehousing use appears to be increasing among many large manufacturers in the nineties. Why would a company like Procter & Gamble, which produces a wide variety of consumer products such as Crest toothpaste, Ivory and Tide soaps, Pringle's snack chips, and Prell shampoo, move toward public warehousing?

6. Movement and storage are the two basic functions warehouses provide. The warehouse type, however, influences which of these two functions a company would emphasize in a particular warehouse. Why is this generally true?

7. Delsey Foods Company's vice president of logistics is evaluating the order picking area's layout in their Cincinnati, Ohio, new warehouse. She has asked you as director of warehousing to provide her with an overview of the alternative layout patterns, to recommend one the three, and to justify your recommendation.

8. Efficient warehouse design is receiving more attention in many companies. Discuss the dimensions of efficiency and why it is receiving so much emphasis.

9. How is the trend toward JIT inventory control systems likely to affect the number of warehouses companies operate? Why?

10. What is contract warehousing? How does it differ from public warehousing? Why are so many companies moving toward contract warehousing?

NOTES

1. Charles Taff, *Management of Physical Distribution and Transportation,* 5th ed. (Homewood, IL: Irwin, 1972), 142.
2. Taff, *Management of Physical Distribution and Transportation,* 145.
3. General Service Administration, *Warehouse Operations* (Washington, D.C.: Government Printing Office, 1964), 2.
4. Kenneth B. Ackerman, *Warehousing* (Washington, D.C.: Traffic Service Corporation, 1977), 162–65.
5. *Public Warehouse Study* (Washington, D.C.: McKinsey, 1970).
6. Denis Davis, "National vs. Regional Warehousing—State Your Case," *Distribution* (Radnor, PA: Chilton Co., February 1985), 55.
7. *Distribution Worldwide* (Radnor, PA: Chilton, June 1970), 60.
8. *Distribution Worldwide,* 62.
9. "Editorial," *Distribution* (March 1983), 83.
10. James Aaron Cooke, "Outsourcing? Who'll do your job?" *Traffic Management* (May 1988), 40.
11. Dr. David L. Anderson, "Contract Logistics," *American Shipper* (February 1988), 46.
12. Benjamin Leeds, "Custom warehousing; distributor services pay (Dakin, Stafford make a winning combination)," *Traffic Management* (January 1990), 11.
13. Michael G. Lepihuska "What is Contract Warehousing?" *Distribution Center Management* 25, 1 (January 1990), 2.
14. "Editorial," *Industrial Engineering* (Atlanta, GA: Institute of Industrial Engineers, June 1981), 56.

CASE 10–1

NITTANY PRODUCTS COMPANY

Nittany Products Company of Spring Mills, Pennsylvania, has been a successful niche player in the pharmaceutical industry, manufacturing needles and syringes which the company sells to large drug-producing companies who actually sell to doctors and other medical practitioners. These companies sell Nittany's needles and syringes separately or "load" them with appropriate drug dosages.

Nittany's success during the eighties was related, in part, to cost efficiency and improving technology. Nittany also has one very large customer, M & M Pharmaceuticals, that purchases almost seventy percent of the company's output. This strategic alliance has had many benefits for Nittany Products, along with a few disadvantages.

Bill Patterson, president and founder of Nittany Products, has recently learned that his patent for a new syringe has been approved. The syringe has tremendous market potential for treating AIDS and other highly contagious diseases.

Bill sees this breakthrough as an opportunity to accomplish two things. First, he can expand his sales to other customers and not depend so much upon M & M Pharmaceuticals. Second, he can expand his international sales.

A key concern for Nittany Products and its director of logistics, Skip Larson, is warehousing. In fact, Bill recently called Skip into his office to discuss Nittany's warehousing situation. Skip reminded Bill that their only warehouse, located in Spring Mills, was utilizing ninety-eight percent of its 25,000 square feet of capacity. While Skip thought that they could squeeze the facility a little more to gain additional output, the warehouse would never have enough space to meet Jack Barry's sales growth forecasts of seventeen to twenty-two percent each year over the next three years.

Jack, Nittany's director of marketing, had recently returned from a sales conference in Philadelphia where another company's representative had mentioned over cocktails his company's success with using Delp Distribution Company of Lansdale, Pennsylvania, as a third-party provider of warehousing and related services including order processing and transportation.

Jack is really excited about this idea. Third-party warehousing can provide initial sales expansion in the big northeast cities that AIDS has hit so hard. And Delp can provide international delivery out of Philadelphia in cooperation with a foreign freight forwarder.

Jack's enthusiasm has Bill excited, which now involves Skip, since warehousing is part of his responsibilities. Skip, a logistics old-timer, has mixed feelings about asking another company to provide Nittany's warehousing services. However, Skip realizes that he must be objective and suggests to Bill and Jack that the C.L.R. Consulting Services investigate this topic. He has heard good things about C.L.R.'s staff.

Case Questions
1. What is your opinion of the situation discussed above? What is your evaluation of Skip's proposal to use a consultant?
2. What advantages do third party companies provide? How about disadvantages?
3. Analyze the pharmaceutical industry's special warehousing problems.

MATERIALS HANDLING AND PACKAGING

At Jaguar's U.S. Parts Distribution Center in Mahwah, New Jersey, the goal is to ship every order at just the right time. In other words, they want to meet their customers' exact requirements and not just set some arbitrary standard such as shipping every order within forty-eight hours. Obviously, this means working with customers to understand their requirements. But it also means having a warehousing system and, more specifically, a materials handling system that can consistently deliver high levels of customer service at high levels of efficiency.[1]

Jaguar's goal is a real challenge because the company has about 13,200 stock keeping units (SKUs), and they process about 125 orders per day at their Mahwah facility. Interestingly, they found that fifteen percent of their items account for about eighty percent of their sales another indication of the importance of ABC analysis.

The parts that move through the Mahwah Distribution Center arrive in containers from Jaguar's warehouses in the United Kingdom, and each container may contain up to 400 SKUs. Jaguar's warehouse personnel unload the SKUs from the containers, place them in a staging area next to the receiving dock, and take them by forklift truck, flatbed cart and/or conveyor just a few short hours after their arrival at the shipping dock to one of four storage areas: Bulk Storage, Rack Storage, Bin Storage, or Fast-Moving Parts (See Figure 11–1).

Jaguar's materials handling system is so efficient that they can ship "hot orders," or VORs (Vehicle Off the Road), within two hours of receiving the order. Doing this with every order is not possible or necessary; in fact, the company ships seventy percent of its orders in forty-eight hours. The important point is that Jaguar can do it in two hours, if necessary.

The ability of Jaguar's materials handling and warehousing system to respond to its customer service policy needs plays a key role in their logistics system's overall success. Our goal in this chapter is to examine materials handling and the closely related activity of packaging in order to understand how companies like Jaguar can achieve such effective customer service levels.

The discussion will begin with a materials handling overview, including a definition, basic processes, objectives, and underlying principles. We should remember that materials handling is tied closely to warehousing, as the previous chapter pointed out. This synergism will become apparent as this chapter unfolds.

MATERIALS HANDLING

Materials handling is very important to any warehouse's efficient operation, both in terms of transferring goods in and out and in moving goods to various locations in the warehouse. The term *materials handling* is somewhat difficult to define. Some people picture elaborate equipment designed to move goods in a warehouse, such as forklift trucks or conveyor equipment. Others visualize

FIGURE 11–1   JAGUAR WAREHOUSE   *Source: Modern Materials Handling,* February 1991.

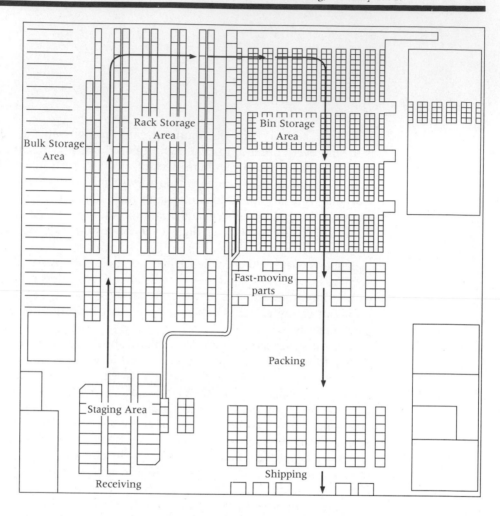

the actual manual handling of the goods. In fact, elaborate mechanical equipment, manual labor or a combination can perform materials handling. We can

definition

think most conveniently of materials handling as *efficient short-distance movement that usually takes place within the confines of a building such as a plant or a warehouse and between a building and a transportation agency.*

In a modern logistics system, specially designed equipment most often performs this short-distance movement; hence, thinking of materials handling from an equipment perspective is not unusual. However, manual movement is also materials handling. The key factor is efficiency, whether the movement is mechanical, manual, or both. Most systems are a combination. Jaguar's system, for example, relies on efficient manual applications of traditional materials handling equipment.

movement

One can gain some additional perspective about materials handling by reviewing basic processes or procedures.[2] First, materials handling involves the *movement* of raw materials, semifinished goods, and finished products into and out of storage facilities and usually within such facilities. Therefore, we can think of materials handling as a means of moving such items as efficiently as possible.

time   A second dimension of materials handling is *time*. Raw materials and semifinished goods must be ready at a certain time for production, and finished goods must be ready at a certain time for customer orders. Materials handling plays an important role in meeting time standards.

quantity   A third aspect of materials handling is *quantity*. The usage ratio of items in the warehouse varies, as does the delivery rate. Consequently, materials handling helps to ensure that the warehouse moves and handles items in the right quantity for manufacturing (physical supply) and for customers (physical distribution).

space   The fourth dimension of materials handling is *space*. The warehouse, the plant, or even the transport vehicle must utilize space effectively. The materials handling system greatly influences the proper use of space.

These four elements represent the basic aspects of materials handling. We must consider them integrated, not independent.[3]

multiple interests   The materials handling area does not usually belong exclusively to the logistics manager. In a manufacturing firm, materials handling activities can occur in several additional areas, but they occur most frequently in the bailiwick of the production or manufacturing manager. Here we also find short-distance movements occurring in conjunction with the manufacturing process. This short-distance movement may also be manual basis or mechanical.

coordination   However, this text will discuss materials handling from the logistics manager's perspective. Most often, the logistics manager's materials handling responsibility occurs in and around warehouses or plants' warehousing sections. Materials handling may require some coordination with individuals, such as the production manager, at least in the purchase of equipment and perhaps maintenance. Manufacturing and logistics may also need to interchange equipment. In designing or purchasing materials handling systems, a firm must look not only at the technology available but also at the entire organization's long-range plans.

Objectives of Materials Handling

Discussing the general objectives of materials handling provides some interesting perspectives. Because the items in this section are general, they apply to areas besides logistics and have varying importance for the logistics manager.

increase effective   One basic materials handling objective is to increase the warehouse facility's
capacity   usable capacity. A warehouse has fixed interior length, width, and height—that is, cubic capacity. Utilizing as much of this space as possible will minimize the warehouse's operating cost.

The use of warehouse space usually has two aspects. One is the ability to use the building's height as much as possible. Many warehousing facilities waste much space by not storing goods as high as possible. Figure 11–2 illustrates the importance of a warehouse's vertical space. Horizontal warehouse space is usually the most obvious and easiest to fill. But the vertical dimension is also a cost factor, and a warehouse operation must utilize this space effectively in order to be efficient. The vertical dimension, is therefore, the biggest challenge. Warehouse managers must focus on cubic space, not just on floor space. This chapter later describes devices to effectively utilize vertical space in a warehouse.

Example—Jaguar   In order to save space and to reduce travel time in their Mahwah distribution center, Jaguar combined the active order picking area with reserve storage. The active picking actually takes place at the two lower levels, with reserve storage above. This enables Jaguar to utilize overhead or cube space and to store inventory up to twenty-two feet high in an area where cubic space is often difficult

FIGURE 11–2   UTILIZATION OF A WAREHOUSE'S CUBIC CAPACITY   *Source:* From *Warehouse Operations,* General Services Administration (Washington, D.C.: Government Printing Office, 1969).

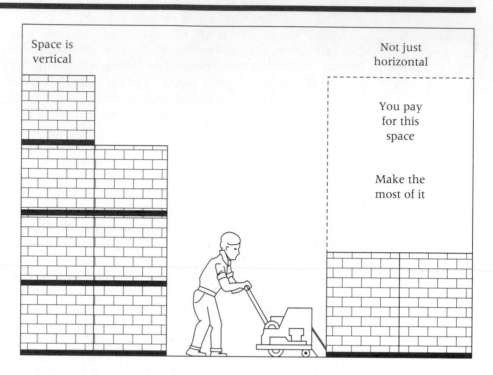

to use. Materials handling equipment and storage aids enable Jaguar to use this otherwise unusable space.[4]

A second aspect of space utilization is to minimize aisle space as much as possible while avoiding aisles narrow enough to impede movement in the warehouse facility. The type of materials handling equipment a company uses will affect aisles width. Forklift trucks, for example, very often require turning space, and they may necessitate much wider aisles than other types of materials handling equipment do. Figure 11–3 illustrates the necessity of aisle space in a storage facility. The illustration which shows items moving out of a rail car into the warehouse, is an example of the warehouse's interface role. From the transportation equipment (rail car or tractor-trailer), the items move to a storage area. The equipment performing this short-distance movement needs adequate turning and maneuvering space. The figure also shows the need to separate items in the storage area, for access purposes.

improve operating efficiency

Another materials handling objective is to reduce the number of times a company handles goods. As we noted in our discussion of warehousing, a company usually moves products into a warehouse and places them in a storage area then moves them to an order selection area to be "picked" and made up into orders and finally moves the products again to ready them for shipment to customers. This process necessitates several unavoidable movements. In some warehouses, however, a company may move goods several times in each area. The company must avoid this additional handling if a warehouse is to operate efficiently. Therefore, the design of any materials handling system and its associated activities should minimize movements to, within, and from a warehouse.

FIGURE 11–3 EFFICIENT USE OF AISLE SPACE *Source:* From *Warehouse Operations*, General Services Administration (Washington, D.C.: Government Printing Office, 1969).

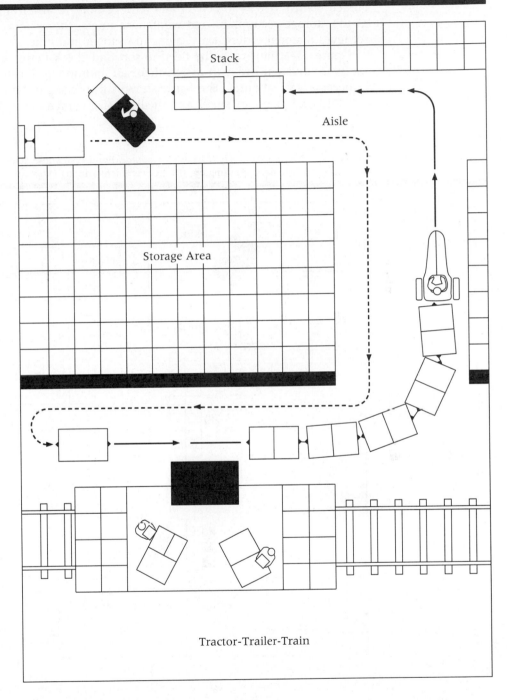

At times, extra movement is unavoidable because of overcrowding, any firm may have to temporarily store and then move products. However, an efficiently designed materials handling system should minimize the number of movements and allow products to flow through the warehouse rapidly and efficiently.

Example–Merck   The key to minimizing movements is "control." Merck Pharmaceuticals has an integrated control handling system which uses a four-unit load-automated guided vehicle (AGV) to deliver and retrieve stock to and from a ten-aisle area in the storage section. In one warehouse move, the system stores stock and retrieves material orders, thus saving movement and time.[5]

Figure 11–4 illustrates the need to sort and check items as they come into the warehouse in order to assign them an appropriate location and to avoid unnecessary rehandling. The figure shows this process to be manual, which is still fairly common in small and medium-size companies. A company could

FIGURE 11–4   EFFICIENT WAREHOUSE OPERATIONS   *Source:* From *Warehouse Operations,* General Services Administration (Washington, D.C.: Government Printing Office, 1969).

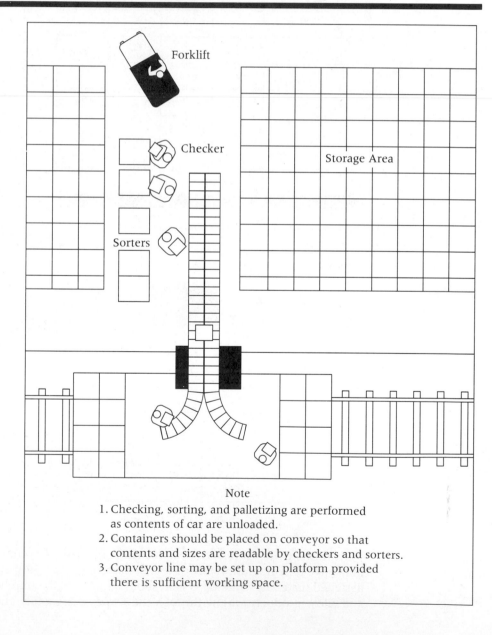

Note
1. Checking, sorting, and palletizing are performed as contents of car are unloaded.
2. Containers should be placed on conveyor so that contents and sizes are readable by checkers and sorters.
3. Conveyor line may be set up on platform provided there is sufficient working space.

highly automate this whole process by using bar coding techniques (discussed later in the chapter). Whether the process is manual or automated, a company has to eliminate unnecessary handling by planning an efficient materials handling system.

Example–Jaguar   Jaguar's Mahwah, New Jersey, facility has a system much more automated than the one in Figure 11–4. Jaguar uses a computer to assign warehouse locations to parts before they leave Great Britain, and the location document is in the parts container when it arrives in the United States. The unloader at the staging area places the assigned items on a series of grid lines in the staging area. This minimizes movement and enables warehouse personnel to take the items directly to a designated warehouse area.[6]

develop effective working conditions   The objective of effective working conditions has a number of significant dimensions in the logistics area, including safety. All materials handling systems, whether in connection with logistics or manufacturing, should minimize danger to nearby workers while enhancing productivity.

As we stated previously, materials handling usually combines automation and manual labor. Most manual effort usually occurs in the order picking area. Therefore, a company has to create an environment that motivates people to get the job done. In this area, Jaguar's Mahwah facility has also had dramatic success; Jaguar parts operation management attributes productivity gains and order filling accuracy to a motivated workforce.

reduce heavy labor   Another part of this objective is to eliminate as much as possible the monotonous and heavy manual labor short-distance warehouse movements. While completely eliminating all routine movements or boring warehouse work is difficult, the materials handling system should perform this work as much as possible.

Taken to its logical conclusion, this objective suggests that companies should automate warehouses as much as possible. For a variety of reasons, including cost efficiencies, firms have attempted to eliminate warehouse labor personnel. Firms may encounter difficulty in minimizing or eliminating order selection personnel in physical distribution warehouses because some companies often receive orders for a small number of a stock keeping unit (SKU). Consider, for example, Hallmark Cards, where the typical order requires only one to three boxes of a certain card. Companies will usually handpick orders requiring small numbers of a large variety of items. This is true of Kinney Shoes, where each shoe length and width is a SKU. In contrast, some companies receive orders for individual SKU pallet loads; these companies find automation quite feasible. Robots are a potential alternative to handpicking small numbers of items from different SKUs.

improve logistics service   Materials handling improves efficiency by making the logistics system respond quickly and effectively to plant and customer requirements. Materials handling plays a key role in getting goods to customers on time and in the proper quantities. By efficiently moving goods into the warehouse, locating stock, accurately filling orders, and rapidly preparing orders for shipment to customers, materials handling is very important to outbound logistics. In inbound logistics terms, materials handling serves company plants in much the same way.

The service objective receives much attention from the logistics manager. He or she must constantly ensure that the materials handling system will respond quickly and efficiently to customers' orders and to a production schedule's requirements. Some companies spend a lot of time and effort trying to reduce transportation time by twelve or twenty-four hours. At the same time, their materials handling systems may be adding several days to the time elapsing after a customer places an order. Customer service improvements that may be possible through materials handling improvements are easy to overlook.

Many firms recognize the need for flexible materials handling within their customer service program. Firms need to integrate materials handling requirements not only with the company's departmental needs, but also with customers' needs.

Example—Xerox

Xerox improved its customer service with a new warehouse that combines forklift trucks, tow tractors, and automated storage in what Xerox describe as a deep-lane storage facility that is capable of shipping error-free. Because this new facility can handle 1000 orders per day, Xerox reduced cost by eliminating two other off-site warehouses: not bad for a facility that prides itself on zero product damage. Key factors in Xerox's success are an automatic storage/retrieval system (AS/RS) and a deep-lane storage rack system for pallets that allows the company to handle 6,391 42-inch pallets on 4,067 60-inch pallets.[8]

reduced cost

Effective materials handling can contribute to a cost minimization program by increasing productivity (more and faster throughput). Also, utilizing space more efficiently and misplacing items less frequently will lead to decreased cost.

Example—Rich's

A good example of a company that emphasizes the logistics service objective is Rich's Department Stores. At its new Haverhill, Massachusetts, distribution center, the company ships ninety percent of the merchandise it receives at the 204,000 square foot warehouse without actually holding the merchandise in a storage area. On the average, unloading, bar coding, transporting, merging, sorting, and a carton loading onto an outbound trailer takes only twenty minutes. The items Rich's does not load in twenty minutes are seasonal products which the company stores in conventional racks until its retail outlets need them. This example also illustrates the improvement of operating efficiency and our next objective—reducing cost.[7]

As the outset of this section indicated, all of these objectives are important and interrelated. In the nineties, materials handling helps companies to minimize warehouse investment and to achieve higher inventory turns.

GUIDELINES AND PRINCIPLES FOR MATERIALS HANDLING

Materials handling requires detailed analysis that can incorporate sophisticated mathematical techniques or modeling. This dimension of materials handling involves complex concepts that are beyond the scope of this textbook. In practice, the logistics manager can ask experts to provide detailed analysis. Therefore, logistics managers do not have to provide such analysis themselves.

However, in order to effectively plan and control materials handling, the logistics manager should recognize some guidelines and principles. Table 11–1 lists twenty of the most commonly accepted principles of efficient materials handling. Asterisks denote principles that deserve special emphasis.

The distances over which a warehouse will handle materials should be as short as possible. This will minimize labor and equipment costs. A company should give the popularity principle some consideration on storing high-volume items at the shortest distance. And items once in motion should stay in motion as long as possible. Stopping and starting are expensive for labor and equipment. Also, routes of materials should be on the same level as much as possible given a particular building configuration. Moving items up and down contributes to higher labor and equipment costs. In addition, a company should minimize the number of times and length of time it handles an item.

TABLE 11-1   PRINCIPLES OF MATERIALS HANDLING

1. *Planning Principle.* Plan all materials handling and storage activities to obtain maximum overall operating efficiency.
2. *Systems Principle.* Integrate as many handling activities as is practical into a coordinated operations system covering vendor, receiving, storage, production, inspection, packaging, warehousing, shipping, transportation, and customer.
* 3. *Materials Flow Principle.* Provide an operation sequence and equipment layout that optimize materials flow.
* 4. *Simplification Principle.* Simplify handling by reducing, eliminating, or combining unnecessary movements and/or equipment.
* 5. *Gravity Principle.* Utilize gravity to move material wherever practical.
* 6. *Space Utilization Principle.* Make optimum use of the building cube.
7. *Unit Size Principle.* Increase the quantity, size, or weight of unit loads or their flow rates.
8. *Mechanization Principle.* Mechanize handling operations.
9. *Automation Principle.* Provide automation that includes production, handling, and storage functions.
*10. *Equipment Selection Principle.* In selecting handling equipment, consider all aspects of the material handled—the movement and the method to be used.
*11. *Standardization Principle.* Standardize handling methods, as well as types and sizes of handling equipment.
*12. Adaptability Principle. Use methods and equipment that adapt to the widest variety of tasks and applications, except where special-purpose equipment is justified.
13. *Deadweight Principle.* Reduce ratio of mobile handling equipment deadweight to load carried.
14. *Utilization Principle.* Plan for optimum utilization of handling equipment and labor.
15. *Maintenance Principle.* Plan for preventive maintenance and scheduled repairs of all handling equipment.
16. *Obsolescence Principle.* Replace obsolete handling methods and equipment when more efficient methods or equipment will improve operations.
17. *Control Principle.* Use materials handling activities to improve control of production, inventory, and order handling.
18. *Capacity Principle.* Use handling equipment to improve production capacity.
19. *Performance Principle.* Determine handling performance effectiveness in terms of expense per unit handled.
20. *Safety Principle.* Provide suitable methods and equipment for safe handling.

---

*Principles that deserve particular emphasis.

Source: Adapted from College-Industry Committee on Materials Handling, Materials Handling Institute, Pittsburgh, PA, 1990.

Companies should use mechanical and automated equipment for materials whenever travel routes, volume, and cost trade-offs justify this investment. In other words, mechanization and automation are not a panacea for low cost and efficiency. Some very effective materials handling systems utilize a fairly high ratio of labor to equipment. For example, at its Camp Hill, Pennsylvania, facility Kinney Shoe Company operates a very cost efficient system with what would appear to be a high labor input.

Materials handling equipment should be as standard as possible and as flexible as possible to lower cost; the equipment should use gravity as much as possible and minimize the ratio of deadweight to payload.

CATEGORIES OF EQUIPMENT

The proliferation of products on the market today makes materials handling selection a very dynamic process. We will now discuss various equipment categories companies could use in a designing materials handling systems. Our objective is to appreciate how and when a company might use such equipment in a logistics system. Keep in mind, however, that because of many new technological advances, logistics managers need much information when making a decision in this area.

Dock Equipment

Materials handling begins at the loading dock when a truck containing the goods arrives and needs to be unloaded. The faster the warehouse unloads the goods, the greater its throughput capability. Due to the constant activity, both the receiving and shipping dock activities need to be efficient. In order to load or unload the goods safely and quickly, the warehouse should utilize the necessary dock equipment. The following section describes important dock equipment such as forklifts, pallets, dock bumpers, dock levelers, dock seals, and trailer restraint systems.

Forklifts   One type of dock equipment common to many materials handling systems is the forklift truck (see Figure 11–5), a very versatile piece of equipment that a company can provide at a very reasonable cost. Able to perform several useful materials handling tasks, the forklift is individually powered and is available with various lift arrangements. Warehouses usually use forklifts in conjunction with pallets.

The forklift truck operates very efficiently, and companies can use it in a variety of ways. Its major disadvantage is that it requires an operator, who may

FIGURE 11–5   FORKLIFT TRUCK   *Source: Modern Materials Handling* (March 1989), 69.

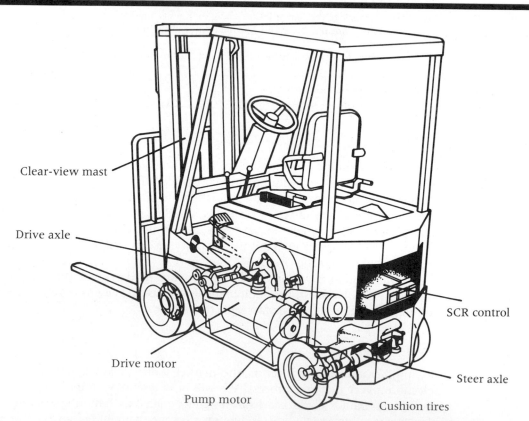

Clear-view mast

Drive axle

Drive motor

Pump motor

SCR control

Steer axle

Cushion tires

very often be idle when the forklift is not in use. But, all things considered, it is probably the most popular and most common type of materials handling equipment in existence. Even the smallest firm with the simplest materials handling system can often afford a forklift truck. Its biggest advantage is its versatility in moving goods from one warehouse section to another or in transferring goods into and out of transportation equipment.

In selecting forklift trucks, a company should consider normal equipment variations such as lifting capacity, lifting height, power source (gasoline, battery, or propane gas), the aisle space the forklift needs, and speed. Manufacturers today offer a wide selection of forklift trucks, including trucks that handle slip sheets instead of pallets, electric trucks, narrow-aisle high-stacking trucks, compact forklifts, and trucks with greater lifting capacity. Computer-controlled lift trucks, designed for use with or without a driver, are also becoming popular for use in the dark, in extreme temperatures, or with hazardous materials.

Dock Bumpers Dock bumpers are molded rubber pieces that protect the building from the impact of a docking trailer backing into it and from a trailer shifting in weight during loading or unloading.

Dock Levelers Dock levelers level out the angle between the dock and the trailer by providing a ramp that enables the forklift to drive into the trailer safely. The greater the ramp angle, the greater the chance of an accident.

Dock Seals A dock seal is a cushioned frame around the dock door opening that connects the trailer to the dock. Its purpose is to create a seal blocking any outside weather, smoke, and fumes from entering the warehouse.

Trailer Restraint Systems Vehicle restraints prevent the trailer from drifting away from the dock during loading or unloading. Since this drifting causes many dock accidents, the Occupational Safety and Health Administration (OSHA) must approve a warehouse's restraining system. While a company can use wheel chocks or wedge molded rubber under a truck's tires, these methods are ineffective on ice, snow, or gravel. The best system is an automated one which uses a lighting or sound system to communicate the trailer's safety status between the dock worker and the truck driver.

Pallets Pallets are both basic and essential to materials handling operations. A pallet's main function is to provide a base to hold individual items together (see Figure 11–6). Once the items are stacked on the pallet, materials handling

TABLE 11–2	THE TYPES OF DOCK EQUIPMENT COMPANIES PURCHASE	
	Lift trucks and accessories	83%
	Dock bumpers	75%
	Pallets	73%
	Dock lifts and levelers	69%
	Dock doors	66%
	Dock shelters seals	62%
	Trailer restraint systems	45%

Note: Percentages add up to greater than 100% due to multiple responses.

Source: Traffic Management (May 1990), 106.

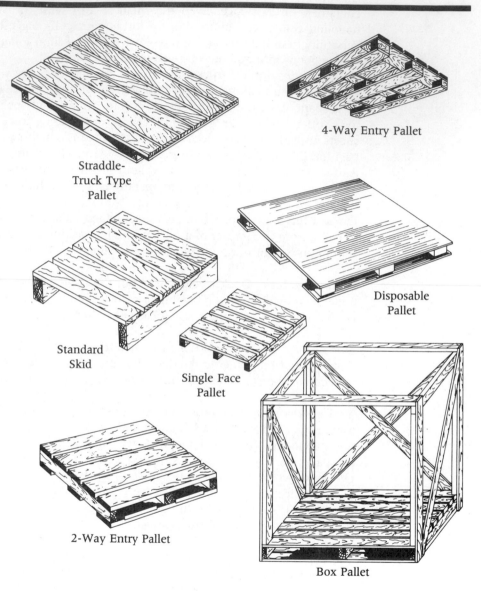

Straddle-
Truck Type
Pallet

4-Way Entry Pallet

Standard
Skid

Single Face
Pallet

Disposable
Pallet

2-Way Entry Pallet

Box Pallet

equipment, most often a forklift, can move the pallet to the proper storage location. Companies also use pallets when shipping products from the warehouse to the customer.

Although pallets play an integral distribution role, their use has one important problem. Most companies do not recycle pallets, even though they can; and many used or unusable pallets go to the landfill. This issue is of growing concern to both environmentalists and logistics managers who must find ways of reducing this waste. Table 11–3 shows the alternative pallet materials and their environmental effects. Wood pallets continue to serve about eighty-five to ninety percent of pallet users' needs. Wood is both biodegradable and recyclable. Shredded wood pallets can be used for mulch, animal bedding, and packaging ma-

TABLE 11–3   PALLET TYPE COMPARISON

Material	Durability*	Repairable?	Environmental Impact	Typical Applications
Wood	Med.	Yes	Material is biodegradable and recyclable	Grocery; automotive; durable goods; hardware
Pressed wood fiber	Med.	Yes	Material is recyclable and can be burned without leaving fuel residues	Printing; metal stampings; plumbing fixtures; building materials
Corrugated fiberboard	Low	No	Material is biodegradable and recyclable	One-way shipping applications in grocery; lightweight paper products; industrial parts
Plastic	High	No	Material is recyclable	Captive or closed loop systems; FDA, USDA applications; automotive
Metal	High	No	Material is recyclable	captive or closed-loop systems; FDA, USDA applications; military

*We define durability as a pallet's expected number of trips.

Source: Modern Materials Handling (April 1990), 53.

terial; however, the market for these products is still limited. In addition, damaged wooden pallets are easy to fix. For example, grocery products manufacturers, the largest users of wooden pallets, currently repair about sixty-eight million pallets each year. Pressed wood fiber pallets, a recyclable alternative to wood pallets, are nail-free, which helps protect products from damage. Corrugated fiberboard pallets reduce weight in the trailer and provide better shock absorbency than wood, and companies can sell the used pallets as recyclable paper scrap. The pharmaceutical, food processing, and chemical industries use plastic and metal pallets because these pallets are easy to clean and keep sanitary. Recycled plastic pallets become products such as orange highway construction barriers or compact discs. All pallet materials have recycling potential. By recycling pallets, the warehouse will receive salvage value from recycling firms instead of paying disposal costs.

Other Materials Handling Equipment

Conveyors   Conveyors, a very popular form of materials handling equipment, play an important role in advancing productivity and improving bottom-line operating results, particularly in the mechanized distribution center or warehouse. These systems decrease handling costs, increase productivity of workers and equipment, and provide an interface with management information systems.

roller versus belt conveyor

There are two basic types of conveyors (see Figure 11–7). The first, a *roller conveyor,* basically uses the gravity principle. The conveyor is inclined, and goods move down the conveyor by force of their own weight, typically at a slow pace depending on the conveyor's incline. The other type is the *wheel conveyor,* or *belt* or *towline conveyor,* which requires power equipment. Such conveyors move goods either on a level or up inclines to a warehouse section. Companies will use a roller conveyor wherever possible to minimize their operating costs.

Many companies consider conveyors advantageous because they can be highly automatic and, therefore, can eliminate handling cost. They also may save space

FIGURE 11–7   MATERIALS HANDLING EQUIPMENT   *Source:* From *Modern Materials Handling* (1987), 107, 381.

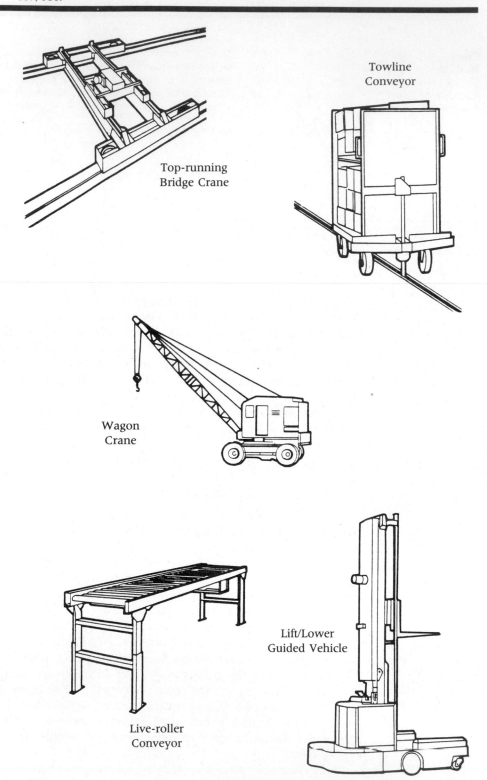

Top-running
Bridge Crane

Towline
Conveyor

Wagon
Crane

Live-roller
Conveyor

Lift/Lower
Guided Vehicle

advantages

since they can use narrow aisles and can operate on multiple levels in the same area. Conveyor systems often have low operating costs.

Conveyors equipped with scanners and other automatic devices enable companies to move goods very efficiently and quickly from one warehouse area to another. Scanners can keep inventory records by recording packages moving on conveyors, and can track storage locations. Finally, scanners enable managers to use computers to rapidly locate goods.

A modern conveyor system is very expensive and requires a large capital investment. It is also fixed in location; that is, it lacks versatility. A conveyor system's design requires much time and effort, particularly with reference to a company's future needs. If conditions change, changing the conveyor system may be necessary, often at a very high cost. Organizations that invest in complex conveyor systems are usually large and successful manufacturing firms. Using conveyors to automate a large distribution warehouse, for example, generally requires a significant investment of funds in a very complex and sophisticated conveyor system. However, companies can install some very simple conveyors at a very reasonable cost.

capital-intensive

In analyzing the possibility of using warehouse conveyor systems, an organization must decide whether its materials handling approach should be capital-intensive or labor-intensive. Many large companies with sophisticated logistics requirements find capital-intensive systems such as elaborate conveyors to be extremely worthwhile because of reduced labor costs and possible improvements in distribution time. However, such approaches are not necessarily right for all companies. More labor-intensive approaches may be much more appropriate. Comparing labor-intensive and capital-intensive materials handling methods is analogous to comparing private and public warehousing. In other words, conveyor systems have a very important fixed cost segment, and a company must have throughput volume sufficient to defray or spread the fixed costs.

One disadvantage of conveyors is the possibility of equipment malfunction, which could cause logistics system delays. However, conveyor users can minimize operational problems. To avoid exceeding the equipment's capacity and causing breakdowns, the company using conveyors must consider the dimensions and weight of each unit the conveyors will carry. The company must consider the load's center of gravity when loads travel on inclined or declined conveyors, are handled in start-stop operations, or are transferred while in motion. To avoid problems, a company must operate a conveyor at the rate for which the company intended it. This rate may vary, depending on unit sizes; and these sizes will be mixed.

Conveyors can handle loads of almost any size, shape, weight, or fragility. However, users must determine, before they purchase equipment, the items a specific conveyor will handle and its expected functions—sortation, for example. Following the guidelines this section suggests will contribute to an effective conveyor system.

No matter an individual firm's solution, trends show that conveyor usefulness will continue to increase as automation technologies develop. Already conveyors can be valuable tools in data generation and product monitoring systems, and their use in computerized inventory control is quite common.

Cranes Companies can utilize a variety of cranes in warehouses (see Figure 11–7). The two basic types are *bridge cranes* and *stacker cranes*. Bridge cranes

ON THE LINE

AUTOMATED EFFICIENCY AT THE LOS ANGELES GENERAL POSTAL FACILITY

The Los Angeles General Mail Facility is one of the United States' most efficient postal operations. The 1.1 million square foot facility, which processes ten million pieces of mail daily, utilizes conveyors, automated sortation equipment, and automatic identification to process the mail. This post office can attribute its efficiency to the reduced manual movement of mail and the increased use of computers. The facility has two sortation systems, one for bulk mail and one for letters (see Figure 11–8). Conveyors transport bulk mail from the receiving docks to the induction stations. At these stations, workers read the address labels and key the zip codes into a computer terminal. The computer system activates a loader conveyor which moves the correct pieces of mail into hampers to go to the shipping dock. In the facility's other sortation system, conveyors move letters through automatic cancelling machines that sort the letters into three processing types: bar code, optical character, or manual letter sortation. After the letters undergo automatic or manual sortation by zip code and address, they travel to the shipping dock for delivery.

are more common in physical supply warehouses or where companies have to move, store, and load heavy industrial goods such as steel coils or generators.

Stacker, or wagon, cranes have become increasingly popular in physical distribution warehouses because they can function with narrow aisles, effectively utilizing a warehouse's cube capacity. This equipment is also very adaptable to automation. Fully automated stacker cranes on the market today can put stock

FIGURE 11–8   MAIL HANDLING AT THE L.A. CENTER   *Source: Modern Materials Handling* (October 1990), 65.

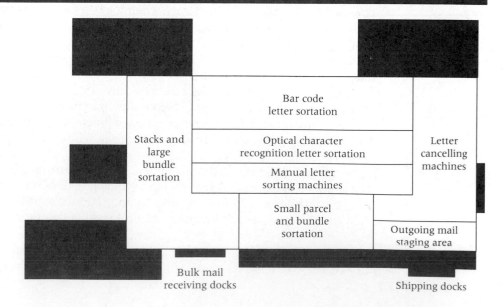

Bar code letter sortation

Stacks and large bundle sortation

Optical character recognition letter sortation

Manual letter sorting machines

Letter cancelling machines

Small parcel and bundle sortation

Outgoing mail staging area

Bulk mail receiving docks

Shipping docks

into and take it out of storage areas without an operator. The computer equipment such systems utilize can select the best storage placement and recall this placement later. Companies stacker cranes are commonly used in conjunction with elaborate shelving systems.

Though not usually as expensive as conveyor systems, cranes are also capital-intensive equipment. Handling very heavy items may require bridge cranes; a company should justify stacker cranes on a cost basis. The advantage of bridge cranes is the ability to lift heavy items quickly and efficiently. The advantage of stacker cranes is the effective use of space and possible automation.

Automatic Guided Vehicle Systems (AGVS)   AGVS are machines that connect receiving, storing, manufacturing, and shipping (see Figure 11–9). Firms can track these vehicles, either roaming freely or on a fixed path, with micro-compressors which make traffic control decisions. Essentially automated guided vehicles (AGVs) travel around the warehouse or manufacturing plant carrying various items to a particular programmed destination. Since these AGVs do not require a driver, reduce labor costs.

The double-pallet jack, another vehicle that does not require a driver, can transport two pallet loads between warehouse areas. As with AGVs, a computer can guide the double-pallet jack to its destination along a floor-wired guide.

Also available is a variety of other, more specialized equipment, including draglines that pull carts in a continuous circle in a warehouse, elevators, hoists, and monorails.

FIGURE 11–9   FRITO-LAY'S NEWEST, MOST AUTOMATED WAREHOUSE   *Source: Modern Materials Handling* (January 1987), 79.

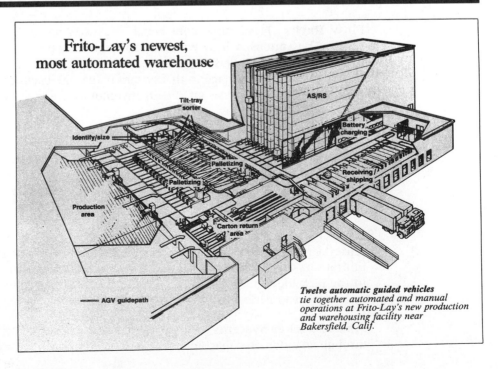

Frito-Lay's newest, most automated warehouse

Tilt-tray sorter

AS/RS

Battery charging

Identify/size

Palletizing

Receiving shipping

Palletizing

Production area

Carton return area

AGV guidepath

Twelve automatic guided vehicles tie together automated and manual operations at Frito-Lay's new production and warehousing facility near Bakersfield, Calif.

Order Picking and Storage Equipment

One of a physical distribution warehouse's main functions is order picking, the process of identifying, selecting, retrieving, and accumulating the proper items for customer orders. Although order picking by nature is labor-intensive, an effectively designed orderpicking and storage system can enhance the order picking process's speed, accuracy, and cost-effectiveness. Most storage systems primarily try to use warehouse space effectively. Because the cost of labor, equipment, and space for order picking equals about sixty-five percent of total warehouse operating costs, any improvement that reduces these costs is greatly important. This section covers two main equipment types: picker-to-part and part-to-picker. Picker-to-part systems include bin shelving, modular storage drawers, flow racks, mobile storage systems, and order picking vehicles. Part-to-picker systems include horizontal carousels, vertical carousels, and miniload automated storage and retrieval systems (AS/RS). Figure 11–10 illustrates these systems.

Picker-to-Part System　In picker-to-part systems, the order picker must travel to the pick location within the aisle.

Bin Shelving　Bin shelving is the oldest and most basic storage system available for storing small parts. The main advantages of bin shelving are the low initial cost and the ability to divide units into various compartments. However, the system underutilizes cubic space by not using a bin's full size and by requiring shelf height to be within a person's reach.

Modular Storage Drawers　Modular storage drawers are cabinets that are divided into drawers and further subdivided into compartments. Their main advantage is a storage capacity able to hold a large number of SKUs. Their main drawback is height: the drawers cannot be over approximately five feet high because the order picker must look into them when picking an order.

Flow Racks　Flow racks store items in cartons having a uniform size and shape. The cartons, which warehouse personnel replenished from the rack's back end, flow on rollers, by gravity, to the rack's front or aisle end for order picking. A main advantage to this system is that the back-to-front item movement ensures first-in-first-out (FIFO) inventory turnover. Flow racks can also hold full pallets of items.

Mobile Storage Systems　Mobile storage systems need only one order picking aisle because a motorized system can slide the racks, shelves, or modular drawers to the left or right. The order picker can slide the racks apart to expose the aisle he or she needs to pick an order. Slower picking speed due to the shift time offsets the advantage of high storage density.

Order Picking Vehicles　Order picking trucks and person-aboard storage and retrieval (S/R) vehicles increase order picking rates and maximize cubic space utilization. The order picker rides or drives the vehicle horizontally or vertically to the pick location. Some of these vehicles move automatically, allowing the order picker to perform another task while traveling.

Part-to-Picker Systems　In part-to-picker systems, the pick location travels through an automated machine to the picker. These systems have a higher initial

FIGURE 11–10   ORDER PICKING EQUIPMENT   *Source: Modern Materials Handling,* 1992 Casebook
Reference Issue (September 1991), 97.

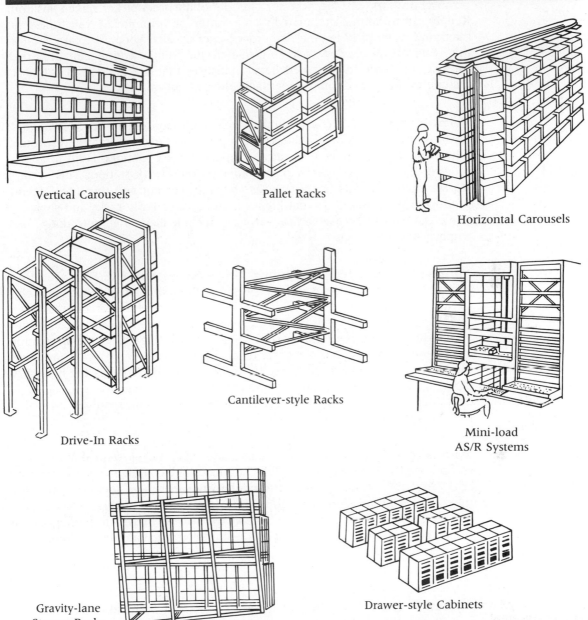

Vertical Carousels

Pallet Racks

Horizontal Carousels

Drive-In Racks

Cantilever-style Racks

Mini-load
AS/R Systems

Gravity-lane
Storage Racks

Drawer-style Cabinets

cost than picker-to-part systems, but utilizing automated storage and retrieval
equipment speeds up order picking operations, improves inventory control, and
increases profits. Part-to-picker systems minimize travel time. By comparison,
in static shelving systems, workers spend up to seventy percent of their time
traveling and only up to eighty percent picking.

Carousels   Carousels are shelves or bins linked together through a mechanical
device which stores and rotates items for order picking. The two main types of
carousels are horizontal and vertical.

Horizontal Carousels   Horizontal carousels are a linked series of bins that rotate around a vertical axis. A computer locates a needed part and rotates the carousel until the part location stops in front of the order picker's fixed position. Keeping in mind that automated systems attempt to minimize wait times and maximize order picking times, an order picker usually works two carousels. In this way, the picker can pick from one carousel while waiting for the other carousel to rotate to a needed item. Industries that use horizontal carousels include aviation, electronic, paper, and pharmaceutical.

Vertical Carousels   Vertical carousels differ from horizontal ones in two ways: the bins are enclosed for cleanliness and security, and the carousel rotates around a horizontal axis. The vertical carousel operates on a continuous lift principle, rotating the necessary items to the order picker's work station. This vertical storage approach cuts floor space use by sixty percent and increases picking productivity up to 300 percent higher than equal capacity racks and shelving. Some industries that use vertical carousels include electronic, automotive, aerospace, and computer.

Miniload Automated Storage and Retrieval Systems (AS/RS)   The most technically advanced order picking system is the miniload AS/RS, which efficiently uses storage space and achieves the highest accuracy rate in order picking. The AS/RS machine travels both horizontally and vertically to storage locations in an aisle, carrying item storage containers to and from an order picking station at the end of the aisle. At the order picking station, the order picker programs the correct item picking sequence. The AS/RS machine retrieves the next container in the sequence while the order picker obtains items from the present container. The miniload AS/RS utilizes vertical space and requires few aisles, but this system is very expensive.

Mezzanines   Mezzanines are a double-layered storage system that utilizes a second level of bin shelving, modular storage cabinets, flow racks, or carousels above the first storage level. Instead of using up square footage space, the mezzanine adds a second level to utilize the warehouse's cubic capacity more efficiently. A steel grating usually divides the two levels which workers access stairs. The mezzanine is not part of the building's actual construction, so its location is flexible (see Figure 11–11).

TYPES OF MATERIALS HANDLING EQUIPMENT—A DESIGN PERSPECTIVE

flexible path

Companies often utilize another materials handling perspective when analyzing equipment needs. This approach contains three categories. The first category is *flexible-path equipment,* which includes manual hand trucks, all forklift trucks, and some other picking equipment. Its design advantages are versatility and flexibility. However, it is customarily more labor-intensive.

continuous-flow fixed-path

The second category is *continuous-flow fixed-path* equipment, which includes conveyors and draglines. These are usually very efficient and highly automated. However, the investment is high; often specializing in certain products they usually have limited versatility; and they have limited flexibility. For a company with volume flow and uniform product size, this approach has many cost advantages.

FIGURE 11–11 MEZZANINES *Source: Plant Engineering* (8 March 1980), 81.

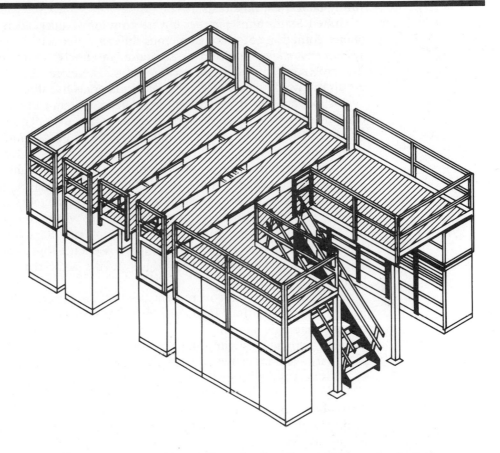

*intermittent-flow
fixed-path*

A third type is *intermittent-flow fixed-path* equipment. Including cranes, monorails, and stacker crane equipment, this category combines the efficiency of continuous-flow equipment with the ability to stop unneeded equipment.

By recognizing the need for equipment able to efficiently move goods within, into, and out of the warehouse, manufacturing firms and equipment manufacturers have revolutionized the whole materials handling area. The number of equipment types available today could overwhelm a materials handling system designer. But these equipment choices also represent an important challenge because of their potential for improving a logistics system.

An interesting question is whether logistics managers should be actual experts in materials handling equipment design. This is very unlikely. Usually, the logistics manager depends on the organization's engineering staff or various equipment managers' advice. However, logistics managers should know about their own systems and their particular needs. This enables logistics managers to establish general parameters for a materials handling system and provides a framework for choosing the best system for a particular company or firm. In the next section, we will discuss some of the logistics manager's equipment selection criteria.

EQUIPMENT SELECTION FACTORS

Several factors affect the type of materials handling equipment a company should use. These factors offers the logistic manager guidelines for analyzing company requirements. He or she must approach this analysis in trade-off terms, measuring benefits against costs.

physical attributes of product and packaging

United States firms produce a vast array of product. Even individual companies sometimes produce numerous different products. A materials handling system that moves books in or around a warehouse is quite distinct from one that stores automobile tires or chain saws. Therefore, the product or product group that we handle affects the type of materials handling equipment we use.

For example, item weight will influence a system's design. Large pieces of equipment that a firm must store in a warehouse may negate using something like a conveyor system and may require overhead bridge cranes. If a product is small and lightweight, usually a firm can use any one or several categories of materials handling equipment. The product and its weight, size, packaging, value, handling ability, and susceptibility to damage all influence the type of equipment a company uses. Therefore, the logistics manager should first consider the product and its dimensions when deciding which equipment options are available and most appropriate for a firm's materials handling system. Because of his or her transportation and inventory experience, the logistics manager will know the company's product or products and the factors that will affect materials handling equipment use.

Since the 1970s, the government has become increasingly interested in the movement of hazardous materials, including radioactive materials and chemicals. A materials handling setting must take this into account. For example, certain raw materials with unique handling characteristics require loose, rather than packaged, movements. Lately, companies have debated the use of slurry systems versus dry bulk systems to move bulk products.

characteristics of physical facility

A warehouse facility's physical characteristics also influence the use of materials handling equipment. Very often we visualize a large, well-lit, one-story facility with very few obstacles, which will be conducive to the use of conveyors, forklift trucks, shelves, or any type of materials handling equipment discussed here. Sometimes, however, this type of facility is not possible. We may have to use a mobile storage facility where conveyors, for example, would not be feasible. We may be dealing with an old warehouse that has low ceilings, negating the use of shelving or containers, or one with floors unable to support a heavy-duty forklift truck. Firms do not always have the option of using the best type of facility, and the facility itself will affect the type of equipment a firm can use.

If we are designing a brand-new warehousing facility, then all the equipment options we talked about here are probably available. If we are dealing with an already-existing facility, particularly if it is old, then we face some constraints on the type of equipment we can use.

time requirements

Time is a logistics system factor in various ways, and it does affect the materials handling. Because customers expect to receive orders in a reasonable time period, time is critical in a market or distribution warehouse where a firm stores its valuable finished goods. These companies will select materials handling equipment that enables them to move goods into, around, and out of the warehouse as fast as possible.

Rapid movement characterizes the distribution or transit warehouse, and we often find the most sophisticated and largest variety of materials handling equipment in these facilities. These warehouses, usually automated, will utilize elaborate and sophisticated conveyor systems, automatic storage placers, and all the materials handling equipment we discussed here.

On the other hand, if we are talking about a storage warehouse or one that a firm uses primarily in conjunction with the manufacturing facility to store semifinished goods and perhaps basic materials, then time is not usually as critical. The equipment would be more basic, and automating such a facility might be unnecessary.

Because of trade-off possibilities, a firm for whom time is critical may be much more willing to invest large amounts of money in sophisticated materials handling equipment. Investing more in a materials handling system enable the firm to increase sales or have savings in other areas.

These factors will provide the logistics manager a basic framework for analyzing his or her particular needs and the materials handling equipment options available to his or her company. After this analysis,the manager can look at what the most likely equipment manufacturers can offer in each category. The logistics manager can also get additional engineering information from the company's own staff, which will help further in designing the system that will best meet the company's particular needs. Although the final selection of a system and its equipment will require a lot of detail, knowing the equipment available and the factors the selection involves provides the basis developing an efficient system for any organization.

Sources of Information

In evaluating materials handling equipment alternatives, a number of sources provide help and insight.

computer program

Computers can estimate storage/retrieval requirements. One recently developed program estimates net cube requirements, storage location requirements, and activity and storage/retrieval configuration, and runs a sensitivity analysis. Often, switching an expensive system is unnecessary. Rather, a firm should try to reduce picking time by increasing the accuracy of storage and inventory information and by optimizing the goods placement for manual retrieval.

internal staff

Many large companies and some small ones have staff engineers who can help the logistics manager analyze the situation. These individuals can provide detailed guidance once the logistics manager has completed an initial analysis.

equipment manufacturers

Equipment manufacturers maintain a staff of engineers who can provide their company cost data on possible alternatives. Equipment has become so specialized today that this may be the best way to get detailed cost information.

consultants

Another possibility is to use consultants to analyze need and select the best equipment. Although such organizations are sometimes expensive, they often provide a very reasonable analysis based upon the costs of using alternative resources.

other

In addition to these, companies can use sources such as trade associations and self-study. While both of these usually provide only simplified data, they often provide a convenient starting place.

PACKAGING

Other individuals, in addition to the logistics manager, may be concerned about a product's packaging. Like materials handling, packaging connotes different things to different people. Since packaging involves a number of organizational areas, these areas will need to coordinate their packaging concerns. The industrial packaging industry will be worth over $80 billion by 1995.[9] Packaging may contribute nothing to a product's value, but its influence on distribution costs is considerable.

marketing

Packaging is of interest to the marketing area. It may be a way of selling a product or of at least providing product information to the customer.

Packaging also concerns production managers, since they are often responsible for placing goods into the package and since a package's size, shape, and type will very often affect labor efficiency. Production managers may look at a package from a perspective somewhat different than the marketing manager's or even the logistics manager's.

production legal

Packaging may also concern the organization's legal section, particularly today, companies must provide information about what a package contains. Thus, some coordination may be necessary between logistics and a company's legal staff.

warehousing

Packaging is especially important to the logistics manager. The size, shape, and type of packaging will influence materials handling and will affect warehouse operations. Also, from a logistics manager's point of view, packaging is quite important for effective damage protection, not only in the warehouse but during transportation.

transportation

Package size may affect a company's ability to use pallets or shelving or different types of materials handling equipment. So the company must consider the package in order to use its warehouse and transportation agencies efficiently. Many companies design packages that are too wise or too high for efficient use of a transportation agency or a warehouse. So coordinating packaging with warehousing and with transportation is quite important. Damaged goods are likely to lower future sales. So packing is quite important to the logistics manager, who must prevent goods from arriving in a damaged condition. Poor packaging can also contribute to handling costs. In short, packaging interacts with the logistics system in a number of different and important ways. The following section discusses more explicitly the role of packaging in logistics.

The Role of Packaging

identification of product and provision of information

A very important packaging function is to provide information about the product the package contains. Looking at this from the perspective of a marketing manager who is trying to sell a product in competition with other products on a supermarket shelf might be easiest. The package should provide information that would make the product more appealing to the customer. The package must also provide handling information. For example, if the package is easily damaged, or if it should be set in only one position, the package should say so.

Information provision is also important to logistics people. Goods stored in a warehouse must bear the proper identification so that warehouse personnel can locate them easily and correctly. When designing a package, firms may spend a lot of time and effort making sure that it provides information to warehouse personnel. Companies can use color codes for placing goods in a warehouse. The company should note weight on the package in order to inform people lifting the package or to determine what can rest on top of it.

Techniques for providing information include color coding, universal product codes, heat transfers, computer-readable tables, symbols, and number codes. A firm's technique or technique combination will depend on the organization's particular circumstances.

A major packaging concern is the ease of handling in conjunction with materials handling and transportation. Large packages, for example, may be desirable from a production perspective; but the contents size and weight might

improvement of efficiency in handling and distributing packages

cause problems for materials handling equipment or for transfer into and out of transportation equipment. So any packaging design should try to maximize handling ease in the warehouse and during transportation. Handling ease is also quite important to the production manager, who places the goods in the package.

The important considerations of package design fall into three areas. The first is the package's physical dimensions. The design must consider space utilization in terms of the warehouse, transport vehicle, and pallets. The product's physical dimension must also take into account the company's materials handling equipment. The second consideration is the package's strength. The package designer must analyze the package's height, handling, and the type of equipment that will handle the package. The final consideration is package shape.

customer interface

With customer service playing an ever-increasing role in logistics planning, companies need to integrate their packages with customers' materials handling equipment. A special package that can interface with our innovative equipment may move products inexpensively through our system; however, a customer's incompatible equipment will impair their ability to receive and store our goods. In this situation, our customer service value may be lost.

protection

A logistics manager's major concern is protecting the goods in the package. In the warehouse, for example, where moving goods could drop from a conveyor or be hit with a forklift truck, the package must provide the product adequate protection. Protection is also important when a transportation agency handles the product. The type of transportation agency will influence the packaging a product requires. Some agencies minimize packaging requirements for products with low damage susceptibility. So the type of transportation agency we use will affect the packaging we need to protect our product from damage. Therefore, one protection objective is to minimize the probability of damage. Protection can also mean protecting products from contamination resulting from contact with other goods, water damage, temperature changes, pilferage, and shocks in handling and transport. Sometimes packaging must support the weight of products stacked above it, and provide even weight distribution within the package to facilitate manual and automatic materials handling.

Changes in federal and state regulations have also affected packaging's protection aspect, especially in food and drug product areas, where companies must design packaging to reduce consumer anxieties about tampering.

What Is Packaging?

We generally discuss two types of packaging: *consumer packaging,* or *interior packaging,* and *industrial,* or *exterior, packaging.* The marketing manager is usually most concerned about the former because consumer or interior packaging provides information important in selling the product, in motivating the customer to buy the product, or in giving the product maximum visibility when it competes with others on the retail shelf. Marketing personnel often refer to consumer packaging, which has to appeal to the customer, as a silent salesperson.

On the other hand, industrial or exterior packaging is of primary concern to the logistics manager. This packaging protects goods that a company will move and store in the warehouse and also permits the company the effective use of transportation vehicle space. It also has to provide information and handling ease, as our discussion of the role of packaging indicated.

Although talking about packaging as a dichotomy is convenient, and quite often we can divide packaging in this way, the two areas do overlap.

We cannot design the interior (consumer) package without considering the exterior or industrial package. Spending a lot of time and effort trying to minimize damage through an exterior package makes no sense if a company does not interior protection. Therefore, marketing and logistics have to coordinate packaging's consumer and industrial dimensions. These areas must also interact with production area people, since they typically join the two packaging types.

Packaging Materials

Many different exterior packaging materials are available to the logistics manager. In fact, as in materials handling, a packaging materials revolution has occurred in the last decade. At one time the use of harder materials, such as wood or metal containers was widespread. But these added considerable shipping weight, which increased transport costs since transportation companies bill customers for total weight, including packaging.

In recent years, companies have tended to use softer packaging materials. Corrugated materials have become popular, particularly with respect to package exterior. However, the plastic materials companies use to cushion the product inside the box have possibly done the most to revolutionize packaging. These materials enable manufacturers to highly automate the packaging area and to maximize protection while minimizing costs. In addition, plastic provides the lowest weight-to-protection shipping ratio.

Cushioning materials protect the product from shock, vibration, and surface damage during handling. Cushioning materials include shrinkwrap, air bubble cushioning, cellulose wadding, corrugated paper, and plastics. We can divide the plastics into expanded polystyrene, polyurethane, foam-in-place, and polyethylene. Figure 11–12 shows a comparison of the various cushioning materials.

Companies often use shrinkwrap for consumer package goods either alone or in conjunction with containers and slip sheets. It provides protection and stability, helps to reduce pilferage, and deters product tampering while items are in a warehouse. Shrink wrap allows companies to stop using corrugated paper boxes. Warehouse personnel places the interior package directly on a pallet and shrinkwraps it. This also displays the item prominently for identification and helps to reduce overall logistics costs. In large warehouse-type retail operations, stores receive pallet loads directly and remove the shrink wrap, making the product immediately accessible to the consumer. Since removing items from a box and placing them on a shelf is unnecessary, the retailer also saves money.

Air bubble cushioning is made of plastic sheets that contain air pockets. Cellulose wadding is composed of tissue paper layers. By forming upright columns in a box, corrugated inserts help prevent a product from getting crushed. Expanded polystyrene (EPS), the most popular cushioning material, is also recyclable. The loose-fill EPS commonly appears as foam peanuts or shells. Polyurethane (PU), the softest foam, provides cushioning for lightweight products. Foam-in-place polyurethane is a mixture of two chemicals which produce a foam that expands and molds to a product's exact shape. Polyethylene (PE) provides lightweight cushioning for heavy products.

These new materials are inexpensive and highly protective. In addition, their light weight helps to minimize transportation costs. If a packaging revolution has occurred, we can probably attribute it to the development of these materials.

FIGURE 11–12 COMPARISON OF CUSHIONING MATERIALS *Source:* "Playing the Protective Packaging Game," *Modern Materials Handling* (April 1989), 65.

Material	Material cost	Static loading	Resiliency	Typical applications
Air bubble	Low	Light to medium	Good	Void fill Wrapping Keyboards Plastic and metal parts Service centers
Cellulose wadding	Low	Light to medium	Fair	Surface protection Furniture Plastic parts
Corrugated	Low	Light to heavy	Fair	Blocking and bracing Rugged parts
Expanded Polystyrene: Loose fill	Low	Light to medium	Fair	Void fill Books Plastic and metal parts
Molded	Low	Light to medium	Fair	Appliances Computers Electronic hardware
Polyurethane	High	Light to medium	Excellent	Computers Electronics Medical instruments
Foam-in-place	Medium	Medium to heavy	Good	Electronics Service centers Spare parts
Polyethylene	High	Medium to heavy	Excellent	Disk drives Fragile electronics Printers

When selecting packaging materials, companies today must consider environmental protection. Consumer advocates as well as government regulations have affected distribution planning. Examples include Food and Drug Administration restrictions on food product packaging. And, with recent consumer panics over pharmaceutical product tampering, the government has implemented stricter packaging materials requirements.

Another concern is the waste containers and packaging produce. Figure 11–13 shows that containers and packaging represent 30.3 percent of America's trash, the largest single trash source. Each year, the United States produces over 160 million tons of waste, which is roughly equal to a convoy of ten-ton garbage trucks lined up halfway to the moon.[10] One way to reduce this waste is to reduce the overall packaging a company uses. Another way is to recycle packaging materials. State and local government has proposed and implemented much legislation to enforce business and community recycling. For example, under Rhode Island's Solid Waste Management Act, businesses must remove seventy percent of all recyclable materials, including corrugated paper, aluminum, wood, and glass, from their waste stream.[11]

FIGURE 11–13   HOW PACKAGING CONTRIBUTES TO U.S. WASTE   *Source:* "Packaging in the 90s—The Environmental Impact," *Modern Materials Handling* (June 1990), 54.

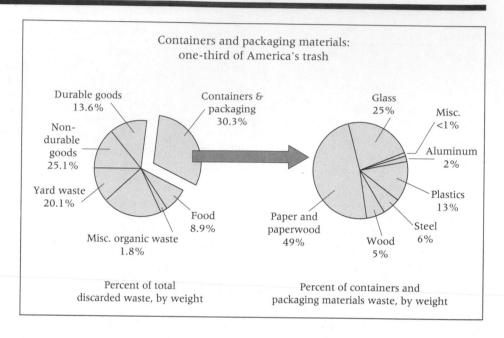

Package Selection

Packaging has two logistics concerns: the physical dimensions (size and shape) and the type of material. These factors establish guidelines for the logistics manager.

physical dimensions   One factor that affects a package's physical dimensions is the product's characteristics—things such as size, shape, and weight. Shoes, which are relatively uniform in size and shape, are much different from glassware, which can vary considerably. Also important are logistics system characteristics: the transportation mode, the number of handlings, materials handling equipment, and storage length. Finally, the logistics-marketing interface will have an impact. Coordination and compromise between these two areas will influence the package's size and shape.

materials   A product's physical dimension will affect a company's packaging material choices. Firms handle small consumer products like glassware differently than computers or auto tires. The transportation mode will also affect the materials a company uses. Airlines and motor carriers require much less packaging than do rail or water carriers. With the advent of deregulation, the common carriers have allowed shippers to experiment with new packaging techniques. Packaging still influences carrier rates, which will be higher for less-protective packaging or for packages that are less dense. Contract and private carriage allow shippers to package goods as they like without rate penalties. Storage time is another factor affecting the material type. Usually, the longer the storage period, the better the packaging. Finally, the production requirements influence materials selection.

unitizing or palletizing   Unitizing or palletizing is the process of accumulating and stacking individual cases or other containers to form a single, larger unit. This process saves handling and transportation costs, utilizes space, better reduces damage and loading and unloading time, and improves customer service. However, the firm faces unitizing/deunitizing costs and requires expensive specialized handling equipment.

Packaging Design Considerations

In developing an appropriate interior and exterior packaging design, we must recognize that a product's package is usually in five basic locations over the product's lifetime. This is particularly true for consumer nondurables or so-called package goods. The five locations are the plant, the warehouse, the transportation unit, the retail outlet, and the home or place of use.

In each instance, we must answer appropriate questions about the packaging. For example, in the home, a consumer may destroy the package immediately or may use it to provide storage until the item is gone. Powdered laundry soap is one product that is stored in its package. Another question is whether the package is returnable and reusable. And we may want to know where the consumer is likely to store the package. The longer the package's potential life cycle and the more hostile the storage area, the more durable and sturdy the package will have to be.

In all the other locations, we must answer similar questions. The responses will provide marketing and logistics valuable package design input.

We may also examine packaging design from the perspective of various logistics area and of other major areas like marketing and manufacturing. From the logistics side, we should consider packaging design questions in terms of warehousing, transportation, materials handling, and procurement. For warehousing, we would want to study factors such as stacking requirements and cube problems. For transportation, we would want to know things such as the mode or modes, the equipment type, and geographic areas. For materials handling, we will need to know the equipment type, if any, and the need to unitize. Designing the appropriate package requires some very important inputs.

Bar Coding

A packaging discussion would be incomplete without a discussion of bar coding. Lineal bar code symbols that an optical scanner can read are having a major impact upon distribution logistics. Representing a technology that caught on in the 1970s and whose use took a huge leap in the 1980s, the bar code industry grew thirty-five percent annually from 1982 to 1989.[12]

A bar code is a series of parallel black and white bars, both of varying widths, whose sequence represents letters or numbers. This sequence is a code that scanners can translate into important information such as a shipment's origin, the product type, the place of manufacture, and the product's price. Bar code systems are simple to use, accurate, and quick; and they can store large amounts of information.

Different industries use different bar code standards. A bar code standard states the language the code uses, the print quality companies expect on the label, the type of information the label contains, and the information format. Over thirty major U.S. industries have developed written standards for bar coding in manufacturing and warehouse operations.[13] For example, different standards include the Automotive Industry Action Group (AIAG) standards and the Universal Product Code the grocery industry uses. With one bar code language standard, suppliers and vendors in a particular industry can easily read each other's package labels.

Bar codes scanners fall into two main categories: automatic and hand-held. Automatic scanners are in a fixed position and scan packages as they go by on a conveyor belt. In contrast, a worker can carry the portable hand-held scanner or wand throughout the warehouse. In order to read bar codes, these optical scanners emit light beams and translate the reflections bouncing off the black and white bars into electrical signals. These electrical signals, which the scanner records as binary digits of 1s and 0s, form the code.

Most of us encounter bar coding in large retail outlets like supermarkets, where clerks now scan individual package bar codes at the cash register. Supermarkets have almost eliminated the practice of labeling every item with a price tag. More importantly, the bar code contributes to much more effective retail inventory control. The scanner and cash register, along with a backup computer system, enable the retail outlet to closely monitor sales and, therefore, inventory levels. The instantaneous transmission of information has allowed companies greater central control and inventory reduction in many retail locations.

Bar coding had its initial logistics impact when companies used it on cartons and monitored or scanned the codes as the cartons flowed into a warehouse. Bar coding at the warehouse improves data collection accuracy, reduces receiving operations time and data collection labor, and helps to integrate data collection with other areas, leading to better database and inventory controls. Companies can assign items more quickly into the warehouse, and warehouse personnel can select and prepare orders much more rapidly.

Containerization

Containers are physical equipment firms use to unify small shipments. Once a firm has loaded shipments into a container, intermodal carriers can move them as one shipment.

The cargo container is usually weatherproof. A company can therefore store it outside or transport it in open cars or on a ship's deck. Typically, the cargo container's construction is rugged enough for movement by mechanical means such as forklifts or cranes and for interchange between or among modes.

With deregulation, more carriers can carry containers intermodally at reduced rates, a factor that logistics planning must consider. Containerization is becoming more popular, despite continuing damage problems in container movements; and industry trade organization conferences on the subject are taking place in most major U.S. cities.

Very simply, containers are attractive to users because of reduced cost. Containerization reduces transportation cost, handling cost, loss and damage, inventory cost, paperwork, and packaging cost.

SUMMARY

This chapter discussed materials handling and packaging. Both areas seriously affect a firm's nodal and link activities. Overall, they are of great importance to the logistics manager and require considerable coordination other organizational areas. Recently, many exciting developments in terms of materials handling equipment and packaging materials have occurred. As a result, the logistics manager's decisions are in a sense more difficult, but more challenging, than they were before. The logistics manager may be able to realize economies and trade-offs in materials handling and in packaging, thereby saving the company money or contributing to the logistics system's overall efficiency, consequently helping to increase the organization's profits.

NOTES

1. Karen Auguston, "How Jaguar Ships Orders on Time, Every Time," *Modern Materials Handling* (February 1991), 74–75.
2. *Basics of Materials Handling* (Pittsburgh: Materials Handling Institute, 1973), 4–6.
3. *Basics of Materials Handling,* 8–10.
4. Auguston, "How Jaguar Ships on Time, Every Time," 74–75.
5. *Modern Materials Handling* (January 1991), 69.
6. Auguston, "How Jaguar Ships on Time, Every Time," 74–75.
7. "Annual Report on Productivity," *Modern Materials Handling* (February 1991), 83.
8. Gary Forger, "Deep Lane Storage," *Modern Materials Handling* (January 1991), 47.
9. "Packaging Costs Will Reach a New High," *Traffic Management* (March 1991), 17.
10. "The Greening of Logistics," *Distribution* (January 1991), 32.
11. "Packaging in the 90s—The Environmental Impact," *Modern Materials Handling* (June 1990), 54.
12. "Auto. I.D.: Reading is Believing," *Purchasing World* (November 1990), 72.
13. Gary Forger, "Bar Code Label Standards," *Modern Materials Handling* (November 1990), 43.

STUDY QUESTIONS

1. We frequently define materials handling as short-distance movement. What exactly does that mean? Where does this short-distance movement take place? Why are logistics managers concerned about materials handling?

2. One materials handling objective is to increase effective capacity, that is, to improve space utilization. How does materials handling help to achieve this? How do materials handling systems differ with respect to this objective?

3. Review Table 11–1—Principles of Materials Handling. How would you prioritize and/or classify these principles if your firm asked you to make a presentation to a group of non-logistics managers to help them understand materials handling?

4. Forklift trucks are generally considered the most popular form of materials handling equipment. Why are they so popular? Analyze forklift trucks in terms of their ability to help companies achieve materials handling objectives.

5. One major area in a physical distribution center is order picking. Compare and contrast this area's two major system types.

6. Companies can use a number of different equipment types for materials handling. From a design perspective, how do these types of equipment differ?

7. Materials handling equipment selection needs to consider three major factors. Select three different products and discuss those three factors in terms of the three products.

8. What functional areas in a company are interested in packaging? What is the nature of their respective interests? What types of disagreements may arise because of these varying interests?

9. How has bar coding affected packaging and materials handling?

10. What are the current trends in packaging? Which of these trends will have the biggest impact upon logistics in the 1990s? Why?

CASE 11–1

RADICAL SYSTEMS

Radical Systems, Inc., located in central Pennsylvania's Nittany Valley, has earned a reputation as an innovative manufacturer of answering machines. Radical Systems has pushed its sales to $250 million and has established a major position in the marketplace.

Jim Tyworth, executive vice president of Radical, was concerned about the company's ability to handle its high growth rate, particularly from a logistics viewpoint. Jim felt that the company needed to change its warehouse and materials handling system.

Tyworth called Bob Sender, director of materials and logistics, into his office to discuss his concerns. Bob listened attentively and indicated that he shared Jim's opinion that they needed to take some steps to change Radical's materials handling system to meet the company's continued growth pattern. Bob told Jim that he had already initiated steps addressing future materials handling needs.

Tyworth was pleased. He asked Sender for a report of the activity thus far and any future plans. Sender subsequently reported that he had assembled a team that combined representatives from marketing, manufacturing, and engineering with logistics personnel.

Sender's initial perspective was that the team would recommend a complex and sophisticated materials handling system, particularly since Radical was a high-tech company. Sender was interested in a flexible system that could expand to accommodate future growth. Sender's team gave their initial report orally. They indicated that they felt that a basic and practical materials handling system was more appropriate for Radical Systems than a complex, sophisticated, highly automated one.

The team wanted some feedback before proceeding to more specific and elaborate plans. Bob Sender discussed the oral report with Jim Tyworth. Tyworth was surprised but quite open-minded about the new system's proposed direction. He requested that Sender give it some more consideration.

Case Questions
1. What would the initial proposal's advantages and disadvantages be?
2. What types of equipment would fit the initial design objectives?
3. What types of equipment would the team not consider?
4. What is your recommendation based upon this preliminary information? Why?

BART DENTAL

Bart Dental is a member of the Sweden-based Delta Medical Group. It is made up of nine divisions: magazine, book, furniture, film, optics, defense, data, medical, and general.

Bart markets frequently used supplies to dentists. It purchases products from outside manufacturers and sells them directly on the basis of mail or telephone orders. Its operations require high volume, efficient handling, computerized routines, and coordinated purchases. For the customer, this form of distribution means lower prices, faster deliveries, and better service. It requires a homogeneous customer base and a well-defined, fast-moving product range.

Invoiced sales during 1992 amounted to $461 million, up thirty percent from the year before. Profit after net financial items was $22 million, as compared to $21 million in 1991. Earnings did not grow as rapidly as sales primarily because of sizable expenses. Return on total assets was sixteen percent, unchanging from 1990.

The growth in the volume of dental care in the Western world has slowed, producing a trend toward depressed prices and narrower margins for companies that sell dental supplies. Companies have to offset this negative trend by increasing volume and raising productivity, as well as by increasing the capital turnover ratio.

Bart is a leader in the mail-order market, a form of distribution that dentists accept. In the United States, Bart is the third-leading mail-order company in its field. Bart has expanded rapidly during the past five years and is now entering a period of concentration and consolidation.

Bart has a huge warehouse located in Baxter, Pennsylvania. Its departments range from receiving to order picking to checking/auditing to packaging to shipping. Bart's offices are located on the warehouse's second floor. The offices contain the sales, tele-marketing, customer service, and purchasing departments, to name a few.

Bart feels that large inventories, quality merchandise, and competitive prices are not enough. The company operates on what it calls its Quick-6 system. This is a six-step, six-hour process Bart employs from start to finish when a customer places an order. Here is how it works:

1. A sales representative enters the order into the computer after calling it in on a toll-free ordering number.
2. The order is on its way to being filled within minutes.
3. Order pickers make sure that what the customer is about to receive exactly matched what the customer ordered.
4. Bart's automated conveyor system speeds the order through the warehouse.
5. The order is checked and double-checked for accuracy.
6. The order is then sealed, banded together, and placed on a UPS truck—all within six hours!

In a complex system such as this, the order picking process is crucial and should therefore be as efficient as possible.

Bart has eight order picking areas, including bulk pricing. Each picker picks a specific number of bin locations. For instance, a picker in station 1 picks bin locations 000–049; station 2 picks 050–099; station 3 picks 100–149, and so on.

On Bart's invoices, a bin location and a product number precedes each product. As the printed orders are pulled off the computer in the warehouse, they are sorted by bin location and passed out to the appropriate order picker for the first item listed. After the first picker receives an order and proceeds to the right bin location, which consists of one shelf, he or she picks the specific product by checking the product number on the invoice and making sure it matches the product number at the bin location. The picker then passes the order on to the picking station for the next item listed. When the order is complete, it is placed on the center belt on its way to the auditing department, where it is checked for accuracy.

All picking stations must have the same amount of work flow. If they do not, certain picking areas may become packed up with work and slow the entire process. The flow rack is one of Bart's busiest picking sections because it contains many popular items.

Two of the biggest problems in the warehouse's order picking section are structural and personnel. The first problem is that the order picking section's structure is inefficient. Some workers do not have enough orders to fill and back up others on the line; other pickers have too many orders to fill and further slow the line. This decreases productivity and warehouse efficiency.

The second problem is the workers themselves. Their work does not motivate them. Their actions are slow, and they seem uninterested in what they are doing.

Bart has no reward system for good order picking. Employee morale is very low, and the company offers no incentive to work harder. Pickers questioning an order's accuracy walk unnecessarily from picking to checking. Order pickers also search endlessly for unstocked items. Stocking is poor and not kept up-to-date.

Case Question   1. What do you recommend?

SELECTED BIBLIOGRAPHY FOR PART 3

TRANSPORTATION MANAGEMENT

Augello, William J. *Freight Claims in Plain English,* 1982 rev. (Huntington, NY: Shippers National Freight Claim Council, 1982).

Ballou, Ronald H., and Daniel W. DeHayes, Jr. "Transport Selection by Interfirm Analysis," *Transportation and Distribution Management* 7, no. 6 (June 1967), 33–37.

Bardi, Edward J. "Carrier Selection from One Mode," *Transportation Journal* 13, no. 1 (Fall 1973), 23–29.

Bardi, Edward J.; Prabir K. Bagchi; and T. S. Raghunathan. "Motor Carrier Selection in a Deregulated Environment," *Transportation Journal* 29, no. 1 (Fall 1989), 4–11.

Beier, Frederick J. "Transportation Contracts and the Experience Effect: A Framework for Future Research," *Journal of Business Logistics* 10, no. 2 (1989), 73–89.

Borts, G. H. "Long-term Rail Contracts—Handle with Care," *Transportation Journal* 25 (Spring 1986), 4–12.

Bowersox, Donald J. "The Strategic Benefits of Logistics Alliances," *Harvard Business Review*, no. 4 (July–August 1990), 36–47.

Brown, T. A. "Shippers' Agents and the Marketing of Rail Intermodal Service," *Transportation Journal* 23 (Spring 1984), 44–52.

Cavinato, Joseph L. "Buying Transportation," *Guide to Purchasing* (Oradell, NJ: National Association of Purchasing Management, 1986).

Coyle, John J. "The Compatibility of the Rule of Ratemaking and the National Transportation Policy," *ICC Practitioners' Journal* (March–April 1971), 340–53.

Coyle, John J.; Edward J. Bardi; and Joseph L. Cavinato, *Transportation,* 3rd ed. (St. Paul, MN: West Publishing, 1990).

Crum, M. R. "The Expanded Role of Motor Freight Brokers in the Wake of Regulatory Reform," *Transportation Journal* 24 (Summer 1985), 5–15.

Flood, Kenneth U.; Oliver G. Callson; and Sylvester J. Jablonski. *Transportation Management,* 4th ed. (Dubuque, IA: Wm. C. Brown, 1984).

Forsythe, Kenneth H.; James C. Johnson; and Kenneth C. Schneider. "Traffic Managers: Do They Get Any Respect?" *Journal of Business Logistics* 11, no. 2 (1990), 87–100.

Gordorn, Jay, "Third Parties: Agents of Change," *Distribution* 89, no. 4 (April 1990), 57–64.

Harmatuck, Donald J. "Short Run Motor Carrier Cost Functions for Five Large Common Carriers," *The Logistics and Transportation Review* 21, no. 3 (September 1985), 217–38.

Harper, Donald V. *Transportation in America,* 2d ed. (Englewood Cliffs, NJ: Prentice-Hall, 1978).

Hoover, H., Jr. "Pricing Behavior of Deregulated Motor Carriers," *Transportation Journal* 25 (Fall 1985), 55–62.

Jackson, George. "A Survey of Freight Consolidation Practices," *Journal of Business Logistics* 6, no. 1 (1985), 13–34.

Jacoby, David. "Implementing Strategic Information Systems in the Transportation Industry," *Transportation Journal* 29, no. 3 (Spring 1990), 54–63.

LaLonde, Bernard J.; James M. Masters; Arnold B. Maltz; and Lisa R. Williams. *Evolution Status and Future of the Corporate Transportation Function* (Louisville, KY: American Society of Transportation and Logistics, 1991).

Lieb, Robert C., and Robert A. Miller. "JIT and Corporate Transportation Requirements," *Transportation Journal* 27, no. 3 (Spring 1988), 5–10.

McGinnis, Michael A. "The Relative Importance of Cost and Service in Freight Transportation Choice: Before and After Deregulation," *Transportation Journal* 30, no. 1 (Fall 1990), 12–19.

Min, Hokey, and Martha Cooper. "A Comparative Review of Analytical Studies on Freight Consolidation and Backhauling," *The Logistics and Transportation Review* 26, no. 2 (June 1990), 149–70.

Muller, E. J. "Using 3rd Parties for International Success," *Distribution* 89, no. 10 (October 1990), 66–68.

Pisharodi, Ram Mohan. "Modeling the Motor Carrier Selection Decision: A Preliminary Report," Council of Logistics Management, *Annual Conference Proceedings* 1 (1988), 237–42.

Raghunathan, T. S.; Prabir K. Bagchi; and Edward J. Bardi. "Motor Carrier Services: The U.S. Experience," *International Journal of Physical Distribution & Materials Management* 18, no. 5 (1988), 3–7.

Taff, Charles A. *Management of Physical Distribution and Transportation,* 7th ed. (Homewood, IL: Richard D. Irwin, 1984).

Temple, Barker & Sloane. *Transportation Strategies for the Eighties* (Oak Brook, IL: The National Council of Physical Distribution Management, 1982).

"Transportation Quality Report," *Traffic Management* 28, no. 5 (May 1989), 37–54.

Tyworth, J. E.; J. L. Cavinato; and C. J. Langley, Jr. *Traffic Management* (Reading, MA: Addison-Wesley Publishing Company, 1987).

Tyworth, John E.; Pat Lemons; and Bruce Ferrin. "Improving LTL Delivery Service with Statistical Process Control," *Transportation Journal* 28, no. 3 (Spring 1989), 4–12.

United States Code Annotated, Title 49, Transportation (St. Paul, MN: West Publishing, 1982).

Vorhees, Roy Dale, and Benjamin J. Allen. "The Test and Failure of a Coordinated Tariff for Rail-Barge Movements," *Journal of Business Logistics* 7, no. 1 (1986), 108–21.

Wilson, George W. *Essays on Some Unsettled Questions in the Economics of Transportation* (Bloomington, IN: Indiana University Business Report No. 42, 1962).

WAREHOUSING

Ackerman, Kenneth B. "Quality Measurement and Improvement in Logistics—Warehouse," Council of Logistics Management, *Annual Conference Proceedings* 2 (1988), 81–84.

Ackerman, Kenneth B. "Value-Added Warehousing Cuts Inventory Costs," *Transportation & Distribution* 30, no. 7 (July 1989), 32–35.

"Are Your Supervisors Doing a Good Job? Measuring Throughput Alone Won't Give You the Answer," *Distribution Center Management* 24, no. 5 (May 1989), 1–5.

Auguston, Karen A. "Leading the Way in Parts Distribution," *Modern Materials Handling* 44, no. 8 (August 1989), 49–52.

Baum, Eric C. "Improving Warehouse Productivity," Council of Logistics Management, *Annual Conference Proceedings* 2 (1988), 137–53.

Bowen, Douglas J. "Partnershipping: It's a Matter of Trust," *Inbound Logistics* 9, no. 9 (September 1989), 20–22.

Bowman, Robert J. "Third-Party Carriers Can Boost Logistics," *Distribution* 88, no. 5 (May 1989), 50–52.

Callari, James J. "Customer Service Prompts Move to Columbus," *Traffic Management* 28, no. 1 (January 1989), 64–65.

Cavinato, Joseph L. "The Logistics of Contract Manufacturing," *International Journal of Physical Distribution & Materials Management* 19, no. 1 (1989), 13–20.

Derewecki, Donald J.; Robert B. Silverman; and Alex Donnan. "Warehouse Planning:

Computer Aided Design," Council of Logistics Management, *Annual Conference Proceedings* 1 (1988), 427–58.

"Distribution Center for the 90's," *Material Handling Engineering* 44, no. 7 (July 1989), 48–56.

"Evaluating Warehouse Costs," *Air Cargo World* 79, no. 7 (July 1989), 27–29.

"Expansion Eases Warehouse Storage Problems, Raises Productivity," *Grocery Distribution* 15, no. 1 (September/October 1989), 11–14, 47.

Fernie, John. "The Role of Contract Distribution in Multiple Retailers' Distribution Strategies," *Focus on Physical Distribution and Logistics Management* 8, no. 3 (April 1989), 31–35.

Foscoe, Mark. "Learning to Live with an Automated Warehouse," *Focus on Physical Distribution and Logistics Management* 8, no. 4 (May 1989), 22–27.

Frosdick, Gordon. "Warehouse Automation—A Financial Case," *Logistics World* 2, no. 2 (June 1989), 107–10.

"Improving Warehouse Fire Protection," *Ackerman Warehousing Forum* 5, no. 1 (December 1989), 1–2.

"Inside Warehousing & Distribution," *Transportation & Distribution* 30, no. 1 (January 1989), 43–50.

Kirk, John A. "Maximizing Productivity Performance and Operational Effectiveness of the Warehouse," *Focus on Physical Distribution and Logistics Management* 8, no. 4 (May 1989), 36–40.

McGinnis, Michael A. *Basic Economic Analysis for Warehouse Decisions* (Oak Brook, IL: Warehousing Education and Research Council, 1989), 8 pp.

Moshavi, Sharon. "When and When Not To Buy Third Party Services," *Inbound Logistics* 9, no. 3 (March, 1989), 27–29.

Nelson, Raymond A. "Integrating the Computer with Warehousing Operations," Council of Logistics Management, *Annual Conference Proceedings* 2, (1988), 349–56.

Price, Richard J. "Changing Logistics," Council of Logistics Management, *Annual Conference Proceedings* 2 (1988), 383–90.

Sheehan, William G. "Contract Warehousing: The Evolution of an Industry," *Journal of Business Logistics* 10, no. 1 (1989), 31–49.

Short, Michael. "Quality in Warehousing," *Focus on Physical Distribution and Logistics Management* 8, no. 5 (June 1989), 29–33.

Richardson, Helen L. "Security Goes Beyond the Gate," *Transportation & Distribution* 29, no 3 (March 1989), 34–36.

Richardson, Helen L. "Stop Damage at the Source," *Transportation & Distribution* 29, no. 3 (March 1989), 30–32.

Tompkins, James A. "20 Strategies for Successful Warehousing," (four-part series) *Material Handling Engineering* 44, no. 3–6 (March–June 1989).

"Warehouse Workers In 1989: Where Will You Find Them and How Will You Keep Them?" *Distribution Center Management* 24, no. 1 (January 1989), 1–4.

"Warehousing—New Services for Shippers," *Air Cargo World* 79, no. 7 (July 1989), 30–41.

"Warehousing: A Review for Management," *Distribution* 88, no. 3 (March 1989), 112.

Weart, Walter. "Cleaning up on the Competition," *Distribution* 88, no. 4 (April 1989), 44–45.

Weart, Wally. "Logistics Tools: How to Automate Your Freight Flow," *Distribution* 88, no. 4 (April 1989), 46–50.

Wilson, Philip R.S., and Steven J. Fathers. "Distribution—The Contract Approach," *International Journal of Physical Distribution & Materials Management* 19, no. 6 (1989), 26–30.

Witt, Clyde E. "New Distribution Center Designed for the Customer," *Material Handling Engineering* 44, no. 4 (April 1989), 32–37.

"Zero Errors: An Impossible Dream?" *Distribution Center Management* 24, no. 7 (July 1989), 1–3.

MATERIALS HANDLING AND PACKAGING

Auguston, Karen A. "Distribution in the 90's: Better Materials Handling, Better Service," *Modern Materials Handling* 44, no. 8 (August 1989), 44–48.

Auguston, Karen A. "Parts Delivery System Takes Off at O'Hare Int'l Airport," *Modern Materials Handling* 44, no. 12 (October 1989), 52–54.

Bowman, Robert J. "B'Gosh, It's Oshkosh!" *Distribution* 88, no. 2 (February 1989), 44–46.

Cooke, James A. "How to Choose the Lift Truck that's Right for You," *Traffic Management* 28, no. 4 (April 1989), 61–64.

Cooke, James A. "Management Briefing: How to Choose the Lift Truck That's Right for You," *Traffic Management* 28, no. 4 (April 1989), 61–64.

"Designing Docks: 14 Tips for Top Productivity," *Modern Materials Handling* 44, no. 7 (July 1989), 64–66.

"Designing for Modular Automation," *Modern Materials Handling* 44, no. 7 (June 1989), 48–49.

Feare, Tom. "Lift Truck Training: Make It Mandatory," *Modern Materials Handling* 44, no. 8 (August 1989), 54–57.

Forger, Gary. "How an AS/RS and Two AGV Systems Saved the Day at Terumo," *Modern Materials Handling* 44, no. 14 (December 1989), 44–46.

Forger, Gary. "Federal-Mogul Streamlines Its Distribution Center," *Modern Materials Handling* 44, no. 12 (October 1989), 48–51.

Forger, Gary. "Weighting Systems: The New Link in Data Collection," *Modern Materials Handling* 44, no. 13 (November 1989), 63–65.

Goetschalckx, Marc, and Jalal Ashayeri. "Classification and Design of Order Picking," *Logistics World* 2, no. 2 (June 1989), 99–106.

"How to Store and Retrieve Parts in an Integrated Carousel and AS/RS System," *Material Handling Engineering* 44, no. 6 (June 1989), 84–85.

"Just In Time on the Dock," *Material Handling Engineering* 44, no. 10 (October 1989), 51–94.

Knill, Bernie. "Small Parts System Makes Big Products Fly," *Material Handling Engineering* 44, no. 8 (August 1989), 86–87.

Knill, Bernie. "Warehousing 89: Focus is on Quick Response," *Material Handling Engineering,* 44, no. 3 (March 1989), 53–60.

Krepchin, Ira P. "Materials Handling in France: A First-Hand Report," *Modern Materials Handling* 44, no. 12 (October 1989), 55–57.

Krepchin, Ira P. "PC's Run This Automated Materials Handling System," *Modern Materials Handling* 44, no. 14 (December 1989), 56–58.

Krepchin, Ira P. "Using Computers for Planning and Control," *Modern Materials Handling* 44, no. 13 (November 1989), 68–71.

"Microsoft Manages Smooth Transition to New Facility," *Material Handling Engineering* 44, no. 7 (July 1989), 62–64.

"Polaroid's Journey to Materials Handling Excellence," *Modern Materials Handing* 44, no. 7 (July, 1989), 60–63.

"RFDC Delivers Tight Inventory Control, High Data Accuracy," *Modern Materials Handling* 44, no. 13 (November 1989), 73.

Schwind, Gene. "Mini-Loads: Doing More in Manufacturing," *Material Handling Engineering* 44, no. 7 (July 1989), 58–60.

Schwind, Gene F. "Turret Trucks: Shrinking Aisles Still Further," *Material Handling Engineering* 44, no 6 (June 1989), 40–46.

"Special Report: Storage," *Modern Materials Handling* 44, no. 14 (December 1989), 47–54.

Torok, Douglas B. "How to Make a Fast Move to Productivity," *Material Handling Engineering* 44, no. 2 (February 1989), 6ll–64.

Torok, Douglas B. "Unitizing Roundup," *Material Handling Engineering* 44, no. 11 (November 1989), 48–81.

Trunk, Christopher. "Gravity Flow Racks Go Paperless," *Material Handling Engineering* 40, no. 8 (August 1989), 82–85.

Trunk, Christopher. "New Horizons for Warehousing Software," *Material Handling Engineering* 44, no. 3 (March 1989), 72–80.

White, John A. "Material Handling in Warehousing: Basics and Evolution," Council of Logistics Management, *Annual Conference Proceedings* 2 (1988), 409–24.

Witt, Clyde E. "Automation Brings Fast, Accurate Service to General Motors' Parts Warehouse," *Material Handling Engineering* 44, no. 3 (March 1989), 82–91.

Witt, Clyde E. "Distribution with a Personal Touch," *Material Handling Engineering* 44, no. 6 (June 1989), 60–64, 69.

Witt, Clyde E. "Flexibility: Sun's Shining Example," *Material Handling Engineering* 44, no. 10 (October 1989), 42–46.

Witt, Clyde E. "Reebok's Distribution on Fast Track," *Material Handling Engineering* 44, no. 3 (March 1989), 43–48.

IV

The first three parts of this book have acquainted the reader with the specifics of the major functional areas of logistics and with the application of the particulars to the immediate short-run decision-making in these areas. In this final part, attention is focused upon the broader (long-run, less-frequent) decision-making areas dealing with the overall management and control of nodal location decisions, logistics quality, organizational structuring, strategic planning and the design of logistics systems.

In the nodal location chapter a discussion of the logistics variables influencing the nodal location decision and an application of logistics-oriented location techniques are presented. The logistics quality chapter examines quality management issues and techniques and the role of logistics in the attainment of a company's overall quality goals. The organization chapter considers the unique problems associated with organizing the logistics function in a company and discusses alternative organizational structures for logistics. The strategic planning process, logistics excellence, leading edge logistics and logistics trends are the topics examined in the final chapter.

FACILITY LOCATION

The location of plants and warehouses in a firm's logistics system establishes constraints upon the efficiency of time and place utility creation. A logistics facility's location directly affects transportation costs, service levels and inventory costs. Once the firm establishes the facility's location, the logistics manager can manipulate logistics variables such as transportation, order processing, and materials handling to maximize the facility's time and place utility at minimum total system cost. The purpose of this chapter is to examine the decision making process firms utilize to determine where to locate a logistics facility.

In the short run, logistics facilities' locations are given; and the logistics manager must operate within the constraints the facility locations impose. Site availability, leases, contracts, and investments make changing facility locations impracticable in the short run. But, in the long run, a logistics facility's location is variable; a managerial decision can change the location to meet the logistics requirements customer, supplier, and competitive changes impose.

Expansion into new market areas, population shifts, development of new product lines, technological changes, competitive pressures, new sources of raw materials, and other external factors motivate firms to analyze a new facility's location or an existing facility's relocation. In addition, corporate downsizing, the development of global markets such as Eastern Europe and the European Community, and global outsourcing of raw materials, parts, and supplies have forced companies to examine their facilities' number and locations.

The facility location decision a firm makes today has ramifications long into the future. A facility properly located under today's economic, competitive, and technological conditions may not be in an optimum location under future conditions. Today's facility location decision will affect the logistics, marketing, production, and finance costs in the future. Thus, the facility location decision must seriously consider anticipated business conditions; and the location must still be appropriate five to ten years in the future.

Firms use both quantitative (cost) and qualitative criteria to make the facility location decision. Generally, a firm considers the quantitative criteria first; potential site locations must meet the quantitative criteria before the site receives further consideration. If the potential sites meet the cost or quantitative criteria, the firm considers the qualitative factors. The following sections examine the location decision process and the criteria firms utilize to select a facility location.

WHY ANALYZE THE FACILITY LOCATION?

The answer to this query is the dynamic nature of business. All businesses operate in a very dynamic environment in which change is the only constant. Consumer demand characteristics, technology, competition, markets, and suppliers are constantly changing; and business must redeploy its resources in response to and in anticipation of this ever-changing environment.

Logistics facilities and their locations are static; firms can not modify them easily in the short run. This static nature presents the logistics manager some difficulty in trying to cope with business environment change. We do not decide to close a warehouse, distribution center, or plant and move it to another site without considering the proposed move's economics as well as the impact on the company's employees and on the community the firm is vacating.

To say the least, firms do not decide facility location or relocation lightly. The decision usually involves considerable capital outlay, cost savings, service improvements, or improved competitive advantages. New plants or warehouses may apply the latest technology to offer cost savings and service improvements even though these new facilities require considerable capital resources. In addition, a relocated facility offers service improvements and a resulting competitive marketplace advantage.

Labor has caused many firms to analyze a facility's location. High labor costs or restrictive union work rules have caused companies to move production facilities from the Northeast to the South, as well as to Mexico and to Pacific Rim countries. Companies balance these areas' lower labor costs against higher logistics costs for transportation, inventory, and communication.

The need to modernize a plant often results in its relocation. A firm deciding to invest millions of dollars in an existing plant must ask, "Is this the proper location for a plant given the current and future customer and vendor locations?"

The steel industry is a good example of relocation in lieu of modernization. Pittsburgh, Pennsylvania, and Youngstown, Ohio, were steelmaking capitals through the 1970s. However, as modernizing existing plants became necessary to remain competitive with domestic and foreign steel producers, the steel industry decided to relocate and build new, more efficient plants at more optimal sites in the Midwest and Southeast, given these sites' raw material sources and markets.

Shifting markets also cause firms to analyze facility locations. The aging U.S. population has resulted in tremendous population shifts to the Southeast and Southwest. New warehouse and distribution centers are following these shifting population patterns and markets. Atlanta, Houston, and Las Vegas have become popular distribution center and warehouse locations for companies serving these increasing population centers.

The auto industry's JIT system's service and cost requirements have forced auto parts suppliers to examine their facility locations. A number of auto parts suppliers serving the Buick Motor Division of General Motors have located warehousing facilities in Flint, Michigan to achieve Buick's service requirements.

Competitive pressures force a company to examine the logistics service level and cost its facility network generates. To remain competitive in the marketplace or to develop a competitive advantage, a company frequently examines its existing facilities' relative locations with the goal of improving service and/or lowering costs. Companies often conduct this network review in light of newly developed transport alternatives.

For example, several air carriers have instituted parts distribution programs at major airports such as Chicago and Memphis. The air carriers maintain an inventory of a company's products and will fill and ship orders at the company's instruction. The resulting service level is higher, and the air carrier sometimes includes the warehousing cost in its transportation rate. This new transportation (logistics) alternative air carriers offer has led many companies to eliminate existing facilities in favor of having an air carrier operate a facility at a major airport.

On the global scene, the collapse of economic walls in Eastern Europe plus the European community's unification have forced U.S. managers to examine facility locations suitable for competition in this rapidly developing market. U.S. companies have purchased existing European companies, established European branches, or entered into joint agreements with existing European companies to gain a presence in this huge marketplace.

Outsourcing of raw materials from foreign countries is another reason to analyze the location of existing facilities. Using Pacific Rim suppliers makes a West Coast warehouse location desirable, whereas an East Coast location would be more desirable for a company outsourcing materials from Europe. As world economies become more interdependent, these facility location decisions are becoming more common.

Following the buyout craze of the 1980s, companies facing huge debt servicing requirements paid this debt by selling warehouses to generate cash. This downsizing of the company-owned warehousing system and the switch to public warehousing forced companies to examine the remaining warehouses' locations.

Finally, changing buyer characteristics have caused companies to grow and to decline. For example, the personal computer industry has faced exploding U.S. demand while simultaneously shifting production and sourcing to offshore points. The reduced demand for U.S.-made autos has caused slow growth for many parts suppliers, forcing these suppliers to close or consolidate production and distribution facilities. Both the computer companies and the parts suppliers must examine the facility location optimal for a changing marketplace.

OVERVIEW OF THE FACILITY LOCATION DECISION

A firm must consider many factors in determining the location of a plant or warehouse. Although this chapter emphasizes the logistics factors in the facility location decision, we should remember that logistics is but one of many determining factors.

The facility location decision is a complex process that numerous factors affect, and the factors' importance varies from industry to industry. In addition, many locational factors are qualitative, representing management's impressions about attitudes of labor, citizens, and public officials in a potential site; these factors are difficult to quantify.

location team   A manager team makes most plant and warehouse location decisions. The team usually will include representatives from manufacturing (or operations), engineering, personnel, logistics, tax, and facilities planning/real estate (if such areas exist in the company).

Steps in the Location Decision*

A typical plant location decision process consists of the following eight steps:

cost/benefit study **1.** Corporate management decides to seek a new plant site basing this decision upon a feasibility study of the cost and benefit of adding a new facility or relocating an existing facility in the logistics system.

team role   **2.** The company assembles a joint divisional-corporate team. The team develops the basic information about the proposed plant, including land re-

*The material in this section is adapted from Roger W. Schmenner, *Making Business Location Decisions* (Englewood Cliffs, N.J.: Prentice-Hall, 1982), 16–20.

quirements, products the plant will produce, labor requirements, transportation needs, required utilities, and environmental concerns.

engineering study

3. A plant engineering group studies the site's engineering aspects (such as the area's topography and geology) that will affect the plant's design.

develop selection criteria

4. The study develops a list of essential criteria for the proposed site. The study teams will customize the specific list to meet the company's unique requirements, but the list will generally consider markets, labor, logistics, raw materials, environmental regulations, and competition.

potential regions

5. The company measures regions of the country against this essential criteria list, reducing the number of potential locations the company will examine in depth. A region may consist of a single state or a group of states—for example, the Sunbelt region of the United States.

potential sites

6. From a list of acceptable regional locations, the team examines particular sites within the regions and selects a manageable number of specific sites (usually fewer than twenty-five) for close scrutiny in the location decision's next phase.

analyze specific sites

7. The location team thoroughly investigates each promising site they identified in step 6, collecting and verifying data for each site and visiting sites to study living conditions, culture, and community attitudes toward business. After comparing the data, the team prepares a final list of recommended plant locations.

select site

8. The company selects the specific site from the recommended site list. Top management or the division responsible for operating the plant normally makes the final decision. The location team does not make this decision.

Most companies follow these decision steps in some form. Smaller companies tend to have a smaller location team and a less formal process. Large corporations organize the location team more formally; the team can range from a highly centralized, corporate-dominated team to a highly decentralized process dominated by the division that will operate the facility.

Major Locational Determinants

One of the facility location team's first tasks is to delineate the new facility location key factors, usually by assessing labor, markets, raw materials, logistics, environment, and competition. Table 12–1 indicates the major locational determinants, in order of importance, for both the region and the specific site.

importance of determinants varies

The importance of the major locational determinants varies among industries and among individual companies within specific industries. For example, labor-intensive industries such as textiles, furniture, and household appliances place greater emphasis upon favorable labor climate and labor rates than do high-tech industries such as manufacturers of engineering and scientific instruments and measuring and controlling devices. For industries such as drugs, beverages, and printing and publishing, in which competition or logistics costs are significant the logistics variable is important.

logistics determinants

Note that, in Table 12–1, the proximity to markets and raw materials represents a logistics factor. Although we may usually implicitly assume that a company would know existing markets and raw materials sources, this is usually not the case when a company is designing a plant or warehouse for a new territory. The marketing and production departments need to analyze the area for potential buyers and suppliers.

TABLE 12-1   MAJOR LOCATIONAL DETERMINANTS

Regional Determinants	Specific Site Determinants
Favorable labor climate	Rail Service
Proximity to markets	On expressway
Quality of life	Special provisions of utilities
Near supplies and resources	Rural area
Labor rates	Environmental permits
Environmental permits	Within metropolitan area
Facility/land already available	On water
Better transportation	Transportation (air and truck)
Taxes, financing	

Source: Roger W. Schmenner, *Making Business Location Decisions* (Englewood Cliffs, N.J.: Prentice-Hall, 1982), 150. Adapted with permission.

site visit

Favorable Labor Climate   Location decision makers consider a number of factors in determining an area's labor climate. In general, those factors delineate the work force's degree of unionization, skill level, work ethic, and productivity, and public officials' attitudes. Existence of state right-to-work laws and the unionization of major area employers reveal the area work force's degree of unionization. Government information regarding work stoppages, productivity (value added per employee), and skill levels is available for most areas.

The location study team visits potential sites to gather impressions and to study attitudes regarding work ethic, absenteeism, labor-management problem resolution, and public officials. These visits will include discussions with major area employers as well as with elected officials, area chamber of commerce representatives, and people on the street. From these visits and the quantifiable labor criteria, the team gives the community a labor climate rating.

transport cost and time

Proximity to Markets   The nearness-to-market factor usually considers both logistics and competitive variables. Logistics variables include the transportation availability, freight cost, and market size within one day's transit time. The market size within one day's transit time indicates the market size available to the proposed location. The greater the number of firms within the market area, the greater the competitive advantage the proposed location offers.

employee well-being

Quality of Life   A particular area's quality of life is difficult to quantify, but it does affect employees' well-being. The quality-of-life factor is more important to companies that must attract and retain a professional and technical mobile work force capable of moving to any location. Such a situation is common in the high-tech industry, especially in a company's research and development operations. The *Places Rated Almanac*[1] rates the quality of life in metropolitan areas in terms of climate, housing costs, health care and environment, crime, passenger transportation, education, recreation, the arts, and economic opportunities.

raw materials availability

Proximity to Supplies and Resources   This determinant considers the availability and cost of raw materials and the cost of transporting those materials to the proposed plant site. The cost and availability of raw materials affect the proposed facility's initial and continued operation. Companies will locate a new plant where raw materials are available in quantities sufficient to permit the plant's continued operation. These companies may trade off higher operation costs against a location with available raw materials.

average earnings by occupation

Labor Rates   Labor cost and availability are significant locational determinants. Companies tend to place labor-intensive production facilities in low-labor-cost areas—for example, the South. But the location of facilities requiring technical expertise will emphasize such labor's availability rather than its cost. The primary cost factor companies consider is the average hourly earnings by industry and occupation, data that governmental agencies provide.

environmental permits

Other Factors   Table 12–1 contains locational determinants we have not yet discussed. Though we would consider these additional factors unimportant in the general location decision framework, any one could be important for a specific firm. Environmental permits are quite important in the decision to locate a plant to produce industrial organic or inorganic chemicals or certain types of drugs. The taxes area includes both business and personal taxes. Business taxes

taxes

affect the operating costs in an area, and personal taxes affect the area's cost of living and the wages a company must pay.

Industrial Development Incentives   A final locational determinant Table 12–1 does not specifically delineate is industrial development incentives communities use to entice companies to locate in their area. Some examples are tax incentives (reduced rates on or tax abatement from things such as property, inventory, or sales), financing arrangements (state loans), reduced water and sewage rates, and rent-free buildings that the community builds to the company's specifications. Most states have an industrial development commission that provides information about state and local inducements.

Company Policy   We must consider our discussion of determinants in light of a company's specific needs. Before undertaking any facility location analysis, the decision maker must receive information from top management about the company's facility location policy. This policy will help the analyst to avoid concentrating upon a location determinant top management deems unimportant.

For example, a company's policy may locate all new facilities in rural areas within fifty miles of an urban center. Thus, the decision maker should exclude all possible locations elsewhere. Or a company's policy may locate warehouses where competitors have located warehouses. These policies may vary for different facilities (plant versus warehouse versus technical center). But whatever the policy, in order to avoid wasting analysis time and money, top management should help the decision makers to establish an appropriate determinant hierarchy.

FACILITY LOCATION AND LOGISTICS

improper location

As we noted earlier, a facility's location directly affects the creation of time and place utility in goods. An improper facility location can result in added costs or unacceptable logistics service levels. For example, an improper facility location may not have sufficient carriers available to provide link service; may be located outside a city's commercial zone, where the rates quote in the city will not apply; may be unable to transport raw materials or finished goods economically; and may increase transit times, reducing customer service or increasing inventory carrying costs.

staff function

Location analysis is a logistics department staff activity. In order to evaluate how alternative sites will affect logistics cost and quality, a company must involve the logistics department in the location decision. The department must accomplish this analysis in light of the firm's service levels policy and in light of the operational constraints production and marketing impose upon the logistics system. The location decision most often begins with determining the facility's least-transportation-cost area—a logistics determinant. The analysis then considers nonlogistic determinants such as availability and cost of land, power, and labor, as well as such nonquantifiable factors as a site's cultural, recreational, and educational opportunities.

transportation starting point

reducing potential sites

The first screening by the logistics determinant will usually eliminate logistically uneconomical areas, thereby reducing the number of alternatives. For example, consider the potential number of warehouse sites available in the Northeast market area. Applying the logistics location determinant, the decision maker may find that the logistically optimum location is in eastern Pennsylvania. This definitely reduces the number of potential sites and enables the decision maker to direct the location analysis toward a specific area.

The decision maker can also use the logistics determination in selecting specific site locations; he or she considers factors such as total logistics costs from various sites in the specific area and transport modes' accessibility from and to the proposed sites (see Table 12–1). Thus, the decision maker generally uses the logistics determinant at various location decision stages.

logistics service

Service level policy statements also significantly affect facility location, especially warehouse location. If corporate policy dictates that a company is to service ninety-five percent of demand within a two-day transit time, the company must establish the warehouse location with this requirement in mind. The company will eliminate any potential location that does not meet this requirement, given the transport mode the company utilizes. However, the decision-maker, who must be aware of various-size warehouses' operating economies, may need to expand the geographic area the warehouse serves to better utilize the facility and thereby reduce warehousing costs. But achieving the desired service level in this expanded area may require a more expedient transport mode (one providing lower transit time); that is, in achieving the desired service level a trade-off exists between warehousing costs and link costs.

service cost trade-off

departmental coordination

The location decision is another example of the required coordination between logistics and other corporate departments. The facility location directly affects logistics costs and the logistics service level the facility provides. These two logistics areas affect product price and competitiveness, manufacturing cost, and firm financing. A decision maker must consider these factors in determining a facility's optimum location.

TRANSPORTATION AND THE LOCATION DECISION

classical theories

As Appendix 12A indicates, the classical location theories considered transportation cost to be the major locational determinant. A facility's location with respect to markets and raw materials sources affected the total transportation cost and, hence, profitability. These theories emphasized selecting the location that minimized total transportation costs and, by implicit assumption, maximized profits.

Many location analyses today emphasize minimizing transportation cost. A new industrial facility's selected location should minimize inbound and out-

minimizing transportation cost

bound transportation costs. Companies apply an average transportation cost per ton per mile to the tonnage they purchase at raw materials sources and sell at markets and to the distance they will move this tonnage to and from a proposed site. The grid technique utilizes this concept.

Grid Technique

nature of approach

The grid technique helps companies with multiple markets and raw materials sources determine a least-cost facility location. Essentially, the grid technique attempts to determine a fixed facility (plant, warehouse) location that is the least-cost center for moving both raw materials and finished goods within a geographic grid. The technique determines the low cost "center of gravity" for moving raw materials and finished goods.

approach

This technique assumes that the raw materials sources and finished goods markets are fixed and that a company knows the amount of each product it consumes or sells. The technique then superimposes a grid upon the geographic area containing the raw materials sources and finished goods markets. The grid's zero point corresponds to an exact geographic location, as do grid's other points. Thus, the company can identify each source and market by its grid coordinates.

Figure 12–1 is an example a supply source and market environment for which a company is to locate a plant. The company, which has located supply sources and markets on the map and has superimposed a grid system over the source-market area, purchases raw materials from sources in Buffalo, Memphis, and St. Louis, Missouri—S_1, S_2 and S_3, respectively. The new plant will serve five markets: Atlanta, Boston, Jacksonville, Philadelphia, and New York—M_1, M_2, M_3, M_4 and M_5, respectively.

grid location

The technique defines each source and market location in terms of its horizontal and vertical grid coordinates. For example, the Jacksonville market (M_3) has a horizontal grid coordinate of 800 and a vertical grid coordinate of 300. The Buffalo source is located at grid coordinates 700 horizontal and 1,125 vertical.

strings, weights, and knot

We can visualize this technique's underlying concept as a series of strings to which are attached weights corresponding to the weight of raw materials the company consumes at each source and of finished goods the company sells at each market. The strings are threaded through holes in a flat plane; the holes correspond to the source and market locations. The strings' other ends are tied together, and the weights exert their respective pulls on the knot. The strings' knotted ends will finally reach an equilibrium; this equilibrium will be the center of mass, or the ton-mile center.

ton-mile center

We can compute this concept mathematically, finding the ton-mile center, or center of mass, as follows:

$$C = \frac{\sum_1^m d_i S_i + \sum_1^n D_i M_i}{\sum_1^m S_i + \sum_1^n M_i}$$

where

C = center of mass, or ton-mile center
D_i = distance from 0 point on grid to the grid location of finished good i

FIGURE 12–1 GRID LOCATIONS OF SOURCES AND MARKETS

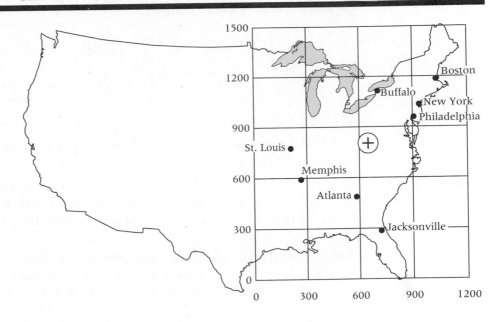

	Grid Coordinates	
Sources	Horiz.	Vert.
Buffalo (S₁)	700	1,125
Memphis (S₂)	250	600
St. Louis (S₃)	225	825
Markets		
Atlanta (M₁)	600	800
Boston (M₂)	1,050	1,200
Jacksonville (M₃)	800	300
Philadelphia (M₄)	925	975
New York (M₅)	1,000	1,080

d_i = distance from 0 point on grid to the grid location of raw material i

M_i = weight (volume) of finished goods sold in market i

S_i = weight of raw material purchased at source i

location and transportation rate

This equation will generate the least-cost location if transportation rates for raw materials and finished goods are the same. But transportation rates vary among commodities, and the ton-mile center equation does not reflect differences in the costs of moving commodities. The transportation rate pulls the location toward the location of the commodity with the higher rate. Thus, finished goods' higher rates will draw the least-cost location toward the finished goods market and thereby reduce the distance the company moves these higher-rated goods. This will increase the distance the company transports lower-rated raw materials.

Thus we must incorporate into our analysis different products' transportation rates. This modification is as follows:

$$C = \frac{\sum_1^m r_i d_i S_i + \sum_1^n R_i D_i M_i}{\sum_1^m r_i S_i + \sum_1^n R_i M_i}$$

where

R_i = finished good transportation rate/distance unit for finished good i

r_i = raw material rate/distance unit for raw material i

linear rates

R_i and r_i are the transportation rates per distance unit, and we assume them to be linear with respect to distance. This assumption does not correspond to the tapering principle of rates, but it simplifies the analysis.

simplicity

Advantages   The grid technique's strengths are in its simplicity and its ability to provide a location analysis starting point. Computationally, the technique is relatively easy to use. A company can generate the necessary data from sales figures, purchase records, and transportation documents (either the bill of lading or the freight bill). More exact market and source location coding is possible, as is modifying the rate-distance relationship quantification. A computer can easily handle such refinements.

starting point

The grid technique also provides a location decision starting point. As we suggested earlier, transportation cost is not the only locational determinant. Using the grid technique can eliminate certain areas, permitting the decision maker to focus on an area more logistically advantageous. For example, the grid technique may suggest Toledo, Ohio, as the least-cost location for a plant to serve the Ohio, Michigan, Indiana, and Illinois market area. This eliminates

eliminates sites

consideration of Chicago, Indianapolis, and other regional cities, and permits the decision maker to concentrate the location analysis in northwestern Ohio and southeastern Michigan. This is a tremendous step forward in the location decision process.

static

Limitations   The grid technique has limitations that the decision maker must recognize. First, it is a static approach; and the solution is optimum for only one point in time. Changes in the volumes a company purchases or sells, changes in transportation rates, or changes in raw materials sources or market locations

linear rates

will shift the least-cost location. Second, the technique assumes linear transportation rates, whereas actual transportation rates increase with distance, but

topography

less than proportionally. Third, the technique does not consider the topographic conditions existing at the optimum location; for example, the optimum site may

direction

be in the middle of a lake. Fourth, it does not consider the proper direction of movement; most moves occur along a straight line between two points, not "vertically" and then "horizontally."

Plant Location Example   Table 12–2 presents relevant data for a plant location example, as well as the grid technique solution using a computer spreadsheet program. The grid coordinates of the raw materials sources and markets correspond to their locations on the grid in Figure 12–1. For simplicity, we will

TABLE 12–2   GRID TECHNIQUE ANALYSIS OF PLANT LOCATION EXAMPLE

Sources/Markets	Rate $/Ton-Mile (A)	Tons (B)	Grid Coordinates		Calculations	
			Hor.	Vert.	(A) * (B) * Hor.	(A) * (B) * Vert.
Buffalo (S_1)	$0.90	500	700	1,125	315,000	506,250
Memphis (S_2)	$0.95	300	250	600	71,250	171,000
St. Louis (S_3)	$0.85	700	225	825	133,875	490,875
		1,500			520,125	1,168,125
Atlanta (M_1)	$1.50	225	600	800	202,500	270,000
Boston (M_2)	$1.50	150	1,050	1,200	236,250	270,000
Jacksonville (M_3)	$1.50	250	800	300	300,000	112,500
Philadelphia (M_4)	$1.50	175	925	975	242,813	255,938
New York (M_5)	$1.50	300	1,000	1,080	450,000	486,000
	TOTALS	1,100			1,431,563	1,394,438

	Horizontal	Vertical
Numerator: $\Sigma\,(r * d * S) =$	520,125	1,168,125
$+ \Sigma\,(R * D * M) =$	1,431,563	1,394,438
Sum	1,951,688	2,562,563
Denominator: $\Sigma\,(r * S) =$	1,330	1,330
$+ \Sigma\,(R * M) =$	1,650	1,650
Sum	2,980	2,980
Grid Center:	655	860

compute two coordinates

assume that this company produces only one type of finished good; so each finished good's rate is the same.

To determine the least-cost center on the grid, we must compute two grid coordinates, one for moving the commodities along the horizontal axis and one for moving them along the vertical axis. We compute the two coordinates by using the grid technique formula for each direction.

Table 12–2 gives this example's computations. The two columns at the far right contain the calculations the grid technique equation indicates. The first calculations column contains the calculations for the horizontal numerator, or the sum of the rate times the horizontal grid coordinate times the tonnage for each raw materials source and market. The calculations at the bottom of Table 12–2 indicate the numerator and denominator of the grid technique equation.

As Table 12–2 indicates, the plant location's least-cost center in this example is 655 in the horizontal direction and 860 in the vertical direction. We measure both distances from the grid's zero point. Figure 12–1 indicates the least-cost center as point +. The least-cost location for the plant is in southeast Ohio or northwest West Virginia in the Wheeling-Parkersburg area.

warehouse application

The preceding example applied the grid technique to a plant location. Companies can use the technique to solve warehousing location problems as well. The company follows the same procedure, but the company's plants are the raw material sources.

Sensitivity Analysis   As we mentioned before, the grid technique is a static approach; and the computed location is valid only for the situation analyzed. If the transportation rates, market and source locations, and volumes change, the least-cost location changes.

what if

Sensitivity analysis enables the decision maker to ask "what if" questions and measure the resultant impact on the least-cost location. For example, the decision maker may examine the least-cost location in light of a five-year sales projection by inserting the estimated market sales volumes into the grid technique equation and determining the least-cost location. Other "what if" scenarios could include adding new markets and/or sources, eliminating markets and/or sources, and the switching transportation modes, thereby changing rates.

rate increase

Tables 12–3 and 12–4 perform two sensitivity analyses for the original problem in Table 12–2. The first "what if" scenario considers switching from rail to truck to serve the Jacksonville market; the switch entails a fifty percent rate increase. The data in Table 12–3 show that the rate increase shifts the least-cost location toward Jacksonville; that is, the new location grid coordinates are 664 and 827, or east and south of the original location (655,860). Therefore, a rate increase will pull the least-cost location toward the market or supply source experiencing the increase.

eliminate source

The second "what if" sensitivity analysis considers the elimination of a Buffalo supply source and increasing by 500 tons the amount the example company purchases from Memphis. Table 12–4 shows this sourcing change's effect. With Memphis supplying all the material the company formerly purchased from Buffalo, the new least-cost location moves toward Memphis, or south and west of the original location. Similarly, a new market or a market experiencing a sales volume increase will draw the least-cost location.

conclusions

We can conclude from these sensitivity analyses that the rates, product volumes, and source/market locations do affect a plant's least-cost location. The least-cost location moves toward a market or source experiencing a rate or volume increase, and away from the market or source experiencing a decrease. Introducing a new market or source pulls the location toward the additional market or source.

TABLE 12–3   IMPACT OF RATE CHANGE ON LEAST-COST LOCATION

Sources/Markets	Rate $/Ton-Mile (A)	Tons (B)	Grid Coordinates Hor.	Grid Coordinates Vert.	Calculations (A) * (B) * Hor.	Calculations (A) * (B) * Vert.
Buffalo (S_1)	$0.90	500	700	1,125	315,000	506,250
Memphis (S_2)	$0.95	300	250	600	71,250	171,000
St. Louis (S_3)	$0.85	700	225	825	133,875	490,875
		1,500			520,125	1,168,125
Atlanta (M_1)	$1.50	225	600	800	202,500	270,000
Boston (M_2)	$1.50	150	1,050	1,200	236,250	270,000
Jacksonville (M_3)	$2.25	250	800	300	450,000	168,750
Philadelphia (M_4)	$1.50	175	925	975	242,813	255,938
New York (M_5)	$1.50	300	1,000	1,080	450,000	486,000
	TOTALS	1,100			1,581,563	1,450,688

	Horizontal	Vertical
Numerator: $\Sigma \, (r * d * S) =$	520,125	1,168,125
$+ \, \Sigma \, (R * D * M) =$	1,581,563	1,450,688
Sum	2,101,688	2,618,813
Denominator: $\Sigma \, (r * S) =$	1,330	1,330
$+ \, \Sigma \, (R * M) =$	1,838	1,838
Sum	3,168	3,168
Grid Center:	664	827

TABLE 12–4   IMPACT OF SUPPLY SOURCE CHANGE ON LEAST-COST LOCATION

Sources/Markets	Rate $/Ton-Mile (A)	Tons (B)	Grid Coordinates Hor.	Grid Coordinates Vert.	Calculations (A) * (B) * Hor.	Calculations (A) * (B) * Vert.
Buffalo (S_1)	$0.90	0	700	1,125	0	0
Memphis (S_2)	$0.95	800	250	600	190,000	456,000
St. Louis (S_3)	$0.85	700	225	825	133,875	490,875
		1,500			323,875	946,875
Atlanta (M_1)	$1.50	225	600	800	202,500	270,000
Boston (M_2)	$1.50	150	1,050	1,200	236,250	270,000
Jacksonville (M_3)	$2.25	250	800	300	450,000	168,750
Philadelphia (M_4)	$1.50	175	925	975	242,813	255,938
New York (M_5)	$1.50	300	1,000	1,080	450,000	486,000
	TOTALS	1,100			1,581,563	1,450,688

	Horizontal	Vertical
Numerator: $\Sigma\,(r * d * S) =$	323,875	946,875
$+\ \Sigma\,(R * D * M) =$	1,581,563	1,450,688
Sum	1,905,438	2,397,563
Denominator: $\Sigma\,(r * S) =$	1,355	1,355
$+\ \Sigma\,(R * M) =$	1,838	1,838
Sum	3,193	3,193
Grid Center:	597	751

Application to Warehouse Location in a City   A special case exists for applying the grid technique to the location of a warehouse in a city. The situation's uniqueness comes from the blanket rate structure, which applies the same rate from an origin to any point within the city or commercial zone. Thus, any location within a city's commercial zone will incur the same inbound transportation cost from a company's mix of suppliers used; that is, the cost of moving supplies to a warehouse within the same city will not affect the location decision.

Since the supply volumes moving into the warehouse do not affect the location decision, the least-cost warehouse location within a city considers the cost of moving finished goods from the warehouse to the customers. We modify the grid technique equation as follows:

$$C = \frac{\sum_{1}^{n} R_i D_i M_i}{\sum_{1}^{n} R_i M_i}$$

If we assume that the cost of distributing (R) the commodity throughout the city will be the same, R cancels out, reducing the equation to a ton-mile center as follows:

$$C = \frac{\sum_{1}^{n} D_i M_i}{\sum_{1}^{n} M_i}$$

As before, this modified grid technique will enable the decision maker to eliminate certain areas of the city and to concentrate the analysis upon sites in the general vicinity of the least-cost location's grid coordinates. To determine a specific site for the warehouse, the decision maker must consider land and facility availability, expressway systems, and highway access in this general vicinity.

Transportation Pragmatics*

The previous discussion showed the transportation factor's importance in the facility location decision. We simplified the rate structure focus on the transportation factor's locational pull. In this section, we will examine how dropping these transportation simplifications affects facility location, directly attention specifically toward tapering rates, blanket rates, commercial zones, and in-transit privileges.

Tapering Rates   As we pointed out earlier in the text, transportation rates increase with distance but not in direction proportion to distance. This tapering rate principle results from the carrier's ability to spread certain fixed shipment costs, such as loading, billing, and handling over a greater number of miles. As Edgar M. Hoover noted (see Appendix 12A), tapering rate in one-source, one-market situations pulls the location to either the source or the market, but not to a point in between.

To illustrate this effect, consider the data in Table 12–5 and Figure 12–2. In this example, we assume the rates to be constant (the same) for raw materials supplied at S and finished products sold at M. The rates in Table 12–5 increase with distance, but not proportionally. For example, the shipping rate from S is $2.00 for 50 miles and $3.00 for 100 miles, a distance increase of 100% but a rate increased of only 50%.

Table 12–5 and Figure 12–2 indicate that a location at either S or M will result in a total rate of $3.70. At any other location the total rate is higher. Thus, the tapering rate pulls the location toward the source or the market.

Dropping rate constancy between raw materials and finished goods draws the location toward M, the market. In Table 12–6 and Figure 12–3 the rates for moving the finished product into the market are higher than those for moving raw materials. The least-transportation-cost location is at M, where the total transportation rate is $3.70.

Blanket Rates   A noted exception to the preceding rate structure is the blanket rate. The blanket rate does not increase with distance; it remains the same from one origin to all points in the blanket area. The carriers establish such rates to

TABLE 12–5   LOCATIONAL EFFECTS OF TAPERING RATES WITH CONSTANT RATE ASSUMPTION

Distance from S (miles)	Transport Rate from S	Distance from M (miles)	Transport Rate from M	Total Transport Rate
0	$0.00	200	$3.70	$3.70
50	$2.00	150	$3.50	$5.50
100	$3.00	100	$3.00	$6.00
150	$3.50	50	$2.00	$5.50
200	$3.70	0	$0.00	$3.70

*Adapted from Edward J. Taaffe and Howard L. Gauthier, Jr., *Geography of Transportation* (Englewood Cliffs, N.J.: Prentice-Hall, 1973), 41–43.

FIGURE 12–2 LOCATIONAL EFFECTS OF TAPERING RATES WITH CONSTANT RATE ASSUMPTION

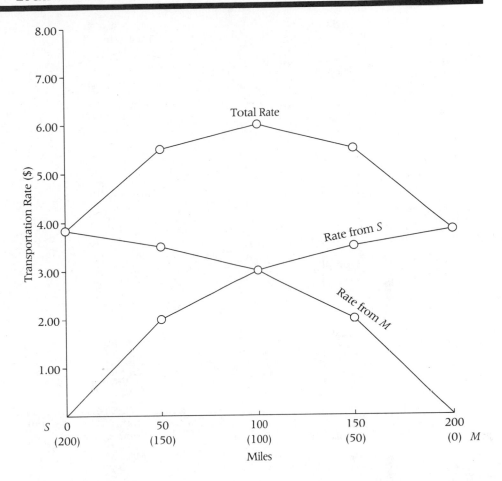

ensure a competitive price for a product in a given area, thereby ensuring demand for the product and its transportation. An example of a blanket rate would be the same rate on wine from the West Coast to all points east of the Rocky Mountains, enabling the West Coast wine to compete with imported wines entering the East Coast.

eliminates transportation factor

The blanket rate eliminates any transportation cost advantage or disadvantage companies associate with a given location. In the case of the wine blanket rates, the West Coast wine producers can effectively compete in the East Coast market area with East Coast and foreign producers. The blanket rate, then, is a mutation

TABLE 12–6 LOCATIONAL EFFECTS OF TAPERING RATES WITHOUT CONSTANT RATE ASSUMPTION

Distance from S (miles)	*Transport Rate from S*	*Distance from M (miles)*	*Transport Rate from M*	*Total Transport Rate*
0	$0.00	200	$5.20	$5.20
50	$2.00	150	$5.00	$7.00
100	$3.00	100	$4.50	$7.50
150	$3.50	50	$3.50	$7.00
200	$3.70	0	$0.00	$3.70

FIGURE 12–3 LOCATIONAL EFFECTS OF TAPERING RATES WITHOUT CONSTANT RATE ASSUMPTION

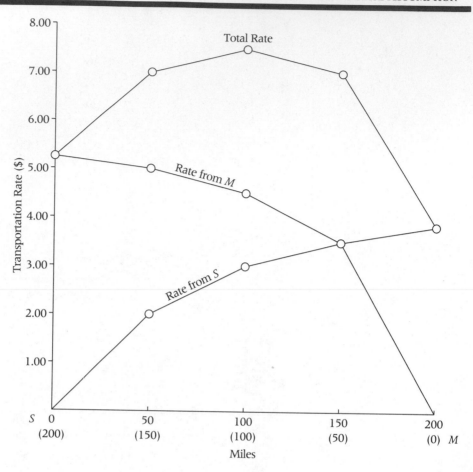

of the basic rate-distance relationship that eliminates the transportation rate as a locational determinant; it is the exception rather than the rule in transportation rates.

transportation definition of a city

Commercial Zones A specific blanket area is the commercial zone, the transportation definition of a particular city or town. It includes the municipality itself plus various surrounding areas. The commercial zone rates carries quote to a particular town or city also apply to points in the surrounding area within the commercial zone.

rates

The commercial zone's locational impact appears near the end of the location decision process when a company selects a specific site. If the specific site is beyond a municipality's commercial zone, rates that apply to the city will not

carrier availability

apply to the site. Also, a site outside the commercial zone reduces carrier availability, especially the availability of motor carriers that define their operating scopes in terms of point-to-point operations.

stop shipment to perform processing

Transit Privileges Basically, the transit privilege permits the shipper to stop the shipment in transit and to perform some function that physically changes the product's characteristic. The lower through rate from origin to final destination (the tapering rate principle) applies, rather than the higher combination of rates from origin to transit point and from transit point to final destination.

MAXWELL HOUSE PICKS JACKSONVILLE: TO CLOSE HOBOKEN

David beat Goliath. At least that's how some people are looking at it. In the battle between Jacksonville, Florida and Hoboken, New Jersey, to keep each city's Maxwell House processing plant open, Jacksonville has to come out the winner.

Americans' changing lifestyles prompted the need to eliminate one of the two plants.

"People aren't drinking coffee like they used to. There has been twenty-four percent decrease in coffee consumption in the United States since 1963," explained Frank Meegan, operations manager for Maxwell House. "Yet, we are still operating the same four plants we operated then, even though we use only fifty-five percent of their production capacity. Therefore, we must eliminate this excess."

And, in eighteen months, that's exactly what they will have done.

Maxwell House will expand the Jacksonville plant to process forty percent more coffee. Meegan indicated that little additional construction would occur outside the existing Maxwell House structure, located across the street from the site of Jacksonville Shipyards, Inc.

The City of Jacksonville, the Jacksonville Port Authority and numerous business groups lobbied to "Keep Max in Jax." The city offered Maxwell House a $4.8 million incentive package to keep its plant open. Hoboken reportedly offered $7.1 million.

But the economics were clear. "It's cheaper to do business in Jacksonville," Meegan said. "We decided to stay in Jacksonville because our total costs were less here, and our assessment is that they will continue to be less in the future.

"Here, we are closer to important supply plants: the Houston plant, which provides decaffeinated beans; our lithography plant in Tarrant City, Alabama, which provides coffee cans; and Central America, which of course is an important source of coffee beans."

In 1988, just over 90,000 tons of coffee moved over Jacksonville's docks. Though that total is only a drop in an annual 4.5 million-ton cargo bucket, the port feels that the coffee trade is important because of the liner trade it represents.

It's too early to tell exactly what effects a bigger coffee processing plant will have on the city and the state, but, if the early economic ripples are any indication, it may well mean millions of dollars in increased business for a variety of maritime and transportation-related firms.

Adapted from James Lida, "Maxwell House Picks Jacksonville: To Close Hoboken," *American Shipper* 32, no. 8 (August 1990), 74. Reprinted with permission from the August 1990 issue of *American Shipper*.

The transit privilege essentially makes intermediate locations, not just origins or destinations optimum. The transit privilege eliminates any geographic disadvantage companies associate with a producer's location. The intermediate point the carrier designates as a transit point enjoys the lower, long-distance through rate that applies at either the origin or the destination.

Like the blanket rate, the transit privilege is not available at all locations or for all commodities—only those sites and commodities the carrier specifies with regulatory sanction. If a commodity benefits from a transit privilege's availability, the limited points the carrier tariffs specify will be prime facility location alternatives.

THE LOCATION DECISION WITH A NETWORK OF FACILITIES

Thus far, the discussion has centered on the relationships between logistics variables and the single facility location decision. For this, we suggested the grid

single facility versus network

technique for determining the least-transportation-cost location. In the system-wide facilities location decision, we must determine the optimum location for a facility network.

The grid technique requires us to identify a facility's markets, the quantities a company sells in each market, supply sources, and the quantity each source supplies. However, in the multiple facilities location decision, these factors are variables. Thus, the grid technique has limited ability to solve the multiple facilities location problem.

Essentially, the multiple facilities location problem is a basic system design analysis. A systemwide facilities location analysis examines the following net-work factors: facility number, size, and location; the market and source areas the network will link; and the items each facility will produce and store.

network factors

These basic questions are interrelated, and a decision in one area affects the decision a company will make in other areas. For example, the fewer number of system facilities, the larger the facility size. The decision to link customers with specific warehouses or plants defines a facility's market areas. The larger the market area, the larger the facility. Market area customers and supply sources determine, in part, the products a company produces and stores at a facility. These seemingly circular interrelated factors are the essence of the multiple facility location decision.

network factors interrelated

Firms have used a number of quantitative techniques to decide systemwide facility locations. These techniques include linear programming, heuristics programming, and simulation.

linear programming

Linear programming (LP)* is a technique that produces an optimum solution within the bounds decision constraints impose. The LP technique is most useful for linking facilities in a network where supply and demand limitations at plants, warehouses, or market areas are system constraints. Through a series of itera-tions, the LP technique defines the optimum facility distribution pattern con-sistent with the problem's demand-supply constraints. A company can then use the LP approach to evaluate distribution patterns and costs in light of existing plants, warehouses, and demand areas alternative locations and their supply-demand constraints. More sophisticated optimizational techniques include mixed integer linear programming and dynamic programming.

defines distribution pattern

Heuristic programming† is similar to the human thought process. Heuristic programming reduces a problem to manageable size and searches automatically through possible alternatives in an attempt to find a better solution. Heuristic programming does not guarantee an optimum solution, but it can provide a good approximation to the least-cost location in a complex location decision problem. To reduce the number of site alternatives, the decision maker incor-porates into the program site characteristics he or she considers optimal.

heuristic programming

simulates thought process

For example, the manager may consider an optimum warehouse site to be 1) within fifty miles of a major market area (a minimum average weekly sales of 25,000 units); 2) at least 250 miles from the company's other warehouses or plants; 3) within three miles of an interstate highway; and 4) within sixty miles of a major airport. The heuristic model searches for sites with these char-

---

*For an application of LP, see R. M. Burstall, R. A. Leaver, and J. E. Sussans, "Evaluation of Transport Cost for Alternative Factory Sites—A Case Study," *Operations Research Quarterly* (December 1962), 345–54.

†For example, see Alfred A. Kuehn and Michael J. Hamburger, "A Heuristic Program for Locating Warehouses," *Management Science* 9 (1963), 643–66.

simulation

acteristics, thus reducing the number of alternative sites those the decision maker considers practical.

Simulation‡ is a highly sophisticated tool with which the decision maker develops a mathematical model of a system. For location analysis, simulation allows the decision maker to test alternative locations' effects upon costs and service levels. The modeling requires extensive data collection and analysis to

system modeling

determine how system factors such as transportation, warehousing, inventory, materials handling, and labor costs interact. The simulation process evaluates the decision maker's selected sites to determine respective costs. Simulation does not guarantee an optimum solution, but it can evaluate the alternatives the decision maker feeds into it.

limitations

These three techniques are all valuable aids to the decision maker, but each has certain limitations. Computer capacity may be insufficient to handle large-size LP problems. Heuristics can handle any size problem, but it does not guarantee an optimal location as LP does. Simulation's mathematical modeling requires considerable (and possibly cost- and effort-prohibitive) data and expertise; it has no size limit, but it does not guarantee an optimum solution.

SUMMARY

This chapter examined the logistics variables that affect a logistics facility's location. A facility's location directly affects the logistics costs of creating time and place utility and the facility's customer service level. Marketplace dynamics change supplier and consumer characteristics, thereby requiring a company to locate a new logistics facility or to relocate an existing one.

A team of managers representing various functional areas makes the facility location decision. The team examines possible sites in terms of facility operating costs such as labor, fuel, taxes, and transportation and in terms of non-cost elements such as quality of life and company policy. Generally, a company gives the logistics variable initial consideration in the location decision process. This initial screening of potential sites reduces the potential locations to a manageable number for more in-depth cost and service analysis. Minimizing transportation costs is the objective in this initial phase.

The grid technique permits the decision maker to analyze the least-transportation-cost location for a facility serviced by multiple suppliers and serving multiple markets. Analyzing a facility network requires more advanced quantitative techniques such as linear programming, heuristic programming, and simulation.

STUDY QUESTIONS

1. Explain the relationship between a logistics facility's location and the efficiency of time and place creation.

2. Discuss the factors that cause a company to analyze a facility's location.

3. Why are most location decisions analyzed by a team of managers instead of merely one logistics manager?

‡For a discussion of simulation, see Martin L. Gerson and Richard B. Maffei, "Technical Characteristics of Distribution Simulators," *Management Science* 10 (1963), 62–69.

4. What are the major locational determinants and how does each affect the location decision?

5. Discuss the logistics variable's role in the decision to locate a plant or warehouse.

6. What is the grid technique? What are this technique's assumptions, advantages, and disadvantages?

7. Explain how tapering rates, blanket rates, commercial zones, and in-transit privileges affect the facility location decision.

8. How would you analyze a new warehouse's location, given a network of existing plants and warehouses?

9. Using the grid technique, determine the least-cost location for the following problems:

	Tons	Rate	Grid Coordinates (H,V)
S_1	200	0.50	2, 14
S_2	300	0.60	6, 10
M_1	100	1.00	2, 2
M_2	100	2.00	10, 14
M_3	100	1.00	14, 18
M_4	100	2.00	14, 6

Customer	Tons	Grid Coordinates (H, V)
A	100	1, 11
B	300	7, 11
C	200	5, 9
D	500	7, 7
E	1,000	1, 1

10. Describe the applicability of linear programming, heuristic programming, and simulation to facility location decision making.

NOTES

1. Richard Boyer and David Savageau, *Places Rated Almanac* (Chicago: Rand McNally, 1989).

CASE 12-1

ROLL FREE TIRE COMPANY

Roll Free Tire Company, a manufacturer of radial tires, sells its tires in the auto aftermarket and distributes them nationwide. It has three plants, located in Allentown, Pennsylvania; Toledo, Ohio; and Macomb, Illinois. The company the U.S. market divides into regions, and each region has a distribution warehouse. Normally, Roll Free ships tires to the distribution warehouse from the plants, but the company sends truckload shipments directly to customers. All shipments to a region move under truckload rates for 400 cwt.

Roll Free management is concerned about the most economical location for a distribution warehouse to serve its southeastern region (North Carolina, South Carolina, Georgia, Florida, Mississippi, Alabama, and southeastern Tennessee; see map). Currently, an Atlanta warehouse serves this region. Roll Free management believes that the Atlanta location is not the most logistically economical location.

To help the logistics department conduct a grid analysis of this region's warehouse location, Roll Free's traffic department developed the following data:

| 1991 Shipments to Atlanta | | | | Grid Coordinates | |
From	cwt	Rate/cwt	Mileage	Vertical	Horizontal
Toledo	15,000	$2.20	640	1,160	1,360
Macomb	5,000	2.43	735	1,070	980
Allentown	11,000	2.52	780	1,150	1,840

| 1991 Shipments from Atlanta | | Grid Coordinates | |
To	cwt	Vertical	Horizontal
Chattanooga	2,700	650	1,350
Atlanta	3,500	600	1,400
Tampa	4,300	220	1,570
Birmingham	2,800	580	1,260
Miami	5,300	90	1,740
Jacksonville	5,100	450	1,600
Columbia	2,200	650	1,600
Charlotte	2,900	740	1,590
Raleigh/Durham	2,200	800	1,700

The traffic department also determined that total freight expenditures from the Atlanta warehouse during 1991 were $217,000 and that the average shipment distance was 330 miles.

Case Questions

1. Based upon the preceding information, is Atlanta the best location for a distribution center to serve the southeast region?
2. The traffic department projects a twenty-five percent rate increase from all sources in 1992. How will this affect the Atlanta location?
3. Marketing anticipates that the Raleigh/Durham market will grow by 3,000 cwt in 1993. Roll Free will serve the growth from Allentown. How will this affect Atlanta as a location?

APPENDIX

12A

CLASSICAL THEORIES OF LOCATION

The purpose of this appendix is to indicate the development of location theory and the importance of transportation factors in this theoretical development. This discussion which provides the basis of the transportation location decision covers the theories of von Thunen, Weber, Hoover, and Greenhut.

VON THUNEN[1]

One of the first writers to theorize the production factors with respect to facility location was Johann Heinrich von Thunen. A German agriculturist, von Thunen was concerned with the location of agricultural production. In his theory, cost minimization (transportation cost) was the locational determinant.

The assumptions von Thunen utilized reduced the problem's complexity and allowed concentration upon the transportation variable. First, von Thunen assumed an isolated city-state that was surrounded by a plain of equal fertility. The plain ended in wilderness, and the city was the only market for the agricultural products. Production of any product would occur anywhere in the plain and at the same cost. Von Thunen assumed equally accessible transportation to all locations in the plain, and transportation costs were a function of weight and distance; that is, transportation cost was a constant rate per ton-mile for all commodities.

Agricultural production would take place where the farmer would maximize profits. Von Thunen determined profits as follows: profits equal market price minus production costs and transportation costs. With a given product's market price and production costs the same at any production location, the transportation cost factor was the major locational determinant.

According to von Thunen, locations farther from the city (market) would incur a greater transportation cost. Such locations would not be economically feasible for producing low-value, high-weight products, which would incur very high transportation costs they could not bear because of their low value-to-weight relationships. Thus, von Thunen concluded, those products should be produced near the city to minimize transport cost.

Another transport attribute von Thunen recognized as a locational determinant was transit time. Perishable products (fresh vegetables) would be produced near the city; the influential determinant was not transportation cost, but the time producers required to move the goods to the markets.* Such perishable products could not sustain long transit time and thus had to be produced near the city.

Von Thunen continued the analysis for various agricultural products and culminated it in by developing a series of concentric rings about the city. The rings, von Thunen's *belts,* delineated the products that should be produced at various distances from the city. Perishable products and products of low value-to-weight ratios would be produced in the belts nearest the city. Products with high value-to-weight ratios would be produced in the rings farther from the city.

The simplifying assumptions and concentration upon agricultural production location make von Thunen's theory seem unrealistic for the modern business firm. But his work remains a major part of the foundation upon which we predicate current location theory and forms a threshold for delineating the relationships between transportation costs and location theory. We also find his general conclusions still valid today. For example, land close to urban areas is expensive, and companies must use it intensively, possibly by building multi-storied warehouses.

WEBER[2]

Alfred Weber, a German economist, developed a theory for the location of industrial production facilities. Unlike von Thunen, Weber started with a given industry and determined its best location. He assumed equally accessible transportation and constant transportation costs with respect to weight and distance. Raw materials points and consumption points are known, and labor is geographically fixed and available at a given dollar amount.

Like von Thunen's analysis, Weber's analysis defines the optimum location as the point that represents the least-cost location. More specifically, the least-cost site is the location that minimizes total transportation costs—the costs of transferring raw materials to the plant and finished goods to the market. Thus, total transportation cost is the criterion Weber used to evaluate alternative plant locations.

Weber recognized that raw materials were different from a logistics standpoint. Raw materials possess two characteristics that directly relate to the total transportation costs they incur: geographic availability and weight lost in processing. With regard to geographic availability, a raw material is either ubiquitous or localized. A *ubiquity* is a raw material that we find everywhere (for example, water and air). A *localized* material is one that we find only in certain locations (for example, coal or iron ore). In addition, a raw material can be either pure or weight-losing. A *pure* raw material does not lose weight in processing (a pure raw material's entire weight enters into the finished product's weight). A *weight-losing* raw material loses weight during production. Therefore, a raw material may be ubiquitous and pure, ubiquitous and weight losing, localized and pure, or localized and weight losing.

---

*Mechanical refrigeration was nonexistent at this time, so this was a practical solution to the problem. Perishability is still a factor today, in spite of advanced technology.

Raw materials' ubiquitous and localized characteristics define their geographic fixity and the need to transport them to and from proposed plant locations. By definition, ubiquities occur everywhere and thus would not require transportation to the plant site. Thus, ubiquities place no constraints upon a production facility's location. However, ubiquities generally favor location in the market, as the following analysis shows.

A localized raw material does not occur everywhere and therefore necessitates transportation (and corresponding transportation costs) for any location other than its supply source. Usually, the greater the plant's distance from the localized material source, the greater the material's transportation costs. But we must recognize the weight lost in processing, since this affects the total transportation cost for localized raw materials and finished goods.

The pure and weight-losing characteristics directly affect the total amount of weight a company will transport and correspondingly affects total transportation costs (for raw material and finished goods) at various plant locations. Since localized pure raw materials lose no weight in processing, their entire weight enters into the finished product's weight. Assuming only one material and one market, a localized pure raw material's total transported weight will be the same both to and from the plant. However, with a localized weight-losing material, a supply-source location can minimize the material's transported weight and consequently minimize transportation costs. That is, by having the location at the weight-losing raw material supply source, a company avoids transporting the weight the material loses in processing.

One Market, One Supply Source

Now let us consider some examples of Weber's location theory. To accomplish this, we will utilize the situation in Figure 12A–1. We will determine the least-cost location for a production facility which utilizes raw materials of different characteristics in the production process. The transportation rate is $1.00 per ton-mile for both moving raw materials and finished goods.

First, if the one raw material the facility uses is ubiquitous, either pure or weight-losing, the least-cost location is at M. At M, no cost the raw material or its finished good incurs no movement cost. This location is possible because the ubiquity is available at RM as well as at M. One example of such a situation is the soft drink industry. With water being the primary raw material and a ubiquity, soft drink bottlers can locate in various local markets and can eliminate transporting water from, for example, New York to the Toledo market area. Since water is available in Toledo as well as in New York, the bottler can minimize total transportation costs by simply locating in Toledo.

FIGURE 12A–1   ONE MARKET, ONE RAW MATERIALS SOURCE

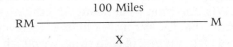

100 Miles

RM ————————————————— M

X

RM = raw materials source
M = market
X = midpoint between RM and M

Second, assume a company uses a pure localized raw material weighing one ton to produce one unit of finished good (FG) weighing one ton. To determine the least-cost location, we must analyze the total transportation cost at the plant's possible locations. If the plant is located at RM, the total transportation cost per unit is $100 (RM = 1 ton, 0 miles or $0; FG = 1 ton, 100 miles or $100); the total transportation cost per unit is also $100 for a plant located at M (RM = 1 ton, 100 miles or $100; FG = 1 ton, 0 miles or $0). If the plant is located at point X in Figure 12A–1, the total transportation cost per unit is also $100 (RM = 1 ton, 50 miles or $50; FG = 1 ton, 50 miles or $50). Thus, the least-cost location using a pure, localized raw material is RM, M, or anywhere in between on a straight line connecting the two. This led Weber to conclude that pure materials cannot bind production to their deposits.

Third, let us assume a company uses a localized weight-losing material weighing one ton to produce one unit of finished good weighing one-half ton. Again, we will analyze the alternative plant locations in terms of total transportation costs. A location at RM will result in a total per-unit transportation cost of $50 (RM = 1 ton 0 miles, or $0; FG = ½ ton, 100 miles or $50). The locations at X and M will result in total per-unit transportation costs of $75 and $100, respectively. The least-cost location for a localized weight-losing raw material is the material's source; at this location, the company does not transport the weight lost in processing.

Considering a situation with one raw material source and one market helps us to grasp the fundamental relationships between transportation costs and a production facility's location under varying raw material situations. However, an industrial firm rarely operates in such a simplified situation. Weber expanded his analysis to consider two sources and one market. We will consider this in the following section.

Two Raw Materials Sources, One Market

Weber approached this problem by considering the advantage of locating the production facility in relation to this situation's three terminals (the market and the two raw materials sources). The two supply sources now complicate the effects of raw materials characteristics upon transportation costs.

Weber formalized the location influence of the relative product weights and resultant transportation costs at the various terminals into a *material index:* the ratio of the sum of the localized raw material weights to the finished product's weight. If greater than one, the least-cost location gravitates away from the market toward the raw materials sources.

To determine which raw material source is the least-cost location when the material index is greater than one, Weber considered the relative pull the weight of the localized raw material exercised. He accomplished this through the location weight index (LWI), which he defined as the ratio of a material's weight at a terminal to the finished product's weight. Then, the least-cost location is the raw material source where the LWI is greater than the sum of the other LWIs. Envision a flat board with the market and raw material sources arranged in a triangle. We drill a hole at each terminal and pass a string through each hole. To one end of each string we attach a weight corresponding to the localized raw material and finished good weight at the terminal. We tie the other ends of the strings together on top of the board. When we release the weights and they transfer their respective locational pulls to the knot, the knot's final resting point is the optimum location.

Consider the four situations in Figure 12A–2. We will attempt to determine the optimum plant location for each, again assuming a constant transportation rate per weight/distance.

In example A in Figure 12A–2, a company combines a ubiquitous raw material weighing four pounds with two localized materials weighing four pounds and two pounds. The material index is 4 + 2 ÷ 8 = ¾, which is less than one. This tells us that the least-cost location is the market. The influence of the ubiquity pulling the location toward the market is evident in this example, as it is in the previous one-source, one-market example. (Justify this example's conclusion as well as those of the following examples by assuming distances between each terminal pair and a transportation rate and then calculating total transportation costs for various locations.)

Example B in Figure 12A–2 offers a situation in which a company utilizes two pure raw materials in the production process. The material index is 2 + 2 ÷ 4 = 1, and we conclude that the optimum location is the market. Any other location would increase the commodities transportation distance and therefore would be a higher-cost location.

In example C, both raw materials are weight-losing. The material index is 2 + 3 ÷ ½ = 10, and we conclude that the location should not be at the market but nearer the deposit source. To determine the specific deposit location, we use the location weight index. The LWI for R_1 = 2 ÷ ½ = 4, for R_2 = 3 ÷ ½ = 6, and for M = ½ ÷ ½ = 1. (The LWI for the market terminal is always one.) Next, we compare the LWI for one terminal with the sum of the others and find that the LWI for R_2 is greater than the sum of the others (6 > 4 + 1). Our conclusion is that the location will gravitate toward the R_2 location.

The last example, D, again involves two weight-losing raw materials; but the optimum location is not at any one of the three terminals. The material index of 4 + 4 ÷ 3 = 2 tells us to not locate at the market. The LWIs are as follows: R_1 = ⁴⁄₃, R_2 = ⅔, and M = 1. No LWI is greater than the sum of the others, and the conclusion is to not locate at any one of the terminals. The optimum location will be somewhere inside the triangle.

We can determine the optimum location for example D by evaluating the total transportation costs our example company would incur at the many alternative sites inside the triangle. However, this is a cumbersome mathematical

---

FIGURE 12A–2   TWO RAW MATERIALS SOURCES, ONE MARKET

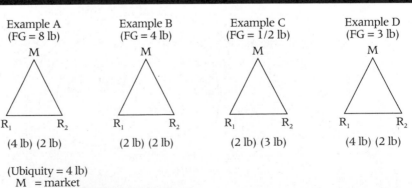

Example A
(FG = 8 lb)

Example B
(FG = 4 lb)

Example C
(FG = 1/2 lb)

Example D
(FG = 3 lb)

(Ubiquity = 4 lb)
M = market
R = raw materials source locations
FG = finished goods
Number in parentheses is the product weight

process. Considering more than two sources is also cumbersome. The grid technique, which basically expands the Weber approach, can facilitate many origins and many destinations in determining a facility's least-transportation-cost location.

Labor and Agglomeration Factors

Thus far, our discussion has concentrated upon how transportation affects the location decision. Weber then considered labor's locational pull by recognizing that labor costs vary at different locations. If labor costs less in a location other than the least-transportation-cost site, the firm will locate at the lower-labor-cost point provided that the labor savings offset the increased transportation costs. In essence, a cost trade-off exists between labor and transportation costs.

We can use *isodapanes* to show the effect of the labor savings or other production cost savings. Isodapanes are lines of equal, though not minimal, transportation costs around the least-transportation-cost site. Figure 12A–3 shows a series of isodapanes drawn around a one-market, two-source situation. Point M (the market) is the least-transportation-cost ($10) location. Any location on the isodapane labeled $12 will incur $12 total transportation costs. At point Y, which is on the $14 isodapane (a transportation cost point $4 greater than the least-transfer-cost point), if a company can purchase labor at a savings of $4 or more over that at M, the decision to locate at Y rather than M would be economically sound. The compound would similarly investigate other alternative sites, analyzing the trade-off between labor savings and increased transportation costs. Using isodapanes enables companies to readily examine these trade-offs.

In a similar trade-off analysis, Weber introduces another locational determinant that he calls *agglomeration,* a net advantage a company gains through a common location with other firms. A common location offers benefits such as a skilled labor supply, better marketing outlets, and proximity to auxiliary industries. (We term a net common location disadvantage *deglomeration.*) Again utilizing Figure 12A–3, point Y will be a desirable location if the agglomeration benefits of $4 or more offset point Y's higher transfer cost.

In summary, Weber's location analysis is a least-cost approach that emphasizes transportation costs. Assuming a constant, linear transportation rate is

---

FIGURE 12A–3   EXAMPLE OF ISODAPANES

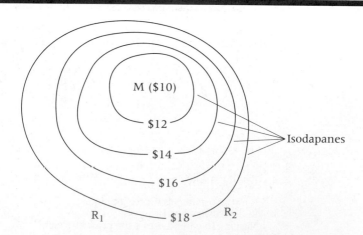

unrealistic, but we can eliminate the constant assumption by applying the actual rate for different raw materials or finished goods. Although Weber's theory inadequately handles more complex location decisions, its benefit lies in its easy application; and it can provide the decision maker with a location analysis starting point. The theory can reduce the alternatives, bringing the decision maker one step closer to determining an exact location. Weber's emphasis upon transportation costs as a locational determinant for industrial facilities is the basis of many other locational works.

HOOVER[3]

Edgar M. Hoover, an American theorist, investigated the optimum location of industrial facilities based upon cost factors. He also dealt with demand factors that von Thunen or Weber did not consider. His demand analysis relates to the definition of what the market area will be after a firm determines a location. His theories recognize distribution cost effects upon a product's price and resultant demand.

In terms of cost factors, Hoover greatly expanded the analysis of previous authors. He considered transportation costs, agglomerative forces, and industrial costs. In all three areas, Hoover's treatment is more inclusive than Weber's.

With regard to transportation costs, Hoover pointed out that rates are not linear with respect to distance. Most rates follow the tapering principle—rates increase with distance, but at a decreasing rate. This alters Weber's conclusions for localized pure raw materials in a one-market, one-source situation. Instead of requiring the decision maker to consider three location choices (market, raw material source, and anywhere in between), rate nonlinearity makes the location at either the market or the raw material source less expensive than one in between. Location in between would cause the two separate movements' rates to be greater than the one rate from raw material source to market.

Hoover also noted that transportation companies are not uniformly available throughout all areas. Companies desire locations in areas that have a high concentration of carriers, since they provide more alternative vendors to meet a logistics system's varied link requirements.

Hoover pointed out that the importance of transportation costs as a locational determinant varies for different firms. Transportation costs may be less important to firms that can ship in carload or truckload quantities than they are to firms that ship in LCL or LTL quantities. Product characteristics also affect carrier rates, and consequently influence the importance of transportation costs as a locational determinant.

Hoover's main contribution to location theory was his more-inclusive analysis of the cost factors affecting the location decision. Basically, he based his approach upon cost minimization.

GREENHUT[4]

Melvin L. Greenhut, another American theorist, emphasized demand as a locational determinant. He pointed out that demand is a variable that enables a company to realize different profits at different locations; thus, the location that maximizes profits is the optimum site, which may not necessarily coincide with the least-cost definition.

Greenhut grouped his important locational determinants into demand, cost, and purely personal factors. Demand and cost factors influence all site selections. Companies should include personal considerations, which partially determine demand or production costs, with demand or production cost determinants.

At this point, you may be concerned with the location difference between the cost minimization and profit maximization criteria. If we assume constant demand, the two criteria will result in the same location. Given differing demand at different locations, a high-cost location may provide higher profits because of its ability to charge higher prices.

NOTES

1. C. M. Warnenburg, trans., and Peter Hall, ed., *von Thunen's Isolated State* (Oxford, England: Pergamon Press, 1966).
2. Carl J. Friedrich, trans., *Alfred Weber's Theory of the Location of Industries* (Chicago: University of Chicago Press, 1929).
3. Edgar M. Hoover, *The Location of Economic Activity* (New York: McGraw-Hill, 1948).
4. Melvin L. Greenhut, *Plant Location in Theory and in Practice* (Chapel Hill: University of North Carolina Press, 1956).

LOGISTICS QUALITY

In their continuing quest for a competitive edge, companies are calling upon their logistics managers to find innovative ways to reduce cost, enhance service, and increase customer satisfaction. As a result, many firms have taken significant steps toward identifying and implementing logistics quality improvement processes. While some of these processes are consistent with corporate-wide quality initiatives, logistics frequently assumes a leadership role in terms of implementing a firm's formal quality process.

CREATING CUSTOMER VALUE THROUGH LOGISTICS MANAGEMENT

A growing number of firms serve as excellent role models in terms of logistics management's strategic impact. At companies such as L. L. Bean, Xerox, Frito-Lay, and McDonald's, logistics helps to create customer value in three important ways: efficiency, effectiveness, and differentiation.

resource utilization

Efficiency refers to the logistics organization's ability to provide the desired product/service mix at a cost level the customer finds acceptable. This emphasizes the need for logistics to manage resources wisely and to leverage expense into customer value whenever possible.[1] Firms have achieved some of the most significant efficiencies by committing themselves to improving and "reengineering" logistics processes.[2] Logistics operations' enhanced efficiencies translate directly into additional value for the firm's customers.

level of service

Effectiveness refers to performance, and whether the logistics function meets customer requirements. An excellent example of a company focusing on effectiveness is L. L. Bean, which has identified seven customer service "key result areas" (KRAs):[3] product guarantee, in-stock availability, fulfillment time (turnaround), convenience, retail service, innovation, and market standing (image).

uniqueness

Differentiation manifests itself logistically by creating value through unique logistical service. For example, The Limited Stores' Distribution Division creates overall system value by marking and tagging all merchandise prior to store delivery. Federal Express's Memphis PartsBank operation also creates customer value by maintaining inventories of repair and emergency parts for immediate shipment to locations throughout the world.

Trend Toward Formalization of Quality Processes

quality process

One of the currently popular trends is for firms to develop a commitment and dedication to a formal quality process. A formal quality process's evolution has four distinct phases (see Table 13–1). A greater emphasis on achieving customer satisfaction through customer—driven quality characterizes the shift from Qual-

TABLE 13–1   IMPLEMENTATION STAGES IN A QUALITY PROCESS

Stage	Characteristics
Quality Control (QC)	■ Defect-free services ■ Management-driven
Quality Assurance (QA)	■ 100% satisfied customer ■ Customer-driven
Total Quality Control (TQC)	■ Significant competitive advantage ■ Management, employees, customers, and vendors work toward a common goal
Customer Value	■ Emphasis on providing best comparative net value for the customer

ity Control (QC) to Quality Assurance (QA). Management, employees, customers, and vendors all working toward a common goal characterizes the evolution to Total Quality Control (TQC). The fourth phase, Customer Value, reflects the need to do things which create the best comparative net value for the customer.[4]

When examining the ways in which business firms have developed and implemented their respective quality processes, we become aware that discussing quality requires a wide range of terminology and a unique vocabulary. Firms may use different names for the phases we described above. For example, many people refer to TQM (Total Quality Management) rather than TQC. This text will rely more on intent and results, rather than on establishing precise, defensible definitions for each term.

Impact of Quality on Profitability

financial justification

An interesting finding of one of the widely–cited PIMS (Profit Impact of Marketing Strategy) studies was that "companies with high quality and high market share generally tend to have profit margins five times greater than companies at the opposite extreme."[5] Figure 13–1, which charts firms' returns on sales and investment (ROS) and (ROI) by the relative quality percentile in which their customers perceive them to be, supports this observation.

benefits

According to the study results, achieving superior quality yields two types of benefits. The first is that lower cost of quality implies overall cost lower than competitor organizations'. The second is that quality is frequently a key attribute in the purchase decision. The study also found that companies which ranked in the top third in terms of relative quality sold their products or services, on the average, at prices five to six percent higher relative to competitors than companies in the bottom half.

The next sections discuss quality concepts, quality "gurus," and a recommended logistics quality process. Then, after examining several quality analysis techniques which are useful in logistics, we will focus on logistics process improvement. Last, the chapter profiles several logistics quality successes and identifies keys to successful logistics quality processes.

QUALITY CONCEPTS

In 1990, *Traffic Management* convened a special roundtable of logistics executives to discuss logistics quality.[6] The participants included representatives of

FIGURE 13–1   RELATIVE QUALITY BOOSTS RATES OF RETURN   *Source: Profit Impact of Marketing Studies,* The Strategic Planning Institute (Cambridge, Massachusetts).

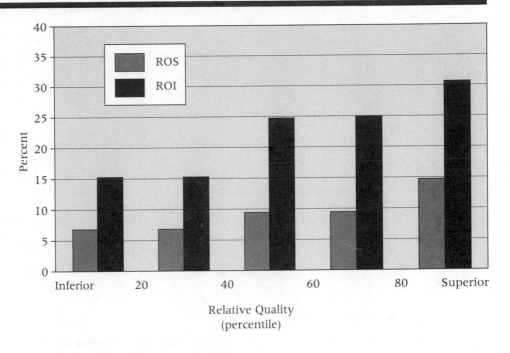

Relative Quality
(percentile)

quality roundtable   Xerox, Motorola, Dow Chemical USA, Westinghouse Electric, 3M, Johnson & Johnson, National Starch, and Xerox Corporation. Among the questions they discussed were the following:

- How do you define quality?
- How do you communicate a quality philosophy and culture to your people?
- How do you get the quality message across to your suppliers of logistics services?

issues   This section will discuss several fundamental issues relating to logistics quality and to quality in general. Examining each of these will set the stage for further investigating logistics quality. The following paragraphs are based on the quality roundtable's proceedings and on a broad base of experience relating to logistics quality.

Definition of Quality

quality defined   The roundtable group defined quality as "consistent satisfaction of customer requirements and expectations."[7] We can enhance this definition by including the notions of exceeding customer requirements, and, as Motorola does, trying to anticipate customer requirements.[8] These elements add a very aggressive and proactive tone to the definition of quality.

Emphasis on the Process

process emphasis   Although the roundtable did not discuss this specifically, firms generally agree that quality efforts should strive for process integrity, and should avoid measuring quality only by measuring output. Firms best serve logistics management's long-term interests by emphasizing sound processes and by developing logistics systems that meet, exceed, and anticipate customer requirements.

Also, firms should consider moving logistics emphasis from productivity to quality and actually achieving productivity through quality. Though this represents a difficult change of mindset for many firms, this shift in emphasis will produce significant results

Continuous Improvement

improvement

This concept requires an outlook that emphasizes continuous improvement at all levels. For example, delivery time windows are becoming shorter as more firms move toward legitimate just-in-time inventory systems. The continual narrowing of these time windows, say from four hours to two hours, can produce significant savings for both supplier and customer.

Cultural prerequisites to successful continual improvement efforts include recognizing internal and external customers; seeing that personnel throughout the organization play key roles; and adopting a consistent vocabulary and terminology that responds to the external customer's language and priorities.

Elimination of Waste and Rework

meeting specifications

For some time, firms have thought of the elimination of waste and rework as essential to a successful quality effort. As a result, logistics managers have increasingly emphasized "doing it right the first time," rather than trying to achieve quality through rework and uneconomical inspection activities. In the order picking area, for example, logistics has focused more on reducing and eliminating "mispicks," rather than on trying to correct such errors once they have occurred.

This issue relates to the concept of quality cost, which suggests that the benefits of taking preventive action will outweigh the expense of quality assurance (inspection) and of internal and external service failures. Table 13–2 provides examples of each of these quality costs.[9]

Measurement and Concern for Variability

process variability

Suggested here is that using statistical methods may be a very effective component of a firm's quality process. Since these approaches (which we will discuss later in this chapter) can help to identify logistics processes that may be statistically out-of-control, they can provide helpful diagnostic value to the logistics quality improvement process.

TABLE 13–2   CALCULATING THE COST OF QUALITY

Component	Logistics Example
Assurance	Inspection, testing, quality data collection
Prevention	Training and education
Internal failure	Expediting, special ordering, substituting
External failure	Production downtime, stockout cost

Total Organizational Commitment

quality culture

The quality roundtable group felt strongly that people throughout the organization, including executives, managers, supervisors, and workers, should promote the total quality effort. Most successful quality processes have benefited from having a "champion" in the form of a top executive or manager who assumes responsibility for assuring the quality process's integrity and implementation.

Dedication to a Formal Quality Process

formal process

Last, firms should consider using a formal quality process to achieve customer value through logistics quality. While some firms have maintained an excellent reputation for product and service quality in their customer's eyes, a greater likelihood of long-term, sustainable improvement will accompany adherence to a formal quality process. This observation applies to the entire firm as well as to the logistics area. Major sections of this chapter dwell on the importance of having a formal quality process and on enumerating the essential steps in such a process.

A structural necessity in the formal quality process will be to identify a firm's requirements and to communicate them to both suppliers and customers of the firm. Understanding suppliers' as well as customers' key processes will help to remove cost from the system, a common objective for firms which have formed partnerships or strategic alliances.

QUALITY GURUS

In recent years, a number of experts and/or visionaries have emerged in the quality area. The list of "quality gurus" includes names such as Deming, Juran, Crosby, Taguchi, and Ishikawa.[10]

This section, which briefly comments on several of the more prominent personalities in the quality area, does not purposely exclude any person or any set of principles or teachings. Rather, the objective is to discuss the prominent contributions of people such as those we have named above.

Dr. W. Edwards Deming

Dr. Deming

Probably the most widely known of the quality gurus, Dr. W. Edwards Deming spent considerable time working with the Japanese on the topic of quality in the post-war 1950s and 1960s. His original involvement was to help the Japanese conduct a population census, but his work quickly expanded into statistical process control, or SPC. This approach utilizes statistical techniques to gain insight into process behavior and represents an invaluable resource in efforts to understand process variability.

Deming's theories center around the distinction between variation due to common causes and that due to special causes. The former is inherent in the system under investigation; we sometimes refer to this as natural variation. The latter is due to specific causes which have resulted in instances of behavior which differ significantly from the behavior desired. Deming's use of SPC and techniques such as the control chart help to determine when "special" causes of variation might be present and to identify and remove these causes.

Deming also advocates customer research and the need to understand the customer and his/her needs. His teachings and philosophies place a high priority on a dedication to continuous improvement, which he considers a structural component of an effective quality process.

Dr. Joseph M. Juran

Dr. Juran

One of Deming's contemporaries, Juran also found the Japanese quite receptive to his ideas on the topic of quality. While he also advocated many of the analytical approaches Deming suggested, Juran had a pronounced interest in quality's managerial aspects.[11] His commitment to translating customers' needs into understandable and actionable terms via his "quality planning roadmap" approach and his guidance for improving on a "project-by-project" basis have served as excellent guidelines for implementing a quality process.

Philip B. Crosby

Philip Crosby

This third guru has established himself through well-known maxims such as "quality is free" and "do it right the first time." Sometimes called "the P. T. Barnum of the quality business," Philip Crosby has made a considerable impact on logistics and on business in general through his teachings and philosophies.

Crosby's main theme is that "quality is conformance to requirements" and that understanding customer requirements is a necessary first step in any quality process. His emphasis on the cost of quality has helped managers to understand that improving quality can actually reduce costs overall. As we discussed previously, this reduction would rely on defining quality cost as the sum of expenses relating to quality assurance, prevention, and internal and external failure.

Others

Numerous others have significantly affected United States and global businesses in the area of quality.[12] Some of these include Genichi Taguchi, who is responsible for developmental work on the quality loss function and the quality function deployment (QFD) approach; Kaoru Ishikawa, who developed the fishbone diagram as well as other statistics oriented quality tools; and Taiichi Ohno, who was instrumental in conceptualizing and implementing the kanban system at Toyota.[13]

Selecting a Suitable Approach

Figure 13–2 places total quality management elements in the context of the teaching and principles of Deming, Juran, and Crosby and illustrates the structural components of these experts' approaches to quality. In practice today, however, it is not unusual for a firm to incorporate elements of various approaches to quality in its own quality process. As a result, the logistics manager must know about all of the approaches to and philosophies of quality, in order to make informed decisions from the available alternatives.

LOGISTICS QUALITY PROCESS AND QUALITY ANALYSIS TECHNIQUES

A recent study at the University of Tennessee found that nineteen of the twenty-two major U.S. corporations the study examined had some formal quality process

FIGURE 13–2   ELEMENTS OF TOTAL QUALITY MANAGEMENT   *Source:* C. John Langley, Jr.; Mary Holcomb; Joel Baudouin; Alexander Donnan; and Paul Caruso, "Approaches to Logistics Quality," *1989 Council of Logistics Management Annual Conference Proceedings* (Oak Brook, IL: CLM, 1989), 85.

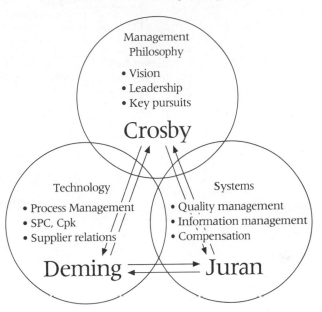

Elements of Total Quality Management

University of Tennessee study

in place.[14] Although some of the processes were more comprehensive and highly structured than others, the fact that this many firms indicated at least some evidence of a commitment to quality was reassuring.

Logistics functions are exhibiting a trend toward identifying and committing to formal quality processes. Firms such as Hewlett-Packard, Xerox, Procter & Gamble, Dow Chemical, Campbell Soup Company, Rohm & Haas, IBM, and General Motors have taken significant quality process initiatives.[15] Inbound and outbound logistics represent key ways for a firm to enhance the value it provides to its external customers. Successfully implementing a logistics quality process enhances not only the value-added for external customers, but also improves internal activities' efficiencies and ease of coordination.

This section outlines a suggested way to look at the overall quality process as it may apply to a firm's logistics function. Before implementing such a process, the logistics manager will want to examine the matter carefully and make an informed decision as to the quality strategy specifics he or she will consider.

Steps in the Quality Process

logistics quality process

Figure 13–3 indicates the six major steps in the development of a logistics quality process.[16] We will discuss each step briefly below.

Step 1: Organizational Commitment   Top management must be the driving force behind the commitment to quality. This applies not only to corporate general management, but also to the vice president or the director of logistics. People at these levels must be fully dedicated to the objectives they must meet

FIGURE 13–3   LOGISTICS QUALITY PROCESS   *Source:* C. John Langley, Jr., "Quality in Logistics: A Competitive Advantage," *Proceedings—R. Hadly Waters Logistics and Transportation Symposium* (University Park, PA: Penn State University, The Center for Logistics Research, 1990), 33.

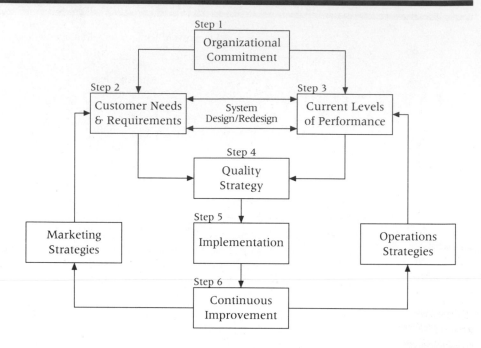

and the initiatives they must take. Also, these executives must provide the resources and encouragement their people need to produce tangible results from the commitment to quality.

Quality processes commonly fail due to lack of top management commitment. An unwillingness to sacrifice short-term productivity, for example, is a telltale sign that a manager may resist necessary improvement efforts. But a logistics function able to engage managerial commitment can usually achieve "productivity through quality," and, by adhering to a formal quality process, actually lower the cost of doing business.

At the outset of a formal quality process, logistics should have meaningful, well-developed statements of mission, goals, and objectives. This step helps logistics to assume leadership with regard to the quality area.

customer needs   **Step 2: Customer Needs and Requirements**   Emphasis here is on specifically and scientifically understanding the needs and requirements of the logistics function's customers. While companies traditionally focus on the logistical needs of the firm's external customers, understanding the needs of the firm's internal customers is equally important. This exceptionally important recognition might include people in areas such as marketing, manufacturing, and finance, as well as logistics co-workers.

Identifying customer needs and requirements is not always straightforward and obvious. More often than not, this step requires a rigorous examination of customers and their needs and the use of approaches such as customer studies, focus groups, and structured interviews.

Besides achieving a one-time understanding of customer needs and requirements, a firm should regularly monitor the marketplace's changing priorities.

While a firm may direct internal resources to such a task, this activity may justify using an outside consultant or service to regularly provide objective information.

Finally, firms desiring a successful quality process should begin to think of their suppliers, vendors, and channel partners as "customers." Firms throughout a truly integrated supply chain must share significant coordination and singularity of purpose. A shortsighted firm's failure to view these other entities as customers will prove counterproductive to the total quality effort.

Step 3: Current Levels of Performance This step includes obtaining accurate and meaningful measures of current performance levels, in direct relation to the specific needs and requirements we identified in Step 2. For this information to be valid and useful, a firm must acquire it specifically and scientifically.[17]

benchmarking

In addition to identifying suitable performance measures in key areas such as transportation, inventory, warehousing, information processing, and packaging, some form of benchmarking will likely prove valuable to the logistics quality process. We will discuss this topic in this chapter's next section, which deals with quality analysis techniques.

Once Steps 2 and 3 are underway, a firm is likely to identify—and immediately implement—short-term initiatives in logistics system design/redesign.

quality strategy

Step 4: Quality Strategy The term "quality strategy" really refers to the specific initiatives the logistics area selects as cornerstones to its overall quality process. Perhaps the first significant step is to study the teachings and philosophies of several of the quality advocates, or gurus, whom we discussed in the preceding section. While the firm should consider many approaches, its ultimate priorities should focus on areas such as

- Understanding the customer's needs;
- Continuous improvement;
- Measuring performance levels and monitoring variability;
- Appropriate initiatives for education and training; and
- Importance of overall organizational commitment

Step 5: Implementation As is the case with any formal quality process, smooth, effective implementation is essential for success. Thus, a firm should direct considerable attention to designing an overall quality strategy which will "roll out" productively and smoothly.

This step has significant logistics implications. Many of the more important people to include in the quality process are inventory control specialists, warehouse and dock workers, vehicle drivers, product packaging personnel, and order entry clerks and staff. These people, who most easily affect the service levels the logistics function's internal and external customers receive, are in a position to make a truly positive contribution to the overall quality process.

A meaningful implementation plan should include a timetable and a comprehensive list of necessary resources. These will help to assure the successes of well-conceived quality process.

Step 6: Continuous Improvement While a dedication to continuous improvement represents the sixth step in the quality process, the real benefit will accrue from modifying and enhancing the firm's marketing and operations strategies. Though we might tend to think of this as the "last" step in the quality process, it is a reminder that the process should be a continuing one and that an effective, meaningful quality process really has no end as such.

In terms of creating value for the customer, a formal commitment to quality represents another way for logistics to deliver the service quality essential to a firm competing in today's marketplace.

Quality Analysis Techniques

Successful logistics quality processes have utilized a number of tools and techniques. Most prominent among these are the flow chart, cause and effect diagram, check sheet, Pareto analysis, histogram, run chart, control chart, and scatter diagram/correlation chart.[18] These approaches can help to identify and understand logistics quality issues and to remove causes of quality failures. In effect, these are the basic tools of process improvement; and they are very applicable to logistics quality issues.

Statistical process control (SPC) refers to the use of statistical methods to better understand process variability. Although SPC is sometimes used generally to refer to the various types of quality approaches discussed in this section, the control chart technique is the only one which truly involves the use of statistical methods.

An interesting logistics quality issue is that of inventory inaccuracy, which may occur when a discrepancy exists between actual on-hand inventory and computer records of on-hand inventory. Using this issue as an example, Figure 13–4 shows how a firm might use each basic quality analysis tool for overall process improvement. The paragraphs below describe the basic tools in additional detail.

flow chart   **Flow Chart** Perhaps the simplest quality analysis technique, the flow chart is probably the most helpful in terms of overall process improvement. Basically, the flow chart is a pictorial representation of a process's components and their relationships. The flow chart represents perhaps the most logical starting point in any quality improvement process.

The flow chart provides an effective way to illustrate sequential activities and to document and gain insight into a process. In Figure 13–4(a), immediately after receiving a shipment at a logistics facility, a firm evaluates whether the quantity received is accurate. If so, the firm enters shipment data and places the incoming product in stock. If not, the firm must notify the vendor and reconcile the matter. The flow chart shows how a firm may receive, fill, pack and ship a customer order; how the customer may accept or return it; and how the parties complete the transaction.

Overall, the flow chart, truly among the more valuable quality analysis techniques, is excellent for identifying problem areas and for generating ideas for process improvement and efficiency.

fishbone diagram   **Cause and Effect Diagram** Sometimes called a fishbone chart, the cause and effect diagram visually represents the relationships between some quality issue, or effect, and all possible causes affecting this issue. Figure 13–4(b) shows how a firm might use a fishbone diagram to represent the problem of inventory inaccuracy. As the figure indicates, the major causes include information systems, company personnel, vendors, and policies and procedures. Subsequently, the firm should refine each major cause into problem sub-causes.

One way to produce a meaningful cause and effect diagram is to utilize group brainstorming to generate ideas and identify possible causes which may relate to the quality issue at hand. The use of brainstorming, either structured or unstructured, helps considerably in clearly understanding the process or sub-process within which the problem lies.

check sheet

Check Sheet   The check sheet, which facilitates the use of other quality analysis techniques, is perhaps the most commonly used method for collecting and compiling data. A technique with significant diagnostic value, the check sheet tells how frequently a phenomenon might be occurring. As Figure 13–4(c) shows, the check sheet represents a useful way to characterize inventory discrepancies by product type.

Pareto analysis

Pareto Analysis   Named after economist Vilfredo Pareto, this technique directs attention toward areas and causes which most relate to the quality issue under consideration. Figure 13–4(d) shows how a firm may apply Pareto analysis to inventory discrepancy and indicates the frequency of each major cause Figure 13–4(b) identifies.

Frequently, firms display Pareto analysis results in bar chart form. The Pareto chart identifies the causes on the horizontal axis and their frequency on the vertical axis. Typically, the chart lists causes from left to right in order of decreasing frequency. Figure 13–5 is an example of a Pareto chart that a firm has constructed for analyzing freight bill error types.

In effect, Pareto analysis, which involves continually breaking down larger problems into smaller ones, helps firms to focus on areas offering the greatest potential for improvement.

histogram

Histogram   This tool displays the distribution of a specific quality issue's measurement data. For example, the data might relate to logistics concerns such as transit times, order or item-fill percentages, damage experience, and information system response times. Using the inventory inaccuracy example, Figure 13–4(e) shows how frequently inventory discrepancies of differing dollar amounts occur. This information is essential to better understanding this quality issue's financial impact.

A histogram's shape can provide useful clues about the causes of quality problems. For example, the histogram might appear to be bimodal, possibly indicating that the firm has gathered data from two separate populations. An example of this would be in measuring transit times between points in a firm's logistics system. The transit time distribution during peak traffic periods might be considerably different from the off-peak distribution. A firm would need to anticipate concerns such as this and make appropriate adjustments to data collection and analysis procedures.

run chart

Run Chart   A forerunner to the control chart, the run chart provides a graphical summary of data in time-order sequence. A firm can use this technique to monitor a system or a process to observe whether its behavior seems to be changing over time. It essentially uses the same type of data as the histogram but exhibits the data in time-order sequence.

Figure 13–4(f) is a run chart showing the behavior of the inventory accuracy percentage over time. Please note that the graph relates to the behavior of inventory accuracy, rather than inaccuracy. This helps the firm to focus on the

FIGURE 13–4   QUALITY ANALYSIS TECHNIQUES   *Source:* C. John Langley, Jr. Reprinted with permission.

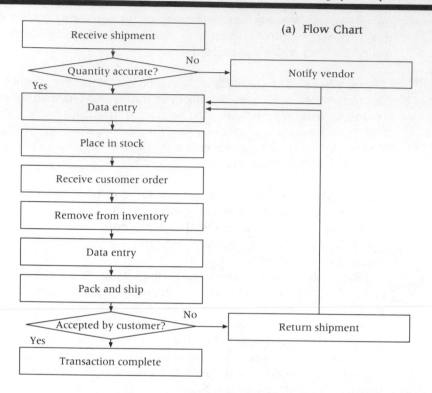

(a) Flow Chart

(b) Cause and Effect Diagram

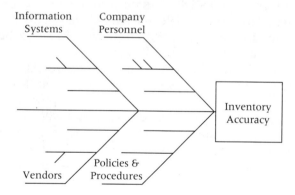

(c) Check Sheet

Product Type	No. of Discrepancies	Total
Canned	ЖТ ЖТ II	12
Boxed-dry	IIII	4
Boxed-frozen	ЖТ ЖТ ЖТ ЖТ III	23
Bagged	ЖТ IIII	9
Total		48

(d) Pareto Analysis

Cause of Inventory Discrepancy	Frequency of Occurrence	Cumulative Frequency
Information Systems	45	45
Company Personnel	25	70
Vendors	20	90
Policies and Procedures	10	100

FIGURE 13–4   QUALITY ANALYSIS TECHNIQUES   *Source:* C. John Langley, Jr. Reprinted with permission.
Continued

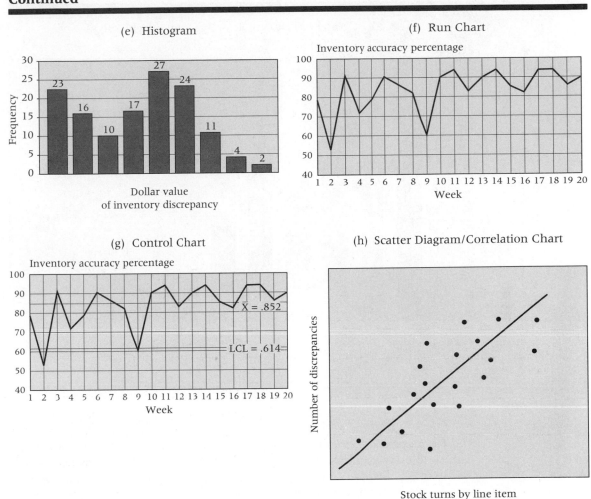

(e) Histogram

Dollar value
of inventory discrepancy

(f) Run Chart

Inventory accuracy percentage

(g) Control Chart

Inventory accuracy percentage

$\overline{X} = .852$

LCL = .614

(h) Scatter Diagram/Correlation Chart

Number of discrepancies

Stock turns by line item

quality issue's positive, rather than the negative, aspects. As this diagram shows, the inventory accuracy ranges from about fifty percent in week 2 to approximately ninety-five percent in weeks 11, 14, 17, and 18. Overall, an upward trend in accuracy seems to be occurring; and this is certainly desirable.

control chart

Control Chart The control chart goes one step beyond the run chart by establishing upper and lower control limits above and below the process average.[19] Statistically determined, control limits are based on the data the firm used to construct the chart. We must not confuse control limits with customer specifications. The firm derives control limits from statistically-based measures of process performance; specifications represent performance standards which the customer sets.

variability

Recognizing that most data will exhibit some degree of variability, a firm must distinguish between (1) variability which is inherent in the process, or which is due to common causes; and (2) variability which is due to special causes, ones that may cause specific points to be out-of-control. The control chart is useful for discovering the presence of any special causes of variability

FIGURE 13–5   PARETO ANALYSIS OF ERROR TYPES ON FREIGHT BILLS   *Source:* C. John Langley, Jr., Reprinted with permission.

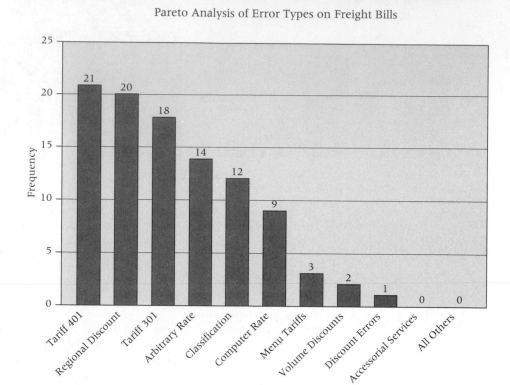

Pareto Analysis of Error Types on Freight Bills

and for judging the extent to which common cause variability exists. Ideally, a firm should set the highest priority on achieving consistent performance, which would imply low levels of variability. After identifying and removing the special causes, the firm can accomplish systemic change by reducing the process's inherent, natural variability.

Figure 13–4(g) is a control chart for inventory inaccuracy. As drawn, it is identical to the run chart except for the lines for the process mean ($\bar{x} = .852$) and the lower control limit (LCL = .614). This implies that logistics management should try to identify the special cause responsible for allowing the inventory accuracy percentages in weeks 2 and 9 to dip below the lower control limit. Although we might expect Figure 13–4(g) to contain an upper control limit as well, no inventory accuracy percentage is so high as to be cause for concern.

Providing an example of a control chart having both upper and lower control limits, Figure 13–6 illustrates a study of transit time performance in which a firm measured transit times in minutes between its logistics system's key points. The subsequent analysis would first identify and remove the causes of the out-of-control points in weeks 3 and 15. Then, the firm should attempt to lessen the inherent variability of the transit time measurements.

scatter diagram   **Scatter Diagram/Correlation Chart**   Figure 13–4(h) shows how a firm may graph the number of inventory discrepancies against stock turns by line item. The theory here is that items that move more frequently into and out of inventory

Figure 13–6   Control Chart   *Source:* C. John Langley, Jr. Reprinted with permission.

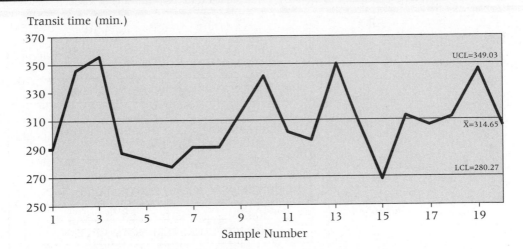

Transit time (min.)

are more likely to have a greater number of discrepancies. The data in the scatter diagram (sometimes called a correlation chart) seem to support this theory.

To further investigate the information Figure 13–4(h) contains, we might wish to conduct a correlation analysis of the data in order to conclude whether any association, or statistical relationship, exists between the two variables.[20] We should not confuse this with concluding whether or not a cause and effect relationship exists.

Additional Tools   Logistics departments use a growing number of quality analysis tools and techniques. Prominent among these are benchmarking, quality function deployment, and customer research.

benchmarking   *Benchmarking* Popularized by Xerox Corporation, competitive benchmarking may be defined as "the continuous process of measuring products, services, and practices against the toughest competitors or those companies recognized as an industry leaders."[21]

Interestingly, Xerox's early competitive benchmarking efforts in 1979 actually preceded its integration into the more comprehensive Leadership Through Quality strategy. As a result of this corporate commitment to a comprehensive quality process, Xerox was recently named a winner of the Malcolm Baldrige National Quality Award.

Figure 13–7 identifies the steps in the benchmarking process. The process requires ten formal steps and several identifiable stages: planning, analysis, integration, action, and maturity. Table 13–3 identifies categories important to benchmarking in logistics and names companies which have achieved success in these areas.

QFD   *Quality Function Deployment (QFD)* Japanese companies such as Toyota principally refined this approach, which originated in 1972 at Mitsubishi's Kobe shipyard plant.[22] Since then, a growing number of U.S. firms such as Digital Equipment, Hewlett-Packard, AT&T, Procter & Gamble, ITT, Ford Motor, and General Motors Corporation have seriously investigated QFD.

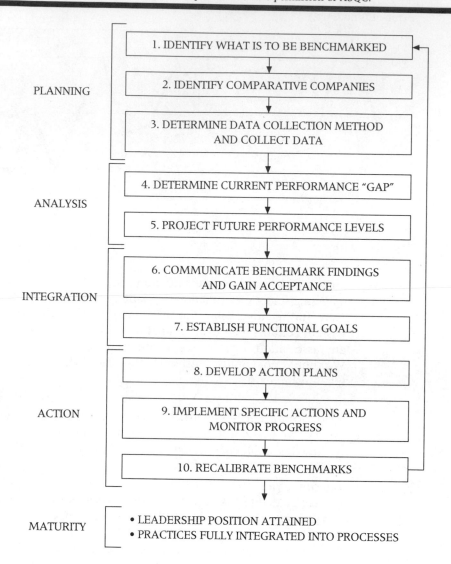

Essentially, QFD focuses and coordinates capabilities within an organization, in order to design, manufacture, and market goods that are desired by the customers. The foundation of QFD is the belief that products should be designed to reflect customers' preferences and priorities. As a result, marketers, design engineers, and manufacturing personnel must work closely together to produce a product which will meet the customer's requirements.

Firms implement the QFD technique through the "house of quality" approach, which helps to determine how well a company has aligned its strengths and capabilities with its customers' needs and helps to make improvements when mismatches are obvious. While QFD logistics applications to date have been exploratory and generally proprietary, more firms are using this tool for quality analysis and improvement.

TABLE 13–3   Companies That Exemplify Logistics Benchmarking

Automated inventory control	Westinghouse
	Apple Computer
	Federal Express
Billing and collection	American Express
	MCI
Customer service	Xerox
	Nordstrom, Inc.
	L. L. Bean
Manufacturing operations management	Hewlett-Packard
	Corning, Inc.
	Philip Morris
Purchasing	Honda Motor
	Xerox
	NCR
Quality process	Westinghouse
	Florida Power & Light
	Xerox
Warehousing and distribution	L. L. Bean
	Hershey Foods
	Mary Kay Cosmetics
Transportation	Japan National Railways
	Singapore Airlines
	Federal Express

Source: Adapted from David Altany, "Copycats," *Industry Week* (5 November 1990), 14.

customer research **Customer Research** This topic involves conducting customer-related logistics research on a continuing basis. A firm adhering to an effective quality process should have competitive information continually available, in order to serve purposes relating to benchmarking and overall logistics service quality.

In addition, good marketplace feedback about logistics activities will help a company to see whether its performance meets its customers' expectations. This chapter's next section, which deals with gap analysis as a means to logistics process improvement examines this type of corporate self-study.

LOGISTICS PROCESS IMPROVEMENT THROUGH QUALITY ANALYSIS

customer service model Figure 13–8 depicts a contemporary model that helps firms to study sales response (or customer response) to logistical customer service. Developed by R. Mohan Pisharodi, and discussed by Pisharodi and Langley, the perceptual process model of customer service suggests that firms may explain market response by analyzing how suppliers and customers perceive actual service levels and by analyzing comparable levels of service among competing suppliers.[23] As Figure 13–8 shows, the bases for the analyses, or perceptions, include past experience, industry standards and norms, standards of competitors, and situational requirements. The model suggests that this approach will help firms to better understand individual suppliers' customer service decisions, as well as customer response in terms of sales revenues firms may attribute to individual suppliers. Empirical testing through the analysis of information from buyer-seller dyads, or matched pairs, has confirmed the validity of this approach.[24]

ON THE LINE

L. L. BEAN, INC.

L. L. Bean, Inc., a speciality merchandise direct marketer based in Freeport, Maine, was founded in 1912 by Leon L. Bean. An avid outdoorsman, Bean started the company bearing his name when he acquired a mailing list of Maine hunting license holders and began advertising a superior lightweight dry boot. In the initial three-page brochure promoting the boot, Bean guaranteed "perfect satisfaction in every way," establishing the beginnings of a company founded on product quality and superior service.

In the following years, L. L. Bean has grown into a company which mails over seventy million catalogs yearly and whose annual sales total over $300 million. In order to meet demand, L. L. Bean maintains approximately 80,000 SKUs and does business with around 2,000 suppliers. The company dispatches approximately 100,000 packages per day during peak business periods.

As important as product quality is to Bean's success, customer service ("treat your customers like human beings"/"provide superior personal service") has probably most influenced the company's ability to attract and retain customers. All of the company's products come with an unconditional guarantee of satisfaction, meaning that if for any reason a customer is dissatisfied with a product, L. L. Bean pledges to replace it or refund the purchase price.

In addition to its 100 percent guarantee, L. L. Bean has used the concept of key result areas (KRAs) to meet objectives in critical areas throughout the firm. In the customer service area, the seven KRAs include product guarantee, in-stock availability, fulfillment time (turnaround), convenience, retail service, innovation, and market standing (image). By setting measurable objectives for each of these logistics and customer service areas, L. L. Bean is able to improve the multiple dimensions of service the company's customers consider important.

Source: Adapted from Bernard J. LaLonde, Martha C. Cooper, and Thomas G. Noordeweier, *Customer Service: A Management Perspective* (Oak Brook, IL: Council of Logistics Management, 1988), 117–121.

---

gap analysis

Figure 13–8 also identifies five critical discrepancies, or gaps, which may exist in this model. Firms should close these gaps in order to achieve customer satisfaction and sales response.[25] We will briefly discuss each in order to show how quality analysis tools and techniques may reduce these discrepancies.

Gap 1: A firm may close the gap between supplier and customer expectations by using better customer research and logistical benchmarking. In combination, these will help to assure greater congruity between the expectations held by suppliers and customers.

Gap 2: A supplier may close the gap between his or her expectations and the system a firm uses to meet those expectations (i.e., customer service decisions) by committing to greater overall service quality and by using quality function deployment (QFD) to help a firm translate supplier expectations into actionable customer service decisions.

Gap 3: Involved here is a discrepancy between customer service decisions and the actual service levels a firm provides. Using statistical methods such as SPC will help a firm to understand variability and to bring actual service levels closer to what the firm designed the system to provide.

Gap 4: Sometimes the customer's service level perception may differ from the actual level a firm provides. This may occur, for example, if the customer has inaccurate measurements of actual service quality, or if the customer

FIGURE 13-8   A PERCEPTUAL PROCESS MODEL OF CUSTOMER SERVICE   *Source:* Adapted from R. Mohan Pisharodi and C. John Langley, Jr., "A Perceptual Process Model of Customer Service Based on Cybernetic/Control Theory," *Journal of Business Logistics* 11, No. 1 (1990), 35.

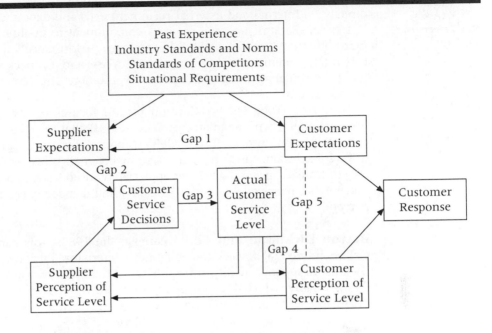

has a different perception of the service levels he or she has received. More effective communication between supplier and customer may close this gap, particularly if the supplier ensures that the customer's service measurement techniques are valid. Also, suppliers may find that providing customers with measurement data (perhaps in the form of statistical process control charts) can help to reduce this gap.

Gap 5: Perhaps the most important gap, this refers to a discrepancy between the logistics service quality customers expect and the service they receive. In effect, this gap's magnitude will depend on the extent to which customers and suppliers perceive gaps 1 through 4 to exist. Thus, closing gap 5 will depend on the meaningful application of quality analysis techniques such as benchmarking, customer research, QFD, statistical process control, measurement accuracy, and communications between suppliers and customers.

KEYS TO SUCCESSFUL LOGISTICS QUALITY PROCESSES

In many firms today the logistics area has taken a leadership role in designing and implementing quality processes. This section outlines several firms' approaches to and accomplishments in logistics quality.

Quality Successes in Logistics

Hewlet-Packard Company[26]   Quality has been a primary focus for Hewlett-Packard (HP), a leader in computers and information systems, since its beginnings in 1939. Although the teachings and philosophies of Dr. W. Edwards

Deming have strongly influenced the company, it has also learned from other sources, essentially creating a unique quality plan customized to HP's needs. The company bases its philosophy on a total commitment to quality and focuses directly on internal and external customer needs and expectations.

quality versus quantity

Hewlett-Packard has reinforced its commitment to quality by replacing the word "quantity" with "quality" in employee performance appraisals. Also, HP is strongly committed to using customer surveys and feedback systems to maintain a continual awareness of customer expectations and perceptions of logistics service quality.

TQC

HP's TQC (Total Quality Control) process focuses on real customer needs. For example, when Canadian customers told HP that they desired exceptionally consistent transit times, HP-Canada's customs and traffic department used TQC to find a solution. Most shipments had involved air transport; by using trucks, HP cut transit times in half. In addition, HP reduced freight costs by sixty-seven percent (a savings of $1 million annually) and damage expense by eighty-four percent.

Becton Dickinson and Co.[27]   Early in the 1980s, this company that specializes in medical devices and equipment, internalized its belief that "at Becton Dickinson, superior quality is the only way." In implementing its quality process, this company, which has principally followed the teachings and philosophies of Dr. Joseph M. Juran, in recent years has organized at least 160 active quality teams in thirty different locations worldwide.

quality projects

The first non-manufacturing quality project at Becton Dickinson involved distribution. In order to maintain low or nonexistent damage levels for finished products, the company embarked on a formal breakthrough project to identify and remove causes of product damage. As a result of this formal commitment to process improvement, Becton Dickinson reduced damage by an estimated forty-five percent. To achieve this improvement, the company installed dock levelers, established written and visual damage standards and truck loading standards, used rack storage in place of bulk storage and "skee" sheets in place of slip sheets, and instituted training for all warehouse employees. Also, the management information system department is developing a damage analysis system for continuous quality improvement.

A major contributor to Becton Dickinson's quality process success has been the company's commitment to team efforts at quality improvement. Experience with this concept has significantly influenced the results the company has achieved.

internal customers

Intel Corporation[28]   The Corporate Logistics Components Network Group at Intel Corporation has defined its mission as a commitment to optimizing the delivery pipeline of Intel products (semiconductor microprocessors) from the inbound internal customer through the outbound customer to the external customer. The group has accomplished this goal by effectively using logistics expertise and resources to provide the customer with a cost-effective, precise delivery process.

The accuracy and flexibility of the company's North American delivery system and Intel's commitment to improving responsiveness reveal the company's logistics quality focus. The quality process involves identifying customers' business requirements and designing a set of resources capable of satisfying those requirements. Because of this quality effort, Intel established a North America distribution center for its products.

Intel has also improved its Asia Pacific operations by reducing throughput time to the customer and by more efficiently controlling freight enroute to destination countries. Increasing delivery frequency has also enhanced customer satisfaction.

Finally, Intel has enjoyed significant success with changes in its product packaging approaches, specifically in going from twenty-three-inch tubes to twenty-inch tubes and in eliminating styrofoam peanuts from its packaging. Results included improved packaging quality, reduced cost, enhanced safety, and significant product/packaging design and freight cost savings.

DuPont Company[29] Implementing total quality management in the complex multinational chemicals producer Dupont, involves sensitizing the organization, setting direction and establishing a business mission, developing a quality management system, and institutionalizing a quality process and philosophy. DuPont believes that cultural change will accompany long-term sustained gain.

DuPont's approach to quality represents a unique response to the collective directions suggested by several of the prominent quality philosophies. This approach reveals DuPont's efforts to customize a quality plan to meet its own needs and the requirements of its external as well as internal customers.

logistics quality successes

DuPont's logistics success included improving supplier-customer coordination (which resulted in on-time delivery), finished product appearance, and product quality.

Federal Express[30] The first service organization to receive the prestigious Malcolm Baldrige National Quality Award, Federal Express is very much involved in the logistics business. A time sensitive transportation service that has grown from handling seven packages on its first night of operation in 1971 to a volume that sometimes exceeds one million packages per night, Federal Express has become one of the best-managed and operated companies in the world.

customer service

Central to Federal Express's quality process success is the company's commitment to its PEOPLE-SERVICE-PROFIT philosophy. Addressing two specific customer service aspects, fast delivery and peace of mind, Federal Express significantly affects customers not only through its high-quality service, but also through technological advances such as COSMOS (Customer Oriented Services and Management Operating System), DADS (Digital Dispatching System), and SuperTracker (for reading barcoded packages at origin and destination).

Federal Express also credits its quality process success its top management's commitment to change, its dedication to employee training and involvement, its belief that Federal Express can use information to differentiate itself from its competitors, and a sincere desire to serve the customer.

Averitt Express, Inc. This $200 million less-than-truckload motor carrier operating principally in the Southeast U.S. has been recognized over the past several years by *Distribution* magazine as one of its "quality carriers." Based on the belief that "Our Driving Force is People," Averitt's founder Gary D. Sasser credits the people of the company as the principal reason for its success in the quality area, and its average growth rates of nearly 35 percent for nearly 20 consecutive years.

Averitt Express has made a significant impression on its customers, as evidenced by the fact that it has been a multi-year winner of the "Partners in Quality" award presented by 3M Corporation. In addition, it has been recognized for its emphasis on quality by The American Productivity and Quality Center, and selected by Saturn Corporation as its indirect materials transportation coordinator.

The success of Averitt can be credited to its customer-driven business philosophies, which see to it that customer needs are foremost in the minds of all of Averitt's associates. Additionally, the company's aggressive programs relating to customer satisfaction, electronic data interchange, and working with a network of other regional less-than-truckload motor carriers have helped to ensure its customer responsiveness.

In addition to the companies we described above, firms such as 3M ("Partners in Quality" program), Campbell Soup Company ("Total Systems" approach), Xerox Corporation ("Leadership through Quality"), and Milliken & Co. have enjoyed logistics quality success.

Suggested Approach for Implementation

To conclude the discussion on logistics quality, this section focuses on steps that can increase the likelihood of a quality process's success. After examining a suggested implementation approach, we will discuss the Malcolm Baldrige National Quality Award.

Besides a formal quality process, such as the one Figure 13–3 indicates, a number of implementation priorities may enhance a company's success. The paragraphs below identify six priorities, listed in suggested implementation order.

quality audit   First, conducting a logistics area *quality audit* should help to identify quality improvement opportunities. This should be a relatively formal examination of the firm's logistics processes and the gaps existing between supplier and customer expectations.

quality education   Second is a *formal two- to three-day course for executives and managers on logistics quality and quality processes.*

quality process   Third, the firm should consider the *elements of the quality process,* including executives/managers', supervisors', and workers' educational needs. The firm should also delineate additional quality process elements, including timing and responsibilities, in this step.

quality projects   Fourth, accomplishing specific *quality improvement projects* will best promote logistics quality. Quality improvement teams should address specific quality issues and communicate these issues to others in the logistics area.

educational sessions   Fifth, after providing executives and managers with formal logistics quality education and completing a few quality improvement projects, a firm should *introduce quality education to supervisors and workers.* The firm must design these educational sessions with the intended recipient in mind and should view them as critical to the overall logistics quality process's success.

implementation   Sixth is *full implementation and continuous improvement.* The logistics quality process should be quite helpful in creating customer value through efficiency, effectiveness, and differentiation in the firm's logistics area.

Malcolm Baldrige National Quality Award[31]

Congress established the Malcolm Baldrige National Quality Award in 1987 to recognize U.S. companies' specific quality achievements and to promote a general awareness of quality among American businesses. Named in honor of the late Malcolm Baldrige, who served as U.S. Secretary of Commerce from 1981 to 1987, the award is presented in three categories: manufacturing, services, and small businesses. The government can give up to two awards yearly in each category.

Both privately owned and public companies incorporated and located in the United States are eligible, and winners can advertise the fact that they have won an award.

Baldrige award criteria

Among award recipient criteria are leadership, information and analysis, planning, human resource utilization, quality assurance, quality assurance results, and customer satisfaction (see Figure 13–9).

SUMMARY

This chapter has presented thoughts and observations relating to logistics quality. Logistics quality represents a key strategy for achieving customer value through logistics efficiency, effectiveness, and differentiation. The chapter intended to provide the reader with a broad overview of logistics quality, a fundamental understanding of quality approaches and techniques, and a suggested implementation approach.

The following list includes critical prerequisites to successful logistics quality processes. Although other considerations may be important, the ones we include here are among the most essential:

- Corporate and logistics mission and objectives
- Priority on creating customer value and on customer satisfaction
- Emphasis on continuous improvement through formal quality education

FIGURE 13–9   MALCOLM BALDRIGE NATIONAL QUALITY AWARD   *Source:* U.S. Department of Commerce, *Malcolm Baldrige National Quality Award Application Guidelines.*

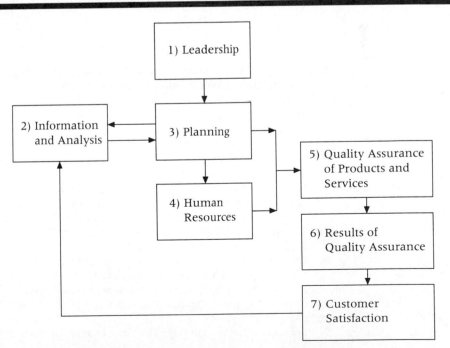

- Critical role of communications
- Identifying necessary quality support resources
- Recognize/reward quality process participants

STUDY QUESTIONS

1. How does logistics create customer value?

2. Identify the key stages in the evolution of quality. Which of these do you feel best represents where most U.S. businesses are today?

3. What evidence supports the contention that positive financial results are likely to accompany a move to a formal quality process?

4. What important concepts are fundamental to any well-conceived quality process? Which of these do you feel are most critical to the success of a quality process?

5. Which quality guru seems to focus more on the issue of measurement? Which seems to be more oriented toward the quality process's motivational aspects?

6. Discuss the elements of a logistics quality process. What elements do you feel an individual business firm should select for its specific quality strategy?

7. Which quality analysis techniques lend themselves more to quantitative analysis? Which seem to be more qualitative?

8. Based on the discussion of gap analysis, which potential gap do you feel a firm should try to close first? Why?

9. Based on the discussion of implementation priorities, do you agree with the order of the six priorities? What suggestions do you have for modifying the order of the priorities?

NOTES

1. For an excellent discussion of reengineering, see Michael Hammer, "Reengineering Work: Don't Automate, Obliterate," *Harvard Business Review* (July–August 1990), 104–112.

2. This topic is addressed in a logistics context in "Reengineering Business Logistics," Cleveland Consulting Associates (1990), 1–9.

3. Bernard J. LaLonde, Martha C. Cooper, and Thomas G. Noordeweier, *Customer Service: A Management Perspective* (Oak Brook, IL: Council of Logistics Management, 1988), 117–121.

4. The issue of customer value is treated comprehensively in *Competing Globally Through Customer Value,* Michael J. Stahl and Gregory M. Bounds, eds. (Westport, CT: Quorum Books, 1991). In particular, see C. John Langley, Jr., and Mary C. Holcomb, Chapter 22: "Achieving Customer Value through Logistics Management," 547–565.

5. The PIMS research program represents an extensive data bank relating to business performance and related factors. The program is conducted by The Strategic Planning Institute, Cambridge, Massachusetts.

6. Francis J. Quinn, "Quality: The Ante to Play the Game," *Traffic Management* (July 1990), 42–49.

7. Francis J. Quinn, "Quality: The Ante to Play the Game," 42.

8. Speech given by A. William Wiggenhorn of Motorola, Inc., at the Annual Conference of the Council of Logistics Management (Anaheim, California, 7–10 October 1990).

9. C. John Langley, Jr., Mary Holcomb, Joel Baudouin, Alexander Donnan, and Paul Caruso, "Approaches to Logistics Quality," *1989 Council of Logistics Management Annual Conference Proceedings* (Oak Brook, IL: CLM, 1989), 87.

10. The content of this section is based on an excellent discussion of quality gurus found in Francis J. Quinn, "The Gurus of Quality," *Traffic Management* (July 1990), 34–39.

11. See Joseph M. Juran, *Juran on Planning for Quality* (New York: The Free Press, 1988).

12. See "The Gurus of Quality," 39, and Kaoru Ishikawa, *Guide to Quality Control* (Tokyo, Japan: Asian Productivity Organization, 1982).

13. Yasuhiro Monden, *Toyota Production System* (Norcross, Georgia: Institute of Industrial Engineers, 1983).

14. C. John Langley, Jr., "Quality in Logistics: A Competitive Advantage," *Proceedings—R. Hadly Waters Logistics and Transportation Symposium* (University Park, PA: Penn State University, The Center for Logistics Research, 1990), 28.

15. We could cite a growing number of companies that have made significant progress in the area of a formal logistics quality process. Those listed in the text only represent the broader number of firms having made significant accomplishments of this type.

16. These steps are described in detail in C. John Langley, Jr., "Quality in Logistics: A Competitive Advantage," 27–33.

17. C. John Langley, Jr., "Quality in Logistics," 30.

18. Excellent sources on these topics include Donald J. Wheeler and David S. Chambers, *Understanding Statistical Process Control* (Knoxville, TN: Statistical Process Controls, Inc., 1986); and Kaoru Ishikawa, *Guide to Quality Control.*

19. See Wheeler, *Understanding Statistical Process Control*, 149–265; and Eugene L. Grant and Richard S. Leavenworth, *Statistical Quality Control* (New York: McGraw-Hill, 5th ed., 1980), 221–316.

20. For further information on correlation analysis, the reader may refer to any basic text on statistical methods and/or quantitative business analysis.

21. Robert C. Camp, *Benchmarking* (Milwaukee, WI: ASQC Quality Press, 1989), 10. Also see David Altany, "Copycats," *Industry Week* (5 November 1990), 11–18.

22. The American Supplier Institute has popularized this approach. Although it applies to many industrial situations, much of its United States experience to date has been in the automobile industry.

23. R. Mohan Pisharodi and C. John Langley, Jr., "A Perceptual Process Model of Customer Service Based on Cybernetic/Control Theory," *Journal of Business Logistics* 11, no. 1 (1990), 34–40.

24. R. Mohan Pisharodi and C. John Langley, Jr., "Measures of Customer Service and Market Response: An Exploration of Interset Association," *Proceedings of the 1990 Transportation and Logistics Educators Conference* (Columbus, OH: The Ohio State University, 1990).

25. Also of interest is a comparable model developed by Valarie A. Zeithaml, Leonard L. Berry, and A. Parasuraman, "Communication and Control Processes in the Delivery of Service Quality," *Journal of Marketing* 52 (April 1988), 35–48. In addition, the use of quality analysis techniques to close logistics service gaps was suggested by James H. Foggin in "Closing the Gaps in Services Marketing: Designing to Satisfy Customer Expectations," Chapter 20 in Michael J. Stahl and Gregory M. Bounds, *Competing Globally Through Customer Value*, 510–30.

26. C. John Langley, Jr., et al., "Approaches to Logistics Quality," 75–76.

27. C. John Langley, Jr., et al., "Approaches to Logistics Quality," 76–82.

28. See Mary C. Holcomb, C. John Langley, Jr., Carl M. Curry, David L. Neff, and William J. DeWitt, "Managing Logistics with a Quality Focus," *Proceedings of the 1990 Annual Conference of the Council of Logistics Management* (Oak Brook, IL: CLM, 1990).

29. C. John Langley, Jr., "Approaches to Logistics Quality" et al., 82–88.

30. LaLonde et al., *Customer Service: A Management Perspective,* 111–16.

31. See "Application Guidelines" for the Malcolm Baldrige National Quality Award, available from the National Institute of Standards and Quality, United States Department of Commerce.

CASE 13–1

HANOVER PHARMACEUTICALS, INC.

Like many American business executives, John Alden thought that he had seen it all. Strategic planning, management by objectives, cash cows, stars, budgeting, leadership . . . It just seemed a matter of time before something else took its place among the popular things for businesses to do. Having received his M.B.A. in the early seventies from a prestigious eastern university, John had been besieged with new approaches and ways of doing business during his twenty-year career. He wondered if it was ever going to stop.

As vice president of logistics for Hanover Pharmaceuticals, Inc., John Alden was very proud of the productivity program he had recently "installed" in the logistics area. Following the advice of a leading consultant, John had made sure that everything in the logistics area was measured, monitored, and controlled. The objective was to see that each available resource performed to its maximum capability and that productivity measures in key logistics areas were at least equal to the industry averages John Alden had seen published.

At a recent meeting, upper management informed John that the company would soon embark on a total quality management (TQM) process that would define quality as "anticipating and exceeding customer requirements." Although he felt somewhat skeptical and tended to think of this new initiative as just another company program, John Alden felt that he should respond meaningfully to this companywide priority.

Case Questions

1. Critique the productivity program Alden recently installed at Hanover Pharmaceuticals. What do you feel are key advantages and limitations of such a program?

2. What do you feel should be done in the logistics area to be consistent with the corporatewide commitment to TQM? Even though details about this process are sketchy at present, try to outline an approach you might recommend for John Alden to consider.

CASE 13–2

NEW ENGLAND TRANSPORTATION, INC.

Greg Batters was vice president marketing for New England Transportation, Inc. (NET), a major provider of transportation and logistics services to customers throughout the Northeast and Mid-Atlantic states. As he watched the Boston Red Sox win easily once again at Fenway Park from the comfort of NET's exclusive corporate box seats, Greg reflected on some rather surprising remarks, Don Jackson, a major shipper customer, made at a recent industry meeting.

"Our experience has been that when a carrier's performance begins to show signs of deteriorating, you call him in and beat on the table to get across the point that this just isn't acceptable," Jackson said. "Generally, he then goes back to his organization and lets his people know that improvement must occur, or else! Usually, there is an initial improvement in service, but it is never sustained."

Although he felt that most transportation firms were sincerely interested in meeting the customers' needs, Jackson observed that very few motor or rail carriers had taken any formal management initiatives in service quality and continual, long-term improvement. He felt that most of the efforts he had seen were superficial at best. As a result, he stated, in the future, his firm would do business only with transportation firms that had adopted a formal quality process. At this juncture, most of the transportation industry executives in attendance felt as though Jackson had read them the riot act.

Greg Batters returned to his company confident that he could take meaningful initiatives to satisfy the requirements Jackson and other customers had established. Batters was also confident that these requirements could result in overall improvement at New England Transportation.

Case Questions 1. Based on this chapter's content, what kinds of initiatives and priorities do you feel would be most appropriate for Batters and New England Transportation, Inc., to consider?
2. How would you incorporate these initiatives and priorities into the overall marketing management process at NET?

14

ORGANIZATION OF THE LOGISTICS FUNCTION

Business logistics management has grown in importance and complexity over the past two or three decades, and its importance will continue to increase in the years to come. The increased attention to logistics management is a result of business environment changes such as high energy prices, transportation deregulation, computer technological advances, volatile interest rates, increased global competition, and product line changes. However, this greater logistics awareness does not automatically translate to improved logistics efficiency. On the contrary, many companies have experienced less-than-desirable results in their attempts to manage the logistics function.

new function

Logistics faces the "new kid on the block" syndrome. In many cases, animosity exists between logistics and the traditional departments, setting the stage for inefficiencies in achieving the economic and service advantages inherent in a coordinated logistics approach. Traditional departments defending their operational turf argue about the functions the firm should locate in a logistics department. In addition, the logistics department's actual design is uncertain.

no best structure

If that is not problem enough, management faces the inevitable conclusion that no one organizational structure is best. Today's business environment is constantly changing; therefore, the logistics organizational structure must be flexible. Increased competitive pressures, global markets and supply sources, just-in-time production management systems, organizational restructuring around product teams, and direct store delivery demand a logistics organizational structure that can deliver efficient service.

Although no one organizational structure for a firm is best, this chapter will attempt to introduce the logistics organization alternatives available and to help the reader appreciate such organizations' fundamental problems and opportunities. Logistics organizations that can deliver efficient and effective service will be critically important in the 1990s as companies compete more vigorously for the coveted preferred supplier status or strategic alliance. As Lee Iacocca, chairman of Chrysler Corporation, said, "The company with the best distribution system and the best service will win all the marbles." [1]

WHAT DOES LOGISTICS ORGANIZATION INVOLVE?

We can define logistics management as "that phase of administration responsible for the effective functioning of the overall logistics process." [2] The logistics organization and logistics management team consist of the following:

- The top logistics executive in the business unit
- The managers of support services reporting through the logistics organization (such as the logistics controller, manager of logistics systems, manager of logistics engineering) and their respective staffs

■ The logistics project services groups, which may or may not fall under one of the support service groups; these may exist as separate staff groups within the logistics organization, or they may be composed of changing groups of line personnel who devote only a portion of their time to staff projects (e.g., planning a new distribution center or designing a new information system)

■ Field operations mangement personnel, such as those responsible for distribution centers, the traffic/transportation activities and the private fleet, and their respective line and staff organizations

For any logistics organization to function effectively, a firm must ensure the effective management of logistical responsibilities at each level.[3]

core activities

Numerous activities are part of the logistics function. Table 14.1, which lists the most common, categorizes these functions into five functional groups: transportation, facility structure, inventory, material handling, and communication and information.

transportation

The transportation functions include inbound, outbound, and international traffic management, that is, the day-to-day management of freight shipments. Also included in the transportation functional group are modal and carrier

facility structure

selection and public and private carriage activities. The facility structure functions involve managing and planning warehouses and distribution centers and se-

inventory

lecting plant sites. Inventory functions include managing raw material, work-in-process, and finished goods inventory; purchasing; post-sale parts/service

---

TABLE 14–1   FUNCTIONAL GROUPING OF LOGISTICS ACTIVITIES

Activities	Functional Group
Inbound traffic Outbound traffic International traffic Carrier selection Mode selection Public versus private carriage	Transportation
Warehouse management Warehouse planning Distribution center management Distribution center planning Plant site selection	Facility structure
Purchasing Raw material inventory Work-in-process inventory Finished goods inventory Parts/service support Return goods handling	Inventory
Salvage/scrap disposal Materials handling Packaging	Materials handling
Order processing Demand forecasting Production scheduling	Communication & information

Source: Kenneth C. Williamson, Daniel M. Spitzer, Jr., and David J. Bloomberg, "Modern Logistics Systems: Theory and Practice," *Journal of Business Logistics* 11, no. 2 (1990), 72.

*materials
handling*

information

degree of control

*prerequisites for
success*

job description

skills needed

*match people to
jobs*

support; and return goods handling. Materials handling functions embrace the short-distance movement of materials within facilities, or materials handling, as well as packaging and scrap/salvage disposal. Finally, the communication and information functions include order processing, demand forecasting, and production scheduling.

In most companies this logistics activities list would create a flurry of dissent. Firms have historically included many of these activities within traditional organizational departments; that is, purchasing within production and order processing within marketing. In practice, the control logistics exercises over these functional groups ranges from dominant-to-total control over transportation, dominant control over facility structure, shared-to-dominant control over inventory and materials handling, and shared control over communications and information.[4]

A firm must meet three requirements to successfully staff its logistics function.[5] First, the firm must formulate accurate job descriptions. Each one should include the job's title, reporting relationship, scope of responsibility, and performance measures. Second, the firm should inventory the skills it needs in the logistics area and assess the extent to which available people meet the various positions' skill requirements. Previous experience in the logistics area will often be helpful, but firms regard multifunctional backgrounds and experience as important qualifications for many senior logistics managers who need a breadth of thinking and perspective as they attempt to successfully coordinate logistics activities and information flows across functions. A third requirement is that the firm should match people to jobs whenever possible, not vice versa. This will require interaction and flexibility in defining the job, inventorying skills, and adjusting jobs and titles to fit available personnel's specific skills and abilities. A firm should relocate existing personnel or add new personnel only when major gaps or duplications in abilities are obvious.

EVOLUTION OF LOGISTICS ORGANIZATIONS

A study reported in *Traffic Management* magazine categorized logistics functions according to the specific responsibilities for which they are accountable. The study identified three phases in logistics organization evolution: traditional responsibilities, extended responsibilities, and advanced responsibilities.[6]

*Phase 1
traditional
responsibilities*

The Phase 1 organization, traditional responsibilities, typically involves activities that directly relate to finished goods' outbound movement and placement. This phase also includes activities such as logistics administration, intracompany transportation, logistics control, and logistics systems planning (see Figure 14–1). These activities strengthen the competitive position of the firm's product in the marketplace, either through improving its availability or through lowering traffic or warehousing costs. This phase tends to emphasize the operational aspects of outbound logistics, principally by controlling finished goods transportation and warehousing.

*Phase 2 extended
responsibilities*

The Phase 2 organization, extended responsibilities, expands the scope of outbound activities that logistics managers coordinate. In addition to the Phase 1 activities, this second phase adds responsibility for customer service, finished goods warehousing, and finished goods inventory management. Firms in Phase 2 also tend to include order processing and inbound transportation within their logistics function and place a priority on integrating the full range of outbound logistics activities as well as on controlling inbound transportation.

FIGURE 14—1   GROWTH RATE OF LOGISTICS RESPONSIBILITIES   *Source:* Jack W. Farrell, "Organization Study: New Clout for Logistics," *Traffic Management* (September 1985), 38.

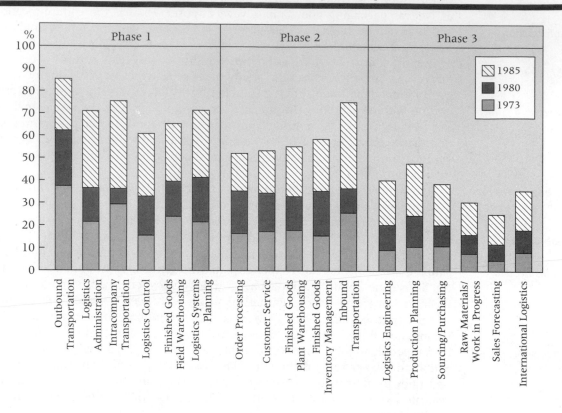

Phase 3 advanced responsibilities

Last, the Phase 3 organization, advanced responsibilities, adds activities such as logistics engineering, production planning, sourcing/purchasing, raw materials/work in process, sales forecasting, and international logistics. Generally, these activities encompass critical marketing and manufacturing functions, as well as logistics. This phase totally integrates the logistics process by joining the management responsibilities for both physical distribution and materials management.

most firms in Phase 1 or 2

Approximately forty-two percent of the United States and Canadian firms the study surveyed were in Phase 1; thirty-eight percent were in Phase 2; and twenty percent were in Phase 3. More companies are in a logistics organization phase in which basic logistics activities form the basis of the logistics organization. Less than one in five companies have reached the stage that encompasses functions critical to marketing and manufacturing as well as to logistics.

The data in Figure 14—2 indicate that logistics departments, in general, have broadened their scope of responsibility. The logistics departments in Phase 3 companies were responsible for thirteen activities, compared to ten for Phase 2 and six for Phase 1 companies. By 1985, Phase 3 companies had added nine activities to their logistics department's responsibility; Phase 2 had added seven; and Phase 1 had added four.

Organizational Issues

historical practices

In trying to develop a logistics organization, the first major problem that usually arises is resistance from other existing departments. Implementing a logistics

FIGURE 14–2   AVERAGE NUMBER OF LOGISTICS RESPONSIBILITIES   *Source:* Jack W. Farrell, "Organization Study: New Clout for Logistics," *Traffic Management* (September 1985), 39.

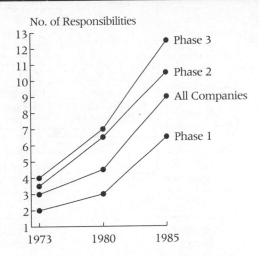

organization may prove, at least in part, to be a political issue. Logistics activities have always existed, but until recently a business's traditional departments handled them. Table 14–2 indicates that in the past, firms located and managed many logistics activities within departments such as production, marketing, and finance. As companies integrate their logistics activities under a single department, this is changing rapidly.

functions removed from other areas

Although many firms have successfully broadened the scope of their logistics functions, the challenge remains for others. To consolidate many of these logistics functions, firms must remove responsibilities from traditional functional areas (marketing, finance, manufacturing) and place these responsibilities under the new department. Many managers who are losing some of their authority will feel threatened by this new organization, and may resist the change. Figure 14–3 indicates how a major chemical company made such a change.

Positioning Logistics in the Firm

high reporting level

To avoid some of the organizational conflicts of creating a logistics department, some companies have established a vice president of logistics or distribution and have charged him or her with consolidating all the diverse activities of logistics under one office. Some early logistics writers have agreed with this method,

TABLE 14–2   TRADITIONAL LOCATIONS OF LOGISTICS ACTIVITIES

Marketing	*Finance/Accounting*	*Manufacturing*
Customer service	Order processing	Inventory control
Demand forecasting	Communications	Materials handling
Warehouse site selection	Procurement	Parts and service support
Outbound traffic	Inventory policy formulation	Plant site selection
Warehousing	Capital budgeting for warehouses, plants, and other logistics assets	Packaging
		Inbound traffic
		Production planning

FIGURE 14–3   HOW ABC CHEMICAL DID IT

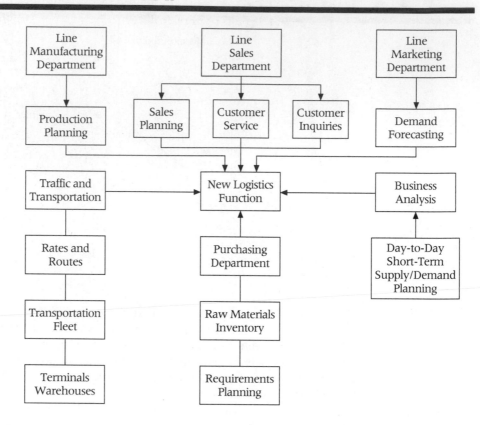

claiming that having such a high reporting level will give logistics the clout necessary to implement new plans. A firm could expect such an executive to make decisions affecting several departments far more objectively than a manager under whose department the firm had subordinated the logistics function. Positioning logistics under a traditional functional area such as marketing, manufacturing, or finance sometimes results in lost balance and skewed goals.

However, having logistics positioned high in the corporate structure is not always necessary for achieving logistics goals. The firm's size may affect this positioning: typically the smaller the firm, the less need for a formal, highly placed logistics structure.

typical reporting relationships

The reporting relationships among logistics executives vary. Commonly, a director of logistics in charge of a logistics division reports to a corporate vice president or president. In another typical structure, a distribution manager in charge of a distribution department reports to a director of operations, who in turn reports to the CEO or the chairman of the board.[7]

LOGISTICS DEPARTMENT ORGANIZATION

Once a firm has decided to create a new logistics department, it must determine the form this department will take. The firm must decide whether the new department's form will be strategic versus operational, line versus staff or, function versus program, and matrix; and must establish its scope of authority.

Strategic versus Operational

overall corporate perspective

Strategic refers to the extent of logistics' high-level visibility within the organization and to the extent to which the firm considers logistics decisions to be significant (i.e., strategic) from an overall corporate perspective. Also implied here is the firm's perception of the organizational relationship between logistics and areas such as marketing and sales, manufacturing/plant management, finance and accounting, strategic/business planning, and data processing/information systems.

tactical operating perspective

Alternatively, *operational* refers to the organizational structure that the logistics department conducts its activities in a manner consistent with logistics goals and the goals of the organization. The operational structure, which emphasizes tactical logistics issues which focus on management-specific logistics functions, directs its attention toward operating issues, not strategic issues.

We can make a strong case for a strategic perspective in today's increasingly competitive environment. Logistics provides the critical link in the vendor-production-customer chain and suggests that firms must integrate various management areas to satisfy customer demand. For example, Coors, which produces beer with a dated shelf life, must respond to logistics service demands from at least three different customers—consumers who want freshness, distributors who demand quick and accurate order response, and retailers who desire order flexibility. As a strategic function, logistics can work with marketing management to sustain sales by satisfying different customers.

Line versus Staff

daily operations

Line management involves making decisions about the department's daily operations. Responsibility for a particular function's operation is delegated to a line manager. Logistical line activities include traffic management, inventory control, order processing, warehousing, and packaging.

analysis

The *staff* function supports the line managers with advice and information. This group develops plans and collects data to support the line managers' decisions. Staff activities include warehouse location analysis, system design, planning, customer service strategies, and cost analysis.

Firms have traditionally divided management into line and staff functions to achieve efficiency through labor specialization. However, a firm organizing the logistics department strictly along one line tends to neglect the other. That is, if line managers completely control the logistics function, a firm will probably suboptimize staff functions. The opposite also holds true. Under these circumstances, the specialization the firm achieves by dividing management into functional concerns may actually undermine the logistics department's goals.

line organization

For example, organizing along a line function pattern (see Figure 14–4) will allow the new department to fit into the firm's traditional hierarchical structure quite easily. However, since either a line manager or another department must now perform logistics planning, this planning is unlikely to optimize the company's logistics goals.

staff organization

Likewise, organizing with a staff function pattern (Figure 14–5) is easy to accomplish; but the daily operational plans the staff approves may not be implemented by the functional departments. One way to overcome this difficulty is to place the logistics staff high enough in the corporate management structure to affect any implementation decisions. Another suggested way to improve on

FIGURE 14-4   GROUPING LINE ACTIVITIES   *Source:* Adapted from John F. Stolle, "How to Manage Physical Distribution," *Harvard Business Review* (July–August 1967), 96.

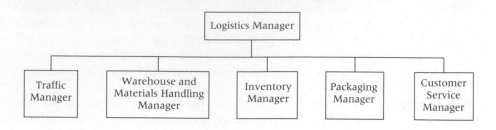

the staff-oriented department is to supplement the staff by allowing it to form permanent advisory committees and ad hoc emergency committees.

combined line and staff

One effective means of overcoming the shortfalls of organizing strictly along a line or staff orientation would be to merge the two approaches (see Figure 14–6), providing the logistics department with all the skills it needs. However, the department, and especially the staff, would have to maintain close contact with the functional departments to ensure that logistics plans meet corporate goals and are feasible. An integrated system such as this does not subordinate any portion of the logistics function, but makes it all functionally dependent on the other departments for information.

Function versus Program, and Matrix

function versus program

Two other approaches to logistics organization treat logistics as a function and logistics as a program.[8] Treating logistics as a *function* isolates logistical responsibilities in a single functional area, as commonly occurs in other corporate areas such as marketing, manufacturing, and finance. This approach's major liability is that it does not typically encourage integrated decision making among

FIGURE 14-5   GROUPING OF LOGISTICS STAFF ACTIVITIES   *Source:* Adapted from John F. Stolle, "How to Manage Physical Distribution," *Harvard Business Review* (July–August 1967), 97.

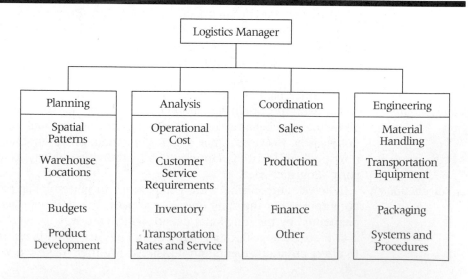

FIGURE 14–6 GROUPING LINE AND STAFF ACTIVITIES *Source:* Adapted from John F. Stolle, "How to Manage Physical Distribution," *Harvard Business Review* (July–August 1967), 98.

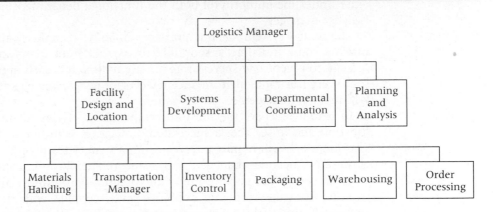

major corporate functions, and suboptimization is often the principal result. A strict functional approach to logistics management generally makes working effectively with other corporate functions for the good of the whole organization difficult.

need for systems approval

In contrast, organizing logistics as a major corporate *program* sensitizes the firm's other functional areas to having an effective logistics *system.* As a result, the organization realizes logistics' ultimate potential contribution to the entire firm's profit-maximizing goals. For a firm to position its logistics program correctly, top management must consider logistical considerations to be of ultimate importance. In theory, the program approach is far more capable of producing appealing results consistent with system goals, and total corporate perspective than is the functional approach.

matrix organization

The *matrix* organization accounts for the fact that logistics activities occur in areas throughout the firm and that they are basically spread *horizontally* throughout the firm. Figure 14–7 illustrates logistics in a matrix organization. The matrix

FIGURE 14–7 LOGISTICS IN A MATRIX ORGANIZATION *Source:* Daniel W. DeHayes, Jr., and Robert L. Taylor, "Making Logistics Work in a Firm," *Business Horizons* (June 1972), 44.

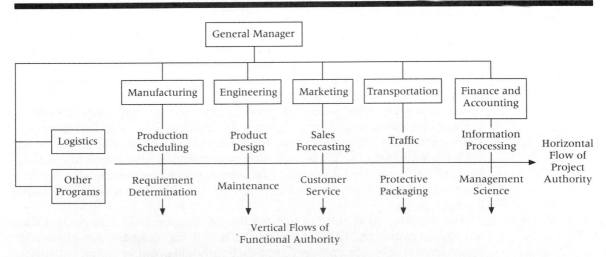

system permits the logistics manager to oversee costs, but leaves the operations in the traditional departments. The logistics activities managers, therefore, operate under the authority of both the functional department manager and the logistics manager.

confusing lines of authority

The matrix system has one primary difficulty: it confuses authority lines by making some functions responsible to two different managers. This has led directly to a very low success rate among matrix approach applications and to some very frustrating performance reviews for people having key responsibilities within such management organizations.

teamwork

In actual practice, the most successful alternative is to treat logistics as a function and to see that it successfully integrates both line and staff activities. This approach will require a heavy commitment to teamwork from the various corporate functional managers and a sincere attempt to integrate activities between areas for the good of the whole organization. Proper guidance and motivation from the corporate executive level, coupled with the availability of competent, progressive functional managers, will increase this approach's chances for success.

Scope of Authority

delegation of authority

Scope of authority, which addresses the degree to which an organization delegates authority to lower management levels, is essentially a question of whether the logistics organization is centralized or decentralized. A centralized structure restricts authority to a few managers; managers commonly refer to this as the home office structure. However, a decentralized structure delegates authority to lower levels of management such as the division or plant level.

more manageable

responsive to customer

Some managers favor decentralization because its smaller size makes it more manageable and because it is more responsive to customer service. Decentralization empowers lower-level managers with the authority to make necessary decisions to improve operations. Providing the person who knows what needs to be done with the authority to do it is extremely desirable. Too often, the centralized manager has the authority to get things done, but does not know what needs to be done.

But decentralization does have limits. For example, a decentralized structure may not give any one division enough volume to negotiate effectively with carriers and to achieve economies of scale with computer systems and warehousing facilities.

economies of scale

negotiating power

Centralization makes coordination among divisions and economies of scale easier to achieve. Taking a systemwide or centralized approach to carrier negotiations results in lower transportation costs for all divisions, and joint use of computer facilities affords economies of scale for information processing, especially in small- to medium-size companies.

parallel company trend

The general trend is to centralize certain functions that will produce savings through improved negotiating power or productivity of assets. For example, firms commonly centralize freight bill payment and information systems to realize economies of scale through increased computer investment utilization. In contrast, firms often decentralize customer service functions to give the individual responsible for performing the service the authority to make necessary changes.

The best way to establish a logistics decentralization level is to parallel the tendencies of the rest of the company. That is, if the company has organized other departments along product lines, then it should organize logistics by prod-

ON THE LINE

DuPont Dismantles Its Traffic Department

At DuPont, "department" has become a naughty word.

A major corporate rethinking, which has been taking shape for the better part of the past decade, has engendered a revolution in how the chemical products giant goes about its business . . . and, in the balance, has done away with the familiar institution, the traffic department.

Instead, DuPont has chosen to gather similar functions under a broad umbrella known as Materials, Logistics, and Services. In line with this new perspective, someone responsible for procuring transportation is also responsible for procuring information systems and organic chemicals.

"We have moved logistics horizontally through the organization, rather than having it be a vertical stovepipe," explained Clifford M. Sayre, one of the three vice presidents of Materials, Logistics, and Services.

By bringing like-minded functions under one roof, DuPont is hoping for some cross-pollination of good ideas. "We have a lot to learn from each other," Sayre pointed out.

The process that has transformed DuPont's logistics approach is part of its supply chain management evolution: the company tailors everyone's job according to the most efficient competitive way to get the end product to the customer when and how the customer needs it.

To make the supply chain operation work, DuPont had to reduce interdepartmental barriers and do away with territorialism. "This meant breaking down turf. The idea of a department was a barrier. We don't call ourselves departments anymore; we refer to a grouping of functions," Sayre noted.

The installation of horizontal functions, rather than vertical departmentalization, has pushed decision making further down in the ranks than it has ever been at DuPont. "By pushing responsibility down the line, we're giving people the responsibility for managing themselves, and getting people to participate in reshaping their jobs," Sayre said. "For the first time people really feel they are in control."

Source: "DuPont Dismantles Its Traffic Department," *American Shipper* (December 1990), 37. Reprinted with permission from the December 1990 issue of *American Shipper*.

---

uct line. Similarly, if a company is decentralized by geographic region, then the logistics organization should be decentralized by geographic region.

A second method is to consolidate centralized staff functions but to decentralize line operations. This approach has some disadvantages, since completely separating line and staff responsibilities is impossible, particularly at the middle-management level. Frequently, firms develop a three-layer structure to implement this approach. (We will discuss the three-tiered approach in a later section.)

advanced companies favor centralization

Table 14–3 illustrates scope of authority according to phases. The table first divides companies into those that are *functional* (or single-business units) and those that are *divisional*. Among the functional firms, advanced companies tend to consolidate logistics activities, rather than having them dispersed throughout the firm. The dominant alternative among advanced divisional companies is to consolidate logistics functions within business units. Now, however, divisional companies show a strong tendency to centralize the corporate staff and policy-formulating functions, but to leave the line organizations relatively decentralized.

Outsourcing or Third-Party Logistics

definition

Outsourcing or third-party logistics involves purchasing logistics services from a service provider outside the company. Third-party providers actually manage

TABLE 14-3   BREAKDOWN OF COMPANY TYPES BY PHASES

	Functional Companies		*Divisional Companies*		
	A *Dispersed* *Logistics*	*B* *Consolidated* *Logistics*	*C* *Logistics Functions* *Consolidated within* *Business Units*	*D* *Centrally* *Consolidated* *Logistics* *Functions*	*E* *Corporate Staff* *Function,* *Decentralized* *Line Functions*
Phase 3 (advanced responsibilities)	21.3%	52.9%	11.8%	9.8%	3.9%
Phase 2 (extended responsibilities)	27.6%	29.6%	14.3%	16.3%	12.2%
Phase 1 (traditional responsibilities)	32.4%	29.7%	7.3%	9.9%	20.7%
All companies	28.5%	34.2%	10.8%	12.3%	14.2%

Source: Jack W. Farrell, "Organization Study: New Clout for Logistics," *Traffic Management* (September 1985), 40.

all or part of a company's logistics system. The outside provider controls the movement and storage of the company's inbound and/or outbound products through activities such as transportation negotiations, shipment routing, warehousing, inventory control, and shipping and receiving.

European import   Logistics outsourcing, a widely accepted management trend in Europe, is just emerging in the United States.[10] In Europe, the concept of outsourcing day-to-day distribution services management is a mature philosophy.[11] Japanese companies also utilize third-party providers to perform specialized distribution functions.

third-party providers   Companies such as IBM and Wang utilize the third party services North American Van Lines (NAVL) provides. NAVL oversees the flow of finished products from plant to customers by controlling line-haul transportation, order consolidation and assembly, and customer delivery.[12] Other companies such as Best Products have converted existing in-house logistics departments into separate corporate entities that provide logistics services to the parent company as well as to other companies. Some of the biggest names in transportation—Federal Express, Roadway, Union Pacific and CSX/Sea-Land, for example—have become major players in the logistics outsourcing market.

cost cutting   The business climate in the United States and throughout the world is forcing companies to seek innovative concepts to make their operations more efficient and thereby more competitive in our global markets. Cost cutting is a major strategy U.S. companies use to survive, to sustain or increase market share, and to realize a profit.

downsizing   Organizational restructuring, or downsizing, is one of the major tools American companies utilize to realize operating efficiencies. To this end, companies are sending legal, engineering, payroll/benefits management, communications, accounting services, and other functions company personnel have traditionally performed outside the company to firms that specialize in these services. Outsourcing enables the company to concentrate its assets and resources on what it does best—manufacturing or retailing, for example—and permits the third-party provider to concentrate on efficiently producing the purchased services.

focus on primary business   U.S. companies downsizing their organizations consider logistics a function a company can outsource to reduce costs and improve service. In many instances, outsourcing enhances the value logistics services add because the third-party provider is a specialist in the service and utilizes economies of scale in providing the services to a number of companies. For example, outsourcing capital-intensive logistics activities such as warehousing and private carriage permits a company to reduce labor and asset requirements and to concentrate on producing and marketing its products. Outside freight payment vendors can replace this function's in-house performance with lower costs, more timely payments, and improved transportation activity information.

managing third party

Managing a logistics organization that utilizes outsourcing entails sophisticated and integrated information systems. The manager must communicate accurate, timely information to the third-party provider who can meet a firm's internal and external logistics service demands. In addition, management will require information to measure and control the third-party service level's effectiveness and economics.

STRUCTURING THE LOGISTICS ORGANIZATION

Up to now, this chapter has focused upon establishing a logistics department. We must also give some attention to the basic principles and steps for planning and structuring the logistics organization and to the generic management functions logistics personnel will perform at various organizational levels. When considering alternative approaches for structuring the logistics organization, the principal objective should be to develop strategies for mobilizing and managing various resources to ensure that a firm accomplishes its logistical mission and achieves its corporate goals.

The first part of this section details a viable approach to logistics organizational design. The second part discusses logistics responsibilities in the context of a three-layer organizational structure.

Key Steps in the Process

No ideal approach is uniquely suited to designing a logistics program, but the following steps have proven useful:[13]

1. Research corporate strategies and goals
2. Organize functions to be compatible with corporate structure
3. Define functions for which you are accountable
4. Know your management style
5. Organize your flexibility
6. Know your support systems
7. Make plans to fit both individual and corporate objectives

The first step ensures that the logistics department's long-term direction is compatible with corporate goals. Organizing functions to parallel corporate structure refers to our earlier discussion of parallelism as a decentralization method. Defining accountability is necessary because of the confusion the horizontal nature of logistics causes. The fourth step basically asks managers to be aware of how their attitudes and actions will affect subordinates' acceptance of change. Concern for flexibility ensures that the organization will be able to adapt to future changes. Knowing your support systems helps you to know exactly what your new system can and cannot accomplish. The last step ensures that the people who are to run the new system accept it, because nothing can torpedo a system faster than user resistance.[14]

Three-Layer Framework

first tier

operational components

The three-layer framework provides the entire organization's basic structure and operational activity (see Figure 14−8). At the bottom are the operational (or physical) systems components, the most elementary system activities. Each of these tasks (a sub-system) has one or more very limited goals. One plant's

FIGURE 14−8   THE THREE-LAYER FRAMEWORK

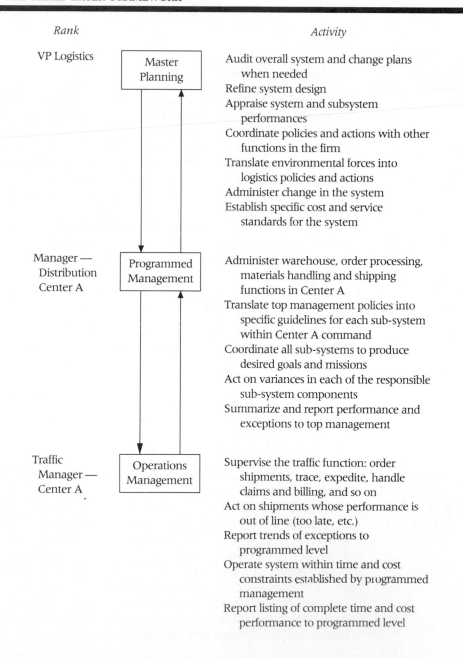

Rank		*Activity*
VP Logistics	Master Planning	Audit overall system and change plans when needed Refine system design Appraise system and subsystem performances Coordinate policies and actions with other functions in the firm Translate environmental forces into logistics policies and actions Administer change in the system Establish specific cost and service standards for the system
Manager — Distribution Center A	Programmed Management	Administer warehouse, order processing, materials handling and shipping functions in Center A Translate top management policies into specific guidelines for each sub-system within Center A command Coordinate all sub-systems to produce desired goals and missions Act on variances in each of the responsible sub-system components Summarize and report performance and exceptions to top management
Traffic Manager — Center A	Operations Management	Supervise the traffic function: order shipments, trace, expedite, handle claims and billing, and so on Act on shipments whose performance is out of line (too late, etc.) Report trends of exceptions to programmed level Operate system within time and cost constraints established by programmed management Report listing of complete time and cost performance to programmed level

shipping department may, for example, have four employees. Its inputs are its personnel and facilities, the orders it ships, and its labeling, shipment, and documentation activities. Processing is the actual shipment, expediting, tracing, miscellaneous carrier contact work, and loss and damage work. The department measures output in terms of tons, shipments, or the number of each product units it ships, their total shipment costs plus losses and damages, and a realistic allocation of overhead costs attributable to the shipping department (supervisor's salary, direct phone expenses, floor space costs, supplies, and tariff book costs, for example).

feedback and control
The supervisor reviews output feedback reports and initiates action on shipments that exceed normal delivery times (tracing and follow-up), compares actual shipment preparation time and costs (wrapping and overall shipping dock throughput time) against a norm or desired standard (for example, all shipments take no more than fifteen-labor-minutes to prepare and must clear the dock within the same day). The actual management activity here is very routine in that it covers only specific control and administrative activities. Very little managerial discretion is required, because each problem has a defined method of approach or solution. The manager's performance is easy to measure since the job goals are specifically defined.

second tier
The second tier of management encompasses the person or group of persons who control and administer two or more individual sub-subsystems. This level, which would include the manager of an entire distribution warehouse or the director of a whole product line, is the programmed level of management; that is, the control activities make programmed decisions on exceptions—the sub-subsystems' problems. Narrow discretionary powers also limit this level's decisions. This manager's responsibility is to manage his or her sector for the firm (several sub-subsystems) under a stated cost, profit, or service constraint. Encountering a problem in one or more sub-subsystems (shipping or warehousing, for example), this manager must take corrective action and initiate investigation to determine why the problem reoccurs. The manager implements changes in the systems under his or her jurisdiction and coordinates related functions within and interfacing the overall subsystems. He or she might also maintain a small support staff that audits the subsystem, conducts continual research to refine and adopt the subsystem to change, and represents the subsystem in dealings with external functions (in negotiating rates, for example).

programmed level

third tier
The top management tier is the master planning level. At this nonprogrammed level managers do very little routine work. Input is the subsystems' performance and problems, and factors external to the entire system (competitive forces and other changed environmental considerations). Processing is mostly analytical work (research and engineering studies). Output is the decisions and orders for correcting subsystem actions; new policies and overall system guidelines; and actions on large distribution system capital acquisition programs. This level typically consists of a top logistics officer (with a supporting staff of controllers, engineers, and analysts who continually audit, consider, and plan system changes) and members of top management who are concerned with the entire firm's policy matters (overall roles, service, return on investment, and corporate strategy).

master planning

strategy

MANAGING THE LOGISTICS ORGANIZATION

A company having implemented a logistics organization must continually monitor and evaluate its effectiveness. This feedback is essential for organizational changes that will increase the company's likelihood of achieving its desired goals.

structural change

A common misconception is that an organizational structure is a permanent fixture. In reality, change is the organization's only permanent trait. Business conditions change, new technologies develop, and firms modify strategic plans and goals, necessitating a structural change in logistics organization. The logistics manager must be aware of these changes and modify the logistics organization accordingly to achieve corporate and logistics goals.

Measuring Logistics Performance

A company may utilize several different methods to measure the logistics organization's performance. In general, these performance measurements compare the logistics organization's output with the various logistics functions' established objectives. Though these objectives may take different forms, they generally deal with cost, productivity, and service.

cost output

Cost Criteria   Companies establish cost objectives for the performance of individual logistics functions. Examples include the cost per pound, per shipment, or per order. The company compares the logistics operation's cost with its established objectives and takes corrective actions if necessary.

Consider the example of a Cleveland department store that charged customers a pre-set cost of $25 for delivering furniture and appliances. The delivery cost became the objective against which the store measured the actual logistics delivery service cost. If the actual delivery cost exceeded the charge, the department incurred a loss on the delivery service. This excessive cost reduced the normal profit built into the product's price. A cost accounting report alerted the department store to such a situation. The report indicated that a problem existed in the delivery area. The logistics manager analyzed the delivery department's operation and productivity performance to locate the problem's cause and take corrective action.

output divided by input

Productivity Criteria   Productivity criteria measure the amount of output a firm produces per unit of input, or outputs divided by inputs. Examples of output measures are tons shipped, pounds loaded, orders filled, and shipments delivered. Inputs are things such as labor hours, the number of employees or trucks, and warehouse space.

Upon analyzing the number of shipments delivered per delivery shift, the Cleveland department store logistics manager discovered that the current delivery rate equalled 4.7 per shift, down from 11.8 the previous year. The conclusion was obvious: increase the number of deliveries per shift, and the increased productivity would lower the cost per delivery.

The real question was why deliveries per shift had decreased from the previous year. To answer this question, the logistics manager established a quality circles program consisting of informational meetings between logistics management and the drivers and helpers. At these meetings, the logistics manager conveyed the problems low productivity and the fixed delivery charge generated; and the drivers and helpers presented reasons for and solutions to this low productivity. The logistics manager solved the problem by purchasing improved materials handling equipment for the delivery vehicles and improving delivery truck routing. (Not all productivity problems are resolved so easily.)

measurable

Service Criteria   Logistics service quality is becoming increasingly important in today's competitive global markets. Firms define service quality in terms of criteria such as time, accuracy, consistency, and damage. A seller's service level provides a competitive advantage (or disadvantage), and service is a criterion that buyers, especially industrial buyers, use in making the purchase decision.

To continue with our Cleveland department store example, the store sold a line of women's clothing that it purchased from a plant in a Pacific Rim country. Because the clothing was very popular, the store experienced increasing numbers

stockouts

of stockouts at its retail outlets. When customers bought competing brands, the stockouts translated into lost profits. Sixty days elapsed between the time the store placed an order and the time it received the order in Cleveland.

Examining the international movement, the logistics manager found that the ocean voyage required twenty-four days and that the truck movement from Long Beach to Cleveland required eight days. During the remaining thirty-eight days, the shipment was sitting in a warehouse at its origin or at Long Beach. Improved communication with the producer and using a new intermediate warehouse at Long Beach reduced the in-transit storage to four days and the total lead time to thirty-six days. Improved store sales monitoring enabled the logistics manager to anticipate demand for the clothing. These actions reduced both stockouts and lost profits.

Measuring Logistics Management Performance

Firms evaluate logistics managers primarily on the basis of three factors: line management ability, problem-solving ability, and project management ability.[15]

Line management ability This criterion considers the manager's ability to manage the department's day-to-day operations and to meet goals that the firm has established for productivity, utilization, and all aspects of performance, including budget.

Problem-solving ability This deals with the ability to diagnose problems within the operation and to identify savings, service improvement, or increased return on investment opportunities.

Project management ability This refers to the ability to structure and manage projects designed to correct problems, improve productivity, and achieve improvement benefits.

Companies also frequently evaluate managers on their ability to motivate and develop their employees' technical and management skills. The company may measure the degree of success here according to individual employees productivity, utilization, and performance.

Figure 14–9 identifies responsibilities that would be typical for a vice president of logistics. The following list sets specific standards against which a company may evaluate performance. Together, these should illustrate the performance companies expect of logistics managers, and ways of measuring the conformity between performance and expectations.

1. Maintain inventory at four-month level during current year. Reduce to three-month level over the course of the next two years.
2. Establish and maintain a customer service level of 92% product availability for all regular line items and have such items ready for shipment within five days of receipt of order.

FIGURE 14—9   EXAMPLE RESPONSIBILITIES OF VICE PRESIDENT OF LOGISTICS

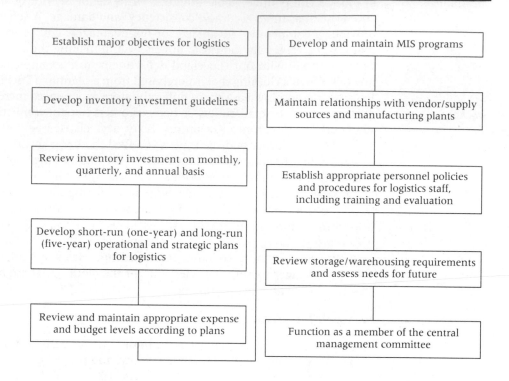

3. Develop procedures to maintain logistics operating expenses at 3.5% of sales during current year.
4. Reduce transportation expenses, including private fleet, to 2.5% of sales during current year, and reduce to 2.4% next year.
5. Reduce freight shipment damage rate to 1% of total sales.
6. Maintain 98% accuracy level in order filling.
7. Maintain employee turnover rate at 12% per year.

Improving Management Productivity and Effectiveness

Companies use a number of programs to improve logistics management productivity.[16] We will briefly discuss each program here.

Organizational Change   This is perhaps one of the most effective means of affecting productivity. The degree of change does not have to be extensive to produce desired results. Simply streamlining functions to achieve a desired level of integration can improve management productivity. So can totally restructuring the logistics organization.

Management by Objectives   The use of management by objectives (MBO) and goal-setting programs give the logistics executive a target to shoot for with the department's operations. Involving the managers in the goal-setting process also develops a pride of ownership in the desired results.

Management by Exception   Management by exception (MBX) programs typically offer many MBO program benefits, but focus managerial attention only on areas where the firm has documented a need. Firms that have committed resources to developing responsibility accounting systems have realized the positive results possible when managers receive concise, relevant information concerning their operations.

Systems Engineering   Many firms' logistics functions have benefited significantly from using available systems engineering techniques for project planning, scheduling, and control. Many of these approaches are available as microcomputer software packages, and the logistics areas of many firms commonly use them.

Capital and Expenditure Management   The logistics function in many firms has benefited from using traditional approaches to capital budgeting and resource allocation. In addition to helping logistics managers to make better capital decisions, such approaches have also increased the logistics function's credibility among corporate general managers.

Use of Computer Technology   While most logistics managers have recognized the value of utilizing available information technology, a significant gap still exists in this area between the ultimate realm of possibility and accomplishments and improvements to date.

Use of Analytical Tools   By using analytical tools such as simulation and various software packages, logistics managers may improve their productivity.

Incentive Programs   Companies are directing resources toward properly motivating managers and employees to achieve desired results. Among the more popular approaches are wage incentive systems and other gain-sharing techniques. These programs are very effective, particularly when a company also emphasizes increasing job satisfaction and improving managers' and employees' self-esteem.

Personnel/Hiring Practices   Many firms have made improvements by implementing programs to ensure that position candidates have the necessary qualifications and talents both before and after the firm hires them. Training logistics managers how to interview and evaluate prospective candidates also helps to improve personnel quality.

Consolidating Logistics Activities across Several Business Units   Although it is not necessarily appropriate in all situations, some companies have achieved positive results by consolidating various logistics activities that may have been spread across various divisions or business units.

Integrated Logistics

fulfill customer service demand

The integrated logistics concept recognizes the links between logistics and other areas of the firm and the need to coordinate logistics activities among other business activities to achieve a high customer service level overall. Logistics' overriding goal is to fulfill customer service demand regardless of departmental responsibility lines.

systems approach

Integrated logistics fosters the team approach to managing the value-added logistics functions. Integrating purchasing, manufacturing, and physical distribution enables logistics to realize a company's maximum efficiency. In addition, integrating these activities improves the logistics performance levels a company can use as a competitive tool in the marketplace. DuPont's elimination of the traffic department is a good integrated logistics example (see On the Line). The DuPont organization eliminated the functional department approach's inherent hierarchy. The company's new organizational structure integrates purchasing, logistics, and customer service.

Logistics integration is basically the application of the systems approach. It generally involves the following organizational principles:[17]

information key to productivity

Using a Networked Information System   The application of new computer technology is critical to achieving integrated logistics. The information system permits a company to move its products faster and to be better informed as to customer demand and inventory levels. Coordinating marketing inventory, production, and purchasing information systems improves productivity, efficiency, accuracy, and customer service.

deviations from norms

Managing by Exception   An integrated logistics system utilizes the information system to alert management of deviations from defined performance standards. Rather than overseeing the details of every operation, managers concentrate on resolving operating problems that performance deviations have identified. Accurate, timely information is critical to the management by exception program.

total product flow pipeline

Thinking from Supplier to Customer   Logistics is a product flow from supplier to customer. This systems orientation recognizes the need to involve suppliers in the logistics process. Vendor partnerships or strategic alliances recognize that efficiencies are possible through a close working relationship that coordinates demand and production information, technology, and engineering.

all employees are customer reps

Seeing All Jobs As Customer Service   A firm must encourage all employees, not just customer service department employees, to do what is necessary to deliver what the customer demands. Firms encourage employees to say yes to customer requests. As global competition increases, attention to customer wants is a key to attaining marketing goals. Periodically discussing customer successes and failures and methods to improve customer service is integral to making every employee a customer service representative.

grant power to do job

Empowering Employees, Flattening Hierarchies   Companies must give employees the authority and tools to do their jobs. So that supervisors can adjust work schedules to meet varying demand, they must have direct access to information such as customer orders and inventory levels. Conferring directly with vendors or customers reduces bureaucratic red tape and improves an employee's efficiency. If timeliness and accuracy are important, then employees must be able to take responsibility for meeting these demands. This empowerment results in flatter organizational hierarchies and in downsizing.

one manager responsible

Changing Management Structures   Managers of functional areas such as purchasing, transportation, or warehousing report to a single individual instead of reporting to functional heads. The individual manager is responsible for the product's complete flow through the channel and this structure emphasizes this responsibility.

change is inevitable

Planning for Change The one constant in organizational structuring is the need to plan for change. The company must be flexible enough to adapt its organizational structure to meet marketplace changes occurring as a result of competition, customer needs, or the economy.

Leading Edge Companies

most advanced

In 1989, the Council of Logistics Management published a study describing the logistics organization, strategy, and behavior of companies on the leading edge of business.[18] These leading edge companies have a logistics competency superior to other firms', and they use logistics as a competitive weapon to gain and maintain customers.

Leading edge companies have the following organizational structures and characteristics:

- Formal logistics organizations exist, and these logistics organizations have been in place longer than those in non-leading edge firms;
- An officer-level executive is more apt to head logistics;
- The company adopts a fluid approach to logistics organization and encourages reorganization to take advantage of opportunities;
- The company favors centralized control and is becoming more centralized as the company adapts the logistics organization to its mission;
- Logistics is responsible for more traditional staff and line activities;
- Management scope extends beyond traditional logistics responsibilities.

Very sensitive to customers' needs, the leading edge companies view logistics as a competitive tool to satisfy these needs. These companies are acutely aware of the product value logistics services add; they also realize the cost of providing these services. The customer is the management's focal point, and the company structures the logistics organization to fulfill customers' needs.

SUMMARY

No one single organizational structure is best for all firms or even for any one firm at all times. Logistics organizational decisions include staffing the function, the functions to be included, the organization's structure and position within the firm, the choice between centralized or decentralized authority, and measuring its effectiveness.

Companies are in different phases of logistics development and consequently have different logistics structures. The more advanced or leading edge companies have a formal logistics structure, tend to favor centralized authority with functional managers reporting to one officer-level executive, empower employees to do what is necessary to deliver the product, utilize networked information systems, and focus on the customer. The flexible organizational structure adjusts to meet ever-changing marketplace conditions.

The logistics organizational structure best for a company depends upon the nature of the company's existing organizational structure, the company's goals, and the resources available.

STUDY QUESTIONS

1. What is so difficult about developing a logistics organization?
2. Discuss the logistics organization's evolution in terms of the three development phases.
3. What activities do firms generally consider part of a logistics organization? Why?
4. What are the advantages and disadvantages of organizing logistics with line activities only? Staff activities only?
5. Where in the organization should a firm position logistics? What justification can you give for this positioning?
6. What types of logistics functions should have a centralized scope of authority? Decentralized? Explain.
7. Describe third-party logistics and the role it plays in a company's logistics organization.
8. What is the three-layer organizational framework of logistics?
9. Discuss the methods available to measure logistics organization effectiveness and management performance.
10. Describe an integrated logistics organization and compare it to the organizational structure leading edge companies use.

NOTES

1. "Organizing Logistics," *Distribution* (April 1989), 29.
2. Council of Logistics Management, *Measuring and Improving Productivity in Physical Distribution* (Chicago: Council of Logistics Management, 1984), 303–4.
3. CLM, *Measuring and Improving Productivity*, 303–4.
4. Kenneth C. Williamson, Daniel M. Spitzer, Jr., and David J. Bloomberg, "Modern Logistics Systems: Theory and Practice," *Journal of Business Logistics* 11, no. 2 (1990) 73.
5. James L. Heskett, "Organizing for Effective Distribution Management," Chapter 29 in *Distribution Handbook* (New York: Free Press, 1985), 828–31.
6. Jack W. Farrell, "Organization Study: New Clout for Logistics," *Traffic Management* (September 1985), 37–43.
7. James M. Masters and Bernard J. LaLonde, "The 1989 Ohio State University Survey of Career Patterns in Logistics," *Council of Logistics Management 1989 Annual Conference Proceedings* (1990), 20.
8. Daniel W. DeHayes, Jr., and Robert L. Taylor, "Making Logistics Work in a Firm," *Business Horizons* (June 1972), 41–44.
9. DeHayes et al. "Making Logistics Work in a Firm," 41–44.
10. K. A. O'Laughlin, "The Progress and Potential of Third-Party Logistics," *Traffic Management* (October 1988), 41–49.
11. Elizabeth Canna, "Contract Logistics for a Mass Retailer," *American Shipper* (August 1988), 32.
12. David L. Anderson and James Gillies, "Third-Party Logistics: What Is the Trend?" *Council of Logistics Management 1990 Annual Conference Proceedings* (1991), 76.
13. James P. Falk, "Organizing for Effective Distribution," *Proceedings of the Annual Conference of the National Council of Physical Distribution Management* (1980), 181–99.
14. "PDM Challenged at Seminar," *Handling and Shipping* (July 1973), 54.

15. Council of Logistics Management, *Measuring and Improving Productivity in Physical Distribution* (Chicago: Council of Logistics Management, 1984), 305.
16. Council of Logistics Management, *Measuring and Improving*, 311–14.
17. "Logistics: Just-Right Delivery," *Enterprise* (Summer 1990), 27–34.
18. Council of Logistics Management, *Leading Edge Logistics: Competitive Positioning for the 1990s* (Chicago: Council of Logistics Management, 1989).

CASE 14–1

SAVANNAH STEEL CORPORATION

Savannah Steel Corporation is one of a limited number of minimills specializing in the manufacture of custom products, specifically a high-quality line of steel joists used throughout the building industry. The product line is narrow, consisting primarily of angles, channels, and bars. Savannah produces these components and then assembles the joists according to the specifics of individual customer orders.

Dale Murphy has recently been named vice president (VP) of logistics for Savannah Steel. With recent increased competitiveness in the custom-structure steel industry, Savannah Steel feels that an enhanced emphasis on the logistics systems concept will help to increase market share by improving customer service and lowering the unit cost of doing business.

The vice president of logistics reports directly to the executive vice president (EVP) of operations, who reports to the president of Savannah Steel. Other EVP positions are in the areas of sales and marketing, and finance. The VP of logistics position is newly created, and an executive search firm identified Murphy as a suitable person to accept the responsibility.

Murphy's predecessor held the title of manager of transportation and distribution. He was basically responsible for the outbound-to-customer transportation of finished product and for managing activities on the shipping and receiving docks at Savannah Steel's single plant. The person holding this job reported to the director of manufacturing, who reported to the EVP of operations. It was common knowledge that he had resigned because he felt that his responsibility was too limited and his contribution too "buried within the organization" to be meaningful.

When Murphy took the job, he understood the president of Savannah Steel that logistics was a top priority for the whole company. The president also made it clear that he expected to see results in terms of improved customer service and a reduced logistics unit cost in the near future.

Even though his tenure with Savannah Steel has been brief, Murphy already has made several significant logistics changes. Logistics has acquired total responsibility for all finished goods transportation and inventory management, production planning, and operation of the company's small private truck fleet. The operations area houses the management of all purchasing activities, with the VP of purchasing also reporting to the EVP of operations. Savannah generally sells finished product to its customers on an F.O.B. delivered basis, and the company purchases most of its raw materials and supplies F.O.B. Savannah's dock.

The EVP of operations has given Murphy his personal assurance that he will do whatever is necessary to help achieve the logistics organization's established goals. While he admits that he really does not know much about the logistics concept, he feels confident that Murphy can achieve significant results without too much trouble.

Case Questions 1. How would you characterize the present status of the logistics organization at Savannah Steel? Specifically, at what phase is this company in the evolution of its logistics organization?

2. What activities should Murphy add to the logistics area in order to maximize its likelihood for achieving its intended goals? What organizational issues and problems may surface if Murphy intends to increase the comprehensiveness of the logistics function at Savannah Steel?

3. Is the logistics area positioned properly within the organization to achieve its intended goals? If not, what alternatives would you recommend? What implementation obstacles would be relevant?

4. If you were Murphy, in what way would you expect the company to measure your performance as VP of logistics? What specific programs would you implement to enhance this company's logistics productivity?

5. In general, what critical factors will determine whether Murphy's performance will satisfy the president?

LOGISTICS STRATEGY

Change is the operative word to describe the economic environment U.S. companies face in the 1990s. Strong competition from foreign sources, coupled with the merger and buyout mania of the 80s and the burgeoning globalization of business, has resulted in greater emphasis upon strategic planning. In some cases, this strategic planning emphasis was born out of the necessity to remain competitive and to survive.

In the late 1980s, by setting in motion a strategy to move away from being a major mass merchandiser in the catalog business to being a speciality store operator, Montgomery Ward undertook a major strategic change in the way it conducted its business. To accomplish this business change and to remain a viable entity, Montgomery Ward called upon its logistics function to produce service improvements and a $100,000,000 cost saving. The resulting logistics strategies reduced inventory levels, consolidated or closed of facilities, reduced head count, eliminated the private fleet, and improved delivery service to the stores.[1]

The success of the strategic change in Montgomery Ward's basic business was largely attributable to the logistics strategies the company implemented. The logistics steering committee worked closely with the chairman of Montgomery Ward to discuss problems that developed in the massive changes embodied in its new approach to retailing. The logistics strategies had to be in concert with those developed for the company as a whole.

Montgomery Ward's overall logistics strategy was to standardize the process and to eliminate exceptions. A JIT system permitted the company to reduce inventory levels (and inventory costs); electronic cash registers which communicate inventory information replaced traditional cash registers; and Wards required domestic vendors to ticket all goods for floor readiness, tagged each product with a bar code; encouraged vendors to use EDI for invoicing, and eliminated direct links between the vendor and retail outlet. These logistics strategies were essential to Montgomery Ward's successful move out of the catalog retail business.

Montgomery Ward's change in basic business indicates the growing recognition of the importance of strategic management and of a very important strategic management component: strategic planning. To be successful a company's strategic process must consider the important roles played by the major functional areas of business. This chapter directs attention toward the key aspects of strategic management and planning, with particular emphasis upon logistics strategy.

DEVELOPMENT OF STRATEGIC PLANNING

early years

During the 1950s and 1960s, strategic planning meant investment planning. The prevailing business doctrine was that diversity led to success and was a hedge against economic downturns. In the 1970s, strategic planning primarily emphasized internal growth opportunities, focusing on the firm's market structure and on research and development. Strategic planning also focused on the cost structure of a firm, primarily designing strategies to reduce costs. During the 1990s, strategic planners will primarily ensure competitive survival and create new opportunities. Also, much attention will focus on the firm's cost structure, primarily cost reduction and control.[2]

new focus

role of strategist

Strategic planning has come a long way from when companies would set up a planning department because it was a current fad—and then ignore all the department's recommendations.[3] Today, most strategic planners do not predict the future. Business and economic conditions are too unstable to allow completely accurate predictions. Instead, strategic planners present alternatives the firm may have to address within given scenarios. The strategic planner is frequently not a decision maker. He or she works closely with management, line managers or executive committees make the decisions regarding the options the planner presents.

OVERVIEW OF STRATEGY

The term strategy and the related concept of strategic planning have become increasingly part of our lexicon. As a result, strategy involves several definitions and some misunderstanding about what it actually means. This section clarifies how this text uses the word strategy.

military origins

The word strategy is a derivative of the Greek word *strategos,* meaning "the art of the general," which indicates its military origins. You probably have heard of military strategy and tactics; differentiating between those two terms would be useful, since they have implications for managers as well as for the military.

strategy versus tactics

Strategy, for our purposes, means a specific action or scheme or a principle idea through which we hope to accomplish a specific objective or goal.[4] In other words, it addresses the question of *how* we are going to achieve something we have identified as being important to our future success. *Tactics* refers to the actual operational aspects of the strategy. *Implementation* would be a good synonym for tactics. Tactics emphasizes short-run and even day-to-day activities or decisions. Strategy emphasizes the long run. Typically, strategies encompass three to five years. However, some strategies can take effect in one to two years.

To help understand the concepts of strategy, tactics, and implementation, consider the following two examples.[5] Both companies wish to increase market share and profitability, but the logistics strategies they use to accomplish these goals are quite different.

Sony Music Entertainment (formerly CBS Records) utilizes increased service as a logistics strategy to accomplish its goals. Their product is market-perishable; a customer wanting to buy a cassette or compact disc will not wait two or three days for the item to arrive from the warehouse. Sony's prior tactics consisted of having sales representatives submit orders every Tuesday, operating two plants, offering a five-day delivery service, and using a private truck fleet. To minimize transportation costs, Sony moved truckloads of product.

improved service

Today, sales representatives submit orders every day; and Sony, which gives regular two-day service to all markets, offers overnight service for case orders of on-hand product. This lower delivery service has increased the number of small shipments and, consequently, transportation costs. Additionally, as part of implementing this improved logistics service strategy, Sony will examine the use of EDI connections with retail outlets to automatically keep inventory levels current and the use of bar coded order entry from sales representatives directly to its three distribution centers. The ability to provide high customer service levels is an essential strategy for Sony Music Entertainment to maintain and improve its market share and profitability.

Avon Products, in contrast, does not face direct competition in the door-to-door delivery of its products. Consequently, Avon does not place the same emphasis upon customer service as a strategy to achieve its market share and profitability goals. Avon uses the same ordering system that it used twenty years ago, and it continues to operate on a two-week delivery service level.

low cost   To achieve its goals, Avon emphasizes cost reduction as a strategy to keep its products' prices comparable to those of similar products distributed through traditional retail channels. Avon has switched from using a private truck fleet plus common carrier LTL trucking companies for delivery to using small, specialized route carriers. The specialized route resembles a newspaper route, with the carriers operating as entrepreneurs. Because the company is under no competitive pressure to provide improved logistics service, minimizing costs to achieve competitive prices is the strategy Avon uses to achieve its goals.

As these two examples illustrate, the economic environment a company faces influences the strategies companies utilize to achieve essentially the same goals. The service level customers demand and differing degrees of competitive pressure require different companies to employ different strategies. Even two companies within the same industry will utilize different strategies to achieve their respective goals.

ELEMENTS OF STRATEGIC PLANNING

planning versus strategy   We should make a distinction between strategic planning and long-range planning. Long-range planning usually begins at the bottom of a firm, in its operating divisions—the separate business units. The focus, usually upon extrapolation from historical performance, often gives external variables minimal consideration.[6] However, some companies make exceptions by using sophisticated forecasting models.

nature of strategy   As indicated, strategic planning involves managing any business unit in the dual tasks of anticipating and responding to changes that affect the firm.[7] Strategic planning, which starts at the top of an organization, evaluates the relationship between the enterprise and its environment. It focuses on fundamental objectives and goals and on deploying resources to achieve them. It also evaluates the relationships among major functional departments in the firm. Though concerned with both short- and long-term factors, strategic planning for logistics usually emphasizes the long run.

contingency plan   Preparing contingency plans is an important part of strategic planning. Such preparation minimizes disruptions in a firm's logistical system by preparing the firm to deal with calamities and lesser problems before they occur. Being prepared will minimize confusion and financial loss if a problem situation occurs.[8] Table 15–1 indicates possible situations requiring contingency plans.

Effective contingency planning requires constant updating to keep the plan current. An obsolete plan may make a situation worse rather than better for the firm.

futuristic   Strategic planning has four general characteristics.[7] First, strategic planning involves looking at alternative courses of action that are open in the future. A

TABLE 15–1   COMMON OCCURRENCES REQUIRING CONTINGENCY PLANS

Calamities	Disruptions	Noncalamitous Occurrences
Windstorms	Infestation by pests	Strikes
Blizzards	Arson	Product recalls
Volcanic eruptions	Revolution	Economic problems
Floods	Railroad wreck	Changes in demand
Earthquakes	Highway accidents	Embargoes
Epidemics affecting people, livestock, crops	Power failures	Regulatory changes
	Fire	Changes in price
	Riots, civil disturbances	Changes in supply
	War	
	Shipwreck	
	Airplane crash	

chosen alternative becomes the basis for making current decisions. Another way of saying this is that planning involves designing a desired future and identifying the means to achieve it.

process   The second characteristic of strategic planning is that it is a process. The process begins by setting organizational goals and objectives; it then defines strategies and policies to achieve them; and finally it proceeds to develop plans to ensure that the firm implements strategies. It is also a continuous process because the firm must continually update plans as environmental changes occur.

approach   The third characteristic of strategic is that planning is an approach to doing business—or even an attitude. In order to be successful, it has to become engrained in managers. It cannot be an exercise that we perform and then forget, and everyone must believe that it is a viable method of doing business.

linking role   A fourth characteristic is that it provides a structure that links three major types of plans: strategic plans, medium-range programs, and short-range budgets and operating plans. Strategic planning is a systematic and usually formalized effort to establish objectives, policies, and strategies and to then develop detailed plans for implementing them. Such an effort requires linkage between a firm's plans and programs.

strategic questions   An element essential to the strategic planning process involves raising questions regarding the company's environment, customers, competition, products, opportunities, historical strategies, future directions, and resources. Table 15–2 provides a list of questions that arise in the strategic planning process. The answers to these questions require considerable examination of the company's basic reason for existing and the direction it should take in the future.

STRATEGIC PLANNING PROCESS[10]

As we indicated, a number of strategic planning approaches are available. Figure 15–1 outlines a several-stage process that a firm can use for strategic planning purposes. Those stages include appraisal, matching, setting priorities, implementation, and evaluation. As the process develops, it becomes apparent that the stages are not really distinct and that strategic planning requires constant monitoring and amendment.

TABLE 15–2	STRATEGIC QUESTIONS

What type of company are we?
What type of company do we want to be?
Who are our customers?
What is the nature of our industry?
What are the opportunities for us?
What are our strengths and weaknesses?
What strategies can we identify?
What strategy is best for us?
What objectives are consistent with the strategy?
What plans are consistent with our plans and objectives?
What are our contingency plans?
What budgets are necessary for our plans?
How shall we monitor performance?
What business or businesses are we in?
What is a logical planning unit?
What is the nature of the environment—the industry and the market?
What is the basis of competition and how does each competitor compare?
What have been our historical strategies and what are our current strategies?
What has been our financial performance and where is our investment?
What assumptions can we make regarding our future environment?
What will be our basic strategic thrust?
What will be our specific strategies to accomplish these thrusts?
What will be our action programs to achieve the strategies?
What is the risk?
What is the expected affect on quantitative performance?

Appraisal

Information and analysis are prerequisites to strategic planning. In the appraisal stage, the manager, or usually the management team, examines external and internal factors that are expected to have a significant impact and assesses them in light of the mission of the company or unit.

mission statement   The mission statement is a declaration about the nature and scope of the business and helps to establish the identity of the company or unit. It should also establish a clear focus and direction for the company. It is usually relatively brief.

external assessment   The management team uses the external assessment to identify external opportunities and constraints that may have important implications for the company or unit. Consider, for example, the situation of many companies in late 1980, after motor carriers and railroads had experienced major changes in the regulations governing their relations with each other and with their customers. Those transportation companies had to develop brand-new strategies, and so did the logistics managers that dealt with them. Not all changes in the external environment are as dramatic as the acts that deregulated airlines, motor carriers, and railroads. More subtle changes usually occur in areas such as demographics, cultural changes, or ethnic influences.

major forces   The major forces that an external assessment should consider are economic trends (federal, state, and local), demographic trends, technological and scientific developments, market trends, and developments within competitive sectors. The assessment should focus upon trends or forces that will affect the company's or

FIGURE 15-1   PROCESS OF STRATEGIC PLANNING

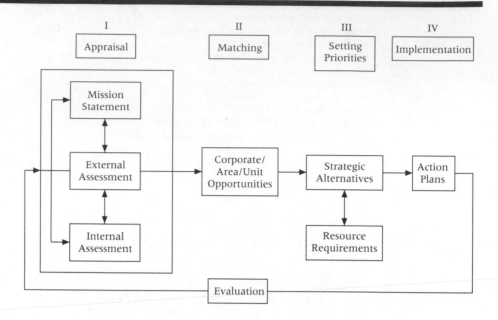

unit's activities. The assessment should help the unit to identify, on a preliminary basis, strategic directions that address the needs, opportunities, and constraints of the relevant external forces.

Table 15-3 shows a number of major external variables (e.g., demographic change), economic factors (e.g., the supply and cost of capital), and supply sources and constraints. The table also indicates possible effects in logistics and related areas.

demographics   We can examine several of these changes to illustrate the strategic planning process. In the demographic area, for example, we cannot question that the United States' population is getting older, families are smaller, more women are working, and more people are moving to Sunbelt areas. Companies have responded to those changes in various ways.

macro level   The macro-level assessment of external factors has implications for overall strategic planning. The appraisal identifies trends and issues that functional areas such as logistics should assess in finer detail. The corporate-level assessment can provide a common information base, a starting point for examining opportunities and threats.

Appraising internal strengths and weaknesses will help a firm to assess what it can accomplish in a quality manner. An appraisal should report on the status of human, financial, and physical resources and should identify internal capabilities and limitations.

Matching

blending   Strategy formulation begins when the management team blends value judgments of the external and internal appraisals with the stated mission. This matching process establishes a framework for relating elements of strength and need, and is essential for identifying areas or products to eliminate or enhance. It may also set the stage for further analyses, both external and internal.

TABLE 15–3   EXTERNAL VARIABLE

Demographic Changes
  Nature of Changes
    Growth rate of population
    Age distribution
    Size of family
    Location of population
    Size of work force
  Possible Impacts
    Location of facilities
    Management mobility
    Labor availability
    Market access
    Delivery costs
    Lead times
    Inventories
Economic Changes
  Nature of Changes
    GNP growth rate
    Inflation rate
    Cost of capital
    Wage rates
    Income distribution
    Differential regional growth rates
    Energy supply and cost
  Possible Impacts
    Inventory carrying costs
    Internal hurdle rates
    Labor costs
    Private versus public warehousing
    Private versus for-hire transportation

Supply Sources and Constraints
  Nature of Changes
    Diminishing supply of basic resources in
      United States
    Distance to new supply sources
    Instability of foreign supply sources
    Trade and tariff relationships
  Possible Impacts
    Transportation costs
    Global sourcing
    Use of intermediaries
    Supply shortages
    Inventory costs
    Warehousing requirements
Political/Governmental Changes
  Nature of Changes
    Tax rates
    Depreciation schedules and rules
    Allowable tax deductions
    Trade policies
    Consumer protection
    Environmental protection
    Farm program
    Industry subsidies
    Transportation regulations
  Possible Impacts
    Plant and equipment investment
    Global sourcing
    Transportation selection
    Research
    Packaging
    Executive travel

Source: Adapted from Theodore E. Pollock, *Distribution Strategy* (New York: McGraw-Hill, 1983), 42.

Frequently, this matching stage identifies logistics as an area for enhancement. Such enhancement may expand logistics activities to include such things as procurement, order processing, and customer service.

From a corporate viewpoint, the process should identify markets, products, and lines of business that will help the company to sustain its viability and to achieve its growth objectives. Other functional areas such as logistics will assist the process in these tasks.

Setting Priorities

alternative strategies

When the matching process is complete, the management team should specify alternative strategies for pursuing prospective changes. Early identification of anticipated resource requirements is critical. A first step in analyzing resource requirements is to reassess existing cost/revenue and cost/benefit relationships.

resources

The matching process usually examines opportunities essentially without considering cost. At the priority-setting stage, the management team may determine that resource requirements are too prohibitive to improve an area significantly. For example, you may be able to reduce average lead time by three days, but this would require adding three new private warehouses in new locations. The expense of the new warehouses plus the added inventory, even with the savings in other areas, may be cost prohibitive.

This stage should result in a limited number of strategies or, perhaps, broadly stated goals from which the team will develop strategies. These will form the basis for specific action plans. As it develops these strategies, the management team should receive thorough documentation of human, fiscal, and facilities requirements and supporting equipment needs.

Implementation

action plans

The implementation stage turns conceptual strategies into action plans. Typically, the action plans encompass several elements, including one- and two-year objectives, specific action plans, determining responsibility, and resource requirements. The team should identify annual objectives, and these should be measurable. For example, as part of an overall strategy to cut costs, logistics may have to reduce inventory levels. The management team can state one-year objectives in terms of percentage reduction, or as absolute amounts. Logistics itself may develop a strategy, such as switching to a JIT system. One-year objectives could focus on factors such as particular locations or product lines.

Evaluation

Figure 15–1 purposely presents the evaluation stage differently than it presents the other stages, and this stage transcends the others. Evaluation is both continuous and systematic. For example, external changes can occur at any time and may require modification or complete change in ongoing activities.

MAJOR TRENDS AFFECTING LOGISTICS STRATEGY

During the past decade, several discernible trends have emerged in the U.S. business environment; and these trends significantly affect logistics strategy. The major trends include transportation deregulation, company restructuring, globalization, quality emphasis, and service flexibility. The following paragraphs will discuss each trend, along with its resulting effect on logistics strategy.

Transportation Deregulation

Beginning in 1980, transportation deregulation created considerable opportunities for logistics managers to lower costs and improve services. Greater reliance on the marketplace to control transportation created an environment that encouraged companies to be creative and to innovatively approach the shipper-carrier relationship. The relaxation of economic regulatory controls over transportation permitted shippers to take novel approaches to resolving transportation needs in terms of both cost and service.

service

Carrier selection in today's deregulated environment focuses increasingly on the service level carriers provide. Shippers are demanding that carriers provide customized, tailored service; and the carriers are responding through a variety of mechanisms, primarily by establishing contract carrier relationships.

proactive

Transportation managers are seeing their job emphasis shift from a passive cost-control-and-tariff-compliance role to a proactive style oriented toward increasing the product value added in the transportation function. Product differentiation is possible with the use of a carrier that provides consistent, low transit times. For the industrial and reseller markets, consistent, low transit times mean lower inventory levels and lower inventory costs for the buyers, thereby giving the seller a competitive advantage.

contracts

Carrier negotiations and carrier contracting are transportation strategies common today. Shippers negotiate with carriers for desired service levels and transportation rates and then finalize these negotiations with a written, bilateral agreement. The duration of these contracts is increasing from the normal one year to an upward limit of five years. The three- to five-year contract is becoming quite popular with railroads and, to an ever-increasing extent, with motor carriers who have formed strategic alliances with shippers.

limit carriers

A related strategy is to reduce the number of carriers a shipper uses. Reducing the number of carriers concentrates the shipper's business and increases the shipper's negotiating power. This increased market power enables the shipper to realize lower costs and improved service. The carrier benefits by receiving a larger portion of the shipper's transportation dollar.

strategic alliance

Finally, many shippers and carriers are developing strategic alliances, which are essentially business partnerships. In a strategic alliance, the carrier recognizes the needs of the shipper and its customers and operates in a manner that benefits the shipper. In turn, the shipper recognizes the carrier's operating requirements and profitability needs. In essence, the strategic alliance is a mutually dependent relationship: the carrier depends on the shipper for revenue to survive, and the shipper depends on the carrier to provide the value-added service that makes the shipper's product competitive. If either partner fails, the other may suffer serious consequences.

Globalization

The world marketplace concept is a reality today. Companies are selling goods and services throughout the world and are purchasing raw materials from far corners of the globe. Increasingly, U.S. companies are feeling the pressures of a foreign competition capturing a greater share of the U.S. market. Likewise, U.S. companies facing maturing markets in the United States see growth opportunities in foreign markets. This globalization trend affects companies large and small.

As the marketplace becomes globalized, so must the logistics function. Logistics costs and service standards are just as important in a global setting as they are in a domestic market. Logistics provides the critical link for achieving a corporate global strategy. Logistics permits firms to connect raw materials sourced throughout the world with production facilities in different countries and to connect these global production sources' output with markets in many countries.

shipping

The obvious impact of globalization on logistics is in the area of international transportation. Voluminous national regulations and the resulting mountainous documentation complicate the international transportation arena. Shippers utilize numerous intermediaries to arrange for inland, ocean, or air transportation; freight transfer at the ports; and customs clearance. The intricacies of international shipping involve more than merely calling a carrier and handing over the freight.

intermodal

Intermodal transportation is a common international transportation system. International moves normally utilize various combinations of truck, rail, water, and air. Consider, for example, the movement of automobile parts from Japan to U.S. automobile assembly plants. The auto parts are loaded into containers at the Japanese manufacturing facility and moved by truck to the port, where the containers are loaded onto a containership. When the containers reach the West Coast the carrier offloads the containers from the ship onto a railroad flatcar. The railroad moves the container into Chicago, where a truck picks it up and moves it to a final destination in Michigan, Ohio, Kentucky, Tennessee, or some other auto assembly location.

logistics network   Maintaining an international logistics network involves developing a working relationship with foreign carriers, intermediaries, warehousing operators, and distribution channel members. Technological advancements in information systems enable an international logistics operation to manage and control inventories throughout a global network of vendors, plants, warehouses, and customers. This international logistics network enables the firm to achieve its global strategy of coordinating supply and demand throughout its world markets and supply sources.

varying service levels   To enable the company to compete effectively in global markets, international logistics must also examine different markets' customer service needs. For example, Japanese food producers and wholesalers can deliver an order in less than one day, whereas U.S. food producers and wholesalers require 7.7 days to deliver an order.[11] To compete effectively in Japan, U.S. food companies would need to modify their logistics systems to achieve the one-day delivery time the Japanese companies offer. Conversely, the Japanese firms' ability to provide one-day delivery time in the U.S. market would give the Japanese companies a distinct competitive service advantage over U.S. companies.

Corporate Restructuring

The 1980s witnessed numerous mergers and acquisitions, both domestically and globally. A vast majority of firms accomplished these business consolidations with heavy financial indebtedness, and, as a consequence, corporate strategy emphasized improved asset utilization and increased operating efficiency. In addition, companies are achieving improved asset productivity by reducing, or downsizing, the fixed asset base and concentrating resources on the company's "core" business.

third party   Corporate restructuring has had a twofold effect on logistics: a reduction in logistics staff and a reduction in logistics assets. The downsizing of U.S. corporations has meant a reduction in middle management throughout the company, including the logistics area. Companies reducing middle management staff rely increasingly on the use of third-party providers of logistics services, or outsourcing. The third-party provider offers expertise in a particular service at reduced costs that result from economies of scale and reduced assets requirements.

Let's say that a manufacturer of an industrial product ships approximately 500 containers per year to the European market. Although this volume of business is quite substantial, when the company was restructured recently, it could not justify the cost of an international transportation manager. Instead, the company decided to use the services of an international freight forwarder, who arranges for inland transportation to the U.S. ports, ocean transportation, inland transportation in Europe, and all of the international shipping documentation.

asset reduction   The second impact of corporate restructuring is a reduction in logistics assets. Companies will eliminate fixed assets not dedicated to the company's core business. For example, following corporate restructuring many companies have concluded that they could use private trucking more efficiently in their core businesses, and so have eliminated private trucking fleets, especially long haul, over-the-road operations. For similar reasons, many companies have eliminated their private warehouses in favor of public warehousing.

As the use of third-party providers increases, so does the adoption of the strategic alliance strategy. Companies employ strategic alliances with third-party providers to ensure the company provides its customers' desired logistics service levels at acceptable costs. The strategic alliance strategy recognizes that partnerships and mutual dependency exist and that both partners must be viable, efficient entities.

Quality

competitive advantage   Quality has become a major goal of most U.S. companies in their flight to maintain or regain a competitive advantage in the marketplace. Attention to quality in the product or service a company offers consumers, as well as in the company's pre- and post-sale support services, is uppermost in corporate leaders' minds; and this attention to quality is spreading from the top of the corporate organization to the bottom. The U.S. government's Malcom Baldrige National Quality Award is a coveted recognition that signals to the marketplace a company's dedication to high quality in all its operations's facets.

logistics service   Logistics quality issues are concerned with customer service levels and the company's ability to provide the logistics service level its customers desire. Providing quality logistics customer service levels requires a concerted effort in all phases of the logistics organization. Companies are developing quality programs to emphasize to their logistics personnel the importance of providing quality service and to define the role each plays in attaining and maintaining the service quality the company's customers desire.

monitor service   Logistics managers are implementing quality concepts within their functional areas. Statistical process control is a typical technique that measures logistics output and compares it to a desired service level. If the output does not meet the desired level, the manager takes corrective actions. Such techniques help to monitor outputs such as on-time pickup and delivery, correct filling of orders, and out-of-stock conditions, with the dual goals of delineating current service levels and recognizing areas requiring corrective action to achieve quality.

Quality management commonly utilizes a participatory management style in which managers ask logistics personnel directly involved with a function not performing to a desired quality level to seek a solution. In addition, companies are empowering lower-level managers to take corrective actions that assure a quality logistics service.

For example, a manufacturer of metal doors component systems had a corporate goal of 100 percent accuracy in filling orders. This goal of quality order filling won the company great marketplace acceptance and resulted in double-digit sales growth throughout the 1980s. However, during 1991, the company fell short of its 100 percent accuracy; and top management made a concerted effort to uncover problems and take corrective actions. To accomplish this, the logistics manager formed a listening group for each materials handling/order picker shift. He presented to them the nature of the problem, using as an illustration an actual shipment that contained errors, and sought their input for solutions.

participatory management

Following several meetings, the listening groups conveyed to management both the problem's cause and its solution. The problem that order entry personnel were bunching orders and that salespeople were pushing end-of-the-month sales to achieve quotas; this situation forced the order pickers to hurry to comply with promised delivery dates. The solution the groups offered was that the company redeploy existing labor to establish a small crew to pick orders during the third shift. During this time no trucks were at the dock for loading and unloading and materials handling personnel could give greater attention to filling orders during the high demand time. In addition, the marketing department changed its sales quota procedures to alleviate the end-of-the-month sales surge; and order entry transferred orders at the end of each day.

Service Flexibility

Being flexible and capable of responding to customer demands is a trend that coincides with the globalization, quality, corporate restructuring, and increased competition trends. Customers are becoming more sophisticated and more demanding of product and service quality, and they are capable of making analyses among suppliers. In addition, customers have different tastes and preferences for products and for services. The logistics area plays a critical role in providing the different service levels a company's customers desire.

heterogenous service needs

Logistics service flexibility recognizes the impact logistics service has on the customer's operation, cost, and sales. The impact is not the same for all customers, giving rise to the need for service flexibility. To establish a rigid logistics service level for all customers assumes, erroneously, that customers are basically homogeneous. As the U.S. market matures, marketing employs the strategy of market segmentation; and logistics must pay greater attention to the different service requirements of the segmented, targeted markets.

A commonly requested service flexibility issue is customer pickup. Many sellers have taken significant steps to develop strategic alliances with contract carriers, who coordinate shipment pickups to coincide with warehouse operating schedules so as to provide maximum service levels at a very low cost. The customer pickup request does not fit into this logistics system design. If the customer pickup vehicles arrive at a time that necessitates paying warehouse employees overtime wages or are of a height insufficient to allow economical loading, such a request may result in higher costs and lower service levels. However, noncompliance with the customer pickup request may result in the loss of the customer.

The logistics manager must examine service flexibility strategy in light of total profitability. Responding to the customer's requirements means keeping the customer, but if the cost of providing the flexible service exceeds the profits the company realizes from the customer, total profitability will suffer.

LOGISTICS EXCELLENCE[12]

profitable logistics

Table 15–4 presents the principles of logistics excellence. These principles, which may apply to any company regardless of its size, products, markets, or industry, provide the fundamental strategic thrusts that are common to companies with

| TABLE 15–4 | PRINCIPLES OF LOGISTICS EXCELLENCE |

Link logistics to corporate strategy
Organize comprehensively
Use the power of information
Emphasize human resources
Form strategic alliances
Focus on financial performance
Target optimum service levels
Manage the details
Leverage logistics volumes
Measure and react to performance

Source: Gene R. Tyndall and Seymour M. Zivan, "Corporate Profitability & Logistics: An Update on Logistics Excellence," *Council of Logistics Management Annual Conference Proceedings 1990) (Oak Brook, IL: Council of Logistics Management, 1991), 286.*

excellent logistics departments. Taken together, these excellence principles enable a company to achieve its full potential for profitable logistics operation.

Link Logistics to Corporate Strategy

support corporate strategy

Logistics is an element of the total company and, as such, is a member of the corporate team that must function as a unity to achieve the company's stated goals. Consequently, the management team develops and deploys logistics strategy in a manner that supports, not undermines, the company's corporate strategy and goals. That is, logistics strategy should assist the company in achieving its corporate strategies and goals.

For example, the company may establish a goal of increasing its market share. One strategy a company may utilize is to create a competitive advantage by providing service superior to that its competitors provide. The company's logistics strategy would aim at providing a high level of logistics service, such as consistent, low lead times and no backorders. To accomplish this strategy, the logistics department might employ the tactics of increasing inventory levels, using faster transportation modes, and utilizing an EDI system to connect order entry with the warehouse and the transportation carrier.

An alternative strategy to achieve competitive advantage in the marketplace is to be a low-price supplier. With a low-price supplier strategy, the logistics function would develop a strategy of low-cost operations. The use of low-cost modes and carriers, minimal inventory levels, and limited customer service levels would be possible logistics tactics for achieving this strategy.

The company's goals and strategies guide its logistics strategies. For example, it would be counterproductive for logistics to utilize a low-cost logistics strategy to achieve a company's goal of increased market share when the company and other functional areas are implementing a strategy of service differentiation in the marketplace. Lower logistics services would offset the service advantages the company gained in areas such as marketing or finance. For the company to achieve its goals, all its areas must operate in unison.

Organize Comprehensively

As we noted in the previous chapter, an organization encompassing all the functional areas of logistics is the optimal structure for achieving logistics ef-

ON THE LINE

CONTRACT LOGISTICS IS A EUROPEAN IMPORT

The trend in international third-party distribution logistics now taking hold in America is a European import, where the market has been developing for the best part of a decade.

The recession of the early 1980s in Great Britain, prompted in no small part by the introduction of Prime Minister Margaret Thatcher's austere economic programs, provoked a radical shake-up of traditional management attitudes towards distribution. Until then, distribution had occupied a kind of managerial twilight zone, existing in limbo between production and sales, largely untrammeled by modern management and accounting practices.

The early recession of the 1980s forced attention on two prime cost-accounting factors: the unnecessarily high levels of stocks that companies were paying large sums of cash to keep sitting in warehouses, and the heavy burdens of running fixed-cost, inhouse distribution departments. Producers and retailers started to take long, hard looks at their fixed distribution overheads, with an eye to trimming costs wherever possible, just as a new service industry started to emerge in the trucking sector.

British trucking, decimated by ten years of rate wars prompted by the deregulation of the late 1960s and 1970s, had started to evolve a new kind of hardened operator who was no longer looking for casual hauls on a one-time basis, but who was offering long-term service contract trucking.

The service contract trucking business proved immediately attractive to many producers for a wide range of reasons. Producers were able to rid themselves of the administrative burdens of running and maintaining their own haulage fleets, or hiring trucks as needed, and could instead concentrate their management and financial resources on the task they perform best—namely, production.

From these relatively straightforward developments in the British distribution market, a whole new international business in third-party logistics has now sprung up across the markets of the European Community, and is now starting to make its effects felt in the U.S. economy.

Source: "Contract Logistics Is European Import," *Traffic World* (26 February 1990), 17. Reprinted with permission.

---

coordinate logistics functions

fectiveness. Logistics organizational structures typically evolve from control of outbound line functions to coordination of all outbound and inbound logistics functions. Close coordination of logistics functions is essential for attaining high customer service levels, low logistics costs, or other logistics goals.

No one organizational structure is best for all firms. In addition, the organizational structure that is best for a given firm will change as the firm, its products, markets, and competition change. To achieve its maximum logistics potential, a firm must constantly monitor and modify its organizational structure.

Use the Power of Information

Companies that have achieved logistics excellence realize the potential and necessity of information processing systems that support transaction-based and decision-support systems. EDI links with vendors, customers, warehouses, and carriers can enable the company to achieve a competitive advantage in the marketplace via improved service and/or lower costs.

link activity centers

Companies usually direct investments in information processing equipment toward attaining economy and efficiency in transaction-based operations as order processing and inventory control. With the advent of computers with enhanced speed and capabilities, companies are utilizing computer information processing abilities to augment the logistics decision-support function.

Emphasize Human Resources

most important asset

Recognizing human resources as the logistics department's most important asset is vital to logistics excellence. Computers, statistical models, statistical quality control, and other quantitative tools will not achieve logistics excellence without well-educated, highly motivated, and creative managers. The challenge is for logistics departments to develop management programs that reward, educate, and enrich logistics personnel. Continuing education that provides logistics personnel with new management techniques and tools is now a common component in human resource management programs.

supplier

In a related area, the supplier's human resource management is of increasing importance to logistics managers. As companies form more partnerships and strategic alliances with vendors and carriers, these partners' ability to provide desired services depends upon their human resources.

Form Strategic Alliances

partnership

Logistics excellence recognizes that close partnerships, or strategic alliances, are vital to achieving a "win-win" linkage between outside service providers such as carriers and warehouses and inside interests such as marketing and production. For example, achieving the benefits of a just-in-time (JIT) operating system necessitates a partnership. Shared information, joint problem solving, and mutually profitable working relationships are critical to a strategic alliance in a JIT environment.

mutual dependency

A strategic alliance is not a substitute form of purchasing power to achieve cost containment. Rather, companies develop strategic alliances with strong partners who will contribute positively to the alliance's success. The partners in a strategic alliance are aware of the mutual dependency that exists and the mutual benefits that accrue to each if the alliance is successful. Thus, a strategic alliance permits both parties to function efficiently.

Focus on Financial Performance

Excellent companies gauge logistics performance on the basis of return on assets, economic value added, cost, and operating standards; and they manage traditional functions such as transportation and warehousing as profit or cost centers. These managerial approaches encourage entrepreneurial logistics managers to develop operational innovations that result in cost and service efficiencies.

return on assets

The return on assets (ROA) is an important financial measure of profitability, and companies are applying this to the logistics area as well. To measure logistics performance, companies are shifting from measuring logistics cost levels to measuring the return on logistics assets. This focus on logistics assets is one reason for using more inexpensive third-party providers for logistics services that require high capital investment. Cutting the use of private trucking fleets and switching to public warehousing are prime examples of strategies companies direct toward reducing logistics assets and improving ROA.

Target Optimum Service Levels

cost versus profit

Targeting optimum logistics service levels is a strategy that excellent companies utilize to improve profitability. A service-at-all-cost strategy does not assure profitability because the cost of providing the service may exceed the profit the company realizes. The optimum service level examines the trade-off between the marginal cost and profitability of providing various customer service levels, with the optimum service level being the one that maximizes the difference between revenue and the service's cost. Increasingly, companies are recognizing the need to determine optimum service levels for inbound materials going to the plant as well as to field support organizations.

Manage the Details

Streamlined operations will improve profitability, but paying attention to details will result in cost savings and bottom-line improvements as well. Companies with excellent logistics departments control an operation's fundamental details and resolve minor issues before they become major problems. The first-level managers and line employees can harness vast amounts of knowledge, experience, and creativity to resolve operating problems and to improve productivity.

Leverage Logistics Volumes

market power

Excellent logistics departments consolidate and coordinate shipments and inventories to increase financial and operating leverage. By handling larger shipment volumes throughout the year, the carrier gains economies of operation which are passed on to the shipper in the form of lower rates. In addition, leveraging shipment volume with a carrier enables the shipper to gain improved service levels from the carrier. An integrated inbound and outbound logistics department enables a company to provide a carrier with a balanced load pattern that precipitates economies to the carrier, who can pass these economies along to the shipper as a lower rate or improved service. Similarly, an integrated logistics approach generates economies in a company's warehousing, inventory, and order servicing areas.

Measure and React to Performance

compare performance to goals

A company cannot live forever on its past excellence accomplishments. Ongoing performance measurement is essential for a firm to take corrective actions that will enable it to maintain excellence in light of a constantly changing environment. Effective logistics operations link operating procedures to logistics strategy, which in turn is linked to corporate strategy. This linkage to corporate strategic goals determines necessary logistics performance levels and the best procedure for measuring performance compliance. Companies with excellent logistics departments require logistics managers to explain performance variations and to analyze standards' appropriateness in light of corporate goals and the dynamic business and logistics environment.

LEADING EDGE LOGISTICS FIRMS[13]

Firms that are operating leading edge logistics functions differentiate themselves from their competition via the logistics strategies they utilize. We may characterize leading edge logistics firms as follows:

Leading edge logistics firms use logistics as a competitive weapon to secure and maintain customer loyalty. They are more responsive and flexible, are more committed to their customers, and more aware of their results, work more closely with their suppliers, are more likely to embrace technology, and are more involved with their firm's overall strategic direction.[14]

value-added service

Leading edge logistics firms tend to manage logistics as a value-added process, and they reflect a stronger commitment to achieving and maintaining customer satisfaction. Such firms place a premium on logistics flexibility, with particular emphasis on accommodating special or non-routine logistics requests; and they are better positioned to handle unexpected events. Leading edge logistics firms make greater use of outside service providers, and these companies anticipate increasing the use of outsourcing. Such firms view third-party provider relationships as strategic alliances, and they emphasize the third-party provider's managing of itself and the service it provides.

outsourcing

planning and technology

In addition, leading edge logistics firms utilize formal logistics planning, involve logistics managers in business-unit strategic planning, and publicize their logistic performance standards and mission statements, and use state-of-the-art computers along with higher quality information system support and new technology such as EDI and artificial intelligence. Finally, leading edge logistics firms use performance measurements such as asset management, cost, customer service, productivity, and quality.

excellence

A close examination of the strategic characteristics of leading edge logistics firms reveals a great similarity to the principles of logistics excellence. In essence, leading edge logistics firms implement the principles of logistics excellence.

STRATEGIC TRENDS OF THE FUTURE[15]

Future logistics strategies are difficult to predict, but a number of discernible trends provide some indication of what is to come. Because of changes in the business environment and in technology, in resource availability and in the economy, the logistics strategies of the future will certainly be different from those of the present. The business world is dynamic, and the strategies companies employ to achieve business success must be adaptable. The following paragraphs estimate the logistics trends of the future.

service focus

The demand for basic logistics services will increase, as will requests for specialized or tailored services. Firms will monitor their customers' service needs and evaluate the profitability of providing various service levels. The attention to service levels will increase the logistics workload in the future.

global infrastructure

The quality of the world's infrastructure will greatly affect logistics productivity. The poor condition of the world's highways, railways, waterways, ports, and airports will limit the transportation system's operating efficiency and result in higher transportation costs and higher product and service prices. Nations must work separately and together to revitalize the deteriorating transportation infrastructure if carriers are to maintain the transportation efficiencies they have achieved during the past decade.

complex problems/ solutions

Future business operations will become more complex, and the solutions to logistics problems will become more sophisticated and more proprietary. Firms will use information technology to solve complex operating problems with tailored services and with solutions developed in conjunction with strategic trading partners. These solutions and systems will be very valuable to the company, which will be more reluctant to share its benefits with other firms.

Companies will evaluate individual functional areas and hold them accountable for the services they provide. The process or means of achieving strategic goals, rather than the end result, will become the focus of accountability. Information technology interconnections will create cause-and-effect cross-departmental accountability.

differentiation

Logistics competency will become a strategic resource that firms will use to establish a competitive advantage in the marketplace. Unlike product, price, or promotion, superior logistics performance is very difficult for competitors to duplicate. Strategies that produce excellent logistics service will earn the company a distinctively differentiated product with the potential for increased market share and profitability.

long-term partners

Strategic alliances and long-term partnerships with logistics service providers will increase. The mutually beneficial strategic alliance, in which a firm and its partner provide one another with dependable, specialized services, will replace adversarial suppliers relationships. Companies will consider these relationships more important than the individual transaction, and the strategic alliance will create a business view longer than the traditional short-term financial perspective of a quarter or year.

centralization

Centralization of logistics authority will continue, and the increased use of sophisticated information systems will centralize the responsibility for performing day-to-day functions. We can expect future organizations to commit to a centralized structure, with day-to-day activities performed within a formalized, decentralized framework. The firm will perform logistics line activities in a decentralized structure with a centralized focus.

transparent organization

Finally, future logistics organizational structures will become more transparent. Companies will diffuse functional responsibility to key personnel who are linked to information systems. Information sharing will coordinate logistics activities, and this information will be the basis for measurement and accountability. The logistics departments of the future will be increasingly information-based, and firms will reduce traditional hierarchical structures.

SUMMARY

While strategic planning is becoming more and more important in business firms, many top managers fail to recognize the important role logistics can play in strategy formulation and implementation. If logistics is to fulfill this role, logistics managers must develop the capability to do integrated logistics planning that covers the flow of materials from suppliers through manufacturing and distribution to the customer—the supply chain.

The development of logistics strategy begins with corporate goals and strategies. Logistics strategies support corporate goals, and logistics tactics support the logistics strategies. The strategic planning process gives attention to the company's mission, its external and internal environment, and its strengths and weaknesses. Such planning also considers contingency planning for catastrophic events.

Transportation deregulation, business globalization, corporate restructuring, an emphasis on quality, and service flexibility all affect logistics strategies. Leading edge logistics companies that have developed excellence in their logistics departments link logistics strategy to corporate strategy, utilize strategic alliances with outside suppliers, emphasize quality service to both internal and external customers, leverage logistics volumes, measure logistics performance, and use computer information systems extensively. In the future, organizational structures will become more transparent. Companies will spread logistics functions to key operating personnel and will make greater use of third-party providers.

STUDY QUESTIONS

1. What is the meaning of strategy? How does it relate to tactics?
2. What is contingency planning? What is its relation to strategic planning?
3. Describe the major steps in the strategic planning process.
4. In what ways has transportation deregulation affected logistics strategy?
5. A U.S. manufacturer has decided to build a production facility in Mexico. Discuss the impact of this corporate decision on logistics strategy.
6. What are the advantages and disadvantages of logistics outsourcing?
7. Describe the strategic effect of corporate focus on quality and service flexibility on logistics.
8. Discuss the major strategic characteristics of logistics excellence companies.
9. What is a leading edge logistics firm? How does it differ from other companies?
10. What are the major trends that will affect future logistics strategies?

NOTES

1. Elizabeth Canna, "How to Save $100,000,000," *American Shipper* (March 1989), 62–65.
2. William L. Shanklin, "Strategic Business Planning: Yesterday, Today and Tomorrow," *Business Horizons* (October 1979), 7–14.
3. John Perham, "The Strategic Planners Take Over," *Dun's Review* (June 1980), 72–77.
4. J. R. Galbraith and D. A. Nathansen, *Strategy Formulation* (St. Paul, MN: West, 1978), 4.
5. Ray A. Mundy, "Evolution of the Small Shipments Problem," *Council of Logistics Management Annual Conference Proceedings* (Oak Brook, IL: Council of Logistics Management, 1990), 285–94.
6. Reuben Gutoff, "Strategic Planning's Failure to Perform," *Public Relations* (March 1980), 32–35.
7. Derek Abell, "Strategic Windows," *Journal of Marketing* (July 1978), 21–26.
8. John F. Spencer, "Contingency Planning: Outflanking Fate," *Handling & Shipping Management* (October 1981), 58–69.
9. G. A. Steiner, *Strategic Planning* (New York: Free Press, 1979), 12–17.
10. Adapted from *Strategic Planning Guide* (Pennsylvania State University, 1984), 6–19.
11. David Ress, "Japanese vs. American Logistics," *American Shipper* (April 1990), 62.
12. The material in this section is adapted from Gene R. Tyndall and Seymour M. Zivan, "Corporate Profitability & Logistics: An Update on Logistics Excellence," *1989 Council of Logistics Management Annual Conference Proceedings* (Oak Brook, IL: Council of Logistics Management, 1990), 284–307.
13. This section is based on Donald J. Bowersox, Patricia J. Daugherty, Cornelia L. Droge, Dale S. Rogers, and Daniel L. Wardlow, *Leading Edge Logistics: Competitive Positioning for the 1990s* (Oak Brook, IL: Council of Logistics Management, 1990).
14. Bowersox et al., *Leading Edge Logistics*.

J & O ROOFING

Located in Florida, J & O Roofing is a small manufacturer of roofing materials, such as shingles. J & O has plants located in Fort Myers and Jacksonville and distributes its products throughout Florida, Georgia, and South Carolina. With the exception of this past year, sales have been consistently increasing by ten percent per year during the past ten years; and currently J & O sales are $26.8 million annually.

The southeastern market area has shown remarkable growth, due in part to the aging U.S. population and the resultant influx of retirees. The construction rate for new homes and multiple dwellings has surpassed the construction rate in all other U.S. areas. This growing market for residential construction has attracted considerable attention from other roofing manufacturers. These competitors have either established distribution centers or built roofing plants in the region.

In the past three years, J & O has seen its competition increase substantially; and for the first time it expects its sales to increase only slightly, if at all. Competition has forced prices down, and is very fierce in multiple dwelling projects. The construction firms' purchasing managers, realize their buying power, are exercising considerable negotiating efforts to extract even lower prices.

J & O's president, John Olmer, met with his senior executive staff to develop a strategy to remain competitive in this market and to return the company to its previous profitability level. Following a series of meetings, the executive staff concluded that the company had to become a low-cost supplier of high-quality shingles in the southeastern market. The low-cost strategy would enable their sales force to offer competitive prices to secure the increased business J & O needed to keep its two plants operating at maximum efficiency. If production dropped below its current level, the plants would experience excess capacity and the cost of the shingles would increase.

The vice president of logistics, Kay Clark, was involved in the executive staff meeting that developed the low-cost supplier strategy. Kay, who has been with J & O for twelve years, has implemented numerous innovations that have resulted in improved service. Kay is extremely proud of the logistics service levels J & O offers its customers and has received numerous congratulatory letters from them. J & O utilizes a private fleet of thirty-five trucks to deliver shingles to the construction site at the time the contractor dictates. The company uses the same trucks to transport shingles from its two plants to its warehouses located in Atlanta, Georgia, and Columbia, South Carolina. Each warehouse maintains a full line of inventory of all makes and styles. Given the slight slowdown in sales growth, each warehouse is full; and J & O is using two off-site warehouses at each plant to store the overflow from the plants, which are operating at full capacity.

Although cost containment has not been a major concern for J & O, the major thrust of its logistics function has been to provide quality service in the delivery of shingles to its customers. Kay has found out that one of J & O's major competitors has no warehouses and uses contract carriers to deliver directly from its plants. Numerous contractors have complained to Kay about the competitor's lack of on-time delivery and driver unloading assistance. Kay knows that if J & O's service level drops, the customer will have the same negative reaction. She is quite concerned about the impact this potentially lower service level will have on J & O's sales.

Case Questions
1. What strategic issues should Kay Clark examine?
2. What logistics strategies would you suggest?

SQUIRE AUTO PARTS COMPANY

Jane Esquire, vice president of logistics, had just reviewed the logistics staff report analyzing the elimination of Squire Auto Parts Company's private truck fleet. The report recommended the use of a contract carrier truck line as a replacement. The direct cost clearly indicated that using the contract carrier was in order, but Esquire was concerned about the staff analysis of the private trucking service benefits that could outweigh the added cost of the private fleet.

Squire is a manufacturer and distributor of auto parts, including filters, spark plugs, lubricants, shocks, and wipers, to the automobile aftermarket. The company has manufacturing facilities in Cleveland and Omaha and three distribution centers located in Atlanta, Dallas, and Los Angeles. The private fleet was started in 1965 and has grown to twenty-five tractors and seventy-five trailers. The fleet's primary use is to move products from the production facilities to the distribution centers and major customers and to transport raw materials from vendor locations to the production facilities.

Squire leases the private fleet equipment from RentUS Truck Leasing Company. Last month, RentUS made a formal proposal to provide contract carrier service in place of Squire's private trucking. The proposal called for RentUS to buy all of Squire's tractors and trailers at the buy-out price the lease contract contained—that is, at no cost to Squire. For three years, Squire would ship by RentUS contract carrier at least forty-five percent of the monthly tonnage moving between the plants and distribution centers, the volume the private fleet typically moved. RentUS contract carrier would charge a rate of $1.19 per mile for basic transportation; RentUS applied a range of hourly charges to a number of special services. The basic charges would be renegotiated at the end of the first contract year. In addition, RentUS would dedicate twenty-five tractors and fifty trailers to the Squire account and would provide one full-time dispatcher to route the shipments.

The logistics staff report concluded that the total cost of operating the private fleet was $1.26 per mile. One major cause for this higher cost was the labor agreement with the drivers. The drivers were members of the union that represented Squire's factory workers, and the wage and benefit agreements the union achieved for the factory workers applied to the drivers as well. During the thirty-one years the fleet has been in existence, there has never been a strike. Driver-management relations are excellent, and the drivers commonly assist in loading and unloading the trucks as well as in routing the loads.

The private truck fleet manager indicated to the staff analyst that the private fleet provided many service benefits that analysis could not quantify. These benefits included the ability to exercise great control over the trucks' routing to enable stop-offs in transit to deliver or pick up shipments; using trailers as short-term warehouses to ease the workload on warehouse personnel; the flexibility to change truck routes and dispatch times to meet emergency orders or plant demands for product and to keep inventory levels low; and controlling the provision of customer service levels at 100% dependability for promised delivery dates.

The staff report did not attempt to quantify the private trucking benefits, but indicated that the so-called benefits may in fact be an added cost that provides with no tangible benefit in terms of improved efficiency or sales. The staff report recommended selling the private fleet and accepting the RentUS proposal. The RentUS proposal would save Squire $105,000 this first year.

Case Question   1. What should Esquire do with the RentUS proposal? Why?

SELECTED BIBLIOGRAPHY FOR PART 4

LOCATION

Bowersox, Donald J.; Omar Keith Helferich; and Edward J. Marien. "Physical Distribution Planning with Simulation," *International Journal of Physical Distribution* (October 1971), 38–42.

Chentnik, C. G. "Fixed Facility Location Techniques," *International Journal of Physical Distribution,* 4, no. 1 (1974), 1–35.

Eiselt, Horst A., and Gilbert Laporte. "Integrated Planning in Distribution Systems," *International Journal of Physical Distribution & Materials Management* 19, no. 4 (1989), 14–19.

Friedrich, Carl J. (trans.), *Alfred Weber's Theory of Location of Industries* (Chicago: University of Chicago Press, 1929).

Geoffrion, Arthur M. "A Guide to Computer-Assisted Methods for Distribution Planning," *Sloan Management Review* 16 (Winter 1975), 17–41.

Geoffrion, Arthur M., and Richard F. Powers. "Facility Location," *Business Horizons* 19, no. 2 (April 1976), 5–14.

Greenhut, Melvin L. *Plant Location in Theory and Practice* (Chapel Hill, NC: University of North Carolina Press, 1956).

Hall, Randolph W. "Heuristics for Selecting Facility Location," *The Logistics and Transportation Review* 21, no. 4, 353–73.

Hoover, Edgar M. *The Location of Economic Activity* (New York: McGraw-Hill, 1948).

House, Robert G., and Jeffrey J. Karrenbauer. "Logistics System Modeling," *International Journal of Physical Distribution & Materials Management* 8, no. 4, 187–99.

Kling, Leslie T. "Strategic Facilities Planning Lets Companies Manage Their Facilities As Corporate Assets," *Industrial Engineering* 21, no. 6 (June 1989), 25–32.

Kuehn, Alfred A., and Michael J. Hamburger. "A Heuristic Program for Locating Warehouses," *Management Science* 9 (1963), 643–66.

Meidan, Arthur. "The Use of Quantitative Techniques in Warehouse Location," *International Journal of Physical Distribution & Materials Management* 8, no. 6, 347–58.

Mentzer, John T., and Allan D. Schuster. "Computer Modeling in Logistics: Existing Models and Future Outlook," special supplement appearing in *Journal of Business Logistics* 3, no. 1 (1982).

Pearl, Jossef, and Sompong Sirisoponsilp. "Distribution Networks: Facility Location, Transportation and Inventory," *Application of New Technologies, Methods and Approaches to Logistics* (James M. Stock, ed.), special issue of the *International Journal of Physical Distribution & Materials Management* 18, no. 6 (1988), 18–27.

Robinson, E. Powell, Jr., and Ronald K. Satterfield. "Customer Service: Implications for Distribution System Design," *International Journal of Physical Distribution & Logistics Management* 20, no. 4 (1990), 22–30.

Robinson, E. Powell, Jr. "Multi-Activity Uncapacitated Facility Location Problem: A New Tool for Logistics Planning," *Journal of Business Logistics* 10, no. 2 (1989), 159–79.

Schmenner, Roger W. *Making Business Location Decisions* (Englewood Cliffs, NJ: Prentice-Hall, Inc., 1982).

Warenburg, C. M. (trans.), and Peter Hall (ed.). *Von Thunen's Isolated City State* (Oxford, England: Pergamon Press, 1966).

QUALITY

Camp, Robert C. *Benchmarking* (Milwaukee, WI: ASQC Quality Press, 1989). Also see David Altant, "Copycats," *Industry Week* (5 November 1990), 11–18.

Chew, W. Bruce. "No-Nonsense Guide to Measuring Productivity," *Harvard Business Review* (January–February 1988), 110–18.

Crosby, Philip, *Quality is Free* (New York: McGraw-Hill, 1979).

Deming, W. Edwards. *Out of the Crisis* (Cambridge, MA: MIT Center for Advanced Engineering Technology, 1986).

Gordon, Jay. "The Evolution of a Quality Campaign," *Distribution* 88, no. 8 (August 1989), 68–72.

"The Gurus of Quality," *Traffic Management* (July 1990), 34–39.

Hammer, Michael. "Reengineering Work: Don't Automate, Obliterate," *Harvard Business Review* (July–August 1990), 104–12.

Holcomb, Mary C.; C. John Langley, Jr.; Carl M. Curry; David L. Neff; and William J. DeWitt. "Managing Logistics with a Quality Focus," Council of Logistics Management, *1990 Annual Conference Proceedings* (Oak Brook, IL: CLM, 1990), 161–70.

Juran, Joseph M., *Juran on Planning for Quality* (New York: The Free Press, 1988).

LaLonde, Bernard J.; Martha C. Cooper; and Thomas G. Noordeweier. *Customer Service: A Management Perspective* (Oak Brook, IL: Council of Logistics Management, 1988).

C. John Langley, Jr., "Quality in Logistics: A Competitive Advantage," *Proceedings—R. Hadly Waters Logistics and Transportation Symposium* (University Park, PA: Penn State University, The Center for Logistics Research, 1990).

Langley, C. John, Jr.; Mary Holcomb; Joel Baudouin; Alexander Donnan; and Paul Caruso. "Approaches to Logistics Quality," Council of Logistics Management *1989 Annual Conference Proceedings* (Oak Brook, IL: CLM, 1989).

Larson, Paul D. "The Integration of Inventory and Quality Decisions in Logistics: An Analytical Approach," *Journal of Business Logistics* 10, no. 2 (1989), 106–22.

Main, Jeremy. "Under the Spell of the Quality Gurus," *Fortune* 114, (August 1986), 30–34.

Novack, Robert A. "How to Calculate the Total Cost of Quality," *Distribution* 88, no. 8 (August 1989), 108–10.

Novack, Robert A. "Logistics Control: An Approach to Quality," *Journal of Business Logistics* 10, no. 2 (1989), 24–43.

Palmquist, James R., and Ray Mundy. "Western Management Process—Are Dramatic Changes Needed?" *Annual Conference Proceedings* I (27–30 September 1987) (Oak Brook, IL: Council of Logistics Management), 141–58.

Pisharodi, R. Mohan, and C. John Langley, Jr. "Measures of Customer Service and Market Response: An Exploration of Intersct Association," *Proceedings of the 1990 Transportation and Logistics Educators Conference* (Anaheim, CA: The Ohio State University, 1990), 92–105.

Pisharodi, R. Mohan, and C. John Langley, Jr. "A Perceptual Process Model of Customer Service Based on Cybernetic/Control Theory," *Journal of Business Logistics* 11, no. 1 (1990), 34–40.

"Quality: The Ante to Play the Game," *Traffic Management* (July 1990), 42–49.

"Quest for Quality," *Distribution* 89, no. 8 (August 1990), 30–62.

Reichheld, Frederick F., and W. Earl Sasser, Jr. "Zero Defections: Quality Comes to Services," *Harvard Business Review* (September–October 1990), 105–11.

Stahl, Michael J., and Gregory M. Bounds, eds. *Competing Globally Through Customer Value* (Westport, CT: Quorum Books, 1991). In particular, see James H. Foggin, Chapter 20: "Closing the Gaps in Service Marketing: Designing to Satisfy Customer Expectations," 510–530; and C. John Langley, Jr., and Mary C. Holcomb, Chapter 22: "Achieving Customer Value Through Logistics Management," 547–565.

Steiner, Thomas E. "Activity-based Accounting for Total Quality," *Management Accounting* 72, no. 4 (October 1990), 39–42.

Walton, Mary. *The Deming Management Method* (New York: The Free Press, 1988).

Wheeler, Donald J., and David S. Chambers. *Understanding Statistical Process Control* (Knoxville, TN: Statistical Process Controls, Inc., 1986).

Zeithaml, Valarie A.; Leonard L. Berry; and A. Parasuraman. "Communication and Control Processes in the Delivery of Service Quality," *Journal of Marketing* 52 (April 1988), 35–48.

LOGISTICS ORGANIZATION

Abeles, Sir Peter. "Logistics: Where are the Professionals?" *Focus on Physical Distribution and Logistics Management* 8, no. 5 (June 1989), 2–9.

Bowersox, Donald J.; Phillip L. Carter; and Robert M. Monczka. "Materials Logistics Management, *International Journal of Physical Distribution and Materials Management* 15, no. 5 (1985), 27–35.

Bowersox, Donald J., and Patricia J. Daugherty. "Emerging Patterns of Logistics Organization," *Journal of Business Logistics* 8, no. 1 (1987), 46–60.

Farrell, Jack W. "Logistics: The Evolution Continues," *Traffic Management* (September 1987), 88–101.

Farrell, Jack W. "Say Goodbye to the Old Organizational Chart," *Traffic Management* 29, no. 8 (August 1990), 57–58.

Herron, David P. "Integrated Logistics Management," *Journal of Business Logistics* 8, no. 1 (1987), 96–116.

Heskett, James L. "Leadership Through Integration: The Special Challenge of Logistics Management," Council of Logistics Management, *Annual Conference Proceedings* 1 (1988), 13–22.

Heskett, James L. "Organizing for Effective Distribution Management," in *The Distribution Handbook* (New York: The Free Press, 1985), 828–31.

"How Logistics Fits In," *Distribution* 88, no. 4 (April 1989), 29–34.

Langley, John. "U.S. Logistics—The State of the Nation," *Focus on Physical Distribution and Logistics Management* 8, no. 6 (July/August 1989), 28–33.

Lynagh, Peter M., and Richard F. Poist. "Assigning Organizational Responsibility for Interface Activities: An Analysis of PD and Marketing Manager Preferences," *International Journal of Physical Distribution & Materials Management* special issue: *Logistics: Interfaces with Marketing and Finance* 14, no. 6 (1984), 34–43.

Murray, Thomas J. "Rethinking the Factory," *Business Month* (July 1989), 34–37.

Pilnick, Saul, and Jo Ellen Gabel. "The Leader: Culturemaker or Crazymaker," Council of Logistics Management, *Annual Conference Proceedings* 2 (1988), 113–25.

LOGISTICS STRATEGY

Bowersox, Donald J., and David J. Closs. "Simulation in Logistics: A Review of Present Practice and a Look to the Future," *Journal of Business Logistics* 109, no. 1 (1989), 133–48.

Campbell, James F. "Designing Logistics Systems by Analyzing Transportation, Inventory and Terminal Cost Tradeoffs," *Journal of Business Logistics* 11, no 2 (1990), 159–79.

Christopher, Martin. *The Strategy of Distribution Management* (England: Gower Publishing, 1985).

Copacino, William, and Donald B. Rosenfeld. "Analytic Tools for Strategic Planning," *International Journal of Physical Distribution & Materials Management* 15, no. 3 (1985), 47–61.

Ernst, Kenneth R. "Visioning: Key to Effective Strategic Planning," Council of Logistics Management, *Annual Conference Proceedings* 2 (1988), 153–67.

Gattorna, John, and Abby Day eds. "Strategic Issues in Logistics," monograph issue of the *International Journal of Physical Distribution & Materials Management* 16, no. 2 (1986).

Germain, Richard. "Output Standardization and Logistical Strategy, Structure and Performance," *International Journal of Physical Distribution & Materials Management* 19, no. (1989), 21–29.

Kearney, Inc. *Measuring and Improving Productivity in Physical Distribution Management—1984* (Oak Brook, IL: National Council of Physical Distribution Management, 1984).

Kleinsorge, Ilene K.; Philip B. Schary; and Ray Tanner. "Evaluating Logistics Decisions," *International Journal of Physical Distribution & Materials Management* 19, no. 12 (1989), 3–14.

Kohn, Jonathon W.; Michael McGinnis; and K. Praveen K. Kesava. "Organizational Environment and Logistics Strategy: An Empirical Study," *International Journal of Physical Distribution & Logistics Management* 20, no. 2 (1990), 22–30.

Langley, C. John, Jr. "Strategic Management in Transportation and Physical Distribution," *Transportation Journal* 22, no. 3 (Spring 1983), 71–78.

Langley, C. John, Jr., and William D. Morice. "Strategies for Logistics Management: Reactions to a Changing Environment," *Journal of Business Logistics* 3, no. 1 (1982), 1–18.

McGinnis, Michael A., and Jonathan W. Kohn. "A Factor Analytic Study of Logistics Strategy," *Journal of Business Logistics* 11, no. 2 (1990), 41–64.

Ploos van Amstel, M. J., and David Farmer. "Controlling the Logistics Pipeline," *International Journal of Logistics Management* 1, no. 1 (1990), 19–27.

Poist, Richard F. "Evolution of Conceptual Approaches to the Design of Logistics Systems: A Sequel," *Transportation Journal* 28, no. 3 (Spring 1989), 35–39.

Rao, Kent; Alan J. Stenger; and Richard R. Young. "Corporate Framework for Developing and Analyzing Logistics Strategies," Council of Logistics Management, *Annual Conference Proceedings* 1 (1988), 243–63.

Wood, Andrew L. "Distribution Strategies for the 1990s," *Logistics World* 2, no. 2 (June 1989), 87–91.

FUTURE

Bowersox, Donald J., Patricia J. Daugherty; Cornelia L. Droge; Dale S. Rogers; and Daniel S. Wardlow. "Leading Edge Logistics Competitive Positioning for the 1990s," Council of Logistics Management, *Annual Conference Proceedings* 1 (1988), 123–32.

Goddard, Walter E. "Are You Ready for the Next Breakthrough?" *Transportation and Distribution* 31, no. 11 (October 1990), 33–34.

LaLonde, Bernard J., and James M. Masters. "Logistics: Perspectives for the 1990s," *International Journal of Logistics Management* 1, no. 1 (1990), 1–6.

Muller, E. J. "TurboLogistics," *Distribution* 89, no. 3 (March 1990), 3, 28–36.

Neuschel, Robert P. "The New Logistics Challenge—Excellence in Management," *Journal of Business Logistics* 8, no. 1 (1987), 29–39.

Sheffi, Yosef. "Third Party Logistics: Present and Future Prospects," *Journal of Business Logistics* 11, no. 2 (1990), 27–40.

Vorhees, Roy Dale, and John I. Coppett. "Logistics for a Service Economy," *Transportation Practitioners Journal* 56, no. 3 (Spring 1989), 286–93.

Voorhees, Roy Dale, and John I. Coppett. "Marketing-Logistics Opportunities for the 1990's," *Journal of Business Strategy* 7 (Fall 1986), 33–36.

Wark, Joe E. "Logistics Issues in the 1990s," Council of Logistics Management, *Annual Conference Proceedings* 2 (1988), 225–30.

Williamson, Kenneth C.; Daniel M. Spitzer, Jr.; and David J. Bloomberg. "Modern Logistics Systems: Theory and Practice," *Journal of Business Logistics* 11, no. 2 (1990), 65–86.

COMPREHENSIVE CASES

ATLANTIC PHARMACEUTICALS (A)

"And finally, transportation costs are out-of-control, Bev. These are the worst year-to-date budget variances in the division." Beverly Roberts listened patiently as Andy Docherty, the division controller, expressed his displeasure. He continued, "We're doing better than target overall, but we'd be doing even better if it wasn't for this freight-in account." Beverly, the vice president of operations for only two months, did not make transportation decisions—they rolled up into a profit and loss statement for her product lines. Bev replied, "All right, Andy. We're under the gun for the upcoming executive committee meeting on Friday. I'll have an explanation by then."

Atlantic is the U.S. subsidiary of Atlantique Pharmachemie S. A. (APSA) of Brussels, Belgium and is dependent on the parent firm for both technology and, in some cases, product. Knowledge of this latter point gave Beverly a starting point, and within minutes she had Larry Moreau, group director of logistics, in her office.

Larry, who had been with Atlantic for twelve years, previously worked for APSA in Europe and knew the parent's worldwide approach to both marketing and transportation. As he listened to Beverly's retelling of the phone conversation with Andy, Larry knew that the principal cause of the budget variance was the airfreight costs of bringing Cefatlan®, their newly reintroduced antibiotic from Europe, already prepackaged for the U.S. market.

Finally Larry spoke. "I certainly cannot deny that the unfavorable variance is of my cause, Bev. We've been paying $3.20 per kilo in airfreight on the incoming Cefatlan®, and that volume has increased to 3,000 kilograms per week. Brussels has been scrambling to keep up with our sales success, so we've been going hand-to-mouth ever since the FDA gave their approval."

"That's okay for product introduction, Larry, but at some point it's got to stop! When do you think Brussels will catch up and give us some breathing room?" Bev asked, clearly frustrated.

"Six to eight weeks, maybe—but I just can't imagine the explosive reaction I'd get from Jake Ellison and his sales group if I ever let him stock out." Jake, the irascible vice president of sales and marketing, was quite protective of his first antibiotic offering to the U.S. market, where he saw a doubling of company sales within two years. That kind of success would get Brussels to allow him to market even more of their newest product developments, which in the past they had been reluctant to do.

Beverly said, "I'll give you and our Belgian colleagues eight weeks to straighten this out. Then I want to see that product arriving by ocean—I know that with a product price of $300 per kilo, everyone sees big dollar signs in front of them, but there is no getting around the fact that this is a high-value product. By the way, how could you structure shipments?"

Larry hesitated, but finally responded, "We could get twenty thousand pounds in a twenty-footer—it'll cube out before maximizing the weight. Our service contract with the North Atlantic Conference currently sets that rate at $2,200 port-to-point."

"That's great! How long does the voyage take? And are there any other costs we need to consider? Maybe you can find additional savings on the nickel-and-dime stuff—you know, customs brokerage and our own order processing."

"Well, it will be a bit more than the three days by air! Assuming we don't encounter too many severe storms at sea during the winter, a voyage will take fifteen days plus additional pier and inland transit time—say twenty-one days in all," Larry replied. "But," he added, "we buy either F.O.B. Brussels International Airport or the port at Antwerp. And, by the way, don't forget that Andy still charges us 20% on in-transit inventories."

Beverly leaned back in her chair with a sinking feeling that the savings that she foresaw only a minute ago were to be elusive. "Yes, you're right, of course. But at least that's better than the outrageous thirty percent that he charges on finished goods in the warehouse," she exclaimed.

"If it's any consolation to you, Bev, my group estimates that an overseas order costs in the neighborhood of $400, if we include the broker's fee."

Confident that he knew his business better than anyone else in the company, Larry finally got up and headed for the door. Just before leaving, he turned and said to Beverly, "Don't worry. I'll get you an explanation, but first I need to make some calculations."

"Don't take too long with those," Bev called after him. "Andy and I are discussing this problem at the executive committee lunch on Friday. Thanks for listening."

Upon returning to his office, Larry Moreau calls you and asks for your assistance in formulating an answer to Beverly Roberts. You don't have much time to prepare a recommendation, as Larry wishes to review it completely before passing it on.

Case Questions
1. Which mode do you believe Larry's calculations will support?
2. What savings do you estimate that choice will yield?
3. What impact would this have on Andy Docherty's profit and loss statement? What accounts are affected?
4. Would you expect that such conversations are representative of the relationships logistics has within some major firms?
5. How do the objectives of these various functions typically differ?

Source: Richard R. Young, "Atlantic Pharmaceuticals (A)" (University Park, PA: The Penn State University, 1990). Reprinted with permission.

COMPREHENSIVE CASE 2

ATLANTIC PHARMACEUTICALS (B)

Hal Lawrence viewed the totals line of his spreadsheet with disbelief. The number was incredible. On just one item he could nearly fulfill his annual savings objective. As traffic manager, he was responsible for seeing that the company paid as little as possible for the transportation services it obtained.

After rechecking his inputs to make certain he was on firm factual ground, Hal printed the spreadsheet and immediately walked down the hall to see his boss, Donna Manning, vice president of distribution, to inform her of his success.

"Hi, Hal. Come on in," she beckoned. "What's going on? Good news, I hope!"

"Wait 'til you see this," he said, putting the printout on the desk in front of her. Hal began to explain: "We've been importing Atlamycin from our Belgian parent already packaged for the North American market. For nearly two years we've been airfreighting this product at a tremendous cost."

"But the new product campaign has been very successful, Hal," Donna countered. "Remember, in the beginning, we couldn't get product fast enough."

"That was nearly a year and a half ago. Things are different now. Look at the savings we can obtain by switching to ocean freight. We've been paying $3.20 per unit by air, but I calculate that we can load 30,000 pounds into a twenty-foot ocean container, which I can move on a door-to-door basis for a flat $1,900 under our service contract with one of the nonconference lines."

"You do seem to have your bases covered," said Donna, looking closely at the sheet in front of her. "We even save money on the customs house broker." Sitting back in her chair, she added, "We've been looking to hit a home run and prove our worth to the product group. This may be it. I'm having lunch with George on Thursday, and I'll be anxious to see his reaction." George Hoffman was the VP and general manager for antibiotics.

"Great," said Hal, adding, "I'll run an extra copy of this for you. Maybe Traffic is more important to the firm than some folks around here think."

Background

Atlantic Pharmaceuticals is the U.S. subsidiary of Atlantique Pharmachemie S.A. of Belgium, a major multinational chemical firm widely recognized for its pharmaceutical research prowess. Atlamycin, a new antibiotic enjoying major success in the United States, is extremely expensive. Each unit weighs 2.2 pounds, which includes extensive protective packaging. With Atlamycin at $300 per unit, these precautions are understandable.

The customer service and shipping departments in Brussels can dispatch an air shipment in three days, but an ocean shipment takes nine days due to the required additional staging and the inland move to the port. Terms of sale were always F.O.B. European port, or Brussels International Airport and Antwerp Container Terminal, respectively. Transit times were three days for air and eighteen for ocean.

The Thursday Lunch

"George, I believe we've come up with a way to save your operation a lot of money," Donna said proudly, showing off Hal's spreadsheet. "The days of product shortage are long gone, and we in Distribution think that airfreight is too rich for our blood. What do you think of this?"

"That's a very big and impressive number, Donna, but does it tell the whole story?" asked Hoffman. "We forecast 160,000 units for this year, and anything which limits product availability adds up to lost sales. I need not tell you what those losses mean when you're dealing life-saving drugs. "Lost sales" is not even in my vocabulary," he added with some emphasis.

"But, you've seen the numbers. We've considered total cost. Just look at the savings in order costs alone. Did you know that it costs us $400 as a company to process each import purchase order from start to finish?" Donna said quizzically, not giving Hoffman a chance to offer a rebuttal.

"Okay, you win, Donna, but I'll take a longer look at this back at the office. By the way, what does this do to my inventory carrying costs? Tony still charges me twenty-five percent carrying costs and fifteen percent on in-transit stocks." Tony Seanote was the company treasurer. "He seems to forget that the prime rate is now down to ten percent," Hoffman grumbled, as he folded Hal's handiwork and put it in his inside jacket pocket.

Case Questions
1. Using what you know about calculating inventory carrying costs, what are the total costs to be compared at Atlantic Pharmaceuticals?
2. Armed with this data, what do you recommend they do? Should Donna Manning still champion Hal Lawrence's cause?

3. What were the savings which Hal saw on his spreadsheet? He was looking at ordering costs and transportation costs.
4. Can you provide some insight into how misunderstandings, if any, could occur?

Source: Richard R. Young, "Atlantic Pharmaceuticals (A)" (University Park, PA: The Penn State University, 1990). Reprinted with permission.

COMPREHENSIVE CASE 3

TREXLER FURNITURE MANUFACTURING CO.

Trexler is a small manufacturer of upholstered furniture located in northeastern Pennsylvania. Although founded by J. Austin Trexler in the early 1990s, ownership has passed to Frank Ryan, who had been an executive at a local division of a larger furniture manufacturer. Although annual sales are $2.1 million, the firm has incurred annual losses or turned only minimal profits over the past five years.

Product

The product line consists of five major styles, all variants of colonial and traditional designs. Trexler, which has a reputation for quality, commands a relatively high price. Sofas, chairs and recliners; typify Trexler's furniture sizes however, some small-volume specialty products are also in the line.

Market

Their market lies primarily within a 250-mile radius of the plant and has 200 active retailer accounts who place orders either for their own showroom floor stock or as customer orders based on floor samples and selections from fabric samples. A typical customer will order two pieces, such as two chairs or a sofa and a chair; but orders for either single or three or more pieces occasionally occur.

Production

A single-plant operation, Trexler employs forty-eight people in trades such as woodworking, sewing, and upholstery. The operation produces nearly custom furniture in a job shop-type environment, given the company's relatively low volume and the permutations possible with three sizes, five styles, and approximately 100 different upholstery fabrics. The company ships finished product each day by uncrated furniture carrier.

The Management Meeting

"These setups are killing us," complained Scott Allen at the monthly meeting. "We change tooling several times a day, if not for style, then for size—sofas are different than chairs, which are different than recliners." Scott, the production manager, had been with the firm for many years, having been hired by Mr. Trexler himself.

"We're just a small operation, though. What do you expect?" replied Frank Ryan, president, CEO, sole stockholder, and sometime salesman. "Maybe you've got a suggestion?"

"As a matter of fact, I do!" Scott exclaimed. "We could run sofas for one week, then chairs for three or four days, letting recliners fill out the second week, depending on what the current orders look like."

"Sounds okay to me, but what about the various styles?" quizzed Frank.

"We'd run more or less one day for each of the five styles. At the end of two weeks we'd begin the size/style cycle all over again," Scott replied.

Frank turned around and gazed out the window, collecting his thoughts. "That's still a lot of changes, but I suppose a style or a size change is still better than a style and a size change. Any idea what your suggestion could save us?"

"A single change only takes seventy-two percent of a double. We'd make thirteen in ten working days, compared to as many as three per day currently," interjected Lou Sciota. Although a foreman in the woodworking shop, Lou, with his long-term familiarity with the antiquated equipment, also served as the plant engineer. He added, "Scott is right on this one. We'll produce more with the same labor costs, but with slightly less material due to improved scrap factors from the fewer changeovers."

"All right, guys, you've sold me," said Frank. "Have at it. I admit I've been on everyone's case to improve productivity, and you seem to have been listening."

End of the Quarter

Carol Muzzi, bookkeeper, plant accountant, and inside salesperson put her spreadsheet down on the desk in front of Frank. "The good news," she explained, "is that our per-seat costs"—units of production were recorded as seats for costing purposes: sofas = 3, chairs = 1—"have been declining. The bad news: inventories are increasing and cash is at an all-time low." Dismayed, she added, "We're going to need a loan against the line of credit just to make payroll this Friday."

Frank looked at the numbers. "Unfortunately, you're right," he said. "What's happening here? If we don't get to the bottom of this and quick, I'll have to get our line of credit extended, and the bank won't be an easy sell. I need some answers right now!"

Case Question 1. Write a report that provides the answers Frank needs. What factors are causing Trexler's inventories to increase while keeping the company's profits at a nimimum?

Source: Richard R. Young, "Trexler Furniture Manufacturing Co. (A)" (University Park, PA: The Penn State University, 1990). Reprinted with permission.

COMPREHENSIVE CASE 4

VELTRI MOTORS*

Company Background

Veltri Motors is the fifth largest automobile manufacturer in Italy. Based in Milan, Veltri produces nine different models under three brand names and exports to many countries in the European Community. One brand targets the economy segment of the market by using small, fuel-efficient engines and front-wheel drive. A second brand serves the sporty car market, making use of high performance engines and convertible tops. The third brand aims at luxury car buyers, producing full-scale cars with all the amenities.

Veltri owns six assembly plants, all of which are located in Italy. Each plant has the capacity to produce 300 vehicles per day; however, the plants have been operating at eighty-five percent of capacity. Sales have increased slowly but steadily over the past five years at around two percent per year. Veltri has no immediate plans to enter the U.S. market.

Purchasing

Purchasing is centralized at Veltri Motors. More than 130 personnel work under the Logistics umbrella. These employees fall into six divisions: Production Purchasing, Facilities Purchasing, Production Scheduling, Transportation, Supplier Quality, and Administration.

The company's distinguishing characteristic is that outside suppliers manufacture approximately eighty percent of the parts on any car Veltri produces. Veltri believes this high degree of outsourcing to be a competitive advantage. Because of the severe competition between suppliers, prices remain competitive and the suppliers maintain technological investment. This permits Veltri Motors to concentrate on assembly.

Veltri Motors employs approximately 100 commodity managers, who are responsible for purchasing. A commodity manager works with engineers, financial analysts, and quality personnel to find suppliers for automotive parts. Three objectives remain atop the buyers' list: supply high-quality parts at the lowest price with a steady supply.

Of the forty-five production buyers, five are responsible for the purchase of stamped parts. These consist of steel and aluminum parts used primarily for the car body and frame. Suppliers purchase their own supply of raw materials. Once in the plant, they slip the material between two dies and literally stamp out parts. The parts are then shipped to the assembly plant, usually just-in-time for assembly.

In choosing the supplier, the commodity manager solicits bids by sending an RFQ (a request for quote) out to a number of suppliers. These suppliers analyze blueprints, projected volumes, raw materials, tooling, and labor. They then submit their quoted price and timing to the buyer for review. After analysis, the buyer awards the job to the winning bidder and sends a PO (purchase order) to the supplier to serve as the business contract between the two companies.

Veltri Motors pays a supplier based on the piece price of each part the supplier delivers. This piece price consists of labor and material. Veltri pays the tooling costs, and they maintain ownership of the tools throughout the life of the job, even though the supplier maintains possession.

The raw material suppliers fall into two categories. First are the large, integrated steel and aluminum mills who produce tremendous volumes of steel and aluminum in massive, capital-intensive operations. Examples of firms in this category are Thyssen (Germany), UXS, LTV, Alcoa, and Mitsubishi. In order to use these raw material sources, a buyer must order a minimum of twenty tons per month and accept a sixteen-week minimum lead time.

The second category of raw material suppliers are the service centers. They purchase steel and aluminum from the large mills and process them into smaller orders. They have no minimum tonnage, and lead times are often by the hour. However, because of this service characteristic, prices are significantly higher when utilizing service centers.

More than 100 stampers are currently shipping parts to Veltri Motors. Most are small operations that do less than $40 million in sales each year, and Veltri represents the greatest portion of their business. As we mentioned before, each stamper is responsible for buying its own raw material requirements and determines how to utilize that material most efficiently. Because of the relatively small order size that each stamper requires, most rely heavily on the service center segment to supply them with raw materials. Therefore, prices are significantly higher than they would be if the stampers could use large steel mills. The stampers then pass this higher cost on to Veltri in the part's piece price; and Veltri ultimately passes the cost on to the consumer.

Case Questions

1. Should Veltri reduce its level of outsourcing? What advantages and disadvantages would this bring?

2. What would a supply base reduction accomplish?

3. How could Veltri integrate backwards, without becoming a raw materials manufacturer, to take responsibility for steel and aluminum purchases for its suppliers and consolidate small tonnages into larger orders to take advantage of mill prices? What organizational changes would be necessary?

*Written by Gregory Stock under the supervision of John J. Coyle.

COMPREHENSIVE CASE 5

LIPPINCOTT COMPUTER*

The Scenario

Steve Kann walked into a meeting with all of the top level plant personnel. Several executives from headquarters were also in attendance. Steve was the youngest level manager in the corporation. Though he had only three years of experience under his belt, the company was beginning to take his ideas seriously. Implementing just-in-time production at the company's made-to-order facility had some serious implications, but Steve thought those problems could be resolved. His boss, Jim Hines, had arranged the meeting after being convinced that Steve had some important ideas that could make a positive difference.

The Company

The Lippincott Computer Company is an international manufacturer of computer systems for various business applications. Having manufacturing operations in eight states and numerous foreign countries, the company produces mainframe systems for large businesses, mid-range systems for medium-sized businesses, and personal computers for all businesses and home users.

The Minneapolis Plant

Their plant in Minneapolis produces the RX-2000, a mainframe computer system for medium-sized businesses. Each RX-2000 is completely custom-made. Sales representatives act as consultants for clients. In most cases, salespeople actually have offices in the client's facility to help implement and maintain Lippincott's computer applications.

Lippincott relies heavily upon batching in the Minneapolis plant. By smoothing the workflow, specializing the work force, and minimizing the average setup time, managers try to realize at least some economies of scale. In reality, however, batching has caused more problems than it has solved. Lead time for the RX-2000 is approximately eighteen weeks from the time final customer design is agreed upon. Lead times are long because work on any order cannot begin until orders are sufficient to fill a batch. This lulls suppliers into complacency and leads to delivery and quality problems. Defects cause extensive rework, triggering further delays and scheduling difficulties. These scheduling troubles produce a high work-in-process inventory. Finally, management has hired legions of overhead personnel to monitor workflow. The end result is that quality and delivery has suffered, and shop floor chaos has spread.

Management's reaction to these problems has been termed the monthly shipment "hockey stick": after a dismal three-week trickle of product, a large volume of product leaves the factory at the end of the measurement period. Company personnel have relaxed quality standards to make quotas and have hidden secret rework in work-in-process. Production priorities are ever-changing, and crises occur daily on the shop floor.

Case Questions

1. Pretend you are Steve Kann and you are preparing for your presentation. What are the benefits of just-in-time production?
2. What problems arise when trying to implement a just-in-time system in a "made-to-order" facility?
3. How would you implement this system? What policies would you implement? What tools would you use to get employees to work with this new system?

*Written by Gregory Stock under the supervision of John J. Coyle.

VEIL CHEMICAL

The Company

The Veil Chemical Company produces industrial and agricultural chemicals and plastics for customers around the world. Their products are used in paints, pesticides, and plastic taillights for automobiles. Based in Baltimore, Veil has carved out an important niche for itself and maintains forty-one manufacturing facilities in the United States and abroad. They have an important relationship with their competitors in that they are both a supplier and customer to most. For example, they supply polymers to and purchase monomers from Dow Chemical. The company has similar relationships with DuPont, ICI, and Ciba Geigy. Veil also feeds its own plants with certain raw materials.

Transportation Department

The transportation department at Veil must coordinate shipments of chemicals to and from its own plants, as well as to its customers. This is a critical department at Veil, considering that eighty percent of its chemicals are hazardous. The department consists of Packaged Transportation, Bulk Transportation, Claims, Carrier Safety, and Packaging. The Packaged Transportation area coordinates moves between nodes for all chemical products packaged before transportation.

Veil's largest manufacturing plant is located in Dallas, Texas. Streetsmart Trucking Company was the single carrier supplying transportation services from the plant. Veil liked the single-source option for the Dallas facility because Streetsmart designated special capital for the business. The chemicals Veil produces at the plant need a slightly modified tank truck, which Streetsmart willingly provides. Over the last nine months, however, Veil had received numerous complaints about Streetsmart's service and delivery. Even after Veil discussed the issue with the carrier, the poor performance continued.

In considering alternative transport sources for the Dallas business, Veil came across Quickfreight, Inc. Veil had worked with Quickfreight on two previous occasions and felt confident about their abilities. Quickfreight was a regional company that had recently decided to nationalize their operations. They had an outstanding industry reputation for fast delivery, excellent reliability, and competitive pricing. In addition, Quickfreight had recently designed their own version of the specialized tank truck. Veil felt that this innovation was adequate for the Dallas business. However, they realized that it would take time for any new company to build a fleet of tank cars and deliver a new service to an unknown facility. Unfortunately, because of its nationalization decision, Quickfreight did not have the capital to build the new tank truck on a scale Veil found acceptable.

In a meeting between Veil and Quickfreight in Baltimore, Quickfreight announced that Green Industries had initiated a takeover of their company. Greene, a holding company that already held four regional carriers, had purchased a large block of Quickfreight's stock and announced their intentions to run the company. In a meeting between the boards of both companies, Greene and Quickfreight decided to join operations. Greene Industries also committed itself to heavy capital investment into Quickfreight to gain the Veil business. But Veil had no previous experience with Greene Industries.

Case Questions 1. If Veil Chemical gives all its business to Quickfreight, what risks come into play?

2. What are the advantages and disadvantages of dual- and single-sourcing for Veil Chemical?

3. Pretend you are Veil's transportation manager. How do you think Streetsmart would react to a dual-sourcing situation? How would you handle Streetsmart?

4. What do you think Veil Chemical should do?

*Written by Gregory Stock under the supervision of John J. Coyle.

COMPREHENSIVE CASE 7

MINIFIX, INC.*

The Company

Minifix, Inc., regionally manufactures and services minicomputers in the northwestern United States. Their logistics department consists of transportation and distribution. Employees under this umbrella are responsible for corporate contract negotiation, site selection, and long-term strategies such as EDI and electronic transmission. Minifix sells directly to users who require office automation for banking, insurance, government; the company also sells to many Fortune 500 companies.

Distribution

Minifix, headquartered in Brockton, Massachusetts, fifteen miles south of Boston, uses a variety of carriers for outbound shipments from their manufacturing plants in the area. These include padded vans (twenty percent), common carriers (thirty percent), and small package shipments (fifty percent). Minifix negotiated contractual arrangements with all carriers through a time-consuming and costly RFQ (request for quote) process.

To distribute products, Minifix used many different and complicated formulas. This resulted in inconsistent transit times for customers, especially those in small market areas. Equipment problems were frequent. Some carriers dispatched to the plants were not equipped to handle sensitive high-value merchandise. In other cases, carriers were incapable of unloading inside.

Communications suffered as well. Messages often became confused because of the legions of carrier personnel involved. Minifix employees wasted too much time performing simple tasks such as obtaining shipment status information. Only about one-eighth of Minifix's carriers had automated shipment tracking capabilities.

Product returns were a disaster. Plagued by a paper-intensive, bureaucratic process, customers were extremely dissatisfied. After a customer contacted Minifix to return an item, Minifix personnel would contact one of thirty local hauling companies to try to arrange for pickup. The cartage company, typically a local agent for a national van line, would then determine a pickup date. This cumbersome process often kept equipment waiting in the customer's office for days, sometimes weeks, before the carrier collected it.

The administrative burdens were staggering. Minifix expended vast resources handling customers' complaints, contacting local carriers, tracking freight, and maintaining carrier contracts with thirty firms.

Case Questions
1. If you were the logistics manager, how would you analyze the potential benefits of a third-party logistics approach?

2. Could Minifix really benefit from a third-party logistics approach? If so, how? If not, what other alternatives would you recommend?

*Written by Gregory Stock under the supervision of John J. Coyle.

SELECTED LOGISTICS PUBLICATIONS

Air Cargo World
6225 Barfield Road
Atlanta, GA 30328

Army Logistician
U.S. Army Logistics Management Center
Fort Lee, VA 23801

American Shipper
P.O. Box 4728
Jacksonville, FL 32201

Container News
6225 Barfield Road
Atlanta, GA 30328

Distribution
Chilton Publications
Radnor, PA 19089

Distribution Worldwide
Chilton Publications
Radnor, PA 19089

Defense Transportation Journal
College of Business Administration
University of Maryland
College Park, MD 20742

EDI News
7811 Montrose Road
Potomac, MD 20854

Fleet Owner
FM Business Publications, Inc.
475 Park Avenue South
New York, NY 10016

Freight Management
Ravenshead Press Ltd.
19-21 Farringdon Street
London EC4 4AB
England

ICC Practitioners' Journal
Association of ICC Practitioners
1112 ICC Building
Washington, DC 20423

Inbound Logistics
Five Penn Plaza
New York, NY 10119

International Journal of Logistics Management
% University of North Florida
4567 St. Johns Bluff Road S.
Jacksonville, FL 32216-6699

International Journal of Physical Distribution and Logistics Management
MCB University Press, Ltd.
62 Toller Lane
Bradford West Yorkshire
BD8 9BY

Jet Cargo News
P.O.Box 920952
Houston, TX 77292

Journal of Business Logistics
Council of Logistics Management
2803 Butterfield Road
Oak Brook, IL 60521

Journal of Purchasing and Materials Management
National Association of Purchasing Management
2055 E. Centennial Circle
Tempe, AZ 85282-0960

Journal of Transport Economics and Policy
University of Bath
Claverton Down
Bath BA2 7AY
England

Logistics Information Management
(formerly *Logistics World*)
IFS Publications
39 High Street
Kempston
Bedford MK42 7BT
England

Logistics Spectrum—Society of Logistics Engineers
125 West Park Loop
Suite 201
Huntsville, AL 35806-1705

Logistics and Transportation Review
c/o University of British Columbia
Vancouver, BC, Canada

Modern Bulk Transporter
874 Chestnut Tree Drive
Annapolis, MD 21401

Modern Materials Handling
Cahnes Publishing Company
Division of Reed Publishing U.S.A.
275 Washington Street
Newton, MA 02158-1630

Modern Railroads
20 North Wacker Drive
Chicago, IL 60606

Naval Research Logistics Quarterly
John Wiley & Sons, Inc.
605 Third Avenue
New York, NY 10158

Proceedings of the Annual Conference of the Council of Logistics Management
2803 Butterfield Road
Oak Brook, IL 60521

Production and Inventory Management
American Production and Inventory Control Society
500 West Annandale Road
Falls Church, VA 22046-4274

Purchasing
Cahnes Publishing Company
Division of Reed Publishing U.S.A.
275 Washington Street
Newton, MA 02158-1630

Railway Age
175 West Jackson Boulevard
Chicago, IL 60604

Traffic Management
275 Washington Street
Newton, MA 02158

Traffic World
1325 G Street NW
Washington, DC 20005

Transport Topics
2200 Mill Road
Alexandria, VA 22314

Transportation and Distribution
(formerly *Handling & Shipping Management*)
1100 Superior Ave.
Cleveland, OH 44114

Transportation Journal
American Society of Transportation & Logistics
1816 Norris Pl. #4
Louisville, KY 40205

Transportation Quarterly
Eno Foundation for Transportation
Westport, CT 06880

Transportation Research Forum
1133 15th Street NW #1000
Washington, DC 2000

SELECTED LOGISTICS ASSOCIATIONS

Air Freight Association of America (AFA)
1710 Rhode Island Avenue
2nd Floor
Washington, DC 20036
202-293-1030
(Also listed as Air Freight Forwarders Association of America)

Air Freight Motor Carriers Conference (AFMCC)
2200 Mill Road,
Alexandria, VA 22314
703-838-1887

Air Transport Association of America (ATA)
1709 New York Avenue NW
Washington, DC 20006
202-626-4000

American Association of State Highway Transportation Officials (AASHTO)
444 N. Capitol NW
Suite 225
Washington, DC 20001
202-624-5800

American Bureau of Shipping (ABS)
45 Eisenhower Drive
P.O. Box 910
Paramus, NJ 07653
201-368-9100

American Institute for Shippers Associations (AISA)
P.O. Box 33457
Washington, DC 20033
202-628-0933

American Maritime Association (AMA)
485 Madison Avenue
New York, NY 10022
212-319-9217

American Package Express Carriers Association (APECA)
2200 Mill Road
Alexandria, VA 22314
703-838-1887

American Production and Inventory Control Society (APICS)
500 W. Annandale Road
Falls Church, VA 22046
703-237-8344

American Purchasing Society (APS)
11910 Oak Trail Way
Port Richey, FL 34668
813-862-7998

American Short Line Railroad Association (ASLRA)
2000 Massachusetts Avenue NW
Washington, DC 20036
202-785-2250

American Society of Transportation and Logistics (ASTL)
P.O. Box 33095
Louisville, KY 40232
502-451-8150

American Trucking Associations (ATA)
2200 Mill Road
Alexandria, VA 22314
(703) 838-1700

American Warehousemen's Association (AWA)
1165 N. Clark Street
Chicago, IL 60610
312-787-3377

American Waterways Operators (AWO)
1600 Wilson Blvd.
Suite 1000
Arlington, VA 22209
703-841-9300

Association of American Railroads (AAR)
American Railroads Bldg.,
50 F Street NW
Washington, DC 20001
202-639-2100

Association of Railroad Advertising and Marketing (ARAM)
3706 Palmerston Road
Shaker Heights, OH 44122
216-751-9673

Association of Transportation Practitioners (ATP)
1725 K Street
Suite 301
Washington, DC 20006
202-466-2080

Automotive Warehouse Distributors Association (AWDA)
9140 Ward Parkway
Kansas City, MO 64114
816-444-3500

Canadian Association of Logistics Management
610 Alden Road
Suite 201
Markham, Ontario L3R 9Z1
416-513-0624

Centro Éspanol de Logistica
Paseo de la Castellana
114-4a 10o
Madrid, Spain 28046
34-1 4116753

Conference on Safe Transportation of Hazardous Articles (COSTHA)
c/o Lawrence W. Bierlein
2300 N Street NW
Washington, DC 20037
202-663-9245

Conveyor Equipment Manufacturers Association (CEMA)
932 Hangerford Dr.
Suite 36
Rockville, MD 20850

Council of Logistics Management (CLM)
2803 Butterfield Road
Suite 380
Oak Brook, IL 60521
708-574-0985

Delta Nu Alpha
621 Plainfield Road
Suite 308
Willowbrook, IL 60521
708-850-7100

Electronic Data Interchange Association
225 Reinekers Lane
Alexandria, VA 22314
703-838-8042

Eno Foundation for Transportation (EFT)
P.O. Box 2055
Westport, CT 06880
203-227-4852

European Logistics Association
P.O. Box 90730
2509 LS The Hague
Netherlands
31-70-1802067

Great Lakes Maritime Institute (GLMI)
Belle Isle
Detroit, MI 48207
313-267-6440

Hazardous Materials Advisory Council (HMAC)
1110 Vermont Avenue NW
Suite 250
Washington, DC 20005
202-228-1460

Institute of Logistics & Distribution Management
4th Floor, Douglas House
Queens Square
Corby, Northampton
England NN17 1 PL
05-36-205500

Intermodal Transportation Association (ITA)
6410 Kenilworth Avenue
Suite 108
Riverdale, MD 20840
301-864-2661

International Association of NVOCCs
3251 Old Lee Hwy
Suite 516
Fairfax, VA 22030
703-691-0900

International Material Management Society (IMMS)
8720 Red Oak Blvd.
Suite 224
Charlotte, NC 28217
704-525-4667

Interstate Truckload Carrier Conference (ITCC)
2200 Mill Road
Alexandria, VA 22314
703-838-1950

Material Handling Institute (MHI)
8720 Red Oak Blvd.
Suite 201
Charlotte, NC 28217
704-522-8644

Motor Carriers Tariff Service (MCTS)
6025 Royalton Road, UP
Cleveland, OH 44133
216-582-0030

National Small Shipments Traffic Conference (NASSTRAC)
1750 Pennsylvania Avenue
Suite 1105
Washington, DC 20006
202-393-5505

National Air Carrier Association (NACA)
1730 M Street NW
Suite 806
Washington, DC 20036
202-833-8200

National Air Transportation Association (NATA)
4226 King Street
Alexandria, VA 22302
703-845-9000

National Association of Purchasing Management (NAPM)
2055 E. Centennial Circle
P.O. Box 22160
Tempe, AZ 85282
602-752-6276

National Association of Rail Shippers Advisory Boards (NARSAB)
American Railroads Bldg.
50 F Street NW
Washington, DC 20001
202-639-2378

National Defense Transportation Association (NDTA)
505 S. Pickett Street
Suite 220
Alexandria, VA 22304
703-751-5011

National Export Traffic League (NETL)
234 Fifth Avenue
New York, NY 10001
212-697-5895

National Freight Transportation Association (NFTA)
P.O. Box 21856
Roanoke, VA 24018
703-774-7725

National Industrial Transportation League (NITL)
1090 Vermont Avenue NW
Suite 410
Washington, DC 20005
202-842-3870

National Institute of Packaging, Handling, and Logistics Engineers (NIPHLE)
6902 Lyle Street
Lanham, MD 20706
301-459-9105

National Private Truck Council (NPTC)
1320 Braddock Pl.
Suite 720
Alexandria, VA 22314
703-683-1300

National Railway Labor Conference (NRLC)
1901 L Street NW
Suite 500
Washington, DC 20036
202-862-7200

National Truck Equipment Association (NTEA)
38705 Seven Mile Road
Suite 345
Livonia, MI 48152
313-462-2190

National Waterways Conference (NWC)
1130 17th Street, NW
Suite 200
Washington, DC 20036
202-296-4415

North American Association of Inventory Services (NAAIS)
1609 Holbrook Street
Greensboro, NC 27403
919-294-2216

Parcel Shippers Association (PSA)
1211 Connecticut Avenue NW
Washington, DC 20036
202-296-3690

Regular Common Carrier Conference (RCCC)
2200 Mill Road
Alexandria, VA 22314
703-838-1967

Society of Logistics Engineers (SOLE)
125 W. Park Loop
Suite 201
Huntsville, AL 35806
205-837-1092

Steel Service Center Institute (SSCI)
1600 Terminal Tower
Cleveland, OH 44113
216-694-3630

Transportation Brokers Conference of America (TBCA)
60 Revere Drive
Suite 500
Northbrook, IL 60067
312-480-1046

Transportation Institute (TI)
5201 Auth Way
Camp Springs, MD 20746
301-423-3335

Transportation Research Board (TRB)
2101 Constitution Avenue, NW
Washington, DC 20418
202-334-2934

Transportation Research Forum (TRF)
1600 Wilson Blvd. #90S
Arlington, VA 22209
703-525-1191

Uniform Classification Committee (UCC)
222 S. Riverside Plaza
Suite 1106
Chicago, IL 60606
312-648-7944

Water Transport Association (WTA)
c/o William P. Morelli
Ohio River Company
P.O. Box 1460
Cincinnati, OH 45201
800-950-7707

Warehousing Education and Research Council (WERC)
1100 Jorie Blvd.
Suite 120
Oak Brook, IL 60521
708-990-0001

GLOSSARY

ABC analysis The classification of items in an inventory according to importance defined in terms of criteria such as sales volume and purchase volume.

accessibility A carrier's ability to provide service between an origin and a destination.

accessorial charges A carrier's charge for accessorial services such as loading, unloading, pickup, and delivery.

action message An alert an MRP or DRP system generates to inform the controller of a situation requiring his or her attention.

agency tariff A rate bureau publication that contains rates for many carriers.

agglomeration A net advantage a company gains by sharing a common location with other companies.

aggregate tender rate A reduced rate offered to a shipper who tenders two or more class-rated shipments at one time and one place.

air cargo Freight that is moved by air transportation.

Airport and Airway Trust Fund A federal fund that collects passenger ticket taxes and disburses those funds for airport facilities.

air taxi An exempt for-hire air carrier that will fly anywhere on demand; air taxis are restricted to a maximum payload and passenger capacity per plane.

Air Transport Association of America A U.S. airline industry association.

Alaskan carrier A for-hire air carrier that operates within the state of Alaska.

all-cargo carrier An air carrier that transports cargo only.

American Society of Transportation & Logistics A professional organization in the field of logistics.

American Trucking Association, Inc. A motor carrier industry association composed of subconferences representing various motor carrier industry sectors.

American Waterway Operators A domestic water carrier industry association representing barge operators on inland waterways.

Amtrak The National Railroad Passenger Corporation, a federally created corporation that operates most of the United States' intercity passenger rail service.

any-quantity (AQ) rate The same rate applies to any size shipment tendered to a carrier; no discount rate is available for large shipments.

artificial intelligence Understanding and computerizing the human thought process.

Association of American Railroads   A railroad industry association that represents the larger U.S. railroads.

auditing   Determining the correct transportation charges due the carrier; auditing involves checking the freight bill for errors, correct rate, and weight.

automated guided vehicle system   A computer-controlled materials handling system consisting of small vehicles (carts) that move along a guideway.

average cost   Total cost, fixed plus variable, divided by total output.

backhaul   A vehicle's return movement from original destination to original origin.

back order   The process a company uses when a customer orders an item that is not in inventory; the company fills the order when the item becomes available.

backup   Making a duplicate copy of a computer file or a program on a disk or cassette so that the material will not be lost if the original is destroyed; a spare copy.

bar code   A series of lines of various widths and spacings which can be scanned electronically to identify a carton or individual item.

barge   The cargo-carrying vehicle inland water carriers primarily use. Basic barges have open tops, but there are covered barges for both dry and liquid cargoes.

basing-point pricing   A pricing system that includes a transportation cost from a particular city or town in a zone or region even though the shipment does not originate at the basing point.

benefit-cost ratio   An analytical tool used in public planning; a ratio of total measurable benefits divided by the initial capital cost.

billing   A carrier terminal activity that determines the proper rate and total charges for a shipment and issues a freight bill.

bill of lading   A transportation document that is the contract of carriage between the shipper and carrier; it provides a receipt for the goods the shipper tenders to the carrier and, in some cases, shows certificate of title.

binder   A strip of cardboard, thin wood, burlap, or similar material placed between layers of containers to hold a stack together.

blanket rate   A rate that does not increase according to the distance a commodity is shipped.

bonded warehousing   Companies place goods in storage without paying taxes or tariffs. The warehouse manager bonds himself or herself to the tax or tariff collecting agency to ensure payment of the taxes before the warehouse releases the goods.

boxcar   An enclosed rail car typically forty to fifty feet long; used for packaged freight and some bulk commodities.

bracing   Securing a shipment inside a carrier's vehicle to prevent damage.

break-bulk   The separation of a consolidated bulk load into smaller individual shipments for delivery to the ultimate consignee. The freight may be moved intact inside the trailer or it may be interchanged and rehandled to connecting carriers.

broker   An intermediary between the shipper and the carrier. The broker arranges transportation for shippers and secures loads for carriers.

bulk area   A storage area for large items which at a minimum are most efficiently handled by the palletload.

business logistics   The process of planning, implementing, and controlling the efficient, effective flow and storage of goods, services, and related information from the point of origin to the point of consumption for the purpose of conforming to customer requirements. Note that this definition includes inbound, outbound, internal and external movements.

cabotage A federal law that requires coastal and intercoastal traffic to be carried in U.S.-built and -registered ships.

cage Can have two definitions in a warehouse setting: (1) a secure enclosed area for storing highly valuable items or (2) a pallet-sized platform with sides that can be secured to the tines of a forklift and in which a person may ride to inventory items stored well above the warehouse floor.

capital The resources, or money, available for investing in assets that produce output.

Carmack Amendment An Interstate Commerce Act amendment that delineates the liability of common carriers and the bill of lading provisions.

carousel A rotating system of layers of bins and/or drawers which can store many small items using relatively little floor space.

carrier liability A common carrier is liable for all shipment loss, damage, and delay with the exception of that caused by act of God, act of a public enemy, act of a public authority, act of the shipper, and the goods' inherent nature.

central processing unit (CPU) The physical part of the computer that does the actual computing.

centralized authority Management authority to make decisions is restricted to few managers.

certificate of origin An international business document that certifies the shipment's country of origin.

certificate of public convenience and necessity The grant of operating authority that common carriers receive. A carrier must prove that a public need exists and that the carrier is fit, willing, and able to provide the needed service. The certificate may specify the commodities the carrier may haul, the area it may serve, and the routes it may use.

certificated carrier A for-hire air carrier that is subject to economic regulation and requires an operating certification to provide service.

charging area A warehouse area where a company maintains battery chargers and extra batteries to support a fleet of electrically powered materials handling equipment. The company must maintain this area in accordance with government safety regulations.

chock A wedge, usually made of hard rubber or steel, that is firmly placed under the wheel of a trailer, truck, or boxcar to stop it from rolling.

city driver A motor carrier driver who drives a local route as opposed to a long-distance, intercity route.

Civil Aeronautics Board A federal regulatory agency that implemented economic regulatory controls over air carriers.

claim A charge made against a carrier for loss, damage, delay, or overcharge.

Class I carrier A classification of regulated carriers based upon annual operating revenues—motor carriers of property: ≥$5 million; railroads: ≥$50 million; motor carriers of passengers: ≥$3 million.

Class II carrier A classification of regulated carriers based upon annual operating revenues—motor carriers of property: $1–$5 million; railroads: $10–$50 million; motor carriers of passengers: ≤$3 million.

Class III carrier A classification of regulated carriers based upon annual operating revenues—motor carriers of property: ≤$1 million; railroads: ≤$10 million.

classification   An alphabetical listing of commodities, the class or rating into which the commodity is placed, and the minimum weight necessary for the rate discount; used in the class rate structure.

classification yard   A railroad terminal area where rail cars are grouped together to form train units.

class rate   A rate constructed from a classification and a uniform distance system. A class rate is available for any product between any two points.

coastal carriers   Water carriers that provide service along coasts serving ports on the Atlantic or Pacific oceans or on the Gulf of Mexico.

commercial zone   The area surrounding a city or town to which rates carriers quote for the city or town also apply; the ICC defines the area.

Committee of American Steamship Lines   An industry association representing subsidized U.S. flag steamship firms.

commodities clause   A clause that prohibits railroads from hauling commodities that they produced, mined, owned, or had an interest in.

commodity rate   A rate for a specific commodity and its origin-destination.

common carrier   A for-hire carrier that holds itself out to serve the general public at reasonable rates and without discrimination. To operate, the carrier must secure a certificate of public convenience and necessity.

common carrier duties   Common carriers must serve, deliver, charge reasonable rates, and not discriminate.

common cost   A cost that a company cannot directly assign to particular segments of the business; a cost that the company incurs for the business as a whole.

commuter   An exempt for-hire air carrier that publishes a time schedule on specific routes; a special type of air taxi.

comparative advantage   A principle based on the assumption that an area will specialize in producing goods for which it has the greatest advantage or least comparative disadvantage.

Conrail   The Consolidated Rail Corporation established by the Regional Reorganization Act of 1973 to operate the bankrupt Penn Central Railroad and other bankrupt railroads in the Northeast; the 4-R Act of 1976 provided funding.

consignee   The receiver of a freight shipment, usually the buyer.

consignor   The sender of a freight shipment, usually the seller.

consolidation   Collecting smaller shipments to form a larger quantity in order to realize lower transportation rates.

container   A big box (ten to forty feet long) into which freight is loaded.

contingency planning   Preparing to deal with calamities (e.g., floods) and non-calamitous situations (e.g., strikes) before they occur.

continuous-flow, fixed-path equipment   Materials handling devices that include conveyors and drag lines.

contract carrier   A for-hire carrier that does not serve the general public but serves shippers with whom the carrier has a continuing contract. The contract carrier must secure a permit to operate.

conveyor   A materials handling device that moves freight from one warehouse area to another. Roller conveyors utilize gravity, whereas belt conveyors use motors.

cooperative associations   Groups of firms or individuals having common interests; agricultural cooperative associations may haul up to twenty-five percent of their total interstate nonfarm, nonmember goods tonnage in movements incidental and necessary to their primary business.

coordinated transportation   Two or more carriers of different modes transporting a shipment.

cost of lost sales   The forgone profit companies associate with a stockout.

cost trade-off   The interrelationship among system variables indicates that a change in one variable affects other variables' costs. A cost reduction in one variable may increase costs for other variables, and vice versa.

Council of Logistics Management (CLM)   A professional organization in the logistics field which provides leadership in understanding the logistics process, awareness of career opportunities in logistics, and research that enhances customer value and supply chain performance.

courier service   A fast, door-to-door service for high-valued goods and documents; firms usually limit service to shipments weighing fifty pounds or less.

crane   A materials handling device that lifts heavy items. There are two types: bridge and stacker.

Critical Value Analysis   A modified ABC analysis in which a company assigns a subjective critical value to each item in an inventory.

customer service   Activities between the buyer and seller that enhance or facilitate the sale or use of the seller's products or services.

cycle inventory   An inventory system where counts are performed continuously, often eliminating the need for an annual overall inventory. It is usually set up so that A items are counted regularly (i.e., every month), B items are counted semi-regularly (every quarter or six months), and C items are counted perhaps only once a year.

decentralized authority   A situation in which a company management gives decision-making authority to managers at many organizational levels.

decision support system (DSS)   A set of computer-oriented tools designed to assist managers in making decisions.

defective goods inventory (DGI)   Those items which have been returned, have been delivered damaged and have a freight claim outstanding, or have been damaged in some way during warehouse handling.

Delta Nu Alpha   A professional association of transportation and traffic practitioners.

demurrage   The charge a railroad assesses for a shipper or receiver holding a car beyond the free time the railroad allows for loading (twenty-four hours) or unloading (forty-eight hours).

density   A physical characteristic measuring a commodity's mass per unit volume or pounds per cubic foot; an important factor in ratemaking, since density affects the utilization of a carrier's vehicle.

density rate   A rate based upon the density and shipment weight.

deregulation   Revisions or complete elimination of economic regulations controlling transportation. The Motor Carrier Act of 1980 and the Staggers Act of 1980 revised the economic controls over motor carriers and railroads, and the Airline Deregulation Act of 1978 eliminated economic controls over air carriers.

derived demand   The demand for a product's transportation is derived from the product's demand at some location.

detention   The charge a motor carrier assesses when a shipper or receiver holds a truck or trailer beyond the free time the carrier allows for loading or unloading.

differential   A discount offered by a carrier that faces a service time disadvantage over a route.

direct product profitability (DPP) Calculation of the net profit contribution attributable to a specific product or product line.

dispatching The carrier activities involved with controlling equipment; involves arranging for fuel, drivers, crews, equipment, and terminal space.

distribution requirements planning (DRP) A computer system that uses MRP techniques to manage the entire distribution network and to link it with manufacturing planning and control.

distribution warehouse A finished goods warehouse from which a company assembles customer orders.

diversion A carrier service that permits a shipper to change the consignee and/or destination while the shipment is en route and to still pay the through rate from origin to final destination.

dock receipt A receipt that indicates a domestic carrier has delivered an export shipment to a steamship company.

domestic trunk line carrier A classification for air carriers that operate between major population centers. These carriers are now classified as major carriers.

double bottoms A motor carrier operation that involves one tractor pulling two trailers.

double-pallet jack A mechanized device for transporting two standard pallets simultaneously.

download Merging temporary files containing a day's or week's worth of information with the main data base in order to update it.

drayage A motor carrier that operates locally, providing pickup and delivery service.

driving time regulations U.S. Department of Transportation rules that limit the maximum time a driver may drive in interstate commerce; the rules prescribe both daily and weekly maximums.

drop A situation in which an equipment operator deposits a trailer or boxcar at a facility at which it is to be loaded or unloaded.

dual operation A motor carrier that has both common and contract carrier operating authority.

dual rate system An international water carrier pricing system in which a shipper signing an exclusive use agreement with the conference pays a rate ten to fifteen percent lower than nonsigning shippers do for an identical shipment.

economic order quantity (EOQ) An inventory model that determines how much to order by determining the amount that will minimize total ordering and holding costs.

economies of scale The reduction in long-run average cost as the company's size (scale) increases.

electronic data interchange (EDI) Computer-to-computer communication between two or more companies that such companies can use to generate bills of lading, purchase orders, and invoices. It also enables firms to access the information systems of suppliers, customers, and carriers and to determine the up-to-the-minute status of inventory, orders, and shipments.

exception rate A deviation from the class rate; changes (exceptions) made to the classification.

exclusive patronage agreements A shipper agrees to use only a conference's member liner firms in return for a ten to fifteen percent rate reduction.

exclusive use Vehicles that a carrier assigns to a specific shipper for its exclusive use.

exempt carrier A for-hire carrier that is exempt from economic regulations.

expediting Determining where an in-transit shipment is and attempting to speed up its delivery.

export declaration A document required by the Department of Commerce that provides information about an export activity's nature and value.

export sales contract The initial document in any international transaction; it details the specifics of the sales agreement between the buyer and seller.

fair return A profit level that enables a carrier to realize a rate of return on investment or property value that the regulatory agencies deem acceptable for that level of risk.

fair value The value of the carrier's property; the calculation basis has included original cost minus depreciation, replacement cost, and market value.

Federal Aviation Administration The federal agency that administers federal safety regulations governing air transportation.

Federal Maritime Commission A regulatory agency that controls services, practices, and agreements of international water common carriers and non-contiguous domestic water carriers.

field warehouse A warehouse that stores goods on the goods' owner's property while the goods are under a bona fide public warehouse manager's custody. The owner uses the public warehouse receipt as collateral for a loan.

fill rate The percentage of order items that the picking operation actually found.

finance lease An equipment-leasing arrangement that provides the lessee with a means of financing for the leased equipment; a common method for leasing motor carrier trailers.

financial responsibility Motor carriers must have bodily injury and property damage (not cargo) insurance of not less than $500,000 per incident per vehicle; higher financial responsibility limits apply for motor carriers transporting oil or hazardous materials.

finished goods inventory (FGI) The products completely manufactured, packaged, stored, and ready for distribution.

firm planned order In a DRP or MRP system, a planned order whose status has been updated to a fixed order.

fixed costs Costs that do not fluctuate with the business volume in the short run.

fixed interval inventory model A setup wherein a company orders inventory at fixed or regular time intervals.

fixed quantity inventory model A setup wherein a company each time it places an order for an item, orders the same (fixed) quantity.

flatbed A trailer without sides used for hauling machinery or other bulky items.

flatcar A rail car without sides; used for hauling machinery.

flexible-path equipment Materials handling devices that include hand trucks and forklifts.

F.O.B. A term of sale defining who is to incur transportation charges for the shipment, who is to control the shipment movement, or where title to the goods passes to the buyer; originally meant "free on board ship."

for-hire carrier A carrier that provides transportation service to the public on a fee basis.

forklift truck A machine-powered device used to raise and lower freight and to move freight to different warehouse locations.

form utility   The value the production process creates in a good by changing the item's form.

freight bill   The carrier's invoice for a freight shipment's transportation charges.

freight forwarder   A carrier that collects small shipments from shippers, consolidates the small shipments, and uses a basic mode to transport these consolidated shipments to a consignee destination.

Freight Forwarders Institute   The freight forwarder industry association.

full-service leasing   An equipment-leasing arrangement that includes a variety of services to support the leased equipment; a common method for leasing motor carrier tractors.

fully allocated cost   The variable cost associated with a particular output unit plus a common cost allocation.

gathering lines   Oil pipelines that bring oil from the oil well to storage areas.

general-commodities carrier   A common motor carrier that has operating authority to transport general commodities, or all commodities not listed as special commodities.

general-merchandise warehouse   A warehouse used to store goods that are readily handled, are packaged, and do not require a controlled environment.

going-concern value   The value that a firm has as an entity, as opposed to the sum of the values of each of its parts taken separately; particularly important in determining a reasonable railroad rate.

gondola   A rail car with a flat platform and sides three to five feet high; used for top loading long, heavy items.

grandfather clause   A provision that enabled motor carriers engaged in lawful trucking operations before the passage of the Motor Carrier Act of 1935 to secure common carrier authority without proving public convenience and necessity; a similar provision exists for other modes.

granger laws   State laws passed before 1870 in midwestern states to control rail transportation.

Great Lakes carriers   Water carriers that operate on the five Great Lakes.

grid technique   A quantitative technique to determine the least-cost center, given raw materials sources and markets, for locating a plant or warehouse.

Gross National Product (GNP)   A measure of a nation's output; the total value of all final goods and services a nation produces during a time period.

gross weight   The total weight of the vehicle and the payload of freight or passengers.

guaranteed loans   Railroad loans that the federal government cosigns and guarantees.

hard copy   Computer output printed on paper.

Hawaiian carrier   A for-hire air carrier that operates within the state of Hawaii.

hazardous materials   Materials that the Department of Transportation has determined to be a risk to health, safety, and property; includes items such as explosives, flammable liquids, poisons, corrosive liquids, and radioactive material.

hi-low   Usually refers to a forklift truck on which the operator must stand rather than sit.

Highway Trust Fund   Highway users (carriers and automobile operators) pay into this fund, and the fund pays for federal government's highway construction share.

highway use taxes Taxes federal and state governments access against highway users (the fuel tax is an example). The government uses the use tax money to pay for the construction, maintenance, and policing of highways.

hopper cars Rail cars that permit top loading and bottom unloading of bulk commodities; some hopper cars have permanent tops with hatches to provide protection against the elements.

household goods warehouse A warehouse that stores household goods.

hub airport An airport that serves as the focal point for the origin and termination of long-distance flights; flights from outlying areas meet connecting flights at the hub airport.

hundredweight (cwt) The pricing unit used in transportation; a hundredweight is equal to 100 pounds.

igloos Pallets and containers used in air transportation; the igloo shape fits the internal wall contours of a narrow-body airplane

incentive rate A rate that induces the shipper to ship heavier volumes per shipment.

independent action A carrier that is a rate bureau member may publish a rate that differs from the rate the rate bureau publishes.

inherent advantage The cost and service benefits of one mode compared with other modes.

interchange The transfer of cargo and equipment from one carrier to another in a joint freight move.

intercoastal carriers Water carriers that transport freight between East and West Coast ports, usually by way of the Panama Canal.

intercorporate hauling A private carrier hauling a subsidiary's goods and charging the subsidiary a fee; this is legal if the subsidiary is wholly owned (100%) or if the private carrier has common carrier authority.

interline Two or more motor carriers working together to haul a shipment to a destination. Carriers may interchange equipment but usually they rehandle the shipment without transferring the equipment.

intermittent-flow, fixed-path equipment Materials handling devices that include bridge cranes, monorails, and stacker cranes.

intermodal transportation Using two or more transportation modes to transport freight; for example, rail to ship to truck.

internal water carriers Water carriers that operate over internal, navigable rivers such as the Mississippi, Ohio, and Missouri.

International Air Transport Association An international air carrier rate bureau for passenger and freight movements.

International Civil Aeronautics Organization An international agency responsible for air safety and for standardizing air traffic control, airport design, and safety features worldwide.

interstate commerce The transportation of persons or property between states; in the course of the movement, the shipment crosses a state boundary.

Interstate Commerce Commission (ICC) An independent regulatory agency that implements federal economic regulations controlling railroads, motor carriers, pipelines, domestic water carriers, domestic surface freight forwarders, and brokers.

Interstate System The National System of Interstate and Defense Highways, 42,000 miles of four-lane, limited-access roads connecting major population centers.

intrastate commerce   The transportation of persons or property between points within a state. A shipment between two points within a state may be interstate if the shipment had a prior or subsequent move outside of the state and the shipper intended an interstate shipment at the time of shipment.

inventory   The number of units and/or value of the stock of goods a company holds.

inventory cost   The cost of holding goods, usually expressed as a percentage of the inventory value; includes the cost of capital, warehousing, taxes, insurance, depreciation, and obsolescence.

inventory in transit   Inventory in a carrier's possession, being transported to the buyer.

inventory management   Inventory administration through planning, stock positioning, monitoring product age, and ensuring product availability.

irregular route carrier   A motor carrier that may provide service utilizing any route.

joint cost   A common cost where a company produces products in fixed proportions, and the cost the company incurs to produce one product entails producing another; the backhaul is an example.

joint rate   A rate over a route that requires two or more carriers to transport the shipment.

just-in-time inventory system   An inventory control system that attempts to reduce inventory levels by coordinating demand and supply to the point where the desired item arrives just in time for use.

Kanban   A just-in-time inventory system used by Japanese manufacturers.

lading   The cargo carried in a transportation vehicle.

laid-down cost   The total cost of a product delivered at a given location; the production cost plus the transportation cost to the customer's location.

land bridge   The movement of containers by ship-rail-ship on Japan-to-Europe moves; ships move containers to the U.S. Pacific Coast, rails move containers to an East Coast port, and ships deliver containers to Europe.

land grants   Grants of land given to railroads to build tracks during their development stage.

lash barges   Covered barges that carriers load on board oceangoing ships for movement to foreign destinations.

lead time   The total time that elapses between an order's placement and its receipt. It includes the time required for order transmittal, order processing, order preparation, and transit.

lessee   A person or firm to whom a lessor grants a lease.

lessor   A person or firm that grants a lease.

letter of credit   An international business document that assures the seller that the bank issuing the letter of credit will make payment upon fulfillment of the sales agreement.

lighter   A flat-bottomed boat designed for cross-harbor or inland waterway freight transfer.

line functions   The decision-making areas companies associate with daily operations. Logistics line functions include traffic management, inventory control, order processing, warehousing, and packaging.

line-haul shipment   A shipment that moves between cities and over distances more than 100 to 150 miles in length.

liner service   International water carriers that ply fixed routes on published schedules.

link   The transportation method a company uses to connect nodes (plants, warehouses) in a logistics system.

live   A situation in which the equipment operator stays with the trailer or boxcar while it is being loaded or unloaded.

load factor   A measure of operating efficiency air carriers use to determine a plane's utilized capacity percentage, or the number of passengers divided by the total number of seats.

loading allowance   A reduced rate carriers offer to shippers and/or consignees who load and/or unload LTL or AQ shipments.

localized raw material   A raw material found only in certain locations.

local rate   A rate published between two points served by one carrier.

local service carriers   A classification of air carriers that operate between less-populated areas and major population centers. These carriers feed passengers into the major cities to connect with trunk (major) carriers. Local service carriers are now classified as national carriers.

locational determinant   The factors that determine a facility's location. For industrial facilities, the determinants include logistics.

logbook   A daily record of the hours an interstate driver spends driving, off duty, sleeping in the berth, or on duty but not driving.

logistics channel   The network of intermediaries engaged in transfer, storage, handling, and communications functions that contribute to the efficient flow of goods.

logistics data interchange (LDI)   A computerized system that electronically transmits logistics information.

long ton   Equals 2,240 pounds.

lot size   The quantity of goods a company purchases or produces in anticipation of use or sale in the future.

LTL shipment   A less-than-truckload shipment, one weighing less than the minimum weight a company needs to use the lower truckload rate.

lumping   The act of assisting a motor carrier owner-operator in the loading and unloading of property; quite commonly used in the food industry.

mainframe   An organization's central computer system.

major carrier   A for-hire certificated air carrier that has annual operating revenues of $1 billion or more; the carrier usually operates between major population centers.

marginal cost   The cost to produce one additional unit of output; the change in total variable cost resulting from a one-unit change in output.

marine insurance   Insurance to protect against cargo loss and damage when shipping by water transportation.

Maritime Administration   A federal agency that promotes the merchant marine, determines ocean ship routes and services, and awards maritime subsidies.

market dominance   The absence of effective competition for railroads from other carriers and modes for the traffic to which the rail rate applies. The Staggers Act stated that market dominance does not exist if the rate is below the revenue-to-variable-cost ratio of 160% in 1981 and 170% in 1983.

material index   The ratio of the sum of the localized raw material weights to the weight of the finished product.

materials handling   Short-distance movement of goods within a storage area.

materials management   The movement and storage functions associated with supplying goods to a firm.

materials planning   The materials management function that attempts to coordinate materials supply with materials demand.

materials requirements planning (MRP)   A decision-making technique used to determine how much material to purchase and when to purchase it.

matrix organization   An organizational structure that emphasizes the horizontal flow of authority; the company treats logistics as a project, with the logistics manager overseeing logistics costs but traditional departments controlling operations.

measurement ton   Equals forty cubic feet; used in water transportation rate-making.

merger   The combination of two or more carriers into one company that will own, manage, and operate the properties that previously operated separately.

mileage allowance   An allowance, based upon distance, that railroads give to shippers using private rail cars.

mileage rate   A rate based upon the number of miles the commodity is shipped.

minimum weight   The shipment weight the carrier's tariff specifies as the minimum weight required to use the TL or CL rate; the rate discount volume.

mixed loads   The movement of both regulated and exempt commodities in the same vehicle at the same time.

modal split   The relative use companies make of transportation modes; the statistics include ton-miles, passenger-miles, and revenue.

MRO items   Maintenance, repair, and operating items—office supplies, for example.

multiple-car rate   A railroad rate that is lower for shipping more than one carload at a time.

national carrier   A for-hire certificated air carrier that has annual operating revenues of $75 million to $1 billion; the carrier usually operates between major population centers and areas of lesser population.

National Industrial Traffic League   An association representing shippers' and receivers' interests in matters of transportation policy and regulation.

nationalization   Public ownership, financing, and operation of a business entity.

National Motor Bus Operators Organization   An industry association representing common and charter bus firms; now known as the American Bus Association.

National Railroad Corporation   Also known as Amtrak, the corporation established by the Rail Passenger Service Act of 1970 to operate most of the United States' rail passenger service.

no location (No Loc)   A received item for which the warehouse has no previously established storage slot.

node   A fixed point in a firm's logistics system where goods come to rest; includes plants, warehouses, supply sources, and markets.

noncertificated carrier   A for-hire air carrier that is exempt from economic regulation.

non-vessel-owning common carrier (NVOCC)   A firm that consolidates and disperses international containers that originate at or are bound for inland ports.

on-line receiving   A system in which computer terminals are available at each receiving bay and operators enter items into the system as they are unloaded.

operating ratio   A measure of operating efficiency defined as

$$\frac{\text{Operating expenses}}{\text{Operating revenues}} \times 100$$

order cycle time   The time that elapses from placement of order until receipt of order. This includes time for order transmittal, processing, preparation, and shipping.

ordering cost   The cost of placing an inventory order with a supplier.

order picking   Assembling a customer's order from items in storage.

order processing   The activities associated with filling customer orders.

out-of-pocket cost   The cost directly assignable to a particular unit of traffic and which a company would not have incurred if it had not performed the movement.

outsourcing   Purchasing a logistics service from an outside firm, as opposed to performing it in-house.

over-the-road   A motor carrier operation that reflects long-distance, intercity moves; the opposite of local operations.

owner-operator   A trucking operation in which the truck's owner is also the driver.

pallet   A platform device (about four feet square) used for moving and storing goods. A forklift truck is used to lift and move the loaded pallet.

pallet wrapping machine   A machine which wraps a pallet's contents in stretch-wrap to insure safe shipment.

passenger-mile   A measure of output for passenger transportation; it reflects the number of passengers transported and the distance traveled; a multiplication of passengers hauled and distance traveled.

peak demand   The time period during which customers demand the greatest quantity.

pegging   A technique in which a DRP system traces demand for a product by date, quantity, and warehouse location.

per diem   Payment rate one railroad makes to use another's cars.

permit   A grant of authority to operate as a contract carrier.

personal computer (PC)   An individual unit an operator uses for creating and maintaining programs and files; can often access the mainframe simultaneously.

personal discrimination   Charging different rates to shippers with similar transportation characteristics, or vice versa.

physical distribution   The movement and storage of finished goods from manufacturing plants to warehouses to customers; used synonymously with business logistics.

physical supply   The movement and storage of raw materials from supply sources to the manufacturing facility.

picking by aisle   A method by which pickers pick all needed items in an aisle regardless of the items' ultimate destination; the items must be sorted later.

picking by source   A method in which pickers successively pick all items going to a particular destination regardless of the aisle in which each item is located.

piggyback   A rail-truck service. A shipper loads a highway trailer, and a carrier drives it to a rail terminal and loads it on a rail flatcar; the railroad moves the trailer-on-flatcar combination to the destination terminal where the carrier offloads the trailer and delivers it to the consignee.

pin lock   A hard piece of iron, formed to fit on a trailer's pin, that locks in place with a key to prevent an unauthorized person from moving the trailer.

place utility   A value logistics creates in a product by changing the product's location. Transportation creates place utility.

planned order   In DRP and MRP systems, a future order the system plans in response to forecasted demand.

police powers   The United States constitutionally granted right for the states to establish regulations to protect their citizens' health and welfare; truck weight, speed, length, and height laws are examples.

pooling   An agreement among carriers to share the freight to be hauled or to share profits. The Interstate Commerce Act outlawed pooling agreements, but the Civil Aeronautics Board has approved profit pooling agreements for air carriers during strikes.

port authority   A state or local government that owns, operates, or otherwise provides wharf, dock, and other terminal investments at ports.

possession utility   The value created by marketing's effort to increase the desire to possess a good or benefit from a service.

primary-business test   A test the ICC uses to determine if a trucking operation is bona fide private transportation; the private trucking operation must be incidental to and in the furtherance of the firm's primary business.

private carrier   A carrier that provides transportation service to the firm that owns or leases the vehicles and does not charge a fee. Private motor carriers may haul at a fee for wholly owned subsidiaries.

private warehousing   The storage of goods in a warehouse owned by the company that has title to the goods.

production planning   The decision-making area that determines when and where and in what quantity a manufacturer is to produce goods.

productivity   A measure of resource utilization efficiency defined as the sum of the outputs divided by the sum of the inputs.

profit ratio   The percentage of profit to sales—that is, profit divided by sales.

proportional rate   A rate lower than the regular rate for shipments that have prior or subsequent moves; used to overcome combination rates' competitive disadvantages.

public warehouse receipt   The basic document a public warehouse manager issues as a receipt for the goods a company gives to the warehouse manager. The receipt can be either negotiable or nonnegotiable.

public warehousing   The storage of goods by a firm that offers storage service for a fee to the public.

pull ordering system   Each warehouse controls its own shipping requirements by placing individual orders for inventory with the central distribution center.

purchase price discount   A pricing structure in which the seller offers a lower price if the buyer purchases a larger quantity.

purchasing   The functions associated with buying the goods and services the firm requires.

pure raw material   A raw material that does not lose weight in processing.

push ordering system   A situation in which a firm makes inventory deployment decisions at the central distribution center and ships to its individual warehouses accordingly.

quality control   The management function that attempts to ensure that the goods or services a firm manufactures or purchases meet the product or service specifications.

random access memory (RAM)   Temporary memory on micro chips. Users can store data in RAM or take it out at high speeds. However, any information stored in RAM disappears when the computer is shut off.

rate basis number   The distance between two rate basis points.

rate basis point   The major shipping point in a local area; carriers consider all points in the local area to be the rate basis point.

rate bureau   A carrier group that assembles to establish joint rates, to divide joint revenues and claim liabilities, and to publish tariffs. Rate bureaus have published single line rates, which were prohibited in 1984.

reasonable rate   A rate that is high enough to cover the carrier's cost but not high enough to enable the carrier to realize monopolistic profits.

Recapture Clause   A provision of the 1920 Transportation Act that provided for self-help financing for railroads. Railroads that earned more than the prescribed return contributed one-half of the excess to the fund from which the ICC made loans to less profitable railroads. The Recapture Clause was repealed in 1933.

reconsignment   A carrier service that permits a shipper to change the destination and/or consignee after the shipment has reached its originally billed destination and to still pay the through rate from origin to final destination.

Reed-Bulwinkle Act   Legalized common carrier joint ratemaking through rate bureaus; extended antitrust immunity to carriers participating in a rate bureau.

reefer   A term used for refrigerated vehicles.

refrigerated warehouse   A warehouse that is used to store perishable items requiring controlled temperatures.

regional carrier   A for-hire air carrier, usually certificated, that has annual operating revenues of less than $75 million; the carrier usually operates within a particular region of the country.

regular-route carrier   A motor carrier that is authorized to provide service over designated routes.

relay terminal   A motor carrier terminal that facilitates the substitution of one driver for another who has driven the maximum hours permitted.

released-value rates   Rates based upon the shipment's value. The maximum carrier liability for damage is less than the full value, and in return the carrier offers a lower rate.

reliability   A carrier selection criterion that considers the carrier transit time variation; the consistency of the transit time the carrier provides.

re-location (Re-Loc)   A situation in which a company must develop a new location for an item whose previously established storage location(s) is (are) filled to capacity.

reorder point   A predetermined inventory level that triggers the need to place an order. This minimum level provides inventory to meet the demand a firm anticipates during the time it takes to receive the order.

reparation   A situation in which the ICC requires a railroad to repay users the difference between the rate the railroad charges and the maximum rate the ICC permits when the ICC finds a rate to be unreasonable or too high.

right of eminent domain   A concept that, in a court of law, permits a carrier to purchase land it needs for transportation right-of-way; used by railroads and pipelines.

rule of eight   Before the Motor Carrier Act of 1980, the ICC restricted contract carriers requesting authority to eight shippers under contract. The number of shippers has been deleted as a consideration for granting a contract carrier permit.

rule of ratemaking   A regulatory provision directing the regulatory agencies to consider the earnings a carrier needs to provide adequate transportation.

safety stock   The inventory a company holds beyond normal needs as a buffer against delays in receipt of orders or changes in customer buying patterns.

salvage material   Unused material that has a market value and can be sold.

scrap material   Unusable material that has no market value.

separable cost   A cost that a company can directly assign to a particular segment of the business.

setup costs   The costs a manufacturer incurs in staging the production line to produce a different item.

ship agent   A liner company or tramp ship operator representative who facilitates ship arrival, clearance, loading and unloading, and fee payment while at a specific port.

ship broker   A firm that serves as a go-between for the tramp ship owner and the chartering consignor or consignee.

shipper's agent   A firm that primarily matches up small shipments, especially single-traffic piggyback loads to permit shippers to use twin-trailer piggyback rates.

shippers association   A nonprofit, cooperative consolidator and distributor of shipments member firms own or ship; acts in much the same way as a for-profit freight forwarder.

short-haul discrimination   Charging more for a shorter haul than for a longer haul over the same route, in the same direction, and for the same commodity.

short ton   Equals 2,000 pounds.

simulation   A computer model that represents a real-life logistics operation with mathematical symbols and runs it for a simulated length of time to determine how proposed changes will affect the operation.

sleeper team   Using two drivers to operate a truck equipped with a sleeper berth; while one driver sleeps in the berth to accumulate mandatory off-duty time, the other driver operates the vehicle.

slip seat operation   A motor carrier relay terminal operation in which a carrier substitutes one driver for another who has accumulated the maximum driving time hours.

slip sheet   Similar to a pallet, the slip sheet, which is made of cardboard or plastic, is used to facilitate movement of unitized loads.

slurry   Dry commodities that are made into a liquid form by the addition of water or other fluids to permit movement by pipeline.

Society of Logistics Engineers   A professional association engaged in the advancement of logistics technology and management.

software   A computer term that describes the system design and programming the computer's effective use requires.

special-commodities carrier   A common carrier trucking company that has authority to haul a special commodity; the sixteen special commodities include household goods, petroleum products, and hazardous materials.

special-commodity warehouses   A warehouse that is used to store products requiring unique facilities, such as grain (elevator), liquid (tank), and tobacco (barn).

spot Moving a trailer or boxcar into place for loading or unloading.

spur track A railroad track that connects a company's plant or warehouse with the railroad's track; the user bears the cost of the spur track and its maintenance.

staff functions The planning and analysis support activities a firm provides to assist line managers with daily operations. Logistics staff functions include location analysis, system design, cost analysis, and planning.

statistical process control (SPC) A managerial control technique that examines a process's inherent variability.

steamship conferences Collective rate-making bodies for liner water carriers.

stock keeping unit (SKU) A single unit which has been completely assembled. In a DRP system, an item is not considered complete until it is where it can satisfy customer demand.

stockless purchasing A practice whereby the buyer negotiates a purchase price for annual requirements of MRO items and the seller holds inventory until the buyer orders individual items.

stockout A situation in which the items a customer orders are currently unavailable.

stockout cost The opportunity cost companies associate with not having supply sufficient to meet demand.

stores The function associated with storing and issuing frequently used items.

strategic planning Looking one to five years into the future and designing a logistical system (or systems) to meet the needs of the various businesses in which a company is involved.

strategic variables The variables that effect change in the environment and logistics strategy. The major strategic variables include economy, population, energy, and government.

strategy A specific action to achieve an objective.

stretch-wrap An elastic, thin plastic material which effectively adheres to itself, thereby containing product on a pallet when wrapped around the items.

substitutability A buyer's ability to substitute different sellers' products.

supplemental carrier A for-hire air carrier having no time schedule or designated route; the carrier provides service under a charter or contract per plane per trip.

supply warehouse A warehouse that stores raw materials; a company mixes goods from different suppliers at the warehouse and assembles plant orders.

surcharge An add-on charge to the applicable charges; motor carriers have a fuel surcharge, and railroads can apply a surcharge to any joint rate that does not yield 110% of variable cost.

switch engine A railroad engine that is used to move rail cars short distances within a terminal and plant.

switching company A railroad that moves rail cars short distances; switching companies connect two mainline railroads to facilitate through movement of shipments.

system A set of interacting elements, variables, parts, or objects that are functionally related to each other and form a coherent group.

systems concept A decision-making strategy that emphasizes overall system efficiency rather than the efficiency of each part.

tally sheet A printed form on which companies record, by making an appropriate mark, the number of items they receive or ship. In many operations, tally sheets become a part of the permanent inventory records.

tandem   A truck that has two drive axles or a trailer that has two axles.

tank cars   Rail cars designed to haul bulk liquids or gas commodities.

tapering rate   A rate that increases with distance but not in direct proportion to the distance the commodity is shipped.

tare weight   The weight of the vehicle when it is empty.

tariff   A publication that contains a carrier's rates, accessorial charges, and rules.

temporary authority   The ICC may grant a temporary operating authority as a common carrier for up to 270 days.

terminal delivery allowance   A reduced rate a carrier offers in return for the shipper or consignee tendering or picking up the freight at the carrier's terminal.

third party   A firm that supplies logistics services to other companies.

three-layer framework   A basic structure and operational activity of a company; the three layers include operational systems, control and administrative management, and master planning.

throughput   A warehousing output measure that considers the volume (weight, number of units) of items stored during a given time period.

time/service rate   A rail rate that is based upon transit time.

timetables   Time schedules of departures and arrivals by origin and destination; typically used for passenger transportation by air, bus, and rail.

time utility   A value created in a product by having the product available at the time desired. Transportation and warehousing create time utility.

TL (truckload)   A shipment weighing the minimum weight or more. Carriers give a rate reduction for shipping a TL-size shipment.

TOFC (trailer-on-flatcar)   Also known as piggyback.

ton-mile   A freight transportation output measure; it reflects the shipment's weight and the distance the carrier hauls it; a multiplication of tons hauled and distance traveled.

total cost analysis   A decision-making approach that considers total system cost minimization and recognizes the interrelationship among system variables such as transportation, warehousing, inventory, and customer service.

Toto authority   A private motor carrier receiving operating authority as a common carrier to haul freight for the public over the private carrier's backhaul; the ICC granted this type of authority to the Toto Company in 1978.

tracing   Determining a shipment's location during the course of a move.

traffic management   The management of buying and controlling transportation services for a shipper or consignee, or both.

tramp   An international water carrier that has no fixed route or published schedule; a shipper charters a tramp ship for a particular voyage or a given time period.

transit privilege   A carrier service that permits the shipper to stop the shipment in transit to perform a function that changes the commodity's physical characteristics, but to still pay the through rate.

transit time   The total time that elapses between a shipment's delivery and its pickup.

Transportation Association of America   An association that represents the entire U.S. transportation system—carriers, users, and the public; now defunct.

transportation method   A linear programming technique that determines the least-cost allocation of shipping goods from plants to warehouses or from warehouses to customers.

transportation requirements planning (TRP) Utilizing computer technology and information already available in MRP and DRP data bases to plan transportation needs based on field demand.

Transportation Research Board A division of the National Academy of Sciences which pertains to transportation research.

Transportation Research Forum A professional association that provides a forum for the discussion of transportation ideas and research techniques.

transshipment problem A variation of the linear programming transportation method that considers consolidating shipments to one destination and reshipping from that destination.

travel agent A firm that provides passenger travel information; air, rail, and steamship ticketing; and hotel reservations. The carrier and hotel pay the travel agent a commission.

trunk lines Oil pipelines used for the long-distance movement of crude oil, refined oil, or other liquid products.

two-bin system An inventory ordering system in which the time to place an order for an item is indicated when the first bin is empty. The second bin contains supply sufficient to last until the company receives the order.

ubiquity A raw material that is found at all locations.

umbrella rate An ICC ratemaking practice that held rates to a particular level to protect another mode's traffic.

Uniform Warehouse Receipts Act The act that sets forth the regulations governing public warehousing. The regulations define a warehouse manager's legal responsibility and define the types of receipts he or she issues.

United States Railway Association The planning and funding agency for Conrail; created by the 3-R Act of 1973.

unitize To consolidate several packages into one unit; carriers strap, band, or otherwise attach the several packages together.

unit train An entire, uninterrupted locomotive, car, and caboose movement between an origin and destination.

Urban Mass Transportation Administration A U.S. Department of Transportation agency that develops comprehensive mass transport systems for urban areas and for providing financial aid to transit systems.

value-of-service pricing Pricing according to the value of the product the company is transporting; third-degree price discrimination; demand-oriented pricing; charging what the traffic will bear.

variable cost A cost that fluctuates with the volume of business.

vendor A firm or individual that supplies goods or services; the seller.

von Thunen's belts A series of concentric rings around a city to identify where agricultural products would be produced according to von Thunen's theory.

warehousing The storage (holding) of goods.

waterway use tax A per-gallon tax assessed barge carriers for waterway use.

weight break The shipment volume at which the LTL charges equal the TL charges at the minimum weight.

weight-losing raw material A raw material that loses weight in processing.

work-in-process (WIP) Parts and sub-assemblies in the process of becoming completed assembly components. These items, no longer part of the raw materials inventory and not yet part of the finished goods inventory, may constitute a large inventory by themselves and create extra expense for the firm.

zone of rate flexibility   Railroads may raise rates by a percentage increase in the railroad cost index the ICC determines; the railroads could raise rates by six percent per year through 1984 and four percent thereafter.

zone of rate freedom   Motor carriers may raise or lower rates by 10 percent in one year without ICC interference; if the rate change is within the zone of freedom, the rate is presumed to be reasonable.

zone of reasonableness   A zone or limit within which air carriers may change rates without regulatory scrutiny; if the rate change is within the zone, the new rate is presumed to be reasonable.

zone price   The constant price of a product at all geographic locations within a zone.

Author Index

SUBJECT INDEX